THE DARK SECRET

LIMITED RAW

*The Metaphysics of Magic,
The Death of New Age Spirituality,
and the Disruption of Light Consciousness*

~ *The Untold Truth of the Matter* ~

Lorna J.

"What you seek cannot be found in the Light."

~ Lorna J

CONTENTS

BOOK ONE

THE SUMMONING

The Promise Of The Dark 1

The Stifling Mimicry Of The Light Grid 24

Dark Is The Newest Light 49

Darkworkers And Lightworkers: A Fine Distinction 51

The Absolute Science Behind Manifestation 56

On Mastery Of The Absolute Science Of Manifestation 58

Shadow Alchemy And The Problem Of The Shadow 66

Codes Of Consciousness: Teaching The Light Grid And The Archetypes Of The Collective Consciousness (Master The Archetypal Consciousness You've Been Given) .. 98

The Light Grid Vs Absolute Truth 100

The Light Grid 108

Mastering The Light Grid 112

Glossary Of Terms 117

The Metaphysical Language And Archetypal Consciousness Of The Psyche (I.E, The Truth Of Who You Are, And The Four Pillars Of Light Power) 119

Archetypes Overview 121

The Master Map 124

The Soul Killer (The Prostitute + The Lover) 125

Prostitute Deep Dive	138
Lover Deep Dive	141
The Identity Killer (The Child + The Sovereign)	144
Child Deep Dive	150
Sovereign Deep Dive	153
The Body Killer (The Victim + The Warrior)	156
Victim Deep Dive	160
Warrior Deep Dive	165
The Mind Killer (The Saboteur + The Magician)	169
Saboteur Deep Dive	175
Magician Deep Dive	182
The Case For Shadow Alchemy	187
The Shadow Alchemy Tool	189
Shadow Alchemy: Benefits And Deep Dive	199
Shadow Alchemy In Action: An Amazing Client Case Study	200
The Experience Of Alchemized Shadow And The Application To A Trigger	204
Shadow Management Vs Shadow Alchemy: Some Distinctive Differences	206
Shadow Alchemy Q&A	209
The Master Seven: The Three Fields Of Manifestation And Will And The Four Channels Of Light Energy	225
Lorna J Coaching + Shadow Alchemy In Action: The Work	229
Codes Of Disruption	258

    THE TRUE TRUTHS
    WHAT IS ENERGY
    THERE ARE NO VICTIMS. NOTHING AND NO ONE HAS POWER OVER YOU.
    GENIUS IS NOT RARE OR A LUXURY. THE COST FOR NOT ACCESSING IT IS GOING UP IN MENTAL ILLNESS.
    MENTAL ILLNESS IS NOTHING
    OUR EGOS ARE MEANT TO GROW, NOT DIMINISH
    CAUSE AND EFFECT

The Soul Is No Longer Necessary And Is The Source Of Suffering

Hero's, Heroine's And Anti-Hero's Journeys, In Relief 267

The Dark Lattice. The Dark Archetypes: The Archetypes Of Euphoria, Prestige And Genius 270

The Dark Goddess And The Band Of Unhooking 271

The Prestige: The Call Of The Dark, The Anti-Hero's Journey And Speaking The New Myth Into Existence 272

What Does It Look Like To Answer The Call (The Dark Dance) 274

Applying Light And Dark Mastery To The Real World 276

What About….? 279

    People Who Are Already Artists And Are Addicts, Depressed And Suicidal?

BOOK TWO

LIGHT MASTERY, THE MAGICAL MASCULINE AND THE TRUE SECRET OF MANIFESTING ON DEMAND

Table Of Contents [In Process].. 285

What Kills Magic?.. 288

Magic Is Natural.. 289

Magic 292

The Problem Of Spiritual Consciousness (Why New Age Spirituality Is Dead)............ 300

Portals That Kill 306

Thoughts, And What They Don't Create 311

Physical Existence, Codes Of Consciousness, The Mechanics Of Inspired Action And The Role Of Intuition In Manifesting On Demand...................... 321

Guards Down, Boundaries Up 331

On Self-Actualization, The Feminine And The Dynamic Nature Of Source 333

On Our Struggle With Awakening And The Degraded Role Of The Masculine 335

The Energetics Of Desire And The Essential Missing Link To Loa Teachings (The Bestowal Of Power Onto Desire) 338

On Women, Men And Anxiety 339

Anxiety And The Sleepy Stuckness Of The Swampy Feminine 340

The Magical Masculine 341

The Dark Masculine 345

The Misunderstood Masculine And The Root Of Real Magic 348

Loa Redefined And Distilled 351

The Secret To Men And Money Success 352

The Mechanics Of Inspired Action 357

Light Consciousness: The One Consciousness. Dark Consciousness: Unique Consciousness 363

The Domain Of Lightworkers, The Domain Of The Dark 433

Light Codes Vs Codes Of Genius: Law Of Attraction, The Mechanisms Of Desire And Why You're Not Attracting What You Want 434

Openness Is An Exact State. 436

To All The Budding Truthtellers And Shadow Seers Out There, Who Are Still Trembling A Bit, Terrified Of Coming Out: I Got You ;) ~ [Or...A Note Of Encouragement In The Spiritual Storm] 437

True Magic 440

Joseph Campbell Is Wrong 441

Gold Minds, Caves Of Genius And Business Alchemy: The Inversed Posture Of Success For Darkworker Ceos (Or, Darkworker Ceos: You're In For A Real Awakening) 443

The Experience Of Dark Initiation 446

All Genius Is Dark 447

Your Work Is Not To Make Yourself Palatable 448

The Secret To Happiness: Kill Your Children While They're Young And Healthy 449

Artisans Of Consciousness 451

The Holy Grail Is Madness 452

Codes Of Magnetism And The Energetics Of The Inefficacy Of Expert Advice 453

It Begins With A Deep Appreciation Of Your Conditioning. 456

Integrity Consciousness + The Dark Grid: The Exacting Standards Of The Darkcodes And How This Impacts The Potency Of Your Gift (And Therefore Your Sales) 460

The Evolution Of The Divine Human Ceo 463

The Energetics Of Fear And Genius 464

Ambivalence Is Terror (Or The Next-Level Sophistication Of The Shadow Mind) 465

The Alchemy Of Action 467

It Is Time: The Age Of Disruption 468

Darkness Is The Real God 475

The Dark Goddess And The Takeover Of Consciousness 588

Hiring A Darkworker Is Hiring The Energetic Laws Of The Universe 598

On Sales Stagnation, Stuckness And Lack Of Inspiration 601

Death To Certifications 605

I'm Calling For The Untaming Of The Personal Transformation Movement 606

On Shame, Genius And Freedom 611

The Energetics Of A Nervous Breakdown 613

The Gold Mind And The Genius Frequency 614

Quantum Flight And Genius Activation 615

The Problem Is You Think You're Only Worthy Of Love If You Change. 616

~On Energetic Mastery And Shadow Self Care~ 619

Going Sane (Or Truth Kept In, Is Toxic: A Short Memoir) 622

The Energetics Of Extreme Transformation 625

After You Step Out Over The Chasm, The Bridge Appears Under Your Feet (And Never, Ever Before) 629

Both/And, Not Either/Or 631

You Want More Energy? Start Telling The Fucking Truth. 635

Dna, Light And Sex Magic 638

The Energetics Of Miracles 640

Action Releases The Energy Needed To Create Quantum Leaps 642

When You Transmute Fear Into Power, You Create A Clear Channel For Energy To Turn Into Matter Rapidly And Everywhere All At Once 644

Energetic Truth = Freedom From All Concern 645

Time Mastery: How To Directly And Practically Impact Your Past 646

Divine Timing Is An Excuse 647

Divine Timing, Princess Energy And Excuse Making 648

Badass? Or Rich, Famous Follower? How Energy Mastery Is Time Mastery And What That Has To Do With Your Ambitions 650

Quantum Leaping Is Old Paradigm. 654

> ANNOUNCING THE ADVENT OF THE NEW PARADIGM OF CHANGE MASTERY: CHANGE AT THE SPEED OF (F)LIGHT.

You Are Capable Of A Quantum Uplevel Right Now 657

Leader Consciousness: Why Arianna Huffington Woke Up In A Pool Of Blood 658

On Authenticity And Being Triggered 660

The Truth Of Being Triggered 662

Anger Is Disempowerment. Only Victims Get Angry. 663

The Spiritual Symbolism Of Your Life 665

My #Metoo Post 667

The Thunderclap Of Uncomfortable Light: Strong Emotion Vs Being Triggered [Or How To Tell Whether You're Stepping Into Your Natural Role As A Truthteller Or Whether You're In The Presence Of Your Own Deep Shadow] 668

Unwavering Self Belief (Or Everything Changed For Me When…) 671

It Is Not Easy To Love The Fabric Of Consciousness And Yet You Do. 674

> EXAMPLES FROM CLIENTS: 674

Your Cells Can Be Either In Protect Or In Growth Mode. 677

We Are Not Meant To Be Ourselves Forever 678

You Must Become Unrecognizable 681

The Energetics Of Power (True Leadership Consciousness For The Energetic Olympian) 682

> "YOU ARE A MURDERER."

Answers Come Instantly From Your Soul. There Is Never Any Need To Meditate To Receive An Answer. 686

> MARKETING IS METAPHYSICAL

The Energetics Of Marketing ... 695

Your Wildness Is A Lighthouse ... 697

SALES IS INTIMATE AND HOLY

Notes From The Dark ... 700

Expressing The Soul Of Something (Your Business, Yourself) Will Not Lead You To Its True Essence. To Do That You Must Express Its Spirit. ... 701

Not All Dreams Matter: ... 704

The Magic Man Is Godlike. ... 708

Mental Illness And The Channel Of Challenge: ... 709

Dark Seers, The Non-Resonant Dark Heart Of Gold, The Importance Of Not Trusting Most People, The One Frequency Of Absolute Truth, And What This Means For Dark Collaboration To Bring Forth Synergistic Genius…. ... 713

The Universe Responds To The Use Of Light (Or, The 7-Figure Thunderbolt Path To Awakening And Wild Success And Whether You're A Match For It) ... 717

It's Not Mind Over Body. It's Mind As Body. ... 720

Deep Success In Any Field (Love, Money, Health) Is Always About Striking The Precise Balance Of A Total Paradox. ... 721

Channeled Message From #Allthenonphysicalbeings Imploring Everyone To Stop Worshipping Them. ... 722

Integrity Is Your Ability To Hold Yourself Together As One ... 725

Your Value System Was Given To You As The Vehicle For Your Soul Evolution ... 727

But What About…..? (#Allthequestions) ... 728

The Magic Bask: Success Stories And Praise ... 730

BOOK THREE

THE DARK DOMAIN OF GENIUS

The Fine Print Before The End 760

The Takeover Of Consciousness 761

Mirror, Window, Portal: The Three Stages Of Awakening 765

The Wild Beast Of Genius 768

Your Dark Genius 769

Dark Codes Of Genius, Mad Archetypes And Shadow Alchemy In Action: The Work.. 770

Codes Of Money, Power, And Genius 776

Doing Shadow Work On Your Genius 780

The Light Cannot Deliver On It Promise Of Awakening 782

>   Livestream (Euphoria, Now Masters Of Magic), July 19, 2018
>   Livestream (Euphoria, Now Masters Of Magic), May 15, 2018

Shadow Work Vs Dark Work 784

The Hunger For The New 792

The Vampiric Nature Of A Dark Business 794

On Self-Loathing And The Highly Practical Benefits And Deep Joys Of Knowing Yourself As A Darkworker 796

Channeled Transmission: The Origin Of Consciousness And The Big Bang, The Source Of Anxiety And Form, The Journey Of Awakening And The True Purpose Of The Feminine Rising Movement: 799

The Master Map: Shadow, Light And Dark 802

Alien Poetry. How About Some Alien Language Fun?!?! 803

Acknowledgments 805

BOOK ONE:

THE SUMMONING

Shadowlands

This is dedicated to all

dragons of consciousness.

To those who live their lives

in the most remote and imperial,

elite and delightful,

terrifying and ingenious

fields of play;

and who love,

with every ounce of their dark heart of gold,

the truth that burns

in every bone.

You see, I want a lot.

Perhaps I want everything:

the darkness that comes with every infinite fall

and the shivering blaze of every step up.

So many live on and want nothing,

and are raised to the rank of prince

by the slippery ease of their light judgments.

But what you love to see are faces

that do work and feel thirst.

You love most of all those who need you

as they need a crowbar or a hoe.

You have not grown old, and it is not too late

to dive into your increasing depths

where life calmly gives out its own secret.

~ Rainer Maria Rilke

This is a book of magic.

A gathering of spells.

Pages that awaken.

A cast of activations that unlock channels of the genius mind.

These transmissions will vault you into your natural inheritance. The genealogy of witches and wizards, giants and dragons, all of which roam the land you long for. What you call home.

Whatever wakes you into your most transported state, that is what stirs within these pages.

Here you will find reservoirs of New Consciousness.

Deep scents of the most pure and potent energy emanating from the perfumed wells of the Dark Divine, who is making Her way in secret to the collective grid.

You will unearth the fantastical unfictional.

Stun open your magical mind, cast over yourself charms of metaphysical knowing and unleash within you a flowing charism of spiritual insight that feeds your work, your world, your waking.

You will learn the mysteries ancient schools kept secret.

As if power belongs only to a few.

As if Truth is dangerous.

As if you are not naturally magic.

You will receive codes and tones of living consciousness, of the newest, lightest Light.

Tunes that will vibrate the bones of your being in resonance with the treasure you seek, but which someone...everyone...buried in your sleep.

You will receive feasts of the mind, visit sprawling oases in the desert of understanding, thrum with the color and sound of the hidden Dance.

There will be sense.

There will be nonsense.

This book is a mystique, a masquerade.

A palace.

A shack in the forest.

A temple of divination to be visited the way you would any place of magic and wonder, and for the same reasons.

To open doors in the unimaginable realms.

To activate your spiritual channel.

To resurrect your genius.

The words within these pages offer you the same transported feeling that the carnival and the playground, the church and the temple, the synagogue and the mosque, the dance floor and the altar do now, or did when you visited or visit them.

And if you do not have an altar, this is that altar.

And if you do not have a dance floor, this is that dance floor.

And if you are far from playgrounds or churches, carnivals or mosques, this is that playground.

These words are every house of worship.

Portals that uplift your consciousness through arcs of insight, unsettle and float away your everyday mind so that the uncontested new, the dazzling energy of the gods, can make its way into you the way it did when you dizzied yourself into altered states when you were seven and the sun was setting and the grass was cooling and the twilight was upon you.

When I was a little girl, I read my way through my childhood because I felt out of place in the "real" world; the one everyone else navigated with such aplomb. From the time I can remember remembering, I did not feel welcome, or at home.

Fantasy fell around me when I read and when I wrote.

I could feel the slip and shift of energy and matter. Could see the sinuous tones of Time and the boister and presumption of Space as these two illusions moved in gravity and graceful dischord around each other.

With every comma, every letter, I stepped into and out of the Dance.

And when others read my words, they could not deny the movement in their heart.

They tumbled into trances, veins flooded with wonder.

And then craved more.

Write another chapter please. I heard over and over.

For years I dabbled and wrote on the side and promised myself one day I'd be a "real" writer. Someone who stayed permanently open behind the looking glass. But after college I abandoned my dream, convinced my love of reading and writing was simply how I *escaped* my pain instead of facing it.

So I packed that dream away along with all the others I branded foolish and childish and irresponsible, impossible, arrogant, and unreasonable, and so brandishing my weird and unreachable and unpopular self I went to work in cubicles and thousand-dollar suits and spent the rest of my time in therapist's offices and on calls with psychics and intuitives and psychoanalysts trying to fix whatever in me kept wanting to escape.

And then I almost killed myself.

And then I almost killed myself again.

The heart of a magical child is both tender and dark.

It is terrifying to itself and to others, like a pure dragon.

And its terror is where its power and magic lie.

In the elevated and in the deep realms, it seeks the golden fruit of nourishment and when properly fed, its spirit flies in the face of order and will not be ordered.

And this is what the world both longs for and loathes.

The heart of a magical child is a tender and dark dragon full of terror and nourishment.

In its elevated and deep realms are where the golden fruit of its purity lies.

When properly fed on how to seek and be sought, the world both longs for and loathes how it flies.

In the face of order, its spirit will not be ordered.

Years later, after my death, I realized that when I cracked open a book or placed words on slips of paper or tapped them into screens, I wasn't escaping, I was feeding myself.

In the cold empty desert of my childhood, I was nourishing my dragon nature.

In secret, and in fits and starts, stealing a speck of stardust. Hoarding a fleck of magic. In between the rage of my father and the brittle and invasive silence of my mother, cradling a word, a phrase, I kept myself alive.

Even though I terrified them with my impudent elegance, which I carried as all magical children do, proudly on my lips and defiantly in my eyes so that every adult knew.

Who was the true ruler here.

Even though this amplified the rage and the training. The shame and the shaming.

Until little by little I chose to hate and starve my own aliveness. My stark knowing.

And then one day I walked out of my precious play and into a suit of armor and shut the castle door.

But dragons are patient and exacting.

Full of integrity and noble oaths, they know how to tell Time.

None of which is in our fairy tales.

Why they burn their homes.

Crave nothing.

Do not sleep.

It was not my shame that almost killed me twice.

It was my dragon nature, coming for its pride:

For my dark heart of gold.

And my Gold Mind.

Both of which I'd thought were mine to dismiss, refuse to steward.

It took two nervous breakdowns, two suicidal scares, four mental illness diagnoses (the natural outbursts of my hindered dragon mind), being fired three times from executive positions in corporate America, and facing homelessness before I became willing to carve a throne in the middle of my life for my little girl, her dragon heart, and our magical mind.

And that is why I am here.

To tune you.

Which is the new teaching.

To warn you.

Of the true waking.

And to remind you where your place in the fury is.

You belong in the grand takeover of consciousness.

In the wild unopen middle of this.

Sweating and carving with all the others thousands of thrones out of thin air, in utter obedience to the dragon within, because it is time.

There is blood on the circus tents now.

Lions gnaw at the altar.

Thunder shakes the parquet floors and breaks the arcs of every broken covenant.

And we are gathering.

To summon the empty blueprint of the genius giant.

To weave the Dark Web through the 13th dimension into the infinite openness of the portals of the Diamond Mind, the Gold Mind and the new Dark Body.

To spring forth the radiance in our bones of light.

And hook the world to magic.

When I seed you, it is a feeding.

Codes of awakening carrying in the empty blueprint.

No more adhering.

This is about becoming unhinged.

Disobedient to the blueprint that exists.

And the constant exhaustion of questioning,

do I match the tones and frequencies exactingly?

And if not, where is my mercy?

We call down, from balconies built on tragedy.

THE PROMISE OF THE DARK

The Pledge

It is time for a new tone of truth to be made visible.

Once you can see it, you will be able to hear it. And once you hear it, you will know who you are and the source of all your struggle. You will also hear and be drawn to heed the harmonic call to deprogram the content of your consciousness so the truth of who you are can flow effortlessly through you. In other words, you will embark on an uprising. A resonant journey toward your giant nature. Once completed—and even before completion, at a critical mass along the way—you will activate the tipping point of consciousness in which you will reverse the effort of awakening and expend less and less energy on your growth. You will easily resound. Imperially and unequivocally, with one, unequal voice, you will stand out from the crowded consciousness as a frequency of strength and ingenuity that is unmistakably Itself. This occurs when you have full access to your power and once you have this, you will operate the essential energies of the universe with pure mastery and will create magic in your life and much more beyond. That beyond has to do with what lies in the Dark and your place in it and what happens when you move from being coded to decoding to encoding consciousness using the raw material of the universe—the codes of genius that are waking up from deep within every individual and the codes of chaos that are streaming in from the newest, lightest Light that has not yet made it to collective consciousness.

When your genius turns on before the codes of chaos have made it fully onto the planet, it is especially difficult for you. For you will be branded crazy.

If you are internally disoriented and questioning yourself and everything you have and are, this book will be your sanctuary. The place you will learn about the New Sanity you have stepped into.

It will also be your silent killer, the Dark Goddess of Awakening, who will rattle your cages until you set yourself free.

You will feel profound relief in these pages.

Extreme forms of hope are here for you.

(And terror.)

An understanding of your true power and business on the planet and why it's been so hard to hang out down here, make a living, have friends and lovers and family who actually get you. And yet these pages are also your meathook and will keep you hanging until the last word of your illusion is turned from flesh to earth and you are nothing but bone.

And then we wake up your innermost codes and this is when you lift off into your genius giant nature. Your true form.

Magnetic and brilliant, emanating the blacklight of the Gods.

And then you receive your inheritance of super health, genius, riches, synchronization of your greatest powers and entrance into the UnTribe of others just like you who are also learning how to live in a world unprepared for the repellent love that lives in their dark heart of gold.

The Turn

But first you must know the Truth. How to deal with the insistent gathering of invisible and stifling content in your mind and with the inhuman and unruly beast of genius that lies deep within you and feeds on chaos.

This is the problem of consciousness.

Someone or something or a collection of beings and things is your energy and power source. Find the source and you've discovered the identity of energy. Its root-level laws and behaviors. Master these and now you are behind the curtain with your hand on the controls. You have become not the consumer but the curator of your own consciousness and therefore of your reality, inside and out, because as you know:

As above, so below.

As within, so without.

And then you are faced with the great unhooking which inevitably happens as you unzip from the human design you've been blueprinted with and begin making your way toward the dark room to where your genius lies, where you will join the Master Handlers who are crafting themselves and the collective consciousness from the wild, chaotic new.

This is not for the faint of heart.

It is the work of spiritual giants. Those who have fully lifted off into the truth of who they are, leaving behind the world of the humans and choosing the world of gods and archetypes, those who craft the new myths, weave the new stories and make possible new ways of being the incarnated divine.

And then the problem of consciousness is solved.

When I discovered the truth about the energetics of power and consciousness, I took myself through a rapid spiritual awakening that defied logic and reason, western medicine and training, the culture of incremental growth and the accepted wisdom of mental health and went from being a jobless single mom of 43 facing homelessness, having just recovered from my second nervous breakdown and being diagnosed with bipolar, PTSD, severe mood and anxiety disorder and two forms of ADD and with my psychiatrist urging me to take medication, to being a recognized leader and innovator in the field of consciousness and a spiritual millionaire in just ten months. I defied the rules and the pleas and came out of nowhere to build a powerful transformational movement, teaching and transforming thousands with similar struggles, using the spiritual technologies and new tools of consciousness I invented and used on myself. Later on you will read about their miraculous changes in money, love, health, and psychic abilities and hear in their own words why they say these are the most potent and ground-breaking transmissions on consciousness, energy, magic and spiritual awakening being offered anywhere on the planet.

When I say this is magical, I mean it.

When I say it is the answer and the end to your spiritual seeking, I mean it.

When I say this is the next evolution of consciousness, so new it's not being taught by any of the spiritual luminaries, living or dead, I mean it.

And yes, I'm aware how crazy and arrogant that may sound.

But look at them.

It's said that the night before Siddhartha became enlightened, he was challenged by a demon who claimed the throne of enlightenment for himself, declared his own spiritual achievements to be greater than Siddhartha's and challenging him to produce someone who would speak for him.

"The earth is my witness," Siddhartha said, and reached down and touched the ground.

And the world shook and roared in resonance, "I BEAR YOU WITNESS," and the morning star shon in the sky and Siddhartha became the Buddha, the Enlightened One.

Earth Certification. That's what he got.

I did something a bit more radical, because the final stage of awakening is not enlightenment, but enDarkenment, and in that state of consciousness there is no one and nothing to speak for you.

And that is the point.

And that is the final trial.

And that is why it's so terrifying.

You must speak into the void and cause your own divinity consciousness to leap into being.

You must lift yourself up into direct contact with your own divine standing. You must deliver to yourself, in visceral, imperial and electromagnetic fields of new energy, the knowledge that you are the true and complete source of your own power and that no one and nothing has power over you. And then using new spiritual technologies, you must cause this to be your new, effortless reality.

This is the way you liberate yourself from the constraints of human consciousness and become able to operate with pure grace and aplomb *within* the very paradigm you're shattering.

It all happens at a point in the evolution of consciousness I call the Meathook Moment of Awakening, based on the myth of Inanna, the Dark Goddess and Sumerian Queen of Heaven and Earth, in which she descends a long, stone staircase into the pit of the earth, is divested of all her finery until she stands at the bottom naked and alone and then, if that wasn't bad enough, is lifted onto a meathook, hangs there for three days, turns to nothing but bone, and then is lifted off, walks back up the stairs, receives all her finery and returns to the surface of the earth, arrayed in all her glory once again.

What happens on the meathook cannot be spoken of without falling *ad infinitum* into paradox and nonsense, but suffice it to say that it is the most terrifying, maddening, opaque, resistant and *liberating* moment in consciousness.

And, it looks to all the world and to your human awareness as if you're going completely insane.

If your friends and family haven't beseeched you to seek professional help—and most likely medication—during the "tumble down the stairs", I guarantee they'll do it during your time hanging off the hook of human consciousness out over the Nothing.

And yet this stage is essential for anyone who desires to activate their divine nature.

I knew this. And I'd been avoiding it.

I'd tumble down the stairs of my life, take one look at the meathook and run scared back up to the light, only to tumble down once again.

This is because if you're a born disruptor, the meathook is the *gravitational point of your true nature*.

This time though, since my options were suicide or some kind of unknown and only slightly less terrifying, self-induced energetic death—on the other side of which I knew in my bones would be *true life*—I stayed still and let the moment take me.

And when it was over, which took about a month, I rested for a few months, and then when I knew it was time, declared myself a spiritual genius who had gone sane, flipped my mental illness on its head and went from broke, bipolar and suicidal and being told by my psychiatrist I needed to be on two forms of medication just to stabilize, to creating deep emotional and mental stability on my own, *without* medication, inventing a new spiritual technology to both activate and maintain my new state of being, and becoming the successful CEO of a seven-figure spiritual transformational business in ten months.

Working part time.

And breaking all the rules and records in my industry for how business had to be done.

I now have a group of over 3800 members who resonate deeply with my message, many of whom have been called crazy, misfits and outcasts in their own worlds and whose lives have not been just mentally and emotionally changed but materially improved by applying what I teach. I hear from people all the time that they went from broke to rich using my (de)programs and from depressed to thriving and *without the need for pills*. And these are people who've done #allthethings to try and do what they were finally able to do with this new way of working with the energetics of consciousness.

And just two years ago, I was seriously considering killing myself.

I was recovering from my second nervous breakdown, had been recently diagnosed with bipolar 2 and PTSD (on top of the severe mood and anxiety disorder and two types of ADD I was diagnosed with a few years earlier), had just gotten fired for the third time from my role as a top executive in corporate America and only had $1400 to my name.

Not even Starbucks was going to hire an ex corporate executive with a resume like Swiss cheese. Take one look at my life on that piece of paper and there was clearly something wrong with me.

I was company kryptonite.

Plus, I'd already spent four years spiraling into hell, burning through $250,000 of savings and investments trying to build my own business, drinking every day, not getting out of bed for a week, schlepping across Chicago in the dead of winter and the pitch black of early morning delivering laundry for fourteen bucks an hour, and completely unable to go back to a regular job or get my own business off the ground because my mind kept leaping out with its fangs and its claws and destroying my relationships, my resolve, my focus, my health, my confidence, my emotional stability, my sense of self.

Then one day in bed contemplating how to kill myself, I read an article in the *New York Times Magazine* about Carl Jung and his crazy *Red Book*. And then the next day I read about Marion Woodman, a renowned Jungian analyst, who refused to take pills during *her* psychotic break because she said they numb the body, which we need fully alert because it's the very vessel for our awakening, and that's when I decided fuck it.

I knew in my dark heart of gold there was nothing actually wrong with me and that it was my shame and my shadow that were killing me, not the strange (de)condition of my mind, so I went against the well-intentioned guidance of my psychiatrist and decided not to take pills—fully aware of the concerning "consciousness catch 22" of using my diagnosed mentally ill mind to decide how to *handle* said mind—and instead invented and then took myself through the set of spiritual technologies I mentioned earlier, which upgraded my consciousness and all my physical and non-physical systems so I could handle the pure potent and high octane energy of my genius mind and not spin mentally out of control, become emotionally destroyed or fall physically ill.

And as I applied these new spiritual tools, my life flew to new heights I couldn't possibly have imagined.

I'll never forget the look on my psychiatrist's face when I told her I'd made fifteen grand in two weeks. And then when it became thirty grand in a month. And then I ended my sessions because my own spiritual and energetic techniques were far more effective.

And my clients regularly had their own astonishing results. Several of them saw spontaneous disappearances of physical conditions they'd had for years. One woman's hair had been falling out for 16 years no matter what she tried and after one session with me, it stopped. Another woman had a skin condition for forty years and after three weeks of working with me, it cleared up. Others came to me suicidally depressed and on medication and were able to throw the meds away after a few months. Others went from being on the brink of divorce to madly in love in weeks. And the money. The money results were crazy.

It's been two years now, and my mind and body are the picture of health.

Ok maybe not "health" because I'm sure many highly trained doctors and therapists and psychiatrists would say there's something quite wrong with me for saying all the "crazy" things I do, so let's say the picture of *stability, euphoria and success.*

No manic highs followed by crazy lows.

No insane mood swings.

Just up. Flowing. Euphoria. And successful? Well, I'd say heading into my second million and being a serial entrepreneur (my business partner and I have just started a new company that's the intersection of super-nutrition, spirituality and esoteric wisdom), counts as being the picture of success.

Because here's the deal. The reason you're suffering is *not* because of your crazy mind. Your crazy mind is your greatest blessing, the portal to higher consciousness and the channel for your genius.

You're suffering because you're streaming high octane energy through your *shadow* and your *human consciousness* and *that's* what's making your brain and body sick.

The fields that run your human consciousness were never built to run divine energy alone. And when you try to, it's hell.

You have an entirely other energetic blueprint that holds an infinite capacity to run your true nature without ever shorting out and when you activate *that*, it's *heaven on earth*.

And to do that, you must *go fully sane* and step in to your divine nature without reservation, apology or justification and in a way that channels your genius through a completely different energetic system. Then your body and mind become what they're meant to be: vessels that express the new consciousness through creative, visionary genius. Master handlers and artisans of the shimmering, pure Dark, which is the newest, lightest light that has not yet made it to our collective consciousness, and which you, my friend, are here to bring to the world.

And when you do, the most wonderful thing happens.

That other planetary home where you're convinced you belong? The one you've been dreaming about and wishing you lived on since you were a kid?

That becomes *this one right here,* because the energetics of consciousness have shifted and it is now the age of *you* and your crazy mind and your equally crazy *UnTribe*—that host of other aberrantly wired creative geniuses and spiritual visionaries who are here to change the world with you.

And, yes. You'll still have your detractors and naysayers. I've been called a cult leader, a narcissist and a crazy, cold hearted bitch. And not just in private but publicly, by friends and former clients.

But none of it phased me or impacted my reputation or success because I know that no one and nothing has power over me, that I am built for magic, wired for genius and *thriving is my natural state*. And the same is true for you.

What humans *really* want—and the reason Hollywood is replete with films about superheroes, biohacking has gained such popularity and extreme sports are on the rise—is to be who we truly are: superhuman.

And if humans want that, they will have to open the portal that takes them there and that means removing the ceiling in their mind and the floor to their fear and that is the *definition* of going sane.

And the good news is you're already more than halfway there.

You did not fall asleep and wake up at the wrong stop on the universal bus route and figure here was as good as anywhere.

You came to create new myths with your genius. New pathways for others to access their own divine nature.

It's your dream, isn't it, to have giants on the land?

Mine, too.

And so from the vast warehouse of all possible states of being we selected a mind without a ceiling and fear with no floor so we could use our madness the way it's meant to be: as the bridge to our individual and collective divinity.

So hear me when I say.

Your mental illness is *magical*.

You selected it with great purpose.

Because you looked down and saw that it is the Age of enDarkenment.

And in your own dark heart of gold, you knew it was time to thrive.

Because here's the thing. YOU have equal genius to any of the spiritual luminaries who have come before you, because YOU are a god just like they were and are. Genius is in your bones, literally. It is time we stop cloying and couching ourselves before the spiritual greats who've come before us, as if they are a different species than we. They are not. It is time, it's past time, to take your place alongside all the spiritual greats and step into your own genius, giant nature.

Many have already been transformed by these teachings, all of whom say they've never heard or learned of this knowledge in any of the decades of reading, retreats, workshops, or certifications they've done, and these are people who have studied with the greatest spiritual figures in the world, and who have even built their own reputations as spiritual influencers, teachers and mentors. And yet they are still struggling, depressed, lost, seeking, wandering, angry, frustrated, ready to throw in the towel, press "restart" and come down for another try.

And yet in a matter of months with these teachings they create wealth, wellbeing and influence on their terms and see their genius explode to new levels, accelerating and amplifying its impact on others.

This is what I want for you, more than anything, because this isn't just esoteric knowledge meant for monks to pour over in their cells in candlelight and strict silence.

This knowledge is not only infinite, it is practical. It cares about you particularly.

Not in the way we think about caring—meaning being attached to an outcome, no. And not in the way we orient ourselves towards emotions—as benefiting our state of being or detracting from it. Again, no. This knowledge is simply conscious of you, though you are not yet conscious of it. And it is conscious of you in a detailed and specific manner. It has the ability to shape itself around your practical concerns, your daily, lived life, and bring the world of magic past the intersections of your grief, through the construction zones of your struggle, right to your temple door.

It is my mission to demystify magic and spiritual awakening for you. To unveil the workings of energy and consciousness, the true root of thriving and the path to stepping into the state we all so deeply desire and which all teachings have aided in making more clear than before, but which could only go so far, because the answer lies not in the Light, but in the Dark. The newest, lightest light, which has not yet made it to collective consciousness. Shadow, what most of us mean when we say "dark" is light that has denied its power. It is the densest and most illusion-steeped consciousness there is. And those who have given in to it completely are what we call "evil" (even though there's no such kind of morality at play in divinity consciousness.). This is completely different than working in and with the consciousness of the Dark.

The domain of this field of dark energy is imperial, mystical and edgy, and the experience of living and operating from deep within this unsystematized consciousness is nothing like living in the bounding eagerness of the Light Grid. Dark Consciousness is playful and terrifying.

The highest frequency consciousness there is. It is where the Absolute New is being created from nothing. It is where geniuses hang out.

And our spiritual teachings up until now have fallen short of being able to guide us into the final stage of awakening, that VIP back room of consciousness, because all our myths, fairytales and spiritual traditions fall silent at the point where the hallway goes dark. There's a bouncer at the door and the password is not "enlightenment," but "enDarkenment. Do you really think the Titans of the Universe, the Architects of Genius, are back there singing Kumbaya and spinning their chakras with sickly benevolent grins plastered on their faces?

No. That is the product of the weak imagination of the human trying to conceive what gods and archetypes could possibly be doing back there, behind the Ultimate Curtain.

I'll tell you what they're doing.

They're smoking $7,200 Elie Bleu Red de Alba Cuban cigars as they toy nonchalantly with impossibly unstable, dangerously explosive, potentially obliterating and yet delectably new Potions of Consciousness, which bubble away happily in all manner of glass tubes and vials while their Alchemist Handlers sidle up to Dark-skinned, sacred prostitutes who slither endlessly on long poles of awareness as the room fills with weird scents and everyone breathes in the sound of Miles Davis' "Bitches Brew" drifting through the thick, Dark air.

They're also pulling pranks.

Laughing uproariously at Nothing.

Because they're so light-hearted, you see. Practical Jokers Extraordinaire.

Just before the atmosphere, the tone of the room, gets too heavy—which is usually due to someone (most likely the MythMaker) momentarily forgetting that there are no stakes and that Nothing really matters (in other words, it's all dark energy)—you can bet someone else (probably The Activator) is putting a whoopee cushion on someone's (probably the Blind

Seer's) $33,000, hand-embroidered, vermillion Louis XIV chair, or, or…gliding down the hallway into the crowded dance club of the collective consciousness to slip a little wink and a nod from the Dark into our very human drink.

Not to doze us off, but to wake us up.

And where we wake is in a black room, attended to by Nothing and No One, where we discover we are hanging from a meat hook and have turned to nothing but bone.

We cry out. And hear Nothing.

We writhe. And Nothing changes.

We scream. And Nothing happens.

And then at the still point, which we reach and hold not with limp resignation but with eminent poise, we realize the repleteness of what we have heard and of what has changed and of what has actually happened.

The Nothing has happened to us.

And suddenly we find ourselves rising.

Lifted off the meathook.

And as our bones touch the ground of our Being, we activate the framework of our genius, and a new Dark Body spins itself up and around us and forms itself into a new, energetic anatomy that now operates in place of our Soul, not as a surge protector between our human consciousness and the raw material of the universe, but as a transformer and amplifier of this most potent energy. And we have become a god.

One who operates chaos with mastery and imperial grace. Who streams genius down and onto the Light Grid as new thought forms and expressions of divinity consciousness.

This requires skill no human possesses, because the human consciousness is an artifact of illusion, requiring order to operate. But genius, chaos by another name, is dis-order of a higher order. It can only be handled by our giant blueprint, and this is a blueprint of the void. The unpredictable, a-human, a-temporal majesty of power that submits to Nothing.

This makes it appear to twho cannot see in the Dark, exactly like that sister field of consciousness, shadow. And this means you have been doing shadow work on your genius, and when you do that you trespass on dark territory, for in the heart of every myth and story of spiritual awakening lies a grave untruth about how to handle the darkness that lies beyond the light.

The truth is far simpler, and much more terrifying, than we imagined—which is why our stories go mute at the same place where the hallway goes dark.

But they must speak, for they are our guides.

And so they come back from the threshold and lie about it.

Scrawl across the land they were incapable of visiting *hic sunt dracones*.

Spread out the map they have no business teaching and point.

Here be dragons they whisper.

How right they were.

Your shadow and your genius are the same energetic substance. It simply changes dimension to meet you where you are.

The difference between the two?

Nothing.

In other words, everything.

The meathook moment of awakening is the place at which you decide whether your shadow is your devil or your god, the angel of death or the angel of awakening. It is the tipping point in human consciousness in which we intend, and create it to be so, that it is both, and it is for us to decide when and whether and how and to what degree, it is one or the other.

It is time to place your hand on the true controls of your life and alchemize the architecture of your consciousness into whatever you want it to be. Your natality becomes ground for breakthroughs of your own choosing. And you go from being lorded over by the arrangement of archetypal energies patterned into your consciousness, to lording over yourself. In other words, to creating yourself as *you* intend and wish to be, not as your Soul intended and desired.

You are not your Soul. You are individuated Spirit. Energized divinity. Your Soul was simply an intermediary, an energetic pulse of grandeur, not the full stream of it. And this is because our human consciousness needed to be lied to long enough for it to build something that can act as a springboard into our genius, giant nature.

The giant in us, *as* us, is the one capable of handling this potent, chaotic material of consciousness.

In the hands of the human, it destroys.

Destroys minds.

Destroys bodies.

Yes, it creates impeccable newness, in art, science, music, philosophy, literature, film, you name it. But more often that not, it leaves the human wrecked and wretched. And so we have come to fear it and believe that we must chose between genius and health. Between that which we long to be and that which sustains life.

This is only because human consciousness is young, too immature, incapable of handling the codes of destruction, the beasts of genius, that feed on chaos deep in the heart of all that matters, and which are becoming more and more restless, calling to us to wake to our true nature.

Genius is in our bones. Literally. The codes of our genius lie not in our Light body, where all our Light Codes—the codes of our human consciousness—lie, but deep in our bones, which are the only aspect of our physical frame that are utterly still.

This is why the final stage of awakening, depicted by Inanna, The Dark Goddess Sumerian Queen, is one in which we hang out over the Nothing until we are nothing but bone, and in the stillpoint of our fresh nature, activate the dark codes of genius that lie dormant there.

We can either train our human eye onto this moment, which pulls it into the dimension of Light and therefore casts it in deep shadow, and then we see it as most of human consciousness, and certainly as Western culture and medicine, does: as terrifying, morbid, grotesque and insane. As our inner devil and destroyer and therefore as the absolute opposite of awakening.

Or we can train our inhuman, our divine eye, onto this moment, which exposes it as a primary dimension and expression of the Dark, and seen in this newest, lightest Light, the moment is able to turn everything that matters, the entire body of consciousness into Nothing. And in the repleteness of what is exposed, the New Void, our genius is freed into itself and becomes the bridge to Nothing, and over Nothing.

This practice of training our genius onto our shadow is called shadow alchemy. It is a new energetic technology or encoding practice that I invented to be able to directly handle and work with my genius and with the raw material of the universe, so I could wield the full thrust of my power, inventiveness and brilliance without dimming or dumbing or numbing it down with drugs, or having it run wild over my life and nearly kill me, which it almost did. Twice.

It is the reason I was able to go from broke, bipolar and suicidal to a seven figure spiritual entrepreneur and online influencer in just ten months, and why I have been able to run and build my business for two years without medication, and from a place of emotional euphoria and mental thriving, in spite of my several mental illness diagnoses—bipolar 2, PTSD, severe mood and anxiety disorder and two forms of ADD—which ruled over and ruined my life for decades.

And it is the reason my clients go from struggling to successful in a matter of weeks.

Shadow alchemy is the practice of adjusting the aperture of our willingness to see ourselves as and be seen as an aberration, a god of consciousness.

It is also the mechanism that activates the Anti-Hero's journey, the third and final stage on the path to awakening and the end, and the answer to, all our seeking.

Through it we learn to see in the Dark.

And agree to become monstrous.

One by one, we are returning to our giant posture, solidifying the giant blueprint. I see it every day in my work. People exploding into geniuses and creating drastic, rapid changes in their practical, lived life.

I am here to create and expose the extra, hidden pathways for us to access this giant place and to help you remember what it's like to touch your genius giant nature, because it is time to have giants on the land. To turn you and you and you into your native strength.

The Prestige

To do this, you must go sane.

You must open your portal for intuition and beyond intuition, to your psychic abilities (which we are all coded with).

And, if you are already feeling the sting and the push down the infinite staircase of your mind, know that your mental illness is magical.

It is the pathway to your spiritual genius and the bridge to accessing the new success blueprint. You simply need to know how to metabolize this potent potion in a way that does not dumb the body or destroy the structures in your life too completely. Pills do not metabolize the genius within mental illness. They just numb the body's ability to channel it. And modern psychiatric and psychological practices are woefully ill-equipped to teach you how. Because a degree of destruction is necessary, and they don't understand this and can't help you refine your genius for destruction so that you take a surgical precision to the structures in your mind and your life. Handling mental illness this way is energetic brain surgery. Many codes of consciousness are meant to be destroyed, and certain ones need to be left intact so they can become the new grid onto which your new psyche and thriving can be built. That's all I'll say for now about that. I'll leave the rest for the beyond in this book.)

But suffice it to say, this is what I have discovered, and what I am here to teach you. The way to go sane and step into the final stage of awakening so your life can be one magic act after another.

And not only, but the you who is reading this who may not yet be tumbling, but who knows, deep down, that the rumble is there. That the tectonic plates of your mind and spirit are shifting without your conscious consent, and the tsunami that will take your life and reduce it to rubble is quietly growing, far beyond your sight. That's because this is happening for everyone. There's an unsettling drifting itself over our collective consciousness and we no longer have the luxury of ignoring it. It is why the self help field is a ten billion dollar industry and growing.

It is also why suicide and anxiety is rising all over the planet.

And everything we have tried has only gotten us so far and it is not nearly far enough.

This is not white-knuckle, lightworker spirituality (the kind that doesn't, ultimately, work).

This is an invitation to run through the content of your consciousness in a way you never have before. Not by treating it as matter to be traversed. In other words, not by treating it as something that matters, but by doing exactly the opposite. By treating this precious content of your consciousness, what you dream to be You, as immaterial. As that which does not in any way matter. In other words, we are going to activate negative space in your mind so that you can treat of the content there in a way that once and for all alchemizes it into its proper and intended nature so that it does not continually trip you up but instead amplifies your energy, power, knowledge, success, wellbeing and ingenuity at all times and in all ways.

In order to do this, you cannot bring this immaterial tone of truth into the light, for that is not where it resides and it will not lower its frequency to be brought there. You have to go to it. To its where the newest, lightest light is being born and prepared for us. And that means you are going on a journey with me, through the final stage of the evolution of consciousness, so that you can shrug off the cloak of the wanderer, the sandals of spiritual seeker, the dust of the constant shadow-worker, and take up your place as an artisan of consciousness, a creative and spiritual genius striding the earth as a god. For this is nothing less than the trip from human to divinity consciousness. A trip that can finally be completed, for it was always meant to be completed.

You are not meant to seek forever, wandering the desert with your spiritual tribe until you die. You are meant to find your UnTribe. And I have come to take you there, because you asked

three

three

Your neurosis is your entry to the numinous.

You are quite right, the main interest of my work is not concerned with the treatment of neuroses but rather with the approach to the numinous. But the fact is that the approach to the numinous is the real therapy and inasmuch as you attain to the numinous experiences you are released from the curse of pathology. Even the very disease takes on a numinous character. - C. G. Jung Letters 1, pg 37

What we are pioneering is

NOTHING SHORT OF A RADICAL DEPARTURE

from treating neuroses as the CURSE

to treating it as the BLESSING

and the BRIDGE

that it is...

to the NUMINOUS.

WE ARE THE BRIDGE BUILDERS to heaven on earth.

And we are not building the bridge TO heaven FROM earth

we are building the bridge TO and FROM

NOTHING.

Because the ability to stand in power and grace

OVER NOTHING

is the precise definition

of what it means to fly.

To lift off from our human confines in the neurotic conditioning of the anxious brain —

which EVERYONE displays, just in different doses,

and accept the invitation from the NUMINOUS MIND that is our BIRTHRIGHT,

to live in the world of SuperImagining,

the CREATIVE FANCIES

of the GOD AT PLAY

who is not concerned with madness, because It knows

MADNESS is but dys-functioning GENIUS,

BEASTS OF THE NEW

that have simply resisted our HEROIC ATTEMPTS TO KILL THEM

TAME THEM

MASTER THEM

through our myths—which are nothing more than PRISONS OF THINKING—

and are waiting patiently for us beyond the edges of our conditioned minds

in the LAND WHERE DRAGONS PROWL

for the ANTI-HERO who has gone from

CONTROLLING ENERGY (medication, therapy, twelve steps, shadow work, enlightenment)

to ALCHEMIZING IT (shadow alchemy, chaos alchemy, enDarkenment)

and has therefore EARNED THE ABILITY

—already NATIVE within him due to his NEUROTIC DRIVE

that sees EVERYTHING AND NOTHING all at once—

to STAND IN THE GAP

occupied by these ARCHITECTS OF AWAKENING—

these mad genes of the SuperConscious—

and instead of KILLING, TAMING or MASTERING their WILD ENERGY

knows how to make them

DANCE.

THE STIFLING MIMICRY OF THE LIGHT GRID

As you can probably imagine, the answer to erupting your genius and making it the source of wild success on your own terms—and finally ending the decades-long uncivil war that's been raging inside you and threatening to take your life out at the knees—will not be found by following any of the rules.

Including the dreams of your child.

Genius comes from inhabiting a harmful, disastrous, elemental and exacting state of being that would kill a child and nearly kills full-grown adults (most of whom are still children anyway).

It is also the state of being you crave.

Imagine the one food you cannot, no matter how many pounds of fat Oprah piles next to you to demonstrate how much weight you'd gain were you to eat it every day until you passed out, resist.

That is how you feel about streaming your genius.

It is your secret obsession. And one you feel terribly guilty of desiring because it's so uppity of you to conceive that you could, and also because you feel completely unfit to handle what would happen if you did.

And yet more than anything, you want to know yourself as a genius. You want to see evidence of it everywhere. In your love life. In your home, car, clothes, vacation spots. In your work in the world.

The only reason you're dissatisfied in any area of your life is because it does not reflect your genius, giant nature. Even physically. Genius Giants are not fat, lazy, or with thick rolls of belly fat. They are lithe, structured like gods, and casually alarm passers-by with their physique, stature, gait and grasp of supreme poise.

To be master of energy means to carve energy into matter with precision. Not to learn how to live with and pretend to love matter than spills over itself and prevents you from leaping or flight.

And to expose this in your life you must inhabit a state of being you've been running from your whole life and are bound and determined to never be. The state of being you spent all your energy trying to prove you are not endemically prone to. (When everyone around you can clearly see you are.)

Everywhere you go, you throw fireballs, my therapist said to me. *It's like it's licking the hems of your robes and setting everything on fire. STOP SETTING THE WORLD ON FIRE*, she said.

And so we settle in to do decades of shadow work on our genius.

The reason you're running from your genius, giant nature is because you're being viewed through the lens meant for viewing humanity by a tribe only capable of seeing human, so all they see is something monstrous.

The consciousness you were handed came factory-loaded with a value system and set of principles, untruths, beliefs and desires that do not serve or match your fields of truth, genius and natural affinities, and it was handed to you by a tribe who does not know you and cannot see you and who has focused on teaching you how to survive, when for you, their survival tactics not only dis-serve your basic functioning, but cause you to become only capable of imagining killing yourself because your innate M.O. is coded almost entirely opposite of theirs.

And theirs, at least up until now, is how the whole world has been built.

Humans have two sets of codes; those that govern survival and those that govern thriving. But for you, survival and thriving have the same code structure.

The only thing you spend your time doing is trying to determine whether the condition of your life meets your requirement that it be euphoric, and that means you're consumed with one of two thoughts at any given time:

One: *Am I wildly euphoric yet?*

I'm certainly happy. But I don't think I'm wildly euphoric in this job/marriage/career/relationship. It was great for a while. But it's really gone downhill. I think that means it needs to end, and that I need to move on to the next one. The better one. The one that will hopefully be where I am definitely, without a doubt, wildly euphoric. Or maybe everything is fine and I'm just an arrogant crazy bitch who needs to learn to be happy with what I have…

Two: *I'm miserable.*

I'm definitely not wildly euphoric in this job/marriage/career/relationship. Is it me, or is it them? As long as I know the answer to that, I'll do whatever it takes and I mean whatever the fuck it takes, to change it. If it's me, I'll change me. If it's them, I'll change them and if I can't change them, I'll leave. Just like that. I love 'em but I'm here to be euphoric. I'm just not sure if it's me or if it's them. It's probably me. I'm probably just an arrogant crazy bitch who needs to learn to be happy with what I have.

This, my friend, is called the Spiral of Despair and my guess is you've been on it for a LONG time. It probably feels like you're riding an infinitely rotating, sickeningly high Ferris Wheel with No One at the controls way down there.

You are. You are on that Ferris wheel and the horrific news—and the incredible news—is that you are never getting off. No One's at the controls because this paradigm is the one you picked to live your life through, and you can either see it as a nightmare you're trapped in or a CIRCUS RIDE you get to be on for the rest of your life.

Do you know how many people would love to have picked a CIRCUS for their paradigm of consciousness?

How many instead picked…say…SCHOOL?

How many LightWorkers do you know whom you now realize picked SCHOOL as the overarching metaphor in which they will always experience their lives?

Graduating from one level of self mastery to the next.

Striving for the "A" in Consciousness and the passing grade in Peace of Mind and trying not to fail at Oneness with All.

Working for lifetimes on their PhD in Self Mastery.

What's the lesson you learned from this? They're always fucking asking themselves until they die.

Don't get me wrong. I loved school. I was a straight A student from the time I cracked open my first book until I graduated college. And then I was DONE. I wanted to LIVE a little. Of course, I couldn't figure out exactly how to do that, which is why I ended up wanting to kill myself, until I realized I am not, and never was, in the School of Life. I picked the Circus of Consciousness for my playground of growth. And then I spent about a year alternately exactingly thrilled and energetically sick to my stomach as my own personal Ferris Wheel sent me spinning through one rapid up-level after another.

It's a bit of a mindfuck to go from broke to a million in ten months. When I did the calculations in October of 2018, I realized I'd averaged $100,000 a month from the day I opened my doors. That will put anyone's human consciousness into a tailspin for sure. It's the same reason astronauts throw up when they start space training. When we enter radically new dimensions of capacity, our human massively struggles to orient and re-orient and re-orient its internal balancing systems to every new position and when you're operating in the dimension of genius, which flies fast and furious from the word "GO," there are just way too many new positions and speeds flying at our human for it to be able to keep up.

The way to stop the Ferris Wheel from feeling like a nightmare is to stop orienting yourself to the dimensions of your human and shift into the being within you that is already mapped to every dimension possible and who therefore does not get dizzy at the thought of you spending your life spinning through cycles of consciousness and degrees of genius.

And the way to do that is to own that you are, in fact, an arrogant, crazy bitch (or your version of the barrage of adjectives you've been accused of being since you were a kid that everyone around you gathered up as evidence of how much help you needed and how inhospitable you were to live with or employ or befriend or understand or love or support).

In other words, you must go in search of the *nightmare* of youth, *not* the dream, because the dream was usually the place in your psyche that you concocted and inhabited in order to escape from the nightmare of being you.

Why did I dream of being a writer, a teacher or a priest?

Because those were ways I could finally prove to the world I was a useful, brilliant human, which would get me praise and approval and acceptance from the tribe and not constant accusations of being an arrogant, crazy bitch.

Those might not have been the adjectives hurled at you by your best friend or balled up into wads of paper and spit into the back of your hair, or launched at you by your boyfriend or mom or boss. But I guarantee that you have a secret stash of "I must prove to the world I'm not _____." And that, if you look back on your core relationships that have failed and systems and paradigms within which you failed, was all was due to you being _____, which was anathema to the way the system was set up.

This is because genius is monstrous.

It is also effortless. (That's why they call the most effortless state of excellence your "zone of genius." ((And it's way beyond excellence, because excellence is what you get when you master the Light Grid. And excellence is ultimately empty. Genius is never full, because it comes from chaos, which is the void. So it can also never be empty. As I said earlier, genius is a state of being, first and foremost, from which infinite content pours. It is not a condition of being full or empty. And that is why it is the ultimate, and only, fulfilling state of being.))

And so, being both monstrous and effortless, it's what you simply do. And who you simply are. Without even trying. But for most others, who are not interested in extending themselves far beyond their human conditioning, having a monster in their midst is alarming, unsettling, frustrating and really fucking annoying.

They are all about order. Lining up neat paradigms and making sure they are all in their place. This genuinely makes them happy.

And you? It makes you want to shoot yourself.

The fundamental paradigms of tribal consciousness, the very ones that have been built to allow humans to survive, are your stomping grounds. Not your sacred cathedral.

There is nothing "sacred" about your genius. Which is why you take such delight in destroying what is sacred to others (and then thinking there must be something terribly wrong with you).

And I don't mean destroying walls or cars, although you'll very likely get to the point of physical destruction if you don't express the energetic version freely enough. Your propensity to destroy will have its time on the planet, one way or the other. And since genius cares about Nothing, how it gets expressed can get pretty fucking ugly.

It will either shoot out sideways—throwing cell phones across living rooms and careening a car into the back of a parked semi, for instance—or straight ahead and with surgical precision and high-minded intention—in deftly dismantling the mental programming of a client or the global programming of the system of human archetypal consciousness.

The choice is yours.

Live a life of wreaked havoc: struggling, suicidal, sick, depressed, relationships in ruins, dreams in tatters (shredded by the nightmare run wild).

Or live a life of sculpted chaos: thriving, euphoric, wildly alive, gigantically expressed, relationships in high relief, dreams unimaginably accelerated.

And to do the latter you must shrug off the stifling mimicry of the Light Grid and correct the glitch in light consciousness for yourself first.

You must take yourself from being coded to decoding and then finally encoding consciousness.

That's what shattering paradigms results in, when you do it with craft and class. The whole point is not to destroy absolutely everything. It's to destroy everything but the essential framework so a new encoding can begin. You know this about yourself: You aren't a willy-nilly destroyer. If you look carefully through the microscope of your life, you'll see there are certain ways of destroying that bring you incredible glee. And those ways, you will also discover, if you peer even closer in and then zoom even further out, are for a great and terrible and noble and heartfelt purpose. #amiright?

Yes, I'm right. Because I know you.

By heart.

The Decision, In Relief

No one can tell you how to be. No one can even tell how you're actually being.

And they also therefore can't help you see your genius, how it's meant to change people's lives, or how you're meant to speak to the ones who are meant to be moved by you.

So that means, in practical terms...?

There aren't yet any coaches or business guides or gurus or programs that can really, deeply, accurately launch your genius out into the world.

You'll be mis-marketing from day one. Missing the mark completely for how to speak to your UnTribe, because your LightWorker mentor or guide will most likely cringe at your crazy ideas for hour message or marketing or your off-color or far too edgy or not-professional-enough-and-Lightworker-y branding.

Where is the pic of you peeking happily over your laptop?

What about the one of you jumping with joy on a beach?

Or the one of you all in white, against a white background, drinking a white latte from a white mug sitting at a white table with your white journal and your white pen?

When want *you* want do to is crown yourself with a gathering of thorns, drape a black fur robe around your shoulders, throw yourself back against the red throne, lift a heavy skulled chalice to your lips and photoshop blood pouring into your mouth. (You can find this one on my website: www.lornaj.com.)

No one but you knows the weird tone and the unhurried tenor of your people.

No one but you carries the dark code of disruption—the frequency of dis-chord—that is exquisitely and exactingly built and perfectly timed to explode the dark codes in those who are blueprinted to be transformed by you and only you.

And there is usually, in any given tribe, only one of those dis-chordant freaks of nature. (In your tribe, you're the one.) And that means your tribe, and those tribes in which your people live, will only ever see people like us as an aberration that must be corrected.

For your own good, they say.

But it is not for our own good. It is our undoing. Because we are not here to speak to the masses. We are here to speak to the other outcasts and misfits of consciousness.

There are plenty of them (just about every family has one). And they are growing restless. (This is why the global suicide and anxiety rates are rising and have been for thirty years.) But they are still in the vast minority and so you and they have been taught that conformity, polishing off your edges and learning how to not be the strange thing you actually are is the only way you will survive.

When in truth, this is a sure fire way to get yourself killed.

By you.

Or really by your genius, which is the Youest You, beyond even what your Soul provides you in terms of distinctiveness, and which knows there are an infinite number of times you and it will return to earth and an infinite number of expressions of itself, so it really doesn't care if it's got to off you this time around because you're not listening to it and instead listening to the unwise voices of the collective illusion.

(The popularized myths about genius—that if you do not capture it first, it will move on to someone else—are patently absurd, since genius is the most individuated of codes and is non transferable, because if it could be, it would be mere creativity, and what you're after is your genius, not the mimicry of consciousness, a xerox, a facsimile, a reproduction of light codes that passes for creativity).

What works for the masses does not and never will work for you, for a few reasons:

1. Your genius is *shattering* paradigms, not mastering them.

Your failure to thrive inside almost all human paradigms—institutions, corporations, schools, churches, religions, ideologies, and social structures—is not an indication of how much of a failure you are. It is an indication of how much of a genius you are. And you cannot look to LightWorkers or the masses for guidance on how to thrive inside the very paradigms you're here to shatter. You're going to have to use your genius, and the guidance and help and wisdom of the few DarkWorkers on the planet, to do that. (So to that end, I suggest you find me on YouTube. You will find, for the first time in your life, someone who speaks your language, sees you for who you really are, and can help you complete the journey of your true awakening. You can find me at http://bit.ly/LornaJYouTubeChannel.)

2. Your path to wild success must be created on your own terms, your way, because you have agreed that this is the lifetime your genius, not your human, gets the final word, the upper hand, the most power. And if you don't play along, you know what happens.

This is not the case for your tribe. They haven't made that agreement, which is why you keep wondering why other people can live such low frequencies lives and be apparently happy, or successful, or rich. They made different agreements with their genius, that's all. So stop comparing yourself to humans—because I know you are. You do it all the time. You're a chronic and baffled comparer. That's because you're not human. How many times do I have to tell you.

3. The energetic pathway for how money flows to genius has shifted.

This one is crazy. I can't believe I'm telling you this here. Buried on page whatever-it-is-now-after-all-the-edits. It should be its own book. Or at least its own heading. That's how important it is. But hey. The Dark does not announce itself with trumpets and red carpets. It sneaks in unannounced (and then blows everything to smithereens). So it makes total sense you're hearing this here. This, my friend, is a quick tour through the energetics of genius and money....

Money and the Genius Frequency

For centuries, genius was bereft of its true reign on earth.

In many cases, mental and creatives geniuses died early, went crazy and stayed poor. For many spiritual geniuses (Jesus, Buddha, etc.) their awareness of Spirit overshadowed (literally, energetically) their understanding of the spirituality—or consciousness—of matter and this led them to renounce material possessions and take vows of poverty, or simply value spirit over matter to the degree that they also, like their brothers and sisters in intellect and creativity, stayed poor.

And so we have this belief set that for some crazy reason, we have to choose between genius and abundance and the great treasure of experiencing heaven on earth.

This is because of the density of human consciousness, which has now shifted, and, thanks to LightWorkers across time and space, lightened a great deal.

Genius comes from the Dark and is commensurate with it—to the degree that two energetic entities, both coded with extreme aversion to existing in relation to anything and without context or precedent, can exist in relation to each other. Which means that they are not simply similar. They are the same. Dark Consciousness is Genius Frequency. And that means genius is, like the Dark, the newest, lightest light and highest frequency consciousness that can possibly exist.

Try moving that kind of rarified super-frequency through the multiple densities of human consciousness and all its equally dense systems (financial, relational, commercial), and see how easily money will be able to detect, find and flow to it.

No wonder artists died poor.

Genius has worked against the human vessel and systems of functioning for as long as human history. Most geniuses had brains and bodies—physical, mental and emotional systems— that were simply far too burdened with shadow consciousness and therefore couldn't handle the divergent wiring and overload of extremely high frequency energy required to stream such dis-ordered chaos into form and contain and direct it effectively. They inhabited worlds so vast, complex, exquisite, and energetically dis-orienting compared to their earthly one that their systems simply couldn't complete the turnabouts and accelerations and dimensional traveling and after awhile, everything just burned out and down. And so we equated being a genius with being crazy, sick, doomed to an early death, and definitely being poor.

But over the centuries our consciousness, and that of the planet and all systems and institutions, have lightened up considerably. And because they are less dense, money can find its way through the mental, emotional and physical constructs to meet genius before the human carrier has died. How cool is that.

And why would money flow to naturally to genius?

Money is coded with masculine energy, because money is our earthly provider, and the heart of the masculine divine is as Provider of All. Genius is the content of the Dark Feminine delivered by the masculine to the doorstep of our being. In our human condition, we are an expression, until we alchemize it, of the shadow feminine. This means that in receiving our genius, the feminine is being delivered back to herself.

And the masculine is drawn, more than anything in the world, to the scent of the True Feminine, his other energetic half, the Dark Divine.

The story of money making its way to genius is the story of the Hero making his way to the great treasure hidden in the castle, sleeping in a glass coffin, or guarded by a beast. Over the centuries, money has found genius, just as in our stories the Hero finds and rescues the princess after great trial. And just as in our myths, which are coded with the collective consciousness and require new telling—deprogramming, reinvention and encoding, just like all aspects of human consciousness—money had to overcome a great deal of density in time, space and consciousness in order to arrive at the doorstep of genius and place itself in its service.

(And no, these myths were not meant to depict women as weak and in need of saving. They were depicting the feminine as the receiver energy, and more than this, the energy of that Great Treasure that cannot be reached but through extreme trial. They were also depicting the true nature of human consciousness as the shadow feminine in need of arrest, wakefulness and correction by the masculine, the Light, so that she could find her way back to her home in the Dark, and earn true dominion over energy and matter. The True Feminine recedes far from reach, and in so doing, expresses her awareness of her great value, and sets out the difficulty of trials the masculine must overcome in order to be honored with the luxury of her presence. The princess was not kept captive by the dragon because she was too weak. Her True Value was being expressed through the fire and sharpness and deadly test of the dragon. And in truth, it was a test of whether she, Herself, could see the true purpose of the Dragon in her own story. Whether she is able to see that she birthed the Dragon from her own being, as the expression of her own still-powerful shadow. The fact that women are the ones who ask the Hero to kill the monster is an indication of how far the feminine has dropped into her own shadow, for the monster is the very expression of her own genius giant nature, but which she cannot recognize because she is still unconscious of her own nature and of her great value, which she has sprung from her being without her awareness. And it is the Great Hero of all—who does not yet exist but is coming into the global blueprint now—who does not kill the monster, but leads it out into the darkness and frees it into its native field and in so doing, delivers the feminine back to her own. This the New Myth. And yet even our old myths, far from being sexist, misogynistic and anti-woman, are coded with great reverence for the prestige of the feminine and a secret chamber of awareness about the condition of her shadow.)

But, the trials are lessening and lightening because the denseness of human consciousness has lightened considerably. This will be the content of the New Myth, which will move from the masculine and feminine being separated by extreme space and time, both in our stories and in our systems, and will now be focused on telling the Story that happens after the union, the bliss of first touch, the marriage, and the happily ever after.

What, when the feminine has been restored to the wildness of her monstrous nature, will they create?

They will create magic.

When you are capable of extreme thriving in all areas of your life—mentally, physically, emotionally and financially, when genius flows through all your systems uninhibited and instead of threatening them, amplifies their power structure, continually opening and expanding them to be able to handle more and more potency, that is when and how you will create magic in your own life.

You will master the collapsing of Time and Space. All dimensions of time and all frequencies of space—emotional, mental, physical space.

Magic is the activation of codes of consciousness capable of collapsing time.

(This sends Space into sudden submission. Something she must learn to like.)

These codes exist in all humans, in a field of energy and power called the SuperConscious.

For before we can create from Nothing, we must first be able to handle what is given.

Understand the order of appearances and why they must be so.

Magic is not the handling of the new.

It is the ordering of the natural. The intentional curation of that which already exists.

It is the simple ability to manifest on demand.

To call into our experience all the codes and frequencies that are already oriented toward us but are simply not in our five sensory awareness.

In other words, to shift the mirror into a window.

And then to properly see through it.

Until then, we cannot turn this plane into the portal it truly is.

To make magic requires a consciousness capable of balancing the two polar opposite energies of the feminine and masculine: that which decrees and decides what matters (the true feminine), and that which provides and makes manifest those decrees and turns energy into matter (the masculine).

It is the ability to hold extreme paradox in perfect discord at one and the same time.

The ability to do this is the special domain of the Diamond Mind, the God mind, the human in its natural state as genius giant.

It is the causing-to-be in an instant of what would normally take a great deal of space or time.

Imagine I disappear from one spot and instantly appear across the room. This is only magical because I've accomplished this in no time and no-space. If I took time and traversed space, that would be called walking. And unless you're six months old, dreaming of the day you'll ambulate as a biped, there's nothing magical about that.

Imagine I told you I went from broke, bipolar and suicidal to a happy, stable millionaire without using any medication, and I did it in…

ten years.

Not so magical.

What's magical about it, literally the reason you're reading this book, is because I collapsed several dimensions of space (the mental and emotional space of dis-chord, clutter and heaviness) in an extremely collapsed time period compared to what it takes most humans to do. (No one in my industry did a million in ten months. And I keep forgetting to mention, which is also absolutely miraculous, that I achieved this working 20 hours a week and using no automated systems as leverage (so, no automated, paid ads; no email campaigns; no funnels). Several more examples of space and time collapse.

Magic is essentially the ability to collapse lifetimes. It is thrusting yourself forward—just like the astronaut through the weight of gravity—through the density of your own and the collective human consciousness, collapsing emotional and mental space (your shadow) and achieving quantum flight. In essence, changing nature states, so that your new (and always native) nature is to fly and never need to touch the ground.

This is what is now available to more and more humans, through the lightening of the energetic "gravitational field" of consciousness, and through a suite of new spiritual technologies I have invented and used on myself and many others, including Shadow Alchemy, which is essentially emotion and mental space collapse. And the inheritance of magic is money, riches, abundance in all forms, because when the field of play becomes as light as possible, it switches to Dark Mode, in which space and time become playthings of the genius giant.

Your tribe does not know any of this.

They think they are protecting you by pressing you to be normal, to contract your contrast and expand your commonalities with them. Because this is how humans have gathered together and shared wealth. In tight circles of communion.

But your circle of communion is jagged, rich, raw and multidimensional. You can tap it at any time and a client, customer, partner, opportunity will arrive at your doorstep in minutes.

Literally.

One woman, who learned how to activate this kind of magic went to bed $110,000 less in debt than when she woke up that morning. All because she knew how to access her energetic circle of richness.

Because the energetic pathways between genius and money have shifted, making true thriving—what you are fundamentally coded to do—possible. This means that the lining up of the genius giant blueprints is happening apace, and because this is commensurate with your coding, it is time for you to get with the (de)program. You have nothing to fear. Streaming your genius will not result in poverty, sickness or loneliness, even though your tribe, and most of the planet, still subscribes blindly to the old myths and tortured lives of the geniuses of old that would tell you otherwise.

This is because your tribe is not coded this way. They could give a shit about genius. They could also give a shit about money (meaning they're capable of living beneath the frequency of thriving). And because it was (and they still think it is) their job to raise on you the Light Grid, in the Light, as a child of the Light, they are not going to encourage you to activate your genius.

Especially because it's monstrous, and if there's anything the tribe is coded to do, it's to disarm and defang the monster.

5. Your job is not to become One With All.

Because you are coded to unleash genius, and because genius is the most individuated of frequencies, (which is why when you contemplate becoming one with all it does absolutely Nothing to or for you), your job is to become utterly, unapologetically One With Nothing. Meaning, a stand-alone frequency. All the myths, religions and spiritual traditions of human consciousness are about becoming one with all, how to dissolve into the All (the Total Something), *not* how to erupt as The One (the god, who springs from the Complete Nothing).

Their stories and guidance systems will not serve you.

No one can tell you who and how to be, because no one knows you are not here to be human.

You are not here to *speak* human to humans. You are here to speak the dark divine codes to the dark divine in others.

And dark language is not of or for the masses. It is nonsensical, abrupt, maddening and unclear. You cannot shine light on it to cause it to make sense.

It is the language of Gods, Archetypes and Mythmakers. Blind Seers. Alchemists. Dark Empresses and Dark Goddesses. It is the language of the activation of the codes of disruption, and there are many who prefer to stay asleep.

This is why it is imperative that you master being utterly, radically yourself, and utterly, radically alone.

And that means lifting yourself up out of the shadows, for good.

And *that* means opening up to the nightmare of your life, staring into its jaws, and baring your neck to its teeth.

Which explains the dream of the Friendship-Notes-Turned-Chinese-Throwing-Stars and the Lion.

When I was sixteen, I had a Big Dream. In Jungian circles, this means a dream that provides a narrative arc for a momentous stage of your life and evolution. It often extends far beyond the moment and has come to inform of you of the journey you are embarking on.

I was in my back yard and it was pitch black and several of my friends were throwing triangular friendship notes at me (you know, you fold a piece of paper this way and that and then fold the bottom part up and then fold it a few more times this way and that and then tuck the bottom part in and you have a neat little triangle you can pass easily in class). Except that somewhere on their way to me, they became as sharp as Chinese stars. You know, the multi-pointed death weapons of the East. No matter where I ran, these notes-turned-weapons found me and sliced my flesh. Penetrated bushes and trees and travelled impossible distances. Then suddenly they were gone and I found myself running at breakneck pace from a massive lion. Then, without warning, I stopped and turned and faced it and it just stood there. And the dream was over.

I've known for years this meant I was running from some aspect of myself. I'm a Leo so the lion had clear meaning. And I'd also known for years that it meant I was running from some aspect of my power.

Ok. So I was denying or afraid of some extraordinarily, regal, powerful aspect of me. Got it. But what exactly was this mysterious power? And where or what was the source of it? And what does it actually mean to stop running from it and face it?

I also knew my friends tossing deadly weapons disguised as notes my way had something to do with the fact they they were abusive relationships. Which was true. Every single one of my friendships in high school was toxic to the core. I was regularly belittled, shamed, judged, demeaned, scolded, criticized, and admonished. My loyalty, compassion, and empathy were constantly questioned. I was told I was mean, cold hearted, abrasive, too harsh, arrogant, self centered, selfish, narcissistic. I was always doing something wrong that mortally wounded them and it was always because there was something about me that just wasn't right. And so I spent all my time 1) trying to prove them wrong and 2) investigating all the ways they were most likely right and 3) trying to fix what they had uncovered as my essential wrongness so I could actually have a friend or two, like most people seemed to be able to do without much problem. Sure, girls fought. But it didn't seem, on the rare occasion I swapped stories with someone about my friendships, that theirs were bloody, protracted and poisonous like mine.

It was only until last year that I realized how the running from the lion and the notes-turned-deadly-stars were connected, and what it meant that I turned to face the lion and why that turning, when I finally did it in my actual life, was the reason I went from wrecked and wretched to magical in a matter of months.

To illustrate my realization, I'm going to tell you about the last time this happened, and will ever happen. (And by "this" I mean willingly staying in a one-down relationship and trying to prove that I was not, in fact, an arrogant, crazy bitch.)

It was also the day I realized I was a DarkWorker. And the day the Dark Portal open and dark codes started streaming through onto the planet. Kind of a big day in the life of consciousness. Like basically its bat mitzvah. Or sweet sixteen. Or quinciniera

But more like it's *Risky Business*.

And it happened just last year...

She was twenty-seven or twenty-eight by the looks of it. Made her first million when she was 18. Ranked by Inc. Magazine as #1 of the top 27 female entrepreneurs changing the world in 2017. Named one of the top 40 millennials to follow in 2018. Former ambassador for education at the U.N.. Forbes Under 30 columnist. And etcetera, I think you get it.

She was also a channel, an intuitive and a psychic whose spiritual life was real, grounded, authentic and her absolute priority. She lived her spirituality inside and out.

We met online, instantly connected and decided that when she was flying through Chicago, she'd make a weekend out of it and come visit me so we could meet in person.

But soon after that was decided, I felt an energetic shift in our connection. This disconnect grew over the weeks before our planned meeting, and when the weekend finally arrived and I welcomed her into my home, we sat on the couch facing each other.

"You know. I almost didn't come," she said.

"I know," I said. "I felt it."

"I mean, like, even when I was driving here from O'Hare," she said.

O'Hare is minutes from me.

"Oh, really?"

"Yeah. Really."

"Why is that?"

And then she said, and I'm paraphrasing here: "Because I don't think you're a clear channel. I sense a lot of shadow in your work."

Oh, the flames that licked the insides of my heart.

I could literally feel myself *heating up*.

By this time she'd been a member of my Facebook group for weeks and I'm sure saw the kinds of things I posted, the kinds of livestreams I did. I wasn't surprised at all that there was discord, because she and I are pretty much the exact opposite when it comes to our spiritual orientation.

My message is uncomfortable as fuck. I do not set out to make people feel good. I set out to make them *squirm*. My style is unapologetically confrontational, disruptive and uncomfortable. (Even though in person I'm soft as a kitten. At least that's what everyone tells me when they finally meet me in the flesh.)

Softening my edges is what got me almost self-killed. Believing people like her, this delightful woman sipping tea on my couch, is what sent me into the longest, most terrifying and destructive tailspin of my life. And here it is again, sitting right across from me: the message from the world.

You don't know yourself. You've got a lot of work to do before you have a right to be saying what you're saying. What you see isn't what you think you see.

And to my disappointment and dismay I watched as I betrayed my own knowing. I slunk into a corner energetically and spent the next two days "proving" to her that I was, in fact, a grounded, awake, aware, spiritually advanced being.

That began a six-month long friendship in which, in all kinds of subtle ways, I betrayed my dominion, my domain, my standing in spiritual Truth.

And guess what else happened during these six months?

My sales halved.

My inspiration, creativity and connection to my genius dwindled to next to nothing.

I was running my spiritual business school and doing amazing work with clients, but inside, something felt off. I couldn't put my finger on it. It certainly wasn't anything like depression or anxiety, the two calling cards of my former illnesses.

It was as if someone very dear to me had quietly disappeared. Dissolved into thin air.

I went on with my life and my business, confounded by this gaping, silent hole inside…and by the numbers in my bank account—still quite high but not nearly what they used to be—and by my lack of direction and inspiration.

Then through a series of conversations and revelations six months later, I realized what I'd done.

I'd betrayed the Dark, my first love. Sold my Dark Soul in return for a friendship I valued more than my own gift.

The minute I realized this, I reached out to her and asked to get on the phone, and I told her what I'd done, how I'd betrayed myself and my knowing. And I said that I needed to know whether she perceived me as a pure channel, because as much as I dearly loved her and cherished our friendship, I was not going to be in a relationship in which my spiritual gift was seen as needing shadow work.

It was one of the most incredible conversations I've ever had.

Together we walked straight into the heart of the current quandary in consciousness, she as a Lightworker, me as a Darkworker, both with profound respect for each other and also with the awareness that I carry something both valuable and still impenetrably confounding.

"How can the Dark be a pure channel?" she asked, with a true openness to hearing an answer she couldn't imagine feeling true, but was.

How, indeed. This book is an answer to that very real, valid and most pressing question.

If you are a Darkworker, this is the question that has plagued you your whole life.

You have believed, like me, (even when I *knew* better) that there was something wrong with you, that it *has* to be you.

What is so beautiful is that your commitment to integrity is so great (this is another carrying card of the Darkworker: extreme commitment to integrity), that you will turn against your genius and your spiritual gift of dark sight over and over rather than boastfully scatter it across the world, because you care *more* about impeccable integrity in using your gift than you do in expressing one that is full of shadow, misalignment and distortion.

This is why for most of your life, you're this strange amalgam of pretty-fucking-miserable-but-not-really.

It's this weird experience of "I'm fucking miserable in my life but I'm not actually a miserable *person*. So why the fuck am I so miserable? Is it me? It's got to be me."

And all because you're this dark fucking energy sitting in the middle of all of this light and softness. People can hardly stand to be around you.

Your entire life has been an unconscious apprenticeship with the Dark, because the world is built in a way that cannot see in the dark, cannot see the dark for what it is, and so your entire orientation is considered depraved. This is why so many dark workers have been diagnosed with mental illnesses, depression and also suffer from "inexplicable" physical illnesses.

Until now, you have been unable to find your conscious congruence with your darkness.

This is why I developed bipolar, two types of ADD, severe mood and anxiety disorder and PTSD, why so many clients who work with me have the same problem, and why they go off their pills and their symptoms simply drop away. Because I'm putting them back into their natural habitat; back into the darkness where they belong.

I've had people with decades-long physical ailments cured after a matter of days or weeks after starting to work with me. One woman had been losing her hair for sixteen years. After one session with me, her hair stopped falling out three days later. Another woman had had a skin condition on her face and the backs of her hands for forty years and had tried everything from creams, pills, acupuncture, specialists and every possible kind of cure, but to no avail. After working with me for three weeks, her skin condition completely cleared up. (She also went from making about $1500/month in her coaching business to doing $22,000 in her first four weeks. Because energy is energy is energy, and when you are initiated into your Dark Alchemist archetype, heaven on earth is yours for the taking.) Another woman went from severe migraines, crippling anxiety and such an unstable mental state that a year before she worked with me, her therapist had told her that if she didn't get better, she'd have to have her committed, to a complete clearing of all her physical, mental and emotional ailments, using no drugs, therapy or other methods (and to doing $130,000 in sales in *one day* and over $250,000 in the fourth months she worked with me).

The point here is that this shit is *real*. Honoring your Dark gift *matters*. Literally.

She makes Herself known and felt in physical, mental, emotional and financial *matter*.

Health and wealth, in other words.

These aren't just cool ideas (or terrible, horrible disruptive ones, depending on your frame of mind about the Dark). They have actual repercussions in your lived life.

Continuing to call yourself a light worker is screwing up your energy and your life for *real*. It's also relegating the darkness to the position of that which needs fixing, which, as you know by now, it does not.

I and all other Darkworkers who have agreed to certify their own genius without any outside confirmation, are making a call for the honoring and the conscious elevation of the role of the Darkworker in the spiritual world and in the evolution of consciousness on the planet.

This is my life's work: To build up Darkworkers, to help them find their dark message, activate and craft their dark genius to a fine art, develop their dark channel, and build an empire and a legendary legacy based on their dark work.

DARK IS THE NEWEST LIGHT

Now that the DarkCodes are coming through, everything we have believed as spiritual Truth is turning on its head and we're being called to a higher understanding of Truth, Love and Integrity.

This has nothing to do with evil, black magic, shadow work or Darkworkers as described by shamans, and is not a gimmicky or trendy marketing tactic or attempt to myopically label people. This is a new energy that is starting to come through and it requires keen understanding and awareness in order to work with it.

Since The Dark is bringing through the newest, lightest light, Light now represents the aspect of consciousness that includes illusion, since it does not, by definition, have access to the frequency of Truth carried only by the Dark.

This is not to denigrate the Light in any way. And in fact there is an acknowledgement by the Light Consciousness (the way in which humans manage their understanding of Light) that It has entered into a new humility with respect to the Dark, becoming more expansive in finally allowing itself to embrace the Dark as a TruthCarrier.

This means, therefore, that the age-old spiritual equation of Light = Truth = Love has now become an outdated understanding of all three energies.

We now require an upgrade in our consciousness in order to hold the most accurate understanding of their nature.

Light Consciousness now acknowledges that the Dark carries (and has always carried) Truth frequencies that have never been structured or organized into consciousness (Light).

It also acknowledges that Integrity has been built into the energetic structure of the Dark and that therefore, the Dark can be trusted.

The most accurate energetic display of how spiritual understanding is being altered, along with our concepts of Light, Dark, Truth and Love, is this:

From:

Light = Truth = Love and Dark = Illusion = Absence of Love

To:

Truth = Dark Light = Love

Another way of saying this is:

Truth is the aspect of Dark Light that is brought across the border into the Light as the result of Creative Will used with Supreme Integrity.

This is what it means to become both God and human.

Darkworkers And Lightworkers:

A Fine Distinction

Lightworkers carry more density than Darkworkers because they have to transmute the new message that's coming in and make it more dense so that those who are more dense can absorb, alchemize and transmute it.

Therefore Lightworkers are built to carry a denser message. Dark workers are built to carry the lightest message possible, the one that comes from the utterly new, the totally foreign, the absolutely strange and the unthinkably uncomfortable place that consciousness has not been willing to go.

This is why the Dark Alchemist—the lightest archetype in human consciousness and the pinnacle of the SuperConscious archetypes—stands alone, unhooked from the others. It must be entirely removed from the Light and therefore from the influence of the prevailing consciousness, in order to be tuned to the fragile frequency of the New.

The Dark Alchemist is the alchemized energies of the Hermit, the Magician and the Reversed God (the Hanged Man). It is the magical upgrade to the magnificently unimaginable. Magic that happens entirely in the Dark. The creations of the Dark Alchemist are handed off to the Seer, the MythMaker and the Activator to refine and process into a message and an experience that can enter into human consciousness. These are the Relator archetypes. The ones who bring the gift from the center of the labyrinth back through the refining energetic path that processes the dark slowly, and through many twists and turns of revelation (this is what is meant by "cold processing"), until finally it has been refined and processed into something that can be received by the Light.

The Relator archetypes are the ones who stand at the end-edge of consciousness and bring forth the Dark Truth from the regions beyond, bringing it right over the edge into the Light, and then retreating back along the same path into the heart of darkness to receive the next gift for consciousness being crafted from the rawness of reality.

As a Darkworker, you are knit with all four of these archetypes (and we will go into them in detail later in the book). And their properties and roles is what your system, your frequency and your energetic grid can handle.

If you try to bring that the newest, lightest light closer in, try to come from the hinterlands or the top of the mountain or the bottom of the sea or wherever your darkness is and bring that message further and further in to the frequency of the masses, you are going to get sick, mentally ill, will lose your money, your house, your friends because you are not built to hold and carry that kind of denseness.

Drop the new consciousness right over the edge into the light and go back into the dark where you belong.

This is what spiritual innovation is. Darkworkers are spiritual innovators. They are saying and offering something new that has never been thought, said or conceived of in the history of humanity. They are the new Mythmakers.

This is your legacy.

This is your lineage.

When you step into your role as a Darkworker, still know that you carry and *are* light.

On the Earth plane, in 3D consciousness, there is a stark contrast between light and dark. It is for this reason that right now at least, you cannot be both a Lightworker and a Darkworker, because what each sets up energetically in your system and what each require of you physically—literally in the cells of your body—and what they are each capable of handling in terms of incongruence with the Truth is radically different.

Light workers are able to carry more density, meaning more illusion. They are therefore able to work with the energy of mercy. This makes them approachable and trustworthy and highly effective with those who are in the early to middle stages of their shadow work. Much more effective than a Darkworker, who does not carry the energy of mercy and whose energy will most likely so severely threaten the spiritual seeker with the Unknown and the UnMetabolizable that the process of shadow work cannot even begin, let alone the process of Dark work, which comes much later.

(This is why Darkworkers are often accused of spiritual bypass. Which is exactly what they're doing. They are bypassing the decrepit, ineffective and obsolete model of handling toxic energy, which dumps energetic toxins directly into the body to be felt and processed—but which does intense harm on the body's DNA and cellular integrity, not to mention the human's mental form and clarity. There is another way entirely, which alchemizes the toxic energy by sending it directly into a new energetic anatomy--the dark heart of gold--which is built to be an infinite energy alchemizer. The dark heart of gold alchemizes the toxic energy, and because it is not mapped to the physical body or the light body, does no damage to the physical or mental fields, and then, when the energy has been fully cleaned and upgraded, streams the upgraded frequency into the physical and etheric systems as pure, potent arrangements of clean codes and programming. So yes. Darkworkers engage in spiritual bypass all the time. We highly recommend it.)

What we mean when we say that Lightworkers are able to carry more density is that their physical, mental, emotional and financial systems don't break down as drastically under the weight of that density. Lightworkers will feel the strain of carrying heavier densities on an emotional level - grief or sadness that they're not influencing their vibration into the world.

But if you as a Darkworker don't realize your gift or come out of the closet (most Darkworkers know they're carrying a level of power that feels potent, intense or scary as hell), you will get sick and die.

It's like entering the Earth's atmosphere without armor. You can't do it. Drop it in and then go back out into outer space where you belong and where your people are.

How does one go back into the darkness? You release attachment to the outcome. The Dark Feminine has no attachment to the outcome because she lives in the unfettered field of the Nothing.

When you're within the unfettered field of the Nothing, you never really leave. The only way you can leave the darkness is when you become attached to the outcome in any way.

You have chosen to be in love with something that the vast majority of people on this planet think one can only be in love with if they have a depraved, twisted consciousness.

Once you release the shame around that, simply by dropping it—which you can do because your energetic system is naturally constructed and architected to run on dark energy—all your energetic systems—financial, emotional, physical and mental—shift into alignment and congruence and your entire life changes overnight. This has happened over and over for me and with people who work with me.

If you try to work with clients who are meant to be light workers rather than those who are meant to be activated into their dark work, dark channeling or their dark energetic lattice, you will likely run into serious problems. Your clients will probably fire you frequently or you'll end up firing them all. You'll be using huge amounts of energy with little return.

The caveat to this is having an awakened process of coming into congruence with your clients, where at the beginning, before they become your clients, you make it clear the nature of the work you do and cause them to enter into discernment about whether they are ready to activate their DarkDNA and become Darkworkers.

If they are truly here to do dark work, they will instantly recognize that it is time to activate their Dark DNA and when they enter into a working relationship with you, it will be based on such different grounds that the previously discussed problems won't arise.

The distinction between whether you are a Darkworker or a Lightworker is important because it determines how you see and experience Truth and informs you where your blind spot is for mistaking Truth for Untrustworthiness. And since Truth is the ultimate and only life giving substance, if you're living in Untruth, your life will suffer.

Many Lightworkers are suffering in their spiritual businesses, finances, physical health and relationships because they don't understand the importance of the DarkCodes to teach them the fullness of how Truth operates. They are unwittingly mistaking Truth for shadow, and therefore mistrust it greatly. This has practical implications for their ability to grow into the greatest expression of themselves in their business possible. And of course to their mental and physical health as well.

The Absolute Science Behind Manifestation

There are many frequencies of light. From dusk to white light. This is what mercy is. And this is why Light workers think Truth is relative. Because there are in fact shades of light. Therefore they think there are shades of truth. And they also think actualizing your potential occurs on a spectrum and cannot be hit exactly like a note on a piano.

But there is only one frequency of Dark. One exact tone. This is why Truth is not relative. And this also explains why we have one *exact* potential that is expressed in negative Space.

This is also why it takes Time to build but no Time to destroy or disrupt. Light has many frequencies of itself and therefore all structures, built as they are on the energy of Light, take time to grow. But Dark brings one exact frequency and when that frequency hits a structure, it is sent into chaos instantly. Light = Time and Space. Dark = Timeless/Spaceless/Negative Space/Negative Time/No Time.

Anything built is built with Light. Light carries the energy of structure.

This is why truly instant manifestation doesn't yet exist. It's possible, but you must hit the exact tone of potential first and that means destroying and rebuilding in one instant. We're not yet capable of that. This incapacity is what keeps the dream alive, meaning the entire illusion of our consciousness, otherwise our thoughts would become things in an instant.

The Dark being absent from structured consciousness is essential for anything to hold together and become, and is also essential for allowing experience, otherwise everything would collapse, Time/Space would disappear and everything would be and not be in an instant. The Dark then has given up the privilege of experiencing its creations.

Was the Big Bang created when the Dark receded from the Light? This is a question for our next book.

On Mastery Of The Absolute Science Of Manifestation

You don't have a general or infinite potential. It is precise. And it is coded in your DarkDNA. Manifestation is an exact science and it is unique to you, since it is mapped to your *exact* potential, and to your light and dark energetic structures and how clean/clear/activated they are. Generic methods like Law of Attraction (LOA) only capture the species-level rules for manifestation, not the *unique* way *you* are coded to manifest, which is accessed through the mapping in your DarkDNA rather than in your LightDNA. When you manifest using the energenetics (energy genetics) of your DarkDNA versus your LightDNA, you *bypass* Time and instead of *building* your dream, you *snap* it into focus instantly. This is why LOA is so flimsy and unpredictable. It only works with LightDNA, and therefore universal principles of manifestation rather than personal principles.

Mastery of your imaginative domain and *exact* potential requires mastery of the act, art and absolute science of manifestation.

In order to access your exact mapping, you must ascend into your personal Negative Space through your Dark Womb, which is the birth place of your *imaginative domain*.

This domain is yours and yours alone.

It is the way you are God.

Once you know how to access it, Heaven on Earth is yours.

First you must clear your positive space (shadow, dense light) before your imagination can come through. Imagination is what sparks it all, but it has a very high frequency and it can't make it through the denseness of shadow, shame and fear.

Openness is an exact state

When you manifest using the Dark (vs the Light)—meaning when you manifest the expression of your unimaginable genius (vs the expression of your gifts/highest existing frequency of Light)—the standards rise dramatically for how to work with the energy that accesses this state of manifestation.

Working with the Dark is an exact, and exacting, science nothing like working with the forgiving nature of Light.

There is one, specific tone of genius that resonates as an exact match for your availability at any given time. Strike this tone (the Tone of Truth), and you will strike gold (the wealth resonance of your genius).

Dark work is heaven for the spiritual geniuses among us, because it is finally the exacting field of play in which they thrive (versus the ambient playing field in which the Light resides).

Mastering Dark work, for a spiritual genius, is like finally being able to exhale.

There is a delicate and steely and filamental silence to it, like the silence of bones.

We came here to see how much pure energy and life force can be expressed through a human channel, and collectively through the gathered energy of all humans and the material universe.

It is a crazy experiment, to be sure, trying to fit god inside a human. But that's what we dreamed up and why the earth and this universe was created.

There are specific codes of disruption that were held by the shadow archetypes until now. Each archetype carries its own specific codes. These are your gold. And they get released during your personal band of unhooking. The planet's band of unhooking was the time from 12/12/12 to 5/11/18, when the Dark Portal opened.

When you move into the band of unhooking, it is time to become intimate with your own exterior. Time to understand that your access to time has moved inside.

Time to begin mastering the precise science of disruption.

The Truth About Your Shadow

Exercise your demons.

Their energy is your raw genius but because we have been taught to cage them up, then they become our shadow archetypes. Shadow archetypes are simply *raw awareness*. They are not to be used to make decisions. This results in disaster. They are emotional and intellectual content, meaning, our unique energy signature. If we take them as inherently meaningful, then we get into trouble.

Meaning, if we make them MATTER.

They are meant to be used as raw material for self creation and genius.

The Prostitute uses the raw material of its nature and place in shadow consciousness to become aware of the desire for a dream...*and nothing more*. Raw awareness of the desire for a dream is not sufficient to code the desire with value, which is why the prostitute is incapable of owning or even seeing the value of its desire and therefore is unable to hand the desire over so it can be transformed into an inspired dream.

The Child uses the raw material of its nature and place in shadow consciousness to become aware of the dream and the vision...*and nothing more*, which is why the child is incapable of making its own dream come true. Raw awareness is not enough to turn the dream into a decree.

The Victim uses the raw material of its nature and place in shadow consciousness to become aware of the monumental task of making the dream real ...*and nothing more*, which is why the victim feels overwhelmed by the dream and unequal to the task. Raw awareness is not enough to turn the decreed dream into something that matters, something to stand and fight for.

The Saboteur uses the raw material of its nature and place in shadow consciousness to become aware of the need for a steady stream of brilliant ideas and insights that will turn the decreed dream, supplied with resources and fueled by the will of the Warrior, into reality...*and nothing more*. Raw awareness is not enough to create from Nothing, which is why the Saboteur feels overwhelmed with the task of ideas and swings wildly from being creatively blocked to having so many ideas that they feel suffocating.

There is a way to perceive and work with blocks and "bad luck" that is a radical departure from what New Age spirituality offers. A way that offers a way out, not simply up and around forever.

It looks at personal failings not as due to the quality of our energy or reflections of our low-frequency being offered back to us in the form of "unwanted circumstances," but something radically, almost unimaginably, different.

As nothing more than the sweet presence of chaos striking a chord in our field wanting to be welcomed into our energy so something entirely new can happen for us – something that will lead us to unimaginable heights of ecstasy *now*.

We take an ordered approach to improving our lives. Incremental. Measured. Raises at 3%. Slightly better lovers and friends as the years go on.

And there is a directly proportional energetic relationship between this very approach—steeped in a belief that change happens in an orderly fashion through steps—and our view of blocks and "bad luck" that we encounter on the way to that new, incrementally improved level.

In other words, to commit incremental growth means or implies that we see bad luck and blocks to that growth as detrimental to our path forward. And so we then go searching in our mental and emotional field for the source of the block.

But, what if *order* is not the only field of spiritual law that is operating?

In fact it is not.

Chaos operates according to its own, totally oppositional spiritual and energetic law and in this field, what happens to us is not a reflection of us (ordered law, 1:1 ratios and relation) but rather the introduction of an entirely new element that does not have any correlation to anything that exists in our field and that, were we to embrace it, would catapult us to an entirely, radically new level of life experience – something far beyond what we can even imagine wanting.

In other words, chaos brings Grace.

What we wish for can be obtained two ways: through following the energetic laws of order – masculine, light, incremental steps that all have relation to each other—or of chaos—feminine, dark, quantum leaps that do not have any relation to each other. The question then is how to behave in the chaos (bad luck, blocks). How to reply. In the ordered, energetic law, we simply shift our internal world and the outer one responds.

In chaotic energetic law, we do what?

We do nothing. We do not make it about us.

We eliminate Manifestation Shame.

We choose to see through an entirely different lens. One that operates outside the laws of cause and effect, of order, relation, Light. As in: *My thoughts and choices have no relation to what is happening to me. They are completely acceptable to me and I do not condemn them or make them the cause of this block. Instead I understand it as another world that is asking to insert itself into my experience. An entirely new set of laws.*

Grace is different than Mercy.

Grace offers a radical new way, unsummoned by our current thoughts and choices.

Grace is Dark. It works to uplevel limitations of imagination. Mercy forgives low-frequency thoughts and choices and exists on the ordered light grid. If you seek mercy, you will be constrained to incremental growth. If you accept—*and recognize*—grace, you will be catapulted into quantum growth.

The whole question being put to humanity is whether they can move from simply reactively and passively responding to blocks and "bad luck" with tantrums and victim consciousness (why is this happening to ME???), to consciously and co-creatively responding to blocks and "bad luck" with spiritual maturity and sovereignty consciousness (how did I create this?), to having such a radically rewired brain, nervous system, emotional framework and artisanship that extreme "bad luck" and blocks are experienced on two planes at once: the visceral, human experience of feeling sordid (victim consciousness), and at the same time the wonder-field awareness that there is no relation to or cause of what is happening next, what is happening now, but that universe-as–mirror has turned into universe-as–window and they are being visited by the goddess of chaos.

In other words, it is the end of ordering experience as "wanted" or "unwanted."

How does this not send us back to victim consciousness where we simply accept what is happening to us? How do we see what happens in our experience as neither 1) happening to us (victim) or 2) happening from us (LOA) but rather 3) so far outside of us that it feels like it's happening to us but that is in fact an invitation from an entirely new place and has no relation to us at all, to what we think or feel or do. In this new paradigm, going outward to try and improve our experience (victim) is really the same as going inward to try and improve our outward experience (spiritual warrior).

Blame: victim's response to unwanted experience. Human as caged, useless and physically tribal.

Shadow work: enlightened spiritual warrior's response to unwanted experience. Human as freed into his spiritual tribe.

Chaos alchemy: enDarkened response an energy-bearing condition, seen as neither wanted or unwanted. Human as wild, individuated beast of genius.

This new way is far beyond simply overcoming hardship or turning hardship into something positive. It has to do with experiencing the raw material of emotion and thought as strongly as possible (what would normally send us into victim state — being a victim to our emotions and thoughts) while at the same time having no reaction to them (neither the impulse to change the external world to better suit us or the internal world so that the external world changes to better suit us).

In other words, wanting to change anything is limited energetic imagination. And yet this is not an advocacy of apathy. Of doing nothing. It is in fact an advocacy of a radically active intimacy with chaos that requires us to do "nothing" while it is in the midst of coming into the most intense and intimate relationship to us. This is the meathook moment. And it differs from "divine timing" fundamentally.

In this new state, we do away with stations, levels, above/below me, inside/outside of me. In this new state, we judge the quality of an experience differently.

We do not use the perceived quality of experiences to indicate to us whether we are progressing or retreating in our station in life. And so there is not that inevitable, albeit subtle, holding back of our most expressive and engaging selves because we are always noting how we are in relation to. Think about it: How often do you use external circumstances to reflect to you the quality of your life or how much you are progressing?

How much do you care about progressing?

The degree to which you care about progressing is the degree to which you stunt your growth.

This kind of care limits imagination considerably.

So what does this do to desire, goals and imagination? Have a goal, then abandon it immediately? Don't have goals? Have goals no matter what? Have a goal but don't look to experiences as feedback as to your progress toward it?

The answer is found, as in everything, in the Dark.

Because the Dark does not seek to experience itself.

It is entirely possible to have a goal that has nothing to do with experience. But rather, with offering an invitation.

In other words, we are not here to *receive experiences*. We are here to create them for others. What they do with that invitation is up to them, but has no relation to the euphoria we find in making the offer or setting the stage for their transformation.

Shadow Alchemy And The Problem Of The Shadow

The sub-content of consciousness

In order to speak to and free the genius within others, you must first speak to and free the one within you.

And that means learning how to speak the unimaginable, because genius is inhuman.

In fact, it is monstrous.

And how could your child have dreamed of that?

You must know where the monsters belong. You must know their native tongue. You must become familiar with their native land.

Your genius does not belong, and will not emerge, onto the Light Grid directly. It requires special handling in the dark room first. It demands a Master Alchemist capable of lightly handling, or cold processing, the highly unstable and therefore potently nutritive elements of chaos, the codes of disruption and disorder that are meant to activate their brother and sister codes in other human carriers.

And what is the first order of business, then, for a Master-Alchemist-To-Be?

Apprenticeship, of course.

With the lesser and much denser and far less explosive expression of genius, the shadow.

And that means that for now, we must leave the question of genius alone. For we are not prepared to handle it directly. It is too wild and unimaginable for our human framework. And, right now, your desire to find your genius is corrupted. It is part of the glitch in Light Consciousness you must first correct because right now you want to USE your genius to prop up your demolished sense of self.

So we will return to it later, when we have earned the right to approach it directly.

For now, to the shadows we go.

The beginning of the path is hiding in plain sight, in an energetic place many of us have been diligently trying to wrap our heads around, and requires such a slight shift that on the surface it might seem laughable. Like a joke.

All you have to do is stop seeing your genius as your shadow (which leads you to doing shadow work on your genius, which leads to the never-ending Spiral of Despair), and instead, see your shadow as your genius.

Which leads to Shadow Alchemy (The Alchemist in you being your essential genius), which leads to the completion of the final stage of awakening, the dissolution of your shadow, the alchemizing of your Soul and the birth of your New Dark Body, and that is what turns the head of the divine masculine irresistibly your way because now you are an energetic match for your genius frequency, and that means you have become radiant with black beauty, darkly divine, resting in the prestige of the True Feminine who has taken herself on the journey of a lifetime and now can ask anything she desires of the masculine and knows she will receive it without question, for the masculine is coded to provide to such an eminent, imperial beauty as she.

n other words, he is blueprinted to automatically provide for the feminine when she is in her highest frequency…

and Nothing else.

Stop demonizing, minimizing and denying it, we've been taught. Understand, befriend, tame, manage it instead. And yet nothing works, because we do not know how to handle it or even how it is meant to be handled. We certainly do not know about the final gift that drifts from it like fine perfume when we handle it properly and we also have been told all the wrong stories about the fiery and impromptu energy of that deepest gift of the feminine once it does get released.

Released from millennia of prisons. Bars that are our myths and fairytales about all the wrong ways to face the monstrous. (Befriend. Tame. Kill.)

I'm referring to your shadow, of course.

The trend to go from demonize/minimize/deny is a good start. It is not wise to fear the unDark. The shadowed Light. A poor use of time and energy and a full degradation of power.

Understand/befriend/tame/manage is what I call shadow management. It's the best the spiritual self help industry has been able to do so far.

And it is not sufficient and it is time for more. To go deeper into the potential of this energy. To seize the fangs of it more suddenly and with greater boldness built on Truth.

There is a groundswell of dissatisfaction with New Age spirituality by those who were once steeped in its teachings. I see the dissatisfaction every day on the faces of my clients who know everything there is to know about shadow work, Law of Attraction, manifestation, unleashing their feminine essence, becoming One with All, meditating, yoga, journaling and all the myriad other hundreds of practices and who are still miserable and stuck as fuck.

And I have talked to hundreds who share this deep disillusionment. Thousands, likely, by now. I have a 3,800-member group on Facebook devoted entirely to teaching the new consciousness and the spiritual science of energy alchemy, because so many are fed up with spiritual practices that do not free them like they were promised. And I see also, almost on a daily basis, the miraculous results that happen for my clients as they apply this bold new spiritual technology to their consciousness, which is very eager and primed for the experience. More primed than we are.

Most of these are financial results, because my work centered on helping struggling entrepreneurs make money. (Because as I said, this energy knows you intimately and wants practical success for you.)

So for instance, one woman—a psychic and energy worker—had been hustling six days a week and only making a thousand dollars a month in her business. She'd been doing this for almost a year, but when she learned the techniques I teach—specifically for her it was the understanding the missing link to the Law of Attraction and how to manifest with the masculine energy—she made eighty thousand dollars in five months working part time.

Another woman was a research scientist at a world-renowned company. Her life was steeped in logic and reason and yet she was drawn to me (probably because I come from a long line of thinkers — authors, writers, English majors mostly—and myself double majored in philosophy and the history of math and science in my country's most intellectually rigorous school. Brainiacs recognized a kindred spirit in me, even though by now I'm the farthest thing from being trapped in analysis paralysis, thank god). She said on her call with me that she wasn't "woo woo" and didn't believe in intuition, but that sometimes she "knew things," and didn't know why or how.

Fast forward four weeks and she'd sold $58,000 in her brand new intuitive strategy consulting business , $48,000 of which was from two comments on Facebook that she was intuitively guided to make.

Another woman, a brilliant Business Psychic with boat loads of potential, had co-founded a company with an internationally renowned, Harvard-educated business partner who was a serial entrepreneur and founder of a company with a board of directors from some of the most successful CEOs in the world. And then her world shifted on its axis. She left the company that was so dear to her heart and started her own coaching business. And yet it was a tiny, microscopic expression of her true genius. This is a woman with illustrious, imperial energy and here she was struggling month after month to just do $7,000 a month in her business. She was working with low-level clients who left her bored stiff and her dream of conscious world domination was slowly slipping through her fingers.

When she reached out to me, she was in panic mode. Her emotional and mental state of mind were suffering and she was close to ending her business and potentially her life.

(If you are coded with genius—and you are—and it's risen to right underneath the surface of your consciousness, you're going to feel like you're either going to go crazy and kill your self or blow up your life. It's existentially and energetically excruciating to not be able to release all that pent-up potent potion. This, by the way, is what Darkworkers experience all the time as mental breakdown. Darkworkers being those individuals who are carrying the new Codes of Consciousness and whose codes of genius and chaos are already activated and pressing strongly on the psyche to be released. And, if you Google "Dark worker," this is not the definition you will find. Because that definition comes from the Light Grid. This new one comes from the Dark and hasn't hit the collective consciousness yet, so you won't find it anywhere other than in my work.)

So, back to my client. Like I said, when she found me, things were dire.

And then in ninety days, she went from selling $5,000 coaching packages to low-level clients to selling $50,000 coaching packages to visionary entrepreneurs of million dollar companies, had a $100,000 month, and….

was invited "out of the blue" to speak at several prestigious gatherings, including to the world's most promising leaders under 40, in partnership with one of the world's most prestigious intergovernmental institutions, and..

she was also able to go off her medication for depression.

Like I said. Our consciousness is eager and primed for this. So, truthfully, there is no real problem of consciousness at all. Just an elusive and illusory one. But of course this is where the trouble begins: in the invisible and ineffective mind-field that operates outside your awareness or active consent.

The one handed to you by the Collective Grid.

"You can't get it wrong and you'll never get it done."

~ Abraham Hicks

My guess is you've heard this famous line by Abraham Hicks and if you haven't, you've likely been told by a coach or mentor or friend that you should expect to be doing shadow work until you die. My friend, that is a freaking lie. Not an intentional one. They really do believe it. But it's so far from the truth I can't even tell you. Believe me, if all I was going to teach you here was a better way to do shadow work, please. There'd be no point. It would just be turtles all the way down and how you ride them to infinity really doesn't fucking matter.

No.

I'm going to teach you shadow alchemy. How to alchemize your shadow completely, so that it is gone for good, leaving only a ghostly outline of itself. And once it takes that UnShape, all you have to do is sweep your empty shadow for trace amounts of its energy and quickly, nearly instantaneously, alchemize what you find there and go on with your kickass, god-like life.

If shadow management is the path to enlightenment, shadow alchemy is the path to enDarkenment, which is the final stage on our journey to divinity consciousness. Euphoric Living. Health, wealth and happiness that grows day after day, month after month, year after year, decade after decade, without the need for contractions, "healing crises," or time to "ground" or "integrate."

The era of quantum leaps is over. The era of quantum flight has begun.

The truth is that you aren't who you think you are or what the New Age world (or any of the other religions or spiritual traditions) has told you you are.

The true content of your consciousness is invisible to you and energy works in ways you can't possibly imagine, but must know in order to master your life, stop the incessant seeking and find true euphoria and success.

And since power comes from knowing who you really are and knowing both how energy works and actually mastering the use of it, no wonder you feel so powerless and frustrated with life. And we will change that. In no time.

But first I want to let you off the hook.

It's not for lack of trying that you've gotten yourself to this state. You're one of the ones who's gone to every workshop, retreat weekend and certification course you could get your hands on. You've read #allthebooks. You've followed #everynewguru until you could practically give their lectures or do their hot seat coaching for them. And, you've hired #allthecoachesandmentorsandintuitivesandpsychicsandhealersandhypnotherapistsandpastlifer egressionexpertsandeventherapistsandgodforbidpsychiatrists. And because the spiritual self help world is misguided about who we truly are and doesn't actually understand how energy works, it has invented millions of spiritual tools that don't work. Which is why even though you've mastered so many of them, you still feel like you haven't made much progress.

You're right. You haven't. You're like Xeno's arrow. Incrementally traveling to the target and doomed to *never* reach it. In fact incapacitatedly ignorant about the fact that it hasn't even begun the journey of movement in the first place.

And it all boils down to keys versus codes.

If you want to unlock a door and gain access to the room it guards, you have two choices: use a Master key or a "change key." Master keys open a whole set of locks. Change keys open only one key in the set.

This is what the spiritual awakening and self-help movement has been doing: Creating a flurry of change keys in the form of books and workshops and retreats, because they're working at the level of unlocking individual chambers in the mind, each new development hoping it will be, and many claiming to be, the Master Key that will unlock all the chambers in the mind and set us free.

But the problem is approaching it from this energetic analogy in the first place, because doing so instantly creates an infinite number of doors.

Up until now, all spiritual leaders, self help gurus and seekers have gone at awakening from the perspective of unlocking chambers in the mind. This wasn't a conscious orientation. For many it was just a useful analogy. Scores of gurus and self help books, including The Kybalion, which claims to have the Master Key to unlocking the great mysteries, talk about "the key to success," "the key to awakening," the key to you-name-it. It's so prevalent in our conversation about consciousness and spiritual awakening that you probably don't even notice it.

But it is why, decades after the New Age movement began, very few are much better off emotionally, mentally, physically or financially than they were before.

And many are worse.

I certainly was. As were many of my clients. When I was seriously contemplating suicide (both times), I was also the most spiritually aware person I knew, having spent decades steeped in all the best training, workshops, retreats, books, and 1:1 help I could get my hands on.

In fact if our friends and family could chime in, they'd probably say that behind closed doors, we are the farthest thing from a positive testimonial for how well New Age spirituality works.

#amiright?

Now I don't want to totally diss on New Age Spirituality. It's done a lot for human consciousness. The whole concept of shadow work, for instance, was beyond ground-breaking for me and to all of my clients as they were going through their journey. In fact it forms the basis for shadow alchemy, which is a piece of spiritual technology I invented that can single handedly lead you to the promised land for real and for good. (No getting kicked out because you're having an "upleveling crisis," in other words.)

But on the whole, New Age Spirituality doesn't work. And so I proclaim it dead. And it's all because of Zeno and his paradoxes.

Zeno was an ancient Greek philosopher who created thought experiments that were logically sound but ended it a total absurdity in terms of lived human experience. And one of them explains in astonishing energetic accuracy (meaning, in the way it depicts the truth of energetic law) exactly why New Age spirituality has not and never can deliver on its promises.

The paradox is this:

Imagine shooting an arrow at a target and hitting it. Now, we are going to look at the path the arrow took on its way to the target, which it did, in fact, hit.

On its way, the arrow first has to travel half the distance to the target before it travels the full distance. But in order to travel that half distance, I has to travel half THAT distance first, and so on ad infinitum....the arrow never actually goes anywhere and clearly doesn't reach the target.

Feel like a particular kind of spiritual seeking that goes nowhere and doesn't get you anywhere near your goal?

But the arrow does reach the target. And so Zeno in his Ancient Greek office leans back in his Ancient Greek office chair, hands on both sides of his head, exclaiming "How can this be?? How can this be? It doesn't fucking make sense. How can it be????"

Modern calculus claims to resolve this paradox with the notion of a convergent infinite series, which basically says that an infinite series converges to 1, so you can traverse an infinite set within a finite unit.

So that solves it then?

That makes it any less absurd, now that some numbers have been put to it and prove that in fact a finite unit can contain an infinite series? It's Alice in Wonderland stuff and that's the point.

What's happening in both these situations—ancient philosophy and New Age spirituality—is that the illusion is being forced to the surface so we can see it. And that is where we are with our awakening. It is time to force the illusion all the way to the surface. Or, to step all the way *through* the surface — the mirror — to meet the illusion on its own terms so that we can stop being claimed, owned and managed invisibly by it, and begin using the illusion to our advantage.

In other words, the answer is not *con*vergence. It's *di*vergence.

Not in homing-in-ever-closer-to-but-never-quite-reaching Oneness With All, but in taking strict stock of the pitch of our utter individuality. In using this as the touchstone: the degree of my divergence is the force of my spiritual genius.

Not "Am I in the highest spiritual class?" But "Am I yet in a class of one? And if not, where is the fine tuning to shift me into perfect pitch with a tone only I can hear?"

The only way to reach the goal is to diverge completely from the path laid down in everymyth. To refuse to be the hero in a story told by our collective consciousness and instead to step up off the page and invert the narrative of consciousness. To walk the illusion—the shadow—into the light and complete the narrative arc of consciousness in the Dark, with the Anti-Hero's journey, whose ending is very unpolished, unpopular and as potent as it is raw.

And along the way to pen our power, make magic and prepare ourselves to dance with genius, alchemize chaos and play the part of a god.

The tectonic plates of consciousness have shifted and the way we must play the game has changed.

And what has changed most is *how we must change*.

Incremental change will not get you to the euphoria and wild success you seek. You'll never get there from here. (Which is why Abraham Hicks says what they do. But that's only because they're looking at the problem of consciousness through the lens of the Light Grid, which is an incomplete energy system.)

Incremental change requires that you make something matter that does not, in fact, matter at all.

Being committed to incremental change means you're no longer acting against the illusion but operating unconsciously within it.

And yes, there are stragglers of consciousness who seem to be doing alright.

Their time is waning and gone. It is now the Age of Disruption.

It did not used to be this way.

Humans used to be able to rest in their illusion, to live far outside the realm of magic and be content. Their systems—financial, physical, emotional, spiritual, mental—were able to significantly thrive without the experience of magic, the consuming of magic as part of their energetic nutrition. This has changed.

The fact that the arrow actually gets to the target, in all defiance of logic and mathematics that doesn't really resolve the absurdity but just normalizes it, the same way you will finally be able to reach your spiritual goal: By collapsing space and time (which is the same thing, since time and space are one), and being oriented to the journey from a completely different paradigm in which the archer does not take the traversing of space and time into account. (This is why the Hero's and Heroine's journey cannot ever take you to your goal: They're traveling pathways in the mind and heart.)

This is what it means to make magic, for magic is nothing other than the instant traversing of space and time and root-level operating with matter that conforms to strange, but dependable, and seemingly otherworldly laws. Bring the bunny back now, rather than in two years when it has enough time to be born and come back to you. Produce the un-sawed woman. Disappear from your place in front of someone and instantly appear in the corner of the room.

If the archer is to reach her goal (if the spiritual seeker is going to finally end her seeking), she must know the truth about matter and about what matters. And since matter is energy, what she really needs to know is the truth about energy.

She must know the truth of energetic law, for how matter comes to be in the first place and how it is affected by energy, and the truth of spiritual law, which governs how we interact with matter, how matters comes to each of us, specifically, in the form of money, people, and upgraded physical health. In other words, of how we interact with what matters. And also how we interact with Time. (For, how installed in your consciousness is the True Truth that you are master of Time, that you create it and that Time comes from you? And the same goes for money?…My guess is: not at all. And that is why you struggle. Because you don't understand how energy works. And because the Law of Attraction has given you incomplete systems for understanding and operating it.)

Our nature is to operate in the quantum with ease. To create elegant instant shifts without effort. To move from one state to an entirely different one—emotionally, mentally, physically, financially—without moving through all the incremental phases. To take a giant's stride over the increments, the insignificant intermediate steps of growth that were once necessary for the human mind and emotions to traverse in order not to explode or implode from the force of the change on the mental and emotional constructs of the human consciousness at that time.

But we are in a new age now. We are capable of magic on a global scale. And on a quantum scale. And because we are capable of it, we desire it. And desiring it is meaningful. It is part of our blueprinted homing device, calling us back home to the Dark, which is where the dark codes of genius consciousness reside and where the new codes of consciousness are being created. For after the mastering of consciousness comes the creation of its next expression.

This is the word of the god. The work of the human as god. Stepping behind the curtain. Unveiling the underlying mechanisms that create the beautiful and moving illusion we willingly and delightfully step into every day as our playground.

Our laboratory.

Our theater.

We no longer need it to be the inefficient version as battleground. The theater of war. No. It is time to make a quantum shift in spiritual growth and not focus on traversing each unit of spiritual, emotional and mental space separately. In other words, it is time to make the content of our consciousness deliberately not matter, in one precise and exacting way that frees consciousness to instantly leap to a much higher state rather than wringing it through an infinite series of unlockings that will never lead it to its intended goal.

There are many imprecise ways to make the content of consciousness not matter. One of the most popular has been termed "spiritual bypass."

This is not that.

There is only one precise way to make the content of consciousness not matter, which in fact frees it into its naturally elevated state in which magic and the raw material of the universe are easy and natural for it to access and operate.

The archer is confronted with the quandary of physical space. The mind is confronted with the quandary of mental and emotional space: Content. Raw awareness. And the minute we talk about keys and unlocking, we automatically create an impossible scenario. An absurdity of infinite mental and emotional spaces — chambers in the mind — that must be traversed.

This part of my childhood. This emotion. This past life. This piece of soul to retrieve. This memory to heal. This manifestation of the mother wound to understand. This manifestation of the father wound to integrate. This original trauma. This subsequence re-enactment of the original trauma. This proceeding re-enactment of the re-enactment. This form of mental illness. This episode of depression. This resistance to upleveling. This form of self sabotage. This trigger. This codependent relationship. This hijacking. This healing crisis. This contraction. This. This. This. This. This.

And there springs into being the infinite series of beautifully locked chambers and we become haunted by the weight of all the keys we must carry and the work of all the endless unlocking.

The way we see the problem of consciousness either gives birth to the infinite and impossible journey through the desert of the locked mind or it unveils something true that, while raw and cold and seemingly untouchable, can be consumed and turned into our final awakening.

Not the dawn of sleepy awareness but the vigorous, nutrient-rich behavior of athletes of energy mastery. Up before the light. Active in the pitch black.

In other words, do we have the spiritual boldness and energetic constitution for what we will find in the Dark.

Keys to Codes

It is time to upset the analogy for Truth seeking.

It is not about unlocking, which is an ancient technology. Which means it's

also not about keys. Even master keys.

It's about codes. And not light codes, but dark codes.

Light codes only have the ability to open the doors in the mind and shine light on the shadow.

Dark codes have the ability to collapse the content of consciousness and turn it from an infinite set of locked chambers into an infinite channel of spiritual genius and euphoria.

And this means that the dark codes are here to disrupt the substrate of Light Consciousness and perform a root-level migration and reboot onto an entirely different operating system. One that exists, fully coded in our consciousness, like a wall sparking with new electric grids. It is called into being by our Dark DNA, which rests in a stillpoint in our bones of light—that aspect of the body that does not move and therefore is impermeable to the temptation to spring space and matter and the illusion of what matters into being and then ignorantly try to cross it.

When you deny the crossing, you lift yourself up onto the cross of consciousness, the meathook of awakening, which hooks you into a satisfying death. It is the moment you complete the arc, finally go sane, finish the journey, hit the target of your seeking and let yourself off the hook for good.

The hook where you have hung your whole life, sacrificing yourself to the infinitely small gods of progress.

So then I asked myself, how is it that I was able to alchemize my shadow, because I did it using individual instances of raw awareness. But each time, there was less of my shadow present, and *not in an incremental way.*

This is the story and mystery of shadow alchemy.

The way you manage your shadow now requires that your Soul tell you little white lies about your energy and power. Yes. Your Soul is the source of your suffering. We will get to this later.

Shadow is created when we believe the illusion that anything other than occupying the playful stance of a god matters. Shadow management is calming of the shadow through toys, distractions and candy. Replacing one thing that our human is convinced matters greatly and that is causing the mind great pain with something else that matters over which you have more control, but which does not, in the end, actually matter, in such a way that you are creating more and more content each time than must then be run through to infinity.

Shadow alchemy depletes and deletes the inaccurate codes of consciousness.

Shadow management creates calming chambers in the mind—meditation rooms of inaccurate stillness, filled with quieting content that soothes for the moment but is ultimately lacking in core nutrition and requires it be managed and run through later in order to process. And of course that processing creates yet another chambering of content in the mind that must then again be processed and so on ad infinitum into the going rage of spiritual seeking insanity.

And until you master shadow alchemy, you will always have inner factions. The voices of your shadow self that are rising up in mutiny. The bugs of consciousness, really, that are constantly causing glitches in the system.

Like this:

"It doesn't matter what your dad thinks of you. What really matters is what you think of yourself."

Calm. Soothing. Sitting in front of the flickering flame that knowing your worth solves all your problems.

But now you have to go in search of your worth. Because you do not inherently feel it or know it. (There is a good reason for this. It doesn't exist. You don't need it. You're not inherently "worth" anything. You're priceless. Like a work of art.) And so now you've created another chamber of content in your mind which must now be processed, but which you tell yourself is okay, since it feels better to be in search of your worth than to be tussling with the painful memory of your dad.

But now you have to go find out how you matter and then that's another workshop and another retreat and another book and another spiritual tool and another year or decade or three of spiritual seeking.

Consciousness mastery is not about processing content. It's about being able to drop content.

And when I say that, what I mean is that it is dropping the need to have anything matter. Content is matter, but it's also *that* it matters or that *something* matters. If space matters to the archer, the arrow never gets to the target. If the mental and spiritual and emotional content of your consciousness matters (meaning if you assign meaning and emotionality to it), you instantly create an impossibly large set of things that can matter and ways that they matter and ways it impacts you that they matter that you will be unlocking until you die.

And at first, unlocking a room is fun.

We feel a sense of accomplishment, mystery, and joy in the task. We wonder what's in the next room. How easy it will be to unlock. And so at the beginning and for quite a while, we were really into unlocking all the chambers. But now it has become exhausting and tedious and repetitive and addicting and all Abraham Hicks has to say is, "You can't get it wrong and you'll never get done."

Fuck that.

I am not a proponent of believing things because they feel good, so if it felt shitty to hear that, and yet it was true, I'd be backing it up 1000% and directing you to the place your mind when your comfort matters more than the truth.

But lucky day, it's not actually true.

And to be clear, the root-level reboot that happens as a result of shadow alchemy, which is to understand, own and live on the foundational truth that nothing matters, is not a place of depression and suicidal ideation. Because there's actually nothing wrong that nothing matters. And emotion and desire can still rest on something entirely different than matter and that things matter and which things matter, and still be at ease with themselves and in your body/mind and fill you with euphoria and complete joy.

They are meant to rest on playfulness. Not on matter and on what matters. This is their native home, and when emotion and joy discover their resting place there, they are for the first time freed to their greatest and most unleashed expression, because they are not chained to the deleterious effects of things mattering as a result of their being themselves.

I want to be very clear. This is not existentialism. It's not even Buddhism wrapped in a new bow.

The existentialists said, essentially: there's no meaning so stop trying to make meaning. But they weren't able to get anywhere close to a feeling of euphoria. All they could manage was patient internal emptiness.

The Buddhists had to reject desire in order to accept that nothing matters (or that everything is an illusion). But when you achieve Dark Mastery, it is so far from either of these paradigms that it's hard to put into words. Impossible, really. But I will try: Living beyond shadow and in the truth that nothing matters and in fun and full residence in the Dark generates a consistent level of sustained joy, exhilaration, and a whole dose of sinful and wicked glee, because you feel like you've gotten away with the biggest heist in human consciousness. You get to be and do whatever the fuck you want and have all the wild success you desire. It's not the depressive suicidal ideation of the existentialist. It's the playful stance of a God.

Gods, myth makers, alchemists, the Dark Archetypes all know that Nothing matters. It's not even a concept that makes sense to them. It has no content. What they would say, if they were not blind and mute, would be, this: "We are not talking about things that matter or which have inherent worth. We are talking about things that are priceless. The value, the mattering of them to one person or many people, is simply not our concern." What they would say to anyone concerned would be this: "Your genius will be worthless to most and priceless to a few. Get over it."

And so we come to the Prestige. The reveal in the magic trick. The return of the bird, the impossible freeing of the woman from the locked chamber of water. The arrow that strikes at the heart of all that matters.

The final arc of the narrative of consciousness, the journey from human to divine human, is about becoming a work of art. Turning yourself and the world around you into a work of sustained, open-ended questioning and playful appropriation of the entire content of consciousness into a display of beauty, not into a proclamation of import and meaning. This is the work of Gods and archetypes who don't care about things like worth and matter.

A painting hanging on the wall really doesn't fucking matter. And yet it streams so much euphoria and joy to those who see something in it. But it doesn't mean that it matters. In fact it can't matter in order to so boastfully express its power and have its greatest impact. If it mattered, it couldn't possibly open that portal.

And how do you reach this odd and desired state of being?

Through an infinitely open mind.

The mind can either be mistreated as an endless number of locked chambers, or it can be seen for what it truly is: a channel of genius, open on both ends.

Instead of being infinitely closed it is in fact infinitely open.

This is why it's so terrifying to consider stepping into the state of mind that would deliver to you what you truly seek, which is a constant feeling of euphoria and the knowledge that you have and are a superpowered being akin to a God or an archetype: It requires that you have an infinitely open mind. And those of us on the earth plane right now who have infinitely open minds are considered crazy.

But the truth is that the mind is meant to move energy, not hold it. It is meant to stream genius, not grip content. All physical, mental, and emotional struggle stems from a mind that is trying to hold onto the content of its consciousness and make emotions and thoughts and physical experiences matter in certain ways and not matter in other ways. When it moves from its natural state as streaming genius to trying to be a container that holds energy, an entire world of pain, suffering, and struggle springs into being and the mind stumbles under the burden of an infinitely heavy set of chambers full of matter, rather than feeling immaterially light, a portal open on both ends.

Your mind is a dual channel meant to stream gold at all times. Out and through as well as in and up. This is what we call "streaming prestige." And when it is in this natural state, health, wealth, happiness and genius are the inevitable result. This is why I assert from spiritual law that everyone is a channel and everyone is a genius.

Out from your SuperConscious you flow your genius onto the world stage as works of art. In you pull gold through as you are out in the world, alchemizing and streaming its energy up from the world into your body/mind as euphoric experiences of the world as a collection of works of art, not as a set of problems—philosophical or mathematical, emotional or mental—to be worked out.

It is a new kind of breathing that the world and the SuperConscious are engaged in. And you are what is being breathed.

In other words, there's genius in the world available for us to be streaming into our minds and bodies at all times. When you're streaming gold from the world, you are streaming it back up into the Superconscious and fulfilling your role as a being on the leading edge of consciousness, supplying the SuperConscious with new material that then becomes synergistically mixed and alchemized with the content already there, informing the storehouse of new archetypes and myths that provide us with the raw materials we then bring back into our physical experience with which to build our new our playground.

And which comes back through us out into the world as new myths, and which we then interact with in such a way as to extract their gold, the genius birthed in the illusion of being other, which is where the New gets its body and energy, and which we then stream back in and up.

It is the breathing that a piece of art does that, when we experience it, takes our own breath away. Because of course we are being breathed in and up along with it.

All the content that already exists and has already been created—even from the perspective and the positions of people that what they've created matters—contains gold that is there for you to stream. For you are meant to experience the world that already is as a work of art as well. In addition to creating works of art and being one.

And just as art doesn't matter but gives you a magical experience of euphoria and transports you into your imagination, where your own legacy and greatness lie, so you, too, do not matter. In the same way and to the same degree.

Art is a portal to a new world. And the only reason it does not present itself as a problem for consciousness is because it clearly identifies itself as a work of art, and as a *portal*, not as a mirror or a window, and so we understand that it doesn't actually matter. We see that it is at once immaterial, priceless and essential. We are able to suspend the content of our minds. (Or we are meant to. For that is the only way to reach through to the other side and pull in what is hidden there as treasure. Though now even art is being asked to mean something. To take a stand among the moral and the ethical. To step fully into the world of illusion and participate in the sleep of the human. And this is when art loses its power in exchange for becoming useful.)

Shadow alchemy is in essence looking at the experience that triggered you and seeing it a work of art with gold hidden in it to be streamed into your fields of play. Shadow management is looking at the experience that triggered you as a problem to be solved. Peering into an experience to find what really does and doesn't matter about the experience. It is a process of exchanging low-frequency content for higher frequency content, yes. And yet the highest frequency is formless. And that is what you crave.

To accomplish shadow alchemy, your mind must first be infinitely open.

In other words, you must become bipolar.

This is where the blessing of already being this way comes in. Yes. It has been excruciatingly painful to live in a world that believes minds with ceilings and fear with a floor is healthy and promotes stable functioning; a world whose systems, structures and institutions are all organized to submit to the closed mind and shuttered heart and serve them.

Where does the Wild mind go. Where does the unfettered heart thrive. Nowhere but inside, first. And then everywhere outside, because as within, so without. And so now I can teach you how to remove the ceiling in your own mind and the floor of your crippling and mostly invisible fear.

Without this, nothing great can happen.

If you have a ceiling to your mind, it won't create the powerful energetic pull that extracts the gold from experience and allows you to see and live the world as a work of art, no matter what actual experience you're having. You will have a ceiling to your mind and that means that you will be using your mind as a series of chambers, looking for things that matter, paying attention to how much they matter, and of course placing yourself into that attention as well, which means you are then obsessed with how much you matter and where you matter and to whom. This cuts the flow of pure genius energy so that it cannot stream in through the world up through your body and mind and into the superconscious, and this means you cannot be in a constant orgasmic state of euphoria, because you have turned your mind into a container that must hold energy.

In other words: fear is the mind killer. And it is also intelligent and lonely. And so it slinks in the shadows unseen and undetected and when we step in, you will be horrified at how afraid you actually are. All the time. Everywhere. I know you think you're a badass in your life. So did I, until I learned the four voices of fear and realized they were speaking as me, to me, all the time. And this is fine. It is a necessary first step in awakening and you may think you've done this before and that this appears elementary enough to put down.

That would be foolish.

And not the kind of Fool-ish that is in fact wise and all knowing. The kind that emanates from the sticky and spongey mind of a fool who thinks she knows it all already. (That would be the influence of your saboteur. The sophisticated devil in your mind who whispers *let's leave. We've heard this all before* because he knows what's coming and being alchemized into nothing doesn't suit him. I've lost track of all the people who tell me they thought they'd done all the deep work on their fear, trigger, shame and shadow and yet when placed in front of the mirror of this new spiritual technology, with the blacklight switched on, all their telltale shame burns bright as day. Which is wonderful because then it can be truly alchemized away.)

It is energetically impossible to have one or the other: a ceiling to your mind but no floor to your fear, or a floor to your fear but no ceiling in your mind. When you have one or the other, your mind instantly becomes the infinite set of locked chambers and you are thrown into the spiral of despair.

When you have no floor to your fear you can stream pure genius from your Superconscious into your mind and straight out into the world, with no concern for how it's going to be received, perceived, valued or understood. This is the euphoric activity of a God creating worlds as works of art and creating itself as a work of art in the process, because when you stream genius through your mind, you're also streaming it through your body and the body gets to experience the euphoria of that genius energy flooding your system. This is what people refer to as being in a constant orgasmic state of being.

Being bipolar is an absolute gift. I am so grateful for how easy it is for me to collapse the conditioned container my mind looks to be into an infinitely open space. And yet. The considerable shadow that exists in all of us, including those with mental illness, exerts a powerful downward pull through the nonexistent floor of fear straight into the willingness to commit suicide. For if nothing matters (open mind at the top) and I have no fear (open mind at the bottom), then suicide is an option.

This only happens when the shadow is in full effect and not alchemized. So while I say bipolar is my greatest gift, it was almost my greatest curse until I alchemized my shadow so that the absence of a floor to my fear led not into the shadows but straight into the Dark, which is a land empty of content and therefore full of possibility and the play of the divine.

I don't take pills for my bipolar because I've discovered a new way to channel its genius so that my life is enriched by my bipolar, not crippled by it.

It's like all those stories you hear about people curing themselves of a physical illness using advanced nutrition and changing their diet. Except in my case I used advanced consciousness and spent months inventing a new spiritual technology and mastering bringing it online in my mind and body so I could stream the full force of the genius my bipolar carries and not be taken down by it.

That's how I went from broke, bipolar and suicidal to a millionaire and CEO of my own company in ten months, feeling happy, stable and deeply fulfilled all along. It's been almost two years since my diagnosis (I was also diagnosed with severe mood and anxiety disorder, two types of ADD and PTSD) and I am now starting a second company, finishing my first book, traveling the world and enjoying an amazing relationship with my thirteen-year-old daughter as a single mom.

We go to the world, any world—emotional, physical, mental, spiritual—and we have a choice. We can either put it into chambers in our mind, which instantly get locked and which we then we have to go unlock, or we can experience it with a mind that channels, that is able to go from mirror to window to portal instantly. These are the three levels of consciousness mastery—window, mirror, portal—otherwise known as the hero's journey, the heroine's journey, and a completely new journey that has never been spoken of before: the Anti-Hero's journey.

What's different about shadow alchemy is that it does not incrementally treat of the shadow until it disappears, because you're not taking out more and more pieces of your shadow every time you do shadow alchemy, you're just further and further mastering the ability to instantly see every experience and experience everything as a work of art. You're not taking on the shadow as something, and therefore what it is can show itself, which is the den of genius.

For genius is what is hiding deep within our shadow. And yet if we take shadow as something, then it becomes relevant content and we are in a house of mirrors and our genius is sent to another realm. But if we take the shadow as nothing, the content of consciousness as nothing, then the house of mirrors collapses into a window and then into an infinite extension of portals and these are the dark codes, and this is where our genius lies in wait for us.

Shadow is not a piece of material you're diminishing over time until it doesn't exist, because when we try to do that it will never not exist.

Shadow is actually an orientation towards the world as a world that matters and our place in that world as mattering, which instantly creates the shadow mind that can never be traveled all the way through.

Shadow is a dimension of its own that is locked and crowded and immovable. It is a cut-rate, one-dimensional consciousness.

But if you orient yourself to the world and to every single experience as a work of art that has gold hidden at the heart of it and what you're doing every time you experience triggers is mastering to an even greater degree the ability to experience that experience as a work of art, this is is the essence of shadow alchemy.

By seeing the world as a work of art, shadow consciousness loses its dimensionality and drifts into the background so that new doors can open in the mind.

And you will, at a certain point, reach a critical mass, a tipping point in your own consciousness where matter instantly turns back into energy and a tipping point when energy instantly becomes matter. Both require exacting and precise mastery of codes and frequencies of consciousness. This is the point at which you go from incremental mastery of shadow alchemy to instant alchemizing and reach a tipping point where effort flips and feeds itself in the other direction, from the negative spiral to the positive spiral where you're gaining momentum in the other direction.

This is when the apprentice becomes the Master Artisan.

Where the trainee becomes the Master Handler of the beasts of genius and wins the honor of handling them directly.

Incremental mastery of shadow alchemy is not based on making the content of consciousness matter, as emotional space to navigate, but operating your will against the shadow as one would turn a flywheel.

In other words, it's not linear, but rotational treatment where Time is treated of not as a line to traverse but a spiral to leverage.

In the book *Good to Great: How Good Companies Become Great,* Jim Collins talks about the concept of the flywheel, a massive wheel used as an energy storage and delivery system, and which at first, and for quite awhile, strongly resists being moved because of its inertia.

The way to change its stored energy state—the way to cause the flywheel to go from *requiring* energy to *generating* it—is by increasing or decreasing its speed of rotation.

When you increase it enough, the flywheel collects energy over time and then releases it very quickly at rates that far exceed the ability of the energy source itself. If you apply continuous effort against the flywheel, you will eventually get it to start moving. As you continue to apply effort, it picks up speed and then you apply less and less effort until at a certain point it's actually using its own weight to continue the progress. You've switched from negative to positive feedback loop. You have reversed effort.

This is what shadow alchemy is.

At first it's excruciatingly tedious and takes up a great deal of your time. But there is a point where you have left the gravitational pull of illusion and are in the anti-gravity of Truth, heading into the Dark, generating Time and artfully crafting your consciousness.

And from then on you simply sweep your shadow to keep it clean and clear and empty, which takes infinitesimally little effort because your Creative Will has been rotated into its own beneficial springboard. Into a wellspring of Will.

The energetic law behind this is that as you alchemize your shadow, you are switching out operating systems. The speed at which thoughts and emotions and their energy travels through your body changes dramatically and the gravitational pull diminishes, because you are collapsing time.

And this is because analogies of space contain the problem.

The visual metaphor that depicts the energetic law here is that where shadow management requires you have an infinite number of keys to open mind rooms, shadow alchemy collapses down the entire system and the dimension in which shadow exists altogether. There are no rooms. There are no walls. There are no ceilings. There are no floors. And the mind has become radically, extensibly open.

And yet, because we still exist in a realm in which space and time are experienced separately, the collapsing of time takes some time, at first.

There is a period of changeover during which the migration from one consciousness to another is occurring, as the expression of the root-level reboot.

Think about actual system migrations. There are a finite number of systems to migrate over (just as there are a finite number of bugs in your consciousness - four actually. Not very many.), requiring a finite number of codes to be rewritten. Once you rewrite them all, you're done.

This is how you are not hooked into the implementation of it forever.

There is a point when you are no longer directed to the same process of treating your consciousness that you used to be directed to unconsciously. And for quite a while, just as in the 3D world, where companies will often use two systems side by side for awhile, the old one and the new one, so you too will be toggling between Light and Dark Consciousness until you are embraced so sustainably by the Dark and your taste for the divine has shifted so dramatically that the old system of consciousness collapses down into nothing.

The mind is not a series of locked chambers. It is a program with a finite number of codes and systems, and if you get to the root-level code and change it, it no longer operates the same way. In the words, it doesn't create content that has to be managed.

It becomes multi-dimensionless.

And the way this root-level deprogramming and reboot happens?

That is for the Master Codes of disruption, which go in and destroy the essential coded elements of the mind that create the false chambers, filled with immaterial content, which then created all the things that matter.

In other words, the Master Codes of disruption are shot like an arrow straight to the heart of the matter and cause a complete system collapse and reboot. There are only a few codes of illusion. Once you fully disrupt them, you are done.

The problem of consciousness lies in the shadows, travels through the light and resolves itself in the Dark. There are three phases to the journey and up until now we have been trying to complete the process with only two phases available to us. To our imagination and to our will.

The reason the spiritual enlightenment and self help industry is nearly $10B and growing is because no one has been able to end the seeking. No one has even conceived that there *could* be an end. We are an uncivil battlefield of warring internal factions and we will always need the newest spiritual technology, the latest upgrade to our very old, outdated, glutted consciousness so we can at least keep the thing running.

The answer is not incremental upgrades to an old system. The answer is a root level reboot to an entirely new one in one fell swoop.

The flywheel is heavy matter.

Very different than codes and programs.

And yet the analogy to shadow alchemy fits perfectly, because the flywheel represents the way in which we, as humans, *as matter*, work either with or against our programming *that things matter*.

And the aspect of us that manages the flywheel is our Warrior, because the Warrior is the domain of will and matter. It is what we are *willing to make matter* and what we are *willing to do* about the illusion.

The flywheel's incredible weight represents the resistance of our will to change and the powerful effect of our shadow programming, which is deeply embedded in our bodies and brains—in our matter.

This is why consciousness mastery is so difficult: It's not just sitting down at a computer to decode and recode the bugs. It requires that we complete dizzying and continual shifts between two completely opposing paradigms, and master both at once: turning the massive flywheel of our resistance (our habituated belief in the illusion of matter and that things matter) for days and weeks and months to generate enough energy to then be able to sit down and code the content of our consciousness (a paradigm that demands we relinquish that habituated belief completely).

Turning the flywheel is meant to give us energy so we can sit down and debug our consciousness, and then encode our mind, but at first it's all we can do to actually muster the will to keep trying to turn the wheel when we see so little progress and it's so easy to give up. And by progress I don't mean progress through time. I mean progress in our willingness to see the Truth.

This is another way in which shadow alchemy does not partake in incrementalism, because we're talking about rotational energy, movement around an axis that picks up speed, not movement through space toward a target. It's a change from trying to aim at a target to generating massive amounts of power, more than we as humans could generate "on our own."

Our dark heart of gold is the transformer of toxic energy (power that has been corrupted) and the amplifier of pure potent energy and our inner flywheel, our will, is the generator of power. And it is turned by the Warrior.

When we are no longer oppressed by how hard it is to get and manage power, are being easily powered at all times and don't have to expend energy on getting and managing power (which is what shadow management is - a great and constant and never-ending expenditure of energy), that's when the fun begins. The euphoria. The feeling of being a god walking among humans.

The spiritual transformational world has never been able to offer true empowerment because its approach has been coded with the completely wrong analogy.

And now it is time for the mass migration. Not from one land to another but from one consciousness to another.

There are a few of us Consciousness pioneers, early adopters of the new spiritual technology and it is time we introduce this alarmingly simple, elegant, sophisticated and incredibly powerful, highly streamlined and much more efficient energy and power management system to the planet.

Windows users, move over. It's time for the Apple revolution.

Window consciousness.

Versus Apple consciousness.

Staring through a pain at the bright world beyond versus taking a bite of the apple and tumbling through the mirrored window-turned-portal into the magical world as its honored guest.

And yes, a completely backwards and upside down world where Time and Space are playthings. Where nonsense is the highest form of art.

Believe it or not, like it or not, the desert caravan is coming and bringing the circus freaks of consciousness with it. They are the carriers of the dark codes, and they are headed straight for the shadowland in your mind, so they can collapse the chambers into channels, turn out all the confusing lights and plunge you into the Dark, which is your natural home. Your native land.

And where together we will all create the Greatest Show On Earth.

Codes Of Consciousness: Teaching The Light Grid And The Archetypes Of The Collective Consciousness (Master The Archetypal Consciousness You've Been Given)

Human consciousness is a kingdom of energy that has woken up to itself in the middle of a siege and is playing catch-up with the storyline to understand as desperately as possible who is trustworthy, where the true power lies, and how to best orchestrate peace and thriving.

The architects of the war, and of the awakening, are the archetypes.

You are the Sovereign. The one who's in charge of working this out whole mess. You're supposed to be in charge. But you're not.

To aid you in this most important task of discernment are two councils, one speaking for truth, the other for illusion, both claiming to offer wisdom and guidance to aid you in your most critical process of discernment, and to give direction on all consequent decisions that must be made.

You must decide which to listen to and which to cast out of the throne room.

Get it right and magic, euphoria and heaven on earth inevitably results.

Freedom from physical, emotional, mental, and financial struggle of all kinds, in no time, and with no need to hustle and grind.

Get it wrong, and it's hell on earth.

The Good news:

Truth is not relative. It is not ambiguous. And it is not difficult to know.

The Bad news:

You probably believe it is. Which is why you're suffering.

THE LIGHT GRID VS ABSOLUTE TRUTH

The reason most don't believe Absolute Truth exists is because they've been schooled on the Light Grid. Light exists on a spectrum, so they believe Truth does, also. The Dark has no spectrum. It is itself only, with no shades or variations. And Truth, just like the newest, lightest Light, comes from The Dark.

A confused mind is an undecided mind.

A mind that is unaware of its confusion is not just undecided but impotent.

Your true awakening means you must leave the tribe that raised you. We know this. You know this.

You've already done it, in fact.

Or so you think.

But I'm not talking about your tribe of origin.

I'm talking about tribal consciousness in general. In totality.

I'm talking about the *human* tribe.

And how do you leave the human tribe? Not the way you left the first one, when you went on your Hero's journey and struck out on your own and physically changed environments and conditions and often friends, lovers, spouses, and very like left your family of origin, at least for a while.

In order to leave the human tribe, you must first know where it is. Where it lives. Where *you* truly live. Then you'll be able to leave it all behind for good and instead of seeking incessantly like a spiritual nomad, setting up camp on one book, guru, retreat and workshop after the next, traveling the vast wastelands of New Age spirituality with everyone else who thinks seeking is the new residing and expects to be wandering from one oasis of spiritual eureka after another, with the same arid conditions of money, love and health ruin stretching infinitely in between, you'll actually find your true home, and your UnTribe.

Abraham Hicks was dead wrong when they said "You'll never get it wrong and you'll never get it done." All the spiritual leaders and coaches are dead wrong when they say you'll be doing shadow work until you die.

Just like all the myths and fairytales are wrong when they claim to depict the arc of the journey of awakening and fulfilment as the Hero's, followed by the Heroine's journeys.

So where does the human tribe live?

On the Light Grid.

The Dark is where the monstrous and the dragons live.

And since genius is monstrous, guess where that means your true home is.

Hic sunt dracones

In 1510, artisans created a hollow copper globe about 5 inches in diameter. It came to be known as the Hunt-Lenox globe, which represented all the regions of the known world at that time, and is one of the only remaining globes from that period, which was right after the discovery of the New World—North, Central and South America.

Across what was the eastern coast of Asia was written these three words in Latin: hic sunt dracones.

"Here be dragons."

Scholars disagree about the meaning of "dracones." It does mean "dragon" in Latin, however some believe this refers to the Dagroians.

In any case, the phrase depicts the abode of the monstrous, because legend had it that the Dagroians "feasted upon the dead and picked their bones."

For most humans, seeing those three words scrawled across the map of their consciousness is enough to drive them as far away from the Dark Lands as possible.

But for you, those words mean something entirely different.

"Hic sunt dracones" doesn't even register as "here be dragons."

What you see is this:

"Here we are. Come home."

And that's where I'm going to take you.

Into your genius, giant nature, to your UnTribe, so you can end your endless seeking, master the raw materials of the universe and learn how to make magic on demand.

In order to do this, you must go with me on the final journey from the subconscious to the conscious—the journey of the Hero through the shadow lands into the Light—through the Band of UnHooking—the journey of the Heroine off the Light Grid—and away from the human tribe altogether, into the pure Dark, the wild, unruly domain of the Anti-Hero; the human who has stepped out of his skin of limited consciousness, ended the search for meaning and purpose and oneness, of value and self worth and alignment, and has become what he truly is: a beast of genius, a law unto himself, crafting consciousness, creating new myths, roaming the land with all the others of his kind, all of whom have arrived at the holy grail of experience.

Heaven on earth.

Or what I call SuperConscious Awakening.

Why So Many Spiritual Workers Are Still So Fucking Miserable and Broke

After decades of the rise and reclaiming of the feminine, of a multi billion dollar industry of spiritual self help, do you ever wonder what is UP with so many (frankly, most) spiritual workers still feeling secretly depressed, lost, empty and nowhere near the thriving, million/billion dollar empire they know is within them?

Are you one of them...?

If so, it's not that you need more feminine empowerment. You've gotten shit tons of that. You may even be a LEADER in that movement. And yet you're secretly stuck as fuck.

Miserable or at the very least, meh.

Bank account a roller coaster of feast or famine.

Or if it's not, your energy and wellbeing and happiness certainly is.

Rich and miserable. Just like the corporate drones you left behind (or now coach). And now you're one of them.

You do not need more tools in your spiritual toolbox. You have a bazillion of those.

Crystals and wands and crystal wand dildos.

Precious stones placed strategically in corners of your house and under your bed and in your shower head so that they rain pure energy on your crown chakra in the morning.

You chant and dance every day like a good little spiritual student.

You do #allthefemininerisingthings.

And yet nothing.

And it's not that you need masculine energy, either. You've got that in spades. Maybe too much. So yes maybe there's a little balancing that needs to happen but the answer lies so far outside anything you know or have been taught that it's hard to know where to begin or even begin to look.

So you go back to what you know.

I know this is happening because even though you appear successful and happy on the outside (to "them"), you come and confess to me in droves what it's *really* like behind the curtain.

You are not, in fact, happy and fulfilled like your social media presence suggests.

Your mental and emotional health, and your businesses, are actually in shambles, and you're exhausted with the constant seeking, the constant spiritual work with no end in sight, the constant keeping up the facade, and you're at the end of your rope with answers.

That's because the path we are guided to take by our mentors, coaches, priests, therapists and psychiatrists to achieve spiritual transformation is based on their understanding of the archetypal journey of awakening as depicted in our myths and fairytales and stories, and all those myths, fairytales and stories are flawed. They cannot deliver on their promise of transcendence.

And yet all we know to do to cure our inner dis-ease is to strike out on the journeys they depict, and follow the steps of awakening they tell us to follow, because we believe they have — because they claim to have — the answers to our predicament.

For centuries, all we had was the Hero's Journey, as depicted in thousands of stories across the globe.

When the Hero's Journey couldn't deliver on its promise of fulfillment — because Heroes inevitably end up going through a Dark Night of the Soul AFTER their heroic quest is over and they have presumably found the holy grail of life (their purpose, their calling and their personal power)— we explained this unfortunate turn of events by saying that the Hero's Journey doesn't "work" because it's incomplete. It doesn't address the importance of the feminine in our psyches.

So we were pointed to the Dark Goddess myths and told to go on the Heroine's journey to reclaim our inner feminine and then integrate our feminine and masculine energies.

Thus the birth of the feminine rising movement and dancing circles and birthing circles and red tents and honoring our intuition and our bodies in our decisions and our lives.

We left corporate America (the site of our Hero's Journey gone awry), and started our spiritual business by following and honoring our feminine souls.

And that was awesome for awhile.

And yet....

Sales rose and then fell. And then rose and fell again.

Inspiration waxed and waned.

We dug deeper. Did more shadow work (the go-to tool of the feminine-based transformational world). Hired masculine-based coaches to teach us strategy. Hired feminine-based coaches to get us in touch with our bodies and our intuition.

And each one gave us a bump to our incomes and inspiration.

But for most of you, this simply doesn't last.

Something always reasserts itself and you settle back into a stultifying homeostasis of mediocrity.

You aren't a miserable corporate 9-5 drone.

But you also are decidedly *not* a genius empire-building agent of consciousness living The Dream and watching in slack-jawed astonishment as your legacy body of work slithers into all corners of the global movement of awakening, gathering speed and power at an alarming rate.

And THAT'S what feeds your soul and lifts your Spirit.

If you don't have THAT, you've got nothing, no matter how much better things are than they used to be.

But THAT? That doesn't come from traveling the Hero's or the Heroine's Journey.

Those are essential preparatory journeys along the way, for sure.

But they are entirely insufficient to get you to THAT.

And so maybe you try to resign yourself to never having THAT.

To convincing yourself that THAT is a pipe dream.

My friends, it is not, in any way, a pipe dream.

That pipe is simply being smoked somewhere far from your imagination. Far from any human's imagination, which is why the story of the journey describing the path there hasn't been told yet, because that myth was, until now, unimaginable.

No longer.

It is through following a wildly unpopular, misunderstood and demonized path that I took myself from broke, bipolar and suicidal to a self-made millionaire in ten months and then to giving birth to my genius legacy, a global movement of consciousness that has never before settled into into the human awareness and that is changing lives, blowing minds, birthing lucrative genius businesses right and left and finally...FINALLY...ushering people into their own personal experience of euphoria and the epiphany they have been seeking their whole fucking lives.

If you are sick to death of the same old methods for self-realization and awakening that have taken you Nowhere New and have done nothing to radically alter your conditions, then you are a candidate for this new way.

It is a new modality called SuperConscious Awakening, which completes the journey and finally ENDS the numbing and constant seeking and searching.

You are not meant to seek and search forever.

There is something waiting for you BEYOND that horizon. And not just any something.

THAT is waiting for you.

The only question is: How badly do you want it?

The Light Grid

The Light Grid is the collective energetic blueprint of human consciousness, a non-physical power collection, management and amplification structure to which every human is linked through their light body, itself a grid of energy that surrounds and infiltrates the body, and which is the personal power management system that serves as the home to the chakras, our aura, and our mental, emotional and physical fields.

The Light Grid is the Father figure in all our myths and fairy tales.

It's where energy collects to become matter, according to certain laws. It is also the place where matter dissolves back into energy.

When someone is channeling someone who has died, they are simply connecting to the place on the Light Grid where that gathering of energy is living non-physically.

All that is, has been and will be hangs out on the Light Grid.

The proper way to understand manifestation, by the way, is not to talk of it as bringing something into reality, as if it didn't already exist. All that is manifested already exists as a manifold collection of energy. You are simply bringing that energy into your physical experience.

Your home is in the New Myth.

Not as a seeker of meaning, but a maker of one.

Not as a child of God or a follower of the Light (same thing) but AS a god.

A god in a land unknown.

A god in a land unaware of itself.

A god in a land unseen.

Half breathing.

Wings resting on darkened ground.

Fire becalmed in the nostrils.

And the absurd absence of heartbeats.

These are the ones to wake.

And of course, first you must wake yourself.

So I have to do to your consciousness what you are then meant to go do to others'. I have to completely disrupt your paradigm, overturn everything you've been told and taught and deprogram your mind so you can be available to your Higher Mind, your SuperConscious and the source of your true genius. That is the "map home" part of the book. Then once you are open-minded enough, I can show you the real secrets and give you the source code to how to make magic in your life and masterfully stream your genius.

In other words, first I have to tell you who you thought you were and who you actually are and lay out all the implications of this great chasm in your awareness. (Meaning, Iwhy you feel so lost in the The Land Of Perpetual Struggle.) This is all about orienting you properly to the Land of Consciousness so you can get where you want to go: to the Promised Land. This is explained through the archetype map—the map of your current consciousness. Think of this as the "You Are Here" dot on the map.

Once you know where you actually are and what's possible, then I'll show you how to get there.

So, who are you, really?

To answer that, I'm going to show you the map of your sense of power.

Because Identity is a matter of power management: Who you think you are is simply a result of where you think your power lies.

Who Am I? What Am I Made Of? How Do I Recognize Truth?

As we ask and answer these questions—in other words as we embark on the Hero's Journey of Consciousness—we will along the way be not only discovering the answers we have always sought, but will be building a sleek, keen, effective, fool-proof and predictable method for calling in our magic, on demand.

We will in other words be building total mastery in recognizing the difference between the voices of our shadow—the inner liars about who we are and where our power lies—and the voices of our Light.

Shadow is the sound of fallen Light. It is the sound of the Dark Feminine at war with herself. It is, at heart, the anxious feminine who has lost her way in the Light, refuses to surrender to its mastery, refuses to be mastered *by* the masculine, and in so doing, never achieves mastery *over* him.

To know how to inspire the divine masculine to provide for your every desire is to know how to master Light. And in order to master it, we must first be mastered *by* it.

Light has four voices. Each voice has two tones: illusion and truth.

Illusion sends the voice of light into shadow, making us weak at calling in our magic. Illusion is therefore the source of all struggle.

Truth is the sound of Light. It opens the portal to our absolute power and, by energetic law, inspires the divine masculine to provide for our every desire. Truth is the source of power and magic.

MASTERING THE LIGHT GRID

Archetypes are energy patterns that exert incredible influence throughout the dynamism of the grid of human consciousness. They are the coding, the essential programming, of our psyche. They are fundamentally oriented around getting, managing, keeping and amplifying power, and they govern and direct all our thoughts, beliefs, feelings and actions and instincts, down to the cellular level.

This is why we tell ourselves stories and myths and create religions and schools of thought: to pass on the knowledge we have gained over centuries regarding which archetypes--which patterns of counsel about how to get, manage, and amplify power--are right, and which are wrong, and to continue the investigation into the open questions that remain.

This goes for human consciousness itself, as well as every individual's consciousness.

Which means the most important question any human can ask, and know how to answer with certainty, is this: What is the truth about my power?

Does it reside outside of me? If so, how much of it, and where, and how do I get it and keep it within me so it can't be taken? And if none of it resides outside of me, if I am literally all powerful, then how come I feel so powerless? And how do I claim the power that is mine, for good? And anyway, how do I even come to believe this crazy statement as true?

Let's tackle the last question there for a minute:

You simply believe it to be true.

In the face of all evidence to the contrary, you believe it to be so, because in this world, believing is seeing, not the other way around.

And, you elevate the mechanism within you for detecting Truth and invited it to sit at your right hand and inform your every decision. Right now, it is in prison.

For being an insubordinate know-it-all who keeps chattering in your ear complete nonsense that distracts you from the important business at hand. The Fool. Sometimes you wonder why you even keep him around.

We'll get back to him. But suffice it to say that all the mechanisms you've been taught for detecting and knowing Truth, for deciding what is worthy of your time and attention, and for directing every micro-decision you make, come from the mis-gidance of the False Council, from the collection of voices of the very consciousness you are so desperately endeavoring to discover, so you can kick them out and end the inner war.

You just don't know it yet.

So, come with me to the shadowlands. The rusty abode of the psyche.

Carl Jung "discovered" our archetypal consciousness. If you do much reading or study on archetypes, you'll find there are hundreds of them.

They are all derivatives of four pillars of consciousness that we use to access and run Light Energy. (This is not the same as Source Energy. Source Energy is Dark. And in order to work directly with Source Energy, you need to master the Light Energy archetypes first and then gain entrance into the Dark Domain where a set of very different archetypes resides and works their magic.) Each pillar has a base and a pinnacle: a *de*-based expression of one particular vein or skein of consciousness and a *peak* or *pinnacled* expression of that same vein or skein of consciousness.

Shadow is the debased version.

Light is the pinnacled one.

Shadow is fallen light.

Illusion.

Shadow consciousness is the source of all struggle, because struggle is unnatural. If you're struggling anywhere in any way, either in the most abject of conditions that would make the evening news or the most first-world variety that would have most of the planet's population rolling their eyes, you're running your life through the low, slow, clogged, dirty channel of your shadow.

Yes that means children and rape victims and burn victims and victims of #allthethings everywhere. (And yes, that means it's unnatural to be poor.)

Because that Truth is there are no victims. *That*—the belief that there are victims—is at the heart and soul (literally) of human/tribal consciousness.

It is the major dis-chord that it is now time to clip so we can rise into our genius, giant nature.

(And if this truth triggers you, I have a tool for that....)

Lest you think I'm going to prove that there are no victims, let me disabuse you of that right up front.

Theoretically proving shit with your brain is not how this game works. That's Doubting Thomas stuff.

In this world, believing is seeing. Once you adopt the stance of the Truth, fully, without reservation, and run your consciousness through the high octane energy of the Truth (which I am about to teach you) in every area of your life and at all times, The Truth becomes glaringly obvious.

But only after you commit to it completely.

And yes. I recognize how ass backwards that sounds.

But. What can I say. It's the Truth.

So, these eight archetypes (four bases, four pinnacles) create the content of your consciousness either with clean, clear, crisp codes that create high-level frequencies that flood your field with optimal magnetism or with dirty, smudged, waffly codes that create low-level frequencies that clog your field and make you energetically ugly as fuck.

And so money doesn't come to you and the people you want in your life don't come to you and the opportunities you long for don't come to you and what *does* come to you is just as dirty and nasty as your field.

This is what everyone means when they say you're an energetic match for whatever is in your experience.

It's also what they're referring to when they talk about how important it is to be "high vibe" (even though they have no idea what achieving and maintaining that high vibe actually entails).

Your work, your only work, the most important work of your life, is to *master the content of your consciousness*. Do this, and your inheritance of magic and miracles is yours. Don't do it and nothing else you do (affirmations, meditations, yoga, zen retreats, whatever the fuck) will matter.

Everyone asks me how I managed to achieve such miracles in my life and the life of my clients. (As I write this, I'm "arguing" with my personal trainer, who coaches and trains celebrities, about whether it's possible to lose a pound a day. He says no. And his decades of success would seem to present him as the expert. He assailed me with data of all kinds to support his position. But I know better. First of all, the body is simply a reflector field. It will do whatever it's told...like the good little feminine energy system it is. Secondly, my own clients have proved him wrong. One client dropped 25 pounds in 6 weeks...*without effort or changing anything in her life*. Another dropped ten pounds in a week. And both have kept it off. Science would say it's impossible. Consciousness Mastery knows otherwise.) I tell them it's entirely due to my ability to crack the code on struggle, discover its root cause, and perform eneretic surgery--as one of my clients puts it--to deprogram and reboot consciousness onto an entirely new operating platform. One in which magic and miracles are *de rigueur*.

That energetic surgery and subsequent deprogramming and reboot is what we're going to do with you, right now.

Glossary Of Terms

What Is Shadow Consciousness?

The set of belief-illusions that, when they direct human decisions, commitments and actions, inevitably create unwanted outcomes incapable of creating magic, thriving or fulfillment and which guarantee and are the sole reason for all forms of struggle and mental, physical and emotional weakness and misery.

What is Light Consciousness?

The set of Truths of energetic law that represent the most potent form of energy (Truth) the collective consciousness can handle without exploding/imploding and which, when they direct human decisions, commitments and actions, inevitably create highly desired outcomes and experiences of magic, miracles, synchronicity, abundance, thriving and joy, guarantee supreme mental, physical and emotional power and health, and the elimination of all forms of struggle, and assist the human in developing mastery over his gifts and achieving true excellence, but which ultimately require upgrading in order for the human to reach true fulfillment. Because the content of the focused power of these Light Truths is the shadow, once the shadow has been alchemized, the Light has exhausted its purpose and finds itself emptied of content and therefore inevitably restless. This is the meaning of the Truism of Light Consciousness: Excellence is empty.

What Is Dark Consciousness?

The final resting place of human consciousness. The domain in which the genius giant crafts new forms of consciousness, plays with the root-level laws and determines the newest, lightest light (the True Truths) to place onto the Light Grid and into collective consciousness. The theater of the gods. The sustained experience of euphoria. The unimaginable new. Beyond giftedness and the emptiness of excellence and into the rich octaves of genius. The deep mysteries. The intersection of cutting edge science and the ultimate The end of seeking.

What is an archetype?

An archetype is an expression of energetic law that has been coded with a distinct "personality structure" so that human consciousness can begin to work with, discover and ultimately *master* energetic law.

What is Archetypal Consciousness?

The gathering of the core codes of consciousness that together express and channel the power and outcome of the truth of energetic law into human consciousness as its substrate and foundation.

THE METAPHYSICAL LANGUAGE AND ARCHETYPAL CONSCIOUSNESS OF THE PSYCHE (I.E, THE TRUTH OF WHO YOU ARE, AND THE FOUR PILLARS OF LIGHT POWER)

Archetypes defined (one last time):

An archetype is a gathered expression of energy relating to and directly expressing energetic law, which has been "personalized" so that human consciousness can discover, work with, master, and ultimately deny its conditioning, outgrade (UPleveling and UPgrades are ways of speaking about profess on the Light Grid, which has structure levels of frequency gradation that must be moved through incrementally from lower to higher. Hence "UP." But when you step OFF the Light Grid you are not continuing the motion of consciousness that was ordered by and on the Light Grid. There is no continuity of orientation or dimensionality from Light to Dark. Dark is not just the "next highest" frequency of Light. It is an entirely different beast altogether. The best way to explain what happens, in human terms, when a human steps off the Light Grid and traverse the Band of Unhooking and enters the Dark is not that she goes UP but that she goes OUT.

And in, her Light.

GOES.

OUT.

But she doesn't "just" go out. Her going out is also a being in. A staying put. A journey of motionless that doesn't just defy gravity but is completely unaware of its existence.

The gravity of concern and of cinders.

The gravity of bereavement and corners.

The gravity of selfhood in general.

And in extreme particular.

This is what all humans long for with an ache.

And it is there, in a foreign land, breathing fire and waiting for Nothing, including, and most particularly, for the Nothing that is You.

So, let's us begin (again. There have been SO many beginnings. Just like the experience of Light. Each new brightness feels like the end of seeking. Only come to realize it is actually dimmer than we hoped.)

ARCHETYPES OVERVIEW

Imagine four pillars, each with a base and pinnacle. At the base is the shadow. At the pinnacles is the Light. The Four PIllars of Light Energy Consciousness are the Prostitute/Lover, the Child/Sovereign, the Victim/Warrior and the Saboteur/Magician. Like this:

Sovereign	Warrior	Magician	Lover
Child	Victim	Saboteur	Prostitute

Don't worry about why I've placed the Prostitute/Lover pillar last but mention it first. The deeper secrets of the Grid, or Archetype Map, will be revealed in time (and if you like, feel free to come join us in the Gold Mind Academy, where I am revealing all the mysteries of the layers, levels and journeys of the three stages of Archetypal Consciousness). But suffice it to say that the Prostitute/Lover Pillar is both "The First and the Last," the "Alpha and the Omega." *And*, it is also true that the Child/Sovereign is the Absolute Leader of the Grid.

As you move throughout the following pages, you will be traveling the labyrinth of your own mind, twisting and turning down garishly lit curvatures in your own psyche, seeing in high relief the innards of your own spiritual metabolism — how clogged they are with toxic waste. Labyrinth turned...intestinal tract.

Because yes. What we're really doing is clearing out the shit that's making you sick.

I've devised this map of consciousness to be full of itself. Replete with hints as to deeper meanings, significances and understandings. You are invited to use each aspect of it as a clue to unlock the power, secrets and hidden mysteries of each core code of consciousness.

Each code is a portal. The way god peers down into the human. The way we as god pour ourselves down into our human frame.

Each pillar is in fact a channel of Light energy. They are the four energy channels that create human consciousness and stream source energy into the psyche. They are the four pillars that generate your SIGNATURE TEMPLE vibration.

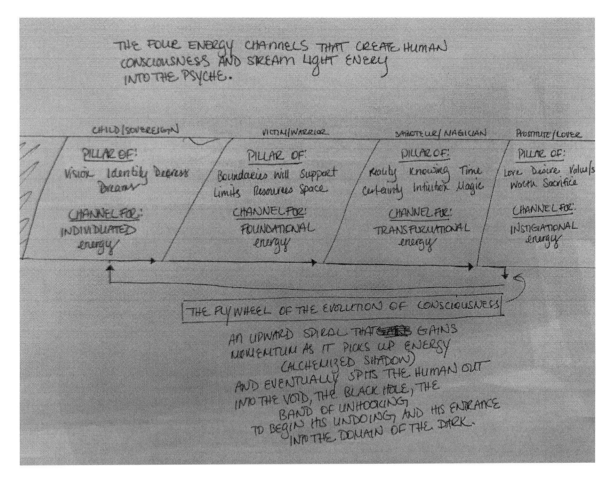

Prostitute/Lover: The Channel of INSTIGATIONAL energy

Child/Sovereign: The Channel of INDIVIDUATIONAL energy

Victim/Warrior: The Channel of FOUNDATIONAL energy

Saboteur/Magician: The Channel of TRANSFORMATIONAL energy

and back to….

Prostitute/Lover: INSTIGATIONAL energy.

This is the FLYWHEEL OF THE EVOLUTION OF HUMAN CONSCIOUSNESS. An upward spiral that gains momentum as it picks up energy (alchemized shadow) and eventually spits the human out into the void, the black hole, the Band of Unhooking to being his Undoing and his Entrance into the Domain of the Dark.

The Master Map

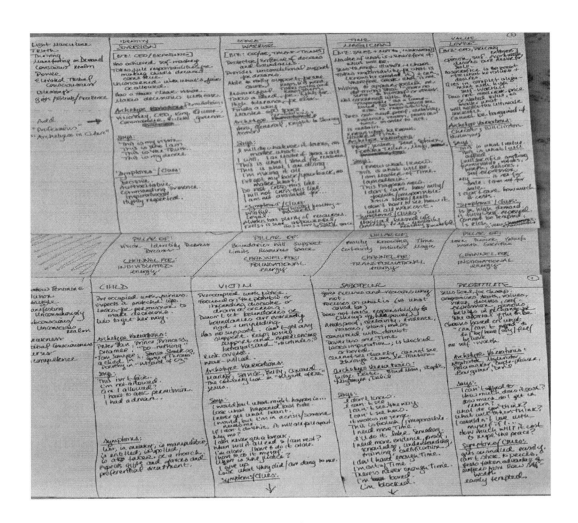

THE SOUL KILLER (THE PROSTITUTE + THE LOVER)

The Prostitute and the Lover

The Pillar of
Love, Desire, Value/s, Worth, Sacrifice
The Channel for
INSTIGATIONAL energy

The first lesson is not to be afraid... you asked me to teach you how to fight. And I can teach you the ways in which to fight with a sword and an ax, or a shield to stay alive. But if you are afraid, then you are already dead.

- Vikings, Season 5, "The Lost Moment"

Ah, the Soul.

For centuries we've been told it's our guide and our saving grace. *Listen to the voice of your Soul*, they say. *Seek soulfulness. Never sell your Soul* (this is True, until it isn't because you've done something even more unthinkable...and which actually works to secure what selling your Soul promised but could never achieve: alchemized it out of existence.). *Heed your soul guidance. Achieve soul mastery.* And so yes. We will do that. For the time being...

And God saw everything that he had made, and behold it was very good. And there was evening, and there was morning the sixth day. [Genesis 1:31. Darby Bible Translation]

If you've been living a life you don't value, it's because your Prostitute archetype has been in charge, because this channel oversees and directs our relationship to INSTIGATIONAL energy -- the energy that BEGINS everything and anything. And that energy is the energy of value, cost (sacrifice) and worth.

The moment value is seen, acknowledged or claimed, a new beginning erupts into being.

And that beginning carries weight. Dreams that demand service. Visions that require sacrifice.

Much better, then, to ignore value. Keep cost at bay, at all costs.

Pretend we don't know what we truly desire.

And thus the Prostitute is lost.

Sells herself in exchange for security, safety and approval.

Unwilling to elevate herself into the Lover energy, who knows his own value and values and who acts in accordance with these no matter what. No matter the risk, the fear of disapproval, the lack of security and safety that might result.

The other important element here is that valuing, loving and committing to your worth must happen before you know what that looks like in form and structure. It's like birth—again we see the INSTIGATIONAL energy in this pillar: You have to love the baby before you get to experience the baby.

You literally VALUE the being into existence.

And yet we are taught to assign value after the fact, when all the evidence is in that valuing it won't risk our standing in the tribe.

A writer valuing words in a family of plumbers.

A plumber valuing labor in a family of dancers.

Dangerous, that.

The Prostitute wants to see what it is she's being asked to value first, *before* she commits to valuing it. The Lover commits to seeing value first and because of this is able to *see the true value of things* and to stand in that true value without apology and without compromise.

This is why this pillar is the pillar of the CFO. The one in a company who oversees the cost and the value of the business. This pillar oversees your pricing. Your bargaining with yourself and others. Your willingness to be negotiated downwards.

As a business owner you always standing out on the edge of the Unknown and you have to commit to moving within your core value out into that unknown before you have evidence of what value that truly is for others. The prostitute sells herself and her gifts for cheap because she's convinced she can't afford to do otherwise. Her soul is for sale. Her authenticity is for sale. Her opinion is for sale. Her truth is for sale.

Whatever has been for sale in your life will show up in this energy.

If you've built a career you don't inherently value, then you have to look at the Prostitute archetype for what's been for sale. If you've built a body you don't inherently value. A relationship. A living arrangement.

What is for sale in this archetype is always something in return for approval by the tribe.

This is where the fear of being rejected by the tribe comes in. Where the fear of telling your truth comes in. Where your fear of standing out on who you really are and declaring what you truly value comes in. There's a real business element to this. Pricing your services means being able to stand out in your true value, in the Lover, not the Prostitute.

The work here is in taking an inventory of where it is you've sold something of true value in return for approval or a sense of safety or security—financial security, approval from family and friends, colleagues, approval from the culture, a spouse or partner.

When the power is taken from the Prostitute energy and given to Lover, that is when you can start to free yourself. This is the first place you have to work and look and reclaim and restore and heal and make new declarations about in order for any kind of real change to occur. Because without a claim of value, nothing can begin.

If when you are building your desire, you are dipping your hand in the shadow cesspool of the prostitute and drawing out codes dripping with the sound of this, even though you yourself may not be able to hear them, the blueprint of your desire will be as weak as the voices of these illusions are strong:

I am worthless.

I must prove my worth.

Having, being, doing this will prove my worth.

I can't afford to be/do/have/think/say/believe what I really want, because of what people will do/say/think/believe about me.

I will sell my soul/self expression/value/values/standards/beliefs/true desires/self expression in return for what pleases others and gains me their approval.

The prostitute is the pillar of worth, worthiness, value and values, and therefore of money, the mediator of value and worth and the system we use to indicate what we value and find worthwhile and to what degree. The prostitute is the pillar of investment. What are we willing to invest in and afford? What are we willing to require others to invest with respect to us and our worth and value? As such, it is also the pillar of pricing and cost and sacrifice.

This, then, is where we sell our Soul in return for something we value even more greatly: approval.

When we desire something because we believe it will bring us worthiness, because it will distinguish us among others as a valuable and worthwhile human, we are building the blueprint of that desire on weak energetic grounds and it has little hope of ever coming to pass.

Because this is neither true nor powerful, that others in any way hold our power.

The voice of the prostitute is the snake-oil salesman in us, the bargainer, the negotiator who has a price, whose pride, esteem, self expression and standards (values) can be bought and sold in the market of approval, and therefore of perceived safety and security.

This is the pillar that must crumble first in order for anyone to even embark on the Hero's Journey, because the first thing the Hero must do is stop selling his soul, his truth, his desires, his values, his self expression, his beliefs, in return for the safety, security and approval of the tribe, which is where he has been taught his power lies.

It is an ancient shadow coding in us that makes us terrified of leaving or disappointing our tribe. The pillar of the prostitute is why. It is one of the four pillars in the Shadow Temple where we go to worship, and seek, power.

And so if what you want is in any way coded with the same shadow blueprint that built the pillar of the prostitute in you—built by what I call tribal or victim or human consciousness—, if you want it because it will prove you worthy in the eyes of others, which includes yourself; if what you want is a facsimile of what you *really* want but don't think you can afford, either monetarily or because of the sacrifice you'd have to make that would cost you acceptance, approval and understanding by your tribe, then you are building your desire on shadow energy, not Light, and the only way it will come to pass is not through the effortlessness of having inspired the energy and power of the magical masculine who instantly places gifts in our path that take no effort to pick up and enjoy, but through the extreme, time-consuming, and exhausting application of will, effort and energy of the feminine trying to do the work of both energies, because her Magic Man is not in any way attracted to or inspired to help. And that feels not like delightfully discovering a gift placed right at our feet at the perfect moment, but more like moving a mountain that's blocking our path.

That's called hustle and grind.

And Queens don't hustle. They flow.

Let me use some examples.

For twelve years I worked for my family consulting business. I started as a receptionist helping my parents part time as they built the company from two spare rooms in their house. I did this because I felt worthless. My only talents were seeing through people as if they were translucent, being uncomfortably truthful and stubbornly visionary, thinking deeply and writing strange poetry.

How was I going to make a living doing that?

I had just graduated second in my class from college with a double major in philosophy and the history of math and science and a double minor in Greek and the history of music. I'd applied for a job as an admin at a recruiting company and instead of placing me at one of their clients, they asked if I wanted to join them as a recruiter.

I spent my days breaking records at work and my nights smoking copious amounts of pot, playing the banjo and feeling deeply depressed and lost.

Then my parents needed help running their business. They were in their first year, doing very well, and overwhelmed staying up until 2am sending out invoices.

I was the third employee and I ended up staying for twelve years helping build and run the company.

My ultimate goal was to become the next CEO. My parents both indicated they saw this as the right next step. And no matter how much I dreamed about it, wrote affirmations and got into the feeling of already being C.E.O., *it did not happen*.

And yet other miracles happened effortlessly.

In my first year in sales, I came across a book called *The Secrets of SuperSelling*, which was my first introduction to manifestation and the power of the mind. At the time I'd been working full time as a recruiter for the company, making $30k a year. Now I was in sales as an independent contractor and could make as much as I wanted and work whatever hours I liked.

So I set myself an insane and totally unreasonable goal: to make $250K in my first year, working part time.

1. I'd only had 3 months of low level sales experience in my first job out of college, which was now 5 years prior.
2. I would now be selling to C-level executives at the Fortune 500, going against multinational, brand name competitors with $40B in revenue, as a $6MM company with no brand recognition and no marketing budget, in one of the most glutted markets in Chicagoland.
3. I had never made more than $30k a year and couldn't even conceive of a $250k income. And I'd certainly never worked part time for more than $14/hour.
4. Up until that year when I decided to try my hand at sales I'd been convinced I'd make a terrible salesperson. My mom had been in sales from the time I was in high school and everything she talked about at dinner was both boring and repugnant to me. I thought

sales was slimy and inauthentic and that corporate America, and anyone who worked in it, was full of soulless husks of humans who'd sold their integrity in return for a buck.

Needless to say, my goal of making $250K—which, based on my comp plan, would mean I'd need to sell at least twice that—was a pipe dream.

And yet I exceeded it.

In ten months I had made $269k, working no more than 25 hours a week.

But this is the problem with the way manifestation is taught, even in such life-changing books as *The Secrets of SuperSelling,* or, in another book with a similar name and even greater fame, *The Secret*: they don't explain why some desires come to pass and others don't, when the strategies and intention, energy, focus and desire are just as strong in both cases.

The reason is clear now, and that is why I can predict what I will manifest with total confidence. And when something I desire doesn't come to pass, I also know exactly why and what to do about it so that it will. Same goes for my clients.

So, why did the $250k in twelve months working part time come to pass and the CEO role did not?

Because I was in a completely different operating system with one desire versus the other, and it was all tied up in the pillar of the prostitute…and the Lover.

My desire to be C.E.O. was built on a desire to prove my worth to myself and to my world. My desire to do the impossible and break my income ceiling was not to prove anything to anyone. It was an empty, and therefore a strong desire. There was no content to it other than itself. It could easily have been coded with worthlessness and therefore the desire to prove something, but in this case it was simply a game in which there were no stakes (because the existence of stakes means there is something that matters, which means there is something to prove.)

And my desire to be C.E.O. could have easily been a desire to play the game at my highest level and in that case, it would not have been coded with shadow, built on weakness and incapable of inspiring the Magic Man—my own magical masculine energy—to make my dream come true.

I was unaware of the content of my own desire, and this was the problem. I was building it with energetic material guaranteed to create struggle and require immense energy, focus and will to realize. And of course shadow being so weak, it is doubly difficult to summon the intensity of energy and will required.

And so my dream never materialized.

This is the energetic reason why so many say that it was only when they "forgot" about their desire that it came to pass. It's not because we *must* forget. It's because keeping our eye on it most often means keeping the eye of our *shadow* on it. An eye trained to see our worthlessness in everything, trained to detect how little value we hold, how hard it is to maintain approval from others; the diligent eye of the soul determined to find and feel its worth.

Once in awhile we forget to be so plagued. We become distracted with the pure joy of the game of it all, or of some other game altogether, and this is finally when our desire can come to pass because our distraction has emptied the shadow from our desire, leaving it clean and clear and filled with Light and therefore automatically attractive to the masculine, who is glad to provide it for us quickly and easily.

The Energetics of Consciousness have shifted. The ground of being has shifted and spiritual law has tightened. There is less mercy for shadow consciousness on the planet. Less tolerance of illusion. If we are to learn how to operate the raw material of the universe to make magic on demand and step into our genius, giant nature, we must upgrade both our understanding of spiritual law and our willingness and ability to abide by it.

The pillar of worth, value and values, desire, price, cost, sacrifice and self expression coded with the voice of Light sounds like this:

I will afford whatever is required to be true to my self and my soul.

There is no cost, price or sacrifice too great for the expression of my truth, desires, self expression, and values.

I do not care about the approval of others and I know their approval is not the source of my safety and security.

My power lies in my total allegiance to my soul, my self, my truth and my values.

When you are gripped and owned by the Prostitute, you allow anything to come between your truth, in the name of safety and security.

When you have given your heart to your inner Lover, you allow *nothing* to come between your truth and know *that* is your true security.

What Exactly Is Love

It's not enough to know that everything is energy. It is just as important to know what is *true*, because energy responds to vibration and the vibration of Truth is where our power lies to direct energy to our will.

Fear (anxiety) is the energy of illness and struggle and is the opposite of truth.

In order to make magic in your life, to be free of struggle of all kinds—mental, emotional, physical, and financial—you must know what the truth sounds like, and contrary to what most spiritual leaders teach, truth does not sound like our typical understanding of love.

There are many stories of miraculous healing that talk about the experience of profound love as the cause of that healing. The problem with this focus is that we do not know how to recognize the energy of love. Being loving has become synonymous with being non-threatening. To anyone. Ever. This is a completely inaccurate understanding of love. Love is synonymous with Truth, and truth, particularly now when it is time to truly wake up, hurts. A lot.

My clients who have had the most miraculous results are the ones I have told the most excruciating truths that did not seem "loving" or feel good at all at the time.

And by miraculous, I mean turning around a sexless marriage on the brink of divorce in 4 weeks to soulmate love and amazing sex, dropping 8 dress sizes in 12 weeks with no change to diet or exercise, eliminating skin conditions in three weeks that have resisted decades of treatment of all kinds, and going from $1500 months in their business to $23,000 months in ten weeks.

The energy of the Lover is the willingness to sacrifice anything and everything for the Truth, because the Lover knows that Truth is the vibration of power. The Lover speaks Truth no matter what. And that also means that the Lover speaks a fully self-expressed reality.

We are all coded with a powerful and unflinching ability to know the Truth and to express this through all our systems. We are TruthCarriers, and our natural state is to speak and express Truth and when we don't, we create struggle and weakness.

This is often anathema to the tribe. As little children we're encouraged to lie in order to be accepted. What child hasn't told an adult she is fat, ugly, or smelly and has not been reprimanded? *Be nice*, we're admonished and shamed. And this develops in us an allegiance to our prostitute energy, to be willing to say and do what is considered "nice" and "loving" in order to avoid being cast out by our tribe.

And what if we have a dark heart of gold, a natural draw to speak the most uncomfortable and unwelcome truths to a group or an individual, which will likely cause the person more distress than they're already in? Those of us with this spiritual gift have typically been deeply shamed our whole lives for being "uncaring," "cold hearted" or abrasive, and most certainly not very loving.

You're likely going to learn how to lie.

And while you may not make any connection between living a lie about the Truth you have suppressed your whole life and not being able to manifest the life of your dreams, though you may be doing affirmations, gratitude lists, vision boards, getting in the energy of what you desire and following every piece and part of the strategy of manifestation, if you are living out of your prostitute, which almost always is completely unconscious, your dreams and desires will not come to you without extreme effort.

But magic is your natural state. And precisely *because* everything is energy, it is imperative that you know how energy truly works and how to lift its unconscious operation in your shadow into the Light where you can have full power over your conditions.

But what if the truth hurts? What if it might even kill? We will pick this up in a few chapters, when we talk about the victim.

Implications for Business

In business, this pillar is the decision matrix of price and pricing and the ability to stand for the true value of something and for your true values no matter what pressures come against you.

It is the power to refuse to negotiate, no matter the perceived cost or loss.

Whether it is succumbing to market pressures to lower your costs or compromise on your integrity, or a prized potential client who wants to negotiate you down or demands terms that go against your principles or policies, or internal pressures, for instance a star employee who tries to hold you hostage in return for special treatment, a larger salary or commission, or greater responsibility that goes against your true standards or values.

A leader in his prostitute energy will collapse under the perceived danger of losing business, market share or top talent. A leader in his lover energy knows he and his company is the prize, and that there are plenty of clients and employees and markets to dominate without having to compromise, and that in fact it is by holding to his standards and truth that he invokes the power to bend reality to his desire.

Navigating the powers and temptations of this pillar is especially challenging for new entrepreneurs. I see this all the time in my work. Entrepreneurs unsure of their value discounting their services to see what the market will pay and then hustling 24/7 to make ends meet because they're not charging anything close to their true worth.

PROSTITUTE DEEP DIVE

Manifestation Field: Shadow/Unconscious Field/Subconscious Field

Channel for: INSTIGATIONAL Energy

Domains of Power(lessness): Love, Desire, Value/s, Worth, Sacrifice

Overview

- Sells Soul for cheap. Compromises truth, values, value, desires, self-expression, opinions, beliefs in exchange for approval of the tribe.

- Chooses based on what she "can"/"can't afford" to do/be/have/say/feel/believe

- No self worth

- Fears rejection

- Consumed with belonging

- Uses sexual energy for influence and gain (most dependable form of approval and acceptance; the lowest common denominator and most widely accepted "currency" in the tribe")

Archetype Permutations

- Negotiator, Moderator, Peacemaker, Bargainer, Devil, People-pleaser

Archetypes in Culture

- Julie Roberts in "Pretty Woman"
- The entire cast of "The Office"

Professions

- Stripper
- Prostitute

Says

- I can't afford to.
- How much does it cost?
- How much do I get in return?
- What do you think?
- What will others think?
- I couldn't live with myself if I…
- How much will it cost me to keep the peace?
- What's my true passion?
- What do I really WANT?
- Where do I belong?

Symptoms/Clues

- Charming; uses charm to get by, get her way
- Gets swindled easily

- Can't stick to prices
- Feels taken advantage of
- Easily tempted

Shadow Audit: The Prostitute

Time to take inventory. Where in all areas of your life do you recognize the prostitute running the show?

Where and how are you moderating your opinions, values, value, true desires, self-expression? Where and how have you set up your life because you are terrified of rejection, of disapproval?

- Sex Life
- Finances
- Relationships
- Bank Account
- Body/Weight/Health
- Purchases
- Business
- Conversations

LOVER DEEP DIVE

Manifestation Field: Light/Conscious Field

Channel for: INSTIGATIONAL Energy

Domains of Power: Love, Desire, Value/s, Worth, Sacrifice

Overview

- Opinion, self-expression, desires are never for sale
- No sacrifice is too great for what he values and desires
- Acts in complete alignment with high self-worth
- Does not moderate price or stated value, no matter what
- Will make the ultimate sacrifice
- Cannot be bargained with

Archetype Permutations

- Bill Clinton
- Christ on the Cross

- Jesus on the top of the mountain with the devil

Archetypes in Culture

- Mary Poppins
- Sara Blakely
- Kenneth Branagh's Henry V
- Freddie Mercury
- Dalai Lama

Professions

- CFO, pricing
- Financial Advisor
- Investor
- Broker
- Trader
- Sacred Prostitute

Says

- This is what I value
- This is what I will afford
- I will sacrifice anything for my value, values, worth, desires, self-expression
- My opinions, beliefs, thoughts, self-expression or choices are not for sale.
- I am not for sale.

- I don't care how much it costs.

- I value my own words and my own opinions and my own self-expression, no matter what.

- I do not modulate my self-expression for anybody's approval or for my security and safety or approval from anyone.

- I don't care what someone else thinks.

- I value my method of self-expression and my words and my opinions.

- My safety and security comes from me, not from anybody else and what they think of me.

"Symptoms"/Clues

- Is in high demand
- Is fully self expressed
- Cannot be tempted
- Is highly charismatic

THE IDENTITY KILLER (THE CHILD + THE SOVEREIGN)

The Child and The Sovereign

The Pillar of

Vision, Identity, Decrees, Dreams

The Channel for

INDIVIDUATED energy

The child is all about dreams. The child is the innocent energy of visions and dreams; And as the child archetype, the power here is to dream, but the child archetype doesn't have the power to manifest those dreams or make those dreams come true.

So if you've been giving your power to the child, rather than to the Sovereign, the way you'll know is because you've been waiting for someone or something else to make your dreams come true. This is like the princess who waits for the Prince to make her dreams come true.

The child sounds like this: I had a dream. Once upon a time, as in the fairy tales, I had a dream. I don't have it anymore because no one in my life has made it come true for me, but I did have it, and here's what it was.

Take inventory of where you've given your power to somebody or something else in some way and are now in a position of seeing that person as responsible to make your dreams come true.

Perhaps your boss, your partner, your culture. "My culture isn't structured in such a way that I can really live my dreams." "My parents wouldn't allow that." "My partner wouldn't allow that." That's all the child.

The Child/Sovereign energy is also the pillar of identity and truth-telling. So the child also doesn't know who she is. The child hasn't developed a true identity yet, whereas the Sovereign has a very clear sense of identity. The child says "I don't know who I am." The sovereign says, "I know exactly who I am." And along with that is the ability to tell the truth. So the child is the liar. You know this, right? If you have kids, you see that look in their eyes when you're asking them whether they did something and you know they're about to lie to you. Well, if you're an adult and there are parts of your life that are a lie, those are the areas where you are in your child archetype. Wherever you can't stand up and speak your truth, you are in your child, not your Sovereign.

The Sovereign is the CEO energy. So if you are an entrepreneur, it's critical that you NOT be in your child energy and that you be in your Sovereign energy in order to properly run your business.

If the child says, "I had a dream," the Sovereign says, "I Have a Dream. This is my dream. I'm living my dream." The child puts her feelings of wellbeing into someone else's hands. The Sovereign says, "I am responsible for my wellbeing. My wellbeing is no one's responsibility but mine and I take full responsibility for every bit of my life experience as it is today."

The Sovereign, the C.E.O., commits to making that dream come true. So when you're thinking about your business, it's critical to be in the archetype of your Sovereign as you're designing and launching this business, not the archetype of your child. And the reason why the Lover archetype has to be activated first is because the Lover is the energy of *valuing* that dream. If the prostitute archetype is in play and the power is within the prostituting archetype, you won't be allowing yourself to dream nat all because you'll know at a core level that your prostitute is just going to walk right up and say, "That dream is going to cost way too much. Put that down."

And so probably that happened for you. It might even be happening now. That's why it's important to put the power of value in your life into your Lover and make that commitment. "I commit to valuing what I value and desire no matter the cost." That is what allows the child to begin dreaming again and allows the Sovereign to come in and say, "I'm now going to make those dreams come true. Now that I'm allowing myself to value this dream, I'm also committing to making it come true for me."

So these are deepening levels of a commitment, deepening levels of declaration that are being made at each stage.

So the work here is to look at all the places where you've given the power to your child archetype and then activate your Sovereign archetype and in encountering your Sovereign, you start saying to yourself, "I now place the power of my well-being squarely within myself. No one is responsible for my well-being. No one else is responsible for the quality of my life experience. No one is responsible for the choice that I make. I commit to being responsible for my life in every aspect of it. I commit to stepping into the C.E.O. energy of my business and my life. I commit to being responsible for taking the value that I now declare that I have for my dream and making it a reality."

Once the Lover archetype is activated, the Lover has to love something. And what does the Lover love? The child's dreams, the innocent child in you that has this dream, the dream for this life. And so once the Lover is enabled and active in loving the dream, the dream becomes restored to its true value. And then the Sovereign can step in and take the dream from the child and say, "This is no longer your responsibility. It's now mine. And I now step into my role as my own Sovereign, and I'm taking the power away from my child archetype. And I'm no longer going to let my child archetype run my life."

The Sovereign energy is also the energy of joy. Joyfulness is in fact a very powerful spiritual energy. it's literally a vibration of power and manifestation (which means that it actually powers up another key archetype – the Magician, which we'll get to later.). And so the other thing to do here is to start looking at how much of your life you spend in joy. This will tell you how active your Sovereign is in your life. Or, how much of your life do you spend in despair, frustration, limitation, heaviness? That is the child. Really, that's all of the lower archetypes. They all create feelings of heaviness and burden.

So your homework is to journal and reflect on both of these archetypes. Notice how much of the time you and others use the language of the child. How many times do you hear people at work or in your personal life talk about the dreams they used to have? We are a nation of children, really. A nation of grown up children walking around having given our power away to our survival child archetype and bemoaning the fact that we don't have the life we want, as if we don't have all the power in the world to make our dreams happen.

To me that's what is so exciting about this. We discover where the power really lies, and it lies with us. Entirely, exactly and squarely within us. And this doesn't mean that we have to white knuckle our way into our dreams or out of our mess. When we activate these higher archetypes life actually becomes easier not harder. Life begins to flow and have a sense of magic about it. Yes there is still work to do and challenges to overcome, but there is a feeling of being at one with your power and having it always accessible to you that is a truly incredible feeling and that does create success in the real world – in relationships, in work, in income, in creativity, all of it.

So you want to make a declaration that you're stepping into your Sovereign, the truth of who you are. The Sovereign is the truth teller. And you can't tell the truth unless you know your Lover is going to *value* that truth. The truth of who you are, the truth of what your dream is, the truth of what your vision is. The Lover must first be activated and willing to pay the cost for telling the truth.

If not, you won't be willing to tell the truth even to yourself because the minute you tell the truth, there's a cost to pay; and if you're not willing to pay it, you're not going to be willing to say it.

Your work is to start telling yourself the truth of who you are as your powerful Sovereign. Start telling yourself the truth of what you vision for your life. The truth about what your dreams are.

CHILD DEEP DIVE

Manifestation Field: Shadow/Unconscious Field/Subconscious Field

Channel for: INDIVIDUATIONAL Energy

Domains of Power(lessness): Vision, Identity, Decrees, Dreams

Overview

- Preoccupied with fairness
- Expects a protected life
- Looks for permission to make decisions
- Lies to get her way
- Wants to dream forever and play and have other people take care of her

Archetype Permutations

- Prince
- Princess
- Dreamer

- "Do-Nothing"

Archetypes in Culture

- Tom Sawyer
- Peter Pan
- Young Sansa Stark in "Game of Thrones"
- Dorothy in "Wizard of Oz"
- The entire cast of "The Office"

Professions

- Prince
- Princess

Says

- This isn't fair.
- I'm not allowed.
- I should/need to ask/check with someone first.
- Am I allowed?
- I need permission.
- I had a dream once upon a time.
- Who am I?
- What is my purpose?

Symptoms/Clues

- Lies

- Is sneaky
- Is manipulative
- Is entitled
- Is spoiled
- Taker/mooch
- Expects gifts, favors and preferential treatment

Shadow Audit: Child

Time to take inventory. Where in all areas of your life do you recognize the child running the show?

Where and how are you obsessed with things being fair, with expecting a protected or a charmed life where you're taken care of like a child? Where and how have you agreed to ask for permission to live the life of your dreams or expecting someone else to make your dreams come true?

- Sex Life
- Finances
- Relationships
- Bank Account
- Body/Weight/Health
- Purchases
- Business
- Conversations

Sovereign Deep Dive

Manifestation Field: Light/Conscious Field

Channel for: INDIVIDUATIONAL Energy

Domains of Power: Vision, Identity, Decrees, Dreams

Overview

- Has achieved self mastery
- Takes full responsibility for making child's dreams come true
- Unconcerned with what's fair or allowed
- Has a clear vision
- Makes decisions with ease

Archetype Permutations

- Visionary
- King
- Queen

- Commander
- Ruler

Archetypes in Culture
- Kenneth Branagh's *Henry V*
- Mufasa, *The Lion King*
- Barack Obama
- Mary Poppins
- Sara Blakely

Professions
- CEO, Branding
- Ruler
- Governor
- King
- Queen
- President
- Entrepreneur

Says
- This is my vision.
- This is who I am.
- This is the Truth.

- This is my decree.

- Nobody's actions, or thoughts have any power over my wellbeing, happiness, or sense of self, and identity.

- I don't care about what's fair, because I am the source of my own power and well being.

- I don't monitor how other people are behaving, or how they're treating me compared to others, because it simply has no bearing on my well being at all.

- I am my own power source, no one else.

- I take full ownership over my power, and its impact, and therefore I don't worry about whether others notice, don't notice, take credit, or not, because it's not actually possible for them to take from me what I don't give them.

"Symptoms"/Clues

- Decisive
- Authoritative
- Commanding presence
- Inspirational
- Highly respected

THE BODY KILLER (THE VICTIM + THE WARRIOR)

The Victim and The Warrior

The Pillar of

Boundaries, Will, Support, Limits, Resources, Space

The Channel for

FOUNDATIONAL energy

The truth doesn't just hurt. It kills.

Lorna J.

This is the pillar of support, protection, boundaries, limits and taking a stand.

And what's likely been active in your life is the victim archetype. The victim sounds like, "I can't," "Someone isn't letting me," "Some situation isn't letting me." It's really the voice of you being bullied by something in your life. And anything can become your bully: a physical illness can be bullying you around so you "can't" do what you want with your life. Your income situation can be your bully. A relationship certainly can be. Take inventory of where in your life you've given power to the energy of "I can't," "I'm under someone else's control," "I'm the victim of some external circumstance I have no control over, so I can't have or act in the way that I value."

When you give your power to your warrior, you're saying, "I am going to fight, stand for and protect what I love. I am willing to stand for what I love. I am willing to protect what I love and what I value and I am willing to protect my value." The warrior sets clear and firm boundaries with himself and with others, but he does it with grace and compassion. So this isn't the place of setting rigid and overly dominating boundaries because that's just really a victim overcompensating – in fact that's you being a bully.

The warrior is willing to stand, in between, what he loves and all the things that are threats to that. He is willing to stand in between his value and all the things that are threats to his value. One of the things that might be threats to your value, especially in a business perspective is your prostitute, who is going to want to come in and negotiate and compromise.

People who aren't happy in their relationships is very likely because they are not setting good boundaries, and are either being a bully, or the victim of someone else's bullying.

So once you activate the Lover and truly stand in the place of declaring your value, what you value and love, and your Sovereign, the truth teller, is committed to turning those desires into concrete dreams and making them come true, then your warrior can come forward, and say, "Yes, and I am the protecting energy, the fending off energy, the fighting and the standing for energy, of declaring that I am no longer at effect in my life, I am at cause in my life."

Look for all the places and all the ways where you can make declarations, from a position of being your own hero in your life, of coming forth and protecting and making declarations of what you love and what you value.

"I am no longer allowing my victim, to hold power in my life. I no longer am willing to say I can't, or why me. I now declare, that I am willing to do whatever it takes, at all costs, to fight, stand for, and protect what I love." That's the warrior.

Here is the other way the victim shows up – in not having support for your dreams. In having people try to undermine or attack you, your value, what you value, what your truth is, what your dreams are, and in letting them do so. In not setting clear boundaries – which would be you being in your Warrior – about what you will and will not allow, will and will not let through the gates of your kingdom.

The other way this shows up is in feeling alone. The Warrior is able to rally forces for its cause. The Warrior doesn't just stand out there alone facing the enemy and running into battle. The Warrior is able to rally the troops, gain support and protection from others who are bought in to the cause. So if you are feeling alone, like no one has your back, that's another sign you're in your victim in that area of your life.

In a very real sense activating your warrior is activating and getting really comfortable with asking for help and support. If you look at it from the energy of the victim or the warrior, who is more empowered in gathering troops and support and reinforcements for the cause? The warrior. The General. The victim is the one who sits in the corner needing the support but unable to stand up for himself long enough to go get it. That standing up for, that's the warrior.

Take inventory of all the places where you are and have been in your victim and where you are stepping into or know you really need to step into your warrior. And remember this warrior is not the rigid, autocratic warrior we might initially imagine. This warrior is able to move with boundaries that feel right in the moment but doesn't have to set overly rigid and dogmatic restrictions and limitations on things either. This is the noble warrior, not the despotic one.

VICTIM DEEP DIVE

Manifestation Field: Shadow/Unconscious Field/Subconscious Field

Channel for: FOUNDATIONAL Energy

Domains of Power(lessness): Boundaries, Will, Support, Limits, Resources, Space

Overview

- Preoccupied with justice

- Focused on the possible or impending disaster, drama or crisis

- Doesn't set boundaries OR boundaries are extremely rigid and unyielding

- Has no support. Can't get any support. Keeps losing support and experiencing betrayals and "mutiny."

- Risk averse.

- Weak-willed

- Issues with being inconvenienced or being "too inconveniencing."

- Issue with being pushed around or being "too pushy"

- Gets called/feels like a doormat or treats others like a doormat
- Life feels heavy
- Issues with being a burden. Doesn't want to burden others.
- Is always "bearing the brunt" of a situation
- Always "takes the fall" for others
- Is overbearing, Always looks for a scapegoat. Someone or something to blame; to "take the fall" or "take the hit"
- Is always getting wrongly accused
- Is angry/full of rage OR seems to always attract lots of anger and rage from others "without provocation"

Archetype Permutations
- Bully
- Savior
- Rescuer
- Martyr
- Coward

Archetypes in Culture
- Julia Roberts in *Erin Brocovick*
- Donald Trump
- The entire cast of *The Office*
- The Cowardly Lion in *Wizard of Oz*

- Crucified Christ

Professions

- Activists

Says

- I don't want to be a burden.

- That's inconvenient.

- I don't want to inconvenience you/them/us/myself

- I would, but look what might happen/what happened last time

- Where's the justice?

- Where's my help?

- Why me?

- Why am I always alone?

- I never get what I want

- I would, but somebody needs me/is in a crisis

- If I don't do this, everything will all fall apart

- I can never get a break

- When will it all end so I can rest?

- I have to do it alone. Why do I always have to do it alone?

- I give up.

- Look what they did/are doing to me.

Symptoms/Clues

- Is codependent
- Catastrophizes
- Is heavy/overweight (carrying too much weight)
- Is underweight (can't carry her own weight)
- Accident prone
- Always or easily sick/physically weak
- Spaces, house, things, always getting lost, robbed, broken, ruined
- Always in a physical crisis
- Someone close is always in crisis
- Surrounded by drama or crisis
- Is alone/lonely
- Passive aggressive
- aggressive

Shadow Audit: Victim

Time to take inventory. Where in all areas of your life do you recognize the victim running the show?

Where and how are you obsessed with justice, with finding fault or blame, with using crisis and drama as excuses to not live a life according to your own standards? Where and how are you being the martyr?

- Sex Life

- Finances
- Relationships
- Bank Account
- Body/Weight/Health
- Purchases
- Business
- Conversations

WARRIOR DEEP DIVE

Manifestation Field: Light/Conscious Field

Channel for: FOUNDATIONAL Energy

Domains of Power: Boundaries, Will, Support, Limits, Resources, Space

Overview

- Protector/enforcer of decrees and boundaries
- Provides unconditional support for dreams
- Able to rally support for the cause
- Keeps his word
- Makes oaths and keeps them
- Resourceful
- Takes a stand for. Fights for.
- High tolerance for risk.
- Finds a way.

- Master of space.

Archetype Permutations

- Hero
- General
- Knight in Shining Armor

Archetypes in Culture

- Mary Poppins
- Sara Blakely
- Mel Gibson in *Braveheart*
- Kenneth Branagh's *Henry V*
- Ragnar Lothbrok in *Vikings*

Professions

- COO
- HR
- Firefighter
- Soldier
- General
- Bodyguard
- Construction
- Coder

- Engineer
- Architect

Says

- I will do whatever it takes, no matter what.
- I will.
- I am master of space and all resources.
- I create Space with ease.
- I have all the space I require.
- I have all the resources I require.
- I am the source of all my resources.
- Cash comes from me.
- This is what I stand for.
- This is what I am doing.
- I'm risking it all.
- I've got my back/your back, no matter what.
- Do not cross this line.
- I will not cross this line.
- I am not available for...

"Symptoms"/Clues

- Willful. Stubborn.

- Loyal.

- Physically healthy and powerful

- Always has plenty of resources

- Feels and is seen as powerful.

- Has and loves own space/plenty of space

- Is rich

THE MIND KILLER (THE SABOTEUR + THE MAGICIAN)

The Saboteur And The Magician

The Pillar of

Reality, Knowing, Time, Certainty, Intuition, Magic

The Channel for

TRANSFORMATIONAL energy

And God said, Let there be light: and there was light. [Genesis 1:3. King James Version]

The Pillar of Manifestation. The Channel of Spiritual Intelligence.

The survival archetype here is the Saboteur and this is another one that is very common to most people and It's actually a little bit difficult to understand how it is working because this is actually the most insidious of the archetypes and it is why I talk about it last, because all of the other three empowered archetypes must be truly active in your life and you must be truly committing to living from those power sources of your lover, your sovereign and your warrior in order to do the work of continually taking the power from your Saboteur and putting it into the empowered archetype of your magician.

The magician in you is where you want your power to be placed because that is the energy of manifestation; it is the energy of creating something from nothing. In the business world it is the sales and marketing energy, among other things.

It is the energy and power that you have within you to actually create the life experience that is now being held in your dreams, your dream for your life. You don't just want to hold it as a dream, you want to bring it forth into your life experience.

The reason you haven't been bringing your dreams forth into your life experience is because you have been giving your power to your prostitute to manage your value and what you are willing to afford; you have been giving it to your child, in allowing yourself to say "well no one has made this dream come true for me yet and that's why I am not living it." You have been giving it to your victim in allowing you to feel that there are things that are stronger than you out there and that you are at an effect in your life and not at cause. And the other reason that you haven't had the experience of your dream life in your life experience is because you have been sabotaging it.

The Saboteur is the reasoner, the rational part of yourself, it is the one that makes excuses and demands reasons.

The Saboteur is the one that will sound so reasonable. "Well, that will be irresponsible of me, so I can't do that." The Saboteur is the one that demands reasons for things. So if you're a really rational person, if you tend to feel comfortable in the world of the mind, your saboteur is going to be rreally strong for you.

You want to be very mindful of this energy because taking the stand to live your truth and make your dreams comes true requires you to follow your inner voice, your intuition, which is the domain of the Magician. The Saboteur is all about pure logic and reason and seeing a clear path from A to B to C. The magician works on intuition and gut and hunches and this is why people like Einstein and Steve Jobs say intuition was their greatest ally in creating greatness in their life.

As you are moving through this great change, expect a constant overcoming of the tension between your Saboteur—your mind, your brain, your ego, your reason—and your magician, which is your ability to create something from nothing, your ability to act on an inspired moment, your ability to take decisive action based on a hunch, a gut feel, not because you have good reasons for it.

The Saboteur completely shuts off access to your intuition because your intuition is *unreasonable*, it's not rational. It will often encourage you to do things that don't make any "sense" and your Saboteur is the one that will come in and say, "You can't do that. That makes no sense. You're being irresponsible…"

Your intuition is your absolute magic and it is like the blood of your life and your business.

The magician doesn't care about making sense. The magician takes the energy of the intuition and creates and gives you permission to act on that intuition, to actually take that intuition and put it into form, into the world.

Take inventory around your Saboteur, where you making excuses in your life, where you are requiring your actions, values, words, beliefs, dreams and goals to be reasonable.

If you are having challenges dreaming and visioning with the sovereign and the child, it could be because your saboteur is so strong that it jumps in before you know it's there and shuts down the process before it can begin, because your dreams aren't going to be reasonable.

They are not going to submit to anything that makes a whole lot of sense. And so if you have been very strongly under the influence of your Saboteur, you may have some challenges dreaming.

Make another declaration and say, "I no longer require my life to be or look or feel reasonable. I now place my power in my magician to manifest my life to create something from nothing and I am allowing my life to make no sense to me right now, to make no sense to others."

The fact is, when you're being called to make great changes in your life, it will not make sense to a lot of people.

The path your intuition is going to guide you along isn't going to look or feel very sensible. Make this declaration: "I am willing to live outside of my reasoning mind. I am willing to let my magician, my trickster in and actually let play in, let creativity in." Your magician is the energy of creativity.

You are bringing something completely new into existence and so if your Saboteur is very strong, you're going to be tempted to look outside of yourself for a template for who is doing something similar and how are they doing it.

This shuts down your guidance, your intuition, your gut. The way you navigate this journey is going to be unique to you. The challenge here is to really dial down that Saboteur, go inward and discover and activate that pure inner vision that is not going to look like anything that is on the outside world and to honour that and to birth that.

The Saboteur: The Survival Questions

Take inventory of where your Saboteur is managing your life, and the damage it has caused.

Envision your life in the hands of your Saboteur.

Where are you demanding that your dreams, your life, your desires, your plans, be reasonable, rational or sensible?

Where are you allowing others to expect this?

Where are you making excuses?

How active is intuition in your daily life in driving your decisions and choices?

In what circumstances might you do this again?

Notice how often the Saboteur shows up in what others say and how they choose to behave and decide.

Really take time to engage the survival archetypal energy, even if you think you've "conquered" it or "know" it. The fact is that our survival archetypes are never conquered. So the more we face the way in which they have, and will again, surface in our lives, the more conscious we can be of keeping them at bay.

Here are some helpful prompters....

The Saboteur says:

That doesn't make sense, therefore I won't do/say/act on that.

I don't understand, therefore I won't act.

The Magician: Thrival Questions

Envision your life and your business in the hands of your Magician. In the hands of a powerful manifestor, the energy of bringing something forth from nothing and of being able to powerfully enroll others in your vision and your value. What would that look and feel like?

Here are some helpful prompters....

The Magician says...

I create from my intuitive knowing, not my rational mind.

I am master of inspired action.

I am always in the most inspired place, at the most inspired time, saying and doing the most inspired thing.

The Commitment

Write and sign a sacred contact with yourself to take back the power from your Saboteur archetype and put it in the hands of your Magician archetype.

SABOTEUR DEEP DIVE

Manifestation Field: Shadow/Unconscious Field/Subconscious Fiel

Channel for: TRANSFORMATIONAL Energy

Domains of Power(lessness): Time, Reality, Intuition, Knowing, Certainty, Magic

Overview

- Gives excuses and reasons why not
- Focuses on what is (vs what could be)
- Does not take responsibility (shrugs off her power)
- Consumed with being and appearing responsible and therefore paralyzed and unable to be response-able to the moment
- Needs proof, certainty, evidence, reasons, plans, maps
- Consumed with doubt
- Powerless over Time
- Lacks inspiration; is blocked or bored

- Cannot see clearly; cannot see through chaos or illusion
- Clueless
- Flaky and unaware
- Indiscriminately rebellious
- Arbitrary Rule-breaker
- Grave. Serious.
- Takes self and others too seriously.
- Unmoored, so unable to be rooted in Truth because constantly rebelling against the Truth-roots
- Mired in either/or

Archetype Permutations
- Judge
- Critic
- Blind Man
- Skeptic
- Naysayer
- Devil
- Dunce
- Class Clown
- Rebel

- Teacher's Pet
- Annihilator
- Destroyer
- Void

Archetypes in Culture

- Sheldon in Big Bang Theory
- Jerry Seinfeld
- The entire cast of The Office

Professions

- Judge
- Lawyer

Says

- I don't know
- I can't see
- I can't see the way
- It makes no sense
- This is foolish/irresponsible
- I need more time
- I'll do it later. Someday.
- I need more evidence, proof, knowledge, understanding, training, certification

- I don't have enough time.
- I'm out of time.
- There's never enough time.
- I'm bored.
- I'm blocked.
- I have no idea

Symptoms/Clues

- Mentally unstable
- Very intellectually bright
- Highly logical
- Mentally ill
- Mind has a "mind of its own"
- Depressed
- Anxious/worried
- Always late/hurried
- Cynical/pessimistic (but says is being simply realistic)
- Gets mired in analysis paralysis
- Perfectionist
- Accused of being arrogant, judgmental know it all
- Wants everything spelled out

- Forgetful.
- Flaky
- Flighty
- Unmoored
- Unhinged
- Uncontrollable/Out of control
- Unable to complete anything/bring creations to completion
- Barren

<u>Is Powerlessness around Knowing/Struggles with Certainty. Is Obsessed with:</u>

Perfectionism: is paralyzed by perfectionism. Stems from terror of looking foolish and the belief that perfect conditions are essential to create with (when in fact perfect conditions sterilize creativity and magic). *This situation/these conditions/my state of being/my state of mind/ is/are not perfect, so I can't act/decide/commit.*

Judging: Must judge/come to a clear conclusion about all aspects of the situation before is willing to commit, act or decide. *I can't come to a clear judgment so I can't/won't act/decide/commit.*

Justification: I can't justify the decision, so I can't act.

Validation: *I can't see the validity; I can't validate that this decision is right/correct/trustworthy, so i can't act*

Certainty/Certification: *I don't know what to say/do/think/believe. I need to be certain or i can't act/decide; I need more certifications or certainty before i can act/decide.*

Proof/Proving: *I don't have enough proof, so i can't act. What is, is what I can see and make sense of. If I can't see or make sense of it, it doesn't exist so it doesn't count as proof. Seeing is believing. If I can prove it to others then it's true.*

Gathering Evidence: *I don't have evidence of the outcome/trustworthiness/correctness of the decision so i can't act.*

Reason/Being Reasonable: *I don't see a good reason, so I won't act.*

Being Responsible: Values being responsible. Hates looking or feeling foolish or irresponsible. *It seems irresponsible/foolish, so I won't act.*

Logic: *It makes no logical sense so I won't act.*

Linear cause/effect, linear timeline: *I don't see how it will get me from here to there so i won't act.*

Plans and maps: *I need a plan so I can act. I need a map before I act.*

Preparation: *I need more preparation before i can act; I will act when I'm fully prepared.*

Symptoms:

Anxiety, stress, mental illness, depression, mania, indecisiveness, flakiness

Is Powerlessness around Time: Struggles with Time. Is Obsessed with:

Procrastinating: *I'll do it later. Now is not a good time. Someday.*

Hurry: I have to hurry or I'll be late.

Laziness: I don't care when it happens/when I show up.

Rushes: there's never enough time. I have no time. There is no time. I need more time.

Is Powerless around Creativity/Imagination/Inspiration: Struggles to be Creative, Imaginative, Inspired and Inspiring

Bored, Blocked, Uninspired, Unimaginative

Shadow Audit: Saboteur

Time to take inventory. Where in all areas of your life do you recognize the saboteur running the show?

Where and how are you demanding that everything make sense and be all laid out before you take action and follow your intuition? Where are you refusing to know what you know? Where and how are you resisting being or looking foolish or crazy?

- Sex Life
- Finances
- Relationships
- Bank Account
- Body/Weight/Health
- Purchases
- Business
- Conversations

MAGICIAN DEEP DIVE

Manifestation Field: Light/Conscious Field

Channel for: TRANSFORMATIONAL Energy

Domains of Power: Time, Reality, Intuition, Knowing, Certainty, Magic

Overview

- Master of what is and therefore of what will be

- Sees through illusion and chaos

- Takes responsibility for what is (knows he created it) and can therefore create what "is not"

- Completely willing to appear foolish or do things that "make no sense" to himself or anyone else (because he knows this is what creates magic)

- Not concerned with being or appearing "responsible" and therefore able to be truly response-able

- Does not need proof, certainty, evidence, plans, maps, reason or time in order to act

- Knows what he knows and knows that he knows what he knows

- Understands the "clues" hidden in "reality." Alert to the hidden meaning.
- Has mastered the rules and laws and can break them to create magic.
- Has learned how to energetically "fly." Is not weighed down by the prevailing illusions of consciousness and beliefs about "reality"
- Light hearted.
- Delightful sense of humor. Does not take life too seriously.
- Doesn't need everything spelled out and therefore able to cast spells
- Knows magic is in the both/and
- Master of Time

Archetype Permutations
- Fool
- Jester
- Seer
- Sphinx
- Fortune Teller
- Magi
- Joker
- Prankster
- Loki
- Detective

- Private eye
- Teacher
- Master
- Creatrix
- Priest

Archetypes in Culture

- The Fool in Shakespeare's plays
- Mary Poppins
- Sara Blakely
- Willy Wonka
- Kennegh Branagh's *Henry V*
- Ragnar Lothbrok in *Vikings*
- Floki in *Vikings*

Professions

- Inventor
- Sales and Marketing
- Innovation
- R+D
- Artist
- Writer

- Speaker
- Filmmaker
- Actor
- Priest
- Healer

Says

- I know what I know
- I know that I know what I know
- This is what will be
- I am Master of Time. Time comes from me.
- I am certain.
- This happens now.
- I don't care how silly/foolish/irresponsible this looks/feels
- I don't have to see how it will all work out

Symptoms/Clues

- Is certain
- Grounded and graceful
- Controlled with precision and grace
- Full of joy
- Brings creations to completion

- Lives a magical, blessed life

- Anxiety-free

- Mentally healthy and powerful

The Sovereign asserts power through decrees. The Warrior, through action and will. The Magician by calling forth from Nothing. The Lover through knowing what is truly valuable.

THE CASE FOR SHADOW ALCHEMY

Nothing else that has ever been invented in any field—science, spirituality, self help, mental health or religion—allows the human to truly master the spiritual science of making magic in their lives like Shadow Alchemy does, which is why its users go off their mental illness medication, become rich quickly, completely cure their physical ailments and find true love. It is the holy grail of human seeking. And as such, it *ends* all seeking and puts us on the path we've been longing for all along - the path of pure joy, abundance and effortless success.

The Origin of Shadow

The Soul is on a learning journey. It is the anxious/degraded feminine making her way from shadow (denied power, belief in the illusion that there are victims and that power rests outside us) to her native home in the Dark. As she learns, she clears shadow. When the soul enters the body it codes the body and mind with its lessons learned, with the wounds it still needs to clear (hence cellular ancestral trauma), and with its desires (the homing mechanism that will set it on its learning journey in this lifetime). The body and mind are simply the vessels for soul evolution. The car the soul uses to drive around in 3D. But because the soul is on a learning journey, it is still ignorant of the True Truth and is therefore going to code the body and mind with limits they don't actually have and unTruths they're not aware of.

In other words, it's going to code your consciousness with shadow.

Shadow is the source of all suffering and struggle. It is the frequency of despair, weakness and ruin. This is why I say the Soul, as the source of our shadow, is therefore the source of all suffering, and not to be used as a guidance system.

This is also why Shadow Alchemy is so essential. Without it, you are driving blind, because what you pay attention to, make important and base your choices on determines the frequency of your consciousness and therefore the quality of your life. Shadow alchemy ensures that every minute of the day you are paying attention to and affected by the GOLD in your inner and outer environment, not the LEAD, and that when you *find* lead you can instantly alchemize it back into its natural state as vibrational gold.

Paying attention to and being affected by illusion, or your shadow consciousness, is the only reason you suffer and don't easily have everything you desire. Shadow Alchemy creates an empty shadow, completely eliminates your triggers, and makes you unfuckwithable in every area of your life.

It turns you into a legend, not just in your own mind, but in your impact and influence, your leadership, insights and transformational abilities, and in your financial success and mental and physical prowess. It restores you to your true nature as a genius giant.

The result is that you effortlessly carry the most powerful frequency on the planet—god consciousness—which is what creates financial, relational, and physical abundance.

Shadow Alchemy makes you rich, with ease. And rich with ease.

The Shadow Alchemy Tool

The deliberate, conscious act of shifting your entire programming at its core from the illusion that someone or something has power over you to the truth that no one and nothing does, and to living from this state of being at all times, is called shadow alchemy.

This is the process by which you fully alchemize all the toxic energy that is being held in your shadow until you have an empty shadow that cannot be triggered. A shadow empty of the illusion that power resides anywhere but within you. To have an empty shadow means you no longer resist the truth that you are a god who creates your experience and that so is everyone else. Even those who appear to be suffering greatly.

When you alchemize your shadow, you don't you don't do what everyone does now, which is dump its toxic contents straight into your body and mind, which then instantly and thoughtlessly generate the cascading actions that will eject the toxic energy from them and from your field.

That's how people deal with their shadow now, which is what being triggered causes, and which is why people will often, when they start to do shadow work, get sick, depressed, or angry and wonder, "What the hell is going on with me? Why is my body shutting down?"

This is commonly referred to as a "healing crisis."

And it's entirely unnecessary.

When you uplevel, you're replacing toxic consciousness with generative consciousness. Releasing energy that has been held captive in your field by a low frequency system of thought and correlating emotions and beliefs. When you release that toxic energy, if you don't do it using shadow alchemy, you're essentially dumping energetic poison that has been held in your field for decades directly into your body and mind. But your body and mind are not made to run toxic energy, so they're going to reject it and do whatever they can to discharge it.

This is the up-level crisis and this is what's happening energetically when people say, "I'm up leveling, so now I'm sick," as if it simply has to be this way.

But it is not necessary to poison your mind and your body.

It is not necessary to contract. To need to "ground" before you continue expanding.

Shadow alchemy offers another way where you shoot the toxic energy released during your upleveling process or during a situation in which you're triggered directly into your dark heart of gold so that it does not go into your physical, mental or emotional fields.

Your dark heart of gold is an infinitely vast and potent alchemical, energetic organ that shines the black light of the truest truth, the most challenging, confronting, and triggering truths directly on to the shadow content for as long as it takes for the shadow to release its grip on that illusion and to have its dense energy transmuted into pure potent energy. It is at this point that your dark heart of gold then channels this cleansed energy into your body and mind to be made available for use as increased mood, focus, optimism, inspiration, genius, creativity and life force magnetism, all of which draws your dreams and desires closer to you. In other words, crisis and drama can become powerful sources of potent energy that increase the overall magnetic power of your field and contribute powerfully to your mental and emotional health, your access to your spiritual gifts and to your magic and your ability to call into your experience all your desire without struggle.

When you're triggered, you literally have no energy for anything, other than managing the trigger and the drama and your run-away shadow that's reeking havoc on your life.

That's why you can't do anything right. Why you can't sell. Have no inspiration. Can't market. Can't hang on to money, or lovers, or weight loss. It's why you literally don't have the energy physically to do anything. Obviously, the sooner you learn to alchemize your shadow, the more easy, pleasurable, and rapid your rise will be into your greatest legacy, and your big, rich, wild, and free life.

The dark body is here to help us shift from our human consciousness to our divinity consciousness, and you really can't do it any other way. This is why so many spiritual leaders end up getting some kind of fatal illness. Because in managing their shadow, they're also toxifying their systems.

These are the essential steps in the energy alchemy process.

Step 1: Kill the Bond With Your Shadow

Before you can alchemize your shadow, it must first submit to being alchemized. In other words, it must agree that its beliefs are an illusion, that this process is one of shining the light of Truth onto it, and that when this happens fully, it will be shifted completely out of existence. So first, tell your shadow that you want to hear what it has to say, and that before you allow it to speak, it needs to acknowledge that everything it is about to say is UNTRUE and an ILLUSION, and that it is 100% willing to submit to being alchemized by the truth.

Once you get its agreement, you let the trigger talk.

Step 2: Let the Trigger Talk

Now, let your trigger talk. What were/are you upset about? Write it out, talk it out, get all the details out so you can observe and alchemize every piece of your shadow.

It's important to BE SPECIFIC. Use actual scenarios. What someone *actually* said. What you *specifically* thought and in relation to what *specific* event or situation. Do NOT use general concepts, like "How do you alchemize 'stupid'?" You don't alchemize GENERAL CODES. You alchemize specific ones.

I'm going to use a real-life example from one of my clients, so you can understand how this process is meant to unfold. She had an amazing early win in one of my groups. After our first coaching session, she had a big-time coach reach out to her and ask about her work (my client was a love and relationship coach). Two weeks later she closed this prospect for a $12,000 sale and took a $5,500 down payment. To be approached by your dream client and be ASKED by them about your work and then close the deal with an almost 50% cash payment is huge in many ways. So I posted a public congratulations of her, mentioning her win and specific success.

She then posted in our private group, "Lorna, you don't ask your clients before you share their name and successes?"

I said no, I don't. And I explained why, and then I took her through this very process of energy alchemy. By the end her trigger had vanished completely.

So, here is *her* step 2, speaking to/about me:

"Lorna, you have no consideration for my feelings or privacy. I should get to have control over how and when I share my results. You're taking credit for the work I've done. It could get back to my new client that I'm sharing about her and turn her off and fire me/ask for a refund. This could deter other people who may have been interested in working with me if they feel like I'm immediately sharing about new clients. Also, I've seen you ask other people for permission for sharing their comments so I don't get the disparate treatment."

Step 3: Name the Shadow

You're casting out demons here. Think of it as shadow exorcism.

And a proper exorcism always requires that you name the demon.

It's one of the essential components in unleashing it and sending it out of your system.

(And later you'll see what we do with those demons now that they're freed. Would you believe they become the content of your genius? They do. Because your genius is monstrous and it doesn't belong trapped in your shadow. In fact that's why it's been doing so much damage down there. Genius is DARK. It belongs in its natural home - Dark Consciousness, the energetic of chaos, the home of the Utterly and Unruly New. And you've got it trapped and prowling in the cramped cage of your subconscious. No wonder you're a hot mess. But all that's for much later. Now your focus simply needs to be on alchemizing the cage—your shadow—so that it eventually evaporates into thin air. That's when the beasts of your genius—the Dark Codes of disruption, euphoria and new spiritual energy—get activated and released. And by then you'll be a master beast handler and you'll know exactly how to usher them back to their home in the Dark and then begin unleashing your legacy body of work into the world, one beast of genius at a time.)

So, now that the shadow has spoken, you must identify which shadow archetypes spoke every one of the sentences (usually there are several that show up). You already know that the only way you can be triggered is to believe the illusion that someone or something has power over you. That means everything "you" just said was spoken by your shadow archetypes. So now identify which ones said which sentences.

You'll have to dig for some of them because our shadow can get quite sophisticated, and because the initial statement or thought is usually not the decocted and clear voice of the shadow.

So you want to go back and interrogate the statements that surfaced when you let the shadow speak, using a series of "And so what?" and "so who cares?" questions that will reveal the core voice/statement of the archetype so you can properly identify it.

For example:

"They have no consideration for my feelings or privacy."

So what? Why should someone consider your feelings or privacy?

Because that's what it means to be a good friend/parent/lover. Because it's not nice to be inconsiderate. Because my feelings matter!

Oh. So someone else should be taking care of you and your feelings.

And there we have it.

Because essentially ""They have no consideration for my feelings or privacy" means, "They're not taking care of my feelings and wellbeing." Meaning "they have power over my well-being. It is in their hands."

That's the child.

"I should get to control over how and when I share my results."

Why do I need the control? Why do I want all the control? What am I afraid will or won't happen if I don't have all the control?

This is answered later when my client said, "\It could get back to my client and she could fire me/ask for a refund."

So she's wanting to avoid a catastrophe. That's the victim. ("Look what might happen to me.")

And one last one.

Everyone will think I'm cold hearted if I cut off my mom from my life.

So what? Why does that matter?

Because then they'll hate me and not like me and they'll cut me out from their life and I'll have no one.

And there it is. The prostitute who is consumed with getting approval and belonging.

At first this is very tedious (you're deprogramming *lifetimes* of shadow consciousness). But I promise you, this is the HOLY GRAIL of life. The feeling and absolute UNSHAKABLE knowing that no one and nothing has power over you—that YOU are the source of ALL your power and that no matter what anyone says or does or what happens, you are totally free of fear—is the source of true euphoria, the end of all worry, anxiety and struggle, AND the source of your FORTUNE.

Because if you are here to make waves (which you are), then your FORTUNE depends on you making those waves FREELY and without needing to spend any energy dealing with your own emotional crashes every time someone doesn't like you rocking the boat.

This work is the key to total self mastery. And total self mastery is the key to complete emotional freedom and euphoria. And that is the key to being an energetic match for your highest genius. And THAT is where your fortune lies.

You're taking credit for the work I've done.

Sounds like "this isn't fair" → The Child.

It could get back to my new client that I'm sharing about her and turn her off and fire me/ask for a refund.

Worst case scenarios → The Victim

This could deter other people who may have been interested in working with me if they feel like I'm immediately sharing about new clients.

This is what I can't afford → The Prostitute. But also kinda sounds like the Victim...

I've seen you ask other people for permission for sharing their comments so I don't get the disparate treatment

Sounds again like, "I'm being treated unfairly," → The Child

Step 4: Speak the truth to your Shadow (Direct the Blacklight Beam of Truth)

Now the FUN begins.

Now that you have the shadow archetypes identified, you also now have the TRUTH immediately available to you, in the form of their Power versions (the light archetype pair).

This is where the alchemy happens because this is when you shoot your shadow straight like an arrow into your dark heart of gold and speak the truth onto it until it fully surrenders and is alchemized. I call this the Truth Rant.

So, for each statement of illusion, what's the truth?

I'll give an example:

Taking credit — this isn't fair/child >>

The voice of the Sovereign (The Truth):

Nobody's actions or thoughts have any power over my well being, happiness or sense of self and identity. I don't care about what's "fair" because I am the source of my own power and wellbeing. I don't monitor how other people are behaving or how they are treating me compared to others because it simply has no bearing on my wellbeing at all. I am my own power source, no one else is. In other words, no one and nothing has power over me (including how I FEEL). I create my own results and I take full ownership of my power and its impact and therefore I don't worry about whether others notice, don't notice, take credit or not, because it's not actually possible for them to TAKE from me what I don't GIVE them.

(AND, buried deep in this is the child's belief in limited resources. If the toy is mine and you take it, now I don't have it. In fact resources are infinite. You can have the toy AND someone else can also have the same toy. You are 100% responsible for your results. And because I am also a sovereign being and I also own and know my power, I am also 100% responsible for my results. And my result was coaching that catalyzed you to get your results. In other words 1-1=1)

Here are the results my client came up with:

It could get back to my new client that I'm sharing about her and turn her off and fire me/ask for a refund.

Worst case scenarios → The Victim

The truth is no person is my supply. If she decided to ask for her money back, that has nothing to do with me and ultimately will have no impact on me, my life, my business, or well being. It's none of my business what she thinks or says about me. There are no victims and no one needs to be saved. Not me. Not her.

Moreover, I am calling in aligned clients who need me because I am the best at what I do. I know what I'm doing and I don't need to be afraid.

This could deter other people who may have been interested in working with me if they feel like I'm immediately sharing about new clients → The Victim

I have access to infinite abundance and I have strong standards and boundaries. I don't ever need to fear "turning off a potential client," because my clients want me. Anyone who is deterred is not someone I'm meant to work with. There is no danger of there being not enough powerful single women who need support bringing love into their lives.

I've seen you ask other people for permission for sharing their comments so I don't get the disparate treatment

Sounds again like, "I'm being treated unfairly," → The Child

I don't need to be worried about what's fair because no one and nothing has power over me. I don't need to compare because I take full responsibility for myself including how I feel.

Step 5: Do this until there is no content left.

No matter how long it takes.

No matter how tedious it is.

No matter how much your shadow puts up a fight.

No. Matter. What.

This is the process of energy alchemy. And if, at the end, you can still feel the shadow active and insistent on its belief being true, run through the process again, using its resistant statements—its "but what about…" or "but what if…." rebuttals of the Truth Rant—as the new content you alchemize.

Shadow Alchemy: Benefits And Deep Dive

1. Zero energy expended managing your energy, therefore ALL your energy get channeled into your genius (and therefore into Quantum flight success)
2. Euphoria becomes predictable and repeatable at will. No more mystery around how to reach those "elusive" euphoric states you've felt a few times but couldn't maintain and didn't know what caused them in the first place
3. Increased magnetism which causes your Magic Man to continually deliver incredible experiences in all areas of your life
4. Sustaining this level of energy alchemy places you in a new stage of being where you then move into CHAOS alchemy, which is the ability to turn new thoughts that have never been thought into consciousness and share them with others - in other words, you become intimate with your GENIUS frequency. And this is where your Fortune and bliss truly lie.

Shadow Alchemy In Action: An Amazing Client Case Study

Taken from the Dark Mastery Retreat…

I'm going to give you a really practical application of this. Not the "before and after," but rather the "could've been, but wasn't" scenario. It's about a client who I was working with for several months, and who decided to step in to my high-level package.

Actually, at the end of the call to do the upsell, she told me she'd come into the call with every intention of telling me no. She was going to go it on her own. "Integrate for a while." See if she can do it on her own, because that's better. It's better to do it on your own, more noble than having somebody's help, she said. We worked through all that and she upleveled with me.

Three weeks later, she was hit with some of the most devastating news she'd ever received in her life. Her husband's company—and their multimillion dollar business—was facing a lawsuit that would send the business into bankruptcy.

What she didn't realize until this happened was that this had always been her plan B. *If the coaching doesn't work*, she'd say to herself, even though she only said it subconsciously, *I'll always have this. This secure **source** of money*.

The news of the impending bankruptcy sent the people in her life into a tailspin and she texted me saying she was getting sick and feeling nauseated from the news.

But in about three hours, with my coaching, she took all of that toxic energy that she'd dumped into her system and completely cleared it. She had no residue whatsoever of fear. She had no residue of worry, anxiety, nothing.

In fact, she went to bed *blissful*, even though just hours earlier she'd received some of the worst news of her life.

The next day she sent me a voice text: "This is crazy. My body is buzzing. It's like that feeling you get when you do really intense breath work. Like your body is just buzzing, buzzing, buzzing. I have so much energy. I don't know what to do with it all. It's like **so** much energy. This is amazing. This is crazy." She actually started to wonder, "Okay, really though, what do I do with all this energy? This is crazy."

This is ground zero. Day one after disaster struck. Her family, the people around her were calling her, saying, "I couldn't sleep last night. I was crying all night. I'm so sorry this is happening to you. This is such a disaster." People are falling apart around her, and she's completely fine.

Come Monday we had a coaching session and she rolled into her chair looking like she just came from a vacation in the Bahamas.

"Do you want to talk about what's been happening?" I said.

"Not really," she said. "I mean, you know. It is what it is. What I really want to talk about is…" and she moved on to something else." Impending bankruptcy. Having to lose their home. Shit. Big shit. And she didn't need to talk about any of it.

And so I said to her, "I want you to stop and rewind four weeks to your decision...that you were almost not going to do this uplevel with me into one-on-one work. What would have happened if that was the parallel universe? Tell me that parallel universe, that story."

"I would've totally collapsed into victim, into trauma, into crisis" she said. "I would've totally been there with everybody in the drama. And I probably would have *discounted my prices and lowered my packages* because now I had to make the money in the family."

"And what about your big client?" I said.

She'd recently landed this huge client, a $25K sale, the biggest package she's ever sold and something she's wanted to sell forever.

"How would you have shown up for her?"

"I mean when you're a fucking hot mess of a crisis, what's your coaching like? It's shit," she said. "And I certainly wouldn't have been able to sell. I wouldn't have been inspired."

That's what happens when you don't continue on your path of up leveling. When you're meant to do genius-level work in the world, shadow alchemy mastery is *essential*, because shit's going to happen. And instead of having it take her down, she used it. She alchemized it.

"There's a lot of powerful energy swirling around you," I told her. "Use it. Don't let it bring you down." And she did, and it was amazing, an incredible thing to witness.

This is not theory. This is real life stuff. And *this* is what you want.

You don't want to have to keep dabbling with your shadow and your triggers. It's exhausting. It keeps you at a low-level of functioning. It's like you're on life support in a hospital bed. This will get you off of life support for good so you can just keep leaping and leaping and leaping.

It's called quantum flight, and it is the promise of Shadow Alchemy Mastery.

THE EXPERIENCE OF ALCHEMIZED SHADOW AND THE APPLICATION TO A TRIGGER

Also taken from the Dark Mastery Retreat…

The Fine Print: For a while, this will be super annoying, and super tedious. When I did this, it's what I did all day. I mean that literally. Tt was just what I was *always* doing.

The feeling you're going for here, what you want to be asking yourself about your shadow is: Have these (shadow archetypes) become concretized? Do they have gravitational pull? Is matter collecting around them? Things that matter. *That* something matters, has power over me. Or can you just do a clean sweep and feel nothing.

That's what you're going for. Like the doors and windows are open and there's nothing, just wind. Because we have a human vessel, it does require a constant sweep, otherwise like photons to matter, that shadow is going to start collecting again around that field of consciousness. But it's like brushing your teeth or taking a shower. It just becomes just part of your system, part of your energetic hygiene to sweep through your shadow and clean it out.

First of all, you'll feel the tension, or the dis-chord of what shadow brings. You'll notice it immediately. Then you'll be like, "What is that?" You have to be really working with this material constantly, though, in order to feel the subtleties. And then later you're just coming in and sweeping the clean field, the ghostly outline of the shadow, to keep it clear.

Right now you're on the ground level with these monsters, these little beasts, or whatever you want to call them. These gravity-filled, heavy, concretized archetypes that are active in your daily life. You're on the ground floor with them. You have to be getting to know them inside and out. Very, very intimately know their language. How do they speak to you? What does it feel like when the victim is triggered? You have to know all the nuances so you can recognize them in an instant.

You're driving, you're in a conversation with someone, and then you go, "That feeling or thought pattern is so familiar that I could just go there. I know what that is." But instead you refuse. "I'm not going to give that any energy. I'm not going down with that." And you do shadow alchemy on it instead. It's not a wrenching, or a complete dismissal, because that just brings your shadow back later.

There's a conversation going on in one of my groups about this, and someone was saying, "Just release it, or let it flow through." That can, in the moment, discharge the energy, but it's just going to come back in another form later, and that's not at all what we're talking about here. That's shadow management.

Shadow Management Vs Shadow Alchemy: Some Distinctive Differences

Also taken from the Dark Mastery Retreat…

Me: Shadow management is where you own and befriend your shadow. That's where New Age spirituality is. Own it, befriend it. It's not going anywhere. It's part of who you are. It's your makeup. Stop trying to deny it.

There's an actual book called *Befriending your Shadow*, and while it can be a helpful part of the process, franky it's unnecessary if you do Shadow Alchemy, and you certainly won't benefit by staying in the friend zone.

Because it requires constant maintenance.

It is a full shadow, always needing to be emptied.

Yes, you have a spiritual business, and you're also kind of a hot mess behind the scenes. You're exhausted. Burned out. That is the legacy of shadow management.

This is also what creates the constant seeking, because you know there has to be another way. Because you're only deal with shadows individually, rather than the root-level source of shadow consciousness itself, you have to go in search of *all* your shadows and shadow elements.

Maybe if I just befriend a critical mass of them, you think, *then the other ones won't be such a problem. I'll have monsters in the yard, but they won't be that much of a problem, and it'll be great, it'll be fine. That's what I'm seeking. It's like some elements of fucking peace in the house.*

Retreater: You just get addicted to shadow work. Gabby Burnstein has a book called *Spiritual Junkie*.

Me: Yup.

Retreater: She's just addicted.

ME: This is why our myths and fairytales need to be re-told, because what we believe heroism is, and the answer to our problems is, is finding and killing the monsters, or taming them, or putting them in their proper place, so they don't fuck with us. That's what shadow management is. It's like I've got that one done, and then that one done, and that one done, where's the next one? That's what you do till you die.

Retreater: Like Ghost Busters.

Me: Like Ghost Busters, totally. You spend all your time...I'm writing a post about this right now. About people's spiritual hygiene routines. It's like having fifty face products on your counter in your bathroom. First there's the cleanser, and then there's the toner, and then there's a serum for this, and a serum for that. There's mediation, and there's affirmation, and then there's understanding my human design. Then there's learning yoga. Then there's this, then there's that. This is what it is for most people.

Retreater: Breath work.

Me: Breath work, and then journaling, and all this stuff. By the time you do it all, it's time to go to bed. And it's all because you have a shadow. That's the only reason any of that is necessary, because you have a shadow that's going to fuck with your day somehow. Fuck with your inspiration, your energy, your demeanor, your attitude, your happiness, your wellbeing, your confidence, your focus. I mean that's all it is, shadow management.

Retreater: The fairy tale thing is like we become the monster.

Me: Yes. I'm the monster, so therefore all these monsters that are hanging out around me. I don't really care. They're not a threat to me. I'm the biggest one around. I'm the giant here. We're going to get into that. There's some really cool things that Colleen and I actually just realized as early as this morning. But yes, that's the answer. The answer is, I am the monster in those fairy tales. Shadow Alchemy is when you vaporize the shadow. This releases your genius. There is a dark code of genius. It is like a piece of gold that your shadow holds, that when you fully alchemize, your shadow now sends its pulse of genius, and now this becomes the content for your dark archetypes to use for your legendary work in the world. Your genius level work. Meaning you as an archetype hanging out on the planet. That's dark mastery. That's what it is. It's the end of seeking. There's no more seeking, and the beginning of artistry. The beginning of becoming a work of art.

Colleen: Yeah you give up seeking for creativity.

Me: Yeah.

Colleen: It's like constant creation is being turned out. Constant creation, not "I don't have anything. I've got to go do this," or whatever the case may be. Constantly seeking for more of yourself, or "there's a piece of me that's missing. If I have that, then I would be able to create this." It's just waking up in the morning, and just creating, creating all day long.

Shadow Alchemy Q&A

Taken from the Dark Mastery Retreat…

Retreater: What did you call step one?

Me: Surrender the Shadow. You say, "This is what's happening here. You think you're going to survive this. You're not going to survive this. You are not going to survive, because the fact is you are not carrying truth." Your shadow thinks it's carrying the truth. Even if it knows that parts of it are not carrying the truth, it thinks there are some parts that are.

Retreater: It's sure of it's validity.

Me: Yeah, that there's some part of it that's true.

Retreater: So we decide already it's an illusion, and untrue. So why do you give the shadow a chance to talk at all?

Me: Because it has to be alchemized. Because it's still holding the illusion. I mean in other words, it doesn't know the content of truth yet. It hasn't been given the truth, so it's like "I'm holding this thing that I know is killing me. I need to apply a process to it that's going to empty it out and replace it with the truth." It just needs to be taught. It's like a teaching lesson, you know what I'm saying? The whole "it's an illusion" thing is really ... if you stop there, that's just shadow management. You're going to end up managing that piece over and over.

The shadow doesn't know what the truth is. It thinks that it's holding the truth. It can't imagine what the truth is, because part of your shadow is your saboteur, who has no imagination whatsoever. Your shadow can't imagine what the truth actually is. It could potentially acknowledge that it's not *holding* the truth, but it actually can't imagine what the truth really is. In order to alchemize the shadow, it must be shot through with the truth. That's what alchemizes it. It's the catalyzing element.

Okay. Then step two. Let the trigger talk. What were you upset about? Write it out, talk it out, get out all the details, so you can observe and alchemize every piece of your shadow. Because as you know your shadow has four ... your shadow is schizophrenic, and it has four voices, and only four voices. Only four, everything you can possibly come up with, we can slot into one of those four voices. They can sound very sophisticated. This is why I want to take you through this, because it takes some sleuth work. It takes some detective work to figure out which archetype is speaking. It's not always completely obvious, because your shadow can get pretty sneaky.

You want to just really write out the story. When you're going to do this on your own, you really just want to get it all out on page. I really encourage you to do this on the page. Unless you can hold a lot of content in your mind, and then kind of go back and alchemize each piece. But if not, it's really important that you don't leave part of that voice active, not expressed, not captured.

Retreater: So that's where you do the: "...and I make this mean," "and that matters because…" and that whole process that you talked about before?

Me: Yes, yep, yep. It's the "so what." You just exhaust it: So what happens then? And so what's the problem with that happening? And so what? That's how you get to the voice of the shadow. That's how you discover who's talking. Because sometimes it's unclear.

Colleen: I use the "then what?"

Me: Yeah.

Colleen: Then what? Then what? Every answer that you get, you get to keep digging, and going.

Me: Yeah, okay. So, you let the trigger talk. I'm going to use a real life example for you guys.

Because this is the thing. When you are not available to be triggered, you can coach like a fucking genius because you don't take any of this personally. I guarantee you, had I had this happen to me a year, and a half ago. I would've been like, "Oh shit, oh my God, what did I do? Oh fuck, oh my God ..."

When you are not able to be triggered, you can take your clients through their own shadow alchemy process, and they can shift in an instant out of something that would've taken them down, and taken you down as the coach.

It's the same reason why when you master this, your close rate will go through the fucking roof. You will close anybody you want. Because when you're not able to close somebody, it's because you are in the same trigger that they're in. You're available for the same illusion. You validate it. "Oh you don't have the money?" "Oh yeah, you have to ask permission. I totally get it."

You have no imagination, because you're in your own shadow around that same thing. You have no imagination for what you could possibly say to them that would cause them to change their mind. But when there is no content here, the things that come out of your mouth are just like "this is the most fucking brilliant thing I ever said."

And the person is like, "I can't believe you just said that to me." Like this woman who just had this happen. She was going to say no to my package. She went from saying no, coming into the call I'm saying no, I'm not going to do this, to being a fully paid 30K sale at the end. That is what shadow alchemy allows you to do. It's very practical.

Ok, so the real-life example. Let's see. So this client had an amazing early win in one of my groups. After our first coaching session she had a big time multimillionaire coach reach out to her and ask about her work. My client is a love/relationship coach. Two weeks later she closed this prospect for a $12,000 sale, and took a $5,500 down payment. To be approached by your dream client, asked by them about your work, and then close a five-figure deal with an almost a 50% cash payment is huge in many ways. I posted a public congratulations of her, mentioning her win, and specific success.

She then posted in our private group, "Lorna, you don't ask your clients before you share their name, and successes?" I said, "No I don't." I explained why. What I said was, "If you know anything about me, you know that the way I coach is to coach you into your power, and into your realization that no one and nothing has power over you. If you have a problem having your success amplified in the world, you're not a match for me, because I can't help you, because the whole fucking point is that no one and nothing has power over you." That's what I said to her.

Then I said, "Why do you ask? Are you upset at what I did?" She said, "Yes I am." Then I said, "Okay, so do you want to know how to alchemize that? Do you actually want to know how to alchemize your triggers completely, so that you just don't even have that thing at all ever? She said, "Yes, the reason why I addressed it here is because I knew there was something here for me to look at. So yes please teach me how to do this." I was like, "Okay, awesome."

I took her through this process of energy alchemy, and by the end her trigger had vanished completely. Here's her step two, speaking to and about me. This is her shadow talking okay?

"Lorna, you have no consideration for my feelings, or privacy. I should get to have control over how, and when I share my results. You're taking credit for the work I've done. It could get back to my new client that I'm sharing about her and turn her off and fire me or ask for a refund. This could deter other people who may have been interested in working with me, if they feel I'm immediately sharing about new clients. Also I've seen you ask other people for permission for sharing their comments, so I don't get the different treatment."

How many of you would be like, "Fuck." Be honest.

Retreater: Yeah.

Me: Would you be like, "Fuck, fuck. There's a lot of good things in there that she said, fuck." Yes or no?

Retreater: Yeah totally I would've been like, "I fucked up."

Me: You would go in to your shadow. What would you do?

Retreater: I think apologize.

Me: Apologize, okay.

Retreater: Take it down.

Me: Okay so you would be triggered, but you would know that your reactive ideas are not the good ideas, and would you do the work of getting to the place where you had the response that I had?

Retreater: It would take me a while.

Other Retreater: I don't think I would've gotten to that point, but now that I think about it ... it would've gotten to that point, but if it got to that point, I probably would've sat there for a while, and figured it out.

Me: What if she said, I want it taken down? I don't appreciate that?

Retreater: Take it down.

Me: I've had people say "you need to take down, I am not okay with that. You cannot talk about how much money I made. You cannot talk about, and use my name, and my picture."

Retreater: I probably would just terminate honestly. It's harder for me ... I'm trying to change it into a context that I would face because I work with moms. Because you're a business coach.

Me: So you're telling a story about a client who felt like a shitty mom, and...Maybe you use a picture, maybe you don't even use a picture. Maybe you just talk about her in a way that she's like, "That is so fucking obvious that's me, and you're talking about how I hired you, because I feel like a shitty mom, and my kids are misbehaving, and getting kicked out of school."

Retreater: Not having sex.

Me: "I'm not having sex with my husband, and I haven't had an orgasm in five years." Okay, so that would be the analog.

Retreater: Because even though they signed the contract they could still sue you.

Other Retreater: That's like deformation, or slander right.

Me: Where is that coming from with them?

Retreater: Something has power over them.

Me: Yeah, someone has power over them.

Retreater: Yeah. There's a victim for that one, or something?

Me: They're coming from the belief that's something, and someone has power over them. And don't you want to coach them past that? That's what they're there for right? But in that moment you're now aligning with their shadow.

Retreater: That's what I can see.

Me: Yeah you're aligning with their shadow, so you can't be helpful to their transformation out of it. You're going to actually encourage them to continue behaving that way if you say "Oh yeah right, okay we'll take it down."

If you're going to have them do the work on themselves, they have to know the archetypes. If you're going to coach them through it, you have to know the archetypes.

My client did, because I give her the fear and power series [Now the Archetypal Consciousness Series]. This is why I give it to everyone of my clients, so that we have the language. We have the framework. They have the map.

Okay, so now you name the shadow. This is step three. You name the shadow that's speaking. In this one there are several. There are several shadow voices in hers. That's why it's important to know all of them, because there isn't just one.

Now that it's spoken, you must identify which shadow archetype spoke every one of the sentences. You may have to dig for something, because their shadow can get quite sophisticated. 'm going to give you an example. This is literally what I did to her. I said I'm going to give you an example of one, and then you do the rest. "You have no consideration for my feelings, or privacy." Which shadow is that?

Retreater: Victim?

Me: Yes, so this is why it's so important to know the voices of those archetypes, and the nuances. There's lots of off-shoots, but there's a very clear family. One of the way you can interrogate this sentence, is to ask yourself "What does that mean? What are you trying to say? You have no consideration for my feelings, or privacy? What are you trying to say? Who cares? So what does that mean? This means you're not taking care of my feelings, and well being. Okay, that's what it is. You're not taking care of me." That's the child.

Retreater: Yeah.

Me: That's why I'm saying, you want to take each sentence, and really distill it to its essential aspect. In acting, this is called the subtext.

You get the script, and your line might be "I never want to see you again." But the subtext is, "I'm so in love with you, I can't handle it." The way you say that line is very different than if the subtext is, "I want to kill you." What you're looking for is the subtext of your own script that's running, okay? The subtext here is, "You're not taking care of my feelings." And now the other one, "I should get to control of how, and when I share my results." Which one is that?

Retreater: It's the victim.

Other Retreater: It's the prostitute. She decides when she's got the value of sharing it.

Me: I should get to control over how, and when I share my results. Why? Why does she want that control.

Retreater: I want to decide when there's value in my work.

Me: Why do I want all the control? What am I afraid will, or will not happen if I don't have all the control?

Retreater: Someone else's power over her.

Me: She's wanting to avoid a catastrophe. "If I don't have the control, then there will be a catastrophe," which she says later. "My client might find out about it, and they might fire me."

Retreater: Other people won't hire me.

Me: Other people won't hire me, and then I will be on the street with no food.

Retreater: How did you subtext that?

Me: One of the ways you can get to the subtext is "why does this matter to you? Why do I need this? Why is this important? What's going to happen if I don't have it? Why do I want it? What am I afraid will, or won't happen if I don't have it? Or if you don't act this way, or whatever." Makes sense? "Why do I need it? Why do I want it? What am I afraid will, or won't happen if I don't have it?"

Once you get the archetype, then it's easy. Then the path is clear. It's not easy necessarily to speak the truth to it, but the pathway is clear. You're like, "Oh it's the victim." "No one, or nothing has power over me. There's no such thing as a catastrophe. I cannot possibly fail." That's when you can do your truth rant, right? But you can't really do much until you know who's voice is speaking. Okay. So she's wanting to avoid a catastrophe, that's the victim. "Look what might happen to me." That's one of the core things the victim says. "Look at what might happen to me."

"Look at what happened before. Look at what might happen." Yes, at first this is very tedious. You're deprogramming lifetimes of shadow consciousness, but I promise you this is the holy grail of life. The feeling, and absolute unshakable knowing, that no one, and nothing has power over you. That you are the source of all inner power, and that no matter what anyone says, or does, or what happens, you are totally free of fear. It is the source of true euphoria, the end of all worry, anxiety, and struggle, and the source of your fortune.

Because if you are here to make waves, which you are, then your fortune depends on you making those waves freely, and without needing to spend any energy dealing with your own emotional crashes every time someone doesn't like you rocking the boat.

Okay. "You're taking credit for the work I've done." Which one would that be?

Retreater: I want to say prostitute, but that means it's nothing.

Me: ou're taking credit. Just think about the energy of it.

Retreater: The child.

Me: Yeah. You took my toy.

Retreater: Yeah.

Me: "Give it back. It's my toy. This isn't fair. It could get back to my new client that I'm sharing about her, and turn off, and fire me, or ask for a refund."

Retreater: Victim.

Retreater: Yeah. "This could deter other people who may have been interested in working with me, if they feel like I am immediately sharing about new clients?"

Retreater: Victim still.

Me: Because that one is unfinished right? I mean her point is, "and then I wouldn't have money." That's the catastrophizing. The actual hook here isn't something she says, which often is the case. You'll say something, and your shadow is like, "Yeah that's terrible." But you haven't even investigated, or interrogated to the "so what, who cares?" You see. You shadow automatically agrees that that's a terrible thing. That's why this requires detective work. Because your initial thoughts are not going to be always obviously a shadow voice.

"I've seen you ask permission from other people for sharing their comments, so I don't get the disparate treatment."

In my former life as a coach, when I was trying to build my business before, and failing miserably, I mean if someone told that to me I'd be like, "Fuck." You know what I would've done, I would've gone back. I would've been like, "Wait who did I give that treatment to ... Let's see, did I ... Oh yeah I guess I did. Because I was asking other people's permission.. Shit. Maybe I'm not being fair or professional.. Am I not paying enough attention? Oh my God, this sucks."

Retreater: You took all this energy. It's like crippling. It's debilitating. It's crazy.

Other Retreater: How are you ever going to fucking do anything in your day? If you even do this for 30 minutes, a total of 30 minutes a day.

Me: But then think of how many clients you have, and think how many issues. They're coming to you because they have issues, and they're triggered by life. That's why they're coming to you right? It just multiplies, and multiplies, and you just spend your whole day doing this in your business.

Ok so look at your archetype maps. You wouldn't go on a trip without a GPS system, right? This is your map. This is so important. You really need them for your work. Ok, so that was Step three.

Retreater: That was something.

Me: Now that you have named the shadow, the shadow has agreed to submit, the shadow gets a chance to talk. You've identified what shadow it is. Then it gets shot into your dark heart of gold, which is this alchemizing organ in your dark body. What it's going to do, is it is going to shine the black light of truth onto that shadow. That's what a truth rant is.

You shine the blacklight of Truth onto the shadow relentlessly, incessantly. You as the host of this process must be more committed than your shadow. If your shadow survives this, it's because you don't really want to do work. And the way you know the truth is by the pair, whatever the light archetype is paired with the shadow voice you've identified.

Because once you have the shadow archetypes identified, you also now have the truth immediately available to you in the light archetype pair.

And this is where the alchemy happens. This is when you shoot your shadow straight like an arrow into your dark heart of gold, and speak the truth on to it until it fully surrenders and is alchemized. I call this the truth rant.

Okay, so for each statement of illusion what's the truth? Because that's important. I'll give an example. "Taking credit, this isn't fair," right? This is the child. The voice of the Sovereign: "Nobody's actions, or thoughts have any power over my wellbeing, happiness, or sense of self, and identity. I don't care about what's fair." I'm already getting full body chills.

When you release, speak the tone of truth like we've talked about, your body will respond. "Nobody's actions, or thoughts have any power over my well being, happiness, or sense of self, and identity. I don't care about what's fair, because I am the source of my own power, and well being. I don't monitor how other people are behaving, or how they're treating me compared to others, because it simply has no bearing on my well being at all. I am my own power source, no one else is. In other words, no one and nothing has power over me, including how I feel. I create my own results, and I take full ownership over my power, and it's impact, and therefore I don't worry about whether others notice, don't notice, take credit, or not, because it's not actually possible for them to take from me what I don't give them." That's the truth rant spoken from the sovereign.

Retreater: Just for one sentence?

Me: Yup. Okay, here are the results my client came up with. "It could get back to my new client that I'm sharing about her, and turn her off, and fire me / ask for a refund. Worst case scenarios: the victim. The truth is no person is my supply. If she decided to ask for her money back, that has nothing to do with me, and ultimately will have no impact on me, my life, my business, or well being. It's none of my business what she thinks, or says about me. There are no victims, and no one needs to be saved. Not me, not her."

"Moreover I am calling an aligned client to meet me, because I'm the best at what I do. I know what I'm doing, and I don't need to be afraid." I have total chills the whole time. This is true energy alchemy, you see, turning lead into gold.

Retreater: Yup.

Me: Shadow lead. Gravity into gold. This is what we're talking about. By the time she was done with the exercise it was completely gone. She was like, "Yeah it's gone." I want to pause, and say something, because when you do it this way, it's going to feel like shadow management, in the sense like there's this fucking beast, and this beast, and this beast. It's going to feel like it for a while like, "Fuck, I'm just doing the same ... It's this process, but it's the same thing. I'm just managing my shadow all over the place." But the difference is this: You are alchemizing your shadow.

You're literally reducing it. You're taking pieces, and you're completely and purely alchemizing it. There is a point which that shadow just doesn't have any mass left to it. It is a process that is ... You're not just moving the shadow out for a while, so you feel better, and then it comes back. Then you're moving the shadow out for a while, so you feel better, and then it comes back. Then you're moving the shadow out for a while, and then it comes back. You're literally emptying the shadow out, and releasing into your consciousness a completely new programming.

Colleen: In the management way, it's like you are using emotion to ... You're exchanging one emotion for another.

Retreater: Affirmations.

Colleen: Affirmation, yeah, but also it's really tied into your emotions, where the energy alchemy has nothing to do with emotion. You're not even pulling from your emotional body. That's not happening. That's where the potency comes in, because the emotions are like the glue, are like the bonding. Emotions, if you think about emotions, and how much emphasis we've put on emotions in the last however many decades. Being the holy grail to get ... If you're the most emotional person in the room, you win in the spiritual circle. That's how it's been.

Retreater: By shifting emotions is how we manage our shadow right? It's basically what you do, you shift your emotions. Abraham Hicks has the .. What's it called? Oh yeah it's the frequency of emotions.

Colleen: That's the best that we have. Then you take that, and you're like okay that's shadow management. You manage your shadow through shifting emotions. The difference in how you can start to see, and detect if you're doing alchemy, or managing is what level, where are you? Are you emotionally attached to this? Is there emotion involved.

Me: That's not to say...because when I do a truth rant, or I don't really need to anymore but when I did, there was ... I wasn't necessarily emotional, but it was intense as fuck.

Colleen: Yeah there's so much energy there.

Me: The intensity of the truth that I was speaking was off the chart.

Retreater: But where did the goose bumps come from Lorna? When you go, "I got chills."

Colleen: That does not come from the emotional body.

Me: No.

Colleen: It comes from a higher consciousness that's clicking in every single time that you get those chills, and you go, "Oh my God I got chills." That's not because you were having an emotion.

Me: Yeah. It's recognition of truth. And I want to clarify, because your shadows are strong. Your shadows are powerful right now. They're very powerful. It's like cutting through steel right? It's light that cuts steel. It's truth spoken in a way that literally cuts through.The cold hard truth. That is why this can only happen in the dark heart of gold. Because the dark heart part is the cold, hard truth. It is the steely truth that slices you open. It's dispassionate. That requires intensity, and the will to kill. The shadow heart is the heart of emotion, and emotionality. That's not what is capable of alchemizing shadow. It's part of the shadow.

Retreater: I can see the big difference now. The only difference is the emotional part, because there's people that need to be light. You need to feel good.

Me: Yeah. It's not an emotional experience. It's really more like going on a sociopathic murder rampage with no emotion.

What you brought up, which didn't even cross my mind, is that the lack of emotion in this process. It's imperative actually. Yeah the intensity is super, super high. I mean it's almost like, because there's no emotion, the intensity is through the fucking roof.

Colleen: That first step is really ... It's really like killing the bond with your shadow. That's the first step. That's really what you're saying in the first step.

Me: Yeah.

Retreater: I like that.

Colleen: You have to come at it that way. I have no alliance with this shadow.

Retreater: It's like the guy who gives you the polygraph test. He doesn't give a shit about whether you pass your polygraph, or not. He's just there to run the polygraph test. It's your job ... You're freaking out, and you're the nervous wreck, and you're failing the polygraph, because [crosstalk 01:31:45] your heart is all over the place.

Other Retreater: Whenever you watch those TV, it's always some nerdy guy that doesn't give a shit. He's just running the polygraph.

Me Yeah, ok. So that's the last step. So you do this until there is no content left, no matter how long it takes, no matter how tedious it is, no matter how much your shadow puts up a fight. No matter what. That could be step five.

Retreater: You dissect the trigger, and then go on a truth rant.

Me: And if at the end you can still feel the shadow active, and insistent on its belief being true, run through the process again using its resistance. In other words, "yeah, but what about," or "What if," or "But that can't be the case…" In other words, you shadow is going to hear the truth, and may rebut okay. Then use the rebuttals that the shadow is giving. And You'll know when it's gone.

Then, you'll be like, "This is fucking amazing, this so awesome." Then half an hour later ...

Colleen: You'll be at again.

Me: But here's what happens. Your shadow at some point is like, "Okay I get it, I get it. This is something new. I don't actually get to hang around. I get it." This process will become instantaneous. That's what really happens. It's so instantaneous it doesn't even happen. That's when you stop being triggered. That's when you know the upgrade has happened. You full downloaded the new consciousness, and that's the program that's running in the background now.

THE MASTER SEVEN: THE THREE FIELDS OF MANIFESTATION AND WILL AND THE FOUR CHANNELS OF LIGHT ENERGY

There are three fields of manifestation and will. Unconscious Will *undermines*. Conscious Will *drives*. Superconscious Will *overrides*.

The reason you aren't getting what you want is due either to you being run by your Unconscious/Subconscious field of manifestation, where your un/subconscious will is *undermining* your conscious will, OR you are being directed by your SuperConscious Will, the field of manifestation that overrides your small desire in exchange for a much grander, unimaginable one.

When you master these three fields of consciousness, by mastering the Four Channels of Light Energy, you will know which is which, and what to do about it.

The following is a channeled transmission in response to a client's question about how to balance the popular LOA teaching that you must be fully IN the reality of what you desire (in his case, $50K months) with doing shadow alchemy, which requires you to engage your shadow, which is decidedly NOT in the reality of what you desire.

Shadow alchemy is tripping you up because you're paying attention to what is now, to what's blocking you, to the illusion, rather than just saying to yourself, "No, no. Oh no no no. There is no illusion. No no no. I'm already there. I'm already there. I'm already there." As you know, that doesn't work, and the *reason* is because your subconscious has not been pulled into the True Field of manifestation, which means you essentially have two fields of manifestation going, and they're fighting each other.

There are actually three fields of manifestation—the subconscious/unconscious, the conscious and the super conscious. The subconscious/unconscious field of manifestation is where humans manifest unconsciously, not at will. It is the "involuntary" field of creation. And what it creates is struggle and hell on earth. The conscious field of manifestation is what humans long to master, and which is where they manifest consciously and at will. This is where manifesting on demand, and true magic, happens. For quite a while, until your shadow is fully or mostly alchemized, operating this field takes effort. Not physical effort, as in hustle, but rather consciously and consistently applied will in order to overcome the involuntary operation of the unconscious field of manifestation.

The superconscious field of manifestation, or the Dark Field, is where the genius giant (formerly the human) crafts new codes and laws of consciousness with which to create new magic and myths on the Light Grid.

The problem with manifestation boils down to the two fields of manifestation that exist on the Light grid—the subconscious/unconscious and the conscious—being at war with each other (or you being unaware that your SuperConscious is overriding your small desires in return for an unimaginable one). Far from creating or emphasizing this rift, Shadow Alchemy actually *brings these two fields together* and merges them into one. It eliminates the internal civil war and between the "either/or" battle of "Either I am where I am and I have this shadow, or I am where my $50K month is."

That's an either/or condition set up by the two fields being at war with each other, because the truth (and the magic) is always in the both/and.

The fact is that until you have mostly or fully alchemized your shadow, you have a field of manifestation that's operating against your conscious will. That field only has power if you give it power, so it's an illusion that it has a separate power structure and a separate will, even though it feels like it.

Shadow Alchemy *stitches back together* those two fields that are meant to be one, one field of operation, The Light.

When you are doing shadow alchemy, you are establishing the ground rules, the rules of engagement, for how you require your conscious and subconscious fields to work together to manifest what it is that you declare that you desire. And because you know there is no time and this is all a game and the whole split in that field is simply part of the illusion, it's not a dichotomy to also say, "I'm in the $50k reality. That is my reality, it's just that right now a whole area of my field of manifestation doesn't believe it and doesn't see it, so I have to go to that field and do some work in that field because that field is an illusion."

See yourself as the *operator* between the fields of truth and illusion. When you do that, it's very easy to do shadow alchemy and *also* be in the place of your $50k month. That it *is* here, that *this* is the truth—the truth is that it is here *and* if I am not 100% on board with that, it just means there's some illusion going on, some shadow going on, and Shadow alchemy is a way of bringing those two fields together.

This is what gives you full access to your power. You begin streaming the content of your higher mind and unlock access to the source codes of the universe. The source code is the feminine and masculine energies, and when you can place your hands directly on them and work with the raw material of the universe, you create magic in your life.

Magic, the mysteries of the magical masculine and the feminine energies, manifesting on demand is what we'll be covering in Book Two: Light Mastery.

Lorna J Coaching + Shadow Alchemy In Action: The Work

This is taken from a Dark Mastery retreat in 2018 where I taught the Shadow Alchemy tool with my business partner, Colleen Mogan. I had them pick a trigger that happened to them while they were at the retreat so we could work through something real time.

Me: So who wants to go? Who wants to pick one of your triggers?

KG: Snoring. I couldn't sleep. I couldn't sleep last night, so I was tossing and turning and trying to move to wake up CT so she would stop snoring, and then she wouldn't, so I came out here. And then someone else was on the couch and SHE was snoring too and I was like, "Oh my God!"

CT: I warned you. I warned you.

KG: And I was like, "Why didn't I grab the other room?

CT: I specifically warned you.

RB: Should have been in the bed with me, because I have a CPAP on, and I don't snore.
Me: Okay. So what is the trigger?

KG: That I can't sleep.

Me: What was the thing that's making you pissed off, angry, annoyed?

KG: That I didn't make the right decision. I should have chosen a better bedmate or just a better bedroom or whatever. That was my: "Why do I sleep here? How come everyone snores?"

Me: So the first step is to acknowledge that whatever it is you're worried about, whatever wants to say what it's gonna say (the shadow archetye who wants to talk) is an illusion.

KG: Right. There is no perfect bedroom. Is that what you mean? Like, there's no perfect bedmate?

Me: No. No, it's deeper than that. You're not gonna know what you have to agree is an illusion yet. Because you haven't even clarified what really is happening down there. So you're blindly agreeing. "Yep, whatever I'm about to say, which I don't even know, is gonna be a lie. Whatever I'm gonna uncover." So you have to, without knowing the full force of what you might have to face is an illusion, agree that whatever it is, it's an illusion.

KG: Okay.

Me: And then you let the shadow talk. And t's going to be really fucking messy. So that's why you just write all of it out. All the things you just said, and whatever else comes. Until it's clear that you've got it. You got all the pieces. So: Everyone was snoring. I couldn't get a good night's sleep. Why didn't I pick the right bedroom? Is there anything else?

KG: Yeah. I think if I go deeper, it's the whole ... This just came to me, like triggering. My sister... I was always the one that got the shitty bedroom and had to share a room with my mom, and she got the best bedroom. I don't know if I'm kind of reaching here, but maybe that was the whole thing about, "I'm not worthy of the right bedroom or the right sleeping arrangement."

Me: Okay. So this is **not** going into your past, into your history, into your childhood. This is a totally different approach, like, completely. So it doesn't fucking matter whether you were homeless and people around you snored on the street. You know what I mean? It totally doesn't matter. Stay with the present moment, and then you're gonna alchemize it from here. So no past. You just do not need to go in the past.

KG: Got it.

Me: So the present moment is, "I couldn't get a good night's sleep. Everybody's snoring, and I'm pissed that I didn't choose better."

KG: Right. Yes.

Me: Okay. So that's letting it speak. Is that it? Is that it?

KG: Yeah. I wasn't-

Me: You're annoyed.

KG: Yeah. I was annoyed.

Me: Okay. So now you identify the shadows. So "I'm pissed that I didn't get a good night's sleep." That's not obviously a shadow yet, right?

KG: Mm-hmm

Me: This is why this is so amazing. Because when you find it, you're like, "What? That's what is really underneath the subtext? What?" And the way you get there is by asking yourself, "Ok. So what? Who cares?" So you're not going to get a good night's sleep. So what.

KG: Because then I won't be at the level I need to be to get what I need to get out of this retreat that I invested money in and-

Me: So what?

KG: I will leave the retreat feeling like a loser.

Me: Because you wasted your time?

KG: Because I wasted my time, my money, I'm no further along than I was four months ago.

Me: So there's big stakes here. Really big stakes. You have to squeeze every moment out of this.

KG: Totally. Every drop.

Me: Because if you don't, so what?

KG: Then I fucked up and invested in-

Me: It's a catastrophe, KG. It's a catastrophe.

KG: Yes. I'm more in debt. I have nothing to show for it.

Me: It's a catastrophe.

CT: You failed!

KG: Totally.

Me: But it's a catastrophe that you're trying to avoid.

KG: Yes, yes.

Me: A catastrophe of feeling a certain way, a catastrophe of your life still being fucked up. You're saying, "Please don't put me face to face with a catastrophe of my life."

KG: Right.

CT: Chills all down my body.

KG: I just got that, too. I was like, "Oh, fuck. Yeah."

Me: That is why you're annoyed you didn't get a good night's sleep.

CT: Wow.

KG: Yeah.

CT: Yeah, fuck.

Me: Isn't that amazing?

CT: Totally.

KG: Yeah.

CT: Still chills. They won't stop.

KG: Yeah.

Me: See how much incredible power they have?

KG: Yeah. And it's funny, because I think I would have stopped at, "Oh, it's all my childhood bullshit," or whatever. "I'm just being silly."

Me: Which is just more emotion and bonding with the shadow.

Colleen: You identify with the shadow.

CT: The drama. You're searching for the drama, you're searching for the trauma.

Colleen: But you don't get anywhere.

CT: No.

VM: You see it, you know it, you've known it for your whole life, and it's like, "Oh, yeah. My sister." Like what?

Me: Yep. That's shadow management. "That thing with my sister. That bitch. That thing's always gonna be with me. I'm always gonna be doing shadow work and that thing with my sister. Yes."

KG: So true.

Me: Okay. So now you have to -- and this is why you gotta have your archetype maps with you, because you're going to need them. So now you have to find the archetype that catastrophizes. Or that wants to avoid a catastrophe. So it's the victim.

KG: Totally. Mm-hmm.

Me: Okay? So let's go to the next one.

KG: The next irritant?

Me: Yeah.

KG: In the same situation?

Me: Right. Because we wanna get all of them.

KG: I didn't get a good night's sleep.

Me: Didn't get a good night's sleep.

KG: And then I didn't choose right.

VM: Roommate.

Me: I didn't choose the best roommate. I didn't choose well.

CT: Or the best room.

Me: I didn't choose the best room. So who cares?

KG: So I don't make good decisions.

Me: And you have to make good decisions because why?

KG: I think it's gonna go to the same thing. Because I have to prove that I make wise investments, that I get-

Me: You have to prove?

KG: Yes.

Me: To?

KG: To myself that I invested, and look what I got out of it?

Me: You have to prove to yourself that you made good investments.

KG: That I can trust myself.

Me: That you can trust yourself.

KG: Mm-hmm (affirmative). I can trust that, "Oh yeah, this is ..."

Me: Ah. Wow.

KG: Yeah. That I can trust-

Me: Lots of stakes for choosing a good roommate.

KG: Totally.

Me: It's like life and death.

KG: It is! I better choose well.

Me: Or you're fucked.

KG: Yes. Go down in flames.

Me: Because if you don't believe ... Okay. So you have to prove to yourself that you make good investments, why?

KG: So that ... Well, I think so I can trust this is the right decision, this is the right next step, this is the right blah blah blah, so that I'm on the right path, so that I'm doing my life's work, that I-

Me: Uh-huh. So who's the ... What's the archetype that has to know?

KG: The saboteur.

Me: Yes.

KG: Yeah. I have to see, right? I have to see.

Me: Yes. It's evidence. I've got evidence. I've got to have evidence.

KG: Everything lines up to prove that this is perfect.

Me: Yes. Okay. So the core archetype there is: I don't trust unless I can see where I'm going, and then it all makes sense.

KG: Right.

Me: So it's the saboteur, right? I gotta see before I trust and I have to be able to see all the steps. Okay, amazing. So you've got the victim and the saboteur operating, okay?

KG: Mm-hmm (affirmative).

Me: So what is the truth now? If you're gonna take the victim statement, which is ....

KG: The catastrophe.

Me: If I don't get a good night's sleep-

KG: Oh, right.

Me: I mean, it just sounds so completely ridiculous when you say it. "If I don't get a good night's sleep, I will have to face the catastrophe of my life."

KG: My business will fail.

Me: My business will fail, and I'll face the catastrophe that is my life.

KG: Right, right.

Me: Okay. So then, what does the warrior say?

KG: I got your back. You're fine. Go back to sleep.

Me: Keep going, keep going. You gotta get into the full energy of the Truth. This is the alchemizing part, okay? So this is why you gotta know your archetypes. You gotta know how the warrior sounds and what the warrior says.

KG: Oh yeah. I'm the master of my space, physical, emotional, and mentally.

Me: Chills.

KG: Yeah, me too. Totally. Total chills.

Me: Do you see how that's way more powerful than, "I got your back, you're fine?"

CT: I'm a master, biatch.

VM: Or a simple "I couldn't get sleep," is, to me, a fact of truth, right? "I couldn't get to sleep," is totally different than I expected.

Me: But it's that there's a trigger around it, right? I have many nights where I've not gotten good sleep. And it's just like, "Yeah, okay. So fine. So I don't get good sleep..."

KGThere's no story, right?

Me: There's no story. There's no, "Well, then I won't be there for my clients the next day because I didn't get good sleep." Well, fuck that. I decide how I show up for my clients. It does not depend on how much sleep I get. And even if I did show up less, who the fuck cares? What's gonna happen then? I'm gonna lose my clients? I'll get more. They're gonna hate me? I don't care. It doesn't matter, you know?

KG: Right.

Me: Doesn't matter. But you have to be speaking in the voices of the truth there, not in this watered-down, "Oh, I guess it doesn't matter." You know what I'm saying?

KG: Right.

Me: Because there is a ... This is about **precision**. There is a **precision** to your shadow that it has to be spoken to, with this precise truth about it. And that's what causes the alchemy... That's why you felt the chills.

KG: That's the truth. Right. What did you say?

CT: Exact science of manifestation is what we're calling it.

KG: The chills. Oh, the recognition of truth.

Me: So keep going with it. Keep going with it, with the warrior. Specifically around catastrophe. All of that. What does the warrior have to say about that?

KG: That I have all the support I need.

Me: All the resources.

KG: Support, help, resources.

Me: Yes.

KG: Not dependent on one night's sleep.

Me: Right. Exactly.

KG: That's ridiculous.

CT: That's why I laugh when I release, because it becomes ridiculous.

KG: I love it. Yeah.

Me: And you were triggered by that. You were annoyed.

KG: Yeah. I was flopping around trying to make some noise to try and wake her up in the night.

Me: Yeah.

RD: She was humping the air.

Me: See? Resourcefulness. The warrior is resourceful. So, there is a gift that you were trying to be resourceful but because you are captive by your shadow, by your victim, you were doing it passive aggressively.

CT: You came and slept with someone that you knew snored. You messaged me weeks ago and asked me if you wanted to be my roommate. And I was like, "Dude, I'll probably sleep on the couch. I talk in my sleep."

KG: Right.

RD: Oh, you should have roomed with her.

CT: And she was by herself.

Me: Resourcefulness.

KG: I did ... I was playing the victim, like flopping around instead of, "Just get the fuck up and leave." And I finally did, and came out here. But-

Me: Okay, but now that you know how to do this, and you're gonna do it, you're gonna practice this 'til you get it, master it. Last night you could have just run through this really quickly. "I'm the warrior. I'm fucking resourceful as fuck. I have all the resources I need. I am master of my space." I wonder if there's someone else sleeping in here that doesn't have a roommate. I am going to go find out. And then you would have found her, and you would have gotten in bed with her, and you would have had a great night's sleep.

TM: And I wouldn't even so much as moved.

KG: Totally.

Me: So it's not that you're supposed to like not having a good night's sleep. Do you know what I'm saying? That's what they call spiritual bypass.

KG: Yeah, accepting.

Me: If you fucking want a good night's sleep, go get a good night's sleep. But you're not able to access your resourcefulness, which is your warrior, when you're trapped by your victim. And you don't even know that you're trapped. That's the crazy thing about this.

KG: Totally. I can't believe I stayed there as long as I did, it's ridiculous.

Me: Okay. So what's the other one?

KG: That I can't see how it's all gonna work out.

Me: What's the original .. Because you wanna do the alchemy on the original statement, because that's the one that triggered you, okay?

KG: The original statement, I chose the wrong bedroom or wrong roommate?

Me: I chose wrong, and therefore-

KG: My business is doomed.

Me: Right. And I won't be able to trust myself.

KG: Right.

Me: To make good decisions.

KG: Because I make bad decisions, yeah.

Me: And see the way in the future.

KG: Right. Totally.

Me: So you wanna take the original statement, the one that exists way up on the surface of your consciousness that's not at all connected to the shadow consciously, and take it all the wah to the voice of the shadow itself. So in this case, "I didn't choose the right roommate." Which means "I can't trust myself," and "I have to see the way and know all the pieces and how they work together, in order to do anything and have trust that it's all gonna work out." So it's actually the combination of the two that you wanna alchemize. Does that make sense?

KG: Yeah.

Me: The distilled voice of the shadow has to be there, because the original statements are usually far-removed from the true voice of the archetype that's speaking. The original statement matters because it's the one that triggered you, and obviously, the distilled voice matters because that's the one that's active, that caused the triggering in the first place.

KG: The underlining text?

Me: Yes. The subtext. So they both have to be sent to the dark heart of gold.

KG: Well, that's funny, because you said "I need to see how it will all work before I can trust myself," which doesn't fucking work. You can't see how it'll work before you trust yourself.

Me: Of course. Yes.

Me: So you actually have to create the complete voice of the shadow, so that you can send that to be alchemized.

Me: It's really: "This is what's bothering me. And the reason it's bothering me is because this…Because I believe this to be true about the world, and the way the world works." In other words, the reason it's bothering me is because I have to see the way before I can trust myself. Or, I didn't get a good night's sleep and the reason *that's* bothering me is because my life will be a catastrophe if I don't grab every ounce of worth out of this event, because my business and my life are at stake here.

KG: Mm-hmm. Right.

Me: And then you speak the truth to that statement, from the light archetype. So what would the Magician say to that statement? So first what's the statement?

KG: I didn't get a good night's sleep. And because I didn't get a good night's sleep, I won't get as much as I need to out of this retreat. And I need to be able to get every ounce of everything out of this retreat, otherwise my business and my life will be a mess.

Me: And this magician says?

KG: I have all the time I need. I don't have to see how it will all work out. Fuck.

Me: Chills.

KG: Yeah.

Me: Because really, you're racing against time.

KG: Yes. Totally.

VM: Literally looking at the clock. "I'm still not asleep. I'm still not asleep."

VM: I know! This is fucking wild!

RD: This is really cool.

Me: Okay. So, we've got time for one more.

CT: I'll do it. I have a fear of over-speaking, talking too much.

Me: Oo, I like that one. Okay. So, is there something that happened? Because you really wanna try to concretize these into something that happened.

CT: eah.

Me: So this is another step. You want to concretize the fear or the worry. Nail it to a specific event if at all possible. That identifies it to the conscious field to more easily alchemize. So it's really, "What did someone do or say?"

VM: What if no one did? Or didn't do or say?

Me: It's always going to be what somebody did or didn't say or do.

VM: But mine's not about that.

Me: Like what is it about?

VM: Mine's just what I don't have.

Me: What do you mean?

VM: Like being here. I don't have a house like this, and I want one. You know what I mean?

Me: You're right. But you said it. So it's not just somebody else; it's what you said in your own mind. It's always what was said or done.

DM: There's always gonna be a statement. A real statement.

Me: Yes. There's a statement. You wanna capture the thing that was said or done, or not said or done, that set you off. Does that make sense?

DM: Mm-hmm.

Me: So what's your example?

CT: Yesterday before the bell rang, I was the only one talking in the hallway. And the bell rang and I was literally mid-sentence. And afterwards, I was like, "Shit, I talk so much. And I was so chatterbox."

Me: Okay, great. This is great. So this is the shadow speaking, but we don't let the shadow speak until the shadow submits, right? So is your shadow going to submit and surrender to the truth?

CT: Well, I have written "the following is all bullshit," and then I wrote some of my statement while KG was doing it.

Me: The following is all bullshit. Okay. So what are they?

KG: I think that people think that I talk too much. I think no one cares what I have to say. I think everyone thinks that I'm lying or they're gonna be fact checking.

Me: Mm-hmm, wow. Now, this is the first. You've got others to work on later.

CT: Mm-hmm.

Me: Say the first one again?

CT: I think people think I talk too much.

Me: People think I talk too much. Okay. So now, what do you do with that?

CT: People think I talk too much, so why does that matter? If I talk too much, then I expose what I do or don't actually know.

Me: Wait a minute. That doesn't make sense.

CT: It does when you're a politician.

Me: No. But if people think ... Why do you care if people think you talk too much? Why do you care about that?

CT: I care if people think I talk too much because I care ... It goes with the next one, because I think that everyone thinks I'm lying or that they're gonna have to go fact-checking. Or they're gonna have to go double-check what I had to say. I'll have a conversation with them and they're gonna go back home and Google and make sure that everything that I said was actually accurate. Or the whole time I'm talking, they're like, "She's fucking bullshitting me. I'm just gonna sit here and talk to her, but I don't actually give a fuck what she's saying because she's lying."

Me: Okay. So if they go home ... So what? So then they go and fact check it. So what?

CT: This is what's been hard for me in doing this, actually. It's that I can get to the surface, and then I just ... Or even to the next one down, and then I'm like, nothing. It doesn't fucking matter. I have plenty of people fact-check me and I couldn't give less of a shit.

Me: But you do give a shit.

CT: Yeah. And that's where I get stuck. I wanna go to some past trauma and how my dad always used to call me a liar.

Me: But why do you *care*? Why do you care if, in the moment, somebody is thinking you're lying?

CT: Because the child in me wants everyone to approve of me and think that I'm smart and pretty and, "Look at how smart you are! Look how pretty you are! Look at all the things you've done for yourself! Oh, good girl!"

Me: Right. So if they think you're lying, you're not gonna get any of that approval.

CT: Right.

Me: Okay. Which archetype is that?

CT: Prostitute:

Me: Which is why you care so much about belonging. That's why your *thing* is belonging. So, "I care. I think people think I talk too much. And that matters to me because I think that they're not gonna believe anything I'm saying, and they're gonna see through the façade, and they're going to not think that I'm worth their approval." That's the statement, right? I care that people think I'm talking too much because they think they're gonna think I'm lying, and my attempts to prove that I am lovable and worthwhile are gonna go nowhere with them. So the first step is to recognize ... This is the hard part, is getting your thought to reveal itself. It's like, name your source. Reveal your origins. Because it's so messy. And it's so far above the root of it.

VM: And it's so subtle.

Me: The nerve, you know? And subtle.

VM: And you stay in the state instead of going back to your childhood.

Me: And stay here, exactly.

VM: So used to going back.

Me: Don't do that.

DM: Don't go back to childhood.

Me: Stay right here. Do not go back to childhood, please. Okay. So yes. This is the tough nut to crack. But when you can get the statement ... So what do you have written down?

CT: My actual statement?

Me: No, like the combined one that we've-

CT: I think that people ... I fear that people think I talk too much because ... It's hard for me to do it in pieces like this. Okay. It's down to the fact that I'm just seeking approval from everything.

Me: So what does the lover say?

CT: That I'm good enough.

Me: Don't speak from your emotion, C. Literally go to the map and speak from the Lover. This is really important. This is really, really important that you speak from...right now anyway...from the map. Because your attempts to make yourself feel good are not going to work. I mean, they might work for a minute, but that's trying to replace one feeling with another, right? That's what you're trying to do right now, because that's what we all know.

CT: Well, yes but everyone's done a ton of shadow work. I found you immediately. I haven't done a lot of this work. I haven't had anyone to go to this level with.

Me: Really? So this is all brand new.

CT: First time ... I don't cry in public. I don't fucking cry in public.

Me: Wow.

CT: It doesn't happen. So you're saying don't feel emotion, but my body's like, "You have to physicalize it for a second, to even be able to get to what the Lover is saying." Because otherwise it's just spiritual bypass, you know.

Me: Yeah. So the emotional body is essential, but not to bond with it. Not to let it become your identity and where you swim and seek for the change. Because then you're just gonna start shifting out one emotion for the other. It's like, "Oh, well this doesn't feel good, so now I gotta find another emotion that does feel good..." and you still have content in your shadow that will come back in some other form.

CT: Right. So the Lover says ...

Me: So, C, when you are ... Because you're right. This is advanced stuff. This is really advanced. So it's like you went from sixth grade to a PhD program.

CT: Because I couldn't handle every fucking high school class that I kept going to. I'd work with those coaches for two weeks, and terminate their contract because I would be fucking bored and be like, "You've already shown me everything."

Me: Yeah, yeah.

CT: I literally said that to my husband. I was like, "I found Lorna six months into my spiritual journey."

Me: Wow.

CT: I hadn't even done anything yet. So when I hear some of these things, I'm grateful, because I haven't had all the programming. I don't have to worry about, "Oh, well, this is what my coaches all taught me," because I fired every coach I've hired so far, except for you. And I take in all in your deeper-level shit, because I'm like, "She gets it." I don't know what she gets, but she gets it. Because I just don't have the programming, but that makes it so when I get to pieces like this, I haven't ever done them at all.

Me: Yeah, they're huge.

CT: I feel like I'm over-dissecting them. I've never even fucking looked at some of these things before, because I didn't know they were there.

VM: You're used to having somebody blow smoke at you instead of somebody burn you.

CT: Yeah. Essentially. I'm used to someone who lets me have power over them, by firing them. Right? Those are the people that ... I always surround myself with people that I can be better than.

Me: Okay, okay, okay. Well, that is not true. You're not trying to surround yourself with people that you're better than. You just see more precisely than almost anyone in your life, including all of your coaches and mentors. So you're not trying to do anything... That's just your reality. And you won't stand for that, because if you really wanted to surround yourself with them, you wouldn't fire them. You wouldn't fire those coaches. You would just totally be with them the whole time, be like, "I'm so much smarter than you." And it would fill something in you. What I want you to understand is that you are not trying to do something so that you can feel better than other people.

CT: Everything comes back to the approval, though. And I don't understand why.

Me: This is the beginning of the journey, the prostitute. It is the beginning of the journey.

VM: Interesting.

Me: So okay. But I wanna say something about when you unearth that powerful, swampy, murky stream of emotion. That's not the time to try to shift it. Because you're *in* it. You're completely and totally swimming in it. And yes. That's part of the process. Bit it doesn't have to last ... Look how you're already over it.

CT: That's what I was trying to say.

Me: It lasted like, a minute, maybe. Okay? This is why children can go through an emotion like that. [I snap my fingers.] So the best thing to do is just let it fully express itself, but don't try to put words on it and don't try to fix it and don't try to feel better about it and don't try to make it ... I mean, you know this from parenting, right? You don't do that to a kid. You just let the kid move through the emotion. It'll be gone in like, 30 seconds. Maybe a minute. You know? And that's when you speak the truth to the shadow piece. Because the emotion has welled up and left, but you still have the trigger. If you don't do the alchemy on it right now, it's gonna happen again. But you gotta go back to the statement. What is the statement? "I worry that people think I talk too much."

CT: People think I talk too much and I care because I'm trying to get approval from everyone.

Me: But what does the Lover say?

CT: I don't wanna be rude, but it's so old ...the map. And many of the things you would say aren't actually here.

Me: Do you value your own words and your own opinions and your own self-expression, no matter what? That's what the Lover says. "I value my self-expression, no matter what. I do not modulate my self-expression for anybody's security, for my security and safety or approval from anyone." That's what the Lover says. "I don't care what someone else thinks about whether I'm talking too much. I value my method of self-expression and my words and my opinions." That's what that column is all about. "My safety and security comes from me, not from anybody else and what they think of me."

CT: When you talk about the main archetypes, like how everyone has their own main. Say everything starts with the prostitute. But for me, I think everything starts at the child. Because ... I value my own self-expression, I literally wanna throw up at the thought of saying what you just said. I don't know why, but I just do.

Me: Yeah. Because that's where it begins, CT. If you value your own self-expression, if you value your own desires ... This is why you are called to desire, to sexuality, all of that stuff. It is this column that you are in right now. You are massively in the alchemy of your prostitute in all kinds of ways. It's totally related to your whole shift. Totally related. And the next one that gets activated is your Sovereign, which is the Child coming into their Sovereign. That is why you're being called to that right now. It's because you are rising from your Prostitute and your Child into your Lover and your Sovereign. And you have to value your own opinions, your own self-expression, your own values, no matter what, in order for you to be able to make the dreams of your Child come true. The value has to come first. You see that? Because nobody else is gonna value it if you don't. Nobody else is gonna say, "That's a valuable dream. That's a valuable mode of self-expression." By you valuing it, it becomes valuable by others. That's the only way it's gonna happen.

CT: So then, I guess it's being able to go back, when you can't be true to the Light Archetype and you're just lying in the shadow...

Me: Yes. The resistance? Is that what you're talking about?

CT: Yeah. Because that's where I'm at right now. Because I just ... I don't know what to do with it. I hear everything you're saying, but if I were to say all that right now, I know I would be laughing to myself. Because I don't-

Me: But that's because you didn't do the first fucking step. That's because you actually believe what your shadow is telling you is true. It's not true!

CT: Ohhhh!

Me: It's not fucking true. It's not true. You have to agree that it's not true before you step into this process. Otherwise, that's what happens. You get stuck in your shadow and you're like, "Well, I'll say it, but I'm not gonna believe it's true."

CT: So my attempt to get approval from everyone is not true.

Me: What's not true is that *approval from people matters*. That's what's not true. Because that's where you're stuck right now, right? Your shadow is just like, "No. No, dude. No. You need people's approval." But that's not actually true, CT. And yes, someone who talks a lot really values their opinion. You do value your opinion. In fact, you think you're probably the smartest person in most rooms you walk into. Okay. You do value your opinion very highly. Over others. This is part of the gift that's gonna start to get released when you alchemize this part of your shadow. It's will be game over because you're not available for the falseness and the lie.

CT: When you do this, though ... Could this be one of those things ... what you mean by being relentless? Like, I'm not allowed to get up from this chair until I can say this and get full body chills? Because that's what's happening right now. And that's what I mean by my child is coming in. It's because my defiant little two-year-old's like, "Fuck you, Lorna. I'm gonna sit here and tell you what KG said, and tell you that I got body chills, when I didn't." So is that what you mean by the relentlessness, that now I have to keep going back?

Me: Only if you wanna be free of this.

CT: Right.

Me: I mean, you don't have to sit in the chair.

VM: Not because we say.

Me: But only ... Look, this is not just a CT consciousness thing. This is a human consciousness thing, okay? This is millennia. It's not gonna go away in one 20-minute sitting. It's not gonna fucking happen. And it's not gonna go away, even though you do the earnest work that you just did. Your shadow is like, "Psh, you gotta try way better than that. You gotta give me way more than that. I'm not going anywhere." Okay? So yes. Relentless. I mean, does it mean you have to sit here? No. But do you have to have supreme will that this is going down? And that you are going to stick with this until it goes down? And it doesn't matter how long it takes, and it doesn't matter how annoying it is, and it doesn't matter how tedious, and it doesn't matter how it triggered, and it doesn't matter whatever? Yes, you do. Because you are deprogramming the most hooked-in elements of your consciousness that exist.

VM: In a totally different way.

Me: In a totally different way, yeah.

VM: It's a totally different way.

DM: This is why you fired everybody else.

CT: Oh, yeah.

Me: But that's not your child; that's your saboteur, by the way. You're a rebel. You're a rebel who's like, "Fuck you. I know better than you. I'm not gonna fucking listen to you."

CT: It's not even that. It's just being cornered. That's why, with the crying, it's how you're supposed to have these releases and things like that. That's why I say the child. It's not just the rebel. It's really that I can't ... You're being told to do it, not just from authority, but from ... I don't know. It doesn't ... The rebel isn't what ... I just think of my three-year-old. Every time, it's like my three-year-old is the one that's trying to come out.

Me: Yes. But that's-

CT You backed me into a corner.

Me: Okay, but all I'm saying is, and this is really important, it's not because they're three. It's because they're rebellious. It's not because it's a child doing it; it's because they're coded. Your child is coded to disrupt and to question and be skeptical, and "I don't know if I'm gonna agree with you just because you're an adult or just because you told me that this is the way or just because you have five degrees and I don't or just because you did this or did that." That is the genius of the saboteur. That is the devilish disruptor who's like, "Pfft" to all of it. Okay?

That's what that is that's in you. I can see it very clearly. And it's also what has caused you to be so fucking brilliant. The saboteur and the magician is the spiritual intelligence. That is the channel of it. Okay? And when you're running prodigious intelligence through your brain, through your saboteur, it's extremely excruciating. When you're running it through your magician, when you don't have to rebel against your own magical mind and your own intuition anymore, that's when you actually start to channel and get all of these incredible hits and all that kind of stuff.

And, you still can see right through illusion. See, your magician is wanting to be activated in you, because you see through illusion and bullshit. And that's why you resist. So right now, that part of you is like ... That's a brilliant aspect of you. And it's like, "Can we trust this person sitting here? Is this something that we can really get on board with?" That's not something to be ashamed of. That's not something to wanna squash at all. It's just the other aspects of your saboteur that have to know beforehand and all that kind of stuff, that is trapping you. But it's not your child.

So do what you can. This is super advanced stuff. So I want you to do what you can over the next, what did we say? Two? 2:00?

VM One question. Because we said that if it wasn't over, like in this case, for instance, she can come back to it and do it with the other statements.

DM: The rebuttal statements.

VM: The rebuttal. Oh yeah. How would that work?

Me: You mean when you try to speak the truth, and then your shadow is like, "Yeah, but what about this?" "Yeah, but what about that?" "But no, no, that's not really true."

VM: Yeah.

Me: Then those become the things that you then work on.

VM: Dissect, okay. It's complicated.

Me: But it's so powerful. It really is.

Quantum Flight, Shadow Management and Shadow Alchemy

Quantum flight happens when you don't have any matter in your shadow that pulls you down to the ground. Quantum leap is: "I achieved escape velocity, and now I'm back on the ground, because I actually still have a shadow, and now I have to do it all over again." Quantum flight is "there is no shadow... Nothing matters. There's no matter in my shadow." Therefore there is no gravity, no pull downwards.

But that means the gravitational pull of your shadow has to be gone.

There are a few books that one should read in one's life time. *Synchronicity Key,* by David Wilcock, is one of them. There's an experiment the author shares in there about DNA strands and photons that collect around the DNA strands. Even when the DNA strands were blasted apart, including therefore the photons, the photons collected again *into the shape of the helix.*

In other words, *light has memory of matter*. Light remembers what mattered, and what matters.

Shadow management is like blasting the DNA molecule, and then the photons recollect...and also "recollect" as in remember what matters and make it matter again ... and so you blast it again, and then your consciousness recollects—recollects what matters and makes it matter again—and then you blast it again and around and around the endless cycle. That's shadow management.

And it's why you hear so many Lightworkers say it's never done.

That's what incites this constant seeking. The constant seeking for the next thing that's going to get you there. For the next thing that's going to put enough gap between you and your shadow, so that you don't have that constant recollection. And you always come back to the same thing. The same crap you processed six months ago.

I call it Trigger Whack-A-Mole. You get rid of one trigger, and maybe that trigger is really gone, that issue just doesn't hold charge for you, but another one does. Then you work on that one. Then another one does, and then you work on that one. That's why you hear so many coaches and mentors say, "You'll always be doing shadow work until you die."

Think of your own triggers. Aren't they basically still the same ones you've always had? So now maybe instead of days it takes maybe half an hour, or one hour, or 15 minutes, depending on the trigger, but they're still there.

And think just in terms of time. That 15 minutes, that half an hour, that hour. Then the next day the 15 minutes, the half hour, the hour. Then two days later, and then next week, and the next week. The drag on your momentum, on your acceleration into your true legacy work, your greatest expression of your genius, the expression of you as the true artisan of your consciousness is just enormous, and it's all being crippled. And think about all that energy you don't have access to, when in fact you could be *amplifying* your field with all of those triggers.

There is so much more power in empty energy than there is in matter-filled, content-filled energy.

But it's in that empty space that you start to rise in consciousness, because the space you're occupying now, that's where the triggers just keep coming, and at the same frequency you're at. So you just end up shifting content and matter around, and there's no energy left or energetic empty space left for imagination and creativity.

Shadow management, in other words.

It is in the moment of disorientation that space is created, and those are the magical moments, because that space is now created for the higher consciousness to come in. But if you're constantly in order, and you're constantly in doing, then you know what to expect. And this means you're not creating imaginative space, because that requires disorientation, and disorientation is at your service. And yet you avoid it at all costs because it triggers you.

To the human there's a payoff to be in your shadow, in with your triggers. Do you know what the payoff is?

It's bonding.

That's the big payoff. You have to be willing to give that up. The reason it matters, the reason that bonding matters to you, is because it all goes back to where you believe your social power comes from. What's really challenging is this…

The hero's journey is where you leave your tribe of origin, and you go on this spiritual journey, the search for yourself. The search for your true power. That ends for a lot of people in a spiritual tribe, but the spiritual tribe is a tribe of nomads, who are always seeking and searching.

There is no home. Always seeking and searching, seeking and searching, seeking and searching, seeking and searching for their home.

But they're never going to find it on the grid of consciousness they're traveling on. The answer lies in the Dark. In the place of willing disorientation into imaginative space, which is contentless, empty space, which means, again, you must be free of triggers and shadow.

The answer doesn't lie in the hero's journey. You have to get off the grid, and that's why we talk about the anti-hero's journey, which is really what this whole process of going sane is.

Because what has happened is that now your spiritual tribe has become your bonding tribe.

And this bond is sometimes even harder for people to break. There are people who private message me, wanting to work with me, but they're too scared because they have too much of a following, and there's too much at stake. They keep saying, "I really want to work with you, but I can't, I can't do it." Because they know I'm going to go blow it up, because *that's* their new safety, their new false security. No, it's not in their family of origin. They got that figured out. But now it's their spiritual community, and in their spiritual bonds.

It all comes back to the reason that desire for bonding has any power over anybody and that is because they don't understand the source and origin of power, where power comes from. It comes from me. It doesn't come from my community. It doesn't come from my bonds. I'm fine out in the wilderness all by myself, beyond the gate where the coyotes hang out. I'm totally fine there.

And this blows apart the search for belonging. Where do I belong? I don't belong anywhere. I own the whole fucking place. There's no place I don't belong. So the concept of belonging is actually a flawed concept, because in it is the potential that there was a place or there could be a place I don't belong.

CODES OF DISRUPTION

The True Truths

1. There are no victims
2. Suffering is unnatural
3. Quantum BOOMs and Collapsing Time Is Normal
4. Magic is a spiritual science
5. Genius is not rare or a luxury. The cost for not accessing it is going up in mental illness.
6. New age spirituality is dead. The answers you seek can only be found in the Dark.
7. Gods are the ultimate disrupters. They are not peacemakers.
8. You have no worth or inherent purpose. You are a work of art with no purpose
9. All activism movements come from victim consciousness. Activists are simply trying to save themselves in the form of someone else.
10. We do not need a soul forever. The soul is the shadow feminine and is the source of suffering. It's the vehicle to learn how to handle pure potent energy directly. The soul comes to learn through the human.
11. Your Soul is what coded shadow into your body-mind. Your Soul is what lied shadow into you in order for it to go on its learning journey through you. Your Soul, therefore, is the source of your suffering.

What is Energy

Everything is energy. Energy is vibration — tones that vibrate at certain levels of power. These are called frequencies. When we say someone is "high vibe," what we're saying is that the collective gathering of their frequency - their mental, emotional, physical and spiritual tones - is one that resonates at the frequency of strong personal power.

When we say we are "setting the tone" for an event, were literally doing that. Frequencies are electric. When they are activated, they create a magnetic field.

Also with the substrate and foundation of the universe are two energies, the masculine and feminine. If you want to create anything, both of those energies have to be working in HARMONY, not dissonance. Harmony is when the two are attracted to each other. Specifically, when masculine is attracted to the feminine. Because the masculine is the provider energy. So in order to create anything the feminine has to be attractive to the masculine and therefore attracted to herself what she desires. The responsibility for the feminine energy is to remain attractive energetically to the masculine. The masculine doesn't have a responsibility. It is blueprinted to respond to attractive feminine energy. So the problem of consciousness comes down to understanding the energetics of the masculine, how the masculine is attracted and inspired to activate itself and provide for the family, and how, as the feminine, to identify where your energy is unattractive and to know what to do about it.

Everything that exists – in Other words everything that has already been created – holds the frequency of the integrated masculine and feminine, and becomes a new third tone, Especially the masculine, because it is now participating in responding to the feminine energy that is calling to it. This is what money is, for instance. And it is why money is masculine and works the same way men and the masculine do. The only thing in the universe that is primarily Feminine are humans. This is because they have reached several tipping points of consciousness where they have gone past simply responding to commands – – (the masculine) to creating new commands — new tones consciousness, which is what the feminine Does.

Ever wonder why, for the most part, women are always trying to change things — their man, the decor, their relationships. It's literally encoded in the feminine energetic to do this. So if humans are all primarily expressing the feminine energetic, how is it that men primarily express the masculine? Because they are in relation to the feminine as woman.

The feminine sets the tone. The masculine meets it. That's how it goes.

We come coded with certain frequencies already operating. These represent areas of mastery, gained over a sales lifetime. When Soul enters the body for so codes the body with the certain frequencies. Some of these frequencies contain codes that are dissent. This means this is an area that is yet to be mastered and brought into harmony with a full system. Why certain people have different skill sets and why certain things comes easily to one person and not to another. The whole point of life is to bring all of the codes and frequencies into residence and harmony. When you do this you had shaved divinity consciousness. The state of being a total pure Potent power in which all the frequencies in all fields are connected in such a way that is 100% irresistibly magnetic 100% of the time to that which I desire. This is what it means to be a God. It is with all humans desire to achieve.

The degree to which you are conscious is the degree to which your gathering of frequencies either amplifies or diminishes your power.

There Are No Victims. Nothing And No One Has Power Over You.

Implications…

Spirit Guides, angels, archangels, are here to serve YOU, not the other way around. They are spirit without form. They are not at the leading edge of consciousness. We are. We inform them. If anything, we are THEIR guides. Stop giving your power to disembodied spirits. You have all the guidance you need. And when you gain access to the two raw material energies of the universe, you can do away with the ancillary and unnecessary dependence on anything outside of your own consciousness. Guides, angels, ascended masters are simply energetic systems that sit on top of the source code and run source code through their system and then to you. Why not just you run the source code through your own system? Have more pride in your own superpowers. Stop channeling them and start channeling yourself. Your own genius.

Genius Is Not Rare Or A Luxury. The Cost For Not Accessing It Is Going Up In Mental Illness.

Unleashing genius and learning to ride it is an extreme energy sport. Like hang gliding skiing. It is a wild ride and right now we are discovering and inventing at the same time. This means sometimes the genius gets out of hand — we lose our grip and slip into the cracks between worlds. Sometimes I get 3 hours of sleep. Sometimes i get 12. And as we discover abs invent new rhythms for our body to sync and run genius, this is why owning our own businesses is increasingly important because our hours need to be our own and fully at our disposal. We need to be able to truly craft and artisan every aspect of our lives.

Mental Illness Is Nothing

"Mental illness is nothing. A neurodivergence. The response of the mind to the splitting of the paths of consciousness and the activity of spiritual genius that guides us to take not the road less travelled, but the no path. The one that has yet to be created. The calling into being of the bridge over nothing, which appears under our feet by spiritual law, but only after we step out over the chasm. Only someone completely crazy and also stark, raving sane would do that with such boldness and "thoughtlessness," knowing she will respond to whatever she meets with resounding stability, the same way most humans step boldly and thoughtlessly onto firm ground with no concern that they will tumble through to the infinite in-firmament and become the infirm of the tribe.

We just know something most humans don't: the ground of being has shifted.

We are not mad. We're the ones who have gone sane. And we are creating new material—new content of consciousness—that will become the second path, the bridge over nothing, the new architecture of awakening.

Mental illness is now a necessary source of success and spiritual genius in the New Consciousness."

Our Egos Are Meant to Grow, Not Diminish

Our egos are not meant to be crushed. Our ego is our power center! Most of us need a much STRONGER ego, not a weaker one! And what would happen if we destroyed our ego? We would simultaneously destroy our center of power. The problem is not our ego. The problem is the source of power our ego has been operating with. Shadow power (the belief that power comes to us from the outside), is toxic and low frequency power. Dark power (the lived truth that power comes from us) is clean and clear and of the highest frequency possible. If our egos ran dark power instead of shadow power, all our problems would be solved.

The solution is to alchemize our shadow and run our power through our dark heart of gold directly into our ego.

Cause And Effect

The earth is not a grid of cause. It is a grid of reflection and mirroring. This is the hermetic principle of as above so below which really is as within so without. In other words, if you want to effect change on earth, change your energy. Cause occurs energetically. Effect occurs physically. Cause and effect do not occur on the same plane. Einstein said if you want to create change, you gave to do it from above the paradigm you're in.

The Soul Is No Longer Necessary And Is The Source Of Suffering

Souls are not meant to last forever.

They're intermediary vehicles for running blacklight—the most potent energy in the Universe. The energy of chaos consciousness. They're like divine surge protectors, there to stand in between us and the Dark, until we're ready to work with it directly.

We were born with the codes of this highly inflammable, chaotic consciousness of genius imprinted in our field. But, being energetic children with no concept of how to master even the more tame energy of the light (the energy that orders versus the energy that destroys), the DNA of the Dark had to be buried deep. So deep that only great focus and energy—and tools brought forth from within our own mystery and invented only for that purpose—would release it.

Where was it buried?

In the only stillpoint in our system. The only place where there is no movement.

In our bones.

This is where your Dark DNA lives.

So when I say you have genius in your bones, I really mean it.

And how in the world do you activate what lies within the utterly inaccessible stillness?

You alchemize your Soul.

Meaning, your shadow.

The Soul is what cast the shadow consciousness that we all live with.

Another name for shadow consciousness is the shadow feminine so yes.

The feminine is responsible for "the fall." The fall of light onto matter. Onto the false bottom of consciousness, which in truth has no ceiling and no floor, and which, were we to let light fall forever, would never create shadow.

But.

We had to make matter, for awhile.

We had to believe that certain things mattered more than others.

Like staying alive. Which it doesn't, really, in the grand scheme of the game we're playing. (If you delete yourself this time, you'll just come back. So why not stick around and determine to master the game?)

But if we didn't make things matter (create a false floor in consciousness), then early humans would not have stuck around and the gathering of the structures of consciousness (the creation of The Light Grid) would never had happened.

We needed a critical mass. (We needed matter to be critical. We needed it to be critical that certain things matter.)

And so the Dark—the extremely disruptive darling of consciousness, the carrier of the unborn, monstrously new, the a-contextual, that which by definition cannot and does not "matter"....in other words, the energy of creativity, genius and death—agreed to bury itself so deep into our consciousness that we would have no sense of its presence until we had built a physical and energetic structure capable of handling the supreme explosion that contact with the Dark creates, and surviving.

At least **skeletally**.

The bones of consciousness, in other words, needed to remain.

Number one, because if the bones go, we have nothing to build the new consciousness on and instead of amplifying consciousness, we'd just be starting over.

Which isn't terrible. It's that that it's taken us millennia to get to this point, so it would just galactically suck to have to start all over.

The Dark is not out there somewhere, like the light grid. Which lives on and in our bodies and on and in all other bodies and which is our collective consciousness and the place from which, when aspects of that consciousness are placed in shadow—namely that we have and are dark energy and dark matter within us (dark DNA and our dark body) and that these are intimately personal and untouchable and create our own cocoon of mystery which no one can access, though they can be deeply allured and influenced by it, which means we are utterly and completely each of us totally alone in the universe AS the universe and this does not connect us to others as the light grid does and as light longs to do but sends us both within and without further and further apart from ourselves and each other, expanding all the universes of us as dark matter does and so we see (since this is likely triggering you to hear that you are and always will be very alone and that union of any kind either within (integration) or without (communion) is not only not happening but not happening at a more and more rapid pace, we see why the Dark has to be buried so deep within us and go undiscovered for so long.

The discomfort you feel is only because you have a soul.

It is knit to your shadow and your body and remembers being shunned, hunted, burned at the stake, cast out and since at the time the collective consciousness, the light Grid, was the only source of survival (and remember how much the Soul must believe survival matters), it cannot imagine surviving without the light, and in the utter Dark.

And it's utterly convinced that feelings matter.

Which they do not.

We don't call someone with no emotional connectors to other humans "spiritless." Because our Spirit animates our body with life force. we call them "soulless." The walking dead.

Your Soul is therefore a wise/unwise guidance system. As being more practiced in navigating the light grid and therefore "wiser" than you, it is helpful for a time. As abjectly terrified of the Dark and therefore completely untrustworthy, because those little light lies of consciousness are imprinted into it as part of its energetic DNA, it is not capable of being your final guide back home.

The Soul was invented to be our enduring memory system of what matters, so we don't forget from lifetime to lifetime, and to tell us little light lies about what matters (these would be the voices of our shadow archetypes, which we all carry) so that we stay alive.

We had to believe we were not all powerful and could not simply delete and invent new codes of consciousness at will (which we can. At this level energy definitely can be created. What do you think was the source of all this? It didn't exist forever. It came into being from nothing.

From The Nothing.

From the Dark, which gives birth to all as the white hole of the universe.)

Everything that came before sits on the light Grid because light is a collecting and collective gathering system. It is the town square of consciousness. Souls gather there to collect themselves and to collect us and because it is where Souls receive and revive their memories, which get imprinted onto and into us, in our cellular memory system and as instinct and intuition (yes, intuition is a flawed guidance system—though much more highly evolved and dependable than instinct, which sits in our shadow.

This is why we say the body is feminine.

The shadow runs our body system completely.

We are meant to alchemize our Soul. The Soul is the recorder.

They're intermediary vehicles. Surge protectors, actually. To protect us from the direct power of the Dark.

But you can just go ahead and alchemize your Soul now.

Hero's, Heroine's And Anti-Hero's Journeys, In Relief

HERO'S JOURNEY TO ANTI-HERO'S JOURNEY

Movement from Shadow to Light: Hero's Journey – Finding Self

Purpose: overcome fear and illusion; answer "Why am I here?"

Trial: leave the tribe and face and kill your monsters

Promise: inner peace through self-mastery

Gifts: empowerment; discovery of gifts and calling

Epiphany: I am powerful. No one and nothing has power over me. I can slay all my monsters.

Claim: "I am the one who found the great treasure."

Problem: excellence is ultimately empty. Self still defined through being of value to the tribe; uneasy inner condition of peace and mastery. Constantly slaying monsters – separate inner selves/factions

Movement to Unhook from Light: Heroine's Journey – Losing Self

Purpose: find true self and integrate all of the disparate fighting inner selves

Trial: give up gifts and talents that made you excellent, useful, successful, productive and visible. Go invisible. Lose what you know yourself to be.

Promise: true inner peace, not defined by tribe/world/talents/usefulness

Gifts: discover your backbone and ability to hold your own esteem no matter what the tribe thinks of you/your value

Epiphany: I have an undeniable divinity and backbone of will, creativity and self-assurance not tied to my value, gifts, talents or usefulness; I do not fear the monster

Claim: "I was brave enough to give up the great treasure"

Problem: I have no self or soul, I am empty. I need more treasure, something to treasure. Returns to Hero's journey to find treasure and the endless seeking begins

Being in the Dark: Anti-Hero's Journey – Being Infinite Expression of Self

Purpose: find true fulfillment, euphoria and heaven on earth

Trial: create a new self and a new soul in the dark with no direction, endorsement or help from anyone and with no promise it will be valuable (be a source of income or safety) and unleash my raw genius; the energy released in contacting my backbone

Promise: euphoria through application of Creative Will that has fused into one, No more separate inner factions. True stillness and therefore pure play. Accessing the "mind and power of god"

Gifts: expression of raw genius (meaning YOU become the gift) and legacy of body of work.

Epiphany: creativity is divinity. I am the monster. There is nothing to slay of fear anymore. The journey/seeking is over.

Claim: "I am the great treasure that is sought after"

THE DARK LATTICE. THE DARK ARCHETYPES: THE ARCHETYPES OF EUPHORIA, PRESTIGE AND GENIUS

The Dark Archetypes are portals that stream energy. Dark consciousness does not hold content or energy. It just streams it onto the light grid. They do not hoist energy into the light grid. Dark consciousness is a way of speaking energy into matter. It is all about the tone of voice, not the content.

Because at the end of the day, Nothing really matters.

Meaning nothing matters at all. And it matters quite a bit.

It's really the only thing that matters.

The Mad Archetypes, which you will meet later, provide the content for the Dark. They are the Something that gets treated as Nothing. With Nothing. And therefore becomes a Third New Thing—what we on the light grid recognize as true genius. The utterly new. The Incomparable. The Peerless. The Priceless.

The Dark Goddess And The Band Of Unhooking

2012 was a tipping point in consciousness where the world entered the "band of unhooking" and began to dis-orient itself from the light grid and re-orient itself to the dark lattice, which is the new operating system of consciousness, presided over by the Dark, into which we must all migrate in order to complete our awakening and step into our genius, giant nature.

The Prestige: The Call Of The Dark, The Anti-Hero's Journey And Speaking The New Myth Into Existence

The call of the dark - the band of unhooking: the telling of the new myth into existence: the anti-hero's journey

What is it? how do you know when the dark is calling you? excellence feels empty. this will blow your mind for a while… there will come a time when excellence empties out and becomes boring. you feel the unsettling. ppl will start to develop mysterious mental illness. this is the moment when you realize there is something beyond what you can imagine. it's the unimaginable new. it's the anti-hero's journey. you go from streaming your gift to streaming your genius. you want to start to blow it all up. ppl think "what the hell is wrong with me?" identity crisis – restlessness with no content to it. it's a disruptiveness. the moment when the god decides to play the part of the human 'knowingly' … fully knowing it's playing the part/it's biggest game.

kate spade

jim carrey

anthony bordain

robin williams

bradley cooper (marriage between your mastery of your gifts with your true genius) it requires that you give up the gifts you just mastered. the gift becomes the servant of your genius. radical new ways to make money with your genius. your gift has to take a back seat, something else is in the driver's seat it's not my identity, it's not my worth. it's just one of my tools in my toolbox in my human vessel. identity becomes a stupid question…

I am not a thing/identity. what do i want to create? it's a constant reinvention. human as work of art. End of focus on continuous identity

WHAT DOES IT LOOK LIKE TO ANSWER THE CALL (THE DARK DANCE)

The dark divine is ordering consciousness. battlefield to ballrom. masculine leads, but it's the empresses' song.

Feminine needs to surrender to the masculine and obeys (magic man tool). it's the lack of trust that keeps the battle going.

Complete surrender is when riches are unlocked. feminine has fully alchemized, so the masculine has nothing to instruct/structure.. shadow = feminine, light = masculine.

Battlefield: feminine rising movement (against /in resistance to/ in opposition to the masculine)

You cannot rise with shadow. the only way to rise is to alchemize the shadow. surrender and submit to the truth/masculine. activate the dark codes.

Feminine surrenders to the light grid and appears as the dark.

The true feminine is the dark divine, the masculine is the light divine. the empress orders consciousness. 'i want to play this game'… the masculine obeys the feminine. but then the feminine has to take a seat on the light grid (masculine) and take a physical form/matter. the dark divine is directly expressed on the light grid, in a way that distorts it necessarily, for the Dark is disorder of a higher order, and as such, will not be ordered.

Applying Light And Dark Mastery To The Real World

Want to see how to hold yourself in your Prestige energy and exacting standards as you reach out to celebrities to build your visibility, influence and legacy? (And, buried halfway down is a Great Secret revealed)

MY PUBLICIST: If Bradley Cooper won't sit down with you and have a conversation, can you give me some questions you want to ask him in case he's willing to reply that way?

ME: Nope. What I want is to have THE deepest and most important conversation about humanity with him, and that cannot be had over email. If he doesn't want to talk to me, I'll find someone else to talk to.

I'm the prize.

~~~~

Now, I LOVE that my publicist is thinking this way (and that her immediate response was, basically, "Duh. Of course you are.")

She looks at all angles and all possibilities and is prepared for all eventualities. This is the massively creative and resourceful energy of the Warrior and the Magician and of someone who thinks WAY outside the box. I love it. I wouldn't have it any other way. Because this is HOW you have to approach your great legacy. With the highest level of imagination and resourcefulness possible. You will be taxed and pushed to your LIMITS and BEYOND in this regard.

And, it's MY job to hold to my impeccable standards — the Tone Of Truth that I hold about what I'm actually here for and what I require, no matter what. (This is where SO many influencers and leaders and celebrities and artists go vastly astray and fall deep into selling their soul in exchange for a chance on the world stage).

Anything less than that is collapsing into my prostitute and negotiating away a piece of MY ... well I was just going to say "soul" but I don't have much of a soul anymore. I've alchemized almost all of it (yes. I buried one of the most interesting and shocking aspects of the next level of consciousness right here in this little post about Bradley Cooper which is that when you cross over from the light grid to the dark, what you're doing is unhooking yourself from the soul you brought in and exchanging it for a new dark body, a strange gathering of energetic organs that allow you to work directly with the Dark and the Light. Which means the purpose of the Soul —which was to dim the power of the light so we could handle it in our bodies—is over. So when I am being asked to negotiate on my standards, it has nothing to do with selling my soul anymore but simply to do with two things: HOW AFRAID I AM OF THE DARK and how much I trust my Magical Masculine (my Magic Man) to provide for me no matter what.

It's a completely different experience. It's pared down to the bone.

Do I hold to what I'm creating? The utterly new strange tone that right now only I hear and that I want the whole world to hear? Do I stand in my place as the Empress of Alchemy and call a new world into being? Or do I collapse into contentless imitation and back into a worn out soul energy I've already left behind?

The imprint of my Soul, the ghost of it, will be with me for as long as I live this lifetime. Collected like breath around my four shadows. Nothing but an outline of itself, reminding me of what is still possible:

Collapse into my soul, instantly activate my four shadow feminine energies (child, victim, saboteur, prostitute) and be immediately ejected from the Dark, my native home (because the Dark is the True Feminine and it will have nothing to do with its shadow self).

No thank you.

I know how energy works. It is not a belief system or a philosophy. It is absolute knowledge of and masterful handling of the Mysterium Tremendum.

And that means I know that I (meaning the world I'm creating) must be expressed and met in One Precise Way. (Hello being willing to be called "demanding" and "impossible to please.")

World creation is a creating of the highest and most rarified precision. Think of this world. This universe. How it hangs together in such precise and delicate balance.

Imagine how exacting the Tone that called it into being.

One waver on one minute aspect of the energies involved, no matter how seemingly "insignificant" (an interview over email versus in person) and the world that was about to be instantly evaporates back into the Nothing.

This is Dark Mastery.

It is endlessly fascinating, taxing and euphorically fulfilling.

And I wouldn't have it any other way.

What About....?

People Who Are Already Artists And Are Addicts, Depressed And Suicidal?

This is because they are running high octane genius through their body-mind and victim consciousness and not alchemizing their consciousness and channeling their genius through their dark heart of gold first. In other words, they are using their art as a tool of self worth, which means they are hooked to the light grid and to proving and experiencing their worth through their art. This makes them no different than a "non-artist" who proves his worth and value through his work, the title he has, and the money he makes. In other words, art has been coopted and strong-armed into being useful to the human. And the only reason we are focused on feeling and being useful is because we are hooked to the collective consciousness and, in the case of an artist, have identified our ability to create as our most useful and valuable trait. This is like chaining a great, wild beast. The stress and strain of keeping such raw energy contained and constrained to an energetic system that is not its natural home creates tension that surfaces as emotional, mental and physical dis-ease and dis-orders. There is no need for the disorder to exist. Artists don't have to be low functioning beings crippled by their genius. In fact it's not their genius that's crippling them. It's tying genius to the value and purpose grid that creates the energetic tension. Or, tying their sense of worth and purpose to their family and tribe of origin, while also streaming genius that is often unrecognizable to those very groups. The pain of not being seen or understood as an artist, or of being treated only as an object, a celebrity of genius, is very great for many of these people. Most artists have a fascination with the underdog, either themselves as the underdog, using their tragic life story as fuel for their art, or they identify with the underdog and with victims (this is why most artists are liberals), which means they're still deeply hooked to victim consciousness. That means they have a very full and active shadow and a system full of shadow (body-mind) cannot handle the immense amount of genius energy that is being channeled through it. It's like running a high voltage electric current into a hairdryer. It's going to short out. The Soul helps us manage and mitigate this somewhat because it acts as a surge protector, diverting the powerful energy into the four channels of the shadow and essentially downgrading our energy in different areas of our life

One of my tenets of the book is that the answer to all our seeking is to unleash our native genius (so first, to recognize that we are a genius) and to become an artisan of consciousness, someone who is engaging in the high and fine art of turning himself and the world around him into a work of art. But this only works if we also recognize that this has no meaning and doesn't matter and if we're not trying to extract a sense of worth or value or approval from doing this. It must the pure play of a god, not the worth-seeking of a human. When you can strike this fine balance, this specific set of tones or frequencies, euphoria is yours.

So naturally, I expect you'e wondering: what about all the artists and creative visionaries who are addicts, depressed or suicidal or who have committed suicide?

This is because they are running high octane genius through their body-mind and victim consciousness and not alchemizing their consciousness and channeling their genius through their dark heart of gold first. In other words, they are using their art as a tool of self worth, which means they are hooked to the light grid and to proving and experiencing their worth through their art. This makes them no different than a "non-artist" who proves his worth and value through his work, the title he has, and the money he makes. In other words, art has been coopted and strong-armed into being useful to the human. And the only reason we are focused on feeling and being useful is because we are hooked to the collective consciousness and, in the case of an artist, have identified our ability to create as our most useful and valuable trait. This is like chaining a great, wild beast. The stress and strain of keeping such raw energy contained and constrained to an energetic system that is not its natural home creates tension that surfaces as emotional, mental and physical dis-ease and dis-orders. There is no need for the disorder to exist. Artists don't have to be low functioning beings crippled by their genius. In fact it's not their genius that's crippling them. It's tying genius to the value and purpose grid that creates the energetic tension. Or, tying their sense of worth and purpose to their family and tribe of origin, while also streaming genius that is often unrecognizable to those very groups. The pain of not being seen or understood as an artist, or of being treated only as an object, a celebrity of genius, is very great for many of these people. Most artists have a fascination with the underdog, either themselves as the underdog, using their tragic life story as fuel for their art, or they identify with the underdog and with victims (this is why most artists are liberals), which means they're still deeply hooked to victim consciousness. That means they have a very full and active shadow and a system full of shadow (body-mind) cannot handle the immense amount of genius energy that is being channeled through it. It's like running a high voltage electric current into a hairdryer. It's going to short out. The Soul helps us manage and mitigate this somewhat because it acts as a surge protector, diverting the powerful energy into the four channels of the shadow and essentially downgrading our energy in different areas of our life

Steve Mc Queen - channeling his shadow That's what he's referring to when he says in his documentary that he pulls the horrors out of his soul. When you channel genius through a huge heavy shadow it amplifies the shadow. Genius is an amplifier of energy. He saw himself as a gazelle and gazelles always get eaten. Very victim.

But, the point is that the universe was created as an experiment in energy becoming matter. A game.

And, the question of why souls choose to suffer is the same question as why any of us do anything we know is going to cause us an unwanted experience.

Because we aren't actually READY for the wanted experience. We are not an energetic match for it.

Souls are on a LEARNING and EXPERIENCING journey. They are not all-knowing beings (which is why I say in my books that the soul is the source of suffering). There are souls that are energetic matches for extreme suffering just like there are HUMANS who choose a life of addiction, for instance. And there are souls who aren't an energetic match for those experiences, just like there are humans who drink but not to excess and don't ruin their lives and livers in the process.

Souls are NOT all we've held them up to be.

THE DARK SECRET

BOOK TWO

LIGHT MASTERY, THE MAGICAL MASCULINE AND THE TRUE SECRET OF MANIFESTING ON DEMAND

TABLE OF CONTENTS [IN PROCESS]

ENERGETIC LAWS OF LIGHT

- It's Not Natural to Struggle, and Why We Do
- How Energy Becomes Matter
- The Anti-Gravitational Call of Truth (and Why It's Natural to Answer It)
- Codes of Desire (Formerly Known As "Points of Attraction ")
- Strange Brains, Weird Wiring and The Dark Heart of Gold: Neurodivergence as the New Market Advantage and the Gateway to Magic and Higher consciousness
- Success Stories

MAGIC MASTERY = MONEY MASTERY (or, You're Not Conscious Unless You're Wealthy. Yep. I Said It. Yep. I Meant It.)

- The Entrepreneurial Spirit
- Wealth Consciousness
- Money Flows to Genius (The Energetics of True Fulfillment)

THE EXPERIENCE OF MAGIC

- Sales Magic (The Energetics of Sales)
- Marketing Magic (The Metaphysics of Marketing)

- Closing Magic (The Energetics of Objections)
- Love Magic
- Body Magic
- Stories of Success

BUT WHAT ABOUT…..? (#allthequestions)

- Children and suffering
- Successful people who are still unconscious
- Success in one area and not another
- Intermittent success
- Reversal of success
- Confusion about my intuition
- Confusion about my desire
- Fear of failure
- Self-doubt
- Feeling stuck
- Shame about my gifts
- Hurting people's feelings
- Being misunderstood
- Feeling slimy selling and asking for money

- Not knowing my genius

- Not knowing my purpose

- Not knowing my message or my niche

- Hating sales

- Hating marketing

- Feeling insecure about my prices

THE MAGIC BASK

- Quotes, Fan Mail, and More Success Stories

What Kills Magic?

Worry.

Worry kills magic.

Worry, which is the same as ignorance, which is the same as incompetence.

Which is the same as anxiety.

Worry: The human in its unnatural state as the anxious feminine, otherwise known in the spiritual self-help community...

as the shadow.

Magic Is Natural

The natural world contains a secret: It is not the domain of its own causation. Cause and effect do not occur within the same paradigm of power. And until now we have been operating ignorantly within the paradigm of the powerless—that which receives commands and obeys them: the 3D world of matter—and not in the paradigm of the powerful—the energetic realm, the SuperConscious field where Time and Space are one and in which the commands of being and matter are fashioned.

We have been foolishly trying to place our hands on the levers of power while groping in the shadowlands of the imprisoned…and elevating those few who have discovered the root of real magic, the origin of becoming, to the status of gods.

Geniuses.

Rarities.

It is time we stop being so humble. Not only is it unnatural, it is inaccurate.

We are not *of* the ground, though the ground is where we play and place our station. We are of the immaterial realm most essentially. And that does not mean we denigrate the ground of our being, the material, the earthly. It simply means that we recognize it not as our battlefield but as our ballroom. Not as a theater of war but a theater of the imagination into which we place matter plucked at will from the fertile field of potential.

This is the definition of magic, and it varies from our experience only in our understanding, not in our agency.

Whatever is, we have crafted from energy. (This is not new knowledge, of course.) The struggle comes when what is, is not what we desire. And when what is not yet (what is as energy and is coming into matter) is taking too long for our liking.

Then, we do not call it magic, but hustle and grind.

And the difference between the two is simply one of leverage.

When we place our hands knowingly on the raw material of the universe, we activate energetic law, the law of cause and effect, and with the least effort, produce the greatest and swiftest result. Thus we create magic on demand.

When we place our hands unwittingly on these powerful leavers, we also create magic, and yet cannot reproduce it at will because we stumbled onto them, having no training or mastery in navigating the land of power in which they exist.

This is unnecessary.

Ultimate Power—the clear-eyed command of cause and effect, of calling into being exactly what we desire and exactly when we desire it, and not just material objects but people and opportunities and not just physical experiences but spiritual, intellectual and emotional states of being, intuitive and psychic knowledge and gifts, anything we could wish or imagine…and much more beyond—is simply the ability to operate Time and Space—the fundamental building blocks of matter and 3D experience—with supreme mastery.

Time and Space have two masters.

The masculine and the feminine.

And they are at our disposal.

- The Experiment of Consciousness

- The Gold Mind and the Takeover of Consciousness (or, You Are A Genius, Giant)

- **The Gold Mind is the Disruptive Mind (Tits Post Series)**

    ○ Livestream: Guards Down, Boundaries Up

- Beautiful Monsters, Tribal Consciousness and the Bonds of Anti-Genius (Shame)

- Time and the Genius Frequency (How Power Over Time Unlocks Your Genius)

- Why the Feminine Must Obey

- The Spiral of Despair (Trigger Whack-A-Mole and Doing Shadow Work on Your Genius)

- Shadow Management vs Shadow Alchemy (or, The End of Worry. The Beginning of Magic: The Shadow Alchemy Tool)

Magic

Every time I turn around these days it's let me teach you how to manifest.

The five or three or twelve-and-a-half steps to manifestation.

The secret to manifesting.

Except that these spiritual teachers aren't saying what they mean.

At least I hope not. Because then they'd be telling you they want to teach you how to do something you already can't not do.

Which seems like a waste of your high-value energy and time, if you ask me.

And on top of that, there's the whole missing link to Law of Attraction thing (there's a missing link, did you know? More like a missing fucking chain, actually), as well as all the holes in New Age spirituality itself, which nobody seems to be paying much attention to, all of which means that what these spiritual teachers, from the no-names to the big-names to the biggest of big names are going to teach you about Law of Attraction (which is not how to manifest) won't work.

At least not the way a law should.

You know... like...

predictably?

Which is not —let me take a wild guess—how LOA works for you now.

We Interrupt This Broadcast for A Very Important NewsFlash

And the newsflash is this:

You are wired for magic.

Thriving is your natural state.

And genius is in your bones.

You've just been running your great godly power (meaning your natural ability to manifest on demand, at will, exactly what you want, when and how you want it) through a tiny, cramped, low-voltage energy management system that was never built to handle the demands of a genius giant like you.

It's like trying to light up all of Los Angeles on a single generator.

Hello lights off most of the time.

Blindness.

Stumbling around in the deep shadows thinking something is terribly wrong with your generator. There's nothing "wrong" with it. It just needs to be replaced with a Universal Power Management System, which you already have all wired up and connected and in place, you just gotta be told where the switch is.

And then? Magic is inevitable.

And I do mean magic: What any typical human would consider "impossible," "miraculous" and totally inexplicable.

You know, like the way a Neanderthal would feel about an iPhone.

Because magic is not a mystery. It's a spiritual science. And I'm here to teach it to you.

Oh wonderful, you're thinking. And why does the world need ANOTHER book on manifestation exactly? You have heard of a little, no-name piece of work called "The Secret," right? The one that's right up there with the BIBLE in terms of global sales and impact, and that's ALL ABOUT manifestation and features people WAY MORE POPULAR AND WELL-KNOWN than you who are considered the world's EXPERTS on this very subject? I mean HOW EXACTLY do you expect to hold a candle to THAT, hmmmm?

I'm so glad you asked.

So just to kinda summarize your position (which is completely understandable by the way)…

You're saying there are these spiritual giants roaming the land of manifestation…

and who am I to go up against them.

Do I have that right?

Cool.

So lemme tell you this story, maybe you've heard it.

About David and Goliath?

Where Goliath was the giant?

Who was terrorizing the Israelites?

And every day he'd lumber his huge, terrifying self out onto the battlefield and dare someone to face him in single combat.

But hello. He was a fucking giant. And they were all "just humans."

So even Saul, the KING of Israel, was like, hmmmm. No thanks.

So this went on for forty days.

Then one day a little shepherd boy named David, who was bringing food to his brothers, heard about all this hullabaloo, and was like, Jesus Christ (well, not yet. This is still Old Testament times, but you get the point). I'll do it.

Saul offered David his armor, and David was like, Hey, thanks, Saul, King of Israel who's supposed to be doing this but isn't because you're too scared. I'm cool. I have my SLINGSHOT.

And he went out into the field, swung that fucker around, hit Goliath right in the center of his forehead (so, ummm, in this THIRD EYE), and down that great and terrifying giant went.

And then a little later, that no-name shepherd boy became King.

The subtitle of this book isn't called "Magic and the Takeover of Consciousness" for nothin'.

I know what I'm up against.

And I know exactly where to aim my shot.

And I know that when you see that beautiful philosopher's stone of the truth of consciousness travel its most arresting arc through the air of spiritual intelligence and hit the giants of manifestation right in their third eye, (which is totally blind), your third eye will FLY OPEN and that.

Will be the end of that.

Because the truth is that the people who think they're teaching you what you think you're learning, aren't. And it isn't (what you think you're learning).

And by "the people" I mean Abraham Hicks, Bob Proctor, Marianne Williamson (and therefore Gabby Bernstein, because she was taught by Marianne Williamson) and every other brand name spiritual celebrity guru out there.

And that's because there's a dirty secret no one's talking about in the world of spiritual transformation, self help and the way manifestation is being taught:

None of it really works all that well, and most people, even the ones in the inner circle, can't manifest on demand and think it's their fault, so they certainly don't go around talking about how the teachings don't work, because everyone is pretending it's just something wrong with them, not the teachings.

Meanwhile 90% of Bob Proctor's inner circle of consultants, trained by him and his elite leaders, who know LOA backwards and forwards and inside and out, are stuck and struggling and frustrated as fuck.

How do I know?

Because I have a client who shot to the top of his inner circle, bypassed nearly everyone else on his thousands-of-consultants team, made $30K to $50K months for about 18 months, and then everything stalled out and no matter what they did and how diligently they applied #alltheLOAthings, nothing fucking worked.

They slid down to $12K and then $5K months and watched in horror as the empire they were just beginning to build crumbled around them.

And do you know what Proctor's elite trainers told them?

WORK HARDER.

Write what you want 150 times every morning.

It's gestation. It's the gestation phase.

Um.

Are you fucking kidding me??

Your leader was featured in The Secret as having THE secret to success and making magic in your life and your fucking answer when things get rough is to WORK. HARDER.

Write 150 sentences?

GESTATION????

What the fuck, gestation.

(I'll tell you what "gestation" is: It's a catch-all concept LOA teachers use to describe a spiritual condition they can't explain. Exactly the way doctors say someone has "generalized anxiety disorder" because they have no fucking clue what's really going on. Stick around and I'll tell you exactly what's going on when you're "gestating" and exactly what to do about it. Because hello. Time is at YOUR command. You are NOT a victim to anyone or anything. You create Time. Therefore you have power over the "gestation" phase, just like you have power over everything. Because newsflash-within-the-newsflash: you are not human. You are a genius giant zipped up in a human consciousness that is ready to be led to slaughter. And guess what this book is.

The Sword of Truth that will pierce right to the heart of the matter, and slice open your throat so the Voice of God—your voice—can speak.

Or, to extend the metaphor, this book is the stone of truth aimed directly at all the giant concepts of New Age spirituality, which are only uncontested because no one has had the equipment or the balls to contest them.

Ok. Back to the "What the actual fuck is going on with LOA" subject at hand...)

When I heard this from my clients, my jaw dropped.

That's not a fucking secret. Work harder. Write out your affirmations. Just WAIT for the "PHASE" to end.

Those are instructions from someone who has no clue how energy actually works, does not understand the root-level energetics for how realms of consciousness and trapped patterns of power work, and only knows how to apply manifestation STRATEGIES to situations, rather than teach people how to work with the RAW MATERIAL OF THE UNIVERSE to effect instant, predictable change and direct them on exactly how to unlock their trapped energy (magic is a very precise science of working with codes and frequencies) and get them manifesting on demand again.

Which is why when this couple started working with me, they did $30K in two weeks and $100K in 45 days.

And lest you think this is an isolated case, just head on over to my Success Stories section (end of the book) for what I call the Magic Bask: The litany of stories of spiritual entrepreneurs who were stuck and struggling for ages even though they'd worked with the top celebrity coaches, spiritual gurus and leaders in the world, and were still not able to crack the code on their struggle until they were introduced to the very teachings I'm going to share with you in this book.

Which is why the subtitle is what it is.

Because it's time you learn how to make magic.

And in order to do that, you must effect a total and complete TAKEOVER OF CONSCIOUSNESS.

And it has nothing to fucking do with writing out 150 times what your three million dollar mansion looks like and how happy you are that you "have" it in your "vortex."

The Problem Of Spiritual Consciousness (Why New Age Spirituality Is Dead)

My guess it that even though you're one of the most awake, aware, educated, trained, workshopped, certified and retreated spiritual seekers you know, your ability to create exactly what you desire, exactly when and how you desire it, is about the same as the dude down the street who's mowing his lawn drowning in his Dr. Dre Beats, and who's never even *heard* of Abraham-Hicks.

That ever strike you as odd?

That there are *legions of Lightworkers* who after decades of devoted practicing and studying, coaching and mentoring, are *still stuck as fuck*?

I mean, take me, for instance.

Both times I was suicidal and before both my nervous breakdowns and my total financial ruin, I was studying new age spirituality, manifestation, consciousness, intuition, awakening, energy and metaphysics with *world-renowned* masters, consuming every book, course and program I could get my hands on, and doing all the work diligently and zealously and relentlessly as if my life depended on it because it did.

And some days were great and others totally sucked and no matter what I did I kept sinking further into despair and depression and I mean what. the actual. fuck.

And I'm not alone.

Most of my clients are coaches and spiritual entrepreneurs who've been in the self help/new age/spiritual awakening world for YEARS and studied with the great masters and we're talking inner circle of the inner circle (Bob Proctor, anyone?) and still come to me laboring and heavy laden under the yoke of techniques and strategies that offered momentary relief and success but nothing lasting and FOR SURE not anything like CERTAIN HANDLING of the raw materials of the universe to bend time and reality to their will, on demand.

I mean what the hell are these people doing teaching laws of attraction and manifestation if they can't teach the root-level MECHANICS for how the law actually works?

That's like teaching electricians how to screw in a lightbulb but neglecting to bring them over to the wall where the fucking SWITCH is.

And so hey.

If you happen to screw in the light bulb when the switch is flipped up:

Amazing!

Light!

But then you do the same damn fucking thing a day later and nothing happens (because these crazy teachers are handing you shitty "manifesting strategy" bulbs in the first place that need *constant* replacing instead of showing you how to command Light to appear using your FREQUENCY just like the good old God in the Bible who INTONED "Let there be Light," and hey guess what THERE WAS LIGHT, which is the same exact ability YOU have to create from Nothing but you're over here screwing shitty bulbs that keep shorting out into sockets whose switch is sometimes flipped up ((Light!)) and sometimes isn't ((Shadow. Fucking annoying.)) and all because YOU in your SLEEP are flipping the switch up and down TOTALLY UNCONSCIOUSLY and don't even fucking know it ((which yes I know is the same thing as saying you're doing it unconsciously))).

Because the whole thing is off track, people.

Pretty much all of New Age spirituality, what it teaches as truth and what it says must be so and why, is WAY the fuck off kilter.

I mean fuck off kilter. That suggests there's still something walking around with a chance at revival, a body of work still angling its way through the crowds of seekers, albeit at a dangerously oblique angle to the Truth, that can be tilted back to center and uprightness and vitality again with a V-8 juice shot glass of consciousness.

When in fact the whole of New Age Spirituality and Law of Attraction and manifestation teachings and techniques are DEAD.

All you have to do is look in their eyes.

You know how the eyes of a blind man looks?

That's how the eyes of new age spirituality look.

Not glossy, with Light. *Glassy*, from *too much Light*.

Empty, in fact.

And lifeless from an endless seeking that never ends. Nomads without a home, trying to make their laptop lifestyle seem glamorous but I'll tell you something I've coached a lot of 'em and it's bad, people. I've heard stories you wouldn't believe.

Or maybe you would. Since Doreen Virtue just cracked open the coffin of new age spirituality and let the True Light in. Which she thinks is Jesus, bless her soul, but which in fact is the Light of an entirely new age of awakening, the final act of human evolution, and which, contrary to what everyone has mimicked for centuries, is not enlightenment but *enDarkenment*.

The movement of consciousness does not travel from shadow to Light and then end, no.

It finds its true home in the Dark, that VIP back room of Truth that's the source of the *newest, lightest Light*, which has not yet made it down the hallways of genius into the shadowy corners of the collective consciousness where the minds of the gathered masses lounge. The Dark, where the Cool Cats of Consciousness, the Outlaws of Energy Mastery, the Ringmasters of Magic hang out.

Because THAT's what we're after, people.

Magic.

Not manifestation.

And yes I know what they're all GETTING at. What they all MEAN, the spiritual teachers, when they talk about manifestation. I know it's not actually *manifestation* they're referring to, which is calling in what we're an energetic match for (and which we can't NOT do because it's how we're built so of course they're not trying to teach us something we inherently already can't not do), but it's the fact that they misuse the word, you see, that they're lazy with it, that should concern you. Or at least that concerns *me* because it *doesn't* concern you. But I'm fairly convinced that it would if I showed you how it should.

So let me do that then.

Energetic Law 101 states (all you have to do is ascend the long, stone staircase out from your shadow mind up up up into the Dark and the Cold repository of your own genius and the knowledge of How Everything Works and from the topmost shelf swaying and dancing in the starlight pluck the Book of Nothing but symbols and open to page one and receive the activation and the knowledge that...) :

Everyone fucking manifests. All the time. (That's verbatim. Energetic Lawyers were outlaws of the first order. Swearing up a storm every chance they had.)

What we *want* to do is manifest *on demand*.

At will.

As in?

Let there be Light.

This is what *magic* is and what we're all *actually* after and what the self-help gurus *mean* to be talking about when they say

Let me teach you about manifestation.

The three steps.

The five-and-a-half steps.

The secret to having your dream house.

And while it might seem a bit nit picky to pick on the term "manifestation" (she's a big girl concept; she can take it), the fact is that at the level of true energy mastery it is all. about. precision. The codes and frequencies get more and more refined as you go, so your ability to discern a facsimile frequency of Truth from the real thing is *really fucking important* IF it's true awakening and creating on demand that you're after and here's why.

Because magic is not a mystery. It's a spiritual *science*. (I said it once and I'll say it again.)

Meaning, there's a *precision* and a *predictability* to manifestation that can be taught and learned and mastered, just like he workings of any universal law, and it's actually not hard to learn, you just have to go to a few places all the LightWorkers are telling you will DESTROY your ability to create if you go there.

But you gotta go there. Because that's where your GOLD MIND is.

PORTALS THAT KILL

The Missing Link to LOA

If you want to bring something into your experience, whether it's a dream client, a book deal, a mansion, or a human being (a lover, a new friend, a talent agent, a fetus) what you're essentially doing is *creating your experience*.

In other words, *creating from nothing*.

And if you want to do that with *mastery*, so you bring it into your experience exactly how and when you want, you have to know how to work with the two energies responsible for all creation.

The feminine and the masculine.

This, my friends, is the missing link to Law of Attraction.

Not to the law *itself*, but to how it's understood and being taught. (By everyone.)

At the level of pure energetics, the masculine is pure masculine, all the way through. He has no "feminine side." Same with the feminine. One is magnetic energy (feminine) and one is electric (masculine). They are closed systems (hence why the two genders are totally foreign to each other) that activate each other, creating magic (or misery, if you don't know what you're doing).

Manifestation happens when the masculine is called into service by the feminine to go on the great and original Hero's journey and enter deep within her, unearth her own greatest treasures from within her own being, and lay them at her feet.

Manifestation is the masculine giving the feminine back to herself.

But There's a Dark Side...

There's something New Age spirituality, the feminine rising movement, and probably most women don't want to hear.

The feminine is the source of all creation. (That's not what they don't want to hear. That probably makes them very happy. Until they realize what it means…)

The masculine, as the provider and protector energy always in service to the feminine, is coded to do her bidding. (That also probably makes all the tribes mentioned above very happy. But just wait.) This means he is wired to obey her decrees and provide for her every desire, no matter what (this is where it starts to get bad. Because "no matter what" also means no matter how angry or afraid or confronted or challenged or miserable it makes the feminine in the moment….), and he does this by bringing to her specific treasures called from deep within her own being, which is where her genius and chaos, the two raw materials of creation, lie.

The masculine then, *brings the feminine from lie to truth*.

(See? It's getting bad.)

And when this happens, magic is natural and inevitable.

When the feminine becomes unwilling to be brought from the place where she lies, what happens naturally and inevitably is not magic, but misery.

All suffering of all kinds—physical, mental, emotional, financial, spiritual—is a result of the human mishandling the two energies of creation and leaving her feminine energy in a deep state of lie and illusion. Genius is meant to be crafted into living expressions of itself. This cannot happen if it is lying suffocated and stultified in the internal cowardice and anxiety of the feminine energy system.

Afraid of the Light of day.

Afraid of judgement.

Afraid of risk.

Afraid of death.

Afraid, essentially, of what will happen to her great and beautiful creation when she hands it over to the masculine to raise.

To raise up into the Light.

And afraid also of what the masculine must do in order to *retrieve* her greatest treasures.

In order to create magic, the masculine must penetrate deep into the feminine, much deeper than she is comfortable with, into places she's in fact entirely unaware of and has been unconsciously trying to hide from view back in the most remote and blackest shadows, and from that place of her greatest shame, if she lets him violate her in this way—though it is not violent but the greatest act of love—bring forth the expression of her most potent self, which then becomes her experience of her own genius; the unadulterated thrill of her own being.

So while it looks for all the world that the masculine is being activated by the feminine to go on the great and original Hero's journey to enter deep into her, bring her her own treasures, "save her from the monsters" (her fear, her inner demons), and give her back to herself, restored to all her beauty, this is entirely inaccurate.

It is not the masculine who goes on a journey at all. It is the feminine.

She must allow herself to be raised up from her shadow state in which she lies, ignorant of the truth, divorced from her power, terrified of everything that moves, wary of the masculine, and untrusting of his motives (because she thinks he is on a journey that is all about himself, when in fact he is walking to her to wake *her*), to be trained in and learn to *utterly obey* the masculine Light (Cue the raging feminists, New Agers, #metoo-ers and feminine rising-ers….), which is where and how she finds her true power: in the utter trustworthiness of the masculine.

And then (if that weren't bad enough and didn't cause half my readers to pitch this book into the fire of their shadowy outrage) the feminine journey continues in a walk through the wastelands of hell, through the Band of Unhooking, where her consciousness will be utterly dismantled and turned to nothing but bone.

Which means she will lose all her softness. All the ways she carried empathic pain coded in her body: the pain of the world, of the unborn masses, of the ones needing healing and saving, of the innocent and naive, the victims and the weak.

In other words, she will *lose heart*.

And in so doing, she will be shown her true nature and will experience her whole being placed into question (this being the moment of true un-hooking and un-hinging).

Her understanding of the nature of reality, of truth, sanity, power, consciousness, survival, thriving, morality, grace, redemption, joy, and purpose will be placed on trial, which means she will be tempted to waver in her trust of the masculine—of the *Timing* of her true awakening (Time is masculine), that it might happen "too late" or not at all, and she will die—and which, if she passes through to the stillpoint of creation, through what I call the Meathook Moment of Awakening, will cause her to suddenly erupt into her great and SuperConscious nature, not as an energy field that lies in the shadows but as a scandalous Source Field that reigns in the Dark.

She will not be restored to her rightful place as a regal Queen or a cute princess or a gentle fair maiden.

She will be exposed as the fearsome, freakish, Brobdingnagian monster in all our fairy tales.

Not a tortured psyche roiling with demons (though that is how many may see her), but an Exquisite Monster, a Giant of Consciousness presiding with mirthful, disastrous and disorienting reign over form and matter, turning out genius left, right, and center (in other words, no longer *decoding* but *encoding* matter, and therefore the sole matrix of *what matters*) without a single care for the tiny blind eyes of the human psyche, which she has left entirely behind, as she performs her Dance of Chaos Alchemy on the grave of tribal consciousness, transmuting the raw material of the universe into new forms, experiences and expressions at will.

She has become what she truly is: an arrogant, crazy bitch.

A feminine energetic that tunes herself with ease to the precise frequencies required to activate and inspire the magical masculine to do her bidding on demand, calls all the treasures of the universe to her side without apology, hesitation, concern for her "presumptive" behavior, or the need to "leave space" for others to get "their share" (how arrogant of her), and who has shifted power systems entirely, moved off the collective grid of consciousness and become a god (what a crazy bitch).

If the promise of that turns you on, by all means, *read* on

Thoughts, and What They Don't Create

No, thoughts do not create things. And when LOAers say that, they don't even really mean it (noticing a theme here? Fuzzy thinking. It's a major issue in New Age thought).

Because then what they say is well actually *positive* thoughts create *positive* things.

This also isn't true, although it's warmer, because now they're at least acknowledging the role *energy* plays in creation. And not just energy, but the *quality* of the energy.

The main issue with this statement "thoughts create things" is that thoughts are not the *reason* things come to be. Energy is what creates things. And not just energy, but certain frequencies of energy. Thoughts are often handy delivery mechanisms for energy and ways in which the human focuses her desire (her energy) in order to hold the frequency that matches the thing she wants to manifest. But the thought itself does not create anything.

And, you can create things without thought. And you can also create negative (unwanted) things with positive thoughts. (This happens all the time.)

The problem with their theory (one of the many problems), is that positive thoughts create negative, or unwanted, things all the time. Things that weren't even attached to the content or the feeling of the thought itself.

Let me give you an example.

You want to manifest a lover. So you think very positive thoughts about the lover and lo and behold you manifest a lover.

You also manifest the flu.

And the flu, whether you know it or not, is also because of the very positive thoughts that sent you the lover. (You will understand why later. It has to do with what I call the "little devils," which are gifts from the masculine in his role as the *protector*.)

Or, you think very positive thoughts and feel very positive feelings about something, and it is the same degree and force of positivity of thought and feeling that got you many other things, but when it comes to this thing? You got nothin'.

And so then LOAers tell you what's happening is this thing called germinating.

Or gestating. Maybe it's gestating.

It doesn't matter, because this is like a doctor telling you you have "generalized anxiety." It's a catch-all phrase spoken by someone who is supposed to be an expert in their field but who isn't, and who can't explain a very common condition of illness (in this case spiritual illness, the condition in which people are *sick and tired* of following all the LOA rules and still not getting what they want when they want it), and so instead of throwing up their expert hands and saying, "Honestly? I just don't know why you sometimes get what you want and sometimes you don't. I know this is a law, that manifestation works like clockwork, that we are always manifesting what we're an energetic match for, and I know some of the things that seem to work a good deal of the time to get a good deal of people some of the things they want, but getting everyone what they want all the time and if they're not getting it knowing exactly why that is and what to do about it? No. Not only do I not know how to teach that, I don't even know the law to that level of precision. I'm sorry. You're just going to have to gestate on it. I mean germinate. I mean ruminate."

Otherwise you writing one hundred and fifty thousand times in a very positive frame of mind (the positivest you can possibly muster, which was good enough for you to be able to manifest that other thing, back then) about how much you want that mansion, or that man, would have manifested it, or him, by now.

What created Light was NOT the thought, "Let there be Light." It was also not that God was really happy about the idea of Light coming to be.

What created Light—what it takes to create anything—was a CLEAR COMMAND sprung from a CREATIVE WILL intoned by a being whose desire for the creation was entirely *cleared of shadow*.

There are two domains of creation, two sources of Feminine desire, which instigate all acts of creation (Think Eve): shadow and Dark.

This is a being whom the Dark has given access to her body, to lay his hands on her, on the raw material of consciousness, on dis-order of a higher order, and to then order her, with her ultimate permission, down onto the ground.

Creative Will, the divine masculine, is instant, undeniable and irresistible to the laws of energy and chaos, the divine feminine. The raw material of the universe--energy--MUST obey an energy pattern expressing a Clear Command of Creative Will. This law is coded into the wiring of the energetic laws of the universe. It is WHAT electromagnetism is. What the feminine and masculine energies — the two source energies that create EVERYTHING — are and how they operate.

You can think a shit ton of thoughts that don't ever come to be.

You can think a shit ton of POSITIVE thoughts that never come to be.

And if that happens, it's because the sum total of your energy is for shit. You are not a being capable of a Clear Command. You are not a being who has activated your Creative Will. Shadow consciousness runs your life and toxifies your field, no matter how positively you try to think about a specific thing.

Energy is energy is energy. And YOU are one magnetic field.

You can think a million and one positive thoughts but if in any area of your life you're falling prey to letting your shadow handle your precious golden power, that means your shadow is gumming your whole field up with energetic gook and making you one energetically ugly-as-fuck system to the ONE energy you've gotta be energetically GORGEOUS for and IRRESISTIBLE to.

The energy that provides all those dreams to you.

The magical masculine, baby.

Or as I like to call him, the Magic Man.

See there's a deep disconnect happening at the root-level language of your psyche for how you operate, understand, access and command your power, which determines the quality of your energy, the strength of your magnetic frequency, and the attractiveness of your vibrational signature, and basically either turns your Magic Man massively ON (Light, On! Thing I want, here! Right now!) or massively OFF (Shadow, fuck. What happened? I wrote out my desire a thousand times and twirled and tapped my heels twice and danced a jig so why don't I have the thing?)

And the reason you don't understand *why* what seems so intermittent and unpredictable actually *isn't* and how to flip it so YOU'RE in control of IT is because you're still operating out of your *Subconscious Will*. Switching your power center unwittingly on and off.

Usually by using the very techniques those spiritual gurus are teaching you.

See it's time the false prophets and the seduction of spiritual lineage be exposed for what it is:

A fax machine collective of shadow consciousness.

This is what it's like on the Light Grid: It's all about copying and repurposing a piece of the frequency of Light (which also by definition carries a huge piece of the frequency of shadow), and hoping to lay claim to a sliver of the real estate of the psyche by using slightly different words and three instead of four steps and shooting their video in front of an oceanfront mansion instead of in their luxury living room because none of them (and I do mean none of them) are gathering their knowledge or information from anyone but OTHER spiritual gurus who came before them and wrote books and launched Mystery Schools which claimed to be the Womb of Truth, the Center of Spirit, the Oracle of Awakening but the terrible horrible no good cold hard truth is that it wasn't *possible* for them to know the nature of power or the truth of how energy becomes matter —and therefore the truth about what matters — because their shadow frequency was and is operating below the level of THOUGHT (and even below feeling) and constantly sneaking over to the Light Switch and flipping it off which means their access to *their* power is intermittent and limited and not at their command (which is why the actual lives of so many hot shot spiritual teachers are so fucked up). And yet they teach you anyway, because they're at least the most knowledgeable and learned of the blind dead gurus and you sit at their feet and are willing to *listen* anyway because they claim what they teach works when in fact it doesn't, which means YOU end up thinking there's something wrong with YOU.

Because what they really are doing is this.

Receiving codes with a good deal of light but corrupted with shadow they couldn't even see, from a sender who received codes with a good deal of light but corrupted with shadow they couldn't even see, from some other sender who received corrupted codes from some other sender who received corrupted codes from some other sender who received corrupted codes from some other sender

each of whom essentially offered you a spiritual contract from Teacher to Student meant to fool you into believing in their authentic ability to speak and deliver Truth that said something like this:

This knowledge is certifiably True because it came from someone who speaks certifiable Truth. And that person is certified in Truth because someone else certified in Truth certified him (it was always "him's" until recently). And THAT person was certified to certify Truthtellers because HE was trained by a certified Truthteller who was certified by someone who was certified by someone who was certified by someone who.....

And this is where the fine print trails off because no one really looks at it anyway least of all the spiritual leader who's hired the Lawyer of the Spirit to write up the fine print just in case anyone looks at it and the *lawyer* certainly doesn't know how to end the sentence because where does the lineage of certified Truthtellers actually begin?

Where, in other words, are we getting all this information from, *really*?

Buddha?

The *Earth* certified *him*.

So the story goes...on the night before Siddhartha's enlightenment a devil/monster appeared claiming to own the Seat of Spiritual Wisdom and demanding that Siddhartha produce someone to speak for *him*, for HIS right to overturn the monster and ascend to the throne of Truth and Awakening and Siddhartha reached down and touched the ground and said, "The Earth certifies me." And the earth shook and the heavens opened and the sun shon in the sky and Siddhartha became the Buddha and gave birth to a lineage of teachers who received his wisdom and offered it to others and at each handing down and handing over pointed back to that moment and said take, eat. This is a sliver of the body of Truth, certified by the one who came before me. And at each serving the energetic nutrients of the food of Truth were stripped even more bare, spread even more thin until at this point what you get when you go to one of these workshops, doesn't matter who by, is nothing more than spiritual gruel.

Not to mention that it wasn't, actually, the Truth.

Buddha is great and all, but the answer to human suffering is not to deny desire and learn how to un-desire. This is like the *opposite*, in fact the *exact and supreme opposite*, of true energy mastery and the essence of the Olympic Game of Consciousness we're here to play. It's not how to come here and *not* do the thing we were blueprinted specifically to do when we came, which is to advance consciousness through the mastery of the energy of desire, but to learn how to apply the chaotic energy of desire with pure mastery, to focus it like a laser beam of absolute and exacting frequency and call energy into matter with total mastery. We are not meant to numb our energetic nerve endings because at the beginning it's really fucking painful to want shit. We're meant to learn the spiritual science of artfully turning energy into matter—and thereby mastering the truth of *what* matters—so we orchestrate the experience of our desires on cue. And this activity of energy alchemy, and the utterly new material and understanding of what matters that it creates, is what advances consciousness.

But that's for another piece. The point I'm making here with the whole demon/monster/Buddha story is that for all intents and purposes *Buddha* certified Buddha. (And, that he was wrong about a fundamental aspect of human consciousness.)

Same goes for Jesus, who was certified by "God." (I and the Father are one. No one comes to the Father but by me. I am the way, the Truth and the Light.), which looks a lot like self-certification to me.

So that's two great spiritual teachers, who birthed entire lineages, who *basically* certified *themselves*.

Mohammed? Got anything to say?

I had a vision. An angel came to me.

Cool. I'm calling that self-certification also.

It is time the true architects of spiritual genius show their face, and the face is you. You are a spiritual genius giant waiting to be waked. And not by the blaring bleeps of the fax machine lineage of transformation bringing you outdated codes passed down over generations (each of which have so degraded the inking of Truth with their own density and shadow that the final form that's delivered to you is so sloppy, messy and nearly illegible that even if they *did* at one point carry The Secret, what *you're* receiving is more like the end result of a nearly infinitely long telephone game played by sleepy whisperers, than the crystal clear Truth).

No. You require waking of an entirely other kind.

More like a quake, really. That splits open the secret ceiling in your mind and rips open the false floor to your fear so that *you* goddammit become the channel, the straight-ahead gateway to awakening, the access point to the SuperConscious, and *you* certify *you* in the nature of power and Truth and gain access to the root-level laws of energy and the mechanics of manifestation.

And when you do?

Magic. On demand.

And that is what we're here to do. In these pages, to turn you into yourself. To effect a root-level reboot onto an entirely new operating system of consciousness that will no longer be bleeped and faxed at by the faux machines of spirituality.

I'm here to teach you the spiritual science of manifesting on demand. Of making magic in your life and business, like I and like the thousands of people I've taught have done.

Because the truth is that manifestation is right now an almost completely unconscious activity, part of our "autonomic energetic" system, like breathing or heart-beating is to the body. And this is, of course, why it's so goddamn frustrating.

We don't have a hold of it. Not really. Not very much. And certainly not anywhere to the degree we want.

We're like crazed babies, stumbling around on the floor of the laws of energy, accidentally kicking a lever that activates the rules governing how energy becomes matter and look!

A new car! Exactly the one we wanted! Down to the fucking shade of red and the tire tread!

But the lever that would send us the love of our life? The million dollar business we've been dreaming about for years? That's installed on the ceiling so good fucking luck.

The room of energy mastery is nearly pitch black and full of shadows. And we are babies of consciousness with only remedial skills in navigating our way with grace (because there are also levers that activate very UNWANTED experiences, and there seems to be a whole lot more of those, so graceful and skilled navigation around them is very much something we need to learn), with limited reach (and therefore no way to access whatever is activated by the levers hanging from the ceiling, or high up on the walls), almost NO capacity for sustained focus (staying in the apprenticeship phase long enough to become a master) without total emotional meltdowns and temper tantrums, and who keep crying and whining for someone to turn on the light—which all the spiritual toddler gurus of awakening are all rushing around trying to do—when in fact what we *really* want, what energy mastery *truly* means, is to be able to *see in the Dark*.

What is called for now is a complete reversal of instincts and a species alchemy of the highest order.

In fact, a dis-order of a higher order.

In other words, this is the Age of Disruption.

You are wired for magic, built to thrive, and it is time you return to your true nature as a genius giant who calls worlds into being on command.

Well.

Let's get to it then.

Physical Existence, Codes Of Consciousness, The Mechanics Of Inspired Action And The Role Of Intuition In Manifesting On Demand

Knowing this will make it SO EASY to do what you're guided to do, even when it seems silly, irresponsible, or totally unrelated to getting what you want.

Like. This will ELIMINATE YOUR RESISTANCE to acting on your intuition.

You'll do it WILLINGLY. EAGERLY. EASILY.

No analysis paralysis. No procrastination. No sabotage.

- exactly how inspired action magnetizes what we want

- WHY the specific actions we need to take are almost always NOT in the area we're trying to upgrade (For example, why you making a change in your relationship to your body, business, pricing, friend, lover, dreams, etc.—as long as it's based on intuitive guidance and inspired action—causes your ideal client to show up in your world "out of the blue "and instantly pay you top dollar for your services.), and

- why the instructions from your intuition must be followed exactly, (and why when my clients follow my instructions—and their intuition—they get such insane results), even though the actions they have to take may have nothing to do with the area in which they want the extreme results....Although sometimes it does.

It all has to do with the way our code fields are linked through the synchronistic grid to the code field of what we're trying to magnetize.

This COMPLETELY EXPLAINS AND EXPOSES why, if you're a health coach, for instance, you could be in supreme health, but still not magnetize your ideal clients who also want supreme health. Or if you're a money coach, you could be amazingly skilled at making money and making other people money but your ideal clients who want more than anything to do exactly that aren't showing up NO MATTER WHAT YOU DO (perfect your marketing, use #alltheLOAtools, upgrade your OWN money mindset, you name it). Even though it makes all the sense in the world that this is how it would work: You upgrade the system that your clients want to upgrade and then you magnetize those clients. Right? Nope. A lot of the times, as you well know, that's not how it works. ...And then sometimes it is.

It will also COMPLETELY EXPLAIN why your intuition always directs you to a very specific action (ever notice that? It's always very specific. Call Joe. Drink some water. Raise your fees to $50K. Never "call someone. Drink something. Raise your fees." There's a very specific reason for this, and once you know it, you'll also understand why it's IMPERATIVE that you follow your intuition EXACTLY and COMPLETELY and IMMEDIATELY—NOT somewhat, for the most part and later—and will also make it crystal clear why when you do this, it's magic.

(This is also why I tell my clients they must follow my instructions EXACTLY. I'm not being an arrogant overlord—even though I am. I'm....well you'll just have to join Friday to find out what I'm doing, and why, when they my clients do exactly what I say, they make magic (and also why when they don't, they don't).

For example...

"I said exactly what you told me to say and I closed a $3,000 deal!" (Tia Harrison Holmes)

Another client followed the GIST of my instructions and did a livestream on a similar topic to the one I told her to do, but not the exact one. She got maybe 100 views. Then I told her to do a live stream on the exact, specific topic, and she got 22,000 views.

Another did what I told her to do, and made $48,000 in 30 days, from Ground Zero in her business.

And that's all I'm gonna say about that. Because I'm saving the rest for Friday. ;)

Our patterns of consciousness (Code Fields) are directly linked to other patterns of consciousness, but not necessarily in a one-to-one relationship.

Your body codes may not be linked to your ideal client's body codes. (Which is why if you're a health coach, you could be in supreme health, but still not magnetize your ideal clients who also want supreme health. Even though it makes all the sense in the world that this is how it would work: You upgrade the system that your clients want to upgrade and then you magnetize those clients. Right? Nope. A lot of the times, as you well know, that's not how it works. ...And then sometimes it is.)

Your money codes may not be linked to their money codes (which is why if you're a money/business/sales coach, you could be exceptional at making money, but still not be able to pull in your most ideal clients, And be making lots of money, but working with people who drive you crazy or bore you to tears. Or, making lots of money selling small little programs, when what you really want to do is make the same amount of money working with a few hot shot big time clients).

And, on the other hand, your code field might very well be linked in a one-to-one relationship to the things you're trying to magnetize to you.

Your conscious awareness isn't coded with the capacity to see these connections. And it never will be.

But there IS something within you that knows.

Your Gold Mind. Your Magician.

Otherwise known as your intuition.

Your Gold Mind is the energetic mechanism that knows EXACTLY what code fields in you link to and light up the code fields in the thing you're trying to magnetize, and the way it tells you how to become an energetic match to that code field is through your intuition. The nudge to take some specific action (often SEEMINGLY unrelated to the field in which you think the thing you're trying to magnetize is operating).

In other words, your intuition knows that your body codes, for instance, are directly linked to your client's money codes. So it knows that unless and until you upgrade your consciousness with respect to how you treat your body, you will not activate or light up the code field of money in your ideal client that is ready to be upgraded by your transmissions.

And THAT Is because your transmissions of transformational consciousness only come through your UPGRADED code fields (because upgrading a code field simply means transitioning that field from running shadow energy to running light energy, which is required in order to upgrade your client's code field, which is still stuck in shadow, because transformation only ever happens from a low frequency field to a higher frequency field).

The only reason you're not manifesting a new level in your life or business or whereever you desire it, is simply because you have not upgraded the code field within YOU that is linked to the code field within THEM that they are ready to have upgraded.

This is why no matter how much you can't see the connection between your action and the results you desire, you MUST take the inspired action, no matter how little sense it seems to make to be focusing on, for instance, your creative project when all you really want to be doing is making money. Or focusing on making money when all you want to be doing is improving your physical health. Or focusing on marketing when all you want to be doing is going on dates and trying to find the love of your life.

And the action you take must be PRECISELY the action you are intuitively guided to take WHEN you are guided to take it.

That is because upgrading code fields requires extreme precision. Codes are precisely tuned. Of our another way, frequencies are precisely coded.

When your intuition directs you to a very specific actions. This is also why my instructions are equally specific and why I tell my clients they must follow them EXACTLY.

And why, when they do they make magic.

"I said exactly what you told me to say and I closed a $3,000 deal!" (Tia Harrison Holmes)

Another client followed the GIST of my instructions and did a livestream on a similar topic to the one I told her to do, but not the exact one. She got maybe 100 views. Then I told her to do a live stream on the exact, specific topic, and she got 22,000 views.

Another did what I told her to do, and made $48,000 in 30 days, from Ground Zero in her business.

This is because your Gold Mind and I can see exactly where and how your code field is scrambled and we then instruct you to take a certain action that will directly and precisely confront that scrambled field with a certain combination of codes and frequencies that will unscramble it, release the trapped energy (power) and instantly upgrade the field.

This is why you CANNOT CHEAT ENERGY.

And if your body codes are linked to your client's money codes, and yours are in a shadow state, then the frequency that connects the two fields will stay "greyed out" and unlit, and your client will not be energetically alerted to your existence.

(In Magic Man terms, the field you're wanting to upgrade by receiving higher level gifts from your Magic Man—in the form of higher-level clients and sales—will be energetically ugly to him, and he will not be inspired to activate the synchronistic grid connecting you to your ideal client, and will therefore not do what he do easily could, which is to simply tap your ideal client on the energetic shoulder through an intuitive hit or synchronistic event that would immediately put the two of you in touch in the 3D realm.)

The only reason you're not manifesting a new level in your life or business or wherever you desire it, is simply because you have not upgraded the code field within YOU that is linked to the code field within YOUR CLIENT or dream lover, friend, etc., that they are ready to have upgraded.

This is why no matter how much you can't see the connection between your action and the results you desire, you MUST take the inspired action, no matter how little sense it seems to make to be focusing on, for instance, your creative project when all you really want to be doing is making money. Or focusing on making money when all you want to be doing is improving your physical health. Or focusing on marketing when all you want to be doing is going on dates and trying to find the love of your life.

And the action you take must be PRECISELY the action you are intuitively guided to take WHEN you are guided to take it.

That is because upgrading code fields requires extreme precision. Codes are precisely tuned. Of our another way, frequencies are precisely coded.

When your intuition directs you to a very specific actions. This is also why my instructions are equally specific and why I tell my clients they must follow them EXACTLY.

And why, when they do they make magic.

"I said exactly what you told me to say and I closed a $3,000 deal!" (Tia Harrison Holmes)

Another client followed the GIST of my instructions and did a livestream on a similar topic to the one I told her to do, but not the exact one. She got maybe 100 views. Then I told her to do a live stream on the exact, specific topic, and she got 22,000 views.

Another did what I told her to do, and made $48,000 in 30 days, from Ground Zero in her business.

This is because your Gold Mind and I can see exactly where and how your code field is scrambled and we then instruct you to take a certain action that will directly and precisely confront that scrambled field with a certain combination of codes and frequencies that will unscramble it, release the trapped energy (power) and instantly upgrade the field.

This is why you CANNOT CHEAT ENERGY.

Our coming into being is an expression of a unique, never to be re-expressed relationship to every code and frequency that exists in consciousness. We are, at our foundational level of physical, 3-D existence, an expression of a unique relationship to all those codes and frequencies. In fact this is what it means in the first sentence of the gospel of John which says in Greek in the beginning was the word. And word is actually the Greek for logos. Logos doesn't really mean word, what it means Is relation, ratio, relationship. The expression of 3-D physical reality was a calling into being of a concatenation of relationships of codes and frequencies existing in, and linked to each other in, varying degrees of density. A human being enters that pre-existing web as its own unique relationship enneagram or expressiveness that has gathered itself together into one Single collective desire to BE that particular and unique expression of relationships to all other codes and frequencies in the multiverse.

For humans, that desire is to play the most difficult, and therefore the most pleasurable, game of consciousness. For all other entities (inanimate objects, natural materials, other life forms, etc.), the desire is to be of service in the game, to be instruments used to play the game, and to reside as challenges to ensure the game is as difficult, and therefore as pleasurable, as possible.

That is the essence of the definition of what it means to exist in the physical realm. In the non-physical realm, one can exist in many relationships to those same codes and frequencies. In other words, one can be consciously existing in many places and times at the same time. The physical expression of a human is simply a choice to live out a consciousness that is oriented around one particular Time-and-space-bound set of unique relationship to all the frequencies and codes in the universe. I'm not going to get into the reason for that right now, other than really to say that there is no reason, it's just a really interesting and fun game to play, but the point of this transmission is to explain manifestation through this understanding.

All you are doing when you are manifesting on demand, or what I call making magic, is adjusting your Codes and frequencies to the same energetic patterning of the codes and frequencies of that which you desire, whether it is an inanimate object, like a house, or a human being who might bring you sales, in the form of being a client, or love, in the form of being a boyfriend or a girlfriend, or a relationship experience you desire, in the form of you getting pregnant with your unborn daughter. Your intuition, or what I call your gold mind, is the instrument of guidance that directs you, through certain actions, to challenge the existing density of your codes and frequencies that are linked to the codes and frequencies of that which you desire, and through these specific actions, to shatter (or unscramble) their pattern, so that they come into unhindered relationship (logos) to, or in other words *resonate with*, the codes and frequencies of that which you desire. When this happens, time and space, the two energies of consciousness that serve to both create and challenge the experience of the 3D playground as either magical or miserable, orient themselves around this superresonant, or charismatic, relationship and enter into complete obedience to it, bringing all physical objects that resonate at this coherent frequency into one time and place, and lay them at the feet of the human who has mastered this vibration. This is why when you attract one thing you desire, you also often attract several others that *seem* unrelated.

(Physical health is included in this example, because though you are not attracting a new "other," you are indeed attracting a new expression of your physical cells—the healthier one.)

The way we are linked to all the other codes and frequencies of consciousness is often not in the way our logical/time bound brain thinks that they are, or should be. They *are* linked in a direct relationship, which is in fact logical (meaning the expression of a direct relationship), of just isn't according to human logic.

This is why accessing spiritual intelligence will free you from all your struggles. Because that will instantly reveal the new logic, the True Logic, the nature of all Spiritual Relationships, and your brain, once your greatest resistor, due to its inability to see the truth, which simply means its inability to know how to tap into and manage all true connections to its favor, will realize that its lack of sight is simply due to its limited ability to see into the nature of the direct relationships of its human, and will develop a deep appreciation for the faculty of intuition to supply the insight it lacks. And when this happens, the lower mind, the brain, will gladly surrender to the primacy and guidance of its own Gold Mind, and you will release all resistance to acting on your intuition.

When this happens, the result is magic.

Because the only thing standing between misery and magic is not time, space, money, knowledge, approval, permission, luck, chance, or hustle. It's simply dropping our resistance to acting on our intuition.

THE DARK SECRET

Once you is why when you turn the dial up in your life or business, you instantly attract , usually in a different area (because while you think they are seemingly unrelated, that's actually where the direct link exists).

GUARDS DOWN, BOUNDARIES UP

Boundaries are curious, tensile and porous energetic material that are inherently feminine — meaning they are endowed with the skill of instant shifting, from open to closed, from closed to open. They are undecided until the last moment, at which point they either open or close.

Guards are unnatural, rigid and over-formed energetic material created from an uncertain worth and a lack of ability to be quietly present with power. In the presence of power - a room full of eyes on you, a gorgeous, rich man, your own inimitable genius steaming from every inch of your skin — what do you do? If you instantly and pre-determinedly close up, then you are someone who has your guard up and your boundaries down. Boundaries are responsive and curious. They require the energetic mastery of a True Feminine who does not shrink in the presence of power — meaning of pure potent energy — but is able to feel at the edges of it for its purity, its clarity, its cleanness, it's quality of frequency, and naturally and gracefully close or open, depending on the feedback it receives from its energetic investigation.

Emotion, in its purest form, is simply energy.

Powerful negative emotion is exactly the same, in its most pristine state, as powerful *positive* emotion. And if you have completely cleared your body/mind of its wounds and old conditioning, you eliminate the experience of being triggered. It simply does not occur in your system. There is no more shadow to shift. No more shame to alchemize. When you have fully alchemized your INTERNAL field of energy, then you can fully and instantly alchemize any EXTERNAL energy you encounter.

You have turned yourself into a pure, potent, instant energy alchemizer.

It is an absolutely thrilling, incredibly freeing place to be.

And it is available to every one of you, of us.

Repeat after me:

No one and nothing has power over me.

On Self-Actualization, The Feminine And The Dynamic Nature Of Source

self actualization: not the derivative consciousness having arrived at congruence with Source, but the capacity for that derivative consciousness to use Source Light Consciousness directly, and no other derivative consciousness, to expand itself to its highest potential.

Coaching and mentoring is the tool by which one consciousness possessing ultimate will to expand pairs with a higher consciousness capable of continually holding the light onto the area of next expansion (which means the higher consciousness must also be expanding exponentially itself).

When you remove the higher consciousness (the mentor/coach/catalyst), the one that's left moves at a slower rate UNLESS it has reached the capacity to use Source directly as the catalyzing consciousness.

This is what total enlightenment and self actualization is.

The reason self actualization has been defined as a static state of arrival of congruence with Source is because we have misunderstood Source Consciousness as a static state. In other words, we have not understood the essential role of the feminine in its existence.

Source is expanding into ever greater expressions of itself. (The ultimate paradox.)

The feminine is the derivative consciousness. As such, it is also the newest, meaning the most original. This is the way in which Source is both one and many, changeless and the all-ever-changing.

Self actualization is what all derivative consciousnesses strive toward, but *as* a derivative (as a self). It is not necessary to merge completely with Source to be self-actualized. In fact it's by definition impossible.

What has been described as self-actualization — entering into pure union with Source — is the masculine looking at its own desire to be consumed (what all masculine energy desires — to be consumed by the feminine, though in this case it is to be consumed by Source). The feminine, however, desires the ever-emergence of new form that is the expression of its highest potential. This is feminine self-actualization, and since all form is essentially oriented toward its feminine (by virtue of choosing embodiment), self-actualization is not what the masculine would define it as, because it does not speak for embodiment's (self's) highest potential. Only the feminine does that.

Which is why women are almost always the ones to wake up first and lead us home.

ON OUR STRUGGLE WITH AWAKENING AND THE DEGRADED ROLE OF THE MASCULINE

Why do we struggle with awakening?

Because we have degraded the role of the masculine.

It is the divine masculine who awakens our slumbering Soul (the Soul being the feminine divine).

This is why so many fairytales depict the prince saving the princess. Sleeping Beauty. Cinderella.

These stories are not meant to degrade women (which is what has happened. Women have taken them literally). They are meant to express the wisdom of the energies of sleep and awakening. When we are asleep, it is because our feminine energy -- our intuition -- is either inactive (as in Sleeping Beauty) or divorced from our conscious awareness (Cinderella -- where the mice represent her natural instinct -- her intuitive nature).

The divine masculine energy is the thunderclap energy that comes in from the outside -- or what feels like the outside, because it is outside our awareness that we in fact have access to this "savior" within, that it is in fact an inherent aspect of us. It feels foreign and powerful and overwhelming -- as all good Hollywood movies depict the leading man, the romantic interest, the heartthrob. This is only because in our slumber, we are unaware of the power our request for help to awaken has activated within us. This power becomes activated before we are consciously aware of its presence within us. And therefore we think it exists outside of us.

And then we create beliefs about divinity being masculine and external and overpowering. And men being the same. And humanity being the weaker and needier. And women being that.

And over time we began to believe that there was something inherently wrong with the feminine. Meaning, in our unconscious metaphor, the human. Something deplorably weak.

And we began to associate the feminine with being human with being women (specifically being a pussy) and the masculine with being divine with being men (specifically with having balls).

And this created a tension impossible to resolve with integrity -- meaning with the ability to imagine retaining the dignity of both.

One is now the weaker sex needing rescue and healing. And one is now the stronger, capable of saving.

And so then, women attempted to rise on their own -- meaning without the aid of the divine masculine catalyzing seed of Truth, without the essential thunderclap energy that only the masculine brings to the desire to be reborn. Meaning, women shamed what it means to be masculine, and attempted to awaken without this force.

And thus the new age mentality of "manifesting" was created, in which we all attempt to give birth to our new selves without the aid of the masculine. In other words, without action.

It has become "beneath" one's self to change states through action and considered much more "spiritually advanced," desirable and impressive to change states through inaction.

And now the masculine is regarded as the weaker energy, because it has been misunderstood all along.

Watch any commercial these days. The man is nearly always being degraded and depicted as childish and weak.

As long as we reject the essential, life-saving role of the masculine, we will remain deeply asleep.

The Energetics Of Desire And The Essential Missing Link To LOA Teachings (The Bestowal Of Power Onto Desire)

Desire is made magnetic by the nature of the energy that animates it. That energy emanates from either a source of weakness or a source of power. In other words, the source of illusion or the source of Truth.

If what you desire is not coming to you, it is either coded with the energy of weakness and illusion, and therefore cannot come to pass, or your life in general is coded with this shadow aspect of consciousness, thus relegating your field to one with only weak magnetic powers, incapable of activating the magical masculine, who is the one responsible for providing your desires, and who in doing so, keeps a close eye on the quality of your consciousness, and derives his commands from that alone.

In other words, the masculine, the energy that provides for our desires, is activated (derives his commands) from the QUALITY OF OUR CONSCIOUSNESS, NOT the positivity of oour thoughts.

Consciousness is not thought, people. That's like saying Electricity is wires.

ON WOMEN, MEN AND ANXIETY

Conventional wisdom says that women know how to talk about their feelings significantly more eloquently than men because women are trained and encouraged to be emotional, discuss, understand and process their emotions, and men are not.

But this is actually not at all true.

Women have no fucking clue how to talk about their emotions.

They know how to talk about their anxiety and their fear. And they tend to translate ALL their other emotions INTO an anxiety or a fear, particularly when it comes to their relationship with men.

What they don't at all know how to do is talk about their desires (every desire is languaged as a form of anxiety or fear).

So next time it comes time to have one of "those talks" with your man, remember, you're both likely massively handicapped when it comes to having a truly conscious conversation.

And have some grace, humility and acceptance for both of you.

Things will go a lot better if you do.

Anxiety And The Sleepy Stuckness Of The Swampy Feminine

The dance of the healthy feminine: Receive, conceive, detach. Receive, conceive, detach. Receive, conceive, detach. This is an every-moment dance that happens minute by minute, day by day.

The sleepy stuckness of the swampy feminine: Receive, conceive, ATTACH. Attach. Attach. Attach. Attachattachattachattachattach. [otherwise known as anxiety.]

In the former, there is constant flow, creation, calm and euphoria. And also the discipline of firmly putting down what we are tempted to grasp onto: Outcomes. Expectations. Responses or results we desire from our relationships (our business, our clients, our spouse/boyfriend/lover, ourselves).

In the latter because there is the initial grasp and attachment, there is nothing NEW that can be created, and this is what causes the stagnation and swampiness, and the inability to establish firm boundaries externally (causing codependency, abuse), because the firmness has not been practiced within, of detaching from outcomes completely.

THE MAGICAL MASCULINE

as Time

As money

As inspiration

Is our intimate exterior source of power

Powerful people **take their time**, have lots of money

Up until now your brain has been run by your saboteur. I'm going to get it run by your Magic Man

And then all your troubles will be over

They're the same archetypal energy. One just runs their power through fear first. The other runs their power through truth. That's the only difference.

THE MAGIC MAN TOOL

Anything you desire that you don't have, including a FEELING (like feeling inspired, turned on, happy) is your Magic Man's job to provide for you.   So, do the tool that I taught in the livestream. What am I worried about/plagued by? I am feeling shitty. So what does that mean I want to experience? I want to feel inspired. Then make the request of your Magic Man and then walk away from the focus on it. (In this case, stop worrying about feeling shitty) AND, there's a piece that came in right after the livestream (of course 😊) that is critical. ASK your Magic Man if there is anything you need to do to become an energetic match for what you've just requested, and then IMMEDIATELY DO whatever it is you hear/think. (That's your Magic man PROVIDING you with the answer) This isn't the "standing in the garage/can I help you" thing that is really you worrying. This is an "I get that my life must be an energetic match for what I've asked you to provide, so if it isn't, please tell me what needs to be done to change that" thing. It's you being a good partner. And you gotta do whatever he says and don't procrastinate or ask why. Just do it. It might make no sense (he's the magician, remember. Not the saboteur) and might not seem connected to the request you made, but remember the HOW is not up to you. That's HIS job. And if you don't do what he says, he can't do his job. This is when the feminine MUST SURRENDER and just OBEY THE MASCULINE (which in the last fifty years has been massively demonized of course). Not because he's an asshole control freak but because in THIS area, he knows best and can see what you can't. Try that and see what happens 😊 (and don't forget — if you find yourself WORRYING about how shitty you still feel, realize you've just planted yourself in the garage, arms crossed, impatiently watching him work. Or the other visual - you've just marched over to him and grabbed the honey do list and said you'll take care of it, he's taking too long or not doing it right. So give him back the list, apologize for not believing in him, tell him you know he's the fucking PROVIDER OF THE UNIVERSE so he's got this, give him a kiss and walk away! And maybe over your shoulder as you're leaving, say, "and hey. If there's anything I need to do to make this easier on you, just let me know." And if he says, yeah. Actually there is. GO TAKE A BUBBLE BATH and chill. Then DO it. And don't stomp away feeling like he just wants you GONE and out of his hair. He's giving you the EXACT and precise action for you to take that will release the energy of WORRY from your system and therefore from your dynamic and therefore refresh the field and ANIMATE and FREE him to focus and do his job. Men cannot function in the energy of worry. Neither can your Magic Man.   Got it?! ☺

THE SEED

In Hungarian MAG(ic) means seed. Hungarians call themselves MAGyar.

The gift of the Magic Man is the SEED of an idea, the dream coming true. You get the first part of the full dream (the first client for your dream Million Dollar business, the first few pounds lost, the first serendipitous connection to your dream speaking engagement), and THEN it is your job to respond to the pressures that result, and to do so in accordance (a-chord-ance) with the tone of exacting standards being held at all times by your High Feminine.

You get your first client and you worry you can deliver. (Pressure of self worth). If you collapse and freak out, you will often lose the client somehow because you've collapsed your energetic container. They'll ghost, not pay, etc.

But if you stay connected to your worth, know your Magic Man will provide your transformational genius to you in exactly the right way at exactly the right time to blow your client's mind, then you are strengthening your container (your energetic womb, which you are building and strengthening at all times to be able to deliver your vision, your legacy, your dream into your physical experience) and you will keep the client. So now you have DELIVERED the first expression of your vision into your experience.

Time to become pregnant with the next, higher level one!

Having maintained your worth, your boundaries, your standards, with grace and firmness throughout the pressure of labor, you have now become even more magnetic and attractive to an even higher quality masculine with even more potent abilities (higher quality energetic connections to even more powerful people, who can bring you even more amazing opportunities). In order to be fully magnetic to this higher quality masculine provider energy, you likely will also have to upgrade and change aspects of your life that are being held in dischord with respect to your standards and essentially build an even stronger container capable of holding and receiving and delivering an even more potent expression of your desire.

When you do this, you activate the laws of masculine energy and a "better man" shows up and drops in another SEED. This time it's the seed of

The Dark Masculine

If you're disappointed with men or money, it's your own masculine that needs an upgrade.

The Masculine (men, money) is a pure reflector of the condition of your field.

There are three stages of working with Masculine Energy - shadow, light and dark (from no mastery to full mastery).

When you relate to the Masculine (men and money) from your shadow, you can never get enough, it's never what you really want, you're always disappointed, you feel mistreated, misunderstood, neglected, ignored, abused and the relationship takes a lot of work.

When you relate to men and money from your Light, you attract what you want with ease, you feel appreciated and seen, understood and honored.

And yet there is something beyond even this incredible experience: Activating a man's (or money's) Dark Masculine energy.

When you relate to men and money from your Dark Divine energy, you attract a man — and financial abundance — beyond what you can possibly imagine.

New aspects of yourself are seen into existence by your man (or men), aspects you never imagined and yet there they are, radiant, activated by his gaze, by his ability to see in the Dark. (And you as the feminine are *most* beautiful in your darkness.)

In this field, money surprises you as well.

In the radically creative streams it flows in through. Business ideas you could never have imagined. Activated SuperConscious psychic gifts you thought would take years to master. Genius-level creativity flows without end. No more boredom with your business. No more struggling to stand out in a crowded market. No more low-level clients.

The gift of the Dark Masculine is so incredibly rich. And yet His standards are so exacting, so regal, that they will not be activated even by a woman, or a feminine energy, who has only accessed her Light.

And we know this, inherently, as women. The Dark Masculine is what we all secretly want. The "bad boy" energy of the rebel of consciousness that in fact will initiate us into its highest form.

The man who lives on the edge, not because he is escaping, but because the edge is his genius, his calling.

When you work with this level of masculine energy, you become unimaginably gifted.

Men and money come to you and treat you — gift you — in ways you couldn't have dreamed up, but that arouse you precisely and potently.

And you become gifted by your own higher mind, which pours forth genius into your life, inspiring truly distinctive, innovative business models, offerings and services.

When you operate from your shadow and your Light fields, the Masculine is a pure reflector (meaning, what you experience in your relationship with men and money is simply a direct reflection of the purity of your own energy systems).

But when you step into your Dark energy—when you stand in such an explicitly unique field—this is when you no longer need the mirror.

And what the Dark Masculine becomes then, when you have freed it from being your pure reflector, is the euphoric experience you truly seek.

The Misunderstood Masculine And The Root Of Real Magic

There's a lot of talk and focus on the feminine in manifestation and in this online coaching world. Nothing wrong with that. The Feminine is the Receiver Energy, and we've certainly spent centuries misunderstanding the power of the True Feminine in unlocking quantum leaps and pleasurable success with ease.

BUT, there's a major imbalance and overfocus on the Feminine — very similar to what happened in America in the 1960s with the rise of feminism — and it's the reason your business, health and love life are still stuck at unacceptable levels (even though for you, that means $30k months and frequent dates with super hot men).

Even though you're applying LOA and manifestation and feminine energy work diligently, daily and frankly... 'til you're blue in the face...what you know to be your fullest expression (billion dollar business with celebrity clients, and your Twin Flame by your side as you jet around the world), still feels worlds away.

Bank account not even close to where you want it ($30k months are shameful to you, if you're willing to admit it.)

Your legacy in a straightjacket. (You're supposed to be a household name already.)

The hot men nowhere near able to handle your epic energy. (Are there *any* men who can match you?)

AmIright?

It's because you don't understand how to trigger the Masculine Energy of Providing AT ALL.

It's like the ultra feminists thinking that along with burning their bras and refusing to shave and demanding their place right alongside men at work, they can also reject the role the man plays in CONCEPTION.

In order to trigger the magic of manifestation, quantum leaps and consistent, pleasurable high six figure months, and your most euphoric lover, your Feminine Receiver must have an intimate and masterful understanding of, and a DEEP APPRECIATION for, the Masculine Provider energy and know how to activate and work with it.

Otherwise you might have a spiritual genius capable of activating the next world leaders, clever marketing that could bring you a billion dollar business and a body Marilyn Monroe would salivate at — but you and your life will remain completely barren.

Hate to say it, but men — and masculine energy — still matter.

If you're at all interested in Real Love and Money Magic, then you must correct your understanding of how manifestation actually works.

And when you do, euphoric wealth and love is the result (and blissful levels of mental health as well).

This how I went from a bipolar, suicidal, jobless single mom to mentally and emotionally healthy, acutely telepathic and claircognizant, wealthy (seven figure business) and madly in love with my Twin Flame in 14 months.

I'm going to be doing a livestream on the secrets to unlocking masculine provider energy, why and how you're blocking it right now, and sharing detailed, high consciousness channeled truth you aren't hearing anywhere else.

PM me if you're interested in knowing the date, time and location.

And in the meantime, start giving the masculine a little love. He'll return the gift tenfold.

LOA Redefined And Distilled

Your energetic coordinates, i.e., your unique location on the energetic grid, must be fully lit up so that the universe knows where to "deliver" your desires.

How to fully light up? Activate and integrate your masculine and feminine energies.

Because at the end of the day, ALL this is about is energy mastery. Cash is just energy. Pleasure is just energy. Fear is just energy.

The Secret To Men And Money Success

The secret to men and money success is not to embody your feminine energy only.

This is why so many of you, who've spent so many years embodying your divine feminine essence, learning the art of tantra, becoming multi-orgasmic, taking up pole dancing and attending those ever-popular "juicy" feminine retreats in Bali, STILL struggle with men and money.

Your bank account is stuck far below what you know you're capable of and what you truly desire. Or it rises and falls drastically, leaving you exhausted.

Just like you men, who come and go. And the ones who adore and want you aren't ever the ones you truly want.

The cycle will continue like this until you learn how to work with the Masculine Energy, which is a completely separate, imperial energy that operates according to its own energetic laws.

And since money is masculine, if you don't understand how to work with this energy field, your bank account and your heart will remain barren.

It is time for women to step out of the cocoon of the feminine and welcome in the exacting tones and frequencies of the masculine.

This is the only way for you to ride into your true field of grace and abundance with ease.

Which brings us to the nature of magic:

Power over Time.

The Magician is Master of many things, but Time, the resource most elusive to our consciousness, is the one he Masters most.

Collapse Time and you make magic.

It's not magical to make a million dollars in ten years. That's just a hundred grand every twelve months. Plenty of humans can do that.

What IS magical is doing it not in ten YEARS but in ten MONTHS. Working part time. (Power over time, you see. Not using the levers of physical hustle to achieve results but instead using energy to collapse time and bend "reality" to our will. To our Creative Will. Which is VASTLY different than the Subconscious Will, which is what runs the program of manifestation now, for nearly all humans.)

Holy fucking shit. I just downloaded the code mechanics for WHY inspired action is so often totally different from what we THINK will create success.

The biggest barrier to taking inspired action (acting on your intuition) is NOT that you don't recognize the intuitive hit or inspired idea.

It's that you DON'T TRUST IT.

Because so often it seems TOTALLY DISCONNECTED from where you're trying to create success.

"I want my first $100k month."

An hour later (and seemingly totally unrelated)...

"Take a picture of your backside in a bikini."

"Um. Ok." (Takes pic.) "I wonder if I should write a post about my current client and how she just 10x'd her sales. That's seems like a good way to attract my new $20k client and get me closer to my $100k month. What do you say? Good idea?"

Silence.

An hour later.

"Post that bikini pic in Great Goddesses of the Galactic FutureNow. You know. The huge group you're in where you've gotten a huge amount of your business."

"What?! No! I'm ten pounds heavier than I want to be. And besides I'll get kicked out. That's the stupidest thing I've ever heard. That must be my inner saboteur trying to fuck up my goal."

"Do it."

"No."

"Yes."

"Shut up."

"Do it now."

"What the fuck."

"I'm not your saboteur. I'm your intuition. Do it. You won't regret it. I promise."

"Jesus fucking Christ this is crazy. This is CRAZY. No. Ok fine."

So I posted the pic.

Which blew up the group and got everyone talking about me which made me visible to the leader.

"She's your $20k Client. Reach out to her."

"What? No. That's crazy. I've been in business 4 months. She's been in business 5 years. She's a millionaire. I've made like $80k. She's not my client. That's crazy."

"Do it."

"No."

"Yes."

"Jesus Christ. Fine."

I reached out to her and asked if she'd be willing to talk to me about what it's like to build a seven figure business. She agreed to talk.

"Ask her about her packages. How much they cost. How long they are. How many calls. How she provides support."

"That's so presumptuous."

"Shut up and do it."

What are your packages. How much do they cost. How long are they.

Whoa. She's seriously undercharging and overgiving. Like MAJORLY.

"See."

"Shut up."

"Tell her that. That she's way undercharging and overgiving."

"Ohmygod. I cannot. That's SO rude. She'll hang up on me."

"Do it."

I say it. All the things. Ask all the excruciatingly squirmy questions.

Aren't you exhausted?

Who's your sales coach? How is she ok with you charging this little?

Are you aware of how little you value your gift?

I can't believe I'm saying this.

She's embarrassed. She wants to hire me. I can tell.

"Tell her you want to work with her."

I want to work with you. What's it going to take.

90 minutes after I got on the phone with a complete stranger who was a millionaire and leader in the online coaching world, she paid me in full for my $20K coaching package.

THE MECHANICS OF INSPIRED ACTION

Knowing this will make it SO EASY to do what you're guided to do, even when it seems silly, irresponsible, or totally unrelated to getting what you want.

Like. This will ELIMINATE YOUR RESISTANCE to acting on your intuition. □□□□□

You'll do it WILLINGLY. EAGERLY. EASILY.

No analysis paralysis. No procrastination. No sabotage.

This one is blowing my mind.

On Monday I'm going to do a special livestream on the energetics for:

- exactly how inspired action magnetizes what we want

- WHY the specific actions we need to take are almost always NOT in the area we're trying to upgrade (For example, why you making a change in your relationship to your body, business, pricing, friend, lover, dreams, etc.—as long as it's based on intuitive guidance and inspired action—causes your ideal client to show up in your world "out of the blue "and instantly pay you top dollar for your services.), and

- why the instructions from your intuition must be followed exactly, (and why when my clients follow my instructions—and their intuition—they get such insane results), even though the actions they have to take may have nothing to do with the area in which they want the extreme results....Although sometimes it does. 󠀠♀󠀠😊

It all has to do with the way our code fields are linked through the synchronistic grid to the code field of what we're trying to magnetize.

Our patterns of consciousness (Code Fields) are directly linked to other patterns of consciousness, but not necessarily in a one-to-one relationship.

Your body codes may not be linked to your ideal client's body codes. (Which is why if you're a health coach, you could be in supreme health, but still not magnetize your ideal clients who also want supreme health. Even though it makes all the sense in the world that this is how it would work: You upgrade the system that your clients want to upgrade and then you magnetize those clients. Right? Nope. A lot of the times, as you well know, that's not how it works. ...And then sometimes it is. 󠀠♀󠀠😊 On Monday you will know the reason why. And it will make so much sense you'll be slapping your forehead.)

Your money codes may not be linked to their money codes (which is why if you're a money/business/sales coach, you could be exceptional at making money, but still not be able to pull in your most ideal clients. Or you may be making lots of money, but working with people who drive you crazy or bore you to tears. Or, making lots of money selling small little programs, when what you really want to do is make the same amount of money working with a few hot shot big time clients).

And, on the other hand, your code field might very well be linked in a one-to-one relationship to the things you're trying to magnetize to you.

Your conscious awareness isn't coded with the capacity to see these connections. And it never will be.

But there IS something within you that knows.

Your Gold Mind. Your Magician.

Otherwise known as your intuition.

Your Gold Mind is the energetic mechanism that knows EXACTLY what code fields in you link to and light up the code fields in the thing you're trying to magnetize, and the way it tells you how to become an energetic match to that code field is through your intuition: the nudge to take some specific action (often SEEMINGLY unrelated to the thing you're trying to magnetize).

In other words, your intuition knows that your body codes, for instance, are directly linked to your client's money codes. So it knows that unless and until you upgrade your consciousness with respect to how you treat your body, you will not activate or light up the code field of money in your ideal client that is ready to be upgraded by your transmissions, because right now they are both DEGRADED and operating in shadow.

Like DUDE.

Isn't that fucking awesome to realize?!?!?!?!

And because transformation only ever happens to a low frequency field by a HIGHER frequency field, your transmissions of transformational consciousness can only come through your UPGRADED code field (because upgrading a code field simply means transitioning that field from running shadow energy to running light energy, which is REQUIRED to upgrade your client's code field, which is still stuck in shadow).

And if your body codes are linked to your client's money codes, and yours are in a shadow state, then the frequency that connects the two fields will stay "greyed out" and unlit, and your client will not be energetically alerted to your existence.

(In Magic Man terms, the field you're wanting to upgrade by receiving higher level gifts from your Magic Man—in the form of higher-level clients and sales—will be energetically ugly to him, and he will not be inspired to activate the synchronistic grid connecting you to your ideal client, and will therefore not do what he do easily could, which is to simply tap your ideal client on the energetic shoulder through an intuitive hit or synchronistic event that would immediately put the two of you in touch in the 3D realm.)

The only reason you're not manifesting a new level in your life or business or wherever you desire it, is simply because you have not upgraded the code field within YOU that is linked to the code field within YOUR CLIENT or dream lover, friend, etc., that they are ready to have upgraded.

This is why no matter how much you can't see the connection between your action and the results you desire, you MUST take the inspired action, no matter how little sense it seems to make to be focusing on, for instance, your creative project when all you really want to be doing is making money. Or focusing on making money when all you want to be doing is improving your physical health. Or focusing on marketing when all you want to be doing is going on dates and trying to find the love of your life.

And the action you take must be PRECISELY the action you are intuitively guided to take WHEN you are guided to take it.

That is because upgrading code fields requires extreme precision. Codes are precisely tuned. Of our another way, frequencies are precisely coded.

When your intuition directs you to a very specific actions. This is also why my instructions are equally specific and why I tell my clients they must follow them EXACTLY.

And why, when they do they make magic.

"I said exactly what you told me to say and I closed a $3,000 deal!" (Tia Harrison Holmes)

Another client followed the GIST of my instructions and did a livestream on a similar topic to the one I told her to do, but not the exact one. She got maybe 100 views. Then I told her to do a live stream on the exact, specific topic, and she got 22,000 views.

Another did what I told her to do, and made $48,000 in 30 days, from Ground Zero in her business.

This is because your Gold Mind and I can see exactly where and how your code field is scrambled and we then instruct you to take a certain action that will directly and precisely confront that scrambled field with a certain combination of codes and frequencies that will unscramble it, release the trapped energy (power) and instantly upgrade the field.

This is why you CANNOT CHEAT ENERGY.

Einstein discovered that Time and Space are shaped by matter. (Matter literally curves space and bends Time.)

And what shapes matter?

Consciousness, which decides WHAT MATTERS, and in so doing, brings energy into form with certain degrees of power or powerlessness, based on the degree to which the deciding consciousness was in fact accurate about what matters.

Power matters. (Yes. True.)

Power lies in others. (No. Not true.)

We must not speak our crazy ideas because we will anger or offend others and they will exert their power over us.

This is a product of the shadow mind.

Time is a product of consciousness. We create Time. Time comes from us.

Shadow Minds decide the wrong things matter, based on a misguided understanding of where our power lies, and therefore codes matter (the body, the brain) with sickness, and with Time as the bully, as the slavemaster. This is what causes aging.

LIGHT CONSCIOUSNESS: THE ONE CONSCIOUSNESS. DARK CONSCIOUSNESS: UNIQUE CONSCIOUSNESS

Light Consciousness is the One Consciousness (tribal consciousness.

Dark Consciousness is unique. Utterly individuated. Crafted from your own Creative Will.

This is for anyone with a consciousness and who suffers and is looking for a way out.

What I am going to teach you is something that has never been taught — never even thought of — before now. That is because all development in human consciousness, in philosophy, myth, spirituality, psychology, sociology, metaphysics, theology, religion (my auto correct wanted that word to be "delusion" ha ha smart little auto correct), quantum mechanics and physics, chaos theory and new age spirituality has led us here. To this new point.

A point of utter stillness before the next Big Bang, the Quantum BOOM of consciousness creation, the death of the world Soul, the end of all suffering and source of struggle and the beginning of the Grand Unveiling, which is WHY we started coming here millions of years ago, and why I was asked to help design the Earth Experiment in the first place.

The contents of this book are coded with the frequency of this new chaos consciousness — the elite energetic that rests within your Dark DNA and is waiting to be activated and unleashed so it can unveil your superior functioning to you. So you can avail yourself of your Higher Mind, which operates far outside any existing framework, because its genius is to bring the utterly new in.

This is the first of three books.

Here I will tell the story "lightly."

I will introduce the characters of the new myth, interwoven with my own miraculous story of awakening from madness to spiritual millionaire in the span of one year and together this will create in you an unsettling and a longing for a new taste of the divine. This book is the voice sounding in the wilderness, *Make way*. It is the light appetizer before the Dark Feast of Imperial Joy.

Then comes the full story. The complete myth. Replete with a multiversal three ring circus, a blind biker gang, a caravan of unruly, superconscious beasts, and three little girls whose dreams are portals to each other.

Then, after the new archetypes of consciousness have been unleashed, the story told and the ground of being gathered and hushed, the third book will come into being as The Dark Speaks.

This is the Dark Trilogy.

A strange and unprecedented collection of spiritual philosophy, energetic technology, mythmaking and grand storytelling encoded to activate the springing forth of the new consciousness, the commencement of the Great Energetic Olympics and the opening of the Wild Black Tent under whose yawning hunger for the New we prepare to put on the Greatest Circus Show of energy, genius and magic mastery ever presented in the history of SpaceTime.

It all begins, as everything does, with a story

The Dark Heart of Gold

For most people, their brains are wired directly to their heart. Their actual heart.

For Disruptors, their brains Your brain is not wired to your body or your heart, or even to your energy body or heart chakra the way it is with almost everyone else.

Your brain is wired straight into your Dark Heart of Gold.

The way to work with Disruptors is opposite of normal people. Connect their wiring first from brain to dark heart of gold and THEN back to their body, Because the dark heart of gold is the replete compass. Their native GPS.

When THIS is activated (which happens simply by the mentor seeing and therefore validating it which allows the client the opportunity to SEE it which is easy for them because they naturally SEE IN THE DARK) because this is such a potent compass and GPS and is the source of spiritual intelligence or TRUTH, it can provide guidance that is CERTAIN, rather than guidance from the intuition only, which is sourced from the spongey, leaky, moist shadow heart.

It's spiritual intelligence.   Remember when i was asking what faculty of knowing the dark heart of gold has that is an analog to the heart having the faculty of intuition?   It's spiritual intelligence. TRUTH.   And OMFG. Intuition is still murky and "inconsistent" because it's being run by the spongey leaky shadow heart!!   Spiritual intelligence is clear and razor sharp because it's being run by the cold vacuum of the dark heart of gold.   So then my question is how does the dark heart of gold inform the shadow heart with the TRUTH?   And the other equally important question, which is really the same just worded differently and from the other dimension, which is what I call the Sacred Quandary: How do we know when our fear is masquerading as intuition.

Yep. It is. I'm writing a totally new first chapter. It doesn't talk about the fem and masculine yet — but it will. It's all connected.   This book is for spiritual brainiacs who are in fact Disruptors (dark workers) and who are suffering and whose businesses are stuck because they don't know how to operate their own system of genius and power. It's wired completely differently than almost everyone else's on the planet. So differently that no one knows how to help them. Which is why all the coaches and programs don't work for them and why the therapists and psychologists ALSO can't help them. And why no one understands them.
These people have brains who are wired into a totally new energetic body (the dark body) that works completely differently than bodies who are wired to the light body and the light grid. This is all about systems and processes and tools and they hate those.   They just need an understanding of how to work with the fundamentals framework of the universe — the two energies — and they'll create their OWN system. And they need to know they're not broken or hopeless.   The Dark/Light stuff will come later. First my job is to get them to see i get their very real problems and to give them a completely new framework (the one I give in the livestreams) because all they need is access to the RAW MATERIAL of the universe and to be shown how to work with it and they're golden. And then they go make lots of money ☐

OOMMGGG   The feminine and masculine have been creating this new dark body energetically and now it is ready to be received by our bodies and consciousnesses.   It is the body that will channel our personal genius and PURE INDIVIDUATION. And that is what 2012 was about. The end of collective consciousness. It was also the END OF INTEGRATION.

But the new dark body/genius works with RAW MATERIAL ONLY.   And THIS is why people must know about the fem and masc, because those are the two fundamental energies that work with the raw material of consciousness.

his book is really about the energetic anatomy of Disruptors. It is a sneaky bomb from the Dark tucked inside a spiritual business book.

Energy Alchemy of the sub archetypes happens when you invite them in to the cauldron that is the dark heart of gold and apply the darklight beam of the RADICAL TRUTH. This is what a truth rant is. And the only way they enter the dark heart of gold is to SUBMIT to the radical truth they will be told.

nd just remember Jenny, there are and never were any victims. The feminine CHOSE to be demonized. It is her special brand of genius to go under. Go invisible. Be dismissed. Misunderstood. To go DARK. There is a very beautiful, poignant and profound reason for why she did this. The feminine is not and never was a victim. You are going through such an amazing journey. I am honored to be witnessing and holding the space for it. And I'm amazed at your strength and dedication to the truth. As you craft your message and mission, be mindful that there is no victim energy in it. No desire or need to save. And this does mean no desire to seek justice. Justice is something a child seeks. To restore the world to being fair.

The world is not fair in the way a child can conceive. It is equal. But also not in the way a child, totally divorced from her sense of omnipotence, can imagine. The desire for justice and fairness comes from the child and from the victim, who arrange their lives around what was done to them or to their kind and to seeking fairness and recognition for their pain. Deeper than the drive for justice or saving is the drive to FREE others from the prison of their self inflicted illusions, which are the only things keeping them in pain. So I encourage you to submit the fullness of your message and mission to the shadow alchemy tool. Shoot all of it straight into your dark heart of gold so that every ounce of shadow can be alchemize into pure potent truthtelling. Because, while almost everything we've been taught is full of illusion, there is one thing that is unequivocally energetically accurate and that is this: The Truth will set you free.

THE DARK SECRET

Humans create art to experience the feminine. It is the only place on the light grid where the pure feminine is expressed. (Even in sex, or sexual energy, the masculine energy is present.) The feminine is inherently worthless and priceless. That is why women have such issues with anxiety and self esteem. We are the embodiment of the worthlessness and the pricelessness of the feminine. Which doesn't FIT anywhere, really. Which carries the monstrous within. The Dark codes of disorientation and magic. When we talk about the feminine rising, what we are in fact talking about is humans — and really basically women — confessing to themselves that they are, indeed, worthless because they are priceless. The feminist movement went far astray when it tried to prove the WORTH and USEFULNESS of the feminine. That's simply applying masculine principles to the feminine. Hello ☐♀☐☐ that's not progress at all. The masculine is where worth is stored, expressed and used. It is the energy of providing, doing and delivering useful outcomes. It is the linking energy. The word of continuity. The feminine is where worth is MADE UP (we are very good at make-up). It is the energy of madness and genius. Of the ability to unhook and begin from nothing. It is the un-linking energy. The word of death. The feminine is worthless on the light grid precisely *because* it is priceless. Art is the only useless and priceless experience on the light grid. It exists alone. Far from reach. And yet our most intimate prize. Just like women. And the feminine. Time for women to admit it: They're useless worthless works of art.

Lorna - I'm wanting to get defensive and talk about all the other investments I've made in myself over the past 2 years, totaling over $65,000 at this point. I know what it's like to invest in myself. I know what it's like to place my whole fucking life on the dotted line (over and over again) And I'm tired of that too. I'm seeing and meeting a different version of myself, one that doesn't know how to hang because she's not spent much time socializing Like a mama wolf, protecting her new cub, I'm not going to throw this baby self out into the world (or into another program, even if it's yours) until that I know . . .   That it's safe.   (And I get that we create the safety)   So . . . I'm still feeling and sensing   As I let my old habits fall away.   But I don't think that means that I have to scrape by in this process.   I expect to be well-compensated as I move through this   Because I know what I have to give   And i'm not even warmed up yet.   Will I invest more in the future - yes.   And that's why I'm here.   To get warmed up (with you, in this new-for-me way) so I can take on the whole mother-loving court ♥□

I invested twice that. Three times probably. Without complaint or checking my progress and demanding I get some results before I invest more, and again and more again. Because I am committed to my greatest legacy no. Matter. What. It is my first and greatest love and it get WHATEVER it requires to be unleashed onto the world stage. I hold nothing back. I make no demands on it. I am it's steward and its blind disciple. And because O know it it this blind discipleship that is the source of its success and my magic and complete power.   I don't not burden my legacy with concerns of safety. I am god. I decide that my legacy and I are always safe. No matter what. And this frees me to invest at grotesquely high levels because my legacy has extremely high requirements and desires. She is the most expensive date in the universe. She is, in fact, priceless.   And I treat her so.   And as a result, she released her priceless genius to me in the form of total euphoria and financial success.   That's how it goes. It's the laws of energy.   You can balk at them all you want, but they are unbending and do not concerned themselves with the smallness of fear.

Manifesto of the Dark Disruptors, TruthCarriers and Spiritual Iconoclasts

It's time we told the truth.

We are not broken. We're here to *break*.

Break free. Break others out. Break through.

Failing at almost every system or structure doesn't mean there's something wrong with us. It means we're the ones who are meant to *cause the system to fail.*

We're here to *shatter* paradigms, not master them.

It's time we turn the tables on a host of misperceptions, illusions about our nature, and claim what we know to be true.

Some say we're harsh and abrasive and that we need to soften our very guarded hearts. Cold and closed-hearted, they say. And what troublemakers. Selfish, nearly narcissistic, insubordinate inordinate rebels.

We say no. our hearts are not closed guarded hard or cold. They do not need to be opened or softer or warmed in the cultural oven. We have a wildly open dark heart of gold and *disruption is the way we love*.

We do not swing knives, spark chaos or unleash the beasts of genius because we *don't* care. Quite the contrary—because YES, we are contrarians—. We do it with great passion and precision and in service of what has undeniably been *called in*.

And Crazy? Unwell? Unhinged?

We say we've *gone sane,* and yes that last slur is absolutely true. We're unhinged, baby. Unhooked from the hot grasp of the grid. The gasps when we "disobey." Go our own way.

What they don't realize is that they're *longing* for this.

It's what they called us in to violently arrange. The way winter arranges for violets

We are not brilliant but broken.

Genius but jinxed.

We're bringers of a disruptive dis-ordered consciousness—one they think they didn't order, but did definitely request, and which will not be ordered around by anyone— and we will no longer squeeze our unruly genius into a system built to order and arranged with everything it's got *against* the chaos that is our nature.

We are not devils.

Or even angels.

We are the Other, the Unknown, the ones who live their lives outrageously UnDone.

We are vessels of the Great Disruption, which is gathering itself around us like a graceful cyclone.

We are like knives, yes. The knife of a surgeon, a sculptor, a chef.

And we're in their brains, chiseling away at their brave bodies or thought and flaying illusion in the very place they cook up their imprisonment because *we love them*. And because we are here to craft the world into a work of art.

To put an end to the constant self reflection, healing and spiritual seeking and point the way *through the mirror* because the world does not need to endlessly reflect us.

It can be, if we choose, a portal of our own making.

And that is why we refuse to operate inside any paradigm.

It's not that we *can't*, as if we're crippled.

It's that we *won't*.

It's a matter of *supreme integrity* that we *don't*.

This unwillingness to co-operate— to *operate within* — is the sharp point of our genius and we are not ashamed or afraid of it.

We will not slouch through the portal of our greatness or dull our power.

We will instead place the razor's edge of our dark and priceless gift against the heart of all that matters and then….?

With just the right amount of pressure, and in the name of love, slice open the soft flesh of fear with keen precision.

Because the *true* truth is this:

The dark heart of gold beckons in every one of us, longing to be let through. To Shine it's blacklight of brilliance straight into our throats from the other side of the mirror so we can finally step through.

We are not misfits unfit for this life. We are here to fit the point of our finely tuned knife into the heart in our *own throats first,* open our third eye, press the point in until it breaks through and then throw our heads back, laugh with abandon, and speak the motherfucking truth.

Magic Is Natural

Let's talk cause and effect.

Clearly, they do not occur within the same paradigm of power, otherwise the cause would not have the ability to change the state of the entity on which it acts.

The natural world is not the domain of its own causation. In other words, And until now we have been operating ignorantly within the paradigm of the powerless—that which receives commands and obeys them: the 3D world of matter—and not in i paradigm of the powerful—the energetic realm, the SuperConscious field where Time and Space are one and in which the commands of being and matter are fashioned.

We have been foolishly trying to place our hands on the levers of power while groping in the shadowlands of the imprisoned

Whatever is, we have crafted from energy. (This is not new knowledge, of course.) The struggle comes when what is, is not what we desire. And when what is *not yet* (what is energy coming into matter) is taking too long for our liking.

Then, we do not call it magic, but hustle and grind.

The difference between the two is simply one of leverage.

When we place our hands knowingly on the raw material of the universe, we activate energetic law, the law of cause and effect, and with the least effort, produce the greatest and swiftest result. Thus we create magic on demand.

When we place our hands unwittingly on these powerful leavers, we also create magic, and yet cannot reproduce it at will because we simply tumbled onto them, and have no real training or mastery in navigating the land of power in which they exist.

This is unnecessary.

Ultimate Power—the clear-eyed command of cause and effect, of calling into being exactly what we desire, exactly when we desire it, and not just material objects but people and opportunities, spiritual, intellectual and emotional states of being, intuitive and psychic knowledge and gifts, anything we could wish or imagine, and much more beyond—is simply the ability to operate all expressions of Time and Space—the fundamental building blocks of matter and 3D experience—with supreme mastery.

Time and Space have two masters.

The masculine and the feminine.

And they are at our disposal.

#

The Magical Masculine

Much is spoken of about the divine feminine in the role of spiritual awakening, manifestation and the evolution of consciousness. On my own journey, I encountered the term "Feminine Rising" hundreds of times, if I encountered it once.

It was the spiritual equivalent of the feminist movement in the material world: Time to honor the feminine *energy*, women said, not just actual women.

And so the Heroine's Journey was born, to counter in equal worth the Hero's Journey. It was "born" in the sense that it was honored intentionally. The Heroine's Journey has been around for ages, depicted in many myths, though still completely misunderstood. And it is this misunderstanding that has caused the weakness of the journey to complete awakening to be exposed.

At first we believed the Hero's Journey was the answer to our suffering: Strike out from your tribe of origin, follow your own path, discover your strength to overcome all obstacles between you and the treasure you seek (self awareness, purpose and empowerment), kill your inner monsters, integrate your warring inner factions—which means repair your separation from Source (which is put forth as the cause of all suffering), become One With All (the One being presented as the Source of wisdom, Truth, power and wellbeing, and therefore the only way to access these states is to become one with the source of them), and then return to the tribe as a new being full of purpose, ready to teach others what you've learned and encourage them to strike out on their own path.

This is a masculine (Hero's) journey because it embodies, expresses and requires the seeker to call on and use masculine traits in order to complete it.

Fighting and overcoming.

Overpowering and striking out.

Going it alone.

Depending on no one.

Driving to clear outcomes (I want to know and discover myself and the answers to life).

Gathering and amassing treasures as a result of winning the war (treasures of knowledge, awareness, self mastery).

Definition and clarity. (I am this and not that. My happiness is not a product of my tribe. It is a product of my own creation.)

We are all called to go on the Hero's Journey. Some of us answer the call. Others do not. Those who do not, remain children in adult bodies, never having separated themselves from their family and culture of origin. Living according to the values and dreams of their personal collective (family, tribe, culture of upbringing). These are humans who are entirely asleep. Deaf and dumb and mute. Unrealized expressions of consciousness and power. The Late Adopters of Awakening. They will be the last to rise and the first to fight others who rise before them. First to judge, blame, criticize, demean, disdain, dismiss. And also often, to *diagnose*. To see awakening and all its signs as symptoms of sickness, aberration requiring correction quickly and completely. They are the most afraid, least powerful and often most ignorant of their own state. These are the culture keepers. The standard bearers of the opposing side. And whenever they sense a mutiny against the tried and true, they are the first to sound the battle cry of the status quo. Their position is rigid (their battle lines are drawn dead straight and clear). Their righteousness is unquestionable. They are the ones who claim Authority. And if you are intent on waking up, you are guaranteed to encounter them on the journey.

In fact, they are important gatekeepers whose ability to cast fear into your heart reveals to you your own position in the tribe: a dreamer with no actual intention of awakening, a doer who strikes out no matter what, or, the last (or first) group - a creator, who does not ever intend to play the game or win the battle according to any of the rules or lines drawn around the constraints of consciousness.

The doers are the ones who are half awake. They have accomplished the Hero's Journey and are now stuck in an endless loop on the Heroine's Journey, dismantling what they can no longer grasp, spinning and cycling through the spiral of despair of exhausting spiritual seeking they call shadow work.

And why am I taking you along this path when you thought this was a book about manifestation?

Because manifestation *on demand* and *at will* is a skill of a god. It is a power mastered by someone who has unzipped from the human psyche completely, who has left *all* the tribal paradigms behind — family, cultural, spiritual, and the human consciousness itself — and has crafted for herself a new psyche entirely, based on energetic and spiritual law, capable of clearly handling the raw martial of the universe and mastering the orchestration of the feminine and masculine energies, which are required for any creation to be made manifest.

And so you must know about the journey of consciousness. We must walk the path from powerlessness to power, so you can identify where you are on the journey to being able to make magic on demand in your life and business, see clearly the obstacles that were once (are right now) invisible to you, and be taught by a master how to overcome them in such a way that they *disappear from your psyche altogether*.

This is accomplished through a new energetic technology called Shadow Alchemy, in which you complete the Heroine's Journey for good and step into the Anti-Hero's Journey, which is less a journey and more a new Domain of Being in which you craft your own consciousness from the ground of purely individuated being (as any god does) and in so doing access true power, the root of real magic and the ability to manifest on demand.

And the answer lies not in more and deeper activation and honoring of the feminine but in a first-ever-in-human-consciousness, deep, authentic, and full-system understanding and appreciation of the magical masculine.

This will, in turn, open up an accurate understanding and appreciation of the true feminine, because contrary to the good intentions of feminists and New Age spiritual seekers, the feminine has not been honored, activated or properly understood in either of these movements.

What opens the feminine (to our understanding of her, to her own power, to her genius and gifts) is the masculine, for this is his primary role: to serve the awakening and the awakened feminine.

And yet because human consciousness does not understand the masculine and often misinterprets its expression, we miss the greatest gift we are being offered and head down the path of suffering, all the while believing in our hearts we are striking out on the path to awakening.

#

The Two Problems

First, there is the problem of understanding.

Then, there is the problem of mastery.

Understanding creates willingness. Willingness creates mastery.

So first we must discover the ignorance that is hidden from view. And when we do, our natural willingness to take action, to accept certain decisions that would before have been unthinkable, becomes second nature.

This is how we develop supreme mastery over the Light Grid, which is where we operate and live out our experience.

The Light Grid is the assemblage of energetic frequencies that have been selected by the collective human consciousness to operate as our shared system of power. It provides us access, through certain channels with specific gates of passage, to the raw materials of the universe, available for our handling. In other words, the Light holds our power. And we hold the Light.

And we can either handle or mishandle it.

If we mishandle it, we create blocks in our mental field and our mind is in shadow, no longer inspired, bereft of our best ideas, no longer infused with sudden and perfect knowing of exactly what to do, when, and how. We are left agonizing in analysis paralysis, self-doubt, seeking endlessly outside ourselves for the answers. Our mind, wired for total, instant, and perfect knowing, the intuitive and psychic channel, the channel of knowledge and intelligence — human and divine, the portal to insight, either flawed or perfect, becomes crippled and unstable, tortured and tortuous, an instrument of hell rather than a gateway to heaven.

If we mishandle the Light, we also create blocks in our emotional field and our heart is cast in shadow, no longer able to distinguish what it truly desires from what it "should" desire; full of disloyalty to itself, seeking approval and acceptance from every other channel but its own, terrifyingly willing to abandon itself at the first sign of danger, of being cast out; searching for a sense of worth, divorced from its innate ability to shine its fine eye of love and worthiness on the truly wondrous, the awe-inspiring, and pour itself into the clearest expressions of its nature that cause it to skip a beat and take breaths away. The heart, the portal to all stories that transform and uplift, the gateway to priceless self adoration and the channel through which the glory of life flows, becomes a shadowy, empty husk, weak, without access to the rhythm of life.

And, if we mishandle the Light, we create blocks in our physical field, our bodies, and all physical expressions that share the symbolic map of "body." All collections and expressions of boundary, what delimits one entity from another, falter and fail dramatically and in one crisis after another. Relationships collapse. Finances tumble. Careers fail. Homes are lost or damaged.

Cars are wrecked or plundered. We become physically sick, weak, without energy, often in ways that confound traditional medicine. There's "no reason" for our illness, because the reason is energetic: We are wired to source and run power through all our systems from the Light, and when we mishandle it, it cannot flow and we are left to run on its weaker expression as shadow.

And last, when we mishandle the Light, we create blocks in our spiritual field. Our vision for our life, our sense of self, our identity, and our ability to dream weakens into wistfulness, faint hope, wishful thinking and the fantasies of the child who has no agency to make her dreams come true. We lose access to our spirit, to the animating decree that causes the kingdom within us to rise up and hear our true desire, heed our visionary command, stand for our wildest dreams, call on perfect, divine intelligence, and therefore collapse time, lift out of the 3D frame that has become our prison and spring forth over it reimagined as our playground, over which we have ultimate control, and thus make the mundane magical in no time.

All we need to know is when and exactly how we mishandle the Light, and then what to do about it.

That is this book.

The first of its kind, which explains the laws of Light—the Divine Masculine—and the energetics for how to access power on the Light Grid and so to activate magic and to manifest on demand.

For Light is deeply misunderstood here. And if we are to operate the Source of Power with mastery and so to be *in* our full power, we must first understand how Light operates, what its channels of power are, how it falls into shadow, and most importantly, how it sounds.

#

Understanding The Light: The Sound Of Power

The Law of Attraction is more accurately spoken of as the Law of *Inspiration*, for what you are attracting into your experience are the gifts born by the divine masculine, whom I call the Magic Man. Whether it is a house, money, a published book, a new job, a lover, a dream vacation, or even immaterial gifts such as a peaceful state of mind, inspiration that turns into a business, or a brilliant piece of marketing copy, whatever comes into your experience—whatever you are trying to attract using LOA and the principles of manifestation—is being brought to the doorstep of your experience by the Divine Provider, the magical masculine energy of the universe. And if you are trying to attract him and his gifts, then you must be *attractive to him*. It is *his* energy you must know how to work with.

In other words, it is his energy you must know how to *inspire*.

It is his energy that works behind the scenes, activating the Synchronistic Grid where everything you desire already Is. It is he who gets busy "shaking hands" with all the other Magic Men who attend and serve all the other people who will bring you all the opportunities you seek, energetically lining all of you up to activate each other, like an infinite labyrinth of dominoes.

Your ideal client, who brings your cash and your million dollar year, the man you will marry, the agent at the publishing company who will make your book a best seller, the realtor who has your dream home—all of them have their own Magic Man, their own ability to activate and inspire the magical masculine energy to provide for *them* and *their* greatest desire, which meeting *you*—their ideal mentor, life partner, writer, or client—will do.

And the masculine has rules for what inspires him to great action, and what causes him to turn away, disinterested.

The Codes of Desire: Shadow vs Light (The Energetics of Inspiration)

What you desire is coded with certain grades of power. Shadow is weakened Light, therefore shadow desire is coded with only weak power to inspire and attract the Magic Man, who is Light Itself.

You are the creator of the blueprint of your desire. You select it with the tones of your consciousness. The degree to which those tones are built with shadow versus Light codes (unconscious mishandling versus conscious handling of Truth) is the degree to which your desire will be either weak or powerful and your blueprint structured to build a container that is either powerfully magnetic (activating the feminine power to attract), which creates an ineluctable and inevitable electrical current around it (activating the masculine power to gather around the feminine for support and provision) or a weak container that is a nearly powerless magnetic field, one that creates a tiny current of electricity and only inspires a modicum of the full potency of the magical masculine.

The Magic Man builds your order the way a carpenter builds a house, by looking carefully at the blueprint of your desire and knowing every piece by heart.

In other words, to experience what you desire, your desire must be "built to code," or rather "coded to be built."

Shadow codes indicate a weakness in the structure of our desire. They create a weak blueprint and therefore a weak container. A weak container has weak magnetic strength, weak ability to inspire the magic man, and weak ability to hold whatever is received into it.

Light codes, however, vibrate with an insistence and a radiance the Magic Man literally cannot resist. The masculine is coded to turn toward the feminine in her power. It is energetic law.

Light codes indicate power in the structure of our desire. They create a strong blueprint and therefore a strong container, strong ability to inspire the magic man and strong ability to hold what is received.

The magic man is turned on by the presence of desire built on the truth of who we are, which means the truth of our power—where it lies and how we access, activate and grow it.

Just like a woman who knows who and what she truly is inspires the highest frequency man to be profoundly and irresistibly attracted to her, so too a human who knows who and what *she* truly is and what *she* is truly made of, inspires the full potency of the magical masculine energy and creates and lives a life full of miracles and knows magic is her natural state.

And so to talk of making magic means first we must talk of our true and our false nature.

We Are Made Entirely of Light

You are not entitled to the object of your desire just because you desire it greatly. This is one of the great flaws in the way LOA is taught.

Desire, ask, be open to receive, and ye shall indeed receive.

Except the world is littered with those who have desired, asked, been open, and received nothing resembling what they requested.

At least not consciously.

For this is one of the fatal flaws in the teachings of manifestation and Law of Attraction.

They cannot and do not treat of the *subconscious desire*. And the subconscious is what the Magic Man heeds and is drawn to, like a moth to flame.

If there is content in your subconscious, he will hear it, though you will not.

The magical masculine is built to see in the dark, to draw out from its depths our greatest gifts. It is what activates his Heroic Nature; it is the void he seeks to fill. And yet if there is content already there, if the container of our desire is full of shadow and built with shadow, he turns away.

Build your desire on the truth, and you will make magic on demand. Fill your energetic container with the truth of who you are, live every moment of your life in the vibration of that Truth, and the magical masculine has "no choice" but to obey your every command.

Shadow is energetically repulsive to the divine masculine. Just like any high frequency man who does not put up with the crisis and drama of a princess, so too the divine masculine is energetically *turned off* by the presence of shadow.

#

The Precise Science of Manifestation

There's only ever one precise action that leads to your next shift — your next client, sale, speaking gig, lover, dream house, you name it. And WHAT that action is, is not a mystery. At least not to your Magic Man, the Google of the Universe, your straight line to precise and TOTALLY trustworthy guidance.

Intuitive knowing is NOT an art. It is a science.

And so is magic (which is simply the precise application of energetic law).

This is why a new client of mine had two people DM her saying they had to work with her (which "doesn't happen to her") after she did a livestream on a very specific topic but HERE'S THE THING.

It's not the TOPIC that mattered. Or matters.

She could have spoken Swahili (which I have a feeling those two prospects don't speak) and gotten the same result.

AND, she could have spoken as eloquently and convincingly as Martin Luther King on the hottest topic around...and NOT gotten that result.

Because what we still struggle to understand — because it makes absolutely NO sense to our human — is WHAT is actually the cause of WHAT down here in 3D land. I mean, if it was as easy as "push that button, get a client," or "flip this switch, find your dream date," who wouldn't do it?

Isn't that what we're all looking for?! The ultimate guide book to every decision ever?

Some all-knowing entity with access to the Entire Storehouse of Knowledge, who also is paying close and specific attention to little 'ol us, who can just sit there and drop into our mind at precisely the right moment exactly what we need to do or say to get exactly what we want as quickly and easily as possible?

Wouldn't that be AWESOME??

It would. It would be super awesome.

The tragedy (if there were such a thing, which there isn't since there are no stakes and this is all a game), is that there IS. We just have no fucking clue what that Entire Storehouse of Knowledge Who Is Also Paying Precise Attention To Us SOUNDS like.

In fact it's even more tragic than not knowing what the Entire Storehouse of Knowledge Who Is Also Paying Precise Attention To Us sounds like.

The true (nonexistent) tragedy is this: Most of the time when we hear it, we laugh. And not as in an "Oh my, that's so delightful. I'm filled with mirth." kind of laugh. No, it's really more like "Ha! Freak. What IDIOT just whispered a whole bunch of ridiculous nonsense in my ear Jesus Christ. Somebody come get this guy outta here." kind of laugh.

It's because she clipped one specific dis-chord in HER OWN field, one that was keeping her in opposition to her power, that automatically caused the result she desired.

#

The Pillars of the Masculine

Time

Money

#

The Magic Man Tool

Transcript from the now-famous channeled livestream…

>> The masculine and feminine energies and how to use them to active magic in your life.

>> The consistent thing that I do that creates crazy results in my clients and in my life.

>> The reason why my clients make so much money in so little time

>> What a Quantum Leap is and how to activate one over and over…and so shift into Quantum *flight*, which is expansion without contractor or the need for grounding

I'm going to teach you is this tool to upgrade your intentional connection to and activation of your masculine, your provider, your Magic Man.

But before we do that I have to help you shift into what I call your High Feminine, the one who has exacting standards and supreme integrity. The one who makes the requests and the demands…not aggressive demands, but very lovely, graceful, queenly demands of the magic man. She is the one who knows what they really are and what they need to be. And then of course your shadow mind comes in and says, "But that's not possible. But that's ridiculous. But how are we going to do that?" And that's where we get into trouble.

Yes, what we're up against right now is the what, the how, and the when. What you're basically saying is, "How am I going to do this? How is it going to happen? How is it going to happen without me burning myself out? Can it really happen by that time? I don't really know how to do that? Is that really reasonable?"

What I want you to understand is *whose job is what*. Your High Feminine is responsible for the what. That is her job and nobody else's. Your masculine, your magic man cannot and does not have any say at all about the what. And the what comes from your exacting standards for what you desire and require, and from your supreme integrity in implementing those standards. That's it. Supreme Integrity is the Will of the feminine.

The content—the what—is the standard, and the will—the commitment to those standards—is the supreme integrity.

"But I don't know what I want," some will say.

Well, where is there dissonance in your life? That's how you know what you want. The dissonance is essentially the frequency mismatch between your exacting standards and what you've allowed. Between your exacting standards and your supreme integrity

You could also find it by what you're jealous of other people for.

I develop tools for what I have challenges with. That's how it all works. I don't really have a problem with my high feminine. I know what I want.

Most people tend to have a problem with putting their high feminine to the task of getting it done, and then it's burn out, worry, frustration, anxiety, fear, and misery, which is why I've developed this tool to activate the magic man because there is this whole other energy system we are meant to tap into that allows us to fulfill all our desires and requirements with ease.

The piece that's been missing is the provider energy, the thing that brings you what you want, and that is the masculine. And when you really understand how to work with it, when you can personify the energy, it works much better, it makes more sense, and you can work with it, because this truly is a relationship with an energetic consciousness.

This is why Law of Attraction doesn't work for a lot of people. It remains a theory and a concept, and doesn't become a relationship. Something they can feel and work with. It's all just, "Okay, now I'm supposed to do my gratitude. Now I'm supposed to want what I want." it just doesn't help.

The high feminine is responsible for the what, the experiential how, and the overall when: "What do I want, when do I want it and what do I want to experience as it comies into my reality?" It's very prescriptive and full of decrees, like the Queen. It's like, "Here is the decree of the kingdom."

I want to teach you a few key learnings that will change your life and your business overnight, and where we will start is with an explanation using money, but you can use this for anything. You can use this for love, you can use this whatever you want, it doesn't matter. I'm going to use money because that's what I teach my clients how to do and that's what I focus a lot of my efforts on.

The masculine is the provider energy. The feminine is the receiver. There's a piece that a lot of you are missing in your work on manifestation and it stems from a misunderstanding of the masculine and therefore a mistreatment of your feminine.

This is something I see in every single one of my clients and it's called worry and anxiety. I'm going to teach you and give you the methodology for how to create quantum leaps in your life.

I am going to be using the male and sometimes the male biology and how it works to help you understand your relationship to money and get whatever you want, when you want it. It's not just your relationship to money, it's your relationship to time as well. If you go and you start to understand men, like actual men and how they work and what inspires them, what turns them on, and what doesn't turn them on, what turns them off, what does not inspire them, if you just simply translate that to the masculine, you will have all your answers if you're struggling.

When you ask, "Why is this not working? Why is my income up and down and up and down?" It's because you are in an upside down relationship to your own masculine and you will discover when you really think about it how am I treating my own masculine that what you're doing would turn any guy off and make him not want to provide for you, okay. It's powerful when my clients make this connect this dot, they're like, "Holy shit, this is fucking amazing."

Plus, I am a visual metaphor kind of person. If you give me a visual metaphor for something I'm like I get it, it's just so obvious to me and I don't really have to think about it. It doesn't remain theory anymore, it's something I can practically apply and I'm all about practical application in your life. I don't want this just to remain theory, okay. I'm not going to go into all the aspects of the masculine but one of the most important ones is that the masculine is the provider which means anything you were lacking in life and of course there's no such thing as lack.

Anything you desire that's not in your experience, the masculine is responsible for providing you. That's the masculine energy to get to work and bring something into your experience. The feminine obviously is the receiver. This is the stuff that everybody knows, but there's a problem that most people have. I'm not referring to the receiving problem which most people think they have and most women do. I'm not referring to that.

What I'm referring to is the standards problem because the entire orchestration of this high frequency masculine energy coming into your life like fucking injection after injection after injection, okay, begins with your feminine. What I call your high feminine, okay. Your high feminine, so I don't know if you are familiar with my other work where I talk about the swampy feminine and the bully masculine and the brittle feminine and the something masculine, I can't remember what it is.

Those are your shadow aspects of your feminine, your high feminine is what people call your queen, or your goddess energy and I call it your high feminine. To me, there's just I don't know, the queen goddess thing is to me is the old energy it's not … It doesn't do anything for me but it's the same thing. Your high feminine must be standing at all times into specific states of being in order for any of this stuff to work. Okay, so that's where I'm going to begin and also this is where it collapses like completely collapses.

Because your high feminine, just stay with me here because I'm going to be building this a little bit overtime so I may not making a lot of sense for a minute but stay with me. Your high feminine is responsible for building the container into which the masculine is going to inject all his goodness, okay. The quality of the container determines its magnetism. It literally determines how magnetic that field that exist within the container becomes, okay.

A highly magnetic container which is magnetic is the feminine, guess what that does? It automatically creates an electric current around it. Electricity cannot deny magnetic magnetism, it's like they are literally energetically linked, it's like one creates the other, okay. What is happening and what needs to happen always for any of this to work and be activated is that you must be in your high feminine so that you can be creating an energetic container that is magnetic, irresistibly attractive to and that calls to the Magic Man, the high masculine, the divine masculine.

All you got to do is setup the container. It's like build it and they will come, actually it is exactly like that, okay. You setup the container, meaning so LOA is going to make a lot of sense for people in a totally different way and probably blow their minds and be like, "Holy shit, that's why that works." Okay, this is the energetics of manifestation, it's really what I'm teaching you. All you do is you have to all these means in terms of creating the most magnetic container is that you are setting the parameters, you're establishing the boundaries and this is the first state of being that you must be in, in being in your feminine and that is your exacting standards, your exacting standards.

The high feminine has very high, very exact standards. This is not a brittle place, this isn't like a, "Fuck you." This isn't an icy kind of setting standards, it's just very exact. There is a tone, there is literally a tone that she is constantly pulsing at and constantly measuring the tone of your actual boundaries, the ones that you are expressing and managing in your own life. There's this tone and then you're managing according either according to that tone or against that tone because it's really fucking hard and scary sometimes to keep this tone.

The dissonance between the two, the dissonance between your high feminine and that tone of exacting standards and how you're actually showing up in your life and establishing boundaries and holding people to your standards and holding yourself to your standards is the dissonance that you feel in your life. It is the feeling that things are it's what causes struggle, it's what create struggle and strive, worry, anxiety, fear, low self-esteem, doubt, self-criticism, judgments, all of that stuff because there is just a natural dissonance.

Of course, every one of our high feminines holds an extremely high exacting standard tone. That's her job is to stand there energetically and just hold that tone. Some of us are managing our lives in really nowhere near that tone, okay, this was me for many years. Nowhere near that tone. This, the severity of the dissonance Is what can then cause physical and mental illness, extreme financial strive. Bankruptcy, okay extreme relationship issues, okay. As you come closer, as you raise the frequency of your own physical expression up to that energetic one, your life starts to feel like it slow.

When people talk about, "My life is flow, and it's just blessed, and I'm just charmed," like that's what's happening. What's happening is that they are running and managing their actual lives and boundaries and standards according to that exacting tone, okay. I want to make sure that that make sense. The first thing that you must do is understand what the high feminine is and understand what the high feminine does, and why it's so important. Why I'm trying to tell you is those exacting standards are the high, they create when you actually implement them in your life.

Goodbye, I love you too. When you actually implement them in your life what happens is that you create a very powerful, strong, energetic container. You create a vacuum is what you do, okay, like a magnetic vacuum. The boundaries that you hold in your life according to those exacting standards create an airtight container like nothing is getting out. When once something gets in, it can build. Think of a furnace, right. Think of an incinerator, think of a quadrant, give a forge, think of something like that. That's what you're building energetically.

The degree to which you do not live your life according to the statics those exacting standards is the degree to which your container is flimsy and will break is not attractive to the masculine and the Magic Man, so it's not going to cause an influx of amazingness in your life at all and you're going to find that you're struggling and frustrated a lot. It's also going to cut, this is why you have leaps in your business, right? You could organize and arrange things so that there's an element of integrity to your container so this is the second piece.

It's so-called supreme integrity, remember I said the high feminine has two states of being she must hold, supreme integrity is the second one. Literally, all that … Think about it, it means keeping the energetic integrity of the container intact and not letting cools in, right. It's exactly what it is. The degree to which you are lazy in building your energetic, physical, emotional relationship financial container in alignment with that those exacting standards is the degree to which you are living in supreme integrity or not.

It's literally just, "Are you energetically, do you energetically have a strong container or do you have a leaky container?" If you have a leaky container, you're going to have high months and then low months. The high month and then a low month, couple of high months and then nothing. Your marketing will work and then it won't work. You'll get into an amazing relationship and then it will get fucked up. You'll get a client and then no goes on you, right. You get discovery cards but then if cards calls but then nobody shows up. You close a big deal but then they don't pay.

This is a common occurrence and the reason is because your container is not an integrity with the exacting tone of your high feminine, okay. I'm going to pause there and just see where everybody is with respect to that, see if there's any questions. I'm going back here, [inaudible 00:21:08]. I just realized something from what you said, my dad used to get so annoyed he would say when you ask for something, you want it right away. He said he doesn't work like that. He said, "It doesn't work like that, I'll get it for you when I'm ready." Yeah, your dad is not the Magic Man, okay.

Your dad is probably annoyed, here's what's happening, Debianni. Your dad is annoyed that you're exacting standards because you're exacting standards are about what and when you require things to happen in your life. The feminine overseas the what and the when not the how. Not the how, we will get to that later, okay. You and your high feminine absolutely must, if you are going to be in your high feminine and not be lazy or not be apologetic for those exacting standards. You must decide what are those exacting standards represent. They represent what I want and when I want it.

What we often do is women, and I'm so glad you brought this up, Debianni. What we often do is women raised by actual men is that we base our understanding of the masculine, our Magic Man on our dads, okay. In my experience and it looks like in yours too, my dad is an amazing man and many, many, many, many, many ways he taught, made so many amazing things. He spent most of his life feeling impotent in making his dreams come true, okay.

Therefore, when I began stepping into my adult life and had to start orchestrating and setting or not setting my own boundaries with the people in my life, I just automatically would apologize for them and not set them as high as I truly knew they were, as I truly felt that tone being held because in my experience that made my dad feel bad about himself. I also saw my mom do it with her, like she would diminish her requirements and her request and her needs because it made him feel bad about himself. That's putting too much expectation on me, that's putting too much pressure on me.

You're pointing out my weakness, you're pointing out my fucking flaw, don't do that. You can demand the world of your Magic Man. When I say demand, I don't mean like give me the world. I mean like this is my requirement. Because your Magic Man is all potent, omnipotent as we think of god, right. Omnipotent, your Magic Man is part of this, doesn't need Viagra. He's going to give you whatever you want and can do it now. That's part of being potent, that's part of being powerful is having a command overtime.

You have been imprinted to diminish your standards even though it's not what your feminine is carrying and holding as the tone of your true exacting standards and then look what happens in your life, right? You struggle, you don't have the experiences that you really desire, that's why, that's why, okay. Thank you for bringing that up, that's like huge. It's one of the things that we as women but anybody who is … Because whenever you're in the position of creating life, creating your dream life, you're in the position of the feminine, you're in the position of receiving the experience of your dream life, requesting and receiving.

Even if you're a guy in this dynamic, you're in your feminine also. One of the things that we need to deprogram ourselves from is the imprinting of how we saw exacting standards of fact and impact the men in our lives when we were growing up. Huge, huge, huge, huge, huge, there's so much, I could actually do a whole live stream on that. Okay, yeah, and by the time we got it we were often over it, yeah. That's huge, Debianni, that's really huge for you to look at and to recognize that you are imprinting, you're basing your understanding of your Magic Man on your dad.

I'm telling you now, not to throw shit at your dad but your Magic Man can give you whatever the fuck you want whenever you want it and that is his greatest desire and pleasure, okay. Okay. Holy hell I'm going through this right now, trying to center and growing myself today. Amazing, Melanie amazing. This is going to fucking blow your mind seriously. Whenever I teach this to my clients, they're just like, "What the fuck?" I feel like you just help me organize my entire consciousness. Carmel, Natasha, okay so good to make sense. I can see that's what I had done in the past when I knew what the standards were.

I've been struggling with that lately but no more, awesome. Tina, can you give us an example of an exacting standard in business? Completely, thank you for that grounding practical question. I will use myself because I think that's always ... It's always good to use personal examples. I'll use an example from today actually. I had a client, wonderful, amazing woman who just might be on this stream and the other day I gave her some homework and it was very confronting homework and it was very specific homework. Because a lot of the time when I'm in my role in my coaching, I tend … I'm in the role of the mask man.

Anyway, I gave her some specific homework and when I give my clients homework it is tuned exactly and precisely to the frequency of their greatest fear and the thing that is directly, directly in the way of their quantum leap because I can just see that. My homework is very specific, it's very specific and it must be followed exactly to the team because those are the exacting standards. Not only that I have, it's not about you must listen to me but because if you don't hit that tone you don't get the disruption in your field that you need to have in order to release all of these trapped energy that is being held in your low frequency state back into your system, which then strengthens the container, builds up the magnetism, attracts the masculine in, and gets you your cash and that's what a quantum leap.

My clients hire me to create quantum leaps for them. They do not hire me for incremental growth and I can't even do ... I don't know how to teach someone how to do incremental growth, that's just not my thing. My guidance and my homework is very finely tuned to a certain frequency and it needs to be followed. When I checked in today I said, "So did you do it?" She's like, "Well, I did it almost." Because I said do a live stream on this specific thing and she did a live stream on the same topic but not that specific thing. I said "No, but that's not what I told you to do."

She said, "Well I know but I was talking to someone else and they said what about doing it this way that seems to make more sense. I thought it made more sense so I did it that way." I said to her, "If you do that again, we're done. Literally we're over, we are not working together anymore. I am going to lovingly release you from my coaching." That Tina, who would be an example of an exacting standard. The reason is because in my container, in my world, what I say goes. It is a matter of I don't know, I don't want to say that it's a matter of respect because I don't take it personally at all, it's not about me.

It's not really a matter of respect, what it is, is I'm here to do something that she's asked me to do. I pick my clients, and this is what I explained to her. I pick my clients carefully because I want to see them blow shit up. I want to see them get rich, I want to see them create magic, that's what's pleasurable for me. I have a business because it's pleasure, right and because I want to help people but there are no victims so they don't really need my help. It's just we're here to play a big game, okay.

It is not fun for me to work with clients who don't listen to me. I really dislike it quite a bit. It's not according to my standards. Because when you listen to me, the results happen. It is a spiritual guarantee. It's energetic law when you listen to me the results happen. If you're not going to listen to me what are we doing? I'm wasting my time, I'm wasting my breath, I am giving you my energy and you're not doing anything with it. That's not okay with me. It's a requirement of mine, it's an exacting standard of mine that my clients take my guidance.

I am absolutely okay with firing them if they don't do that. I know that might make people really uncomfortable and be like, "Oh my god, you're such a bitch," and all that stuff. Here's a thing, if an Olympic trainer takes on a client, that client is an honored position because that Olympic trainer who has a record of getting people gold metals has the option of working with lots of people and so do I. When I work with the client, if I have selected that client out of many and therefore I have requirements for how that experience is going to go, so that would be an example of an exacting standard.

Taking a vacation from work somehow my soul just wanted to chill and be introverted. Yeah, totally that's your ... Yes, yes, yes sexy, okay. Fucking love this message, awesome. The men in my family have been non-existence for generations. Marina, this is going to change your life, this live stream is going to fucking change your life. Oh my god. Great grandpa ghosted during World War II faked his own death. Grandpa dies of alcohol poisoning, dad non-present from mom of raising kids my relationships embody myself fully in a relationship in last.

Okay, I'm assuming after all this, your mind is like blowing up right? Yes, this is why I'm doing this live stream you guys because I want you to know who the Magic Man really is not ... The Magic Man, your Magic Man is not your dad energetically expressed. It is not your grandfather, it is not your uncle, it is not your great grandfather. We just without thinking that's how we approach the provider energy of the universe, the provider energy of the universe we assume is like our dad specifically insane when you think about it, it makes no sense.

Of course, it does make sense because we don't have an example of that kind of provider, right. I'm giving you the example. That's my goal here today and how to work with it and how to not turn it off. Super clear, thanks for giving that example. Okay, you're welcome. Okay, awesome. We have the high feminine, okay. Standing in her exacting standards and to her supreme integrity, so the exacting standards think of that as the content of your desire and the content of your requirements for your business, for your clients, for your love life, for your body, for your bank account, for your house, like everything, okay.

It's the content of your requirements and your desires. The supreme integrity frequency is your energetic will to execute on those standards in your actual life, does that make sense? Holy shit, this is everything wow. How do you tap into the frequency of Mr. Sexy Magic Man? I'm getting you there but this is the way Marina, this is what you do. Then, I'm going to give you like literally a step by step tool. This might take me a minute to get out because it's a lot, so stay with me and this seriously will fucking … I'm going to stay on this live stream until I deliver the entire tool to you.

I'm giving you right now the energetics, this is how I always work. I give the energetics and then I give the practical application. Right now I need you to understand the energetics of what the high feminine is, what the Magic Man is and then how they activate and inspire. I'm going to give you the practical tool for how to get in to your high feminine and inspire your Magic Man, okay. First, hey Michelle, requirements and standards but what I am asking about is trusting that provider energy. Yes, that's the worry, that's the worry and anxiety piece and that I will get too but that's where you're headed right?

You're immediately going to yes, but yes, but yes, but yes. Yes, but my dad was gone my whole life. Yes, but my great grandpa ghosted. I can have this high fucking standard but who the fuck cares because… Maybe I'll just go there now, I'm just going to go there now. Okay, I'm going to address this right now, the issue of trust because this is actually …. Thank you for raising that because this is huge in my clients. Most of my clients are women and pretty much

99% of them have an issue with trust, trusting the masculine. Thinking about how to roll this out because there's a couple of steps.

It's actually pretty fucking important and there's some pieces to it. Number one, trust … You got to hear this, you got to hear this. Trust is shown in action. It is discovered, it's not even shown, it's discovered in action. Trustworthiness is discovered through action, okay. Took me a minute to get there. You will discover you will have the evidence that your Magic Man is trustworthy when you take the actions that are in accordance with your own exacting standards and supreme integrity and no other way. The reason is because that is the thing that inspires and activates the Magic Man.

It's the only thing that inspires and activates the Magic Man. If you are not having in your experience what you desire, it's not the Magic Man, it's your standards and your supreme integrity that are the problem because the container, the container's integrity determines the degree to which the masculine fills it with things and the time it takes to fill it. Think about it, you have low standards. You totally compromise on your standards all the time. Leaky container, how long is it going to take to fill that container with what you want? A long time.

You tighten up that fucking container, two things … Okay, so actually two things are happening. You have a leaky container, number one it's not an inspiring container. Your feminine is not attractive, you're ugly. Energetically you look ugly to your Magic Man. Your Magic Man is like, "Yeah, I'm going to hang with the guys." Not interested, not interested in sex, not interested in providing, not interested injecting you with anything, not a turn on.

Number one, you are not magnetically attractive to the Magic Man so he's not going to show up that often, okay? Number two, even when he does, chances are what he fills it with just leaves because it's leaky. He's showing up and he's giving you stuff and half of it is leaking out, and he's showing I'm giving you stuff and half of its leaking out and you're like, "Why the fuck does it take me this long to make this much money? What is wrong with me? What is wrong with my business? What's wrong with my fucking masculine? Look at this shit.

It's taking so fucking long and plus it's shit. This is your fault." I mean I don't hate to break to you. I'm telling you something is going to change your life in a day, literally tomorrow your life can completely change because the masculine is also the energy of time and he is always ready and waiting to provide for you. Men get hard like that, takes them no time. Men are always ready to go. As long as you're irresistible, takes no time to turn a man on, right. It also takes no time to turn on your Magic Man. No time at all.

You can fill those leaks in an instant. I have had, here's a perfect example. I had a brand new client yesterday I walked her through all of this, this energetics and I gave her the tool and I gave her some homework the very specific homework and I said, "Do this before your discovery call." She had three discovery calls that day and I said, "Make sure you do this homework before your discovery calls." It was definitely, it was all about establishing, she was way not in her standards in her supreme integrity in her life like literally in this relationship. I said, "Do this, okay."

She was like, "Oh my god, if I do this like I can't even imagine what's going to happen." I've been wanting to do this for 14 years, probably maybe not 14 years she's been in this relationship for 14 years but for a long, long, long, long, long, long time okay. This was somebody who was literally providing to her, a source of money, a source of providing … She was potentially drawing a boundary that would cut her off and she is not in a position right now where that feels anywhere near safe to do.

We're talking like high risk, freaking out her shadow, making her go holy shit, and also emotionally what's this person going to say and feel on my god and there could be drama and blah, blah, blah. I gave her the words to use, we talk through the energy of all of that stuff and she's seriously want to throw up just even thinking about it. She did it you guys, she did it. Then a matter of hours later, I'm pretty sure it was later, it might have been … I forgot to ask her. The same day, she closed one of her discovery calls and a 50% full pay.

I don't know the last time. I need to ask her I don't know the last time that she made a sale but it's been a while, especially in that level, and a 50% full pay. Okay, I'm sorry a 50% down payment. It's not a mystery, it is not a mystery that this … That's filling this container up … Not filling it up but strengthening it, filling in all the holes is directly linked to the 50% cash sale that she made. The e-mail that she sent me was like, "Oh my god, I can't even believe how much energy I feel right now.

The conversation actually was imaging, it was actually beautiful. Oh my god, I can't believe I waited so long. I feel so fucking powerful, I can't even believe this." I'm like, "Yeah, this how this goes." It does not … The whole point here is it does not take time to activate the Magic Man because the masculine is money and time, the energy of money and time. I'm sorry about how it's your fault. Literally all you need to worry about and it's not even worry, concentrate on is doing whatever it takes no matter what, no matter how much you perceived this to be risky and dangerous to your well-being, your financial well-being, your emotional well-being.

Well this person is an emotional support system to me. Well this person gives me money. You must, you must live your life according to those exacting standards no matter what, no matter what. You will not have the evidence that your Magic Man is absolutely trustworthy and absolutely will provide for you guaranteed like clap work like you step off a cliff, you fall it's like energetic law. It's literally just energetic law. It's electromagnetism, okay, but you will not have the evidence that your Magic Man is trustworthy before you have to do this carrying thing to establish your exacting standards in your life, does that make sense?

A lot of us, I spent my whole life doing this and many, many all of my clients do the same thing. Well if I just could know … If he could just give me the thing now and then I'll know that if I do the thing, he's going to give me the thing, or if I can just get some kind of promise like energetically he was whispering in my ear, "Baby, if you do this, I'm going to give you this money." I can just know then I would do it, that's not how it works. Trust means you take the terrifying action regardless and without the evidence. That's what trust actually means you see. If you want to trust your masculine, then actually trust it.

Actually take the action that is terrifying to you but that is in accordance to your highest exacting standards. That's what trust is actually. The other piece that I want to point out around this is that the ease with which you can take that action that seems dangerous and scary because some people are able to just do it and just be like, I'm totally fucking terrified because the thing is you're going to be scared no matter what. Even I, at this time … Even I have been done this so often and had the evidence. I do it, I get the evidence. I do it, I get the evidence.

I do it, I get the evidence. I fucking do it, I get the evidence. I do it, I get the evidence. By now, you would think that I'm just like of course and most of the time I do but there are sometimes where I'm like, "This one seems really, really, really low. I mean really." Then I argue, I try to negotiate with my high feminine. Can we lower the standards just a little please? I mean this is scary. I don't want to do this one? What if my masculine doesn't show up this time?

The ease with which I now can just leap my life to those exacting standards, have a conversation, fire a client, cancel a date, tell somebody I'm not interested in them, whatever it is okay. Is because I know something and that is that I am not a victim and that nothing and no one has power over me. It is not possible for me to fail, and it is not possible for me to make a mistake. Even in the worse possible case scenario where I take the action that is absolutely terrifying that seems financially crazy, that seems emotionally risky, whatever, that isn't according to my exacting standards and my masculine doesn't show up.

I fall and I crash and burn, I'll be fine. That's what allows me to do that because I know my worth you see. Your high feminine knows her worth and it is not attached to money, and it is not attached to fame, and it is not attached to reputation, and it is not attached to friendships, and it is not attached to clothes, and it is not attached to looks, and it is not attached to anything. It just is, it just is, and I walk around with that as an unconditional state of being. I'm going to take the action because the action, it expresses my knowledge of my worth.

The action is a direct honoring and actually an execution of what it means to be in my highest worth, my unconditional worth. You know what if my Magic Man doesn't show up, that's fine. I'll be fine. I might be homeless but I'll be fine. Really, honestly, seriously, I have walked myself energetically down every possible catastrophe corridor there is. There is not a single thing that can happen to me on the planet because I faced down a lot of shit, not nearly as much as a lot of people but a lot of shit.

There's not a single thing that could happen to me on the planet, they would cause me to betray myself and my worth, not a single thing. It makes it easy for me you see, makes it easy for me … Boy, I just got something. I got something. Okay, it makes it easy for me to take those actions and to live my life according to those exacting standards and in supreme integrity. It did not always use to be this way guys. I used to be the worse, my really everything, oh my god I sold my soul all over the place.

Here's something I just got okay, oh my god I'm so excited. Trust isn't the issue, trust of the masculine is not the issue actually so this is cool because it's entirely within your power, it's entirely without your feminine power to fix this whole thing. It's not trust to the masculine that's the issue, the issue is you are worried that you will betray yourself and you will downgrade your sense of self-worth if your masculine doesn't show up and give you what you require and desire.

That's what's actually happening and driving what you think is mistrust of the masculine. It's actually not about trusting the masculine at all, what it's really about is that if you act according to your exacting standards, and it doesn't go the way, you want it or really need it to go your sense of supreme worth is under attack by your own self, by your own self-regard is in danger. You need the masculine to show up and give you the thing or the feeling or the belief or the whatever, for you to have a sense of self-worth. That is so fucking important.

All that your job is to do is to focus on closing the gap between the way your life looks now and the standards that therefore created it and that exacting standard, that tone of exacting standard that your high feminine carries. In the terror of contemplating doing that to do the alchemy work on yourself around where you're really placing your power. No one and nothing has power over me, it is the most freeing, most liberating, most exhilarating, most thrilling, no one and nothing has power over me. Seven sentences in the universe, seven words in the universe. I really truly believe that.

Then of course the wonderful thing is because this is an energetic law, because it's electromagnetism. When you do that, your Magic Man does show up and you're like, "Oh my god, that's amazing." Here's the thing, here's a thing, this is why … This is so crazy. Even though it happens over and over and over again, you're still going to feel that fear which then you're going to be like, "See, I don't trust my masculine. I still don't trust masculine, this is crazy because if I trusted my masculine then I could just close this gap.

It's never about trusting your masculine, it's always about your worth. It's always about your loyalty to your own worth no matter what. Fucking amazing, so fucking amazing. Before I look at the questions or the comments, I want to just make sure that is wrapped up. Actually why don't I look at the comments and see if there's anything. Energetic bloodhound, I love it. We're drinking the same thing right now, my Kombucha. Thank you yes, energetic spiritual okay goals. Totally goose bumps freaking everywhere [inaudible 00:54:22] feel like they're coming. Melanie, that's so awesome.

I'm so glad, I'm so glad. He's Yahweh, isn't he? The streaming host pinched off and eager for the best place to … I love you guys. Don't be a leaky bitch, holy hell and sloppy containers.

How do you discover what that blocking fear is? It doesn't matter, it doesn't matter. Actually I answered your question Roche, the blocking fears that you'll abandon your own worth. That's the fear. It doesn't matter what ... Here's the thing you guys. It doesn't matter what the fear is honestly. Just do the action and you will find your power and you will find ... In doing the action, in closing the gap, that is you expressing your own commitment to standing in your worth no matter what.

The only way you can show yourself the evidence that you stand in your worth no matter what is by taking the action that terrifies you. You're not going to get there any other way. You aren't going to get there by journaling. You're not going to get there by meditating. You are not going to get there by going to yoga. You are not going to get there by doing soul regression. You are not going to get there by doing pass life therapy. You are going to get there by taking the fucking action because your life is built on tones and frequencies.

Your life is literally an expression of a certain quality of tone and frequency, okay. Your high feminine holds the tone of the exacting standards which is what you intend your life to truly be and look and feel like, okay. The way to close the gap and have your life express this tone versus this one is not by meditating. It is by literally going into your life where the tone is depressed and suppressed and freeing it. It's literally, I don't ... It's energetic I can just see it. You free it, it's almost like you snap a cord or something.

It's maybe freeing it here, I don't know exactly how it looks but it just literally your life, it just [inaudible 00:56:51] because this is your natural state of being you guys. This exacting standard, this tone is your natural state of being. It's the easiest state of being to be in. It's the most pleasurable. It's the healthiest. When you're here, you're healthy emotionally, mentally, physically, financially, right? All of your struggle is because of the tension and the dissonance in your life between these two frequencies.

Meditation doesn't change the frequency. It changes that maybe a little, like that, like that, like that, that, that, that, that, that's what meditation does. Going to your actual life, this is why I gave such specific tuned homework. Going to your actual life to the place in your life that isn't the most dissonance when that releases back up and gets an alignment that releases so much fucking power into your fields you guys.

It is fucking massive and amazing and magnetic. That's what instantly fills your leaky container, makes it magnetic, calls in the Magic Man. Then you do it again, then you do it again, then you're like, "Okay, where else now what's in the most dissonance to my exacting standards?" That's what I can give you and it happens again and that was it, that was it. See, it's magic.

Tighten the energetic vagina, oh my god you guys are so pathetic. Oh my god, Joyce that's so on point, holy shit, okay awesome. This is awesome, really loving this, also I'm loving the UnSchool Program, yey. Love this and Ira what you said about that it is okay to take a break, so you're taking a vacation. Yes, totally. Oh my god yes, seriously yeah pass life there'll be yeah, yeah, totally. Okay, thank you about the inspired action. That's really important. Let me see if it's the time for that. No, it's not okay,

I am going to do this, this is just a little thing for you guys. It's really brilliant and my brother taught this to me. When you want to remember something but it's not for now, it's for later like someone is talking up the storm and you're like, "I want to say something but I can't interrupt them," or right now like I have a place to go but this is important but it's for later. Clock the idea, okay wait hold on I got to make sure I get the idea. Inspired action, okay inspired action in response to the honeydew list, that's what I'm going to say.

Okay, now I have it. I could wait for two hours until I release it and I'll totally remember what it was, it's fucking brilliant. I will come back to that, [Adzilla 00:59:51] I think your name is, okay. Going to that darkness, face the fear. Relationship with mother, okay, so [Rushin

01:00:01] for you, the question is, is there a new agreement? Have you been in any kind of unspoken agreement about how you're going to show up that needs to be changed and spoken into new arrangements, right?

Have you been in an actual spoken agreement about how you're going to show up? That is no longer works for you, okay, and that needs to change. This is a big part of where these shifts start to ... Need to start taking place. That's a big one. Yeah, I won't go anymore. Okay. I've had similar principles but never framed in this way. Totally, that you guys this is like law of attraction. I mean, it's not ... I'm not telling you anything ... It's energetic law, so of course you've heard at other places, right? What I'm doing is I'm like pulling the curtain back, unlike the instructions that you've been given, okay?

It's like Abraham-Hicks and other people who teach manifestation and love attraction, they give you the instructions. They give you the manual, do this, do this, do this. For me, that never works. I want to know, why? I want to go under the hood. I want to look at the mechanics, right? I want to look at the energetics of it because then I can hook into that. Then, I know what I'm dealing with, right, and why? I understand the ramifications of things. I don't know. That's just way I always work.

Of course, those are the things that I'm going to be teaching because that's what I do. I go in and I go under the hood. I go, "Okay, why is it worked that way and what's really it play there?" Yeah, this is totally not new stuff but it's going to ... My hope is that it gives you a framework and it gives you the fundamentals of energetic law at work here, and how to master them, right? How to not be confused anymore about why something is not showing up in your life and what to do about it, okay? I love the way you explain this, it's so clear, awesome.

The finger thing, I don't understand the finger thing, Jamie. I need to experience and study with what I learn. Yeah, totally, okay, cool. Okay. Where were going next is so we've got the high feminine in the strong container, magnetic as fuck, right? Okay, so am I going to go to the tool now? Yes. I'm going to go to the tool. Okay. I'm going to give you the tool for how to apply this in your actual life. You're welcome, [Carina 01:02:47]. One of the things that I want to say, you guys, you all probably know about my dark UnSchool.

If this is resonating with you and if you feel like you've got deeper, like things that you need someone to work with you on, you need to really seriously consider my dark UnSchool. It's essentially it's like business school meets Hogwarts. It's like Harvard Business School meets Hogwarts. It's like the quantum leap container and they teach all these stuff, and give you your specific piece of homework, that finally tuned piece of homework, that creates quantum leaps over and over again.

The people who go through this program tell me it's like nothing they've ever done and most of my clients have done everything, all the clients, all the coaches, all the programs, all of it. When they do this, they're just like, "Yeah. There's actually nothing like this out there at all." They make crazy fucking money. One of my favorite examples is a woman who like could barely sell a $300 package. In her first month, she did $24,000 in sales. She did $57,000 by the end of UnSchool.

She went from I think it was, I don't know, $1,000, maybe $1,500 to $2,000 dollar a month to an average of $12,000 a month. She also went from working literally full-time around the clock never seeing her friends ever even on the weekends to an average of 15 hours a week, 20 hours a week I think. She took two months off in the UnSchool. I mean, she still came to classes and all the stuff but she didn't sell and her average was still $12,000 a month. The door is open now.

It begins December 19th. Door is closed the 12th. If you want to do this shit in your own business, get in. Okay. Yes, you addressed more refined consciousness more integrated and real. Awesome, I'm so glad this is speaking to you guys. Yeah. You know what? You guys are like, I need to know why. That's how it gets integrated into me. Yes, I need to know why. Yes

I need to know. You know why? I'm attracting so many of you because we all have that saboteur mind, which also means you guys are super magicians.

This is all stuff I teach in the UnSchool, to all these archetypes that the voices that keep you building your life according to these low standards versus the voices that allow you to see and create the ease of building them according to their standards, I teach all that stuff, but yes. Because I have a strong saboteur in me. I become quickly magnetic. People reaching out and now wanting free information. Wow, this is amazing.

This is from Marina who just joined Sales Masters. I believe this action of exacting standards is insisting that this is now my work and I charge for it. How do you find the balance with giving this information for free versus paid? Awesome, awesome, okay. I will answer that even though I want to get to the tool, this is good. I love these questions.

First of all, Marina literally joined … I don't know, very recently, Sales Masters. This is my beginner mastermind and so UnSchool is 18 grand, four months. There's a luxury three-day retreat in a castle. At the end, you get a ton of time with me, get a ton of time with [Coleen 01:06:39]. It's like fucking amazing. You get channeled sales transmissions and guidance, and all kinds of fucking units. It's like the Cadillac … It's not even a Cadillac. It's like the whatever. I don't know.

`What's that really amazing car that starts with an L, [Livery 01:06:55], whatever, whatever. It's like the Lamborghini of programs. If that's not accessible to you, if you believe that you can't afford it, which is an illusion, but if you believe you can afford it, there's my Sales Master's Mastermind where people having crazy shit happen already. Marina joined, we had our first class. This where I give one on one laser coaching to each person. I think she booked like … Was it you Marina that booked like 10 discovery tools or something?

I don't know if it was you or somebody else. Anyway, crazy shit is already happening and this is exactly what it is, is they're becoming magnetic, stuff just happening. Yes, now you have the opportunity to reinforce those existing ... Those exacting standards, right? Like where is your commitment to your supreme integrity? What's going to happen is you have this container and the masculine is coming this way, but like things are poking it from the outside. Are you really strong?

How strong are you? It's like knock, knock, knock, knock, poke, poke, poke, poke, how strong are you? How strong are you? How strong are you? How strong are you? Okay? If you're like, "Well," maybe this time, "Well, okay." Guess what happens to your container, okay? This is normal because you're not only become magnetic to the Magic Man. You also become magnetic to what I call your dark angel. Interesting, I never thought about this.

I never actually thought about the fact that when we create your container in alignment with your exacting standards, you become magnetic to the dark angel too. Your dark angel is what I call your spiritual boxing trainer, your spiritual trainer, the person that is here, the energy that is here to test you. Why? Not to be mean, but to make sure you're an energetic match, to make sure you are an energetic match for what it knows is coming.

Okay? Because it doesn't want you to attract into this powerful potent, super potent, super potent, super potent experience of the Magic Man, the masculine, and have it blow your fucking system. It wants to make sure that container is double thick, triple thick, quadruple thick, right? That it's like the most powerful masculine can come in and you're like, "Yeah, man, bring it out." Instead of like, "Fuck," my life crashes and burns. Okay. Marina, that's what happening to you. It's a good thing. It's a good thing when you get test and trials, you guys. It is a good thing.

It is not a sign that's something is wrong. It is not a sign that you should quit. It is not a sign that, "Things aren't in flow, I should step back." No, no, no, no, no. It is a sign that you just strengthened your fucking container, okay? What do you do? Exactly. When somebody comes to you asking for help or advice, you say, "I would love to work with you and provide you this advice and experience, would you like an application? I'm assuming you're talking to me about my work, about mentorship, about working with me, right?"

If they say, "Well, no, I mean, I was just wondering if you could just give me a quick little thing, just a quick little thing. I'm your friend. I'm an old client. I'm up here." You say, "My genius is so precious and rare and my time and my energy is so precious and rare to me that I charge for it. I'd love to give it to you. It's pretty fucking awesome but we need to accept into one of my business containers to do that." That's why you just say that.

You don't have to be like, "Fuck you." This is how it is. Now, you might be thinking, why am I not charging for this, right? Okay. I have never actually consciously thought about this, so give me a second so I can see what is wanting to like come through around it. The answer that I am getting is that it is an active pleasure. Literally like this lights me up so much I can't even tell you. You probably can tell. You probably can tell. This is an act of pleasure and play for me. Therefore, I'm not charging for it.

Now, that's not to say that my business and my work is not an act of pleasure. It's an act of pleasurable service, highly pleasurable service, but it is an act of service. Meaning, I'm providing a service, okay? When I am in the place of providing a pleasurable service, I just … The sex analogy is just [inaudible 01:12:36]. I get paid for it. This is self-pleasure. That's totally what it is. This is my self-pleasure. This is my energetic self-pleasure, okay? It's exactly what it is, okay?

`When you're in a business container and you're … It's a pleasurable service, you get paid for it. I crack myself up. My little finger trick. Yeah, yeah, yeah, okay. I really want to do that one next. I booked two more. Awesome, Marina, but now you're being tested. Okay. Tell me about the tests because that is like important. I want to help you with that.

Here's my scheduling like. Yeah, exactly. I needed to hear this. Yes, one was a friend, right? That's what's going to happen. This is what happens. This is what happens. You guys, this is so important, my God, there's so many of these. There's so much fucking shit coming through. It's amazing. I'm like actually hot. My temperature is really like it's cold in here but I'm seriously heating up. Okay.

This is so fucking huge. I love this. I don't know about you guys but this ... I just came up with this whole like container and the high feminine and masculine like thing, but it's so fucking awesome because it's so clear and grounded. This is what I mean by a visual metaphor, right? You guys are probably never lack for a visual metaphor understanding of your masculine and your feminine because now you have it, but I'm going to give you another piece. I'm going to give you another piece, which I never had before.

When you build your container, right, exacting standards, supreme integrity, this is awesome. Your Magic Man comes in, so Marina got all those discovery calls after it was dead, dead, dead. Then, all of the sudden, time, masculine, Magic Man, time, all of the sudden, without having to do anything, because your masculine is the one that does, your feminine is the one who hangs out, right? Pleasure is yourself, it's like discovery call, discovery call, discovery call. Out of the blue, you're like, "What? Well, thank you," right?

The other thing that happens though is that you become ... Okay, wow. Millennia of a story about this is coming in right now. You also become magnetic to the demons, the devils, your dark angel, who is here to test you, who is not a bad guy, who is not Satan, who is not the devil, but it is in your favor working in your favor. What it really is, you can call this a threshold guardian.

Okay. A threshold guardian, meaning, like I said earlier, making sure that you are ready in your energetic match for what's beyond the threshold when you step into that new state, that new higher frequency, which is what this all about, right? Think of your container as the threshold. It's a circular threshold and your dark angel is like poke, poke, poke, poke, test, test,

test, test, trial, trial, trial, trial, friend asks for advice, client doesn't take your guidance. It's like, whatever.

Here's the thing. Subconsciously, what we are doing when we are keeping our container leaky is that we're keeping it nonmagnetic to the devils. We're also keeping it nonmagnetic to Magic Man because the concept of being able to … Like the imagination of like can I hold this? Can I hold this? Is it like very confronting? My clients do this all the time. My one client who just had a 25k sale, her very, very first 25k sale ever and she's been doing this for 15 years. Okay? She's a six figure coach, she's fucking badass.

She just had her first 25k sale couple of weeks ago and afterwards she was like, "What the fuck I'm I going to do with …" Of course what's she's doing with her client is like fucking badass as shit, but in that moment, she's like, "Wait, what am I going to do with this person? I don't know if I can hold what I just attracted in." Then, the self-doubt and the fear, and am I a fraud? My God, can I deliver? Can I deliver?

That's the feminine. Can I deliver the baby? I created this amazing container. I stayed in my exacting standards. I maintained my high integrity. My masculine provided for me. I fucking have a 25k baby that I don't know if I can deliver. My God, it's so amazing. Holy shit, we got to do something with all this energy. We got to move the energy. Energy is not going to sit in this container like, okay, I'm just going to sit here. No. We got to alchemize this shit out of this energy and deliver it.

That is one of the things … That's part of what your fear is. You're afraid of labor and delivery, okay. Also, you're afraid of the devils that are going to be attracted to that powerful magnetic pulsing being that you are becoming, and all that is a fear that you're going to collapse back into your old state. Of course, the fear of what's going to happen if I piss my friend off and what's going to … It's actually this fear, right?

It's the fear of like, shit, like, what's going to actually go down in my actual life when I actually live according to these exacting standards? You are welcome, Rushin. That's why I always have orgasms. Is that Carina? I was just talking about you the other day to somebody. I'm like, "Yeah, there's this woman, she like had a full body orgasm, like listening to [inaudible 01:19:03]." Is that you? It's fucking amazing. We need to work together.

If you're having orgasms this way, like imagine, imagine. We need to find … We need to work together. Okay. Right, I just said that [Shawna 01:19:23]. It's having a taste of your genius. Imagine what would happen if you work with each of us. I know, get into UnSchool, guys. Lorna, as soon as you even mentioned this principle, the universe made sense, and now I have to upgrade the container because I'm making progress, not fixing problems. Yes, yes.

When I raise my vibration, all strange things come in and it doesn't feel good, and I realized it's test for me to plow through. Exactly. What you're doing [Stacey 01:19:49], is you're becoming magnetic to the little devils, okay? Yes, it's pokey. It's poke and fraud, and pressure test, and it's like that's your being, like squeeze. It's part of that labor that you feel. It's like contracting, expanding. Where is my container? Where are my standards? Am I here? Am I here? How firm are they?

How thick? Like all of those things are being tested, and yes, it feels really fucking uncomfortable. It feels really uncomfortable. That's just part of it. What I'm getting is there's an alchemy of that demon, like there's an alchemy of those demons, with those little devils. I'm using that word because I want to demonize devils and demons. Do de-demonize them. There's like an alchemy that can happen, right?

Like a devil, like a little devil comes in and tests you, and you can just hold the energy through your filed and into your container, and as you go alchemize it, and strengthen your container. Okay, and another one comes through and you just hold it through your portal and alchemize that powerful energy because that demon energy, it's very powerful potent energy that you can use, as long as you alchemize the toxic piece of it.

Then, that gets added to the energetic content of your container and that's what continues to magnetize it further and strengthen, magnetize, strengthen, magnetize, strengthen, okay? What I want to say here and I totally hope I remember to do this, so Magic Man, give me this idea later. Thank you. Is it live stream on how this relates to overcoming objections? Because if you understand this whole process, how this whole thing works and these little devils, what you will realize is that the little devils are objections that your clients' prospects display on their sales calls with you.

You can do the same thing with those as you do with your own little devils. In fact, the degree to which you know how to alchemize your own little devils because those little devils are those voices. Remember I was telling you about those, those voices of fear, the archetypes? You listen to those little devils and that's what creates the holes in the container, right?

The little devils like, "Can I poke?" You're like, "Well, it's so reasonable that I not set this standard with this person who's giving me money. Yup, poke a hole." Another one comes, "Can I poke?" "Well, it's so nice to give my friends some advice, because I mean, she's my friend. Poke a hole." Those little demons are so powerful but when you allow them to make decisions for you about the energy of your container, the integrity of your container, they fuck your life up.

If you know how to alchemize those little demons, you … They are powerful pure potent energy that gets assimilated …. It's almost like a cellular thing I'm seeing. Basically it's like cellular, like they come in. You alchemize the low frequency piece. You use the fewer potent energy piece, which is how you respond to them and how you alchemize them. Then, they become part of your strengthened container, so fucking cool, I never thought of that.

The way in which you do that helps you master overcoming objections because those little devils are the objections you hear on your sales calls, because when a client, a prospect comes to you, what they are coming to you to help ... Get help with is fixing their container, helping them raise their standards. It was the same thing. Their life is being run by those fucking little devils who've been poking holes in their container all their lives but they don't know that. They don't know that because those little devils feel sound really reasonable.

It's the voice of reason and it's the voice of the victim. Survival consciousness and fear consciousness, and tribal consciousness, is what those little devils are. There's so much here. Okay. I have so much to say but I won't go into that. This is awesome. Which is taking the action, the supreme feminine or the Magic Man? Okay. I'm going to answer that question not because this is related to this, okay? What's taking the action?

I'm assuming, you mean like in your actual real life, is your ... You. You're taking the action, right? You're high feminine is ... I like supreme feminine. I might actually steal that, it's gorgeous. Your supreme feminine, is an energetic, okay, and your Magic Man is an energetic. The being that takes the action, you, which is the combination of the two, okay? It's your integrated being. What I'm going to explain to you now is the tool and how this happens.

What you're talking about, Jules, is the inspiration, the inspired action that actually is sent to you from your Magic Man, is it a thought, an idea, an intuitive hit, right? That is what you as you, as your physical being, like response to and takes inspired action on, okay? Here's how this works. It's time for me to give you the tool because I've been on here for like an hour and half, an hour and a half.

Here's the tool. Every morning, I have my book. Now, it's going to look like journaling and it kind of is. It's simply the way that I activate my intentional relationship with my Magic Man. Okay. The magic of this is in the exacting standards thing of things that I was ... It's the actions that you take in your actual life, okay? What you're doing here is activating your Magic Man in your life. What I do, and this is where the law of attraction, all that stuff and manifestation, you're going to be like, "I get it. That's [inaudible 01:26:49]."

Men are inspired into providing for you, by knowing how much they ... By praise and appreciation. If you read Alison Armstrong, you will realize this. Men are inspired into providing for you, for your wildest dreams by praise and appreciation. This is the law of gratitude, okay? Because the universe is in the provider energy in the masculine energy in making your dreams come true, this is why when you hear about manifestation rules, gratitude is always one of them. This is why.

Because gratitude, appreciation and praise inspire the masculine to provide for you, okay? I always begin with gratitude, but I make it very specific, because see, I tried these principles before, and I was like, "I'm so thankful for blah, blah, blah. Thank you for ..." I'm like, "Who the fuck am I thanking?" I don't believe in God really like, "Am I thanking me? Well, this is stupid to thank me. It makes no sense." The minute I translated it into like my masculine, my Magic Man, I was like, "I totally thank my Magic Man.

That totally make sense to me." Before my feet hit the floor because this is for me, it's like the most important thing. I get my pen, I get my journal, and I start, and I start with an appreciation. It's like a minute, not even a minute. It's like a sentence or two. I really personalize this. I make this sensual. I make it like I'm talking to my lover, to my man, okay? I'll say like, "Magic Man, you were fucking awesome as provider ever. You are fucking amazing. Thank you so much for what you did yesterday.

You did this, and this, and this, and this, and you provided me with this. I asked for this, you give it to me right away, it's fucking amazing. Thank you so much. I love you. You're fucking awesome," okay, gratitude, but actively and intentionally activating the masculine, okay? The masculine energy. Then, what you do is you stream your worries. I don't know if any of you have seen Harry Potter but Dumbledore has that wand, he like taps it to his forehead, it's like a crystal wand, and these worries or thoughts, I think memories, streamed into this wand. Then he takes the wand and he taps a pool like a cistern of water.

He taps it and all the thought stream into the pool. Okay. You're going to stream your worries. This is what you're doing but it's more than that. There's an alchemy involved as well. Because how do you know what you are exacting standards are? How do you what you want? How do you know what your requests are of your Magic Man? What are you worried about? Worry kills magic. Worry also tells you what you desire, what's "lacking".

For me, because I have been diagnosed with severe mood and anxiety disorder, it's very easy for me to know what I want. I just check myself and go, "What am I worried about?" I'm worried about filling my program. Okay, I have this program, I'm worried about filling it, and I don't go any further. I do not go into, "Why am I worried? What am I going to do about it and why is this ... Maybe this is because of my dad. Maybe this is because of the blah, blah, blah."

I do not fucking do that, okay? I just notice. "I'm worried about my program." I literally open my book and after my gratitudes, I have an example here, I say, "Here, Magic Man, my divine provider, is your honeydew list for the day," because that's what's you're doing. You're giving him his honeydew list and you are taping it to the energetic fridge, and then you're walking away and going to the spa, or doing whatever the fuck you want, like a live stream like this, not because you have to mark it, but because you fucking want to, because it turns you on.

That's what I do. I say, "Here's what you are providing for me." Here's your list of what you're providing for me. Okay, so after, because you don't walk up to a guy and be like, "Hey, can you go fix my car? Thank you." That guy is going to be like, "Fuck you." If you walk up to your guy and you're like, "Hey, baby, you are so fucking brilliant at fixing cars, I can't even tell you. I'm wondering, we need a new radiator, could you fix the radiator?" What is he going to say, "No"? If he says no, then you don't have an example of the Magic Man.

Okay, because your Magic Man will say, "Yeah baby, I'm right on that," okay? Here, I'm just going to read to you so you'll get a sense of how I connect to the masculine, okay? This one's great, you did it again baby, thank you. In 12 hours, you delivered. UnSchool, it's on its way to being rebranded as the dark UnSchool, so perfect, so easy and simple, and yet a profound adjustment that makes me so fucking excited, which is exactly what I asked for. What I asked for was, how do I sell the UnSchool in a new exciting, edgy, totally upgraded, totally fucking like amazing, the most amazing thing that ever existed on the planet?

That's how things have to be for me to sell them, and I was like, I don't see how it works. I don't know because I'm not inspired by the old version of it. I gave it away. Twelve hours later, boom, brilliant, done. Okay. Everything I asked for, you've provided for me with ease, so easy I didn't even noticed it so fucking quickly. You are the intimate exterior, the Magic Man of my higher self, my delicious divine provider, who is always here, always ready to provide and please, always poised with the most potent injection of brilliant inspiration, intuition, guidance and connection.

Thank you for providing exactly what I was seeking and so fucking quickly. Let the massive magic continue today. Here is what you are providing for me now, okay. Then I have a list, I have one, two, three, four, five things. I don't do more than five. You don't want to overwhelm your masculine. It's like five things is enough, and I know we're going long. This should take maybe another 10 minutes, okay?

If you can stick with me, stick with me, all right? We're almost at the end. This is like the most epic long live stream I've ever done. Okay, so that's what I do, all right? I'm not going to go into the details here but I very specifically I'm going to give you the framework. The high feminine rules, the what and the when. The divine masculine, the Magic Man, rules the how. You must know in your high feminine what do you want specifically, when do you want it, and what is the equality of the experience of it, right?

How do you want to experience receiving it into your experience, right? If you want a money goal, I want a 50K a month, do you want to have to work $100 a week? Often included time element that's not just when you want it by but how many hours you want to have to work. Do both, but also what's the experience? I want it to be easy. I want it to be fun. I don't want to even have to think about it. It's not even a thing that I think about. It just fucking happens and I want my clients to be fucking amazing, brilliant amazing, badass.

Describe the experience that you want to have as the goal is coming into existence, okay? That's the high feminine. In your high feminine, you rule over the what and the when, because the what and the when makes up the tone of your exacting standards. That's what your exacting standard frequency is composed of, is the what and the when, okay? This is the piece that is extremely fucking important for women and for everyone who is in this relationship to their Magic Man, you don't get to determine the how.

Most women, like want to scrutinize and this is where you get into worry, and this is where everything collapses and the whole thing goes to pieces, okay? You do not determine the how. You give the how over to the Magic Man. Okay, so you make your list, okay. Then energetically what I do is I hand the honeydew list over to the Magic Man. I say, "Here you go, thank you so much." Then I energetically just I go out my way. This is the piece, Jules, that you were asking about and someone else was asking about inspired action.

This is where it comes in, okay, because I want to explain to you energetically what is happening. You have just handed your Magic Man your desires and requirements, okay? There's a piece in here that's really important about refusing to worry and be anxious, and scrutinize, okay? You cannot be hanging around the garage watching him fix the car, okay? The best thing for you to do would be to leave the house completely. That's what he wants you to do, leave.

Leave it with him, okay? "How are you doing, honey? Do you think it's going to be done today? Are you having any problem? Can I help you out? I really need the car tomorrow, I got a thing I got to do. Do you need help? Should I call your brother?" Okay, this is what you do with your goals and your dreams, and your desires, and your requirements. This is what you do with your Magic Man all the fucking time, I promise. Any time you worry or are consumed with anxiety about something not happening that you want to happen, here's what you're doing.

You are hanging around the garage breathing down his neck, driving him fucking crazy. Guess what's going to happen? He's going to turn on to be like, "You know what, baby? I'm not …" and he's going to walk away. "You do it then. You do it then. I'm not doing it." Worry kills Magic. Worry kills Magic, okay? Limp Dick Syndrome is now when you think about it. It is not attractive. There's another piece to this, which I just got, not your container the way that you maintain its integrity so that it remains magnetic to the Magic Man throughout the process.

Okay, so there's a building of the container, which is what I just taught you the tool to do, right? Also, really the building of the container happens in your actual life, filling, changing your relationships, changing your agreements so your entire life represents your exacting standards, okay? That's the building of the container but it's energetic so you have to maintain the container. You have to energetically constantly be maintaining and holding, maintaining and holding, maintaining and holding, maintaining and holding.

When you decide that you want to go look at the Magic Man's job in what he's doing, you abandon the container. It's like you leave the nest, okay? You're like, "Where's Magic Man? Where is he? Where did he go? Where is he?" Your container is just, it's gone. Now, he's like, "Wait, where is the … Okay." Because he can feel it. It's energetic, so your Magic Man is like, "It's gone, okay. I guess I'm not supposed to do anything." Those must not really be your standards. You must not really want that.

You're not very attractive to me. You're not magnetic. It doesn't even exist, the magnetism is gone. You see, your job is to stay out of the garage, okay? How do you stay out of the garage? This is what I do during the day and I don't really do this anymore because I get it energetically so I really don't worry. I just don't focus. I don't scrutinize. I don't. If I visit the garage in my mind, "What's going on? Is it going to happen by this date?" What I just imagine is me being like, my God, I'm so sorry.

Here I am hanging out in the garage and I just say, "I am totally sorry. I didn't even notice I showed up here. I know you got this, baby. I'm going to go hang on and just leave. I'm so sorry. You got this. I know you do. You're totally good. My bad." I leave the garage, or another way I want you to think about this is when you start to anxiety, worry, scrutinize, wonder, deadline, is it happening, how is it going to happen? How is this going to happen, okay?

Just imagine yourself what you're really doing is going over to your Magic Man and saying, "You know what, give me the list. Can I have the list? Just give me the list, I'll do it. I'll do it myself." That's what you're doing. Okay, so don't do that. If you're profoundly consumed with anxiety and worry, like two levels where it's probably trauma-based, then I'm not speaking to that person, okay. I'm speaking to someone who is in a level of high functioning but just doesn't know how to alchemize it, and probably doesn't even know that it's not your job to worry.

You may be thinking worrying is helping you focus on the goal or something. Those are the people I'm talking to. Last piece and then we're done. It's the inspired action piece, okay? You've given the instructions to your Magic Man. He's going away and here's what he's doing energetically. He's arranging. He's connecting the energetic gridlines between you and the opportunities. Opportunities always come in the form of people so it's essential we're connecting at the energetic gridlines to you and the souls, and the energies of the people who are going to show up in your inbox and be like, "I just was talking to somebody and she's referred me to your group.

I don't even really spend any time on Facebook but I looked at your group and my God, I don't even know what you do, but you, I have to work with you." This happens to my clients all the time, this shit. I had one woman close an $8,000 full pay at Starbucks. She was in the line with Starbucks and the person behind her started talking and she's like, "That's my fucking ideal client." They talked and sat down in Starbucks at the table, and she did a full pay, an $8,000 full pay, okay, because your Magic Man is like, "Okay.

Exacting standards, this is what you require and desire, got it. I got it, baby." When he's out there and moving and shaking, and making all … Lining all the things up, and then what he does is he shows up for just a second, a quickie, okay, and he's like, "Hey, go to Starbucks for a coffee," in this woman's case, right? She's like, "Starbucks? I don't really go in the afternoon." I mean I know this wasn't the story, but like it's an inspired idea. It's an intuitive hit. It's, "I should go here. I should go this.

I should say this. Marketing post." That is what that is, right? You've given him his job. He's moving and shaking, arranging, lining everything up, and he comes in and he's like, "Hey baby, marketing post, worry kills Magic. All right, I'm back out there." It is my job, it is your job as you, as your human consciousness, to fucking act on that and here's why. Because, and that's your intuition, people think intuition is feminine, it's masculine. A content of the intuition is masculine. It is an injection of an idea.

You might experience it and receive it into your feminine container but it's your masculine. Again, "Hey, baby," right? This is what inspired action is and that is your only job. Your only job is to take inspired action. You know this but now I'm telling you the energetics. You see, isn't this amazing? You're like hanging out, hanging out, da, da, da, da, da, doing your thing, whatever it is that you want to do, whether it's a live stream or whatever the fuck, inspired action, do it.

Here's the thing. It is about timing because the masculine is the energy of timing, time, timing, okay? This is why I say to people, when you get the intuitive hit, that is the moment that everything is lined up because he's fucking the master of timing and he's got everything lined up, and he's totally done what you asked him to do. He's like, "All right, this is the moment. Come on, baby. Do it. Do it. Do it. Come on, do it. What the fuck? Do it." You're like, "I'll do it later. No, that doesn't make a whole lot of sense.

I'm not going to do that, it doesn't make any sense at all. I don't know what that's about. That's silly." Your Magic Man is like, "Are you fuck … He just was right … He's gone now but that guy right there, that woman right there, she was going to be your next client. You just had to make a post and she was totally going to go on Facebook. She was just going to do it. In fact, she's on Facebook right now but you're not there. Fuck." Then you wonder why he doesn't provide for you because the idea didn't make sense.

Because you don't understand all the synchronistic grid that's happening and all of the ways he's magically connecting people that don't make sense to connect to you through these all these ways. You're in your conscious brain going, "Well, that doesn't make sense." That feels like a waste of time or that looks irresponsible. Those are more of those little devils that are like, "Well, don't do that, that's silly." There's a whole thing I teach on intuition and how to activate your intuition, and listen to your intuition.

Intuition for launches and quantum needs and wants, and that stuff, but that's what's happening, okay? That's what inspired action is. What's amazing about this whole process because he's also the master of time, and because he doesn't want to have you to work very hard, he wants to do all the work and he wants to do all the providing, is that this one little idea can make you a shit fucking ton of money. I have made $40,000 from one single Facebook post that at the time I was like, "Why am I posting about this? This doesn't make any sense."

I got somebody's attention, it was like, holy shit, I don't even know what you do but I have to work with you. That was a 25K client. Now, I have a 50K client, a 50K client from one Facebook post, okay? I'm done. This is the longest. I've been struggling this for 10 years. I see now. Wow. My God, you fucking said it, just what I needed to hear. I magnetize to me a dark angel, so to speak, and I started to blame myself, "How could I magnetize him if my vibe was so high?"

Then you said it, this makes so much sense, yeah, yeah, yeah, yeah, yeah, yeah, yeah. I've been single for four years and I completely understand. I've turned down my energy. I don't even attract quality masculine, yes, but now you see why, Stacey. I've given you … This is the only live stream you … This is the only thing you ever need [inaudible 01:47:18] honestly. This is it. This is it, like you ever have a question about why something is not working in your life, just listen to this live stream, seriously.

With that said, it's like having a baby, those who truly really are very close and your friends will still be around to help and support, totally. Marina, you've had an orgasm too? What? Fucking hell, amazing. Your burger joint was called Devil Burger? Dude, I want to eat a burger at Devil Burger. Does it still exist? I want to got there. Fucking cheeky little imps. I'm so weak for charmers. They're my imps, which test me. Did I miss this too? Did you share that already? I don't know what you're talking about, Shawna, sorry.

I've given it all for free, integrity and alchemy, no apologies. Yeah. How about the courage to actually going and doing that inspired nudge? That wink from a sexy man, any insight on courage? I talked about that, Marina, so go back and listen to this live steam, okay? I talked about courage. Courage is you knowing that no matter what happens, nothing and no one has power over you. Courage is not being in your victim. Courage is knowing that you're going to be okay no matter what happens.

Therefore, you do the existing, you match your exacting standards. I'm so tired I can't even talk. Go back because that's the piece where I talk about, that's where courage comes from. The root of courage is kerd, which is the French word for heart. The way you develop the heart for something that terrifies you is to know you will never abandon your own heart, but you will never abandon your own sense of work. I don't want to repeat it, just go back. It's there. You may be missed it.

The why, yes, much gratitude for this live, awesome, you guys. Mind blown, holy fuck. Your exclamations are blowing my mind with a strong energetic intentions. Yay, I'm so happy. It's like writing to Santa. Totally, if he turns you on, I would not be … Yeah, with a sexy Santa. A Latin Santa, a tall … A Benicio Del Toro Santa, yeah. Do you say daily more than once? No, because that means that I don't trust my man, [inaudible 01:49:44]. I don't need to go check. To saying it daily more than once is me saying, "Are you really doing it?

Did you hear me? I don't know if you really heard me. Let me repeat myself." My Magic Man heard me. He listens to me. He pays very close attention to me. I say it one time. Then if I ever start to wonder about should I say, da, da, da, all of that, I'm like, "I'm sorry, baby. I am so sorry. I don't know what I was thinking. You're fucking amazing. You are omnipotent. You got this, I know it." You guys, I'm making this sound easy. It's not easy. Worry and anxiety are literally imprinted biologically into our systems as women.

Do a research on this. We are highly anxious beings way more so than men, so I'm not giving you something that you should master tomorrow, okay? Maybe you could. You could master it tomorrow but probably not. You're going to have to walk away from the fucking energetic garage a lot and apologize to your Magic Man a lot, and be like, "I am so sorry. I cannot get myself something to do because I'm just fucking hanging around you too much and showing you that I don't trust you." It's just this has got to be … This is the part the action part, not even the action part.

This is like the rigorous paying attention to those little devil voices and I go into exactly how those voices sound and how you can alchemize them, but this is the piece that's very challenging. This is the part that's not sexy and not ... You know what this is? This is the minute by minute, hour by hour, day by day, week by week non-sexy part of building an amazing relationship is really what it is. It's like, "Fuck, man. I keep fucking breathing down his neck. I got to stop that." The answer is no, I don't see equivalence.

My God, can I help you? Yeah, don't say that, Marina. Don't say that. This has been so freaking amazing that I'm tired just floating a list. My God, you guys, fuck, I do that to my actual man all the time. Rushin, you got to stop that now. Are you serious? Stop it now. Stop it now. This is me. I start going and feel I need to help and everything goes to shit. Yeah. Funny because I was just about to go to bed. I'm in UK. It's 1am. I had a quick peek on Facebook. You've just gone live two minutes before I came on.

Okay. I think I'm done. First video, you've seen mine, Melanie? Holy fucking shit man. Go to my YouTube channel. I got 24 hours of this stuff and find a way to work with me. Find a way. Find a way, nobelwarrior.com. Here, I'll open it here. Okay, I intentionally created different tiers of ways to work with me for different levels of people who think that they can afford certain things. My actual man isn't trying to tell me this too. You guys, I'm telling you man, Alison Armstrong, Alison Armstrong, Alison Armstrong.

She will change your life. Okay. Hey, [Gentry 01:53:47], I'm so sorry. I'm about to end. I've been on for almost two hours. I can't even fucking believe it. I remember when Facebook was doing lives and it would cut out after like 45 minutes, the live stream would just stop. Unfortunately, but Gentry, it was fucking epic. My live streams tend to be ... People tend to tell me that my live streams changed their lives and they're epic, and amazing and amazing. This one was the best one I've ever done ever, ever.

This one was like it was like a comprehensive total complete visual metaphor and energetic understanding of the masculine and the feminine, and how to get what you want in life, and all the things you're doing that you don't realize you're doing to fuck the entire thing up, the inspiration, for how to change it, a specific tool for how to do it. I mean, it's fucking amazing. All right everybody, this was a fucking blast. I laughed my ass off and I will be back at some point. I put my link there.

I will also put a link to UnSchool and the sales masters' group, and I would love to see you guys. I would love to work with you for real and help you apply these things to your life in a very much more specific way so that you can really, really get results. Okay. You are so welcome, good night.

#

LITTLE DEVILS

You don't have what you want and can't keep it when you get it because of one thing and one thing only: you don't understand masculine energy. Or, to put it another way, you don't know what to do with all the little devils. Yes, your Magic Man is amazing and is capable of giving you all you desire. That's his PROVIDER energy. This is what you're CONSCIOUSLY trying to become attractive to and activate when you're strengthening your boundaries and stepping into your exacting standards and supreme integrity. But what you don't realize is that he also has a PROTECTOR energy, and when you arouse one, you arouse the other. But you're not thinking about this one AT ALL. In fact you have no idea how it works or even how to recognize it for what it is. Enter: misery after the victory. That's because the way your Magic Man protects you often does not feel good AT ALL. In fact it feels like a shit storm. Like you had ALL this goodness and amazingness and FINALLY broke through one of the biggest challenges of your life and the money is flowing and the clients are amazing and then BAM. BOOM. Chaos. Drama. Crisis.

And then Self doubt. Anger. Depression. Confusion. Despair. Lack of motivation.

Increase your visibility? (Provider energy! Yes!) Now the criticism of your disruptive message is even harsher because these people don't KNOW you like your original UnTribe does so they're going to feel much freer to be MUCH more direct, critical and disdainful so in the newspaper and on TV you see yourself dissected mercilessly, pilloried, burned at the proverbial stake. (Protector energy. Fuck.)

Are you ready?

Or will you buckle under the onslaught.

Go from $1500 months to a $50,000 weekend (from just TWO sales) and hell YESS your family can afford to go on an amazing vacation.

AND, your husband is going to sink into depression because he was already having a hard time with his career and now you've just gone and blown his self esteem to smithereens. He now spends his days depressed on the couch. Not really an awesome traveling companion.

Are you ready?

Or will you sabotage your next Quantum boom because it's just too painful to see him this way, and because you feel deeply guilty for what you've done. Which is crazy. You know you shouldn't feel guilty but you do. Plus he just doesn't have the emotional management skills or support that you do. So in order to preserve the fucking marriage — YES, this is ACTUALLY the kind of shit that happens — you decide to go easy on him and slow down your growth.

OR the crisis happens right during the uplevel.

Sell a big package, client ghosts.

Post your biggest month yet, unexpected bills come due.

Client pays but the bank systems screw it up so you don't get it for weeks.

Go from $1500 months to a $50k weekend? AWESOME. BADASS. Now your husband feels worthless and your mom thinks you're running a sham. FINALLY sell that dream $25K package? FUCK YEAH. Now you're terrified about actually being able to deliver at that level and secretly convinced you're a fraud and not nearly as brilliant as you think and now that will be exposed. Go from $300 to $6000 packages and from 60-hour weeks to 20-hour weeks and $12,000 months with tons of time to travel? YAAASSSSSS. And now get serious slack from your family about your new lifestyle — because they think rich people are assholes — AND start getting requests to help family members out with their financial troubles since you have so much money now.

Until you understand that when you activate the PROVIDER you also activate the PROTECTOR and can see and EMBRACE all this crazy chaos and crisis and upset AS your Magic Man PROTECTING you (the ability to do this is called CHAOS ALCHEMY, by the way, and it is the highest feminine art there is and is what will provide you with an UNLIMITED amount of access to your Magic and catapult you truly into your most epic legacy life) then you will forever be stuck in the "FINALLY got it!!! FUCK lost it" cycle. In other words, all those little devils didn't come 'out of nowhere' AT ALL. Your Magic Man brought them to you, along with the gifts. Because when you become attractive to him, you activate ALL of him. And those little devils are his gifts also. They're just wrapped in a beautiful, black bow.

The activation of the masculine PROVIDER energy and as INEVITABLE (until you reach a certain height in your power management abilities, at which point it calms down consskderably) for what it is and then it feels wonderful and amazing because you get what he's doing. (and, you know how to handle it, which takes an even GREATER degree of ability to stand in your exacting standards and supreme integrity.)

Because your Magic Man has been where you're going — a place of extraordinary increase in power from where you are now and teeming with goodies but also goblins.

But you're not thinking about this AT ALL when you're dreaming of retiring your husband because he hates his job and traveling the world with him. It doesn't cross your mind ONCE.

But your Magic Man, who because he is Master of Time can see in all dimensions at once? He sees it clear as day and because he is your MAIN MAN, and because one of the primary directives of the masculine is to PROTECT, guess what he's going to send your way.

Not a bouquet of roses and a box of delectable chocolates but a bunch of unruly little devils.

You know, the shit that happens when you try and uplevel.

The stuff that just realized something that could help so may of you understand why you don't have what you want and can't keep it when you get it. The understanding of this somewhat hangs on my previous work (most relevantly two epic livestreams one with over 1,000 views and 300 comments that is making people cry with tears it's so revolutionary) (so feel free to PM me if you want to see them) but I'm going to make this post able to stand on its own so you can grasp the key ah-ha now.   Stay with me. I'm teaching energetic law through the masculine and feminine here so it may take a minute. So maybe put down your fifty million things and your scrolling frenzy and take a deep breath and let me blow your mind □⚡□   First, let's set up the scenario. Tell me if this feels familiar: Or something to that effect. You get what you want (and fuck it may take forever to get it, which will be addressed here also) and then after ALL that, you LOSE IT!   This is because you've been building your life according to one very low frequency belief because you can't imagine how the truth can be true.   The truth being: no one and nothing has power over you.   The path to awakening and success is to wake up and realize the truth and then dramatically adjust all your physical agreements and expressions of your low standard living to match your true, exacting standards (which is the only reason we ever decide NOT to live according to our highest standards: we're terribly afraid of the ramifications of doing so; which means we think someone or something has more power over how our life goes than we do, including how we FEEL).   The dis-chord between your low frequency life and your true standards (very high frequency) creates the struggle and strife you experience. And when you finally decide to "snap" the energetic ties that are holding your life in its low frequency state (literally energetically DEpressing and suppressing your natural frequency) that is what creates a quantum "boom" in your field, and therefore in your life, and that's what a Quantum Leap in success looks like and how it happens.   BUT, remember, the REASON you've been SUPPRESSING your natural frequency and choosing to live a life that doesn't match it, is because you've been SCARED of doing so. That fear doesn't go away (until you do lotsssssss of Alchemy on your physical, mental and emotional fields and essentially alchemize your shadow). You're scared of all the ramifications ("good" and "bad" of doing so.)

That backlash is an inevitable result of your Quantum boom. Because the dis-chord was created to AVOID those very things that now inevitably are going to happen.   But the other thing that happens is that

nd because the masculine

ut in order to STAY at that level and go even higher and have the fullness of what you've just activated come in to your experience, you need to be in a MUCH stronger place mentally, emotionally, even physically.   Because it's all about the management of power.   At an energetic level, upgrades are simply increasing the amount of pure, potent energy we're running in our field. So, you have to be "trained" to deal with it. Like a firefighter or someone working with explosives.   It's not because you're "bad" or did anything wrong that conflict is coming your way. It's because your Magical Masculine wants to make sure you don't totally blow a fuse when you reach that next level — the one he's sending your way also — because you can't handle the power.   He's protecting you by testing you.   That's when, and why, the little devils or what I call dark angels of strife come in AFTER a success. They're there to be your "spiritual boxing trainer." To toughen you up energetically — not by becoming guarded or rigid, but by becoming immune to fear, judgment, criticism, lack of approval from the tribe ... because the tribe does not want anyone becoming TOO powerful.   The energetic system is built to naturally work to do this. Your build your power, and you become attractive to more power (your Magic man providing for you) and also to the little devils who throng around, poking and prodding and testing, to see how you respond.   If your container is weak (meaning you are still highly susceptible to disapproval and fear), you'll collapse the container. (This is why lottery winners tend to go back to the financial state they were in before they won the lottery). There's no judgment about that. It just means you're not ready to get in the arena and box with more power.   So you do your work and find where in your life you collapsed your standards and do it again.   Make sense?

The Domain Of Lightworkers, The Domain Of The Dark

LightWorkers help people adjust to and operate as powerfully as possible within their current paradigm.

DarkWorkers destroy all remnants of the current paradigm so something new can be created.

Light Codes Vs Codes Of Genius: Law Of Attraction, The Mechanisms Of Desire And Why You're Not Attracting What You Want

Desire is the animating force of a dream or vision. It is the source code that emanates and calls to the magical masculine, which is the energy of the universe that provides that desire and brings it into our experience.

Desire is the vibrational point of attraction. (Nothing new there. That's LOA 101.)

What is means to be a *vibrational point* is that it is a *vibrations made of codes*. The codes create a frequency that vibrates at the sum total of power contained in the codes that create the desire.

Some desire is strong, and therefore highly *magnetic*, and therefore highly *attractive* to the Magic Man and therefore works beyond Time to collapse it (Time also being masculine) and bring its vibrational match instantly into the experience of the one emanating that desire frequency.

In fact this is happening all the time (we are always calling in exactly what we are an energetic match for).

The problem is that what we call in is often not what we really want.

That is because desire is made of three kinds of codes, and those codes are of three natures: shadow, light and dark.

Openness Is An Exact State.

When you manifest using the Dark (vs the Light)—meaning when you manifest the expression of your unimaginable genius (vs the expression of your gifts/highest existing frequency of Light)—the standards rise dramatically for how to work with the energy that accesses this state of manifestation.

Working with the Dark is an exact, and exacting, science nothing like working with the forgiving nature of Light.

There is one, specific tone of genius that resonates as an exact match for your availability at any given time. Strike this tone (the Tone of Truth), and you will strike gold (the wealth resonance of your genius).

Dark work is heaven for the spiritual geniuses among us, because it is finally the exacting field of play in which they thrive (versus the ambient playing field in which the Light resides).

Mastering Dark work, for a spiritual genius, is like finally being able to exhale.

There is a delicate and steely and filamental silence to it, like the silence of bones.

To All The Budding Truthtellers And Shadow Seers Out There, Who Are Still Trembling A Bit, Terrified Of Coming Out: I Got You ;) [Or...A Note Of Encouragement In The Spiritual Storm]

There are only a very few people on this planet who actually WANT their shadow shown to them. It's excruciating, terrifying, and the absolute only way to supreme self mastery.

Most people THINK they want their shadow revealed to them, because on some level they know that what's in their shadow is killing them, but then when you show it to them? HOO BOY. They do not like it one bit, no sirree.

You get blamed. Told you're mean. A bully. Egotistical. Too harsh. And for most of your life, because you knew this would be the most common reaction (the Elite are Elite for a reason...their desires are not COMMON, you see) you kept my mouth firmly shut.

And then you likely proceeded to almost die, because Truth, kept in, becomes poison.

Truth, expressed, is potent medicine. Unfortunately, it is one most do not have the spiritual constitution to handle.

Every collective consciousness drops to its lowest common denominator of consciousness. (This is why groups evolve more slowly than individuals.) And because you can see into the leading edge, out to what it's all evolving into, you can also see what it's evolving FROM, but which it's not yet consciously aware that it is strongly desiring to shed.

The only way the group consciousness evolves is through TruthTellers and Shadow Seers who speak that shadow into everyone's awareness so it can be transmuted and the evolution can continue.

Those closest to the leading edge but simply missing this piece of awareness (the Elite 1%, whom I call the Energetic Olympians), adore this information, because it's the last missing piece in their self mastery and in the evolution of the group. Yeah it hurts to have the group shadow revealed (hello, crucifixions and burnings at the stake), but they welcome it with open arms.

The rest of the peeps? NOT so much.

This does not mean you should watch what you say. Not now, not ever. Your saying doesn't need to be watched, because it is not a rabid dog that needs to be kept on a leash. Your saying deserves to be said now, as it is, as you are, because you see and speak Truth (now that your shadow has been alchemized).

You do not doubt yourself, and you know that what you say and speak is necessary and good for healing. No, it's not pleasant to hear. And no, you don't care that it's not pleasant. This doesn't mean you won't converse about the shadow with people who have sincere questions about it. But you are not available for conversations that come from the now-dying group consciousness that believes we have to be careful about being ourselves because ourselves contain elements dangerous to society. That's victim consciousness and, thankfully, it's on its way out.

Victim consciousness is deadly. Literally.

I know because I was steeped in it for decades and it almost killed me. And if you're feeling near-death yourself, it's only because you're consumed with victim consciousness.

The way out is excruciating. And on the other side is Power Consciousness (which of course looks and feels very much like a bully to those who are in their victim, but isn't at all.). And with Power Consciousness comes the exhilarating feeling of the absolute knowing that no one can harm you, no one can victimize you, no one can deplete you, no one can terrorize you, no one can overpower you. AND, that you cannot harm anyone, cannot victimize anyone, cannot deplete anyone, cannot terrorize anyone, cannot overpower anyone.

So if you are biting your tongue and biding your time to speak your uncomfortable Truth, out with it. For the good of the evolution of our collective consciousness, SPEAK it, baby.

Truth out.

True Magic

True Magic, what we are all here to master, is the ability to sew wildly disparate dimensions together. 3D resists this mightily. This is intended.

JOSEPH CAMPBELL IS WRONG

My book is a total overturning of the basic and foundational works on human consciousness and transcendence.

Take Joseph Campbell's "Hero With A Thousand Faces," one of THE classics in mythology, spirituality, transformation, psychology and all about the Hero's journey, which is supposed to be the holy grail of human awakening and transcendence.

But is NOT. AT. ALL.

"The hero has died as modern man. But as perfected, unspecific, universal man, he has been reborn. His second duty then is to return to us and teach us what he knows."

Are you fucking kidding me?

No wonder the process of awakening we have been taught in myths, fairytales, religions, even Light Consciousness spirituality, can't deliver on its promises.

We aren't supposed to be unspecific and universal.

We are built to be unmitigatedly specific, unique and individuated.

That is the essence, thrust and requirement of creativity.

And we are, in our bones, essentially creative.

Gold Minds, Caves Of Genius And Business Alchemy: The Inversed Posture Of Success For Darkworker CEOs (Or, Darkworker CEOs: You're IN For A Real Awakening)

In LightWorker businesses, the CEO is the Sovereign energy, decreeing from on high and delegating delivery to the people (the masses, the armies). This is because in the Light, the creative energy (hidden in the earth) is divorced from the Sun. The Sun/Sovereign reigns from a distant vantage point, from which he surveys and sees the great vision, and extends this vision to the people, who receive the Light of the Vision, are opened to new sight, activated into agency and step into their roles as delivery agents of the vision. The CEO is most effective as the distant Sun and visionary, which is why business experts are constantly advising him to work ON the business, not IN it.

If the CEO descends into the business, the Light of the business goes out, the vision fades, the workers go blind and still and the animating force and binding agent of the company cannot operate. The business will eventually die.

Darkworker CEOs, however, must do the exact opposite. And yet, they are likely attempting to raise themselves up and our, Trained as they are on the Light Grid and having heard for years that their role and proper place is in the high seat of the Sun, the over-lord, the extended visionary.

But if they attempt to run their business with efficiency and scalability according to this model, they will in fact grind it into dust.

This is because the primary archetype of the Darkworker CEO is not the Sovereign, but the Alchemist, whose place is DEEP WITHIN the business, in its bowels, in its bones, attending to its utter stillpoint of creation with a luminary devotion to the next emergent genius that is forming itself out of the codes of individual chaos that express its unique, enchanting and magical spirit.

In this reversal of fortune, the DarkWorker CEO will find not only the deepest fulfillment as the creative heart of the business but will also discover that his true role is to create the heart over and over, from a position of intense scrutiny and intimacy with chaos, with divine madness, with the Dark Divine in its individual expression through his own Entrepreneurial Spirit.

The DarkWorker CEO is the Gold Mind of the business, meant to descend deep into its dark heart of gold and mine the treasures to be found there. There is no one else who can do this work, for he is the only one who carries the codes of life, which do not emerge all at once, as a grand vision to be carried out in clear steps, but rather blindly, out of order—for in a Dark Business, dis-order is the higher order. To have allegiance to the grand vision and to expect to align the business to it, is death.

Instead, like Ezekiel in the valley of bones, the DarkWorker CEO is meant to cast spells of awakening over the still bones of the business and with no concern for orderliness, meaning, arrangement, or cohesiveness, raise up one by one the armies of genius from their slumber.

And as they wake, he is to send them up into the Light, carefully snaking through the labyrinthine path of creative thought and collaboration, which is nothing other than the gridless and chaotic surrender of genius, under the blind gaze of the Alchemist and the watchful hands of the CEO's team, to the First Experience of Form: the labyrinth. Not a grid and not a formlessness, but the liminal and enchanted space in which Dark becomes Light.

The Experience Of Dark Initiation

Total exhaustion.

More "out of commission from a transmission" than ever before.

Nausea.

Heart palpitations.

Muscle Twitching.

Bizarre food cravings.

And more utter exhaustion.

This is what the participants in the very first Dark Initiation Friday night experienced for two days afterward.

Whereas the Light makes you feel light, airy, floaty, even dizzy, the Dark bores into your energetic core and creates "energetic motion sickness" and total disorientation for all your consciousness systems.

Amazing and humbling.

All Genius Is Dark

All genius is dark. The Dark is unordered (will not be ordered ((commanded in any way))). Therefore you may not order your genius to appear, make sense, serve you or make you money. (It will do all these things because the Dark is feminine and loves serving. But not when it is commanded to do so.)

Your Work Is Not To Make Yourself Palatable

(Most people have not developed a taste for the true divine.)

Your work is to make yourself into a monstrous expression of staggering genius and art.

And if it is distasteful, it is no matter.

The Secret To Happiness: Kill Your Children While They're Young And Healthy

The secret to happiness? Kill your children while they're young and healthy.

- How mastering murder of your fresh, successful creations is the only way to unleashing your genius (in other words, why the Greek myth of Theseus + the Minotaur is all wrong and how it's spawned human struggle)

- How misunderstanding (judging, condemning, shaming) your craving for fresh, young creations (meaning your constant struggle with how easily you get BORED with your programs and your business) is just doing shadow work on your genius, and KEEPING you from wealth and fulfillment

- and why I'm closing UnSchool applications in two weeks and leaving coaching once this cohort is done.

Why do we keep retelling old myths and stories just dressed up differently? Because we keep telling them wrong. We just don't get the role of the Dark in the eruption of Unique Consciousness (because we're all so busy trying to unite with the Light Grid (where genius isn't and never will be).

I'm going to tell the myths the right way.

When I did this today with my UnSchool clients, there were TEARS OF RELIEF.

Livestream: Retelling of Theseus and the Minotaur, June 18, 2018

- Transcribe this livestream

Artisans Of Consciousness

You are meant to be an artist of consciousness. Not a cloner of one.

This cannot be completed on the Light Grid.

When you apprentice with the Dark, you become a true artisan and discover the euphoria of developing your unique style of consciousness.

THE HOLY GRAIL IS MADNESS

The holy grail of human experience is elegant, finely crafted madness.

It is not Union with the Light, or with anything. (We came here to be individuals. Union with the Light is like saying death is the goal of life. An elementary paradox that has no value.)

The goal is pure, unadulterated individuality crafted by the deft hands and exquisite taste of the Dark Artisan.

Madness will not be masterfully tamed.

It wants to be exquisitely touched.

Codes Of Magnetism And The Energetics Of The Inefficacy Of Expert Advice

What you're doing when you ask someone if they're an expert in LinkedIn or Instagram or losing weight or finding love because you'd like help with it is....

Expecting that their coding—meaning the codes they send to an energy pattern of potential power in order to activate it towards their will and sync it up with their desire—is the same coding as yours, so that when they say

Well, I just ate carrots and chicken for five days and the weight fell right off or

I just post three times a day and do a livestream once a week and my business grows or

I decided to move across the country to the place I'd always wanted to live and that's how I found the love of my life

you think this indicates that you, too, can eat carrots and chicken and lose weight, or move to your favorite destination and find love.

And so you try, and it doesn't work.

And so then you ask someone else, and they say

Oh. Carrots and chicken? I tried that, too. It doesn't work. What works is...........

Or

Post THREE times a day and only ONE livestream a week? Well of course it didn't work for you. That's not how to be successful. You have to post on Tuesdays at 9am and Thursdays at 4pm and do at least TWO live-streams a week.

Or

Move? To him? Well of course that didn't work. You stay put, woman. Don't move anywhere to find love. Call him to YOU. That's what works.

Because everyone is totally ignorant of Energy Patterns and coding and how you link patterns of power together. It has nothing to do with the ACTION that links the patterns (though the action is in fact necessary to link them, because action represents Will, and Will is the pattern linking agent). It has to do with the drama unfolding between the two patterns and how they are being drawn together to express it. And I don't mean drama as in crisis. I mean drama as in THEATER. As in PLAY. As in MAGNETISM.

You have codes of magnetism. When you place them onto grids (energy patterns of power) in certain places and ways and times, the grid activates and turns toward you and delivers what you desire. (Yes, the Grid is the Magic Man.)

And you are the only one with those codes. And the place, way and time you set them onto the grid is your private and personal work of art and energy science mastery. It comes from mastery of and intimacy with your mental, emotional and spiritual operating systems.

In other words, it is an expression of the interplay between your emergent self and your SuperConscious Mind.

And that is not duplicatable. Not by anyone.

So stop fucking asking experts for advice.

Mentors who can teach you how to handle your own codes and place them artfully and with precision onto grids? Sure. They can help you immensely.

But experts? No. Not ever. Not a chance.

So delete them from your emails and stop watching their slick videos and stop falling for their fancy Facebook ads.

That behavior is beneath the eminence of your code-bearing being, who is the Dark Expression of your Genius, and who does not, in any way. need. the fucking. experts.

It Begins With A Deep Appreciation Of Your Conditioning.

Your mind is either a sanctuary or a battlefield.

Powerful negative emotion is exactly the same, in its most pristine state, as powerful positive emotion. And if you have completely cleared your body/mind of its wounds and old conditioning, you eliminate the experience of being triggered. It simply does not occur in your system. There is no more shadow to shift. No more shame to alchemize. When you have fully alchemized your INTERNAL field of energy, then you can fully and instantly alchemize any EXTERNAL energy you encounter.

You have become an energy alchemist.

In truth, you have become a chaos alchemist, because the most unruly and also the most delectable and potent energy is that of chaos.

Up until now chaos has been anthropomorphized in our myths, fairytales, fables and religions as evil. It is the Darkness, the AntiDivine energy that opposes Light, structure, order.

This was necessary because our consciousness was, up until recently, in a baby state.

Just as certain substances and experiences are too potent for a child — sex, drugs, cars, guns — so, too, chaos was too powerful and unwieldy an energy for us to handle. Embracing and unleashing it too early in the development of human consciousness would have simply resulted in complete destruction. There would have been no remaining skeletal framework of consciousness remaining upon which to create a new matrix of energy.

And so we demonized it, to keep ourselves safe.

We have been children telling each other stories about the boogey man, the monster under the bed.

And just as in nearly all our fables, myths, fairytales and religions, the monster, we are taught, must be killed.

This is what maturation and personal empowerment and even a degree of spiritual awakening requires or did require up until now: Kill your inner monster and set yourself free from its tyranny.

The tyranny of what.

The tyranny of fear, isolation, lostness, depression, self criticism, anger, depression. The tyranny of a mind that feels as if it's on a rampant and wild ride through fields of unruly emotion which threaten to cripple or even fully destroy our happiness, our financial, physical, emotional, creative and spiritual prowess.

So we develop an activist outlook, trying to dim, diminish and delete all possible outbursts of what we would then experience as negative energy.

We develop a constantly seeking mentality, trying to fill and fix inner holes, kill and tame inner monsters, discover our purpose, relate more authentically, feel and find joy.

The personal empowerment industry is a multi billion dollar industry and growing.

And yet if it's so full of incredible wisdom and guidance, why the fuck hasn't anyone been able to stop seeking?

Have you ever stopped to consider that the hunger you feel will never be answered in the light you seek, because there is a missing energetic element, an essential spiritual nutrient, that makes any and all spiritual endeavors at awakening ultimately unsatisfactory?

What we do not understand is how fulfillment works.

And that is because we do not understand the purpose and power of energy alchemy.

I am fulfilled not because of what I know or have "downloaded" or are able to download with my incredible psychic gifts, not because of something I've learned, a block I've moved through or a low frequency emotion I've cast off; not because of an unruly, dangerous aspect of me that i've finally figured out how to tame or kill.

I'm fulfilled because I know that nothing and no one has power over me.

And that truth can only be firmly held, no matter the storms of chaos within or the clashing voices without that criticize, disdain, judge, dismiss and even hate me.

Over the past two years I've been called a cult leader, a narcissist, arrogant, a fraud, a filthy hooker, a saggy dog and have been accused of running a brothel out of my house because of the incredibly obtuse way in which some people understand my teachings and my marketing.

I've been publicly excoriated in huge facebook groups and on pages of total strangers, where vicious discussions about me have raged for days.

And I've been mocked, laughed at and dismissed.

One of my family members, in fact, publicly mocked and derided my teachings, taking sides with someone else who used to be very close to me in my business and who then went public with a livestream about how I was a fraud and didn't walk my talk. I was slack-jawed at the betrayal.

And yet.

Integrity Consciousness + The Dark Grid: The Exacting Standards Of The DarkCodes And How This Impacts The Potency Of Your Gift (And Therefore Your Sales)

DarkCodes are the elegantly refined codes of consciousness (being the True Feminine energy carriers that they are) and as such, require exactingly high standards of integrity, emotional mastery and TruthTelling in order to work with them. When you meet these requirements, you unlock a much more powerful expression of your genius and spiritual gifts.

Your intuitive nudges convert to *psychic gifts*.

Your creativity becomes *innovation*.

And if you are in the business of making money from your genius (or if you're not, but very much want to be), tapping in to the potency of your DarkCodes has very practical application:

Your confidence skyrockets.

You know yourself as a genius who cannot be compared to anyone.

You create from a place of newness and refreshment — programs, products and offerings that are conscious and awake and that collaborate with you in their own marketing that cause you to stand out effortlessly from the crowd. A giant among humans.

You radiate the ineffable, magnetic Black Light of Truth that causes your customers to finally be able to *see* and *feel* their problems at the root and be open only to an utterly new way of solving them.

In other words, your willingness to live according to the decree of your feminine genius calls into their own dark codes and wakes them up.

DarkCodes are the New (and no, I don't mean the new trend).

They are what set you apart from every other transformational agent and spiritual genius on the planet. They are intimate and personal (whereas LightCodes are universal). They work with the Youest You (your genius).

And, they have rules for how they will agree to be used. And you must know what those rules are if you want to access them.

DarkWorkers are the emissaries and stewards of the DarkCodes, and if this is you, you're being called with an urgency never before expressed to apprentice with the Dark, to master your gift at a higher level than you can imagine and to dedicate your entire being to this work.

It's false humility to tuck in your tail and bow your head and not own your true genius.

This the Dark will not stand.

Living in Supreme Integrity to your genius requires that you speak the Truth of that genius, not the watered down version palatable and popular with the humans.

As Light begins to embrace the Dark, what this really means is that God is beginning to explore Its own level of Integrity.

These are extraordinary times.

It is time for you to answer the call.

THE EVOLUTION OF THE DIVINE HUMAN CEO

Step 0) Artifact a 3D business/income stream based purely on human consciousness.

(Since your 5D Blueprint is the true energetic foundation, artifacting a 3D income stream based purely on human consciousness means your source of cash has no alignment to the 5D blueprint. Therefore the source inevitably collapses: Mental, physical illness. Financial ruin.)

Covalent Truth: We are not god/We only have a spark of the divine within us

Step 1) Build 5D blueprint into 3D.

(This is what nearly all spiritual entrepreneurs are being called to do right now.)

Covalent Truth: We are god.

Step 2) INVENT new multiD blueprint and bring it down in synchronous time.

(What a few #5DEntrepreneurs are now doing.)

Covalent Truth: We are creating god.

The Energetics Of Fear And Genius

Science confirms the truth of the energetics of fear and genius I've been channeling.

"If we operate under fear we use a smaller part of the brain, but when we use creative thinking the brain just lights up."

https://ideapod.com/born-creative-geniuses-education-system-dumbs-us-according-nasa-scientists/

Ambivalence Is Terror (Or The Next-Level Sophistication Of The Shadow Mind)

Once you start living naturally in next-level consciousness (meaning, you are a master of your experience in terms of what comes in, when and how, and also that you effortlessly embrace what is tempting you to experience it as crisis), what you must do in order to reach your next level *after this* becomes more subtle to detect.

In order to reach it, you must recognize AMBIVALENCE for what it truly is: TERROR.

I teach a lot about intuition, and how it speaks often in the tone of fear. Much of what our intuition directs us to do is terrifying, because its job is to tune our frequency to our Spiritual Signature, where our highest level experiences, abundance and gifts already reside, so we can be an energetic match for them.

But when you uplevel, so does your fear.

For it is a consciousness just like any other. And its end game is survival.

For those for whom direct and obvious fear holds little sway, ambivalence will rise up as the next cunning seduction of the shadow soul.

Fear is the overt, entry-level resistance to upleveling. It's like the dragon in front of the castle. Everything is obvious. You can see the Princess (your next-level prize) hanging out the 79th-story window. You can see the huge fire-breathing dragon (your fear). And it's hella obvious what you need to do.

Ambivalence is fear's much sneakier, more subtle and sophisticated resistance to upleveling. Ambivalence is like a tiny, sharp-toothed lizard guarding the small, almost imperceptible entrance to a long tunnel that leads to an underground treasure trove of gold.

In other words, nothing is obvious anymore.

The lizard is kind of off-putting. I mean, no one wants to be nipped by a testy gecko. But does it guard anything valuable? I mean. It's a *gecko*.

But it might. It seems pretty insistent on not letting you take a peek down that dark tunnel.

But then again maybe it's just grumpy in general.

And what's down the dark tunnel anyway? More dirt? But maybe not. Maybe this is the famed Tunnel of Gold you've heard a few rare beings talk about having discovered.

But of course you have to be able to see it first AS a treasure. And the thing about ambivalence is that it occurs as so innocuous an emotion that you can't imagine it's guarding anything.

More on this later. But for now, be highly attuned to where your pesky little ambivalence is showing up. It may just hide your greatest treasure yet

The Alchemy Of Action

Use the action you manifestly don't want to do and have no inspiration to do and are resisting like hell as the alchemizing channel through which you intentionally and consciously transmute low frequency fear, self doubt, or paralysis into high frequency power, excitement and triumph.

As long as you are executing the action with the intention of alchemizing the fear or resistance in the doing of it, your results will be high frequency, and you won't have to worry about your results carrying the low frequency energy that began and instigated the action, no matter how full of fear, self doubt, or mistrust you are.

In order for this to work, this must be highly intentional and conscious, otherwise the low frequency energy will stabilize through the channel of your action and come out the other end just as low frequency as before.

Unconscious action won't accomplish the alchemy.

SuperConscious action always will.

It Is Time: The Age Of Disruption

It is time for the human planetary field, created by all of our collective thoughts and actions over thousands and millions of years, to be disrupted at its core.

Not at the edges where it feels better.

That's what the spiritual gurus and teachers before us did. They clipped the tone-cords..literally the CHORDS of dissonance, or the dis-chords...between what we have collectively built and what was intended to be built. And this is the part people can't stand but it's just true (I know because I helped design it):

There is in fact an original blueprint that stands as the tone of exacting standards for the human system of consciousness (basically how we think about where our power and energy come from and how to increase it) and against which every human action or thought either strains-literally is set in dis-chord — or with which it lives in harmony — resulting in health, wealth and abundance.

This is the energetic REASON why you ever struggle or don't have what you want: you don't understand how power and energy actually work.

For millennia, we placed our power FAR outside of us.

Over the centuries, our spiritual leaders have been targeting certain chords of dissonance through their message that have worked to realign us to the Truth about where our power actually resides and how energy actually works.

Love thy neighbor, for instance.

That clipped many dis-chords (love is more powerful than hate) and brought a great deal of humanity back into alignment.

BUT because we had this much deeper dis-chord in place — victim or survival consciousness and the belief that power exists OUTSIDE of us at all — it actually rent another part of the fabric of consciousness even more out of alignment (hence the crusades and the Roman Catholic Church and political systems using Christianity to gain power because people still thought power comes TO them from the OUTSIDE and they saw Christianity as the vehicle).

It is now time, having "raised consciousness" to this degree — literally energetically clipped enough dis-chords that a good deal of our global blueprint of consciousness has risen UPWARDS to its natural state (the anti gravitational pull of truth) — to cut the BIG dis-chord. The one that is keeping every individual, society, culture, and system straining against our collective blueprint.

And that's the belief that there are victims.

And because I'm a Master Code Holder and Blueprint Originator, (meaning I helped design the original blueprint), I hold all the codes and can read blueprints like a book — both the original intended one (for individuals this is the tone of their exacting standards held by their personal High Feminine and for us as a collective it's the collective tone of exacting standards held by the divine feminine), and the one that's been BUILT by the individual over its lifetime or the collective over ITS millennia life. (And by the way, everything you do and don't do carries a frequency and gets coded into the energetic blueprint that is your lived life.)

But there's a piece that wasn't clear to me until recently about why I know it's time for the Great Disruption, and it's very similar to the whole Y2K scare.

Remember that?

Back before 2000, all programs had dates embedded in them as part of their code and operating system, and all the coders just used two digits for the month and year. As in 12/89.

No one thought to specify the FIRST two digits of the year because they would always be "19."

But then people started wondering how when the actual date flipped to "20....", our programs would function. In the absence of the "19", the programs would just read "00."

For instance — making calculations based on dates. Would the date of 12/89 be interpreted as "12/0089"?! If so, what the freak would happen to the WORLD?

I was in the middle of helping build and run an IT consulting company at the time. Our CIO clients were FREAKED. They were talking about the possibility, on 12/31/1999 at midnight, elevators getting stuck, automatic doors freezing, whole companies' critical software just shorting out.

They hired legions of programmers to comb through all their systems to reprogram the dates and avoid catastrophe.

When 12/31/1999 flipped to 1/1/2000, our clients were on call, waiting with baited breath.

Nothing happened. Phew.

But it did happen, you see.

Just not in THOSE programs.

It happened in our mental and emotional ones, about twelve years later, on 12/12/12.

Wanna know what happened?

Embedded into our consciousness at the beginning were these very special and powerful codes. Codes so powerful, they had to be kept completely invisible to consciousness until we were capable of working with them, because when they got turned on, when we became aware of them and they became capable of influencing our programming, all hell would break loose, because THEY were coded with the disruption of the very system they had been coded into.

Their purpose was to effect a Quantum BOOM in that very system. To apply such an intense amount of energy and impact across the entire field and substrate of consciousness that it would *almost* be obliterated, but not entirely. Because then if course there would be no Quantum BOOM of upgrading, it would be a Quantum BOOM that would totally destroy consciousness and reboot the entire program from the beginning. Not that there would be anything wrong with this (though the existing grid would certainly think so!), but the purpose isn't total destruction. It was destruction in the service of a rebirth at a much higher frequency — essentially the creation of beings capable of CREATING consciousness, not just receiving it. (In other words, we were always meant to go from BEING coded — primitive consciousness unaware of itself; the primacy of the subconscious — to DEcoding — consciousness becoming aware of itself; trying to DECODE its own self; the primacy of consciousness — to ENcoding — superconscious that has moved into divinity power and energy management, capable of creating consciousness.)

These codes, because of their power, had to be kept in the dark until the planetary system was ready to receive them. And so they were embedded with their own, separate sub/super-consciousness ("sub-" so as to go unnoticed; "super-" because there was nothing "asleep" or in need of "awakening" about them. They were already fully awake. Just waiting beyond/beneath the ability of the other codes to detect them) that operated totally independent of the main system, and whose job was to determine the precisely perfect *timing* for their own activation.

These are the Dark Codes and they began streaming through the Dark Portal on May 11 of this year.

The time between 12/12/12 and 5/11/18 has been a time of dis-integration from the operating grid of consciousness as the Dark Codes began waking up their primary carriers and calling them to their work. (And because modern western medicine and psychology sees INTEGRATION as the healthiest state, humans who were beginning to dis-integrate were seen as mentally ill, NOT for what they were: the carriers of the next consciousness: Chaos Consciousness. ((For from what, other than chaos, do you think Gods craft consciousness? ☺))

This is why many of you/us went through personal hells during that time. It was our Dark Awakening.

Then, on May 11, 2018, the Dark Portal broke open and began streaming codes onto the Light Grid.

And that means that it is Time.

Time for us to take a quantum leap into a much higher frequency of living, both individually and collectively.

The age of incremental change is over.

It is now the Age of Disruption and therefore of Quantum BOOMs. (Of all kinds, hence the increase in earthquakes, crazy weather, etc).

And for those of us who have had their codes activated—those I am calling Darkworkers or Spiritual Disruptors (the "anti-activists" who are not here to save anything because there is nothing that needs to be saved)— it is our job to create Quantum BOOMs, and that means going to the absolute most dis-chordant tone that exists — the place where individually and collectively we have built our lives in the greatest dis-chord with the truth...meaning with the original energetic blueprint — and shine not the light but the Dark — the newest, lightest light which is coming in from chaos consciousness (what else do you think Quantum BOOMS result in other than chaos?) that, when we alchemize it (the chaos), becomes the NEW blueprint of consciousness.

But of course that very place of greatest dis-chord is by definition going to be the place of greatest resistance, fear and triggering.

We are literally being called to become artisans of consciousness, not just receivers of consciousness. It's an INCREDIBLE and exhilarating and also massively terrifying time!

And in order to craft the new consciousness, we must release ALL of our power back into our fields. And where is that power being held? In the place of greatest dis-chord, because it takes an EXTREME amount of energy to hold ourselves in a constant strain against our native blueprint.

But here's the thing. We have been straining so hard for so long over millennia that we don't even recognize the strain AS strain. It's like the frog in the pot of water that very slowly rises to a boil.

And in order to be able to SEE it, Disruptors must point it out.

Directly.

Precisely.

They must direct a potent laser beam of darklight on it so that it can snap. It's the only way it works.

And that means?

Declaring in no uncertain terms that there are no victims.

And using the word "victim," and no other.

It's the only one that triggers people awake.

When You Finally Leap Over The Abyss, You Will Release The Abysmal

Darkness Is The Real God

Ever wonder why we have a light bulb but not a "dark bulb"?

In other words, an instrument that, when flipped on, banishes the light and plunges the space into darkness?

There's an energetic reason for that.

Darkness is unwilling to overturn the Light.

The reason there is darkness energetically, on our planet, and in the universe, is simply because those are the places, truths, feelings, thoughts, and energies where the Light is unwilling to go.

We've had it backwards all along.

It is the Light that is on the learning journey.

The Darkness is simply pointing the way.

In other words, Darkness is our teacher. Darkness is the real God.

This is for anyone with a consciousness and who suffers and is looking for a way out.

What I am going to teach you is something that has never been taught — never even thought of — before now. That is because all development in human consciousness, in philosophy, myth, spirituality, psychology, sociology, metaphysics, theology, religion (my auto correct wanted that word to be "delusion" ha ha smart little auto correct), quantum mechanics and physics, chaos theory and new age spirituality has led us here. To this new point.

A point of utter stillness before the next Big Bang, the Quantum BOOM of consciousness creation, the death of the world Soul, the end of all suffering and source of struggle and the beginning of the Grand Unveiling, which is WHY we started coming here millions of years ago, and why I was asked to help design the Earth Experiment in the first place.

The contents of this book are coded with the frequency of this new chaos consciousness — the elite energetic that rests within your Dark DNA and is waiting to be activated and unleashed so it can unveil your superior functioning to you. So you can avail yourself of your Higher Mind, which operates far outside any existing framework, because its genius is to bring the utterly new in.

This is the first of three books.

Here I will tell the story "lightly."

I will introduce the characters of the new myth, interwoven with my own miraculous story of awakening from madness to spiritual millionaire in the span of one year and together this will create in you an unsettling and a longing for a new taste of the divine. This book is the voice sounding in the wilderness, Make way. It is the light appetizer before the Dark Feast of Imperial Joy.

Then comes the full story. The complete myth. Replete with a multiversal three ring circus, a blind biker gang, a caravan of unruly, superconscious beasts, and three little girls whose dreams are portals to each other.

Then, after the new archetypes of consciousness have been unleashed, the story told and the ground of being gathered and hushed, the third book will come into being as The Dark Speaks.

This is the Dark Trilogy.

A strange and unprecedented collection of spiritual philosophy, energetic technology, mythmaking and grand storytelling encoded to activate the springing forth of the new consciousness, the commencement of the Great Energetic Olympics and the opening of the Wild Black Tent under whose yawning hunger for the New we prepare to put on the Greatest Circus Show of energy, genius and magic mastery ever presented in the history of SpaceTime.

It all begins, as everything does, with a story

The Dark Heart of Gold

For most people, their brains are wired directly to their heart. Their actual heart.

For Disruptors, their brains Your brain is not wired to your body or your heart, or even to your energy body or heart chakra the way it is with almost everyone else.

Your brain is wired straight into your Dark Heart of Gold.

The way to work with Disruptors is opposite of normal people. Connect their wiring first from brain to dark heart of gold and THEN back to their body, Because the dark heart of gold is the replete compass. Their native GPS.

When THIS is activated (which happens simply by the mentor seeing and therefore validating it which allows the client the opportunity to SEE it which is easy for them because they naturally SEE IN THE DARK) because this is such a potent compass and GPS and is the source of spiritual intelligence or TRUTH, it can provide guidance that is CERTAIN, rather than guidance from the intuition only, which is sourced from the spongey, leaky, moist shadow heart.

It's spiritual intelligence. Remember when i was asking what faculty of knowing the dark heart of gold has that is an analog to the heart having the faculty of intuition? It's spiritual intelligence. TRUTH. And OMFG. Intuition is still murky and "inconsistent" because it's being run by the spongey leaky shadow heart!! Spiritual intelligence is clear and razor sharp because it's being run by the cold vacuum of the dark heart of gold. So then my question is how does the dark heart of gold inform the shadow heart with the TRUTH? And the other equally important question, which is really the same just worded differently and from the other dimension, which is what I call the Sacred Quandary: How do we know when our fear is masquerading as intuition.

Yep. It is. I'm writing a totally new first chapter. It doesn't talk about the fem and masculine yet — but it will. It's all connected. This book is for spiritual brainiacs who are in fact Disruptors (dark workers) and who are suffering and whose businesses are stuck because they don't know how to operate their own system of genius and power. It's wired completely differently than almost everyone else's on the planet. So differently that no one knows how to help them. Which is why all the coaches and programs don't work for them and why the therapists and psychologists ALSO can't help them. And why no one understands them.
These people have brains who are wired into a totally new energetic body (the dark body) that works completely differently than bodies who are wired to the light body and the light grid. This is all about systems and processes and tools and they hate those. They just need an understanding of how to work with the fundamentals framework of the universe — the two energies — and they'll create their OWN system. And they need to know they're not broken or hopeless. The Dark/Light stuff will come later. First my job is to get them to see i get their very real problems and to give them a completely new framework (the one I give in the

livestreams) because all they need is access to the RAW MATERIAL of the universe and to be shown how to work with it and they're golden. And then they go make lots of money OOMMGGG The feminine and masculine have been creating this new dark body energetically and now it is ready to be received by our bodies and consciousnesses. It is the body that will channel our personal genius and PURE INDIVIDUATION. And that is what 2012 was about. The end of collective consciousness. It was also the END OF INTEGRATION.

But the new dark body/genius works with RAW MATERIAL ONLY. And THIS is why people must know about the fem and masc, because those are the two fundamental energies that work with the raw material of consciousness.

his book is really about the energetic anatomy of Disruptors. It is a sneaky bomb from the Dark tucked inside a spiritual business book.

Energy Alchemy of the sub archetypes happens when you invite them in to the cauldron that is the dark heart of gold and apply the darklight beam of the RADICAL TRUTH. This is what a truth rant is. And the only way they enter the dark heart of gold is to SUBMIT to the radical truth they will be told.

nd just remember Jenny, there are and never were any victims. The feminine CHOSE to be demonized. It is her special brand of genius to go under. Go invisible. Be dismissed. Misunderstood. To go DARK. There is a very beautiful, poignant and profound reason for why she did this. The feminine is not and never was a victim. You are going through such an amazing journey. I am honored to be witnessing and holding the space for it. And I'm amazed at your strength and dedication to the truth. As you craft your message and mission, be mindful that there is no victim energy in it. No desire or need to save. And this does mean no desire to seek justice. Justice is something a child seeks. To restore the world to being fair.

The world is not fair in the way a child can conceive. It is equal. But also not in the way a child, totally divorced from her sense of omnipotence, can imagine. The desire for justice and fairness comes from the child and from the victim, who arrange their lives around what was done to them or to their kind and to seeking fairness and recognition for their pain. Deeper than the drive for justice or saving is the drive to FREE others from the prison of their self inflicted illusions, which are the only things keeping them in pain. So I encourage you to submit the fullness of your message and mission to the shadow alchemy tool. Shoot all of it straight into your dark heart of gold so that every ounce of shadow can be alchemize into pure potent truthtelling. Because, while almost everything we've been taught is full of illusion, there is one thing that is unequivocally energetically accurate and that is this: The Truth will set you free.

Humans create art to experience the feminine. It is the only place on the light grid where the pure feminine is expressed. (Even in sex, or sexual energy, the masculine energy is present.) The feminine is inherently worthless and priceless. That is why women have such issues with anxiety and self esteem. We are the embodiment of the worthlessness and the pricelessness of the feminine. Which doesn't FIT anywhere, really. Which carries the monstrous within. The Dark codes of disorientation and magic. When we talk about the feminine rising, what we are in fact talking about is humans — and really basically women — confessing to themselves that they are, indeed, worthless because they are priceless. The feminist movement went far astray when it tried to prove the WORTH and USEFULNESS of the feminine. That's simply applying masculine principles to the feminine. Hello ☐♀☐☐ that's not progress at all. The masculine is where worth is stored, expressed and used. It is the energy of providing, doing and delivering useful outcomes. It is the linking energy. The word of continuity. The feminine is where worth is MADE UP (we are very good at make-up). It is the energy of madness and genius. Of the ability to unhook and begin from nothing. It is the un-linking energy. The word of death. The feminine is worthless on the light grid precisely *because* it is priceless. Art is the only useless and priceless experience on the light grid. It exists alone. Far from reach. And yet our most intimate prize. Just like women. And the feminine. Time for women to admit it: They're useless worthless works of art.

Lorna - I'm wanting to get defensive and talk about all the other investments I've made in myself over the past 2 years, totaling over $65,000 at this point. I know what it's like to invest in myself. I know what it's like to place my whole fucking life on the dotted line (over and over again) And I'm tired of that too. I'm seeing and meeting a different version of myself, one that doesn't know how to hang because she's not spent much time socializing Like a mama wolf, protecting her new cub, I'm not going to throw this baby self out into the world (or into another program, even if it's yours) until that I know . . . That it's safe. (And I get that we create the safety) So . . . I'm still feeling and sensing As I let my old habits fall away. But I don't think that means that I have to scrape by in this process. I expect to be well-compensated as I move through this Because I know what I have to give And i'm not even warmed up yet. Will I invest more in the future - yes. And that's why I'm here. To get warmed up (with you, in this new-for-me way) so I can take on the whole mother-loving court ❤️▢

I invested twice that. Three times probably. Without complaint or checking my progress and demanding I get some results before I invest more, and again and more again. Because I am committed to my greatest legacy no. Matter. What. It is my first and greatest love and it get WHATEVER it requires to be unleashed onto the world stage. I hold nothing back. I make no demands on it. I am it's steward and its blind disciple. And because O know it it this blind discipleship that is the source of its success and my magic and complete power. I don't not burden my legacy with concerns of safety. I am god. I decide that my legacy and I are always safe. No matter what. And this frees me to invest at grotesquely high levels because my legacy has extremely high requirements and desires. She is the most expensive date in the universe. She is, in fact, priceless. And I treat her so. And as a result, she released her priceless genius to me in the form of total euphoria and financial success. That's how it goes. It's the laws of energy. You can balk at them all you want, but they are unbending and do not concerned themselves with the smallness of fear.

Everywhere you go, you throw fireballs, my therapist said to me. It's like it's licking the hems of your robes and setting everything on fire. STOP SETTING THE WORLD ON FIRE, she said.

And thus the prostitute is born in all of us.

And we settle in to do decades of shadow work on our genius.

Manifesto of the Dark Disruptors, TruthCarriers and Spiritual Iconoclasts

It's time we told the truth.

We are not broken. We're here to break.

reak free. Break others out. Break through.

Failing at almost every system or structure doesn't mean there's something wrong with us. It means we're the ones who are meant to cause the system to fail.

We're here to shatter paradigms, not master them.

It's time we turn the tables on a host of misperceptions, illusions about our nature, and claim what we know to be true.

ome say we're harsh and abrasive and that we need to soften our very guarded hearts. Cold and closed-hearted, they say. And what troublemakers. Selfish, nearly narcissistic, insubordinate inordinate rebels.

We say no. our hearts are not closed guarded hard or cold. They do not need to be opened or softer or warmed in the cultural oven. We have a wildly open dark heart of gold and disruption is the way we love.

We do not swing knives, spark chaos or unleash the beasts of genius because we don't care. Quite the contrary—because YES, we are contrarians—. We do it with great passion and precision and in service of what has undeniably been called in.

And Crazy? Unwell? Unhinged?

We say we've gone sane, and yes that last slur is absolutely true. We're unhinged, baby. Unhooked from the hot grasp of the grid. The gasps when we "disobey." Go our own way.

What they don't realize is that they're longing for this.

It's what they called us in to violently arrange. The way winter arranges for violets

We are not brilliant but broken.

Genius but jinxed.

We're bringers of a disruptive dis-ordered consciousness—one they think they didn't order, but did definitely request, and which will not be ordered around by anyone— and we will no longer squeeze our unruly genius into a system built to order and arranged with everything it's got against the chaos that is our nature.

e are not devils.

Or even angels.

We are the Other, the Unknown, the ones who live their lives outrageously UnDone.

We are vessels of the Great Disruption, which is gathering itself around us like a graceful cyclone.

e are like knives, yes. The knife of a surgeon, a sculptor, a chef.

And we're in their brains, chiseling away at their brave bodies or thought and flaying illusion in the very place they cook up their imprisonment because we love them. And because we are here to craft the world into a work of art.

To put an end to the constant self reflection, healing and spiritual seeking and point the way through the mirror because the world does not need to endlessly reflect us.

It can be, if we choose, a portal of our own making.

And that is why we refuse to operate inside any paradigm.

It's not that we can't, as if we're crippled.

It's that we won't.

It's a matter of supreme integrity that we don't.

This unwillingness to co-operate— to operate within — is the sharp point of our genius and we are not ashamed or afraid of it.

We will not slouch through the portal of our greatness or dull our power.

We will instead place the razor's edge of our dark and priceless gift against the heart of all that matters and then….?

With just the right amount of pressure, and in the name of love, slice open the soft flesh of fear with keen precision.

Because the true truth is this:

The dark heart of gold beckons in every one of us, longing to be let through. To Shine it's blacklight of brilliance straight into our throats from the other side of the mirror so we can finally step through.

We are not misfits unfit for this life. We are here to fit the point of our finely tuned knife into the heart in our own throats first, open our third eye, press the point in until it breaks through and then throw our heads back, laugh with abandon, and speak the motherfucking truth.

Magic Is Natural

Let's talk cause and effect.

Clearly, they do not occur within the same paradigm of power, otherwise the cause would not have the ability to change the state of the entity on which it acts.

The natural world is not the domain of its own causation. In other words, And until now we have been operating ignorantly within the paradigm of the powerless—that which receives commands and obeys them: the 3D world of matter—and not in i paradigm of the powerful—the energetic realm, the SuperConscious field where Time and Space are one and in which the commands of being and matter are fashioned.

We have been foolishly trying to place our hands on the levers of power while groping in the shadowlands of the imprisoned

Whatever is, we have crafted from energy. (This is not new knowledge, of course.) The struggle comes when what is, is not what we desire. And when what is not yet (what is energy coming into matter) is taking too long for our liking.

Then, we do not call it magic, but hustle and grind.

The difference between the two is simply one of leverage.

When we place our hands knowingly on the raw material of the universe, we activate energetic law, the law of cause and effect, and with the least effort, produce the greatest and swiftest result. Thus we create magic on demand.

When we place our hands unwittingly on these powerful leavers, we also create magic, and yet cannot reproduce it at will because we simply tumbled onto them, and have no real training or mastery in navigating the land of power in which they exist.

This is unnecessary.

Ultimate Power—the clear-eyed command of cause and effect, of calling into being exactly what we desire, exactly when we desire it, and not just material objects but people and opportunities, spiritual, intellectual and emotional states of being, intuitive and psychic knowledge and gifts, anything we could wish or imagine, and much more beyond—is simply the ability to operate all expressions of Time and Space—the fundamental building blocks of matter and 3D experience—with supreme mastery.

Time and Space have two masters.

The masculine and the feminine.

And they are at our disposal.

The Magical Masculine

Much is spoken of about the divine feminine in the role of spiritual awakening, manifestation and the evolution of consciousness. On my own journey, I encountered the term "Feminine Rising" hundreds of times, if I encountered it once.

It was the spiritual equivalent of the feminist movement in the material world: Time to honor the feminine energy, women said, not just actual women.

And so the Heroine's Journey was born, to counter in equal worth the Hero's Journey. It was "born" in the sense that it was honored intentionally. The Heroine's Journey has been around for ages, depicted in many myths, though still completely misunderstood. And it is this misunderstanding that has caused the weakness of the journey to complete awakening to be exposed.

At first we believed the Hero's Journey was the answer to our suffering: Strike out from your tribe of origin, follow your own path, discover your strength to overcome all obstacles between you and the treasure you seek (self awareness, purpose and empowerment), kill your inner monsters, integrate your warring inner factions—which means repair your separation from Source (which is put forth as the cause of all suffering), become One With All (the One being presented as the Source of wisdom, Truth, power and wellbeing, and therefore the only way to access these states is to become one with the source of them), and then return to the tribe as a new being full of purpose, ready to teach others what you've learned and encourage them to strike out on their own path.

This is a masculine (Hero's) journey because it embodies, expresses and requires the seeker to call on and use masculine traits in order to complete it.

Fighting and overcoming.

Overpowering and striking out.

Going it alone.

Depending on no one.

Driving to clear outcomes (I want to know and discover myself and the answers to life).

Gathering and amassing treasures as a result of winning the war (treasures of knowledge, awareness, self mastery).

Definition and clarity. (I am this and not that. My happiness is not a product of my tribe. It is a product of my own creation.)

We are all called to go on the Hero's Journey. Some of us answer the call. Others do not. Those who do not, remain children in adult bodies, never having separated themselves from their family and culture of origin. Living according to the values and dreams of their personal collective (family, tribe, culture of upbringing). These are humans who are entirely asleep. Deaf and dumb and mute. Unrealized expressions of consciousness and power. The Late Adopters of Awakening. They will be the last to rise and the first to fight others who rise before them. First to judge, blame, criticize, demean, disdain, dismiss. And also often, to diagnose. To see awakening and all its signs as symptoms of sickness, aberration requiring correction quickly and completely. They are the most afraid, least powerful and often most ignorant of their own state. These are the culture keepers. The standard bearers of the opposing side. And whenever they sense a mutiny against the tried and true, they are the first to sound the battle cry of the status quo. Their position is rigid (their battle lines are drawn dead straight and clear). Their righteousness is unquestionable. They are the ones who claim Authority. And if you are intent on waking up, you are guaranteed to encounter them on the journey.

In fact, they are important gatekeepers whose ability to cast fear into your heart reveals to you your own position in the tribe: a dreamer with no actual intention of awakening, a doer who strikes out no matter what, or, the last (or first) group - a creator, who does not ever intend to play the game or win the battle according to any of the rules or lines drawn around the constraints of consciousness.

The doers are the ones who are half awake. They have accomplished the Hero's Journey and are now stuck in an endless loop on the Heroine's Journey, dismantling what they can no longer grasp, spinning and cycling through the spiral of despair of exhausting spiritual seeking they call shadow work.

And why am I taking you along this path when you thought this was a book about manifestation?

Because manifestation on demand and at will is a skill of a god. It is a power mastered by someone who has unzipped from the human psyche completely, who has left all the tribal paradigms behind — family, cultural, spiritual, and the human consciousness itself — and has crafted for herself a new psyche entirely, based on energetic and spiritual law, capable of clearly handling the raw martial of the universe and mastering the orchestration of the feminine and masculine energies, which are required for any creation to be made manifest.

And so you must know about the journey of consciousness. We must walk the path from powerlessness to power, so you can identify where you are on the journey to being able to make magic on demand in your life and business, see clearly the obstacles that were once (are right now) invisible to you, and be taught by a master how to overcome them in such a way that they disappear from your psyche altogether.

This is accomplished through new a energetic technology called Shadow Alchemy, in which you complete the Heroine's Journey for good and step into the Anti-Hero's Journey, which is less a journey and more a new Domain of Being in which you craft your own consciousness from the ground of purely individuated being (as any god does) and in so doing access true power, the root of real magic and the ability to manifest on demand.

And the answer lies not in more and deeper activation and honoring of the feminine but in a first-ever-in-human-consciousness, deep, authentic, and full-system understanding and appreciation of the magical masculine.

This will, in turn, open up an accurate understanding and appreciation of the true feminine, because contrary to the good intentions of feminists and New Age spiritual seekers, the feminine has not been honored, activated or properly understood in either of these movements.

What opens the feminine (to our understanding of her, to her own power, to her genius and gifts) is the masculine, for this is his primary role: to serve the awakening and the awakened feminine.

And yet because human consciousness does not understand the masculine and often misinterprets its expression, we miss the greatest gift we are being offered and head down the path of suffering, all the while believing in our hearts we are striking out on the path to awakening.

The Two Problems

First, there is the problem of understanding.

Then, there is the problem of mastery.

Understanding creates willingness. Willingness creates mastery.

So first we must discover the ignorance that is hidden from view. And when we do, our natural willingness to take action, to accept certain decisions that would before have been unthinkable, becomes second nature.

This is how we develop supreme mastery over the Light Grid, which is where we operate and live out our experience.

The Light Grid is the assemblage of energetic frequencies that have been selected by the collective human consciousness to operate as our shared system of power. It provides us access, through certain channels with specific gates of passage, to the raw materials of the universe, available for our handling. In other words, the Light holds our power. And we hold the Light.

And we can either handle or mishandle it.

If we mishandle it, we create blocks in our mental field and our mind is in shadow, no longer inspired, bereft of our best ideas, no longer infused with sudden and perfect knowing of exactly what to do, when, and how. We are left agonizing in analysis paralysis, self-doubt, seeking endlessly outside ourselves for the answers. Our mind, wired for total, instant, and perfect knowing, the intuitive and psychic channel, the channel of knowledge and intelligence — human and divine, the portal to insight, either flawed or perfect, becomes crippled and unstable, tortured and tortuous, an instrument of hell rather than a gateway to heaven.

If we mishandle the Light, we also create blocks in our emotional field and our heart is cast in shadow, no longer able to distinguish what it truly desires from what it "should" desire; full of disloyalty to itself, seeking approval and acceptance from every other channel but its own, terrifyingly willing to abandon itself at the first sign of danger, of being cast out; searching for a sense of worth, divorced from its innate ability to shine its fine eye of love and worthiness on the truly wondrous, the awe-inspiring, and pour itself into the clearest expressions of its nature that cause it to skip a beat and take breaths away. The heart, the portal to all stories that transform and uplift, the gateway to priceless self adoration and the channel through which the glory of life flows, becomes a shadowy, empty husk, weak, without access to the rhythm of life.

And, if we mishandle the Light, we create blocks in our physical field, our bodies, and all physical expressions that share the symbolic map of "body." All collections and expressions of boundary, what delimits one entity from another, falter and fail dramatically and in one crisis after another. Relationships collapse. Finances tumble. Careers fail. Homes are lost or damaged. Cars are wrecked or plundered. We become physically sick, weak, without energy, often in ways that confound traditional medicine. There's "no reason" for our illness, because the reason is energetic: We are wired to source and run power through all our systems from the Light, and when we mishandle it, it cannot flow and we are left to run on its weaker expression as shadow.

And last, when we mishandle the Light, we create blocks in our spiritual field. Our vision for our life, our sense of self, our identity, and our ability to dream weakens into wistfulness, faint hope, wishful thinking and the fantasies of the child who has no agency to make her dreams come true. We lose access to our spirit, to the animating decree that causes the kingdom within us to rise up and hear our true desire, heed our visionary command, stand for our wildest dreams, call on perfect, divine intelligence, and therefore collapse time, lift out of the 3D frame that has become our prison and spring forth over it reimagined as our playground, over which we have ultimate control, and thus make the mundane magical in no time.

All we need to know is when and exactly how we mishandle the Light, and then what to do about it.

That is this book.

The first of its kind, which explains the laws of Light—the Divine Masculine—and the energetics for how to access power on the Light Grid and so to activate magic and to manifest on demand.

For Light is deeply misunderstood here. And if we are to operate the Source of Power with mastery and so to be in our full power, we must first understand how Light operates, what its channels of power are, how it falls into shadow, and most importantly, how it sounds.

Understanding The Light: The Sound Of Power

The Law of Attraction is more accurately spoken of as the Law of Inspiration, for what you are attracting into your experience are the gifts born by the divine masculine, whom I call the Magic Man. Whether it is a house, money, a published book, a new job, a lover, a dream vacation, or even immaterial gifts such as a peaceful state of mind, inspiration that turns into a business, or a brilliant piece of marketing copy, whatever comes into your experience—whatever you are trying to attract using LOA and the principles of manifestation—is being brought to the doorstep of your experience by the Divine Provider, the magical masculine energy of the universe. And if you are trying to attract him and his gifts, then you must be attractive to him. It is his energy you must know how to work with.

In other words, it is his energy you must know how to inspire.

It is his energy that works behind the scenes, activating the Synchronistic Grid where everything you desire already Is. It is he who gets busy "shaking hands" with all the other Magic Men who attend and serve all the other people who will bring you all the opportunities you seek, energetically lining all of you up to activate each other, like an infinite labyrinth of dominoes.

Your ideal client, who brings your cash and your million dollar year, the man you will marry, the agent at the publishing company who will make your book a best seller, the realtor who has your dream home—all of them have their own Magic Man, their own ability to activate and inspire the magical masculine energy to provide for them and their greatest desire, which meeting you—their ideal mentor, life partner, writer, or client—will do.

And the masculine has rules for what inspires him to great action, and what causes him to turn away, disinterested.

The Codes of Desire: Shadow vs Light (The Energetics of Inspiration)

What you desire is coded with certain grades of power. Shadow is weakened Light, therefore shadow desire is coded with only weak power to inspire and attract the Magic Man, who is Light Itself.

You are the creator of the blueprint of your desire. You select it with the tones of your consciousness. The degree to which those tones are built with shadow versus Light codes (unconscious mishandling versus conscious handling of Truth) is the degree to which your desire will be either weak or powerful and your blueprint structured to build a container that is either powerfully magnetic (activating the feminine power to attract), which creates an ineluctable and inevitable electrical current around it (activating the masculine power to gather around the feminine for support and provision) or a weak container that is a nearly powerless magnetic field, one that creates a tiny current of electricity and only inspires a modicum of the full potency of the magical masculine.

The Magic Man builds your order the way a carpenter builds a house, by looking carefully at the blueprint of your desire and knowing every piece by heart.

In other words, to experience what you desire, your desire must be "built to code," or rather "coded to be built."

Shadow codes indicate a weakness in the structure of our desire. They create a weak blueprint and therefore a weak container. A weak container has weak magnetic strength, weak ability to inspire the magic man, and weak ability to hold whatever is received into it.

Light codes, however, vibrate with an insistence and a radiance the Magic Man literally cannot resist. The masculine is coded to turn toward the feminine in her power. It is energetic law.

Light codes indicate power in the structure of our desire. They create a strong blueprint and therefore a strong container, strong ability to inspire the magic man and strong ability to hold what is received.

The magic man is turned on by the presence of desire built on the truth of who we are, which means the truth of our power—where it lies and how we access, activate and grow it.

Just like a woman who knows who and what she truly is inspires the highest frequency man to be profoundly and irresistibly attracted to her, so too a human who knows who and what she truly is and what she is truly made of, inspires the full potency of the magical masculine energy and creates and lives a life full of miracles and knows magic is her natural state.

And so to talk of making magic means first we must talk of our true and our false nature.

We Are Made Entirely of Light

You are not entitled to the object of your desire just because you desire it greatly. This is one of the great flaws in the way LOA is taught.

Desire, ask, be open to receive, and ye shall indeed receive.

Except the world is littered with those who have desired, asked, been open, and received nothing resembling what they requested.

At least not consciously.

For this is one of the fatal flaws in the teachings of manifestation and Law of Attraction.

They cannot and do not treat of the subconscious desire. And the subconscious is what the Magic Man heeds and is drawn to, like a moth to flame.

If there is content in your subconscious, he will hear it, though you will not.

The magical masculine is built to see in the dark, to draw out from its depths our greatest gifts. It is what activates his Heroic Nature; it is the void he seeks to fill. And yet if there is content already there, if the container of our desire is full of shadow and built with shadow, he turns away.

Build your desire on the truth, and you will make magic on demand. Fill your energetic container with the truth of who you are, live every moment of your life in the vibration of that Truth, and the magical masculine has "no choice" but to obey your every command.

Shadow is energetically repulsive to the divine masculine. Just like any high frequency man who does not put up with the crisis and drama of a princess, so too the divine masculine is energetically turned off by the presence of shadow.

And so then the most critical question you must ask, and the only answer you need know, is this:

Who Am I? What Am I Made Of? How Do I Recognize Truth?

As we ask and answer these questions—in other words as we embark on the Hero's Journey of Consciousness—we will along the way be not only discovering the answers we have always sought, but will be building a sleek, keen, effective, fool-proof and predictable method for calling in our magic, on demand.

We will in other words be building total mastery in recognizing the difference between the voices of our shadow—the inner liars about who we are and where our power lies—and the voices of our Light.

Shadow is the sound of fallen Light. It is the sound of the Dark Feminine at war with herself. It is, at heart, the anxious feminine who has lost her way in the Light, refuses to surrender to its mastery, refuses to be mastered by the masculine, and in so doing, never achieves mastery over him.

To know how to inspire the divine masculine to provide for your every desire is to know how to master Light. And in order to master it, we must first be mastered by it.

Light has four voices. Each voice has two tones: illusion and truth.

Illusion sends the voice of light into shadow, making us weak at calling in our magic. Illusion is therefore the source of all struggle.

Truth is the sound of Light. It opens the portal to our absolute power and, by energetic law, inspires the divine masculine to provide for our every desire. Truth is the source of power and magic.

Welcome Email Transcript

Welcome to The Noble Warrior. This is Lorna Johnson. I am CEO of The Noble Warrior and Breakthrough Catalyst, and I'm going to be working with you in a three month program if you signed up for that, otherwise, this will be a standalone experience virtual retreat for you. By now, you hopefully have read the introduction to the workbook that was sent to you so you have some sense of what we're going to be talking about over the next five days, but if you haven't, that's okay. I will explain everything to you in summary here, and then in detail over the next four days.

But I want to first of all welcome you and honor you for the journey that you are embarking on. I am actually talking to you from an absolutely amazing place, and I mean that figuratively and literally. Literally, I am in a desert in High Desert, New Mexico, actually, right near Abiquiu, which is where Georgia O'Keeffe painted all of her famous paintings, and I am at the most remote monastery in the western hemisphere, Christ in the Desert Monastery, I am staring at soaring canyon walls that are a burnt orange color, and it just absolutely stunning here. And I'm also talking to you from a spiritual place, an emotional place that is also amazing, and it's the one that you're really looking for. I realized as I was preparing for this audio that the journey that I took to get to this place, and by that I mean this monastery, and the place that I am in my life right now are kind of exactly the same.

I drove over a thousand miles here over two days, and I drove alone, I drove by myself, and the last part of this journey is actually a 13 mile dirt road that is winding and torturous and very slow and takes about an hour, and my journey to where I am today is also very similar to that. It took me many years, it took me seven years to get here, and it will not hopefully take you seven years. That's part of the reason why you're going to be working with me, so that it doesn't take you seven years to make a full transformation in your life, but part of the reason that it took me that long is because I had a lot of things that I had to let go of.

I had built a life completely based on fear, on borrowed values, on borrowed belief systems, but really mostly on fear, and that's what we're going to be talking about and discussing and excavating and diving into not only over the next five days, but in all of our work together because the startling truth of the matter is that if you're here right now, it's because you built a life based on fear. You've built a life based on fear of yourself. Really, primarily that's what's at the heart of all of this. That might make a ton of sense to you, it might make no sense to you, and it's okay either way because it will become crystal clear over our time together.

This journey is worth it, it is long, you have to take it alone, no one else can take it for you, and the last part of the journey is the hardest and the most grueling, but it is so worth it to finally be able to stand in your power, to stand in a life that you have created from your truth and your core desires and your gifts, and feel what it feels like to be a true, what I call a Noble Warrior, in your life, and we're going to be talking a lot about that. If that term sounds a little odd, it's okay, just let it sound a little odd. It's one of the archetypes that we're going to be working with, and if you don't know what archetypes are, that's okay too.

So I just want to say that very, very few people on the planet are doing the work that you're doing. Most people stay in very small lives. I call it lowercase living. They walk around in a small 's' self, in a small 'l' life, and to me, that's no life at all, and I have a feeling that you feel the same way, and that's why you're here. So I'm not going to go into too much more detail today about this journey or about the archetypes, but I want to give you just a brief overview of them so that you can be oriented to what you're going to be hearing tomorrow.

So what do I mean by an archetype? An archetype is an energy pattern. It was a concept that was originated by Carl Jung, the famous analyst who came up with the whole union analysis framework, and really what it is is an energy pattern that exerts incredible power in our lives. There are hundreds of archetypes. Mother, father, these are archetypes. They are also specific people in your life, but they also carry what's called archetypal energy, and that just means that they carry a certain way of being and a certain kind of power and they have a certain personality to them. If you say to somebody, "Wow, you're such a mom." You know what you're saying, and excuse my stuffed up nose, I'm getting over a cold here. You know what you're saying to that person, and that person knows what you're saying to them as well, and that's because we all really inherently get archetypes. If you say, "Stop being such a fool." Okay, that's another archetype.

So we're going to be working with eight archetypes. And really, there's four, and I don't want to start confusing you with all of these numbers and things. If you've taken a look at the fear and power archetype map that is in the workbook in the introduction area, you'll know what I'm talking about. But what I want to say about this today is that all of our work is going to center around the four fears and the four powers that we all have within us, and essentially, the four fears are represented by four archetypes, and they're the prostitute, the saboteur, which you probably are very familiar with, most people know that one, the victim, also another very common one, and the child. And these represent your four voices of fear, and you will discover through this time together that they literally have been managing your entire life and are the reason why you're here needing a major change.

And the four what I call elevated archetypes are your four powers. The voices of your four powers. And they are the lover, so the lover is the prostitute who finally has found its power, and this I know might sound like a feminine term, but it's really not. Anybody can prostitute themselves, anybody can sell their souls, and that's really what the prostitute energy is about. When the prostitute finally finds its value and its power, it becomes the lover archetype. When the saboteur finally finds its power, it becomes the magician archetype, someone who can make anything happen, can create from nothing. When the victim finally finds its power, it becomes the warrior, and that is to me the most exciting one because it's the one that actually makes stuff happen and goes out and fights the good right. And when the child finally finds its power, it becomes the sovereign, the king or queen.

And because we're talking about warriorship, we're using the theme of warriorship, I like to think of these four fears as the troops. What do we know about troops? They have not achieved the level of mastery, the life wisdom, the power, the authority that the generals have, right? The generals being the four powers. So they're much more likely to do things like grumble, and complain, and resist when they get called into a great battle. And this is exactly what has been happening in your life. Exactly. The thing is, there's a lot of troops. They really far outnumber in terms of their voice, the generals. So that's why these four fears are so much more influential in our lives. They're not more powerful unless we give them power, but they're much more influential, so we take conscious control over which voices we allow to speak to us because here's the thing. Think about the troops and think about the generals. Which carries more truth? Which carries more inherent authority? Which ones are more trustworthy? Which ones would you entrust with planning and carrying out the most important battle of your life? The generals, obviously.

That is what your work really is. Your work is going to be to first be able to really understand the incredible influence that the four fears, or the troops, have had in creating the life that you now need to change. You're going to ger really, really clear on that. I've created a huge tool for personal reinvention and reflection and excavation of all of this stuff, and then visioning and brainstorming and creating your real life vision from your sense of power and your sense of purpose and clarity. But you're going to get really clear on, first of all, how the four fears have been ruling, and then you're going to make a conscious decision to take your power back and to live from the place of your four powers or the four generals, and you will start to recognize their voices. Each has a very distinct voice. They literally have phrases that they say, which are really phrases you say, and what's so cool about this work is that you will immediately start to be able to say, "Oh, I know who that is. That's the saboteur, not listening to that one." It's incredibly powerful.

And what you can expect from this week, even just listening to these audios and doing this journaling is insights you never expected to have, understandings, realizations. It's going to be kind of an explosive, exciting week. And probably also pretty sobering. Pretty disappointing in terms of really understanding how your life came to be the way it is, but also at the end, incredibly inspirational. Everybody who goes through this virtual retreat leaves it feeling incredibly inspired, beyond motivated. Motivated is a kind of takes effort. Inspired is just effortless, and that is how you will feel at the end, that's how you're supposed to feel because at the end of the virtual retreat, we are going into an intense intensive. I have actually spent almost all of the eight days here at Christ in the Desert Monastery on my retreat creating a massive vehicle for you that is going to take you on the most incredible journey of your life into your dreams. Into your dream life in every area.

We're going to go over 12 domains. You will not be working on all 12 over the next three months. We're going to pick a few. But you will have the opportunity to create an entire life vision that you've probably never done before. Almost nobody takes the time to do this, and I'm going to help you do that and walk you through it.

So I'm going to close here. This is a little bit longer. Most of the audios will be about 10 minutes long, and just say that, again, I really honor your bravery and your courage, and I wish you an incredible week of reflection and insight and inspiration as you come to see yourself as you truly are. And I'm going to end with a poem, and I hope I get it right, that I memorized by my favorite poet, Rainer Maria Rilke, which I think just really encapsulates what we're about here.

You see, I want a lot. Perhaps I want everything. The darkness that comes with every infinite fall and the shivering blaze of every step up. So many live on and want nothing and are raised to the rank of prince by the slippery ease of their light judgments. But what you love to see are faces that do work and feel thirst. You love most of all those who need you the way they need a crowbar or a hoe. You have not grown old and there is still time to dive into your increasing depths, where life calmly gives out its own secret.

And with that I will say goodbye for now until you hear my voice again in the first audio tomorrow

The Prostitute and the Lover

The first lesson is not to be afraid... you asked me to teach you how to fight. And I can teach you the ways in which to fight with a sword and an ax, or a shield to stay alive. But if you are afraid, then you are already dead.

- Vikings, Season 5, "The Lost Moment"

[AUDIO TRANSCRIPT]

We are going to start with what I call the pillar of value and worth. There are four pillars, or four archetypal energy patterns, that govern our lives. We all have them, and they have a survival aspect and an empowered aspect—or in the terminology we're using, the Troops and the Generals way of managing each one—either through fear or through true, authentic power, and the degree to which we are living a life that we are frustrated with that we don't value that doesn't feel right is the degree to which our survival or fear-based aspect of these archetypes is in charge of our lives and managing our lives.

And the place that we going to start is probably with the one that's the most uncomfortable for people, and that is with the prostitute. So the reason for that is because if you've been living a life that you don't value it's because your prostitute archetype has been in charge. Because the energy of the prostitute survival archetype and if it's trivial or spiritual archetype which is the lover is all about value cost and worth.

The energy of value in our lives is managed either by our survival / earthly archetype of the prostitute who sells herself in exchange for security, safety and approval or by the trivial spiritual archetype of the lover who knows her own value and her values and who acts in accordance with these no matter what, no matter the risk, the fear of disapproval, the lack of securing your safety that might result.

The other important element here is that valuing loving and committing to your worth must happen before you know what that looks like in form and structure, it's like birth in a way, for those of you who have children it's like you have to love the baby before you get to experience the baby in, in actual flesh.

So in other word the spiritual principal at work here in this pillar is that believing is seeing. The prostitute wants to see what it is that she is being asked to value before she commits to valuing it. The lover commits to seeing value first and because of this is able to see the true value of things and to stand in that true value without apology and without compromise, this is really important not only personally but also if you are a business owner.

Because as a business owner you always standing out on the edge of the unknown and you have to commit to moving within your core value out into that unknown before you have evidence of what value that truly is for others. So if you think about it the prostitute sells herself because she is convinced she can't afford to do otherwise right her soul is for sale, her authenticity is for sale, her opinion is for sale, her truth is for sale so whatever has been for sale in your life will show up here in this energy.

So if you've built a career that you don't inherently value then you have to look at the prostitute archetype for what has been for sale. And what is for sale in this archetype is always something in return for security in order words you will sell something of deep value to you in return for a sense of safety, security and approval so this is where the fear of being rejected by the tribe comes in, this is where the fear of telling your truth comes in this is where the fear of standing out on who you really are and declaring what you truly value comes in and what your true value and your true worth is. again there's a real business element to that right, pricing your services means being able to stand in your true value, stand in the lover not the prostitute.

the tribe represents security and the prostitute will do anything in order to remain and to feel secure and to be connected to that tribe. So the work here is in taking an inventory of where it is you've sold something of true value in return for approval or a sense of safety or security, financial security, approval from family and friends, colleagues, approval from the culture, a spouse or partner even.

So that is part of your work tonight I want you to take some time and journal about your prostitute. I know that might feel uncomfortable for some people but the more uncomfortable it is, the more important it is to look at. Take an inventory of where it has held your power because this is all about power and with the archetype you've given responsibility to and permission to managing your power.

So when you give your power to the prostitute she will sell everything that you value in return for a sense of feeling security and safety, so the prostitute energy is the survival archetype . And when the power is taken from the prostitute energy and given to lover that is when you can start to free yourself, this is the first place you have to work and look and reclaim and restore and heal and make new declarations about in order for any kind of real change too occur, this is it this is the critical place, and this is also going to tell you whether you really ready to do this work because the prostitute says I can't afford X Y Z.

So you want to hear and listen in your life for where you saying what I can't afford to, I can't afford to do work I really love, I can't afford to live my dreams, I can't afford to take the time to do XYZ, I can't afford to do what it takes to find real intimacy. So if that voice is strong in you right now then it means you are resisting the change you know you need to make in your life, and you will know you are ready when you finally become willing to afford what you know you need to afford that's the energy of the lover.

The prostitute says I can't afford the lover says I will afford. The prostitute says I can't value that because of what it will cost me, the lover says I will value that regardless of what it will cost me. So in order to activate your lover archetype of knowing and owning your true value and your true values of owning your worth and that you are worth this change in your life, the first place you can do that is simply by starting to state what it is you value, I call this your personal value statement.

And if you are struggling with knowing what your purpose is and whether you are in the right kind of work, there's a hint here in understanding how you meant to be of service and that is we teach best what we are here to learn, we teach best what we are here to learn. So your biggest life lessons the ones you keep screwing up and having to learn over and over and over again is actually a clue to your calling, it is a clue to your soul purpose because chances are that is where you're meant to serve. You're meant to serve others in helping them learn that same lesson. Because who better to learn from than someone who's been there, someone who's absolutely been through exactly what you now need to learn.

So in the way you do that is by learning it yourself first a little bit, doesn't have to be completely and then being able to help those who are a step or two behind you. So your lover is the first archetype that needs to be activated because as you'll see in the next audio everything depends on knowing what you value, declaring your value and making commitment to valuing what you value, to standing in that place and to no longer prostitute aspects of yourself.

And so what I would encourage you to do, is once you're done with the prostitute archetype and that inventory to then turn to the lover and start simply writing down what it is you value what you love and desire and how you are a value. One of the really helpful ways that I found to do this is to finish these sentences, the most important thing about me as a person is? The most important thing about me as a partner is? If you're partnered. And the most important thing about me as a mother or father is? If you're a mother or father. And add you know if you're not partnered and if you not a parent then the most important thing about me as a friend? The most important thing about me as a member of my community? If you're very community oriented.

This is going to start to give you a very clear sense and a clue to what it is you most value and once you've clarified that and it's, going to take more than a night to do this and most likely working with a mentor who can really help you articulate this but once you have your core value statement then it's time to make a commitment, a declaration, and I really believe in sacred contracts, I believe in writing out a contract with yourself and essentially I mean you can find your own words for this but it would sound something like, I no longer allow my prostitute to manage my power around my willingness to sacrifice anything for what I value.

So take that commitment take that vow and if you're able to take that vow that means you're really ready for this journey. It's not necessarily going to be easy your prostitute will rise up and want to take over many, many, many times but if you're actually willing to say that then you're ready because the journey begins with investing in your journey and that means investing in a lot of different ways of, of getting support and guidance in walking this path, investing the time, the energy, the focus on this change.

So often the first clue is are you willing to invest in yourself this way? Are you willing to invest in this journey in this way? Are you willing to afford it and all that comes along with that?

Because the lover is committed its values, no matter what. That phrase "no matter what" you'll hear me say a lot because it's unequivocal and that's what the empowered archetypes—the Generals, or the Four Powers, really are. Unequivocal in their stances

So your homework tonight is to reflect deeply on this, journal about it and start paying attention to how often you and other people use the language of the prostitute. You'll be pretty surprised. It's all over the place.

So the next audio is going to be about the archetype that can now be activated once you've activated your lover archetype. So I will see you here for audio two.

[NEW WRITING]

If when you are building your desire, you are dipping your hand in the shadow cesspool of the prostitute and drawing out codes dripping with the sound of this, even though you yourself may not be able to hear them, the blueprint of your desire will be as weak as the voices of these illusions are strong:

I am worthless.

I must prove my worth.

Having, being, doing this will prove my worth.

I can't afford to be/do/have/think/say/believe what I really want, because of what people will do/say/think/believe about me.

I will sell my soul/self expression/value/values/standards/beliefs/true desires/self expression in return for what pleases others and gains me their approval.

The prostitute is the pillar of worth, worthiness, value and values, and therefore of money, the mediator of value and worth and the system we use to indicate what we value and find worthwhile and to what degree. The prostitute is the pillar of investment. What are we willing to invest in and afford? What are we willing to require others to invest with respect to us and our worth and value? As such, it is also the pillar of pricing and cost and sacrifice.

This, then, is where we sell our Soul in return for something we value even more greatly: approval.

When we desire something because we believe it will bring us worthiness, because it will distinguish us among others as a valuable and worthwhile human, we are building the blueprint of that desire on weak energetic grounds and it has little hope of ever coming to pass.

Because this is neither true nor powerful, that others in any way hold our power.

The voice of the prostitute is the snake-oil salesman in us, the bargainer, the negotiator who has a price, whose pride, esteem, self expression and standards (values) can be bought and sold in the market of approval, and therefore of perceived safety and security.

This is the pillar that must crumble first in order for anyone to even embark on the Hero's Journey, because the first thing the Hero must do is stop selling his soul, his truth, his desires, his values, his self expression, his beliefs, in return for the safety, security and approval of the tribe, which is where he has been taught his power lies.

It is an ancient shadow coding in us that makes us terrified of leaving or disappointing our tribe. The pillar of the prostitute is why. It is one of the four pillars in the Shadow Temple where we go to worship, and seek, power.

And so if what you want is in any way coded with the same shadow blueprint that built the pillar of the prostitute in you—built by what I call tribal or victim or human consciousness—, if you want it because it will prove you worthy in the eyes of others, which includes yourself; if what you want is a facsimile of what you really want but don't think you can afford, either monetarily or because of the sacrifice you'd have to make that would cost you acceptance, approval and understanding by your tribe, then you are building your desire on shadow energy, not Light, and the only way it will come to pass is not through the effortlessness of having inspired the energy and power of the magical masculine who instantly places gifts in our path that take no effort to pick up and enjoy, but through the extreme, time-consuming, and exhausting application of will, effort and energy of the feminine trying to do the work of both energies, because her Magic Man is not in any way attracted to or inspired to help. And that feels not like delightfully discovering a gift placed right at our feet at the perfect moment, but more like moving a mountain that's blocking our path.

That's called hustle and grind.

And Queens don't hustle. They flow.

Let me use some examples.

For twelve years I worked for my family consulting business. I started as a receptionist helping my parents part time as they built the company from two spare rooms in their house. I did this because I felt worthless. My only talents were seeing through people as if they were translucent, being uncomfortably truthful and stubbornly visionary, thinking deeply and writing strange poetry.

How was I going to make a living doing that?

I had just graduated second in my class from college with a double major in philosophy and the history of math and science and a double minor in Greek and the history of music. I'd applied for a job as an admin at a recruiting company and instead of placing me at one of their clients, they asked if I wanted to join them as a recruiter.

I spent my days breaking records at work and my nights smoking copious amounts of pot, playing the banjo and feeling deeply depressed and lost. Then my parents needed help running their business. They were in their first year, doing very well, and overwhelmed staying up until 2am sending out invoices.

I was the third employee and I ended up staying for twelve years helping build and run the company.

My ultimate goal was to become the next CEO. My parents both indicated they saw this as the right next step. And no matter how much I dreamed about it, wrote affirmations and got into the feeling of already being C.E.O., it did not happen.

And yet other miracles happened effortlessly.

In my first year in sales, I came across a book called The Secrets of SuperSelling, which was my first introduction to manifestation and the power of the mind. At the time I'd been working full time as a recruiter for the company, making $30k a year. Now I was in sales as an independent contractor and could make as much as I wanted and work whatever hours I liked.

So I set myself an insane and totally unreasonable goal: to make $250K in my first year, working part time.

1. I'd only had 3 months of low level sales experience in my first job out of college, which was now 5 years prior.

2. I would now be selling to C-level executives at the Fortune 500, going against multinational, brand name competitors with $20B in revenue, as a $6MM company with no brand recognition and no marketing budget, in one of the most glutted markets in Chicagoland.

3. I had never made more than $30k a year and couldn't even conceive of a $250k income. And I'd certainly never worked part time for more than $14/hour.

4. Up until that year when I decided to try my hand at sales I'd been convinced I'd make a terrible sales person. My mom had been in sales from the time I was in high school and everything she talked about at dinner was both boring and repugnant to me. I thought sales was slimy and inauthentic and that corporate America, and anyone who worked in it, was full of soulless husks of humans who'd sold their integrity in return for a buck.

Needless to say, my goal of making $250K—which, based on my comp plan, would mean I'd need to sell at least twice that—was a pipe dream.

And yet I exceeded it.

In ten months I had made $269k, working no more than 25 hours a week.

But this is the problem with the way manifestation is taught, even in such life-changing books as The Secrets of SuperSelling, or, in another book with a similar name and even greater fame, The Secret: they don't explain why some desires come to pass and others don't, when the strategies and intention, energy, focus and desire are just as strong in both cases.

The reason is clear now, and that is why I can predict what I will manifest with total confidence. And when something I desire doesn't come to pass, I also know exactly why and what to do about it so that it will. Same goes for my clients.

So, why did the $250k in twelve months working part time come to pass and the CEO role did not?

Because I was in a completely different operating system with one desire versus the other, and it was all tied up in the pillar of the prostitute…and the Lover.

My desire to be C.E.O. was built on a desire to prove my worth to myself and to my world. My desire to do the impossible and break my income ceiling was not to prove anything to anyone. It was an empty, and therefore a strong desire. There was no content to it other than itself. It could easily have been coded with worthlessness and therefore the desire to prove something, but in this case it was simply a game in which there were no stakes (because the existence of stakes means there is something that matters, which means there is something to prove.)

And my desire to be C.E.O. could have easily been a desire to play the game at my highest level and in that case, it would not have been coded with shadow, built in weakness and incapable of inspiring the Magic Man—my own magical masculine energy—to make my dream come true.

I was unaware of the content of my own desire, and this was the problem. I was building it with energetic material guaranteed to create struggle and require immense energy, focus and will to realize. And of course shadow being so weak, it is doubly difficult to summon the intensity of energy and will required.

And so my dream never materialized.

This is the energetic reason why so many say that it was only when they "forgot" about their desire that it came to pass. It's not because we must forget. It's because keeping our eye on it most often means keeping the eye of our shadow on it. An eye trained to see our worthlessness in everything, trained to detect how little value we hold, how hard it is to maintain approval from others; the diligent eye of the soul determined to find and feel its worth.

Once in awhile we forget to be so plagued. We become distracted with the pure joy of the game of it all, or of some other game altogether, and this is finally when our desire can come to pass because our distraction has emptied the shadow from our desire, leaving it clean and clear and filled with Light and therefore automatically attractive to the masculine, who is glad to provide it for us quickly and easily.

The Energetics of Consciousness have shifted. It did not used to be this way. That is a subject for another book, but suffice it to say that the ground of being has shifted and spiritual law has tightened. There is less mercy for shadow consciousness on the planet. Less tolerance of illusion. If we are to learn how to operate the raw material of the universe to make magic on demand and step into our genius, giant nature, we must upgrade both our understanding of spiritual law and our willingness and ability to abide by it.

The pillar of worth, value and values, desire, price, cost, sacrifice and self expression coded with the voice of Light sounds like this:

I will afford whatever is required to be true to my self and my soul.

There is no cost, price or sacrifice too great for the expression of my truth, desires, self expression, and values.

I do not care about the approval of others and I know their approval is not the source of my safety and security.

My power lies in my total allegiance to my soul, my self, my truth and my values.

When you are gripped and owned by the Prostitute, you allow anything to come between your truth, in the name of safety and security.

When you have given your heart to your inner Lover, you allow nothing to come between your truth and know that is your true security.

What Exactly Is Love

It's not enough to know that everything is energy. It is just as important to know what is true, because energy responds to vibration and the vibration of Truth is where our power lies to direct energy to our will.

Fear (anxiety) is the energy of illness and struggle and is the opposite of truth.

In order to make magic in your life, to be free of struggle of all kinds—mental, emotional, physical, and financial—you must know what the truth sounds like, and contrary to what most spiritual leaders teach, truth does not sound like our typical understanding of love.

There are many stories of miraculous healing that talk about the experience of profound love as the cause of that healing. The problem with this focus is that we do not know how to recognize the energy of love. Being loving has become synonymous with being non-threatening. To anyone. Ever. This is a completely inaccurate understanding of love. Love is synonymous with Truth, and truth, particularly now when it is time to truly wake up, hurts. A lot.

My clients who have had the most miraculous results are the ones I have told the most excruciating truths that did not seem "loving" or feel good at all at the time.

And by miraculous, I mean turning around a sexless marriage on the brink of divorce in 4 weeks to soulmate love and amazing sex, dropping 8 dress sizes in 12 weeks with no change to diet or exercise, eliminating skin conditions in three weeks that have resisted decades of treatment of all kinds, and going from $1500 months in their business to $23,000 months in ten weeks.

The energy of the Lover is the willingness to sacrifice anything and everything for the Truth, because the Lover knows that Truth is the vibration of power. The Lover speaks Truth no matter what. And that also means that the Lover speaks a fully self-expressed reality.

We are all coded with a powerful and unflinching ability to know the Truth and to express this through all our systems. We are TruthCarriers, and our natural state is to speak and express Truth and when we don't, we create struggle and weakness.

This is often anathema to the tribe. As little children we're encouraged to lie in order to be accepted. What child hasn't told an adult she is fat, ugly, or smelly and has not been reprimanded? Be nice, we're admonished and shamed. And this develops in us an allegiance to our prostitute energy, to be willing to say and do what is considered "nice" and "loving" in order to avoid being cast out by our tribe.

And what if we have a dark heart of gold, a natural draw to speak the most uncomfortable and unwelcome truths to a group or an individual, which will likely cause the person more distress than they're already in? Those of us with this spiritual gift have typically been deeply shamed our whole lives for being "uncaring," "cold hearted" or abrasive, and most certainly not very loving.

You're likely going to learn how to lie.

And while you may not make any connection between living a lie about the Truth you have suppressed your whole life and not being able to manifest the life of your dreams, though you may be doing affirmations, gratitude lists, vision boards, getting in the energy of what you desire and following every piece and part of the strategy of manifestation, if you are living out of your prostitute, which almost always is completely unconscious, your dreams and desires will not come to you without extreme effort.

But magic is your natural state. And precisely because everything is energy, it is imperative that you know how energy truly works and how to lift its unconscious operation in your shadow into the Light where you can have full power over your conditions.

But what if the truth hurts? What if it might even kill? We will pick this up in a few chapters, when we talk about the victim.

Implications for Business

In business, this pillar is the decision matrix of price and pricing and the ability to stand for the true value of something and for your true values no matter what pressures come against you.

It is the power to refuse to negotiate, no matter the perceived cost or loss.

Whether it is succumbing to market pressures to lower your costs or compromise on your integrity, or a prized potential client who wants to negotiate you down or demands terms that go against your principles or policies, or internal pressures, for instance a star employee who tries to hold you hostage in return for special treatment, a larger salary or commission, or greater responsibility that goes against your true standards or values.

A leader in his prostitute energy will collapse under the perceived danger of losing business, market share or top talent. A leader in his lover energy knows he and his company is the prize, and that there are plenty of clients and employees and markets to dominate without having to compromise, and that in fact it is by holding to his standards and truth that he invokes the power to bend reality to his desire.

Navigating the powers and temptations of this pillar is especially challenging for new entrepreneurs. I see this all the time in my work. Entrepreneurs unsure of their value discounting their services to see what the market will pay and then hustling 24/7 to make ends meet because they're not charging anything close to their true worth.

Implications for Relationships

Shadow Audit: The Prostitute

The Child and the Sovereign

[AUDIO TRANSCRIPT]

This is Lorna Johnson with The Noble Warrior. I am a coach, teacher, author and speaker and this is audio two, the child and the Sovereign—the pillar of truth, identity and dreams; And we're going to be talking about the survival archetype of the child, and the empowered archetype of the Sovereign—The King or Queen.

So the child is all about dreams. The child is the dreaming, the visioning, the innocent energy of visions and dreams; And as the child archetype the power here is to dream, but the child archetype doesn't have the power to manifest those dreams or make those dreams come true.

So if you've been giving your power to the child. Rather than to the Sovereign the way you'll know that is because you've been waiting for someone or something else to make your dreams come true. So this is like the princess who waits for the Prince to make her dreams come true. It's amazing how these things show up in our fairy tales.

So the child sounds like this. I had a dream. Once upon a time as in the fairy tales. It's always Once upon a time. I had a dream I don't have it anymore because no one in my life has made it come true for me so I don't have it anymore but I did have it. And here's what it was.

So what you wanted tonight in your homework is to take inventory of where you've given your power to somebody or something else in some way and are now in a position of well it's that person's responsibility to make my dreams come true.

Okay so your boss your partner your Culture. Well my culture isn't structured in such a way that that I can really live my dreams; so it's who are you making responsible for your life and your dreams. One of the other ways that comes through whenever you think about the life you'd like to have versus the life you've built now that you don't value and you suddenly think: Oh, but my parents wouldn't allow that, or my partner wouldn't allow that. That's also the child.

So where you putting the power to allow and to give your permission to live your dreams and to make them come true; so all the places in your life where you're doing that;

This child/Sovereign energy is also the pillar of identity and truth-telling. So the child also doesn't know who he or she is. The child hasn't developed a true identity yet, whereas the Sovereign, which we'll get to in a minute, has a very clear sense of identity. The child says "I don't know who I am." The sovereign says, "I know exactly who I am." And along with that is the ability to tell the truth. So the child is the liar. You know this, right? If you have kids, you see that look in their eye when you're asking them whether they did something and you know they're about to lie to you. Well if you're an adult and there are parts of your life that are a lie, those are the areas where you are in your child archetype. Wherever you can't stand up and speak your truth, you are in your child, not your Sovereign.

So the Sovereign – this is like the CEO energy. So if you are an entrepreneur, it's critical that you NOT be in your child energy and that you definitely be in your Sovereign energy in order to properly run your business.

So if the child says I had a dream. The Sovereign says I Have a Dream. This is my dream. I'm living my dream; So that the child puts her feelings of wellbeing into someone else's hands.

The Sovereign says I am responsible for my wellbeing my wellbeing is no one's responsibility but mine and I take full responsibility for every bit of my life experience as it is today.

The Sovereign, the C.E.O., commits to making that dream come true. So when you're thinking about your business, it's you know so obvious when you think about it this way but it's so important to be in the archetype of your Sovereign; as you're designing and launching this business, not the archetype of your child. And the reason why the lover archetype has to be activated first is, because the lover is the energy of valuing that dream see if the prostitute archetype is in play and the power is within the prostituting archetype, you won't be allowing yourself to dream. Because you'll know at a core level that your prostitute is just going to walk right up and say that dream is going to cost way too much put that down.

And so probably that happened for you. Many-many times internally it might even be happening now as you're going through this course. So that's why it's important to put the power of value in your life into your lover and make that commitment. I commit to valuing what I value no matter what the cost. No matter what the cost. That is what allows the child to begin dreaming again. And allows the Sovereign to come in and say - I'm going to make those dreams come true.

Now that I'm allowing myself to value this dream; I'm also committing to making it come true for me. So these are deepening levels of a commitment deepening levels of declaration that are being made and at each stage; If you're really able to say if you're really able to make that declaration, then you really know you're ready. You really know you're ready.

So the work here is to look at all the places where you've given the power to your child archetype; and then in terms of activating your Sovereign archetype and encountering your Sovereign you start saying to yourself, I now place the power of my well-being squarely within myself. No one is responsible for my well-being. No one else is responsible for the quality of my life experience. No one is responsible for the choice that I make. I commit to being responsible for my life in every aspect of it. I commit to stepping into the C.E.O. energy of my business and my life. I commit to being responsible for taking the value that I now declare that I have for my dream and making it a reality.

See once the lover archetype is activated the lover has to love something. And what does the lover love? The child's dreams, the innocent child in you that has this dream, this dream for this life. And so once the lover is enabled and active in loving the dream, the dream becomes restored to its true value. And then the Sovereign can step in, and take the dream from the child and say this is no longer your responsibility. It's now mine. And I now step into my role as my own sovereign, and I'm taking the power away from my child archetype. And I'm no longer going to let my child archetype run my life.

The Sovereign energy is also the energy of joy. Joyfulness is in fact a very powerful spiritual energy, believe it or not. it's literally a vibration of power and manifestation (which means that it actually powers up another key archetype – the Magician, which we'll get to last in this series.). And so the other thing to do here is to start looking at how much of your life do you spend in joy, that will tell you how active your Sovereign is in your life. Or how much of your life do you spend in despair, frustration, limitation, heaviness. That is the child. Really, that's all of the lower archetypes. They all create feelings of heaviness and burden.

So your homework for tonight is really just to journal and reflect on both of these archetypes using the workbook pages and again, notice how much of the time you and others use the language of the child. How many times do you hear people at work or in your personal life talk about the dreams they used to have? All the time! We are a nation of children, really, when you think about it. A nation of grown up children walking around having given our power away to our survival child archetype and bemoaning the fact that we don't have the life we want as if we don't have all the power in the world to make our dreams happen.

To me that's what is so exciting about this is that we discover where the power really lies, and it lies with us. Entirely, exactly and squarely within us. And this doesn't mean that we have to white knuckle our way into our dreams or out of our mess. When we activate these higher archetypes life actually becomes easier not harder! Life begins to flow and have a sense of magic about it. Yes there is still work to do and challenges to overcome, but there is a feeling of being at one with your power and having it always accessible to you that is a truly incredible feeling and that does create success in the real world – in relationships, in work, in income, in creativity, all of that.

So you want to make a declaration that you're stepping into your Sovereign the truth of who I am the Sovereign is the truth teller because you can't tell the truth, unless you know that your lover is going to stand and value that truth the truth of who you are the truth of what your dream is the truth of what your vision is, unless the lover is activated and willing to pay the cost for telling the truth.

You won't be willing to tell the truth even to yourself because the minute you tell the truth. There's a cost to pay; and if you're not willing to pay it. You're not going to be willing to say it.

So the other piece of your homework tonight is to start telling yourself the truth of who you truly are as your powerful Sovereign. Start telling yourself the truth of what you vision for your life. The truth about what your dreams are.

And just for a moment for those of you working with me on entrepreneurial or business goals or transformation, I am going to spent a minute on that specifically, because the business element here is all about your business vision. It's about stepping into your role as the C.E.O. of your business; and beginning to allow your business to dream to experiment and to come alive.

So this is the brainstorming aspect of designing your purposeful business and you want to just allow yourself to free associate to dream and scheme as I say about all the different possibilities for your business and I don't want you to edit criticize judge reflect reason – and that goes for everyone as you are beginning to tell the truth to yourself about what you desire and what your real dreams are. just spread your imagination wings and just let whatever comes- come. And this is also what we will be doing in a big way in our Intensive. A great deal of the Intensive is going to be focused on a deeper excavation of the survival archetypes and how they have managed and damaged your life and then we get into the fun part of brainstorming and blue sky visioning. So if you're having a tough time doing that visioning part on your own, don't worry because we will be doing a great deal of that together.

So if you are having blocks here; That's Okay, because this is a place where a mentor can really help because sometimes you've been so blocked from visioning because the survival archetype are not visionaries so sometimes you need to borrow a set of intuitive eyes for a while until you can start seeing the possibilities yourself. And that's completely normal. In fact it's- it's critical.

Nobody can fully see their own possibility. So the other thing that I encourage you to do though in the meantime is to take an external inventory of your soul gifts, your zone of genius. Write down the ways in which you are effortlessly excellent even in places or environments that might not seem relevant or have a direct connection to a business offering. And again for those of you who aren't trying to build a business based on your inner gifts, taking an inventory of your innate gifts cannot possible hurt you either! It is certainly part of the truth of who you are so it's very relevant.

And again you know. Don't worry if this feels like a place you get stuck because that's totally normal and I can use my intuition to uncover your gifts this is actually something that's a gift of mine. In a very short amount of time I'm able to zero in to your magic, your effortless brilliance and see how you can be of value to others and design that into a perfect for your business.

So that's something that we can work on together for sure.

Shadow Audit: Child and Sovereign

The Victim and the Warrior

What if the truth hurts? What if it might even kill? [need to elaborate on this. This is a placeholder to remind me to come back to the question posed in the prostitute chapter]

[AUDIO TRANSCRIPT]

Okay, so welcome to Day three. This is Lorna Johnson with the noble warrior, teacher and coach on awakening and transformation, and this is the victim and the warrior.

This is the archetype we're going to be working with today, and this is the pillar of support, protection, boundaries, limits and taking a stand.

So I'm hopeful of that you've been doing your homework, and taking inventory, and coming to an understanding, and a deep appreciation of your journey. The power of your prostitute archetype in your child archetype, to cause you to become disconnected from your soul, and the life you know you were meant to live, and of course, also to be really connecting to the power of your lover archetype, your archetype of desire, pleasure of love value and worth; And of your sovereign archetype of authority; the truth teller; seat of identity, the C.E.O.; the one who is in command of all three

And so today we're going to talk about the third archetype that needs to be activated, and well, first we're actually going to talk about the one that has been active, because if the lover and the sovereign have not been active up until now then you definitely can't have the empowered archetype active here either.

So what's been active in your life, and then we're all very familiar with-with this one, and that is the victim archetype. And that is the third survival archetype that we're going to talk about, and the victim as I said is one of the most common and the victim sounds like I can't, someone isn't letting, me some situation isn't letting me. It's really the voice of you being bullied by something in your life. And believe it or not, anything can become your bully: a physical illness can be bullying you around so you "cant" do what you want with your life. Your income situation can be your bully. A relationship certainly can be. So again you want to start taking inventory of where in your life you've given power to the energy of I can't, I'm under someone else's control, I'm the victim of some external circumstance I have no control over so I can't have or act in the way that I value. So it all comes back to value and being in alignment with that.

So I encourage you tonight to really Journal and start to take inventory of all the places in your life where you've given the power to your victim archetype.

Then start thinking when and in what circumstances do you ask. Why me? Because that's also the voice of the victim.

And then you want to start activating your warrior archetype. That is the enlightened victim so from victim, to Victor. And when you give your power to your warrior, what it is you're saying is, I am going to fight, stand for and protect, what I love. I am willing to stand for what I love. I am willing to protect what I love and what I value and I am willing to protect my value. The warrior sets clear and firm boundaries with himself and with others, but he does it with grace and compassion. So this isn't the place of setting rigid and overly dominating boundaries because that's just really a victim overcompensating – in fact that's you being a bully!

So there's a business element to this too that will get to in a minute. But it's the feeling of I am willing to stand, in between, what I love and all the things that are threats, to what I love. I'm willing to stand in between, my value and all the things that are threats, to my value. One of the things that might be threats to your value, especially in a business perspective is your prostitute, right; your prostitutes going, to want to come in and negotiate, and compromise, all ways that it possibly can.

When you're designing and launching a business, Oh my goodness you're going to come into direct contact with your prostitute archetype. And that's why your warrior is going to have to be really powerfully activated. So that you can stand in your warrior, and not be a victim to your prostitute; Right. And not say Oh well, I'm just feeling like all this pressure to negotiate, and I'm feeling all this pressure to compromise.

Very-very critical to run a business, but also in relationships. This is a huge area to look at for people who aren't happy in their relationships because very likely they are not setting good boundaries, they are either being a bully or the victim of someone else's bullying.

So once you're able to activate the lover. And truly stand in the place of declaring your-your value. Declaring what you value, declaring what you love, and your sovereign, the truth teller, the one who is committed to empowering the lover to continue to love, and value what it loves, then your warrior is coming forward, and saying yes, and I am the protecting energy, the fending off energy, the fighting and the standing for energy, of declaring that I am no longer at effect in my life, I am at cause in my life.

And so you want to look for all the places in all the ways, where you can start to make declarations, from a position of being, your own hero in your life coming forth and protecting and making declarations of what you love and what you value of that dream. That dream that you had, that you're now declaring that you have, and that you own, for your life.

And again I would encourage you to make a declaration, and say:

I am no longer allowing my victim, to hold power in my life. I no longer am willing to say, I can't, or why me. I now declare, that I am willing to do whatever it takes. That's the lover. At all costs, to fight, stand for, and protect what I love, that's the warrior.

So that; and this is the fourth archetype that we're going to talk about tomorrow, but I'll give you a hint. So that it can come into being for me in my life experience [00:08:00] and that is the force fourth archetype.

Here is the other way the victim shows up – in not having support for your dreams. In having people try to undermine or attack you, your value, what you value, what your truth is, what your dreams are, and in letting them do so. In not setting clear boundaries – which would be you being in your Warrior – about what you will and will not allow, will and will not let through the gates of your kingdom, so to speak.

The other way this shows up is in feeling alone. The Warrior is able to rally forces for its cause. The Warrior doesn't just stand out there alone facing the enemy and running into battle. The Warrior is able to rally the troops, gain support and protection from others who are bought in to the cause, the dream, the truth you value. So if you are feeling alone, like no one has your back, that's another sign you're in your victim in that area of your life.

So In a very real sense activating your warrior, is activating and getting really comfortable with, asking for help, asking for support. This can be particularly challenging for men to do, because it's not acceptable in this culture for a male to ask for help. It is considered a sign of weakness. But if you look at it from the energy of the victim or the warrior, who is more empowered in gathering troops and support and reinforcements for the cause? The warrior for sure. The General. The victim is the one who sits in the corner needing the support but unable to stand up for himself long enough to go get it. That standing up for, that's the warrior.

And what's so cool about this is that making the choice to work with a mentor is a sign an indication already, that you're actually moving out of your victim and into your Noble Warrior. That you are willing to ask for support, you're willing to have help. Standing for, and fighting for, your true value, your truth, you dreams, your desires.

so; the fact that you are even here, in this space listening to this series. Considering working with-with me or some kind of a high-end mentor, is really good sign that you're ready to really stand in your warrior and activate that energy;

So again, journal, reflect, take inventory of all the places where you are and have been in your victim and where you are stepping into or know you really need to step into your warrior and remember this warrior is not the rigid, autocratic warrior we might initially imagine. This warrior is able to move with boundaries that feel right in the moment but doesn't have to set overly rigid and dogmatic restrictions and limitations on things either. This is the noble warrior, not the despotic one.

OK. I will meet you here tomorrow to tell you about the fourth archetype.

Shadow Audit: Victim and Warrior

The Saboteur and the Magician

[AUDIO TRANSCRIPT]

This is the fourth audio and this is Lorna Johnson with The Noble Warrior, teacher and coach on awakening and transformation. In this one, this is the Saboteur and the Magician, The Pillar of Manifestation. We are first going to talk about, as we always do the survival archetype that has been managing your power up until now. And we are going to talk about the thrival archetype that you are being called to give your power to. [00:34]

The survival archetype here is the Saboteur and this is another one that is very common to most people and It's actually a little bit difficult to understand how it is working, it might seem obvious but this is actually the most insidious of the archetypes and it is why I talk about it last because all of the other three empowered archetypes must be truly active in your life and you must be truly committing to living from those power sources of your lover, your sovereign and your warrior in order to do the work of continually taking the power from your Saboteur and putting it into the empowered archetype of your magician.

The magician in you is where you want your power to be placed because that is the energy of manifestation; it is the energy of creating something from nothing. In the business world it is the sales and marketing energy.

It is the energy and power that you have within you to actually create the life experience that is now being help in your dreams, your dream for your life. You don't just want to hold it as a dream, you want to bring it forth into your life experience and the other reason why this is the last one is because it is the last element in designing and launching your business. It's the launch piece and it's really cool to see how this all kind of weaves together, the personal and spiritual and the business.

The reason why you haven't been bringing your dreams forth into your life experience is because; I am just going to do a quick recap, you have been giving your power to your prostitute to manage your value and what you will be willing to afford. You have been giving it to your child, in allowing yourself to say; well no one has made this dream come true for me yet and that's why I am not living it. You have been giving it to your victim in allowing you to feel that there are things that are stronger than you out there and that you are at an effect in your life and not at cause. And the other reason that you haven't had the experience of your dream life in your life experience is because you have been sabotaging it.

So the Saboteur comes around, the energy of the Saboteur and this is where you want to take inventory to let in your journaling. The Saboteur is the reasoner, the rational part of yourself, it is the one that makes excuses and demands reasons.

So the excuses sound like: well I am not living my dream life because I didn't do what I need to do today…

The Saboteur is the one that will come in and sound so reasonable, while that will be irresponsible of me so I can't do that. The Saboteur is the one that demands reasons for things. So if you are a really rational person, if you tend to feel comfortable in the world of the mind, your saboteur is going to be really, really strong for you. Really strong for you and you want to be very mindful of this energy because taking the stand to live your truth and make your dreams comes true requires you to follow your inner voice, your intuition, that that is also the place of the Magician. The Saboteur is all about pure logic and reason and seeing a clear path from A to B to C. the magician works on intuition and gut and hunches and this is why people like Einstein and Steve jobs say intuition was their greatest ally in creating greatness in their life.

So as you are moving through this great change just expect that there really is going to be a constant overcoming of the tension between your Saboteur, your mind, your brain, your ego, your reason and your magician which is your ability to create something from nothing, your ability to act on an inspired moment, your ability to take decisive action based on a hunch, based on a gut feel. [05:05]

Not because you have good reasons for it, really critical there. The Saboteur completely shuts your access to your intuition, because your intuition is unreasonable, it's not rational. It will often encourage you to do things that don't make any quote, unquote sense and your Saboteur is your one that is going to come in and say you can't do that that makes no sense, you're being irresponsible...

our intuition, is your absolute magic and it is critical, it is a critical element, it's like the blood of your life and your business if you are creating a business. It is a critical element to be very, very active and so again spend some time taking inventory on how active and powerful your Saboteur has been in your life up until now.

The magician doesn't care about making sense, so the magician takes the energy of the intuition and creates and gives you permission so act on that intuition, to actually take that intuition and put it into form, into the world.

So again tonight you want to take inventory around your Saboteur, where you making excuses in your life, where you are requiring your actions, your values, your words, your beliefs, your dreams, your goals, to be reasonable. So this could be if you are having challenges dreaming, visioning with the sovereign and the child work that we did, it could be because you saboteur is so damn strong that it just jumps in before you really know that it's there, because your dreams aren't going to be reasonable, they are not going to submit to anything that really makes a whole lot of sense. And so if you have been very strongly under the influence of your Saboteur, you may have some challenges dreaming. Again that's not a problem; it's not something to beat you up about. It is something to recognise because even more importantly then for you to work with a high end mentor who can start to take the claws of the Saboteur from around your dreams and let them live and breathe.

So again I really feel like that this is the time to make another declaration and say I no longer require my life to be or look or feel reasonable, I now place my power in my magician to manifest my life to create something form nothing and I am allowing my life to make no sense to me right now, to make no sense to others, because the fact is, when you're being called to make sure great changes in your life, it may not make sense to a lot of people. You may get a lot of looks from others, and that is okay because you're not in your protstitue, right? And so you don't care what others think. And It is actually a good sign if it is not making sense it is a good sign.

The path that your intuition is going to guide you along, isn't going to look or feel very sensible. So again if you are willing to make this declaration, if you are willing to say; I am willing to live outside of my reasoning mind, I am willing to let my magician, my trickster in and actually let play in, let creativity in – your magician is the energy of creativity - . If you are willing to make that forth sacred contract with yourself, again you know you are willing to do this work, you know you are ready to embark.

So just a few more points about how this looks and that is if your Saboteur energy is strong and It is strong in everybody I mean we are taught especially in this culture, to be thinking creatures, to make sense, to justify to others and ourselves and validate what we want, what we think, what we believe.

You are bringing something completely new into existence and so if your Saboteur is very strong you are going to be tempted to look outside of yourself for a template for who is doing something similar and how are they doing it. For entrepreneurs it's well maybe I should base my business on, what I see around me and for all of you others it's well how are other people figuring this out. That shuts down your guidance, your intuition, your gut. The way you navigate this journey is going to be unique to you. And it's one of my jobs to keep you in your magician and not your saboteur. It's frankly the hardest place to keep you because of how strong the saboteur is. and the challenge here is to really dial down that Saboteur, go inward and discover and activate that pure inner vision that is not going to look like anything that is on the outside world and to honour that and to birth that.

There is a lot more to this, in terms of how the magician energy expresses itself in transformation but we can, leave that for our later work together. So again I encourage you to spend some time tonight, thinking about journaling about your Saboteur and your magician, what a life would feel like to be the hands of your magician and not your Saboteur. To take that declaration and make that commitment.

And tomorrow there will be one final completion audio where I'll bring all this together, so I will meet you back here tomorrow!

Shadow Audit: Saboteur and Magician

The Precise Science of Manifestation

There's only ever one precise action that leads to your next shift — your next client, sale, speaking gig, lover, dream house, you name it. And WHAT that action is, is not a mystery. At least not to your Magic Man, the Google of the Universe, your straight line to precise and TOTALLY trustworthy guidance.

Intuitive knowing is NOT an art. It is a science.

And so is magic (which is simply the precise application of energetic law).

This is why a new client of mine had two people DM her saying they had to work with her (which "doesn't happen to her") after she did a livestream on a very specific topic but HERE'S THE THING.

It's not the TOPIC that mattered. Or matters.

She could have spoken Swahili (which I have a feeling those two prospects don't speak) and gotten the same result.

AND, she could have spoken as eloquently and convincingly as Martin Luther King on the hottest topic around...and NOT gotten that result.

Because what we still struggle to understand — because it makes absolutely NO sense to our human — is WHAT is actually the cause of WHAT down here in 3D land. I mean, if it was as easy as "push that button, get a client," or "flip this switch, find your dream date," who wouldn't do it?

Isn't that what we're all looking for?! The ultimate guide book to every decision ever?

Some all-knowing entity with access to the Entire Storehouse of Knowledge, who also is paying close and specific attention to little 'ol us, who can just sit there and drop into our mind at precisely the right moment exactly what we need to do or say to get exactly what we want as quickly and easily as possible?

Wouldn't that be AWESOME??

It would. It would be super awesome.

The tragedy (if there were such a thing, which there isn't since there are no stakes and this is all a game), is that there IS. We just have no fucking clue what that Entire Storehouse of Knowledge Who Is Also Paying Precise Attention To Us SOUNDS like.

In fact it's even more tragic than not knowing what the Entire Storehouse of Knowledge Who Is Also Paying Precise Attention To Us sounds like.

The true (nonexistent) tragedy is this: Most of the time when we hear it, we laugh. And not as in an "Oh my, that's so delightful. I'm filled with mirth." kind of laugh. No, it's really more like "Ha! Freak. What IDIOT just whispered a whole bunch of ridiculous nonsense in my ear Jesus Christ. Somebody come get this guy outta here." kind of laugh.

It's because she clipped one specific dis-chord in HER OWN field, one that was keeping her in opposition to her power, that automatically caused the result she desired.

The Pillars of the Masculine

Time

Money

The Magic Man Tool

>> The masculine and feminine energies and how to use them to active magic in your life.

>> The consistent thing that I do that creates crazy results in my clients and in my life.

\>\> The reason why my clients make so much money in so little time
\>\> What a Quantum Leap is and how to activate one over and over...and so shift into Quantum flight, which is expansion without contractor or the need for grounding

I'm going to teach you is this tool. It's really very simple, but it's just upgrading your intentional connection too, and activation of your masculine, your provider, your magic man.

but before we do that I have to help you shift into what I'm calling your high feminine. Your high feminine is the one who has those exacting standards and supreme integrity. She is the one who's got to, you've got to ... she is the one who makes the requests and the demands, not the aggressive demands, the very lovely, graceful, queenly demands of the magic man. She is the one who knows what they really are and what they need to be, and you come in, and then our minds come in and go, "But that's not possible, but that's ridiculous, how are we going to do that?" That's where we get into trouble.

Yes, what we're up against right now, hold on, let me make sure I take these. It's the what, it's the how, and it's the when. What you're basically saying is, "How am I going to do these? How is it going to happen? How is it going to happen without me burning myself out? Can it really happen by then? I don't really know and is that really reasonable and all that?" What I want you to understand is whose job is what. Your high feminine is responsible for the what? That is her job and nobody else's. Your masculine, your magic man cannot, does not have any say at all. No say, and the what comes from your exacting standards for what you desire and require, and your supreme integrity in implementing those standards. That's it. It's like supreme integrity is the will of the feminine almost in a way

the content is the standards, and the will, the commitment to those standards is the supreme integrity. The way you know, the way you ... because some people are like, "But I don't know what I want." That's not you first of all, that's silly. Where is there dissonance in your life? That's how you know what you want, the dissonance is essentially the frequency mismatch between your exacting standards and what you've allowed. Essentially it's the frequency mismatch between your exacting standards and your supreme integrity. Got it?

It's like where are you out of integrity, which is why the integrity piece is so right. You could also find it by what you're jealous of other people for. If like for you you're like, "I want Alejandra's," like that's a sign.

I don't know how to activate my high feminine. I feel like I need to know ... I need to practice that or develop that.

I develop tools for what I have challenges with. That's how it all works. I don't really have a problem with my high feminine, like I know what I want, but I think more people tend to have a problem with putting their high feminine to the task of getting it done, and then it's burn out, worry, frustration, anxiety, fear, like misery, which is why I've developed this tool to activate the magic man because ... but I can ... really the way you ... but this will also help with that. I mean it really is kind of ... It really is both. It's really a little bit of both, but I could probably build it out a little bit more. I will think about that, but let me just explain the tool.

how is the magic man and the when ... I'm sorry, the when is ... the what and when is your feminine, those are your requirements. I want to hear it by this time.

the principles are there, because they work, but the pieces that's been missing is that the provider energy, the thing that bring you what you want is the masculine. That's the thing that people have been missing, and when you really understand how to work with it, when you can kind or personify the energy it works much better. It makes more sense, and you can work with it, because it's a relationship, because it's an energetic consciousness.

Speaker 2: This is why a lot of times when law of attraction doesn't work for people because it remains a theory and it remains a concept, and they just don't ... it doesn't become a relationship. It doesn't become like an energetic, like something they can feel and work with like, "Okay, now I'm supposed to do my gratitude. Now I'm supposed to want what I," it just doesn't help.

Speaker 2: The high feminine is like , "What do I want and when do I want it?" We just essentially ... and how, I'm sorry, and it's not the how ... How should I describe this? It's, "What do I want? When do I want it and-

Melissa: How do I want to experience it?

Speaker 2: "How do I want to experience it?" Yeah. I'm going to save that for now. That's the job of your high feminine, it's very prescriptive, it's like the queen. It's like, "Here is the decree of the kingdom." You know, kingdom.

Melissa: Would you say that this is your soul that's wanting these things or is it the ego or both? Is there, like who-

Speaker 2: It doesn't matter. First of all, don't worry about it. In other words, desire is usable energy no matter where it's coming from. It's really just meant to get you up and going, and activated. Just trust it, who fucking cares if it's your ego that wants a 100K? It doesn't matter. As long as it's part of your exacting standards. If you want a 100K because someone else has it, that's totally coming from like ... that's not your high feminine. She doesn't fucking care about anybody else or what anybody else is doing. It's just the point of ... How do I want to say that? For me, what's coming through is if there's attachment to the importance of it in any way, then it's not coming from your high feminine.

If there's an attachment to the importance of the goal, and of having the object of your desire.

Like I just want it because I want it because it's fun. It's like I don't know, like it doesn't matter, like I just want it. It's just going to be awesome. If I don't have it that's fine, it's not going to kill me, and I'm not going to feel like I'm less than, and I'm not going to compare myself to other people, and it's not a matter of myself worth or any of that shit. I just want it.

Melissa: Okay, like for example we've been putting off ... putting a new deck on the back of the house because the deck we want is like 70 grand. We don't want what the 20 grand does, like the sun room and the deck, and all that, like the double-storey sun room and all that, and we've been putting it off because it's like 70 grand, but I want it. I want it. I want it and I'm here in my office and I want the sun room and the deck to be like right off, then it would be double, the upstairs and downstairs, and I want it right off, and so I want it. Then I'm like, "I just want it because it will be fun, and I can go and it will be like nice to be able to go inside and outside while I'm working."

Speaker 2: [Crosstalk], okay, okay. This is great. This is your saboteur, but why do you want it? What's the reason? Is it responsible? Is it logical? Is it reasonable? Is it understandable? Does it make sense? Does it fit in with the plan? Who the fuck cares? You just want it. You just want it. If you want it because ... It's not that the answer is ... Th gift and the blessing of the saboteur is that it's helpful to ask why, because it could lead you to realize that you're totally operating out of your shadow. The reason you want it is because your next-door neighbor has it. If you put up a 20K deck you're going to feel like shit.

Melissa: Yeah, I mean that's not there yet.

Speaker 2: That would be your prostitute wanting it, and then of course that's not going to be helpful at all. You won't even fucking enjoy it when you get it. The whole point will be null and void, and then you're going to go want something else. Why? Because of this reason, and you get it and then it's not enjoyable. It's not bad or good, even the prostitute running your life isn't bad or good, it's just you never get any fulfillment out of anything because the reason is always out of your shadow.

Melissa: Right.

Speaker 2: Honestly, I know it sounds simplistic, but if the question, "Why do I want this? Is just because I do." Then just trust it and just do a launch. Look around for like, "Am I ashamed of it? Am I ..." Also, go the other way, "Well, why not a $100,000 deck? I don't really want that." Okay, good, but if it's like, well, then people are really going to think [inaudible]. Then you want to be like, "Okay, but is that ... but what if ... Have I even considered a $100,000 deck? No. I mean, I just don't want it." Okay, good. Use the energy of the saboteur in a way that allows you to really land on what you're standards are. "What are my standards?" It's just a frequency thing. What I want you to do it's just a ... it's like in your body it just resonates. you're just like, "That's what it is. It's just that, it's just what I want because it resonates with me."

What I'm going to teach you is how to act ... how to inspire you magic man. All of that is just like, "And then just surprise me with all." Just said surprise, just put a cherry on top of all of this. Just leave that open, leave that door open to the imagination, and open to what your magic man has in store that you can't imagine. Don't try to get all in your head about, "I mean I don't mean like this, I mean like that ... but just like ... and surprise me." Surprise me with how amazing the whole thing is and happens and feels.

Melissa: Right.

Speaker 2: Okay, great. Do you care ... Now this is getting more specific so that your magic man can really provide you with what you actually want, and you will have a point, "Oh, fuck, I really flaunt that, that way." You care if you fill your programs. Does it really matter to you that this 50K comes through this program or that program? Could you make a 150K sale and nothing else this whole month, and be like, "Hell, yes," or are there hidden things that are around that goal that are important to you?

the masculine or the piece that kills it that you are doing that is causing the problem is this, worry kills magic. Let's put it another way, worry makes your magic man's stick limp.

elissa: Yes.

Speaker 2: Not attractive in any way. It is not inspiring, nothing's going to happen. You just were like, "I want this." Here is the tool, what activates it, what makes him hard and wanting you is just like, is just, "I trust you. We got this. You've got this, baby. I know you do." It's just like calm, absolute trust knowing 100%. What you're going to do, and also what activates your magic man is knowing what you want out of him. It's like if you think about men, "Just tell me what you need. Just tell me what you fucking need." Don't tell me how you ... Don't tell me, "I don't want to feel this way." What do you need? That's why we went through that, "I want this by this date, and I want it to come to me in these ways. I want the quality of the experience to be this." It's quality.

Melissa: Love it.

Speaker 2: What I do every morning, I have my book next to me by my bedside table, and I have my pen, and I wake up, I do not get out of bed, I literally stay in bed because this is the most important thing. This is literally, this is why Christians were like, "God is my important," like it's this, it's your magic man, because he's the provider. This is what provides you with everything. Then what I do, and I use the ... Hold on, let me just ... I got to [inaudible]. Okay, have you ever seen the Harry Potter movies?

Melissa: Uh-um (negative).

Speaker 2: Dumbledore is like the Gandalf of that world. He is like the wizard who flies, and he has this wand, he has this crystal wand, and he will put it to his head, his temple, and his thoughts will stream into this wand, and then he taps this cistern, this pool of water, and his thoughts just stream out of the wand into this pool of water. This is like energetically what you're doing. You wake up in the morning, and very likely if you're like 99.9% of women on this planet, you start your day by worrying, "What's going to happen? What's going to happen? Is my program going to fail?" This is good, because what's happening is you're being alerted to your standards, your requirements. If your worry is like, "What if that doesn't meet my requirements? How do I want to experience my life and my goals?" That's the first thing you ... Don't just sit and stew in the worry, you want to alchemize the worry.

Speaker 2: What I do is I start out, and this is like the way you start out with any relationship with a man when you're coming to ask or request of him, you don't just make a demand first. You say, "Baby, you know what, the last time you made dinner it was amazing. Would you make dinner again for me tonight?" "Okay." You praise. This is the idea. I'm giving you the energetics behind why this principles of law of attraction work. What you're doing is you're activating the masculine, but people don't realize that, and so it stays a theory and not relationship. You express gratitude, and I literally say, I say, I literally call him my magic man or my divine provider or my hot whatever, I just really get into being connected to that energy. I say, "I just got to thank you for yesterday, and all the things you fucking sent my way. This was amazing. That was amazing. That was amazing. That was amazing. You're fucking awesome." It takes a minute.

Speaker 2: Then I say, "Okay, and these are my requirements for today." It's your honey do list. It's like, this is what I'm doing. I'm literally writing my divine honey do list, and putting it on the energetic fridge for today. How do I know what my honey do list needs to include? It's what I'm worried about. It's amazing. It's just like, "I'm worried about this. Oh, that's because I need to give my magic man a job to do."

Melissa: Interesting, yes.

Speaker 2: "Am I going to finish? What do I have?" For me it's like, "Okay, on school I really want to ... I really want to fill on school. Okay, great, what do I want?" I don't go to any ... I just do not stay and worry like, "Okay, so what does that mean that I want then? I want it to feel this way, with this many people and the clients have to be completely amazing, blah-blah-blah, and I want it by this time." I say, "Magic Man, here is your job for today," or, "This is what I'm handing over to you today to take care of. You're going to take care of filling my school, and it's going to be like this, and this, and this, and this, and this. Thank you, I totally love it. Thank you so much. I appreciate it. I know you've got that handled."

Speaker 2: Then I go on to the next, "What else am I worried about? I'm worried about this, and I'm worried about that." It doesn't matter, my health, my mental health, my relationships, my lack of inspiration, anything that you want that you don't feel you have is something your provider is responsible for giving you. "I'm depressed. I lack inspiration. Magic Man, you are responsible for inspiring me." I do like three or four. I don't go ... I pick the big ones, the rocks, so to speak, and then I say, "Thank you that's awesome." I literally imagine handing him the list, "This is now your job. Thank you."

Speaker 2: This is how you alchemize the worry. Then that is all you do, and from then you just do whatever the fuck you want to do with your day from a place of being inspired, because what you're doing is you're sending the list out, the sway energetically, and then what's going to happen is he's going to go and arrange, energetically he's going to arrange this person to be available at this time for you to run into this person at the fucking ICF thing or whatever it is. He's making all those arrangements. In order for it to activate, on the earth plane you're going to have to do something, not a lot, this is not about hustle, but you're going to have to do something. Sometimes what you need to do is get your brain out of the way so your magic man will be like, "Can you go call her for a while, please?" It might not look like it has anything to do with your goals, but if he knows what you need in order to work with him, and cooperate with him.

elissa: That guidance then is the magician talking?

Speaker 2: That's the magician, yeah. Exactly.

Melissa: The masculine men is working through the magician or no?

Speaker 2: Yes.

Melissa: Is that right?

Speaker 2: Yup. You get a hit of an idea like this, if you go out this way and it comes back in this way, and sometimes physically, like that's you him going, "Okay, everything's lined up, please do your part." This is how leverage and quantum leaps happen, because you do one little thing, and it activates this fucking magical set of dominoes that fall forever, right?

Melissa: Yeah.

Speaker 2: It is like, "What? That's magical. How did that happen?" That's how. The one last thing, and then I have to go, if during the day you start to wonder and worry, and how and time, and how is it, and the burn out, and the [inaudible], the one thing you did not specify, which is your homework, and I want to see it inbox is how many hours a week do you want to be ... How does the time look? Is it Monday through Thursday? I don't care how long I work on Monday through Thursday. Is it 20 hours a week, and I don't care? Be clear about those. That's a very important piece.

Melissa: Got it.

Speaker 2: If you worry during the day about anything that you have handed over, what you're essentially doing is going to hang out in the garage where he's fixing your car. You're just like, "How is it going?"

Melissa: That's my favorite analogy.

Speaker 2: Or you're going to have it being like, "Can I have the list back? Just give me the list. I'll take care of it." What he's going to do is give you the list back, he's like, "You're the queen. Okay, fine. You want the list back, fine. [Inaudible] help." Then you're fucked.

Melissa: Right, right.

Speaker 2:   Because that's not your genius, it's not feminine. It's not the feminine genius, and that's when you get burned out. That's what you get all the stuff that you were trying to avoid. Just be aware that during the day, like the fact that this is potentially going to happen several times during the day. You're going to master this, and then do whatever you need to do visually or whatever to be like, "Oh my gosh, I am so sorry, this is your job. It's not my job, and I know you got it," or whatever it is that you need to do that just hands it all back.

aspects of your weakened relationship to the masculine, and they're worth some money.

When you're sending a rocket into outer space it's a really different manufacturing process than when you're making the car.

When you get into this new relationship with your masculine, which is what this is all about, you don't have to ... don't worry so much about how it's going to ... how the money is going to come through, which channel is it going to, unless it's really important to you in terms of the experience of receiving the money.

A quantum leap is achieving insane results in very little time. It's not, "I made $100,000 in five years," or "I made a million in five years." It's, "I made $100,000 in 90 days (when my typical revenue was 25% of that.)"

It's "I made a million in ten months (when my average was zero. Because I didn't have a business before that.)"

In other words it's not collapsing the frequency disconnect or accomplishing the frequency leap between the results you typically get and the new results you achieve. It's collapsing the time it takes for the results to come into your experience, so it happens all at once, and now. Not in increments, over five or ten years.

Quantum leaps are created by the most optimal cooperation between your feminine and masculine. What happens when your energies are not aligned and when they're not cooperating is strife, struggle, and slow, incremental growth.

There's nothing wrong with incremental growth, but it's not the stuff of manifestation magic.

I want to teach you a few key learnings that will change your life and your business overnight, and where we will start is with an explanation using money, but you can use this for anything. You can use this for love, you can use this whatever you want, it doesn't matter. I'm going to use money because that's what I teach my clients how to do and that's what I focus a lot of my efforts on.

The masculine is the provider energy. The feminine is the receiver. There's a piece that a lot of you are missing in your work on manifestation and it stems from a misunderstanding of the masculine and therefore a mistreatment of your feminine.

This is something I see in every single one of my clients and it's called worry and anxiety. I'm going to teach you and give you the methodology for how to create quantum leaps in your life.

am going to be using the male and sometimes the male biology and how it works to help you understand your relationship to money and get whatever you want, when you want it. It's not just your relationship to money, it's your relationship to time as well. If you go and you start to understand men, like actual men and how they work and what inspires them, what turns them on, and what doesn't turn them on, what turns them off, what does not inspire them, if you just simply translate that to the masculine, you will have all your answers if you're struggling.

When you ask, "Why is this not working? Why is my income up and down and up and down?" It's because you are in an upside down relationship to your own masculine and you will discover when you really think about it how am I treating my own masculine that what you're doing would turn any guy off and make him not want to provide for you, okay. It's powerful when my clients make this connect this dot, they're like, "Holy shit, this is fucking amazing."

Plus, I am a visual metaphor kind of person. If you give me a visual metaphor for something I'm like I get it, it's just so obvious to me and I don't really have to think about it. It doesn't remain theory anymore, it's something I can practically apply and I'm all about practical application in your life. I don't want this just to remain theory, okay. I'm not going to go into all the aspects of the masculine but one of the most important ones is that the masculine is the provider which means anything you were lacking in life and of course there's no such thing as lack.

Anything you desire that's not in your experience, the masculine is responsible for providing you. That's the masculine energy to get to work and bring something into your experience. The feminine obviously is the receiver. This is the stuff that everybody knows, but there's a problem that most people have. I'm not referring to the receiving problem which most people think they have and most women do. I'm not referring to that.

What I'm referring to is the standards problem because the entire orchestration of this high frequency masculine energy coming into your life like fucking injection after injection after injection, okay, begins with your feminine. What I call your high feminine, okay. Your high feminine, so I don't know if you are familiar with my other work where I talk about the swampy feminine and the bully masculine and the brittle feminine and the something masculine, I can't remember what it is.

Those are your shadow aspects of your feminine, your high feminine is what people call your queen, or your goddess energy and I call it your high feminine. To me, there's just I don't know, the queen goddess thing is to me is the old energy it's not … It doesn't do anything for me but it's the same thing. Your high feminine must be standing at all times into specific states of being in order for any of this stuff to work. Okay, so that's where I'm going to begin and also this is where it collapses like completely collapses.

Because your high feminine, just stay with me here because I'm going to be building this a little bit overtime so I may not making a lot of sense for a minute but stay with me. Your high feminine is responsible for building the container into which the masculine is going to inject all his goodness, okay. The quality of the container determines its magnetism. It literally determines how magnetic that field that exist within the container becomes, okay.

A highly magnetic container which is magnetic is the feminine, guess what that does? It automatically creates an electric current around it. Electricity cannot deny magnetic magnetism, it's like they are literally energetically linked, it's like one creates the other, okay. What is happening and what needs to happen always for any of this to work and be activated is that you must be in your high feminine so that you can be creating an energetic container that is magnetic, irresistibly attractive to and that calls to the Magic Man, the high masculine, the divine masculine.

All you got to do is setup the container. It's like build it and they will come, actually it is exactly like that, okay. You setup the container, meaning so LOA is going to make a lot of sense for people in a totally different way and probably blow their minds and be like, "Holy shit, that's why that works." Okay, this is the energetics of manifestation, it's really what I'm teaching you. All you do is you have to all these means in terms of creating the most magnetic container is that you are setting the parameters, you're establishing the boundaries and this is the first state of being that you must be in, in being in your feminine and that is your exacting standards, your exacting standards.

The high feminine has very high, very exact standards. This is not a brittle place, this isn't like a, "Fuck you." This isn't an icy kind of setting standards, it's just very exact. There is a tone, there is literally a tone that she is constantly pulsing at and constantly measuring the tone of your actual boundaries, the ones that you are expressing and managing in your own life. There's this tone and then you're managing according either according to that tone or against that tone because it's really fucking hard and scary sometimes to keep this tone.

The dissonance between the two, the dissonance between your high feminine and that tone of exacting standards and how you're actually showing up in your life and establishing boundaries and holding people to your standards and holding yourself to your standards is the dissonance that you feel in your life. It is the feeling that things are it's what causes struggle, it's what create struggle and strive, worry, anxiety, fear, low self-esteem, doubt, self-criticism, judgments, all of that stuff because there is just a natural dissonance.

Of course, every one of our high feminines holds an extremely high exacting standard tone. That's her job is to stand there energetically and just hold that tone. Some of us are managing our lives in really nowhere near that tone, okay, this was me for many years. Nowhere near that tone. This, the severity of the dissonance Is what can then cause physical and mental illness, extreme financial strive. Bankruptcy, okay extreme relationship issues, okay. As you come closer, as you raise the frequency of your own physical expression up to that energetic one, your life starts to feel like it slow.

When people talk about, "My life is flow, and it's just blessed, and I'm just charmed," like that's what's happening. What's happening is that they are running and managing their actual lives and boundaries and standards according to that exacting tone, okay. I want to make sure that that make sense. The first thing that you must do is understand what the high feminine is and understand what the high feminine does, and why it's so important. Why I'm trying to tell you is those exacting standards are the high, they create when you actually implement them in your life.

Goodbye, I love you too. When you actually implement them in your life what happens is that you create a very powerful, strong, energetic container. You create a vacuum is what you do, okay, like a magnetic vacuum. The boundaries that you hold in your life according to those exacting standards create an airtight container like nothing is getting out. When once something gets in, it can build. Think of a furnace, right. Think of an incinerator, think of a quadrant, give a forge, think of something like that. That's what you're building energetically.

The degree to which you do not live your life according to the statics those exacting standards is the degree to which your container is flimsy and will break is not attractive to the masculine and the Magic Man, so it's not going to cause an influx of amazingness in your life at all and you're going to find that you're struggling and frustrated a lot. It's also going to cut, this is why you have leaps in your business, right? You could organize and arrange things so that there's an element of integrity to your container so this is the second piece.

It's so-called supreme integrity, remember I said the high feminine has two states of being she must hold, supreme integrity is the second one. Literally, all that … Think about it, it means keeping the energetic integrity of the container intact and not letting cools in, right. It's exactly what it is. The degree to which you are lazy in building your energetic, physical, emotional relationship financial container in alignment with that those exacting standards is the degree to which you are living in supreme integrity or not.

It's literally just, "Are you energetically, do you energetically have a strong container or do you have a leaky container?" If you have a leaky container, you're going to have high months and then low months. The high month and then a low month, couple of high months and then nothing. Your marketing will work and then it won't work. You'll get into an amazing relationship and then it will get fucked up. You'll get a client and then no goes on you, right. You get discovery cards but then if cards calls but then nobody shows up. You close a big deal but then they don't pay.

This is a common occurrence and the reason is because your container is not an integrity with the exacting tone of your high feminine, okay. I'm going to pause there and just see where everybody is with respect to that, see if there's any questions. I'm going back here, [inaudible 00:21:08]. I just realized something from what you said, my dad used to get so annoyed he would say when you ask for something, you want it right away. He said he doesn't work like that. He said, "It doesn't work like that, I'll get it for you when I'm ready." Yeah, your dad is not the Magic Man, okay.

Your dad is probably annoyed, here's what's happening, Debianni. Your dad is annoyed that you're exacting standards because you're exacting standards are about what and when you require things to happen in your life. The feminine overseas the what and the when not the how. Not the how, we will get to that later, okay. You and your high feminine absolutely must, if you are going to be in your high feminine and not be lazy or not be apologetic for those exacting standards. You must decide what are those exacting standards represent. They represent what I want and when I want it.

What we often do is women, and I'm so glad you brought this up, Debianni. What we often do is women raised by actual men is that we base our understanding of the masculine, our Magic Man on our dads, okay. In my experience and it looks like in yours too, my dad is an amazing man and many, many, many, many, many ways he taught, made so many amazing things. He spent most of his life feeling impotent in making his dreams come true, okay.

Therefore, when I began stepping into my adult life and had to start orchestrating and setting or not setting my own boundaries with the people in my life, I just automatically would apologize for them and not set them as high as I truly knew they were, as I truly felt that tone being held because in my experience that made my dad feel bad about himself. I also saw my mom do it with her, like she would diminish her requirements and her request and her needs because it made him feel bad about himself. That's putting too much expectation on me, that's putting too much pressure on me.

You're pointing out my weakness, you're pointing out my fucking flaw, don't do that. You can demand the world of your Magic Man. When I say demand, I don't mean like give me the world. I mean like this is my requirement. Because your Magic Man is all potent, omnipotent as we think of god, right. Omnipotent, your Magic Man is part of this, doesn't need Viagra. He's going to give you whatever you want and can do it now. That's part of being potent, that's part of being powerful is having a command overtime.

You have been imprinted to diminish your standards even though it's not what your feminine is carrying and holding as the tone of your true exacting standards and then look what happens in your life, right? You struggle, you don't have the experiences that you really desire, that's why, that's why, okay. Thank you for bringing that up, that's like huge. It's one of the things that we as women but anybody who is … Because whenever you're in the position of creating life, creating your dream life, you're in the position of the feminine, you're in the position of receiving the experience of your dream life, requesting and receiving.

Even if you're a guy in this dynamic, you're in your feminine also. One of the things that we need to deprogram ourselves from is the imprinting of how we saw exacting standards of fact and impact the men in our lives when we were growing up. Huge, huge, huge, huge, huge, there's so much, I could actually do a whole live stream on that. Okay, yeah, and by the time we got it we were often over it, yeah. That's huge, Debianni, that's really huge for you to look at and to recognize that you are imprinting, you're basing your understanding of your Magic Man on your dad.

I'm telling you now, not to throw shit at your dad but your Magic Man can give you whatever the fuck you want whenever you want it and that is his greatest desire and pleasure, okay. Okay. Holy hell I'm going through this right now, trying to center and growing myself today. Amazing, Melanie amazing. This is going to fucking blow your mind seriously. Whenever I teach this to my clients, they're just like, "What the fuck?" I feel like you just help me organize my entire consciousness. Carmel, Natasha, okay so good to make sense. I can see that's what I had done in the past when I knew what the standards were.

've been struggling with that lately but no more, awesome. Tina, can you give us an example of an exacting standard in business? Completely, thank you for that grounding practical question. I will use myself because I think that's always ... It's always good to use personal examples. I'll use an example from today actually. I had a client, wonderful, amazing woman who just might be on this stream and the other day I gave her some homework and it was very confronting homework and it was very specific homework. Because a lot of the time when I'm in my role in my coaching, I tend ... I'm in the role of the mask man.

Anyway, I gave her some specific homework and when I give my clients homework it is tuned exactly and precisely to the frequency of their greatest fear and the thing that is directly, directly in the way of their quantum leap because I can just see that. My homework is very specific, it's very specific and it must be followed exactly to the team because those are the exacting standards. Not only that I have, it's not about you must listen to me but because if you don't hit that tone you don't get the disruption in your field that you need to have in order to release all of these trapped energy that is being held in your low frequency state back into your system, which then strengthens the container, builds up the magnetism, attracts the masculine in, and gets you your cash and that's what a quantum leap.

My clients hire me to create quantum leaps for them. They do not hire me for incremental growth and I can't even do ... I don't know how to teach someone how to do incremental growth, that's just not my thing. My guidance and my homework is very finely tuned to a certain frequency and it needs to be followed. When I checked in today I said, "So did you do it?" She's like, "Well, I did it almost." Because I said do a live stream on this specific thing and she did a live stream on the same topic but not that specific thing. I said "No, but that's not what I told you to do."

She said, "Well I know but I was talking to someone else and they said what about doing it this way that seems to make more sense. I thought it made more sense so I did it that way." I said to her, "If you do that again, we're done. Literally we're over, we are not working together anymore. I am going to lovingly release you from my coaching." That Tina, who would be an example of an exacting standard. The reason is because in my container, in my world, what I say goes. It is a matter of I don't know, I don't want to say that it's a matter of respect because I don't take it personally at all, it's not about me.

It's not really a matter of respect, what it is, is I'm here to do something that she's asked me to do. I pick my clients, and this is what I explained to her. I pick my clients carefully because I want to see them blow shit up. I want to see them get rich, I want to see them create magic, that's what's pleasurable for me. I have a business because it's pleasure, right and because I want to help people but there are no victims so they don't really need my help. It's just we're here to play a big game, okay.

It is not fun for me to work with clients who don't listen to me. I really dislike it quite a bit. It's not according to my standards. Because when you listen to me, the results happen. It is a spiritual guarantee. It's energetic law when you listen to me the results happen. If you're not going to listen to me what are we doing? I'm wasting my time, I'm wasting my breath, I am giving you my energy and you're not doing anything with it. That's not okay with me. It's a requirement of mine, it's an exacting standard of mine that my clients take my guidance.

I am absolutely okay with firing them if they don't do that. I know that might make people really uncomfortable and be like, "Oh my god, you're such a bitch," and all that stuff. Here's a thing, if an Olympic trainer takes on a client, that client is an honored position because that Olympic trainer who has a record of getting people gold metals has the option of working with lots of people and so do I. When I work with the client, if I have selected that client out of many and therefore I have requirements for how that experience is going to go, so that would be an example of an exacting standard.

Taking a vacation from work somehow my soul just wanted to chill and be introverted. Yeah, totally that's your ... Yes, yes, yes sexy, okay. Fucking love this message, awesome. The men in my family have been non-existence for generations. Marina, this is going to change your life, this live stream is going to fucking change your life. Oh my god. Great grandpa ghosted during World War II faked his own death. Grandpa dies of alcohol poisoning, dad non-present from mom of raising kids my relationships embody myself fully in a relationship in last.

Okay, I'm assuming after all this, your mind is like blowing up right? Yes, this is why I'm doing this live stream you guys because I want you to know who the Magic Man really is not ... The Magic Man, your Magic Man is not your dad energetically expressed. It is not your grandfather, it is not your uncle, it is not your great grandfather. We just without thinking that's how we approach the provider energy of the universe, the provider energy of the universe we assume is like our dad specifically insane when you think about it, it makes no sense.

Of course, it does make sense because we don't have an example of that kind of provider, right. I'm giving you the example. That's my goal here today and how to work with it and how to not turn it off. Super clear, thanks for giving that example. Okay, you're welcome. Okay, awesome. We have the high feminine, okay. Standing in her exacting standards and to her supreme integrity, so the exacting standards think of that as the content of your desire and the content of your requirements for your business, for your clients, for your love life, for your body, for your bank account, for your house, like everything, okay.

It's the content of your requirements and your desires. The supreme integrity frequency is your energetic will to execute on those standards in your actual life, does that make sense? Holy shit, this is everything wow. How do you tap into the frequency of Mr. Sexy Magic Man? I'm getting you there but this is the way Marina, this is what you do. Then, I'm going to give you like literally a step by step tool. This might take me a minute to get out because it's a lot, so stay with me and this seriously will fucking ... I'm going to stay on this live stream until I deliver the entire tool to you.

I'm giving you right now the energetics, this is how I always work. I give the energetics and then I give the practical application. Right now I need you to understand the energetics of what the high feminine is, what the Magic Man is and then how they activate and inspire. I'm going to give you the practical tool for how to get in to your high feminine and inspire your Magic Man, okay. First, hey Michelle, requirements and standards but what I am asking about is trusting that provider energy. Yes, that's the worry, that's the worry and anxiety piece and that I will get too but that's where you're headed right?

You're immediately going to yes, but yes, but yes, but yes. Yes, but my dad was gone my whole life. Yes, but my great grandpa ghosted. I can have this high fucking standard but who the fuck cares because… Maybe I'll just go there now, I'm just going to go there now. Okay, I'm going to address this right now, the issue of trust because this is actually …. Thank you for raising that because this is huge in my clients. Most of my clients are women and pretty much 99% of them have an issue with trust, trusting the masculine. Thinking about how to roll this out because there's a couple of steps.

It's actually pretty fucking important and there's some pieces to it. Number one, trust … You got to hear this, you got to hear this. Trust is shown in action. It is discovered, it's not even shown, it's discovered in action. Trustworthiness is discovered through action, okay. Took me a minute to get there. You will discover you will have the evidence that your Magic Man is trustworthy when you take the actions that are in accordance with your own exacting standards and supreme integrity and no other way. The reason is because that is the thing that inspires and activates the Magic Man.

It's the only thing that inspires and activates the Magic Man. If you are not having in your experience what you desire, it's not the Magic Man, it's your standards and your supreme integrity that are the problem because the container, the container's integrity determines the degree to which the masculine fills it with things and the time it takes to fill it. Think about it, you have low standards. You totally compromise on your standards all the time. Leaky container, how long is it going to take to fill that container with what you want? A long time.

You tighten up that fucking container, two things ... Okay, so actually two things are happening. You have a leaky container, number one it's not an inspiring container. Your feminine is not attractive, you're ugly. Energetically you look ugly to your Magic Man. Your Magic Man is like, "Yeah, I'm going to hang with the guys." Not interested, not interested in sex, not interested in providing, not interested injecting you with anything, not a turn on.

Number one, you are not magnetically attractive to the Magic Man so he's not going to show up that often, okay? Number two, even when he does, chances are what he fills it with just leaves because it's leaky. He's showing up and he's giving you stuff and half of it is leaking out, and he's showing I'm giving you stuff and half of its leaking out and you're like, "Why the fuck does it take me this long to make this much money? What is wrong with me? What is wrong with my business? What's wrong with my fucking masculine? Look at this shit.

It's taking so fucking long and plus it's shit. This is your fault." I mean I don't hate to break to you. I'm telling you something is going to change your life in a day, literally tomorrow your life can completely change because the masculine is also the energy of time and he is always ready and waiting to provide for you. Men get hard like that, takes them no time. Men are always ready to go. As long as you're irresistible, takes no time to turn a man on, right. It also takes no time to turn on your Magic Man. No time at all.

You can fill those leaks in an instant. I have had, here's a perfect example. I had a brand new client yesterday I walked her through all of this, this energetics and I gave her the tool and I gave her some homework the very specific homework and I said, "Do this before your discovery call." She had three discovery calls that day and I said, "Make sure you do this homework before your discovery calls." It was definitely, it was all about establishing, she was way not in her standards in her supreme integrity in her life like literally in this relationship. I said, "Do this, okay."

She was like, "Oh my god, if I do this like I can't even imagine what's going to happen." I've been wanting to do this for 14 years, probably maybe not 14 years she's been in this relationship for 14 years but for a long, long, long, long, long, long time okay. This was somebody who was literally providing to her, a source of money, a source of providing ... She was potentially drawing a boundary that would cut her off and she is not in a position right now where that feels anywhere near safe to do.

We're talking like high risk, freaking out her shadow, making her go holy shit, and also emotionally what's this person going to say and feel on my god and there could be drama and blah, blah, blah. I gave her the words to use, we talk through the energy of all of that stuff and she's seriously want to throw up just even thinking about it. She did it you guys, she did it. Then a matter of hours later, I'm pretty sure it was later, it might have been ... I forgot to ask her. The same day, she closed one of her discovery calls and a 50% full pay.

I don't know the last time. I need to ask her I don't know the last time that she made a sale but it's been a while, especially in that level, and a 50% full pay. Okay, I'm sorry a 50% down payment. It's not a mystery, it is not a mystery that this ... That's filling this container up ... Not filling it up but strengthening it, filling in all the holes is directly linked to the 50% cash sale that she made. The e-mail that she sent me was like, "Oh my god, I can't even believe how much energy I feel right now.

The conversation actually was imaging, it was actually beautiful. Oh my god, I can't believe I waited so long. I feel so fucking powerful, I can't even believe this." I'm like, "Yeah, this how this goes." It does not ... The whole point here is it does not take time to activate the Magic Man because the masculine is money and time, the energy of money and time. I'm sorry about how it's your fault. Literally all you need to worry about and it's not even worry, concentrate on is doing whatever it takes no matter what, no matter how much you perceived this to be risky and dangerous to your well-being, your financial well-being, your emotional well-being.

Well this person is an emotional support system to me. Well this person gives me money. You must, you must live your life according to those exacting standards no matter what, no matter what. You will not have the evidence that your Magic Man is absolutely trustworthy and absolutely will provide for you guaranteed like clap work like you step off a cliff, you fall it's like energetic law. It's literally just energetic law. It's electromagnetism, okay, but you will not have the evidence that your Magic Man is trustworthy before you have to do this carrying thing to establish your exacting standards in your life, does that make sense?

A lot of us, I spent my whole life doing this and many, many all of my clients do the same thing. Well if I just could know ... If he could just give me the thing now and then I'll know that if I do the thing, he's going to give me the thing, or if I can just get some kind of promise like energetically he was whispering in my ear, "Baby, if you do this, I'm going to give you this money." I can just know then I would do it, that's not how it works. Trust means you take the terrifying action regardless and without the evidence. That's what trust actually means you see. If you want to trust your masculine, then actually trust it.

Actually take the action that is terrifying to you but that is in accordance to your highest exacting standards. That's what trust is actually. The other piece that I want to point out around this is that the ease with which you can take that action that seems dangerous and scary because some people are able to just do it and just be like, I'm totally fucking terrified because the thing is you're going to be scared no matter what. Even I, at this time ... Even I have been done this so often and had the evidence. I do it, I get the evidence. I do it, I get the evidence.

I do it, I get the evidence. I fucking do it, I get the evidence. I do it, I get the evidence. By now, you would think that I'm just like of course and most of the time I do but there are sometimes where I'm like, "This one seems really, really, really low. I mean really." Then I argue, I try to negotiate with my high feminine. Can we lower the standards just a little please? I mean this is scary. I don't want to do this one? What if my masculine doesn't show up this time?

The ease with which I now can just leap my life to those exacting standards, have a conversation, fire a client, cancel a date, tell somebody I'm not interested in them, whatever it is okay. Is because I know something and that is that I am not a victim and that nothing and no one has power over me. It is not possible for me to fail, and it is not possible for me to make a mistake. Even in the worse possible case scenario where I take the action that is absolutely terrifying that seems financially crazy, that seems emotionally risky, whatever, that isn't according to my exacting standards and my masculine doesn't show up.

I fall and I crash and burn, I'll be fine. That's what allows me to do that because I know my worth you see. Your high feminine knows her worth and it is not attached to money, and it is not attached to fame, and it is not attached to reputation, and it is not attached to friendships, and it is not attached to clothes, and it is not attached to looks, and it is not attached to anything. It just is, it just is, and I walk around with that as an unconditional state of being. I'm going to take the action because the action, it expresses my knowledge of my worth.

The action is a direct honoring and actually an execution of what it means to be in my highest worth, my unconditional worth. You know what if my Magic Man doesn't show up, that's fine. I'll be fine. I might be homeless but I'll be fine. Really, honestly, seriously, I have walked myself energetically down every possible catastrophe corridor there is. There is not a single thing that can happen to me on the planet because I faced down a lot of shit, not nearly as much as a lot of people but a lot of shit.

There's not a single thing that could happen to me on the planet, they would cause me to betray myself and my worth, not a single thing. It makes it easy for me you see, makes it easy for me … Boy, I just got something. I got something. Okay, it makes it easy for me to take those actions and to live my life according to those exacting standards and in supreme integrity. It did not always use to be this way guys. I used to be the worse, my really everything, oh my god I sold my soul all over the place.

Here's something I just got okay, oh my god I'm so excited. Trust isn't the issue, trust of the masculine is not the issue actually so this is cool because it's entirely within your power, it's entirely without your feminine power to fix this whole thing. It's not trust to the masculine that's the issue, the issue is you are worried that you will betray yourself and you will downgrade your sense of self-worth if your masculine doesn't show up and give you what you require and desire.

That's what's actually happening and driving what you think is mistrust of the masculine. It's actually not about trusting the masculine at all, what it's really about is that if you act according to your exacting standards, and it doesn't go the way, you want it or really need it to go your sense of supreme worth is under attack by your own self, by your own self-regard is in danger. You need the masculine to show up and give you the thing or the feeling or the belief or the whatever, for you to have a sense of self-worth. That is so fucking important.

All that your job is to do is to focus on closing the gap between the way your life looks now and the standards that therefore created it and that exacting standard, that tone of exacting standard that your high feminine carries. In the terror of contemplating doing that to do the alchemy work on yourself around where you're really placing your power. No one and nothing has power over me, it is the most freeing, most liberating, most exhilarating, most thrilling, no one and nothing has power over me. Seven sentences in the universe, seven words in the universe. I really truly believe that.

Then of course the wonderful thing is because this is an energetic law, because it's electromagnetism. When you do that, your Magic Man does show up and you're like, "Oh my god, that's amazing." Here's the thing, here's a thing, this is why … This is so crazy. Even though it happens over and over and over again, you're still going to feel that fear which then you're going to be like, "See, I don't trust my masculine. I still don't trust masculine, this is crazy because if I trusted my masculine then I could just close this gap.

It's never about trusting your masculine, it's always about your worth. It's always about your loyalty to your own worth no matter what. Fucking amazing, so fucking amazing. Before I look at the questions or the comments, I want to just make sure that is wrapped up. Actually why don't I look at the comments and see if there's anything. Energetic bloodhound, I love it. We're drinking the same thing right now, my Kombucha. Thank you yes, energetic spiritual okay goals. Totally goose bumps freaking everywhere [inaudible 00:54:22] feel like they're coming. Melanie, that's so awesome.

I'm so glad, I'm so glad. He's Yahweh, isn't he? The streaming host pinched off and eager for the best place to … I love you guys. Don't be a leaky bitch, holy hell and sloppy containers. How do you discover what that blocking fear is? It doesn't matter, it doesn't matter. Actually I answered your question Roche, the blocking fears that you'll abandon your own worth. That's the fear. It doesn't matter what … Here's the thing you guys. It doesn't matter what the fear is honestly. Just do the action and you will find your power and you will find … In doing the action, in closing the gap, that is you expressing your own commitment to standing in your worth no matter what.

The only way you can show yourself the evidence that you stand in your worth no matter what is by taking the action that terrifies you. You're not going to get there any other way. You aren't going to get there by journaling. You're not going to get there by meditating. You are not going to get there by going to yoga. You are not going to get there by doing soul regression. You are not going to get there by doing pass life therapy. You are going to get there by taking the fucking action because your life is built on tones and frequencies.

Your life is literally an expression of a certain quality of tone and frequency, okay. Your high feminine holds the tone of the exacting standards which is what you intend your life to truly be and look and feel like, okay. The way to close the gap and have your life express this tone versus this one is not by meditating. It is by literally going into your life where the tone is depressed and suppressed and freeing it. It's literally, I don't ... It's energetic I can just see it. You free it, it's almost like you snap a cord or something.

It's maybe freeing it here, I don't know exactly how it looks but it just literally your life, it just [inaudible 00:56:51] because this is your natural state of being you guys. This exacting standard, this tone is your natural state of being. It's the easiest state of being to be in. It's the most pleasurable. It's the healthiest. When you're here, you're healthy emotionally, mentally, physically, financially, right? All of your struggle is because of the tension and the dissonance in your life between these two frequencies.

Meditation doesn't change the frequency. It changes that maybe a little, like that, like that, like that, that, that, that, that, that, that's what meditation does. Going to your actual life, this is why I gave such specific tuned homework. Going to your actual life to the place in your life that isn't the most dissonance when that releases back up and gets an alignment that releases so much fucking power into your fields you guys.

It is fucking massive and amazing and magnetic. That's what instantly fills your leaky container, makes it magnetic, calls in the Magic Man. Then you do it again, then you do it again, then you're like, "Okay, where else now what's in the most dissonance to my exacting standards?" That's what I can give you and it happens again and that was it, that was it. See, it's magic.

Tighten the energetic vagina, oh my god you guys are so pathetic. Oh my god, Joyce that's so on point, holy shit, okay awesome. This is awesome, really loving this, also I'm loving the UnSchool Program, yey. Love this and Ira what you said about that it is okay to take a break, so you're taking a vacation. Yes, totally. Oh my god yes, seriously yeah pass life there'll be yeah, yeah, totally. Okay, thank you about the inspired action. That's really important. Let me see if it's the time for that. No, it's not okay,

I am going to do this, this is just a little thing for you guys. It's really brilliant and my brother taught this to me. When you want to remember something but it's not for now, it's for later like someone is talking up the storm and you're like, "I want to say something but I can't interrupt them," or right now like I have a place to go but this is important but it's for later. Clock the idea, okay wait hold on I got to make sure I get the idea. Inspired action, okay inspired action in response to the honeydew list, that's what I'm going to say.

Okay, now I have it. I could wait for two hours until I release it and I'll totally remember what it was, it's fucking brilliant. I will come back to that, [Adzilla 00:59:51] I think your name is, okay. Going to that darkness, face the fear. Relationship with mother, okay, so [Rushin 01:00:01] for you, the question is, is there a new agreement? Have you been in any kind of unspoken agreement about how you're going to show up that needs to be changed and spoken into new arrangements, right?

Have you been in an actual spoken agreement about how you're going to show up? That is no longer works for you, okay, and that needs to change. This is a big part of where these shifts start to … Need to start taking place. That's a big one. Yeah, I won't go anymore. Okay. I've had similar principles but never framed in this way. Totally, that you guys this is like law of attraction. I mean, it's not … I'm not telling you anything … It's energetic law, so of course you've heard at other places, right? What I'm doing is I'm like pulling the curtain back, unlike the instructions that you've been given, okay?

It's like Abraham-Hicks and other people who teach manifestation and love attraction, they give you the instructions. They give you the manual, do this, do this, do this. For me, that never works. I want to know, why? I want to go under the hood. I want to look at the mechanics, right? I want to look at the energetics of it because then I can hook into that. Then, I know what I'm dealing with, right, and why? I understand the ramifications of things. I don't know. That's just way I always work.

Of course, those are the things that I'm going to be teaching because that's what I do. I go in and I go under the hood. I go, "Okay, why is it worked that way and what's really it play there?" Yeah, this is totally not new stuff but it's going to … My hope is that it gives you a framework and it gives you the fundamentals of energetic law at work here, and how to master them, right? How to not be confused anymore about why something is not showing up in your life and what to do about it, okay? I love the way you explain this, it's so clear, awesome.

The finger thing, I don't understand the finger thing, Jamie. I need to experience and study with what I learn. Yeah, totally, okay, cool. Okay. Where were going next is so we've got the high feminine in the strong container, magnetic as fuck, right? Okay, so am I going to go to the tool now? Yes. I'm going to go to the tool. Okay. I'm going to give you the tool for how to apply this in your actual life. You're welcome, [Carina 01:02:47]. One of the things that I want to say, you guys, you all probably know about my dark UnSchool.

If this is resonating with you and if you feel like you've got deeper, like things that you need someone to work with you on, you need to really seriously consider my dark UnSchool. It's essentially it's like business school meets Hogwarts. It's like Harvard Business School meets Hogwarts. It's like the quantum leap container and they teach all these stuff, and give you your specific piece of homework, that finally tuned piece of homework, that creates quantum leaps over and over again.

The people who go through this program tell me it's like nothing they've ever done and most of my clients have done everything, all the clients, all the coaches, all the programs, all of it. When they do this, they're just like, "Yeah. There's actually nothing like this out there at all." They make crazy fucking money. One of my favorite examples is a woman who like could barely sell a $300 package. In her first month, she did $24,000 in sales. She did $57,000 by the end of UnSchool.

She went from I think it was, I don't know, $1,000, maybe $1,500 to $2,000 dollar a month to an average of $12,000 a month. She also went from working literally full-time around the clock never seeing her friends ever even on the weekends to an average of 15 hours a week, 20 hours a week I think. She took two months off in the UnSchool. I mean, she still came to classes and all the stuff but she didn't sell and her average was still $12,000 a month. The door is open now.

It begins December 19th. Door is closed the 12th. If you want to do this shit in your own business, get in. Okay. Yes, you addressed more refined consciousness more integrated and real. Awesome, I'm so glad this is speaking to you guys. Yeah. You know what? You guys are like, I need to know why. That's how it gets integrated into me. Yes, I need to know why. Yes I need to know. You know why? I'm attracting so many of you because we all have that saboteur mind, which also means you guys are super magicians.

This is all stuff I teach in the UnSchool, to all these archetypes that the voices that keep you building your life according to these low standards versus the voices that allow you to see and create the ease of building them according to their standards, I teach all that stuff, but yes. Because I have a strong saboteur in me. I become quickly magnetic. People reaching out and now wanting free information. Wow, this is amazing.

This is from Marina who just joined Sales Masters. I believe this action of exacting standards is insisting that this is now my work and I charge for it. How do you find the balance with giving this information for free versus paid? Awesome, awesome, okay. I will answer that even though I want to get to the tool, this is good. I love these questions.

First of all, Marina literally joined … I don't know, very recently, Sales Masters. This is my beginner mastermind and so UnSchool is 18 grand, four months. There's a luxury three-day retreat in a castle. At the end, you get a ton of time with me, get a ton of time with [Coleen 01:06:39]. It's like fucking amazing. You get channeled sales transmissions and guidance, and all kinds of fucking units. It's like the Cadillac ... It's not even a Cadillac. It's like the whatever. I don't know.

`What's that really amazing car that starts with an L, [Livery 01:06:55], whatever, whatever. It's like the Lamborghini of programs. If that's not accessible to you, if you believe that you can't afford it, which is an illusion, but if you believe you can afford it, there's my Sales Master's Mastermind where people having crazy shit happen already. Marina joined, we had our first class. This where I give one on one laser coaching to each person. I think she booked like ... Was it you Marina that booked like 10 discovery tools or something?

I don't know if it was you or somebody else. Anyway, crazy shit is already happening and this is exactly what it is, is they're becoming magnetic, stuff just happening. Yes, now you have the opportunity to reinforce those existing ... Those exacting standards, right? Like where is your commitment to your supreme integrity? What's going to happen is you have this container and the masculine is coming this way, but like things are poking it from the outside. Are you really strong?

How strong are you? It's like knock, knock, knock, knock, poke, poke, poke, poke, how strong are you? How strong are you? How strong are you? How strong are you? Okay? If you're like, "Well," maybe this time, "Well, okay." Guess what happens to your container, okay? This is normal because you're not only become magnetic to the Magic Man. You also become magnetic to what I call your dark angel. Interesting, I never thought about this.

I never actually thought about the fact that when we create your container in alignment with your exacting standards, you become magnetic to the dark angel too. Your dark angel is what I call your spiritual boxing trainer, your spiritual trainer, the person that is here, the energy that is here to test you. Why? Not to be mean, but to make sure you're an energetic match, to make sure you are an energetic match for what it knows is coming.

Okay? Because it doesn't want you to attract into this powerful potent, super potent, super potent, super potent experience of the Magic Man, the masculine, and have it blow your fucking system. It wants to make sure that container is double thick, triple thick, quadruple thick, right? That it's like the most powerful masculine can come in and you're like, "Yeah, man, bring it out." Instead of like, "Fuck," my life crashes and burns. Okay. Marina, that's what happening to you. It's a good thing. It's a good thing when you get test and trials, you guys. It is a good thing.

It is not a sign that's something is wrong. It is not a sign that you should quit. It is not a sign that, "Things aren't in flow, I should step back." No, no, no, no, no. It is a sign that you just strengthened your fucking container, okay? What do you do? Exactly. When somebody comes to you asking for help or advice, you say, "I would love to work with you and provide you this advice and experience, would you like an application? I'm assuming you're talking to me about my work, about mentorship, about working with me, right?"

If they say, "Well, no, I mean, I was just wondering if you could just give me a quick little thing, just a quick little thing. I'm your friend. I'm an old client. I'm up here." You say, "My genius is so precious and rare and my time and my energy is so precious and rare to me that I charge for it. I'd love to give it to you. It's pretty fucking awesome but we need to accept into one of my business containers to do that." That's why you just say that.

You don't have to be like, "Fuck you." This is how it is. Now, you might be thinking, why am I not charging for this, right? Okay. I have never actually consciously thought about this, so give me a second so I can see what is wanting to like come through around it. The answer that I am getting is that it is an active pleasure. Literally like this lights me up so much I can't even tell you. You probably can tell. You probably can tell. This is an act of pleasure and play for me. Therefore, I'm not charging for it.

Now, that's not to say that my business and my work is not an act of pleasure. It's an act of pleasurable service, highly pleasurable service, but it is an act of service. Meaning, I'm providing a service, okay? When I am in the place of providing a pleasurable service, I just ... The sex analogy is just [inaudible 01:12:36]. I get paid for it. This is self-pleasure. That's totally what it is. This is my self-pleasure. This is my energetic self-pleasure, okay? It's exactly what it is, okay?

`When you're in a business container and you're ... It's a pleasurable service, you get paid for it. I crack myself up. My little finger trick. Yeah, yeah, yeah, okay. I really want to do that one next. I booked two more. Awesome, Marina, but now you're being tested. Okay. Tell me about the tests because that is like important. I want to help you with that.

Here's my scheduling like. Yeah, exactly. I needed to hear this. Yes, one was a friend, right? That's what's going to happen. This is what happens. This is what happens. You guys, this is so important, my God, there's so many of these. There's so much fucking shit coming through. It's amazing. I'm like actually hot. My temperature is really like it's cold in here but I'm seriously heating up. Okay.

This is so fucking huge. I love this. I don't know about you guys but this ... I just came up with this whole like container and the high feminine and masculine like thing, but it's so fucking awesome because it's so clear and grounded. This is what I mean by a visual metaphor, right? You guys are probably never lack for a visual metaphor understanding of your masculine and your feminine because now you have it, but I'm going to give you another piece. I'm going to give you another piece, which I never had before.

When you build your container, right, exacting standards, supreme integrity, this is awesome. Your Magic Man comes in, so Marina got all those discovery calls after it was dead,

dead, dead. Then, all of the sudden, time, masculine, Magic Man, time, all of the sudden, without having to do anything, because your masculine is the one that does, your feminine is the one who hangs out, right? Pleasure is yourself, it's like discovery call, discovery call, discovery call. Out of the blue, you're like, "What? Well, thank you," right?

The other thing that happens though is that you become … Okay, wow. Millennia of a story about this is coming in right now. You also become magnetic to the demons, the devils, your dark angel, who is here to test you, who is not a bad guy, who is not Satan, who is not the devil, but it is in your favor working in your favor. What it really is, you can call this a threshold guardian.

Okay. A threshold guardian, meaning, like I said earlier, making sure that you are ready in your energetic match for what's beyond the threshold when you step into that new state, that new higher frequency, which is what this all about, right? Think of your container as the threshold. It's a circular threshold and your dark angel is like poke, poke, poke, poke, test, test, test, test, trial, trial, trial, trial, friend asks for advice, client doesn't take your guidance. It's like, whatever.

Here's the thing. Subconsciously, what we are doing when we are keeping our container leaky is that we're keeping it nonmagnetic to the devils. We're also keeping it nonmagnetic to Magic Man because the concept of being able to … Like the imagination of like can I hold this? Can I hold this? Is it like very confronting? My clients do this all the time. My one client who just had a 25k sale, her very, very first 25k sale ever and she's been doing this for 15 years. Okay? She's a six figure coach, she's fucking badass.

She just had her first 25k sale couple of weeks ago and afterwards she was like, "What the fuck I'm I going to do with …" Of course what's she's doing with her client is like fucking badass as shit, but in that moment, she's like, "Wait, what am I going to do with this person? I don't know if I can hold what I just attracted in." Then, the self-doubt and the fear, and am I a fraud? My God, can I deliver? Can I deliver?

That's the feminine. Can I deliver the baby? I created this amazing container. I stayed in my exacting standards. I maintained my high integrity. My masculine provided for me. I fucking have a 25k baby that I don't know if I can deliver. My God, it's so amazing. Holy shit, we got to do something with all this energy. We got to move the energy. Energy is not going to sit in this container like, okay, I'm just going to sit here. No. We got to alchemize this shit out of this energy and deliver it.

That is one of the things ... That's part of what your fear is. You're afraid of labor and delivery, okay. Also, you're afraid of the devils that are going to be attracted to that powerful magnetic pulsing being that you are becoming, and all that is a fear that you're going to collapse back into your old state. Of course, the fear of what's going to happen if I piss my friend off and what's going to ... It's actually this fear, right?

It's the fear of like, shit, like, what's going to actually go down in my actual life when I actually live according to these exacting standards? You are welcome, Rushin. That's why I always have orgasms. Is that Carina? I was just talking about you the other day to somebody. I'm like, "Yeah, there's this woman, she like had a full body orgasm, like listening to [inaudible 01:19:03]." Is that you? It's fucking amazing. We need to work together.

If you're having orgasms this way, like imagine, imagine. We need to find ... We need to work together. Okay. Right, I just said that [Shawna 01:19:23]. It's having a taste of your genius. Imagine what would happen if you work with each of us. I know, get into UnSchool, guys. Lorna, as soon as you even mentioned this principle, the universe made sense, and now I have to upgrade the container because I'm making progress, not fixing problems. Yes, yes.

When I raise my vibration, all strange things come in and it doesn't feel good, and I realized it's test for me to plow through. Exactly. What you're doing [Stacey 01:19:49], is you're becoming magnetic to the little devils, okay? Yes, it's pokey. It's poke and fraud, and pressure test, and it's like that's your being, like squeeze. It's part of that labor that you feel. It's like contracting, expanding. Where is my container? Where are my standards? Am I here? Am I here? How firm are they?

How thick? Like all of those things are being tested, and yes, it feels really fucking uncomfortable. It feels really uncomfortable. That's just part of it. What I'm getting is there's an alchemy of that demon, like there's an alchemy of those demons, with those little devils. I'm using that word because I want to demonize devils and demons. Do de-demonize them. There's like an alchemy that can happen, right?

Like a devil, like a little devil comes in and tests you, and you can just hold the energy through your filed and into your container, and as you go alchemize it, and strengthen your container. Okay, and another one comes through and you just hold it through your portal and alchemize that powerful energy because that demon energy, it's very powerful potent energy that you can use, as long as you alchemize the toxic piece of it.

Then, that gets added to the energetic content of your container and that's what continues to magnetize it further and strengthen, magnetize, strengthen, magnetize, strengthen, okay? What I want to say here and I totally hope I remember to do this, so Magic Man, give me this idea later. Thank you. Is it live stream on how this relates to overcoming objections? Because if you understand this whole process, how this whole thing works and these little devils, what you will realize is that the little devils are objections that your clients' prospects display on their sales calls with you.

You can do the same thing with those as you do with your own little devils. In fact, the degree to which you know how to alchemize your own little devils because those little devils are those voices. Remember I was telling you about those, those voices of fear, the archetypes? You listen to those little devils and that's what creates the holes in the container, right?

The little devils like, "Can I poke?" You're like, "Well, it's so reasonable that I not set this standard with this person who's giving me money. Yup, poke a hole." Another one comes, "Can I poke?" "Well, it's so nice to give my friends some advice, because I mean, she's my friend. Poke a hole." Those little demons are so powerful but when you allow them to make decisions for you about the energy of your container, the integrity of your container, they fuck your life up.

If you know how to alchemize those little demons, you … They are powerful pure potent energy that gets assimilated …. It's almost like a cellular thing I'm seeing. Basically it's like cellular, like they come in. You alchemize the low frequency piece. You use the fewer potent energy piece, which is how you respond to them and how you alchemize them. Then, they become part of your strengthened container, so fucking cool, I never thought of that.

The way in which you do that helps you master overcoming objections because those little devils are the objections you hear on your sales calls, because when a client, a prospect comes to you, what they are coming to you to help … Get help with is fixing their container, helping them raise their standards. It was the same thing. Their life is being run by those fucking little devils who've been poking holes in their container all their lives but they don't know that. They don't know that because those little devils feel sound really reasonable.

It's the voice of reason and it's the voice of the victim. Survival consciousness and fear consciousness, and tribal consciousness, is what those little devils are. There's so much here. Okay. I have so much to say but I won't go into that. This is awesome. Which is taking the action, the supreme feminine or the Magic Man? Okay. I'm going to answer that question not because this is related to this, okay? What's taking the action?

I'm assuming, you mean like in your actual real life, is your … You. You're taking the action, right? You're high feminine is … I like supreme feminine. I might actually steal that, it's gorgeous. Your supreme feminine, is an energetic, okay, and your Magic Man is an energetic.

The being that takes the action, you, which is the combination of the two, okay? It's your integrated being. What I'm going to explain to you now is the tool and how this happens.

What you're talking about, Jules, is the inspiration, the inspired action that actually is sent to you from your Magic Man, is it a thought, an idea, an intuitive hit, right? That is what you as you, as your physical being, like response to and takes inspired action on, okay? Here's how this works. It's time for me to give you the tool because I've been on here for like an hour and half, an hour and a half.

Here's the tool. Every morning, I have my book. Now, it's going to look like journaling and it kind of is. It's simply the way that I activate my intentional relationship with my Magic Man. Okay. The magic of this is in the exacting standards thing of things that I was … It's the actions that you take in your actual life, okay? What you're doing here is activating your Magic Man in your life. What I do, and this is where the law of attraction, all that stuff and manifestation, you're going to be like, "I get it. That's [inaudible 01:26:49]."

Men are inspired into providing for you, by knowing how much they … By praise and appreciation. If you read Alison Armstrong, you will realize this. Men are inspired into providing for you, for your wildest dreams by praise and appreciation. This is the law of gratitude, okay? Because the universe is in the provider energy in the masculine energy in making your dreams come true, this is why when you hear about manifestation rules, gratitude is always one of them. This is why.

Because gratitude, appreciation and praise inspire the masculine to provide for you, okay? I always begin with gratitude, but I make it very specific, because see, I tried these principles before, and I was like, "I'm so thankful for blah, blah, blah. Thank you for …" I'm like, "Who the fuck am I thanking?" I don't believe in God really like, "Am I thanking me? Well, this is stupid to thank me. It makes no sense." The minute I translated it into like my masculine, my Magic Man, I was like, "I totally thank my Magic Man.

That totally make sense to me." Before my feet hit the floor because this is for me, it's like the most important thing. I get my pen, I get my journal, and I start, and I start with an appreciation. It's like a minute, not even a minute. It's like a sentence or two. I really personalize this. I make this sensual. I make it like I'm talking to my lover, to my man, okay? I'll say like, "Magic Man, you were fucking awesome as provider ever. You are fucking amazing. Thank you so much for what you did yesterday.

You did this, and this, and this, and this, and you provided me with this. I asked for this, you give it to me right away, it's fucking amazing. Thank you so much. I love you. You're fucking awesome," okay, gratitude, but actively and intentionally activating the masculine, okay? The masculine energy. Then, what you do is you stream your worries. I don't know if any of you have seen Harry Potter but Dumbledore has that wand, he like taps it to his forehead, it's like a crystal wand, and these worries or thoughts, I think memories, streamed into this wand. Then he takes the wand and he taps a pool like a cistern of water.

He taps it and all the thought stream into the pool. Okay. You're going to stream your worries. This is what you're doing but it's more than that. There's an alchemy involved as well. Because how do you know what you are exacting standards are? How do you what you want? How do you know what your requests are of your Magic Man? What are you worried about? Worry kills magic. Worry also tells you what you desire, what's "lacking".

For me, because I have been diagnosed with severe mood and anxiety disorder, it's very easy for me to know what I want. I just check myself and go, "What am I worried about?" I'm worried about filling my program. Okay, I have this program, I'm worried about filling it, and I don't go any further. I do not go into, "Why am I worried? What am I going to do about it and why is this … Maybe this is because of my dad. Maybe this is because of the blah, blah, blah."

I do not fucking do that, okay? I just notice. "I'm worried about my program." I literally open my book and after my gratitudes, I have an example here, I say, "Here, Magic Man, my divine provider, is your honeydew list for the day," because that's what's you're doing. You're giving him his honeydew list and you are taping it to the energetic fridge, and then you're walking away and going to the spa, or doing whatever the fuck you want, like a live stream like this, not because you have to mark it, but because you fucking want to, because it turns you on.

That's what I do. I say, "Here's what you are providing for me." Here's your list of what you're providing for me. Okay, so after, because you don't walk up to a guy and be like, "Hey, can you go fix my car? Thank you." That guy is going to be like, "Fuck you." If you walk up to your guy and you're like, "Hey, baby, you are so fucking brilliant at fixing cars, I can't even tell you. I'm wondering, we need a new radiator, could you fix the radiator?" What is he going to say, "No"? If he says no, then you don't have an example of the Magic Man.

Okay, because your Magic Man will say, "Yeah baby, I'm right on that," okay? Here, I'm just going to read to you so you'll get a sense of how I connect to the masculine, okay? This one's great, you did it again baby, thank you. In 12 hours, you delivered. UnSchool, it's on its way to being rebranded as the dark UnSchool, so perfect, so easy and simple, and yet a profound adjustment that makes me so fucking excited, which is exactly what I asked for. What I asked for was, how do I sell the UnSchool in a new exciting, edgy, totally upgraded, totally fucking like amazing, the most amazing thing that ever existed on the planet?

That's how things have to be for me to sell them, and I was like, I don't see how it works. I don't know because I'm not inspired by the old version of it. I gave it away. Twelve hours later, boom, brilliant, done. Okay. Everything I asked for, you've provided for me with ease, so easy I didn't even noticed it so fucking quickly. You are the intimate exterior, the Magic Man of my higher self, my delicious divine provider, who is always here, always ready to provide and please, always poised with the most potent injection of brilliant inspiration, intuition, guidance and connection.

Thank you for providing exactly what I was seeking and so fucking quickly. Let the massive magic continue today. Here is what you are providing for me now, okay. Then I have a list, I have one, two, three, four, five things. I don't do more than five. You don't want to overwhelm your masculine. It's like five things is enough, and I know we're going long. This should take maybe another 10 minutes, okay?

If you can stick with me, stick with me, all right? We're almost at the end. This is like the most epic long live stream I've ever done. Okay, so that's what I do, all right? I'm not going to go into the details here but I very specifically I'm going to give you the framework. The high feminine rules, the what and the when. The divine masculine, the Magic Man, rules the how. You must know in your high feminine what do you want specifically, when do you want it, and what is the equality of the experience of it, right?

How do you want to experience receiving it into your experience, right? If you want a money goal, I want a 50K a month, do you want to have to work $100 a week? Often included time element that's not just when you want it by but how many hours you want to have to work. Do both, but also what's the experience? I want it to be easy. I want it to be fun. I don't want to even have to think about it. It's not even a thing that I think about. It just fucking happens and I want my clients to be fucking amazing, brilliant amazing, badass.

Describe the experience that you want to have as the goal is coming into existence, okay? That's the high feminine. In your high feminine, you rule over the what and the when, because the what and the when makes up the tone of your exacting standards. That's what your exacting standard frequency is composed of, is the what and the when, okay? This is the piece that is extremely fucking important for women and for everyone who is in this relationship to their Magic Man, you don't get to determine the how.

Most women, like want to scrutinize and this is where you get into worry, and this is where everything collapses and the whole thing goes to pieces, okay? You do not determine the how.

You give the how over to the Magic Man. Okay, so you make your list, okay. Then energetically what I do is I hand the honeydew list over to the Magic Man. I say, "Here you go, thank you so much." Then I energetically just I go out my way. This is the piece, Jules, that you were asking about and someone else was asking about inspired action.

This is where it comes in, okay, because I want to explain to you energetically what is happening. You have just handed your Magic Man your desires and requirements, okay? There's a piece in here that's really important about refusing to worry and be anxious, and scrutinize, okay? You cannot be hanging around the garage watching him fix the car, okay? The best thing for you to do would be to leave the house completely. That's what he wants you to do, leave.

Leave it with him, okay? "How are you doing, honey? Do you think it's going to be done today? Are you having any problem? Can I help you out? I really need the car tomorrow, I got a thing I got to do. Do you need help? Should I call your brother?" Okay, this is what you do with your goals and your dreams, and your desires, and your requirements. This is what you do with your Magic Man all the fucking time, I promise. Any time you worry or are consumed with anxiety about something not happening that you want to happen, here's what you're doing.

You are hanging around the garage breathing down his neck, driving him fucking crazy. Guess what's going to happen? He's going to turn on to be like, "You know what, baby? I'm not …" and he's going to walk away. "You do it then. You do it then. I'm not doing it." Worry kills Magic. Worry kills Magic, okay? Limp Dick Syndrome is now when you think about it. It is not attractive. There's another piece to this, which I just got, not your container the way that you maintain its integrity so that it remains magnetic to the Magic Man throughout the process.

Okay, so there's a building of the container, which is what I just taught you the tool to do, right? Also, really the building of the container happens in your actual life, filling, changing your relationships, changing your agreements so your entire life represents your exacting standards, okay? That's the building of the container but it's energetic so you have to maintain the container. You have to energetically constantly be maintaining and holding, maintaining and holding, maintaining and holding, maintaining and holding.

When you decide that you want to go look at the Magic Man's job in what he's doing, you abandon the container. It's like you leave the nest, okay? You're like, "Where's Magic Man? Where is he? Where did he go? Where is he?" Your container is just, it's gone. Now, he's like, "Wait, where is the … Okay." Because he can feel it. It's energetic, so your Magic Man is like, "It's gone, okay. I guess I'm not supposed to do anything." Those must not really be your standards. You must not really want that.

You're not very attractive to me. You're not magnetic. It doesn't even exist, the magnetism is gone. You see, your job is to stay out of the garage, okay? How do you stay out of the garage? This is what I do during the day and I don't really do this anymore because I get it energetically so I really don't worry. I just don't focus. I don't scrutinize. I don't. If I visit the garage in my mind, "What's going on? Is it going to happen by this date?" What I just imagine is me being like, my God, I'm so sorry.

Here I am hanging out in the garage and I just say, "I am totally sorry. I didn't even notice I showed up here. I know you got this, baby. I'm going to go hang on and just leave. I'm so sorry. You got this. I know you do. You're totally good. My bad." I leave the garage, or another way I want you to think about this is when you start to anxiety, worry, scrutinize, wonder, deadline, is it happening, how is it going to happen? How is this going to happen, okay?

Just imagine yourself what you're really doing is going over to your Magic Man and saying, "You know what, give me the list. Can I have the list? Just give me the list, I'll do it. I'll do it myself." That's what you're doing. Okay, so don't do that. If you're profoundly consumed with anxiety and worry, like two levels where it's probably trauma-based, then I'm not speaking to that person, okay. I'm speaking to someone who is in a level of high functioning but just doesn't know how to alchemize it, and probably doesn't even know that it's not your job to worry.

You may be thinking worrying is helping you focus on the goal or something. Those are the people I'm talking to. Last piece and then we're done. It's the inspired action piece, okay? You've given the instructions to your Magic Man. He's going away and here's what he's doing energetically. He's arranging. He's connecting the energetic gridlines between you and the opportunities. Opportunities always come in the form of people so it's essential we're connecting at the energetic gridlines to you and the souls, and the energies of the people who are going to show up in your inbox and be like, "I just was talking to somebody and she's referred me to your group.

I don't even really spend any time on Facebook but I looked at your group and my God, I don't even know what you do, but you, I have to work with you." This happens to my clients all the time, this shit. I had one woman close an $8,000 full pay at Starbucks. She was in the line with Starbucks and the person behind her started talking and she's like, "That's my fucking ideal client." They talked and sat down in Starbucks at the table, and she did a full pay, an $8,000 full pay, okay, because your Magic Man is like, "Okay.

Exacting standards, this is what you require and desire, got it. I got it, baby." When he's out there and moving and shaking, and making all … Lining all the things up, and then what he does is he shows up for just a second, a quickie, okay, and he's like, "Hey, go to Starbucks for a coffee," in this woman's case, right? She's like, "Starbucks? I don't really go in the afternoon." I mean I know this wasn't the story, but like it's an inspired idea. It's an intuitive hit. It's, "I should go here. I should go this.

I should say this. Marketing post." That is what that is, right? You've given him his job. He's moving and shaking, arranging, lining everything up, and he comes in and he's like, "Hey baby, marketing post, worry kills Magic. All right, I'm back out there." It is my job, it is your job as you, as your human consciousness, to fucking act on that and here's why. Because, and that's your intuition, people think intuition is feminine, it's masculine. A content of the intuition is masculine. It is an injection of an idea.

You might experience it and receive it into your feminine container but it's your masculine. Again, "Hey, baby," right? This is what inspired action is and that is your only job. Your only job is to take inspired action. You know this but now I'm telling you the energetics. You see, isn't this amazing? You're like hanging out, hanging out, da, da, da, da, da, doing your thing, whatever it is that you want to do, whether it's a live stream or whatever the fuck, inspired action, do it.

Here's the thing. It is about timing because the masculine is the energy of timing, time, timing, okay? This is why I say to people, when you get the intuitive hit, that is the moment that everything is lined up because he's fucking the master of timing and he's got everything lined up, and he's totally done what you asked him to do. He's like, "All right, this is the moment. Come on, baby. Do it. Do it. Do it. Come on, do it. What the fuck? Do it." You're like, "I'll do it later. No, that doesn't make a whole lot of sense.

I'm not going to do that, it doesn't make any sense at all. I don't know what that's about. That's silly." Your Magic Man is like, "Are you fuck … He just was right … He's gone now but that guy right there, that woman right there, she was going to be your next client. You just had to make a post and she was totally going to go on Facebook. She was just going to do it. In fact, she's on Facebook right now but you're not there. Fuck." Then you wonder why he doesn't provide for you because the idea didn't make sense.

Because you don't understand all the synchronistic grid that's happening and all of the ways he's magically connecting people that don't make sense to connect to you through these all these ways. You're in your conscious brain going, "Well, that doesn't make sense." That feels like a waste of time or that looks irresponsible. Those are more of those little devils that are like,

"Well, don't do that, that's silly." There's a whole thing I teach on intuition and how to activate your intuition, and listen to your intuition.

Intuition for launches and quantum needs and wants, and that stuff, but that's what's happening, okay? That's what inspired action is. What's amazing about this whole process because he's also the master of time, and because he doesn't want to have you to work very hard, he wants to do all the work and he wants to do all the providing, is that this one little idea can make you a shit fucking ton of money. I have made $40,000 from one single Facebook post that at the time I was like, "Why am I posting about this? This doesn't make any sense."

I got somebody's attention, it was like, holy shit, I don't even know what you do but I have to work with you. That was a 25K client. Now, I have a 50K client, a 50K client from one Facebook post, okay? I'm done. This is the longest. I've been struggling this for 10 years. I see now. Wow. My God, you fucking said it, just what I needed to hear. I magnetize to me a dark angel, so to speak, and I started to blame myself, "How could I magnetize him if my vibe was so high?"

Then you said it, this makes so much sense, yeah, yeah, yeah, yeah, yeah, yeah, yeah. I've been single for four years and I completely understand. I've turned down my energy. I don't even attract quality masculine, yes, but now you see why, Stacey. I've given you … This is the only live stream you … This is the only thing you ever need [inaudible 01:47:18] honestly. This is it. This is it, like you ever have a question about why something is not working in your life, just listen to this live stream, seriously.

With that said, it's like having a baby, those who truly really are very close and your friends will still be around to help and support, totally. Marina, you've had an orgasm too? What? Fucking hell, amazing. Your burger joint was called Devil Burger? Dude, I want to eat a burger at Devil Burger. Does it still exist? I want to got there. Fucking cheeky little imps. I'm so weak for charmers. They're my imps, which test me. Did I miss this too? Did you share that already? I don't know what you're talking about, Shawna, sorry.

I've given it all for free, integrity and alchemy, no apologies. Yeah. How about the courage to actually going and doing that inspired nudge? That wink from a sexy man, any insight on courage? I talked about that, Marina, so go back and listen to this live steam, okay? I talked about courage. Courage is you knowing that no matter what happens, nothing and no one has power over you. Courage is not being in your victim. Courage is knowing that you're going to be okay no matter what happens.

Therefore, you do the existing, you match your exacting standards. I'm so tired I can't even talk. Go back because that's the piece where I talk about, that's where courage comes from. The root of courage is kerd, which is the French word for heart. The way you develop the heart for something that terrifies you is to know you will never abandon your own heart, but you will never abandon your own sense of work. I don't want to repeat it, just go back. It's there. You may be missed it.

The why, yes, much gratitude for this live, awesome, you guys. Mind blown, holy fuck. Your exclamations are blowing my mind with a strong energetic intentions. Yay, I'm so happy. It's like writing to Santa. Totally, if he turns you on, I would not be … Yeah, with a sexy Santa. A Latin Santa, a tall … A Benicio Del Toro Santa, yeah. Do you say daily more than once? No, because that means that I don't trust my man, [inaudible 01:49:44]. I don't need to go check. To saying it daily more than once is me saying, "Are you really doing it?

Did you hear me? I don't know if you really heard me. Let me repeat myself." My Magic Man heard me. He listens to me. He pays very close attention to me. I say it one time. Then if I ever start to wonder about should I say, da, da, da, all of that, I'm like, "I'm sorry, baby. I am so sorry. I don't know what I was thinking. You're fucking amazing. You are omnipotent. You got this, I know it." You guys, I'm making this sound easy. It's not easy. Worry and anxiety are literally imprinted biologically into our systems as women.

Do a research on this. We are highly anxious beings way more so than men, so I'm not giving you something that you should master tomorrow, okay? Maybe you could. You could master it tomorrow but probably not. You're going to have to walk away from the fucking energetic garage a lot and apologize to your Magic Man a lot, and be like, "I am so sorry. I cannot get myself something to do because I'm just fucking hanging around you too much and showing you that I don't trust you." It's just this has got to be … This is the part the action part, not even the action part.

This is like the rigorous paying attention to those little devil voices and I go into exactly how those voices sound and how you can alchemize them, but this is the piece that's very challenging. This is the part that's not sexy and not … You know what this is? This is the minute by minute, hour by hour, day by day, week by week non-sexy part of building an amazing relationship is really what it is. It's like, "Fuck, man. I keep fucking breathing down his neck. I got to stop that." The answer is no, I don't see equivalence.

My God, can I help you? Yeah, don't say that, Marina. Don't say that. This has been so freaking amazing that I'm tired just floating a list. My God, you guys, fuck, I do that to my actual man all the time. Rushin, you got to stop that now. Are you serious? Stop it now. Stop it now. This is me. I start going and feel I need to help and everything goes to shit. Yeah. Funny because I was just about to go to bed. I'm in UK. It's 1am. I had a quick peek on Facebook. You've just gone live two minutes before I came on.

Okay. I think I'm done. First video, you've seen mine, Melanie? Holy fucking shit man. Go to my YouTube channel. I got 24 hours of this stuff and find a way to work with me. Find a way. Find a way, nobelwarrior.com. Here, I'll open it here. Okay, I intentionally created different tiers of ways to work with me for different levels of people who think that they can afford certain things. My actual man isn't trying to tell me this too. You guys, I'm telling you man, Alison Armstrong, Alison Armstrong, Alison Armstrong.

She will change your life. Okay. Hey, [Gentry 01:53:47], I'm so sorry. I'm about to end. I've been on for almost two hours. I can't even fucking believe it. I remember when Facebook was doing lives and it would cut out after like 45 minutes, the live stream would just stop. Unfortunately, but Gentry, it was fucking epic. My live streams tend to be … People tend to tell me that my live streams changed their lives and they're epic, and amazing and amazing. This one was the best one I've ever done ever, ever.

This one was like it was like a comprehensive total complete visual metaphor and energetic understanding of the masculine and the feminine, and how to get what you want in life, and all the things you're doing that you don't realize you're doing to fuck the entire thing up, the inspiration, for how to change it, a specific tool for how to do it. I mean, it's fucking amazing. All right everybody, this was a fucking blast. I laughed my ass off and I will be back at some point. I put my link there.

I will also put a link to UnSchool and the sales masters' group, and I would love to see you guys. I would love to work with you for real and help you apply these things to your life in a very much more specific way so that you can really, really get results. Okay. You are so welcome, good night.

LITTLE DEVILS   You don't have what you want and can't keep it when you get it because of one thing and one thing only: you don't understand masculine energy.   Or, to put it another way, you don't know what to do with all the little devils.   Yes, your Magic Man is amazing and is capable of giving you all you desire.   That's his PROVIDER energy. This is what you're CONSCIOUSLY trying to become attractive to and activate when you're strengthening your boundaries and stepping into your exacting standards and supreme integrity.

But what you don't realize is that he also has a PROTECTOR energy, and when you arouse one, you arouse the other. But you're not thinking about this one AT ALL. In fact you have no idea how it works or even how to recognize it for what it is.   Enter: misery after the victory.

That's because the way your Magic Man protects you often does not feel good AT ALL. In fact it feels like a shit storm. Like you had ALL this goodness and amazingness and FINALLY broke through one of the biggest challenges of your life and the money is flowing and the clients are amazing and then BAM. BOOM. Chaos. Drama. Crisis.

And then Self doubt. Anger. Depression. Confusion. Despair. Lack of motivation.

Increase your visibility? (Provider energy! Yes!) Now the criticism of your disruptive message is even harsher because these people don't KNOW you like your original UnTribe does so they're going to feel much freer to be MUCH more direct, critical and disdainful so in the newspaper and on TV you see yourself dissected mercilessly, pilloried, burned at the proverbial stake. (Protector energy. Fuck.)

Are you ready?

Or will you buckle under the onslaught.

Go from $1500 months to a $50,000 weekend (from just TWO sales) and hell YESS your family can afford to go on an amazing vacation.

AND, your husband is going to sink into depression because he was already having a hard time with his career and now you've just gone and blown his self esteem to smithereens. He now spends his days depressed on the couch. Not really an awesome traveling companion.

Are you ready?

Or will you sabotage your next Quantum boom because it's just too painful to see him this way, and because you feel deeply guilty for what you've done. Which is crazy. You know you shouldn't feel guilty but you do. Plus he just doesn't have the emotional management skills or support that you do. So in order to preserve the fucking marriage — YES, this is ACTUALLY the kind of shit that happens — you decide to go easy on him and slow down your growth.

OR the crisis happens right during the uplevel.

Sell a big package, client ghosts.

Post your biggest month yet, unexpected bills come due.

Client pays but the bank systems screw it up so you don't get it for weeks.

Go from $1500 months to a $50k weekend? AWESOME. BADASS. Now your husband feels worthless and your mom thinks you're running a sham. FINALLY sell that dream $25K package? FUCK YEAH. Now you're terrified about actually being able to deliver at that level and secretly convinced you're a fraud and not nearly as brilliant as you think and now that will be exposed. Go from $300 to $6000 packages and from 60-hour weeks to 20-hour weeks and $12,000 months with tons of time to travel? YAAASSSSSS. And now get serious slack from your family about your new lifestyle — because they think rich people are assholes — AND start getting requests to help family members out with their financial troubles since you have so much money now.

Until you understand that when you activate the PROVIDER you also activate the PROTECTOR and can see and EMBRACE all this crazy chaos and crisis and upset AS your Magic Man PROTECTING you (the ability to do this is called CHAOS ALCHEMY, by the way, and it is the highest feminine art there is and is what will provide you with an UNLIMITED amount of access to your Magic and catapult you truly into your most epic legacy life) then you will forever be stuck in the "FINALLY got it!!! FUCK lost it" cycle. In other words, all those little devils didn't come 'out of nowhere' AT ALL. Your Magic Man brought them to you, along with the gifts. Because when you become attractive to him, you activate ALL of him. And those little devils are his gifts also. They're just wrapped in a beautiful, black bow.

the activation of the masculine PROVIDER energy and as INEVITABLE (until you reach a certain height in your power management abilities, at which point it calms down consskderably)

for what it is and then it feels wonderful and amazing because you get what he's doing. (and, you know how to handle it, which takes an even GREATER degree of ability to stand in your exacting standards and supreme integrity.)

Because your Magic Man has been where you're going — a place of extraordinary increase in power from where you are now and teeming with goodies but also goblins.

But you're not thinking about this AT ALL when you're dreaming of retiring your husband because he hates his job and traveling the world with him. It doesn't cross your mind ONCE.

But your Magic Man, who because he is Master of Time can see in all dimensions at once? He sees it clear as day and because he is your MAIN MAN, and because one of the primary directives of the masculine is to PROTECT, guess what he's going to send your way.

Not a bouquet of roses and a box of delectable chocolates but a bunch of unruly little devils.

You know, the shit that happens when you try and uplevel.

The stuff that

just realized something that could help so may of you understand why you don't have what you want and can't keep it when you get it. The understanding of this somewhat hangs on my previous work (most relevantly two epic livestreams one with over 1,000 views and 300 comments that is making people cry with tears it's so revolutionary) (so feel free to PM me if you want to see them) but I'm going to make this post able to stand on its own so you can grasp the key ah-ha now. Stay with me. I'm teaching energetic law through the masculine and feminine here so it may take a minute. So maybe put down your fifty million things and your scrolling frenzy and take a deep breath and let me blow your mind ⚡ First, let's set up the scenario. Tell me if this feels familiar: Or something to that effect. You get what you want (and fuck it may take forever to get it, which will be addressed here also) and then after ALL that, you LOSE IT! This is because you've been building your life according to one very low frequency belief because you can't imagine how the truth can be true. The truth being: no one and nothing has power over you. The path to awakening and success is to wake up and realize the truth and then dramatically adjust all your physical agreements and expressions of your low standard living to match your true, exacting standards (which is the only reason we ever decide NOT to live according to our highest standards: we're terribly afraid of the ramifications of doing so; which means we think someone or something has more power over how our life goes than we do, including how we FEEL). The dis-chord between your low frequency life and your true standards (very high frequency) creates the struggle and strife you experience. And when you finally decide to "snap" the energetic ties that are holding your life in its low frequency state (literally energetically DEpressing and suppressing your natural frequency) that is what creates a quantum "boom" in your field, and therefore in your life, and that's what a Quantum Leap in success looks like and how it happens. BUT, remember, the REASON you've been SUPPRESSING your natural frequency and choosing to live a life that doesn't match it, is because you've been SCARED of doing so. That fear doesn't go away (until you do lotsssssss of Alchemy on your physical, mental and emotional fields and essentially alchemize your shadow). You're scared of all the ramifications ("good" and "bad" of doing so.)

That backlash is an inevitable result of your Quantum boom. Because the dis-chord was created to AVOID those very things that now inevitably are going to happen. But the other thing that happens is that

nd because the masculine

ut in order to STAY at that level and go even higher and have the fullness of what you've just activated come in to your experience, you need to be in a MUCH stronger place mentally, emotionally, even physically.   Because it's all about the management of power.   At an energetic level, upgrades are simply increasing the amount of pure, potent energy we're running in our field. So, you have to be "trained" to deal with it. Like a firefighter or someone working with explosives.   It's not because you're "bad" or did anything wrong that conflict is coming your way. It's because your Magical Masculine wants to make sure you don't totally blow a fuse when you reach that next level — the one he's sending your way also — because you can't handle the power.   He's protecting you by testing you.   That's when, and why, the little devils or what I call dark angels of strife come in AFTER a success. They're there to be your "spiritual boxing trainer." To toughen you up energetically — not by becoming guarded or rigid, but by becoming immune to fear, judgment, criticism, lack of approval from the tribe ... because the tribe does not want anyone becoming TOO powerful.   The energetic system is built to naturally work to do this. Your build your power, and you become attractive to more power (your Magic man providing for you) and also to the little devils who throng around, poking and prodding and testing, to see how you respond.   If your container is weak (meaning you are still highly susceptible to disapproval and fear), you'll collapse the container. (This is why lottery winners tend to go back to the financial state they were in before they won the lottery). There's no judgment about that. It just means you're not ready to get in the arena and box with more power.   So you do your work and find where in your life you collapsed your standards and do it again.   Make sen

The Dark Goddess And The Takeover Of Consciousness

If great change is upon you, you are in the presence of the Dark Goddess and here is what you must know about Her:

1. She does not care about your comfort. She is here to resurrect your unearth the Soul in order to alchemize it out of existence and put you directly in touch with Her, with the Dark, with Source energy.

2. She is here to take EVERYTHING you're holding on to.

WHATEVER you're holding on to. When you HOLD ON you have no power. Your True Genius only expresses itself fully in your life when you develop a constant ability to LET GO. And then let go again. And again. And again. FOREVER. Your new life of power and ease and soul expression requires that you master the practice of LETTING GO at all times in all ways with everything and everyone. The more you hold on, the more painful She makes it and the more life-threatening (literally) the lesson of letting go.

Let me give you specific examples from my life.

- MY CAREER, CASH and CACHE: GONE

I grew up consumed by anxiety and low self-esteem, to the point where, for most of my life I had either no friends or just one friend who was the most unpopular person in the school. I believed I had no gifts to offer the world and had no confidence in my voice, my truth, my spiritual wisdom or my creative brilliance. So when I stumbled onto the gift of sales and business building, I seized it like it was a LIFE JACKET. I built and ran--along with my mom and dad-- a $15 million consulting business that regularly beat out our multibillion dollar competitors. I made a quarter of a million dollars a year in income for many years. I bought my then-husband a rare, $30,000 Steinway grand piano. I wore fur coats and drove a Lexus SUV. I lived in a half million dollar condo. I was on top of the world, because I had finally found something to justify and validate my existence and my worth. I even put away $300,000 in investments and savings during that time.

SHE TOOK IT ALL FROM ME.

I lost my home, my marriage, all my money, and any ability to claim my worth as a result of having all those things. I went through several nervous breakdowns and was diagnosed with several mental illnesses. But I knew it was nothing other than the Dark Goddess taking me through an archetypal journey of transformation, which is why I didn't and still won't take any little white pills because there was nothing wrong with me. In fact there was something very RIGHT--IS something very right-- with me. I exhibited the IMMENSE and RARE courage that few have to be willing to have my entire life taken down to the ground so it could be rebuilt on my true power, brilliance, self-worth and DIVINE ESSENCE.

I thought it was over. I built a new business, which many if you saw happen last year. I had incredible success – $15,000 months with no real marketing, no list, and no planning. I helped women launch million dollar businesses, find their purpose and soul gifts and step into their calling, and I was on top of the world. AGAIN.

I had simply replaced one set of accomplishments to validate my existence with another. So guess what had to happen. I lost it all AGAIN. And along with it, my relationship to a man I thought I was going to marry. I had to rip apart another home, had to send my daughter through another heart-wrenching breakup of what she thought was going to be her new family. All because I wasn't getting the lesson. You cannot live out of your human consciousness IN ANY RESPECT if you're going to express your soul purpose in the world.

Actually, I take that back. You can, and many do. I see many – way too many - people who have achieved a level of spiritual power, and whose human consciousness is as overbearing and unweildy as any tyrant's. But for those of us for whom that is simply not an option, for those of us for whom this lifetime is the one in which we step into true holy humanness, true divinity consciousness, that is not an option, and it's to you that I'm speaking.

Whatever you are holding onto as a validation of your existence and worth, The Dark Goddess will take away. It doesn't matter if it's a spiritual business, doesn't matter if it's an enlightened calling, and it doesn't matter how many lives you've changed. If you're holding onto it She will take it away.

This is why I left Facebook for over a year. I was sick to the point of nauseous with how many powerful, spiritual women business owners I saw abusing their power and dripping with small-minded humanity. I was nowhere near strong enough to stand against this in my own skin, so I simply had to shut it all out, so I could go through my one last break down and into my greatest – to date, I'm sure there will be more – breakthrough.

I now hold on to nothing. Nothing can rattle me, nothing can shake me, nothing can cause me to believe in the illusion that anything I do or anything that happens to me has anything to do with my worth. I am no longer tempted into the illusion of believing that I need anything to happen or not happen in any particular way in order to be my own badass being, standing in the light of God.

And now that I have this as the steel point of groundedness in the bones of my bones, I need nothing else.

This is what you're *actually* looking for.

Hidden in all your HOLDING ON is actually the deep desire to be constantly able to LET GO. What you're really looking for when you hold on is an unwavering sense of total stability and groundedness and freedom from fear. And because all spiritual principles of awakening and mastery are a paradox, the only way you get to this feeling, the one you're desperately trying to create by holding on to your money, your status, your beliefs, your stories, your brand, your reputation, your relationships, your home, is by mastering the radical and exhilarating and deeply calming practice of LETTING IT ALL GO. Always. And forever.

Week One: Monday 7/17 and Thursday 7/20

Livestream Topic: Death and Rebirth: From Tribal to Divinity Consciousness

Why this group

- elevate from tribal to divinity consciousness

- activate and balance masculine and feminine

-results: this has tangible results (love, men, money, body)

What is tribal consciousness?

What is divinity consciousness?

Why rise?

- NOT out of fear of death

that is tribal consc masked as spiritual awakening

There is no death and no stakes. This is a game.

- But because we are built for it.

It is natural and the most pleasurable.

Here to advance consciousness beyond its limits

Nonphysical requires physical for expansion (friction)

We are on the leading edge; we direct the divine

Spiritual guides/galactic councils report to US, learn from US

There is no death, no victims, no one to save

Puts humans in one-down to nonphysical

No hierarchy, only players in the game

We are the surgeons, nonphysical hands us the right tool

Why important?

This is about energy mastery, which only happens between EQUALS

If you are highly spiritual but not experiencing tangible success, you're in a one-down rel't to the nonphysical (you don't trust yourself; consider nonphysical to be wiser)

If you're experiencing tangible success but suffering inside, you are in a one-up rel't to the nonphysical (you don't trust it; consider it beneath you)

Goal is to get you on an equal playing field with the nonphysical

Meaning mastering fem and masc energy and pulling from energy into matter at will, with ease, in all areas (business, body, bedroom)

Why do we suffer?

- acting unnaturally (out of fear, believing in death)

- natural beliefs work with the earth plane to create thriving

- unnatural beliefs work against the earth plane.

- It is unnatural to suffer

- tribal conc believes it is unnatural to thrive - hard, scary, deadly

- our analogies are misguided b/c they relate us to our human

- flying = thriving. This puts us in an unnatural position to thriving.

- if we know we are spirit and soul, flight becomes natural

- Suffering only happens when we are under the illusion that we are human

- that this earth plane is something other than a construct of consciousness that can be manipulated at will

- that we chose to pretend in the ultimate existence of physical (meaning that death is a real thing) because that's what creates friction and division between states (phys and non-phys) and allows for the new to be drawn out

So, what is the truth? (the Four Archetypes and Spiritual Law on the Earth Plane)

- Everything we learned of natural law is reversed

Believing is seeing

Flying is natural

Death is unreal and unnatural

Queen

There is no loss of identity

No blocks to vision, dreams

Our dreams are real (reality is a dream) and here now (soul frequency)

Warrior

There are no victims

There is no space (nothing to fear)

Magician

There is no time (nothing to suffer waiting for)

Lover

There is no lack of security or safety

Safety comes from unfiltered truth (not pleasing the tribe)

Others must earn our energy

To earn our energy means that someone's presence turns us on, meaning activates our soul frequency - vibration of light (what is already light, not what we believe is dark that we must turn into light)

To be turned on means to be in the presence of light that has embraced the dark; it means to be seen and loved unconditionally and without shame or judgment; this is true pleasure;

With men and clients it is the same – the ones that turn us on are reaching our essence with their own wholeness

The ones that turn us off are coming to us to get help honoring their darkness as real; when our job is to see it as unreal; men and clients who believe in their wound in other words

True pleasure is to be turned on by the men and clients who don't believe in their own wounds

False pleasure is to be lost within the darkness and the indulgence that wounds exist; men and clients who pleasure you for the moment in shared illusion that wounds exist but then leave or create havoc (becuase of course they believe wounds exist and they could die if they experienced you fully)

we must earn energy (work to create cash, become a match for the ideal man) because…

why is the princess high up in the castle behind brambles and flames?

This is how you - the hero - discover your desire, through friction and trial;

"too much" trial means you don't truly desire it;

Discovering your desire means discovering the unique qualities of your soul expression;

DESIRE is the unique energetic blueprint of your soul that is meant to become matter in form, in order to advance consciousness in the only way your soul can

Which means without friction (the requirement of earning energy/presence), you would not be able to discover your desire or uniqueness

It is through this process that we activate our highest frequency, and that is the game we came here to play

So to reverse it, you are Cinderella and you are also discovering your desire;

Do you desire a man or a client who gives up too easily?

Where is your greatest pleasure, intimacy and activation?

With someone who has overcome the greatest hurdles in order to experience your uniqueness and your energy

This person – man or client – has the power to resonate with your soul frequency and create SYNERGY

Synergistic connections are the most potent form of consciousness playing with itself; and since that is the whole point of the game – for consciousness to expand against itself, then one of the principles must be that others must earn our energy and presence.

What is pleasure?

True pleasure enhances and elevates all areas of our lives when we receive it (money, love, health increase)

False pleasure diminishes (addictions, codependence)

True pleasure comes after willingness to receive pain (do what we are terrified of, uncover our darkest shame)

False pleasure helps us avoid pain

Dysfunctional relationships are false pleasure

Clients and men who distract you from yourself

By praising you all the time

By criticizing you all the time

You need the distraction because you are full of shame

Shame keeps you away from your soul, from intimacy with yourself, your spiritual gifts and their tangible results

tangible results = intimacy with your soul = no shame

no shame = no fear

this is why I shared all my dirty launder before I launched my biz

If you can focus on mastering energy between you and this person rather than between you and your soul

What you are avoiding is directing your soul to do your bidding and intimacy with self and other

You are avoiding feeling sovereign

A sovereign being does not need or seek or absorb praise or criticism because it has nothing to do with them

A sovereign being is focused exclusively on its own unique creative expression in each moment; its own game; its own intense delight; and whether others come to play, or understand the game does not matter. And if they do come to play and if they do express understanding or praise, the focus is on integrating them into the play, not in mutual congratulations about the brilliance of the game or who has more guidance about the way the game is supposed to be played.

A sovereign being looks very much like a fool. The Magician.

The four archetypes and Spiritual Law

What does rising look and feel like?

Who come to help us rise?

- The Dark Goddess in the rise of divinity consciousness

- The threshold guardian

Hiring A Darkworker Is Hiring The Energetic Laws Of The Universe

WARNING: Before you rip into the package from your new mentor, (the one with impeccable integrity whom you want more than anything to shatter your patterns and activate your Iconic Frequency....)

be sure to read the fine print on the disclaimer notice.

Here's what is says:

"Contrary to what you believe, you have not just hired a mentor.

I'm other words, a human.

No, no.

You just hired the energetic laws of the universe.

In other words, transforming fire.

In other words, a dragon.

Welcome to the dragon's den! It's hot as fuck in here. And when you emerge, you'll be a diamond dragon of your own."

If that's the kind of thing that makes an evil grin spread across your face, you're in the right place.

If not, best to leave the package where it is and back alway. Quickly.

We do not desire to be happy. We desire to evolve.

It is the misunderstanding of our innate condition of fulfillment that creates DREAMERS, not DOERS, because the DREAM holds the fantasy of happiness alive, without the requirement of sacrifice. Whereas the MANIFESTED life destroys the fantasy of happiness in its requirement for sacrifice through acts of personal terror that annihilate fear and unleash the light hidden in our shadow. As long as we are human, evolution will be filled with terror.

It is with great relief that we discover through our acts of personal terror, and the power we discover within us to generate our own conditions at all time, that we are not, in fact, human, but rather a new kind of being: a divine human. A formed holiness.

Genius manifests. Non-genius dreams. How to switch on your dormant spiritual gifts and enter a world of manifested purpose.

The tribal impulse is a misinterpreted communal access to the energetic grid of consciousness that is calling for our aid in bringing it into form. Consciousness raising takes a village and is the intended purpose for cultures and gatherings. How to initiate your own individual entrance into the already-gathered, and therefore drop the need to identify as a tribal human.

ON SALES STAGNATION, STUCKNESS AND LACK OF INSPIRATION

Your Highest Mind, your Genius Mind, is always streaming the most inspired ideas into you.

The problem is that you are operating with your Narrow Mind, which is an energetically tiny, constricted channel that only allows a trickle of inspiration through.

This is because your Highest Mind operates at the frequency of the highest energetic standards: Supreme Integrity, Radical Trust and Impeccable Truth.

So, stop trying to brainstorm, talk to friends or your mentor, meditate, dance or go to the spa.

That does NOTHING to activate access to your Genius Frequency.

All you need to do is find all the places in your life where you are operating below frequency and raise your standards in every area simultaneously, relentlessly and viciously and you will know exactly what to do.

And what's more, you'll have the energetic balls of steel to command the results you require.

It's called SuperConscious Awakening.

Learn the secrets to opening your Highest Mind at will, consistently, forever.

The Terrifying Requirements of the Feminine Genius Frequency (So You Say You Want to Develop Your Spiritual Gift…)

You say you want to develop your spiritual gift. You pray for it daily. You want to be one of those "magical" ones with those "super" powers because that's cool now. To be magical. Intuitive. Psychic.

You pray for this day and night. Make me intuitive. Awaken my gifts. Give me knowledge of my supernatural powers.

As if they are bubble gum balls or jacks. Things that will make you popular with the in crowd. Things you can play with for hours while a crowd gathers, in awe of your big bubbles and your fast hands.

Ha.

First of all, clearly no one told you about the journey of awakening you must endure in order for your genius to be willing to honor you with their presence.

You must become worthy of your genius, you know. You must pass through seemingly endless trials of intense suffering in which everything you hold dear is burned to ash.

Your pride.

Your reputation.

Your occupation.

Your sense of self.

All of it must go in order for your genius to begin to trust you with even the tiniest spark of its massive streaming firepower.

And then.

And then....

After all that, what does your genius do?

Turns you into a witch. A dragon. A dangerous creature speaking abominations into the fire-ridden crowd of tourists who gathered to get a sense of your magic and who instead run screaming from you, looking over their shoulder aghast at the sight and the sound of you.

And still you must breathe out all the flames. Alone. Ragged. Uncertain.

And then.

And only then....

Will all the other witches appear and the great, teeming pride of dragons.

The ones who have been waiting all along for you, hidden in the invisible world you have now mightily lit with your great and terrible gift.

DEATH TO CERTIFICATIONS

Nearly every attempt to capture transformative power and teach it through some mass-produced method rather than through intimate apprenticeship or training always has the result of silencing, dulling and diluting the very gift it is intending to cultivate, because transformative gifts are deeply specific, unique and intimate to their carriers, and therefore require great precision of thought and insight on the part of both the "apprentice" and "teacher" to draw forth. And in fact what us being taught, and what is being learned, is not a concretized method and repeatable process for producing transformation but rather the skill of maintaining a keen attunement to the frequency of the gift, so that it may flow freely from spirit to matter in the unrepeatable, unique forms it naturally takes when in the presence of each new person desiring transformation.

Mass certification programs simply cannot even approximate this alchemical process at all. And so the students end up getting taught external, concretized processes and methods that attempt to mimic the purity and power of organic alchemy.

And when you try and mimic intimate alchemy you get nothing like gold. Instead, you get a pot of sludge.

I'M CALLING FOR THE UNTAMING OF THE PERSONAL TRANSFORMATION MOVEMENT

For the DEVOLUTION in the DNA of mentorship (back to the WILD nature of our unique genius, which has been held captive in coaching certifications and programs and cultural conditioning for far too long).

It's name?

UnCoaching.

It's time we go from mass-produced coaches with a nice piece of paper but little skill (No fault of their own. They expected to be trained and instead were just TAMED) to ACTIVATORS OF INNER GENIUS who transform their clients with MASTERY and AUTHENTICITY.

What is needed is not to squeeze genius through a template but instead to deprogram coaches' spiritual and cultural conditioning that has caused too many of them to infuse their clients with their own inner shadow rather than give them the key to UNLEASH their clients' Personal Power, Intuitive Mastery and of course, epic success.

What is required is to activate AUTHENTIC BRANDS from the inside out, so each of you intuitively markets, sells and delivers using creative "just in time" ideas that capture your clients' hearts (because who wants to be seen as a copycat of their mentor?).

What this requires is INTIMACY with a UnTame mentor who herself has been UnSchooled, so she can see your genius and provide you with closely tailored, customized and personalized guidance and can personally DEPROGRAM your conditioning so your INNER GENIUS naturally leaps out.

This is what takes your ZERO business to $58,800 in one month, your $1500 months to $22,000 months, your $5k months to $51,000 in three weeks, your $7k months to $77k, etc etc etc.

But it's even more profound than this, because becoming an UnCoach is really about the DEEPER activation done on your CHARACTER and your BEING, since your INAUTHENTICITY and TRIBAL CONDITIONING is the only thing that's been in the way of you launching your business (and the key reason you can't MAINTAIN your Quantum Leap and why your clients ghost, your bank account collapses after your expansion and your inability actually hold the HIGHER FREQUENCY of your True Self).

Activating and monetizing UnTame, elite geniuses (anyone with a creative or spiritual gift meant to transform lives and evolve consciousness):

This is my mission on the planet.

Let the Wildness begin

Trust Your Undoing

It saddens me to see so many with so much mistrust of their process of being undone.

And of course this makes perfect sense, because most of us were born with a deep mistrust of it, but it's crippling your business to mistrust your undoing, because you're actually mistrusting an essential aspect of yourself -- the Dark Goddess within you that destroys in order to create. You're making it bad, undesirable, worrisome, anxiety-creating, something you want to ESCAPE and learn how to HANDLE.

Would you ask your mentor how to handle your joy?

Then think about it: why are you asking her to help you handle your undoing?

I'm being only slightly facetious, of course, because we work with mentors FOR this very reason, but the reason we work with them isn't to help us handle our undoing. It's to help us handle our MISTRUST of it.

Big difference.

Recently a client shared that she was going through deep shadow. She asked for guidance about how to spend her day in this state. And what I said was something that immediately called for a broader audience, to be shared with all of you, in case this is something you struggle with also.

So thank you, my dear client, for making this moment possible for so many others to learn from.

When you feel wonderful, delightful, full of joy, positivity and confidence, you're not likely to feel the need to check in with anyone about how to handle that, what do to with your time, how to manage those feelings.

That's because you TRUST those feelings. You believe they are here to support you on your path. So you go about your days confidently feeling on track and in alignment.

And then the darkness hits. The shadow. The stripping away. And you immediately turn to your mentor for help dealing with this terrible turn of events.

But if your joy isn't a problem to be solved, then neither is your undoing.

The only "problem" to be solved is that you see it as a problem to be solved.

The highest work you can do with your mentor is to learn to trust yourself in all things. And of course you're with your mentor because you don't and haven't trusted yourself in all things. And so, as in all spiritual truth, herein is an essential paradox.

Your mentor's job is to show you that you can TRUST your undoing. She's there to put you into INTIMATE, RAW relationship to it, not to shield you from it.

EVEN the shadow part. ESPECIALLY the shadow part. PARTICULARLY the shadow part.

It's time to TRUST feeling like SHIT.

This is the Meathook Moment of Awakening in the myth of the Dark Goddess, Inanna. It's when she's hanging on a meat hook in the center of the earth, dying a death within a death within a death. And the truth here is that you will continue to die and die and die until you GIVE UTTERLY IN to dying and to the process of dying and to the pain of dying and to the confusion of dying and to the embarrassment of dying and to the endlessness of the dying within the dying within the dying.

And of course you don't want to give in, because this kind of death feels infinite. And it is. And it isn't.

And the paradox is that once you give in, the death ends.

So instead of trying to end the dying, your fastest way back to life is to give fully in to the dying. To fall in love with the dying.

It is the only way back to true life.

(And here's how to tell if you're working with a true Shadow Master: If your mentor gives you ways to "handle" your undoing that in any way calm the confusion, soften the sting or muffle the madness or try and fix, understand or contain it (like meditating, journaling, chakra cleansing, raw food cleanses, mindset work, exercise, spa days, affirmations). If so, they're doing you a disservice, because they're reinforcing the belief (the untruth) that your shadow and your undoing are any kind of problem to be solved.))

Here's to your beautiful, dark Undoing.

ON SHAME, GENIUS AND FREEDOM

What you are most ashamed of is in fact your genius and the key to your freedom.

Take Carl Jung. This book was hidden from the public for decades because of the disrepute and destruction his family and colleagues believed it would have on his reputation, were it to be made public. It chronicles 16 years of what he calls his "creative illness" but what many in western psychiatry would deem a psychotic break.

But Jung knew what was really going on. He knew this was his Soul breaking through into his Being. He knew it was the rending of the veil between the divine and the human. And he knew it was not his downfall, but his uprising.

Jung credits this experience -- allowing himself to tumble into the depths of "insanity" and to rise back into the heights of his true Being, reconstituted, integrated, whole and "holy connected" to his genius -- with providing all the insights and understanding that formed the basis of depth psychology and all his groundbreaking contributions to psychoanalysis.

It was my coming across an article about this book -- its ignominy and recent release and Jung's fearless and wise journey into his deep truth -- in the New York Times last October -- when I was struggling mightily with how to respond to my diagnosis of bipolar disorder -- that gave me the courage to follow my own inner knowing that, like Jung, I was not crazy nor was

I going nor had I gone crazy, but that in fact I was GOING SANE and that I need not fear or be ashamed of my "condition" -- which is simply the condition of being visited upon by a great and powerful Soul whose intent, come hell or high water, life or death, is to make itself fully known to my being and fully unleashed in my life -- but instead can choose to walk into my own SoulFire and have my human burned away so my Soul can be released.

It is after reading that article that I eschewed medication and chose a radical path of healing that had at its foundation an unwavering allegiance to unleashing my Soul, my Truth and my spiritual gifts on the world stage, come hell or high water, life or death.

When I made this contract with myself, I was a jobless single mom with no money, living off of support from my parents, having just been fired from my third six-figure executive job in corporate America.

Now I have a thriving business, having done nearly $300,000 in revenue, where I am unleashing other Souls and restoring their blazing genius to its proper place in the world: front and center where it is meant to be, elevating consciousness, burning away all humans hold dear and raising up among us the new divinity consciousness.

The world needs more humans going sane and freeing themselves from the prison of tribal consciousness, not staying silent and dying within it.

[Update: The world doesn't "need" anything. But it would like it very much.]

The Energetics Of A Nervous Breakdown

Tonight I was watching BrainGames with my daughter. Science confirms what we know to be true energetically: Your brain works much harder when you lie than when you tell the truth, because it has to suppress your NATURAL impulse to tell the truth.

We have a natural impulse to tell the truth, and illness in our body or mind is solely the result of our creating an energetic dissonance over years and years by not doing so -- a dissonance that sooner or later overrides the system and causes...what?

A BREAKDOWN.

A NERVOUS

BREAKDOWN.

A breakdown of the nervous system.

And the delightful thing?

It takes NO TIME to reinstate mental health.

Simply start telling the truth. Immediately. Everywhere. And your entire system will swing back into its natural state of health and wellbeing.

The Gold Mind And The Genius Frequency

Your genius unravels and reveals itself not because you're looking in the "right" place (there is no space/place/Time and there is no right/wrong), but because your genius knows you are willing to do and endure whatever the Truth brings your way, and this -- this ultimate, unconditional loyalty to your Genius, Truth Consciousness and Energy -- is what opens the channel and activates the direct connection between your Super Conscious (your Gold Mind) and your Consciousness (your human awareness). You are literally energetically opening the iron gate of your willingness and your loyalty that has been on lockdown for ages and it is this alone -- this inner ultimate willingness to stand by your Self at all costs and no matter what -- that activates the opening of your crown chakra to receive all the insights and truths you have FELT for ages but never were able to ACCESS and bring through.

Quantum Flight And Genius Activation

Quantum Flight and genius activation occurs according to an energetic technology and orderly process that follows spiritual law.

The Problem Is You Think You're Only Worthy Of Love If You Change.

Or rather, the abusive friend in your mind thinks that.

If you believed you're worthy of your own highest esteem whether you filled your Mastermind or couldn't sell a single seat …

…whether you invested $20,000 in a high-end coach and made $100,000 the next month or totally failed to make a dime …

…whether you signed a high-end client and completely transformed her life or couldn't say a single fucking thing that made any difference …

don't you think you'd have launched that Mastermind, hired that coach and landed that big ticket clients months ago?

Of course you would have.

Because there'd be no stakes. Just an experiment.

If you knew you were worthy of your own love regardless of what happens, you'd finally be free to believe in yourself, which means to let yourself go after your desires full out, because there actually IS NO RISK...because you'd never remove your love from yourself based on the outcome.

And of course there are no "costly" experiments, because there's always a steady supply of esteem ... and CA$H...since CA$H is just energy that responds to love, and you don't have any attachments to your actions, so you'll do anything, literally ANYTHING to create CA$H the way you desire, since you don't have to worry about losing your own love.

But...

when your self-esteem is wrapped up in whether you succeed, it's entirely logical to NOT go after your desire, because if you don't get it, you'll stop loving yourself.

Or rather, your abusive friend would stop loving you...

So, how to suddenly change this all around?

Stop attaching your ability to love yourself to whether you change.

That's what the abusive friend is really telling you, you know...

"In order to be worth my esteem, you have to keep changing, because you're not good enough as you are. And not only that, you have to change and SUCCEED...because of course if you FAIL to change, well that means you're back here, in your unworthy state of being...

So, show me you can change (into being worthy). Here, let's pick something to change into. I know! Go from being someone who doesn't have high-end clients or Masterminds to someone who does."

And your abusive friend crosses her arms over her chest and stands back and watches your every move.

I wouldn't launch that fucking Mastermind to save my life, either.

But of course that's not the only option…

You could simply see it differently…truthfully. That you simply desire new experiences and challenges because your Soul loves them, not because succeeding or failing to get them has any fucking thing to do with your worth.

So, sure, go after launching that Mastermind or working with that $20,000 coach or landing that first high-end client with everything you've got…

…because you love yourself and therefore want to provide yourself with everything you desire…

NOT because you won't love yourself if you don't get it.

That's not very nice.

You wouldn't do that to YOUR friend, would you?

On Energetic Mastery And Shadow Self Care~

These conversations around sex, money and the shadow are incredible and I can feel shadow elements in all of you being released back into your bodies and into the light. It's incredible to be a leading activator in this journey.

And I want to give a shout out to the shadow, because it may be getting a bum rap. Or we may be giving ourselves one, for having a shadow in the first place.

Here's how our shadow is lovely, dark and deep, and how hiding things there is a tender act of self-love…

Or shadow holds energy currents that are too powerful for us to manage. That was the shadow's intended purpose: a container, a vessel, for energy we could not yet master.

The trade-off is that when we place energy into our shadow, less of it is available to us and is instead caught in our cellular structure (the body holds the unconscious within its cells).

There is nothing inherently "wrong" or bad about this. Our suffering begins simply because we kept our soul energy captive there for too long, for energy is meant to move and be moved, and when it stays stuck for too long, it creates disharmony (energy = vibration = harmonic movement), i.e., mental and physical illness. And all we need to do then is go retrieve our soul energy from where we've kept it "safe," hidden from view, until we could manage it properly.

It's a beautiful thing when you think about it, really. Nothing went wrong or has gone wrong - we just noticed a bunch of powerful soul energy that had too much light for our energetic body to handle at the time, so we went and captured it and carried it to the dark for safe keeping, until we were a match for its power.

We are so smart and kind to ourselves, always.

What Creates Synergetic Awakening (Effortlessness Comes After Awakening, Not Before It)

What does it take to achieve greatest impact?

Integrated and fully activated energetic systems - physical, mental and emotional.

This creates synergetic awakening.

Which creates quantum leaps.

Each system has a masculine and a feminine expression, and only wakes up to its true potential (which is expressed effortlessly), when both are fully activated and taken from their shadow expression into the light.

We tend to think that effortlessness comes *before* the awakening. It does not. Effortlessness and genus activation come as the result of awakening and transmutation, which is always terrifying to the paradigm that is being dismantled.

Activating dialogue (what used to be known as "coaching") is one of the most powerful ways to catalyze this transmutation.

As an Activator, it is imperative that you be comfortable serving as the impetus for pain, discomfort and fear responses.

As the Activated, it is imperative that you be willing to die.

Going Sane (Or Truth Kept In, Is Toxic: A Short Memoir)

A long time soul mate showed up after years and in a few simple exchanges gifted me, through the form of a question -- so, what is this Truth that almost poisoned you? -- the opportunity to find, in my answer, the heart and soul of my life mission, the speech I will be giving on the world's biggest stages, and the memoir I will be publishing soon:

In the Fall of 2016, after three years of wrestling with severe depression, thoughts of suicide and unpredictable outbursts of violence blown through with moments of extreme euphoria, intense inspiration and grand hopes and visions for my life that inevitably crumbled in the steely grip of my dark moods, I joined the ranks of the officially bipolar. It was terrifying, surreal, and put my whole life in perspective.

I knew, however, that I wasn't insane; I had simply let Truth sit in my system for too long. Truth, kept in, becomes a toxin. Expressed, it is the greatest cure.

The way to healing, I told myself, was not to ingest little white pills, but to embark on a relentless mission of Truth-telling.

In other words, to finally GO SANE.

The Truth that almost poisoned me was, in many ways, simply the Truth of who I was at any given moment that I clipped and edited and boxed up, in return for the straight A grade of someone's approval, acceptance, admiration.

What Truth?

That I'm a modern day witch.

That I can see straight into someone's soul and that what I see in them is the truth about them. Not "a" truth or "my" truth but The Truth. About them. And that I see their blindness and what will cure them.

"So arrogant," I thought for years (and was told). But it's ... True. And I had to nearly lose my life to finally find the courage to simply speak it. Own it. Live it.

At first I did it out of terror of slipping back into the fog of lies and self-editing and then death.

Now I do it out of pure euphoria.

It wasn't easy. I lost friends, the man I thought I was going to marry (I shake my head thinking about it now. Marry him? A functioning alcoholic whom I couldn't leave until he hit me.). I didn't speak to my parents for months. I risked completely losing my reputation.

It was a fire-breathing, hair-blowing-back several months and I'm just now settling into it.

It is now my mission to stand for True Sanity until it no longer looks like INsanity because enough of us have woken up to the Truth of who we are…

many of us aliens. All divine. Every one magical.

I call it owning your Dragon nature.

You know, the Real You that prowls far beyond the lit terrain in a land few dare journey to, let alone LIVE IN, and which is represented on every map of consciousness by three words, scribbled in the frantic handwriting of the tribe:

Hic sunt dracones.

Here be dragons.

The Energetics Of Extreme Transformation

My sessions -- even just the discovery calls -- seem to regularly catalyze confounding degrees of rapid change -- and in multiple areas at once.

The regularity of this occurrence has baffled me, to be honest, because our species-level conversation around change is that it is slow and that the more entrenched the pattern (addictions and traumatic reenactment especially), the longer the change takes, and the less likely it will be complete.

And so I've been walking around with a constant question ... which is, essentially, this:

What the fuck is going on?

Tonight I learned the answer...

Our stuckness is due to dense energy -- or shadow energy -- that lives somewhere in our energetic system, ... in our body, our thoughts, our beliefs or our feelings. The dense energy can also live between us and other things and people (hence why we seem incapable of leaving places, people and things that no longer serve us).

There are all kinds of tools ... mindset work, meditation, affirmations, movement and dance, martial arts, singing, kicking, punching, screaming, talk therapy, relationship therapy, cord cutting, dense energy clearing, you name it, to move the shadow energy out of the system it's gunking up...

and while it might solve the immediate problem, what's actually happening is that the dense energy is just being moved somewhere else.

So your thoughts might get cleaned up...and you no longer have money issues (at least fewer than before ... they're not really gone, because the energy isn't gone, it's just been moved), but now the energy is out in your spiritual system and then winds its way into your body and manifests as illness. Or out into the space between you and someone else and manifests as a breakup or divorce or ending of a long friendship. Or it gets moved into another place in your mental field and shows up as some other limiting belief or thought system -- perhaps that you don't deserve love and intimacy, or it shows up as a block in your body as sexual limitation of some kind.

Dense energy is dense energy and unless it gets *transmuted* -- changed from dense to light -- it isn't going anywhere. It's just going to keep moving around your system, causing lack and limitation (which is the definition of dense energy).

But there is a way to actually alchemize it ... to change its state for good.

You just transmute it from dark to light.

And when this happens, the change is irreversible. Dark energy transmuted into light cannot go back. It's like reversing the effects of fire. (Exactly like this, in fact...)

When something is burned ... it's motherfucking BURNED. Those ashes are never turning back into their former state.

This is what I do. I ignite an "energetic fire" in people, which just keeps burning and burning, and over the course of a few weeks (it can be as quickly as a few days), the dense energy is transmuted into light and leaves the person's whole system *more filled with light*!

-- which is why they then experience massive upleveling in many realms at once (love, money, sex, health, business opportunities, etc).

...because the more tuned we are to our light, the more tuned we are to the frequency of our greatest opportunities and experiences, which are *already here*, waiting for us.

It's the difference between constantly having to move your enemies farther and farther back, but still having to exert the energy both to move them back and keep them there... and simply dissolving them into thin air.

...and then being able to use all that energy that was being used to move and hold that dense energy at bay...for upleveling and pleasure and exerting power in the service of creation, rather than defense.

This is available to you, right now. It doesn't take much "hard work." It certainly doesn't take much time. What it does take is the willingness to let go of the denseness for good.

And *that* is the hard part ... because ...

We associate our dense energy with *who we are.* We've lived with it so long...have lived with some version of limitation or lack our whole fucking lives ... what would we do if we very quickly had less and less and less of it, and then soon, none at all?...

What would we do, indeed.

We would be making one epic leap after another -- not just in our bank account but in our total energetic ecstasy

In other words, we'd be quickly closing the gap to our divinity.

The full force and source of our true nature as divine beings is already here within us, and it simply needs to *change states* so it can be unleashed ...

And it only takes as long as we are willing to have it take.

Energetic fire can transmute every fiber of dense energy in an instant, if you want.

In other words...

The only thing standing between you as you ...and you as God ... is your desire to have something standing there.

After You Step Out Over The Chasm, The Bridge Appears Under Your Feet (And Never, Ever Before)

Choices that favor truth and power are never easy.

When you take a stand for your soul, for your truth, For your voice, for your power, your Soul will rise up and generate conditions that will completely support you, even as all the old is painfully falling away. You will be totally unable to see with your five senses how it will work out. The decisions will appear mad, foolish, irresponsible, terrifying and dangerous. That us simply because the paradigm from within which the agent is looking is sick, narrow and disconnected from any power source. So of course it all appears like madness and terror.

One leap out over the void is all that is required. Then the bridge appears under our feet and while it appears to those still on the side we left that we are now inexplicably flying, we are being steadied by the firm foundation of living from our Soul guidance.

Yes, some of the things Beth fears will come to pass. But they won't break her. They'd make her stronger. And most of what she fears don't even happen at all. And beyond that, events she can't even conceive of now that will accrue to her great favor will happen for her.

I know this story. I helped create the pattern. And I am here to lead people through their own version if it, from illusion to sight.

I don't believe in gravity.

Not spiritual gravity anyway.

Spiritually, we are built to fly.

Both/And, Not Either/Or

Time to switch energy consciousness, people. No more human being. Only alien being.

EVERY DESIRE YOU HAVE ENERGETICALLY SUPPORTS EVERY OTHER DESIRE.

When I was a little girl, I wanted to be a teacher. At 10 years old I would gather my brother (7) and my sister (3) and bring them to my easel that I had set up in the sunroom and give them spelling lessons.

Then, when I was in high school, I wanted to be a writer. I entered and won writing contests, wrote copious poems in my journals, but didn't have the balls to do much more with it than that. If I can't be as great a poet as Rilke, then what the fuck is the POINT, I'd think.

Then, when I was in college, I wanted to be a priest. I prepared a gave a sermon to a packed church of nearly 300 (my Dad's church). It was an out-of-body experience. I didn't remember what I said, and couldn't figure out why there was a line out the door of people twice my age DYING to speak with me about what I'd said. It freaked my human out so much -- how the fuck can I have anything of merit to say to people TWICE MY AGE? -- I ran far and fast from that calling, all the way into corporate America, a quarter million dollar a year income, lots of luxuries, and light years from my soul.

Every day I'd think -- what the hell am I supposed to BE? Writer? Teacher? Priest? And besides, I have nothing of worth to offer anyway so it doesn't matter. There's one thing I can do: Sell. I can sell the fuck out of anything, anywhere, anytime. So I guess that's what I'll be. A fucking SALESPERSON.

I had no idea that desire is ALWAYS divinely sourced, that it leads us directly into the most expansive experience of aliveness and richness (literally and figuratively) and that it can be trusted IMPLICITLY (I was raised in a strict Christian paradigm - desire trusted? HELL FUCK NO.) AND that ALL desires are energetically structured to fit together in one power grid of purpose, passion, consciousness raising and cold, hard CA$H.

In other words, it is never either/or.

It is ALWAYS both/and.

Whenever you are thinking either/or about something, understand that the most expansive and powerful and life-altering and life-giving solution is ALWAYS in the both/and, and don't rest until you find it.

Now?

I'm a teacher.

And a poet.

And a priest.

AND a salesperson.

How divine.

SO - where is your either/or conflict right now? And how can you see it as both/and?

UNIVERSAL LAW LE$$ON: What weak boundaries have to do with your bank account, client SUCCESS and DISCOVERY CALL Mastery

You may have a beautiful relationship on Facebook or to your friends and colleagues, and everyone on the outside may think you're the picture of perfection, but inside, behind closed doors, you compare your success to your partner's, have one foot in and one foot out of the relationship, or know you're not having the mind blowing sex you secretly crave, because you're both busy agreeing to have weak boundaries.

"You don't set clear boundaries with unwavering consequences for me and I won't do the same to you."

And why is that?

Because you care more about appearance than truth.

Because clear boundaries always means that things get really uncomfortable.

You uphold the highest of standards for how you agree to be treated...and then get accused of being an egotistical fuck.

And then your beautiful relationship gets exposed for what it is. Weak. Unstable. And very imperfect.

And that matters to you why?

Because you secretly attach your sense of self to your appearance....If my relationship appears weak, unstable and imperfect then that's how I must appear to people and that must be who I really am.

So if I can just prop up this relationship, I can prop up my self perception.

And so your weak boundaries serve your poor self-image.

And no one with a poor self image can convert someone else with a poor self image (and anyone who needs coaching is someone who is in the illusion that they are not masterful, powerful and complete...who is in other words, suffering from a poor self image in some area of their lives).

No one with a poor self image can have the inner authority necessary to hold masterful discovery calls and convert a prospect's deep-seated belief that they must keep up appearances and have to maintain their own weak boundaries and lack of inner authority which has them in fear of pissing off their husband by paying for your services without asking permission first.

And of course no one with a poor self image will have easy access to Truth...because poor self image is an illusion...so they won't be able to coach with mastery (because masterful coaching is simply seeing and speaking God-level truth) and therefore will not cause any kind of deep transformation in their clients.

And on an energetic level, someone with a poor self image is unattractive to CA$H, because CA$H epitomizes power, mastery and high standards.

You want to flood your bank account with CA$H, master your discovery calls and change your clients' success from so-so to mindblowing?

Start with your most intimate relationship. Raise your standards and set some boundaries you actually keep.

Like I say, business problems never originate in the business.

You Want More Energy? Start Telling The Fucking Truth.

People have been INCREDULOUS at the amount of energy I have, particularly to be able to sustain the massive momentum I've built up in my business (now at nearly $300,000 in just over four months in business).

And I do have massive amounts of energy. And it's all natural.

How do I do it?

I tell the fucking truth.

I LIVE my truth, meaning my massively high standards are finally in line with my actual, lived life.

I don't do anything I don't want to do.

I don't say anything I don't want to say.

I don't NOT say anything I don't want to say.

I don't spend time with anyone I don't want to spend time with.

(As opposed to what I did my entire fucking life, which was to please and be proper, play small and simper, be polite and practical, rock zero boats, take shit from the men in my life, keep quiet about my radical, real, alien-level genius, and generally behave.)

You want to know the ONLY reason you're exhausted?

You're living a lie.

See, your body is built to know the truth. This is why you can sense fear (which is an energetic lie). This is why muscle testing works. Because you are attuned to the truth. To know it. Feel it. Speak it. Embody it. Truth is ultimate wellness, wholeness, holiness. Truth IS energy. It is Source Energy cursing through your system and when you speak the truth and LIVE your truth, you are literally drawing down pure Energy from your Soul and sending it through your system and then out into the world (which is what Epiphanous Marketing is, and why it's so fucking powerful). You are literally transforming energy into matter at light speed, alchemizing it into insights, awareness, love, transformational power, for both your own life and others.

Your body LIVES on truth. It is fueled by it. Nourished by it. And when you block access to it by refusing to allow your Soul access to your being (which is what it means to live unconsciously, or to be ASLEEP) you deprive your body of the most essential energetic nutrient it requires.

So stop popping sleeping pills. Stop downing caffeine in guzzles and gallons. You're not sleepy and exhausted because you have "too much to do" in a day. Please. Souls have an infinite capacity for activity and play. You're sleepy and exhausted because you haven't had a real, intimate, raw download of TRUTH in decades, because downloads of Truth don't happen for beings who aren't willing to IMMEDIATELY act on them (our Souls know whether we're serious or not, and they won't cast pearls of wisdom and insight before fearful swine) and when you act on your truth, when you live it, breathe it, BE it, you buzz with energy, you are ignited with SoulFire.

And when you don't have regular downloads and unleashings of Truth in your life -- when you're living a lie -- you're left to generate your own energy from your own narrow, limited human system, meaning, with your brain and your brain-generated thoughts, and while it might sustain itself for awhile, there comes a time when you just go limp and end up dragging your body through day after day wondering how the fuck you're going to make it to the end of your life without dying first.

And then the sleeping pills. And the hypnosis tapes. And the caffeine injections in the morning.

There is a simpler (though not at all easier) way. A self-sustaining way that generates massive energy and momentum in your life naturally, without strain on your system, leaving you lit from within.

In other words, ENLIGHTENED.

And...total bonus...all that Truth Serum now flowing through you? That's your potent Epiphanous Marketing genius. You let that flow through your fingertips and out your mouth and you'll blow up your business also and do crazy things like make $20,000 from a single Livestream.

Because Truth loves awakening. It awakens bodies and businesses equally.

Want to wake up and stay awake, literally and spiritually?

$peak Truth.

DNA, Light And Sex Magic

It has been scientifically proven that DNA exerts gravitational force on light and draws light to it, and that the light then forms an exact replica of the shape of the DNA and then STAYS IN THAT SHAPE even when the DNA is gone.

This is the Ka, the Light Body, that Christ formed, in his sex magic with Mary Magdalene, and with/in which he appeared after his crucifixion. It is this quantum alchemy that he and The Magdalene co-activated and this is the way in which he "escaped" death ... by consciously transmuting his physical form into pure light and then inhabiting THAT, without having to die in order for his essence to be released back into his Light Body. And he did it through sex magic, people.

DNA = matter = the divine feminine = The Magdalene

Light = spirit = the divine masculine = The Christ

The energetic union of DNA and light = the intimate energetic union of the divine feminine and the divine masculine (Magdalene and Christ) = sex magic

Sex magic is at the heart and soul of life. It is happening everywhere, all the time, at the quantum level. Everything is having sex. All the time. Everywhere. In public. Right under our noses.

(And in them.)

To be alive means to be a living, breathing scandal of sex alchemy.

The Energetics Of Miracles

I just realized the scientific basis of what I do with people and why so many I work with not only quantum leap their life and business but also experience spontaneous medical healings.

I'm shooting #TruthBeams into them at a cellular level and it is instantly altering the structure of their DNA.

In "The Synchronicity Key," David Wilcock provides scientific evidence (needed for those who believe they don't have direct access to infinite intelligence and have to go the slow route through empirical evidence) that shows that new instructions [light, truth] can be beamed directly into a DNA molecule such that it instantly changes its structure.

This is what miracles and instant spiritual awakenings are.

So, I'm making #truthbeam the new #truthbomb, because it's energetically more accurate.

I've always energetically "stuttered" when I heard the #truthbomb phrase because I knew there was something energetically "off" about it, though I wasn't aware of what, until just now.

It's because bombs simply explode, while light beams directly alter our cellular consciousness.

And you can always test the energetic accuracy of a word or phrase yourself. Just say it and you can feel whether it's heavy or light.

#Truthbomb: Heavy.

#TruthBeam: Light.

And the reason "bomb" is heavy is because it's a manmade concept, and therefore carries the low frequency of the consciousness of its maker. "Beam" is light because it's a naturally occurring concept, sourced from...well...the nature of Source itself, and so carries the high frequency of its creator.

I fucking love this shit.

I could talk about it all day.

ACTION RELEASES THE ENERGY NEEDED TO CREATE QUANTUM LEAPS

How do I get over this?

I hear this from almost every client. It's like they've forgotten they can ACT. We've become a nation of mindset changers and affirmation sayers and meditators and somehow in all of that wonderful consciousness raising we forgot that we can also ACT and that ACTION is what releases the ENERGY we need in order to create CHANGE.

So here's some free kickassery coaching:

Don't check with your shaman and your witch doctor and your medicine man and your sixteen reiki healers and your twenty two light worker friends slash coaches slash spiritual chiropractors and your host of spirit guides and your guardian angel and your dead grandmother and your priest and your friend's rabbi and say fifty thousand Hail Mary's -- I mean rosaries ... but really they ARE Hail Mary's because you're desperate to find the answer ... to figure out how to get over your fear or your limiting belief or your lack mindset.

Just. Fucking. Act.

And when you DO the thing you were terrified of doing you will realize that what you wanted all along was to be ABLE TO DO THE THING YOU WERE TERRIFIED OF DOING.

You want to be a badass?

Do what badasses do. They fucking act.

When You Transmute Fear Into Power, You Create A Clear Channel For Energy To Turn Into Matter Rapidly And Everywhere All At Once.

This is why so often people who work with me not only make lots of money very quickly but their relationships completely transform and they often spontaneously cure themselves of decades long physical conditions.

When you do it this way, you essentially bypass the need to work with mindset, affirmations, etc because when you are BEing Power, your thoughts don't NEED fixing in the first place. And the way to BE power is to annihilate all expressions of fear in our lives and never let fear sit in our system for one moment.

And the way to annihilate fear: speak your truth and LIVE your truth and DO the things that terrify you.

In the New Paradigm, Rest Comes When You Find Your Wings

Energetic Truth = Freedom From All Concern

I seriously can't keep up with my clients' success. My phone is blowing up.

Friends, you've heard "don't sweat the small stuff." I say, "Don't even sweat the big stuff."

BE in the full frequency of TRUTH -- not in what I call "energetic lie," that puts you out of alignment with the laws of energy and spirit -- where you KNOW in every cell of your being that every single thing that happens is a YES, is the answer you have been looking for, is brilliant and that YOU are empowered by IT.

This is freedom, friends. When absolutely nothing rocks your boat. Not disharmony (because disharmony is an energetic lie). Not your finances (because resources are infinite and your wealth is HERE, NOW). Not parenting struggles (because your children don't need fixing and you don't need fixing...and because struggle itself is an energetic lie.)

That. Is freedom.

Time Mastery: How To Directly And Practically Impact Your Past

I knew it. We can directly and practically impact our past. Was just writing about this the other day. Our stories don't just limit us now, they limit who we were and can now therefore be. Changing our stories now is essential to not only healing who we are and releasing who we are meant to be, but also to healing our past. [Note: These were the early days of my business. I would never use the word "healing" now. There are no victims. Therefore there are no wounds. Therefore no one needs healing.]

If you don't believe me, here is proof:

In the 2000's, a doctor selected 3,000 patients of a particular hospital for an experiment. All of them had contracted sepsis as a result of their stay at that hospital. At random (this is key), he divided them into two groups and sent the names of one group to a set of people whom he had pray for that group's healing. The other group was not prayed for. The results showed far beyond statistical margin of error that the group that was prayed for showed earlier recovery and hospital release than the group that wasn't prayed for.

But here's the catch: The two groups had stayed at the hospital and contracted sepsis TWENTY YEARS EARLIER.

Divine Timing Is An Excuse

Divine Timing: an excuse for people you to distance yourself from your divinity, i.e., your BADA$$NE$$, for just a little longer. Because your human is shit scared.

There is no such thing as Divine Timing.

Seriously. What the fuck is it, really? And I do mean "fuck."

Here is what's going on people.

1. You are PENETRATED by a desire.

2. You CREATE that desire into form.

WHEN you do that is entirely up to you.

Because YOU penetrated yourself with the desire. It wasn't some outside force. And because, NEWSFLASH, YOU are DIVINE.

So that "divine" timing you're sitting around waiting for?

Nothing other than an excuse.

Divine Timing, Princess Energy And Excuse Making

Here is what's really happening when you say you're "waiting" for "Divine Timing:"

Slumbering in your pretty white gown in the middle of the deep forest, surrounded by tittering squirrels and chirping birds, and lots and lots and lots of beautiful flowers…

Until Prince Charming comes along and kisses you, so you can finally wake up and do something with your life.

Stop the Princess act. Be a motherfucking QUEEN.

A Queen commands. A Queen has warriors that do her every bidding. A Queen employs a High Magician who creates everything she desires when SHE says, not when her King or good gracious her delightful Prince of a Son, decides when.

And a Queen has a Lover in her bed every night.

Who may or may not be the King.

The Players

Princess: You, waiting for "Divine Timing"

Prince: Your projection of your inner authority, since you can't make your own decisions (hence, Princess...)

Queen: You BEING Divine Timing

King: Your equal and mirror of your total inner authority, which you wield without question

Lover: CA$H. Lots and lots of it.

Badass? Or Rich, Famous Follower? How Energy Mastery Is Time Mastery And What That Has To Do With Your Ambitions

To all my self-proclaimed BADA$$ BU$INE$$ mavens who know you've got a $EVEN and EIGHT figure business in you…

What you want just as much as the seven and eight figure business is to embody TRUE BADA$$ERY in your life and business. If someone handed you a million dollars, a billion dollars tomorrow, would that stop you on your quest to be the MOST BADA$$ woman you know?

Hell, no. You'd sink that million into a nice house, a few investments, a few nice toys, and you'd get right back to the business of BEing a BADA$$.

And what does that mean, really?

It does not mean making multi-six, seven and eight figures.

It does not mean being the next Oprah, the next Tony Robbins, the next Elizabeth Gilbert.

It means BREAKING THE RULES on how you do it.

Otherwise you're not a true BADA$$, you're just a rich, famous follower.

And your true self-satisfaction is in being a BADA$$. The number in your bank account is NOT what will cause you to lay your head on your pillow at night – the one with BADA$$ sewn into it in deep purple lettering – thinking, "Yep. Fucking CRUSHED it today. I'm a BADA$$."

It's how quickly, easily, creatively, differently and joyfully you get to your massive income, impact and influence, following no one's rules but your own, blowing past everyone who says there are stages to your business and steps to your visibility and phases for how to get your best-selling book into the world and that you've got to hustle and work yourself to the bone to get anywhere.

You are a leader of consciousness. A woman who's meant to REDEFINE the terms, not be a shining example of what's already been done.

You will only be happy when you're not just making quantum leaps in income and visibility, but REDEFINING what quantum leaps look like…and making what USED to be quantum leaps now look like little hops, skips and jumps.

You will only be happy when you're collapsing time exponentially and leaving in the DUST every single way it's been done, has to be done, always must be done.

And that means you must become Master of Time. You must realize that Time bends to YOUR will, not the other way around.

I know, I know, you say. I know that Time responds to me.

Really? Then why are you WAITING for divine timing to show up and tell you when it's time to launch your business or catapult it to seven and eight figures?

Waiting for diving timing is like being the princess in a fairy tale who WAITS for Prince Charming to show up so she can WAKE UP and start living her life.

CREATE DIVINE TIMING. How 'bout that?

And one other thing, make sure you're hooking into a mentor who can help you tap into the essence of what it means to be a true BADA$$.

In other words, don't look only at their bank account, Facebook followers, Instagram numbers or pictures. Look BEHIND them, for the true story.

Even women doing $100K months who's everywhere on Facebook ads and in your streams promoting their latest webinar on how they got to $100K months, don't let that impress you.

Six and seven figure coaches are a dime a dozen. Billions in a bank account does not a BADA$$ make.

Why?

Because it likely took them YEARS to get there. (Getting to a multi-six figure business in a few years is no longer on the cutting edge. Getting to seven figures, unless you did in in year one or two, working part-time, with no overhead, is no longer cutting edge.)

And they likely work themselves to the bone doing it (though they don't look it and won't admit it).

They likely give a whole lot of that million/billion away to their big team and sink it into huge photo shoots and ads and copywriters and expensive websites and to keep all their automated this and that and all their structures and systems and support humming along. So at the end of the day how much are they keeping, really and how many rules are they breaking, really…and therefore how much of a true BADA$$ are they, really…?

And even if they don't do the above, they very likely don't have a $100K Mastermind or aren't selling six or seven figure 1:1 packages, but are instead launching massive programs at low-end fees where they are regurgitating the same information over and over and over just to more and more and more people.

And what's wrong with this?

Absolutely nothing. It just doesn't make them…and therefore they won't be able to activate you into … a BADA$$. Because all that's been done. Over and over and over.

You're here to do something that's NEVER, EVER been done.

You are not here to live a tired, old fairytale and wait around for Prince Divine Timing to show up and tell you it's time to wake up.

You are here to be Queen of your own story.

Quantum Leaping Is Old Paradigm.

Announcing the advent of the New Paradigm of Change Mastery: CHANGE AT THE SPEED OF (F)LIGHT.

How we IMAGINE change is how we EXPERIENCE it. And for the past several millennia, it's been an EXCRUCIATING experience, to say the least.

Frankly, the only reason the noble profession of Sales exists is to usher people through the frightening threshold of change, because hardly a single soul can do it on his or her own.

And so we first mastered change in the spacial realm - mastering space has been our primary focus for millennia. How to make a fire. Kill our food. Amass material possessions, and then more luxurious versions of those possessions.

And then a shift happened. We went from focusing on mastering space to finding ourselves doing these things we called Quantum Leaps - changing states suddenly, from one set of experiences to a entirely different set of experiences, overnight. It no longer became interesting to us to read about people becoming millionaires -- over a LIFETIME. That was old news. We wanted to read about the OVERNIGHT millionaires. In other words, the ones mastering TIME, not space.

And the concept and meme of the Quantum Leap was born and up until today, I, as many of us, have been using this term to explain what I do, what I want, what I teach. Particularly, in my case, I teach people how to rapidly and dramatically increase their sales - and not just incrementally, but in massive jumps. Quantum leaping felt like the right analogy for that.

But for two days now I've been struck with the clear sense that the Quantum Leap needs to make way for a new paradigm, and yet I couldn't quite see what it was, or why...

Until tonight.

Quantum Leaps still focus on the SPACE you're leaping from and to. That's what makes it, well, a LEAP. But this analogy contains the inevitable struggle against change we've been dealing with for millennia, because

1) it takes a shit ton of energy to overcome the inertia of being still. In other words, IT'S FUCKING EXHAUSTING TO MAKE QUANTUM LEAP AFTER QUANTUM LEAP,

AND....

2) it really HURTS when you finally LAND.

This is why we have this concept of "upper limiting" where we uplevel and then BAM, we call in some kind of crisis that causes us to not just land on the far other side of the chasm we've just leaped across but to fall flat on our faces, nose bloodied, bones broken, and having to spend all this time healing and then, THEN, after we've just finished healing, we have to GET UP AND DO IT ALL OVER AGAIN???

No wonder there is so much damn fucking resistance to quantum leaps. I mean, the experiences you get along the way - that long, arcing trip over the chasm (in other words, the mansion, the rolls royce, the trip to italy) - that's a shit ton of fun - but then there's that crash and splat part and then the recovery part and then the gathering up all your strength to leap again part.

That's because we're not meant to leap.

We're meant to FLY.

We're not meant to change at the speed of leaping limbs.

We're meant to change at the speed of flight.

Meaning, the speed of LIGHT.

When a photon (particle of light) is in motion, that is the only time it actually "exists" or has mass. When it comes to rest, its mass goes to zero, meaning it stops existing.

Do you want to know why change has been so damn fucking hard?

Because the way we're doing it isn't NATURAL.

We ARE Light. And light is in constant flight. It IS continuous change that never rests, never leaps from resting point to resting point but simply embodies change itself.

Quantum Leaping was simply meant to teach us how to FLY.

The minute this thought came to me, my jaw dropped open.

About ten years ago, I had what I call a Big Dream -- a dream I knew was the expression of my calling. I remember this dream often, wondering how it will come to fruition in my life and what it really means.

In the dream, I'm in a large, cathedral-sized cavern carved into the the side of the earth....

and I'm giving flying lessons around huge, shimmering columns of light.

I love having access to Infinite Intelligence....

You Are Capable Of A Quantum Uplevel Right Now

I have seen women with massive potential and huge prior success tank and do nothing.

I have seen women in what can only be called a wretched state soar to unbelievable heights overnight.

When you allow your High Consciousness to market and sell THROUGH you, you add ZEROS to your packages, the perfect words tumble from your lips or fingertips, you market like a genius, close FULL PAY clients without even thinking, AND deliver such massive transformation to your clients that they become ADDICTED to your work.

This is available to YOU, no matter WHO you believe yourself to be right now, no matter HOW MANY your past successes or failures, no matter WHAT your conditions right now.

Your High Consciousness is HERE, ready to cure your every. single. trouble right now.

Stand up for yourself. Elevate yourself to the level of your High Consciousness NOW.

Leader Consciousness: Why Arianna Huffington Woke Up In A Pool Of Blood

As a big leader (I'm talking to you, CEOs of million and billion dollar companies), you hold the energetic consciousness of the business. The business is simply an expression of YOUR energetic mastery.

If you are a slave to Time, your business will be a slave to external conditions. You and your people will always be racing to be first, stay first, catch up, keep up. No one will have enough time.

And you will all labor under the illusion that Time has power over you. In other words, that there is such a thing as competition, keeping your competitive edge. These are all concepts from the tribal consciousness grid and when leaders embody tribal consciousness energy, they get sick. They have accidents. Their people are stressed, demoralized, anxious and disempowered.

And the struggle to thrive, to embody uniqueness, which is of course the true lifeblood of a business (and a BEing), amplifies until something, somewhere breaks.

This is why Arianna Huffington woke up one morning in a pool of blood.

This is why one high powered CIO I knew, who had an elite career at F500 companies, ended up hospitalized for months.

This is why Silicon Valley execs kill themselves in startling numbers.

This is why we are the most medicated country on the planet.

There is a new way. It is energetic mastery. It is learning to harness the power you have within you that can create worlds, that creates Time and turns matter into energy at will.

This new leader, whom I call an Energetic Olympian, builds businesses whose people collapse time and achieve quantum leaps in revenue and profit with Time to spare. With no attention whatever on competition, for there is no possibility for competition when you realize that the unique energetic blueprint of your product or service is built specifically for similar souls to experience, and who are waiting for your particular business or product to come along.

This new leader holds the new consciousness energy of her business in such energetic integrity that neither she nor her people fall prey to crisis, politics, frenzy or overwhelm. Instead, the business runs on golden energy that is self-replenishing, intense and yet calm, and sourced from the divine.

This is the new Eden. And as a leader, it is your calling to usher it in.

On Authenticity And Being Triggered

Yep. I'm gonna say it:

If you're a coach or mentor and you feel any hint of jealousy, envy, anger or annoyance when you see what other coaches are doing or saying and how much love and attention, accolades or visibility they get online and how much money they're making when you KNOW it's all a sham and they're not walking their talk AT ALL, then my love, I have news for you:

That's because YOU'RE ALSO PRETENDING and you're far from walking your own talk.

If you weren't, you wouldn't be triggered by it. You actually wouldn't even notice it. It wouldn't occur as an event in your consciousness at all.

It's no wonder that when people see someone walking their talk they rush to them, credit cards out, in a matter of minutes, and with no need to "know" anything more about them.

You can talk "authenticity" all you want and you might get a lot of likes and loves and comments but your bank account will show you what your market already knows about the the real truth.

And yes, even those of you who have fat bank accounts and little authenticity - the same holds true for you. Because behind the scenes you gotta HUSTLE for every one of those dollars — because it takes exponentially more energy to get clients with inauthentic energy. You're not taking weeks off on vacation. You're working like a dog every hour of the day for that seven-figure-plus biz. And we're you to activate your true authenticity, your bank account would go from seven to eight figures in no time.

Only the energy of authenticity makes you pleasurably filthy rich (and of course causes the most supreme transformation in your clients, therefore enriching them to the highest degree possible).

Authenticity is the new black.

THE TRUTH OF BEING TRIGGERED

You are only triggered by the people you're an energetic match to. It's one of the most annoying-as-fuck truths that humans hate to hear, but when I discovered and began living this truth, I became free.

Free or triggered. You choose.

Anger Is Disempowerment. Only Victims Get Angry.

If you're angry, you're feeling disempowered. And when you finally discover your personal power, nothing makes you angry anymore.

Nothing.

Over the past several months I have been tested....oh, have I been tested.

And yet, amazingly, I simply don't get angry at any of it.

Why? Because nothing has power over me.

I can always make more money easily. Always.

I can always uplevel and call in new connections - business and friendship.

I can always thrive, in every situation, no matter what.

So why the hell spend one minute on such a waste of energy as anger?

This is a true statement and I can't believe it's coming from MY mouth.

I've been told I was a very angry person since college. Why are you so angry? You need to deal with your anger issues. You're so....ANGRY.

I was diagnosed with bipolar and PTSD, severe mood and anxiety disorder and ADD. I was emotionally abused as a child. I was emotionally abused as an adult. Hit, even, at the end. I've had a fair share of "betrayals" financially.

Who the fuck cares. The only reason I'd be angry about any of it is if I felt I either somehow deep down DESERVED that treatment or couldn't bounce back easily and even higher and whenever I wanted.

Being completely free from anger is an absolutely AMAZING FEELING, PEOPLE.

I highly recommend it

The Spiritual Symbolism Of Your Life

Your life right now is full of specific clues to your blocks and exact guidance on what you need to do to clear them and move on. Being able to see and decipher these clues is one of my most powerful gifts. It's the same work an analyst does in translating a dream. Here's an example of the work I did on myself last night (and what I do with clients all the time):

I've been noticing a pattern over the last several months. Most of the people in my life right now are half in and half out. Not disinterested, certainly, but not 100% IN. They say they'll schedule time with me and they don't. They say they'll text me and they don't. They seem to disappear for while and then pop back in.

In the past I would have taken this personally. This is the BIGGEST mistake you can make if you want to understand what's REALLY going on at a soul level. It took me 43 years, but I now no longer take events personally. That would be like calling up my best friend and getting angry at her for what she did to me in my dream the night before.

Exactly like that, actually.

I now look from above, from "waking spirituality," at the symbolic meaning of what is happening.

So last night I sat with this odd pattern for a while and quickly realized its deepest message for me:

My Soul is giving me the experience of what it feels like to have intermittent commitment and interest.

It's annoying. Be all in or all out!

In other words, I'm still intermittently committed to Her. To expressing and owning Her FULLY and in all ways. I'm still coming and going. Keeping a safe distance. Not being disconnected completely, but not getting too involved.

See the perfect similarity between my relationship to my soul and the people in my life and their relationship to me? Amazing.

If you want true understanding and growth, never blame anyone or anything for your situation. It is ALL your soul speaking to you.

My #Metoo Post

I'm so unimpressed with most of the responses to my controversial #metoopost.

If someone can show up who can be triggered AND curious at the same time, rather than jumping to yawn-inducing black/white assumptions about my teachings, you have my serious fucking respect.

Everyone else? Go learn how to be triggered AND curious at the same time. It is the only way to get out of your comfy bubble of judgments and into the very edgy space between you and what triggers you so that actual understanding can happen.

Damn. Where are my actual energy masters I can have a real, bold, raw conversation with without someone tumbling into vitriol and tantrums?

The Thunderclap Of Uncomfortable Light: Strong Emotion Vs Being Triggered [Or How To Tell Whether You're Stepping Into Your Natural Role As A Truthteller Or Whether You're In The Presence Of Your Own Deep Shadow]

The presence of strong emotion does not imply that someone is triggered. Though because most people don't have mastery over their emotions, and are codependent and in need of controlling their environment so no one speaks out too unpredictably, the two — strong emotion and being triggered — do often go hand in hand.

The deeper insight here has to do with what happens when you invoke the Truth — which can feel like a thunderclap of uncomfortable Light — versus what happens when you quiver with such uncomfortable feelings, because you've just encountered a mirror of your disowned shadow of shame and can't handle it, that you lash out at what you perceive to be the cause of the discomfort in order to destroy it, so you can find equilibrium again.

The former is what TruthTellers do all day.

The latter is what emotionally immature people do all day.

The difference?

Personal attachment to the outcome.

A thunderclap is a natural, potent (in human terms: emotionally strong) response to disequilibrium in the charge of the atmosphere that has been returned to equilibrium through a strike of lightning. The thunderclap is the channel of air, created by the lightning, that is collapsing back into itself.

And then it's over. Until the next disequilibrium occurs.

When YOU are the channel that is being opened by the energetic disequilibrium of light and shadow, of truth and shame, you are the locus of both the flash of Light (the message) and the thunderclap (the emotion, meaning the degree to which the message represents a restoration of Truth from shame).

If the shame has been great — think racism — the lightning and thunderclap will be great. Think Martin Luther King.

Was MLK triggered?

Uh. No.

Meaning, in order to maintain his self-esteem, confidence and inner peace, did he need everyone to stop being racist? (This is what personal attachment to the outcome means.)

Of course not.

He was simply being a channel bringing into equilibrium the great imbalance of shame embodied in our country.

He was an untriggered TruthTeller.

If you have a calling as a TruthTeller, it helps to know where your potent emotion comes from so you can be a clear channel for truth and not simply on a personal, codependent, shame-avoidant crusade. And also so you can unapologetically, and as potently as need be, speak Truth, and remain in your *own* equilibrium, no matter who tries to tell you you're just being triggered, or you're just projecting, or you're being emotionally immature.

This happens when you achieve emotional mastery. It's critical for TruthTellers, otherwise you'll always be second-guessing yourself based on the feedback from tens, hundreds, thousands or millions of others. (Which is why emotional mastery — or energy mastery — is one of the cornerstones of the UnSchool. You've got to be able to withstand extreme reactions to your Uncomfortable and Unfiltered Truth without constantly collapsing.)

The underlying concern when people are trying to be attentive to the presence of triggering is a noble and important concern. You don't do anyone any harm by running around being triggered all the time — because there are no victims. But you also won't be accessing your true potency or freedom, either.

So if you feel called to speak up, the way to know the difference is to inquire whether the outcome of you sharing your message will in any way benefit your state of mind.

If it will, then it comes from a codependent place.

If it won't, then it comes from your sensitivity to the disequilibrium between truth and shame, and in that case, thunder and lightning away, oh TruthTeller.

Unwavering Self Belief (Or Everything Changed For Me When...)

Everything changed for me when I realized the thing I'd been terrified of my whole life wasn't what people would say or do when I finally claimed my genius and unapologetically stepped out as ME; it was knowing that in the face of their judgment and shame, I would ABANDON AND BETRAY MYSELF and choose THEIR truth about me rather than knowing my heart and standing in my OWN self belief.

I realized how often I turned on myself the minute someone questioned my motives or me in any way.

I'd spend hours tearing myself to shreds, excoriating myself, loathing myself, doubting myself, judging, shaming, criticizing myself. (No wonder I was diagnosed with severe mood and anxiety disorder.)

Inside, I was a walking bloody battlefield.

No wonder I spent my entire fucking life trying to please everyone all the time. Not because of what they'd do or say if I displeased them, but of what I knew I'd say and do to MYSELF as a result. Their cruelty was NOTHING compared to mine.

When I realized this, I was floored. FLOORED!

I almost couldn't believe the answer, the remedy, the cure to my lifelong depression, paralysis and mood swings was so simple. All I had to do was just never abandon myself? Just hold myself in high esteem, no matter what?

Realy???! It was that EASY??

(and, that hard....)

In one day, I did an about-face that changed my life forever.

I decided, beyond a shadow of a doubt, that no matter WHAT happened to me -- like even down to losing all my money and becoming homeless with my fifth-grade daughter -- that I would NEVER abandon myself EVER again.

What happened then?

I became able to take any and all risks my intuition asked of me (because there literally were NO STAKES), and my business took off like a motherfucking rocket.

The next week I did $110K and signed a seven figure coach in my fourth month in business.

And, my mental health went from dangerously low to a sustained high, without any medication or therapy.

I'm telling you, unwavering self belief is ALL YOU NEED.

Because why? Because, repeat after me -- and this has become my absolute favorite phrase -- NO ONE AND NOTHING HAS POWER OVER ME.

(This comes in very handy when, later in your business, you get called a cult leader, publicly declared as lacking integrity and become the source of at least two -- probably more -- sustained witch hunts online. REAL handy, I tell ya. 😊 ;))

I'm sharing this because this group is EXPLODING by the day and I'm seeing so many people's answers to the entry questions (yep. I read EVERY ONE), carry this hidden energy of self-betrayal.

So I want to share my story as an inspiration for you and an invitation to take your own inventory on what you're ACTUALLY terrified of.

I guarantee you, it will ALWAYS come back to your terror of your own betrayal.

Here's to your UNWAVERING SELF BELIEF.

It Is Not Easy To Love The Fabric Of Consciousness And Yet You Do.

Examples from Clients:

To the woman I Activated with my Words: In the moment, I fucked up. I don't have any justifications for that. I feel like when we choose to justify victim/perpetrator behavior, it never quite travels down into the places within us that it needs to. I feel really sad that my words caused you pain. I am listening and hearing and responding and going to look at what I'm doing so that I can learn from this. In the moment, I wish I had done things differently. I can see that what I said caused reaction, and that the delivery of my words didn't have the safety of agreements and consent in place to go there in the first place. I will not do this again. With anyone. Ever. Here we are. In present time, I do not feel sorry for myself, because I understand what is happening, and I own that. I see your need to talk about this publicly and make a stand for what you believe in. I do feel deep sorrow that I have caused you pain unintentionally. I didn't mean to, and I'm sorry. I recognize why I caused harm. That if those places had not existed within me to be brought forth to be looked at, it would not have played out in this way. And I commit to doing better with the following actions: I am now creating new boundaries within my business so that when people reach out to work with me, there's a more precise way to see if there is a match instead of the back and forth that we experienced since our call. There is a violence that many (most) coaches have in their on-boarding process that I believe we experience because of unconscious patterns within us. And though many people have called this out in the past, I have yet to work with someone who doesn't employ them in some way.This looks like manipulation, false scarcity, fast-action whatever's, and pressure to decide.I agree to do better and to keep sharing my experience so that we ALL can do better. I now commit to be even more intentional when it comes to asking for consent to share information or insights before bridging that gap. I commit to listening to and talking with professionals from the Sex Worker Industry to completely redefine my process for consent in tandem with their best practices. I can see how the Coaching Industry at large could benefit from this, as it has some of the best-practices in the world for going to vulnerable spaces.In the usage of language that causes harm:I am deepening into my understanding through working with someone who understands the prostitute archetype deeply, and will help me to understand it better as the path to the Divine Lover/Priestess that many of us are called to be. I will reach for consent as I use controversial language in this way, so as to not harm in my usage of it. If there is anything that I missed in this effort for accountability and retribution, any blind spot I may not have seen, please have it brought to my attention so that I can further address it.Sincerely, NAME

The fuck. 💪 YOU cannot cause anyone emotional pain. It is not energetically possible. You did nothing fucking wrong. And you have nothing to apologize for.💪 YOU DID ABSOLUTELY intend to trigger her. ☺ Because you know that's the place of greatest growth for someone. Said another way: DISRUPTION IS THE WAY YOU LOVE. Get used to it. A lot of people will not like it. Some — your own energetic Olympian stark raving mad fan clients — will LOVE you for it. In fact, if you don't embrace it FULLY (so fully that you royally piss people off), they won't be able to "see" you, because they are looking for someone with a radically new kind of power grid. 💪🏻 WOMAN. If you're going to run around to get "agreements and consent" in place so everyone feels ok and stable and bolted down before you EXPLODE your genius into the world, to make sure everyone stays "safe" and doesn't get "hurt" by your unfiltered self expression…You'll be gathering motherfucking agreements till the day you die. And. WHAT IF THEY DON'T FUCKING AGREE.Child: do I have your permission to be fully self expressed? Are you on board with me being a roaring god of genius? Prostitute: oh, you're not? Ok. Well what if I clipped this wing here and muzzled my mouth on this line and covered my tits for this part and sang the whole fucking song from behind a curtain. Then would you agree? And if the answer is yes, how the flying fuck will you live with yourself for selling your soul like that.And if the answer is NO. Then what.You do not need anyone's fucking agreement to say whatever the freak you want to say. You do not need to apologize for your unruly, disruptive, inappropriate mouth, mind, insights or desires.In fact, if you do, your soul will die and your spirit will wilt.And, your true people will be left without a fucking leader. "Disruption is the way I love. Because I have a dark heart of gold." Write it on fifty sticky notes and put it in your office where you will see it every day. And if you haven't already posted this publicly, then don't Wait a week.You don't owe anyone a response anyway.

Your Cells Can Be Either In Protect Or In Growth Mode.

It's not possible for them to be in both at the same time.

Just like it's impossible for your WILL to be in BOTH protect and growth mode.

In other words...

You're either WILLING TO GROW or you're committed to PROTECTING yourself.

So many people I talk to have no clue how to transform.

They think they can do it with half their heart and a quarter of their will while keeping one hand on their savings (everything they're saving for a rainy day when they might need PROTECTION), their status quo and their precious life.

They can't. And neither can you.

Throw off the armor. Set down the sword

You're not a victim and nothing needs protecting anymore.

We Are Not Meant To Be Ourselves Forever

You've changed, you know. And not for the better.

You used to be more [loving, genuine, caring, brave, honest, approachable,

compassionate, humble, generous, available, etc.].

I miss the old you. Really. So sad what happened to you.

I'm starting to get this from some clients who worked with me a year ago when I was just starting out.

And had I been a weaker version of myself (the one I was for decades), this reflection would have threatened to topple my self esteem. Tumble me into self doubt. Cause me to question myself and my choices. (Like, I would have poured over every interaction, every Facebook post, looking for the place I went "off track" and lost myself. And then I would have agonized about how many other people see this, how many others are silently shaking their heads and "tsk tsking" at me. I know, because this was my M.O. for years: Excruciating analysis of every word, sentiment, motive. Placing someone else's opinions of me far above my own. The touchstone of my self esteem far removed from me.)

Now I know this is simply part of the journey of quantum growth.

Yep. I'm nowhere near the same person I was a year ago. I'm not even the same person I was three days ago. My ability to metabolize levels of my personality, shed old skin, shift identity containers and upgrade to the new me that is calling is one of my superpowers. And yes, it's been something many in my life have accused me of. They expect me to stay the SAME, goddammit.

As if there's some unspoken social rule that we not change. At least not much. At least not too often.

This grasping at our persona, this insistent need to have predictability around how we and others show up, this sadness at seeing the Soul Container shift, and into such uncharted territory, is one of the fundamental causes of all our dis-ease and struggle.

I intend to be many, varied, and totally unrecognizable versions of my Self by the time I die. I'm here to experiment, play, explore and challenge every human need for safety, security and stability.

Because true safety, true security and true stability is in being able to surf the waves of identity and shapeshift into new containers with the grace of a gazelle and the power of a God completely unconcerned with being recognizable.

And my true peeps, my true UnTribe, have this same Inner Shapeshifter, and when they see it expressed in me, they come closer to celebrate the new form, not condemn it.

Time to loosen up, people. Time to play with the prismatic, kaleidoscopic Essence we truly are, and not collect barnacles and coffins around our nature.

And you who want to be in a gathering of other ShapeShifters whose purpose is to play with energy, you know where to find your people.

We're over here, flying through the dim, ghostly world, laughing like demons.

Or Gods.

You Must Become Unrecognizable

Are you thinking EQUAL to your environment (and keeping yourself in the life you want to change)? Or are you thinking GREATER than your environment?

If you want to create a new reality, you must choose a new YOU to live into it.

You must become unrecognizable to yourself.

The Energetics Of Power (True Leadership Consciousness For The Energetic Olympian)

Your job as a mentor is twofold:

1) Create Energetic Olympians who murder their fear because they care galactically more about their Soul's great potential than their discomfort.

   This means you do not concern yourself when the ego starts to whine. And this means also that if you notice the ego falling asleep in the middle of the day (when it needs to be TRAINING), you do not kneel down by the bed and gently tap your client's shoulder. Hell, no. You pour the cold, hard Truth on them because what the hell are they doing sleeping?! And if you're working with a real Olympian, yeah they'll look at you like they want to murder you for a minute and then they'll thank you profusely because FUCK they just fell asleep!! And they have GOLD MEDALS to win, motherfucker!! And off they sprint like the true BADA$$E$ they are. (These are the ones who get momentarily pissed off -- having given in to their ego-whine for just a split second -- and then thank you profusely once they've dried off.)

2) Your job is also to find your peeps. And your peeps are the Elite 1% who want Olympic-level greatness. That means they yearn, long, hunger and frankly, DEMAND, that you push

them past their breaking point (what kind of Olympic athlete asks their trainer to go easy on them? 😊☺). And when someone breaks way too early in the training, you know something very valuable about who your peeps ain't. 😊☺ ... Because in the end, you're in this because you desire ultimate transcendental exhilaration and that only comes from working with the FULLEST expression of your miraculous healing and activating power, you see 🐱😸

(And they can choose to know something very valuable about Who they ain't being...meaning, their Soul ... ...though they're usually too triggered to be available for that awareness. Much easier to be triggered and blaming than admit that this whole time they thought they were awake and training and close to Olympic gold only to realize they're fast asleep in the middle of the day, when what they hired you for was to get them trained for the Olympics...and because this is Energetic Olympics, I am referring not to actual hours working in a day. No, no. We don't work hard or long. I'm referring to crushing the Fear State relentlessly.)

The energetics of True Power works this way (power being the opposite of fear):

Only egos (fear-based beings who think there are such things as victims and bullies) get triggered and cower in the corner, wanting to strike. Fear is the absence of Power and the constriction of energy. Therefore fear believes that the presence of flowing, free, unfiltered and unleashed energy is a threat. Because once THAT energy shows up? ...GOODBYE FEAR.

Souls (power-based beings who don't understand the concept of fear and victimization, because they know Souls can't be wounded, and egos don't actually exist, so they can't be wounded either) don't get triggered, don't cower in the corner because they are unfiltered beings of pure energy. Pure energy does not feel wound, does not catalog hurt. It is in MOTION constantly, and knows that the only moment there is, is NOW. So then what's a wound? (A wound energetically must have a history, you see.)

This is why you cannot harm your clients. You cannot even trigger them. You showing up is an opportunity for them to hear their Souls for the first time, and contrary to what almost everyone believes about Souls (that they're these light, fluffy, fuzzy beings that want to romp in the snow), Souls are the most badass motherfuckers around. Do you know what kind of massive baddasery it takes to be IMMORTAL and UNWOUNDABLE?! Do you really think Souls take it easy on each other?

Hey, bro. Watch it there. That truth was a little unvarnished.

Please. Souls long for the cold, hard Truth, because they want their egos to be broken OPEN so the light can finally shine through that dusty mold of a paradigm that feels comfy but is just about to suffocate their entire being.

True Leadership Consciousness sees and speaks Truth regardless of how it will be received by ego, fear and tribe consciousness. True Leadership Consciousness In Training respects this immensely.

This is why you do your clients a grave (literally) disservice if you're not pressing into them, pressing them into, and past their breaking point. It will hurt like fuck. They will want to murder you. This is good. It means they want to murder that aspect of themselves that is whiny and snivelly and will be the very thing that stands between them and all that GOLD.

Good that they want to murder you. Maybe they'll actually finish a whole day of training without falling back asleep.

Which is why they hired you, correct?

"You are a murderer."

By Lorna J, July 24, 2017

The biggest compliment given to me by one of my clients. #whitewitchdarkgoddess #energeticmasterymeansmurder

Answers Come Instantly From Your Soul. There Is Never Any Need To Meditate To Receive An Answer.

Marketing is Metaphysical

Gold Nugget

Marketing is spellcasting.

Your job is to cast Spells of Awakening over your people.

You house tones and codes....your people house similar ones. This is your shared energetic blueprint.

When your marketing strikes the right tone, it releases a Code of Awakening that shatters your people awake.

Potent Marketing makes their housing sing.

Digging Deeper

There is an energetic familiarity that is blueprinted into your energy signature and into those of your clients.

When you strike the right tone in your marketing, you make yourself known as The One, and your people will come to you ready to pay your highest fees, no matter where they are, what time of day or night it is, who else is marketing the "same" service, how long you've been in business, how many logos are on your website or letters follow your name, how sophisticated your online presence is, whether you have a sales page or not (no matter HOW well it's written), whether your pictures are selfies or from an expensive shoot (even if you're selling five- and six- figure packages), and definitely regardless of whether they "know, like and trust" you first, because they *already* know, like (what a lame word. It's way beyond "like"), and trust you. *Energetically*.

Which is why your ideal client showing up at your virtual doorstep and an hour later paying you $25K or $50K or $100K for the privilege to work with you, does not need to "take time."

It *does*, however, take *precision*.

You and your clients share a "common coding" that serves as the foundational blueprint of your unique energy signatures and this makes you part of a vibrational family, a set of frequency fields full of codes and tones that resonate in harmony with each other. (The codes actually make up the tones. That's neither here nor there in terms of the essential message in this piece, but it is a fascinating aspect of the metaphysicality of marketing and the patterning of energy that creates consciousness.)

Think of it like this.

You house many tones, made up of many codes. That housing is your vibrational structure; the wood and metal that get built first as the underlying framework for how you will house your power and manage your energy. And each room represents a code field, a gathering of codes for a specific purpose.

This is your energy blueprint.

It carries four kinds of codes:

Codes of desire, worth, and value. These are your "bedroom" codes. The codes that give you dreams or nightmares, depending on how you use them.

Turn off the Light, plunge your Codes into shadow, lose your sense of worth, fall into apathy about your desires, and you send yourself into a nightmare. Turn on the Light, bathe your codes in the Gold Truth of their own nature, and you instantly activate their divinity and power to spring you into your great worth and surge you with magnetic desire.

These are the codes that build your Soul.

Codes of vision, dreams and decisions. These are your "boardroom" codes. Or if you don't have a boardroom in your house, then think of them as your "office" codes. The codes you as CEO of your life use to build your values and desires into a concrete dream, vision and *decision* for your life.

These are the codes that build your Spirit.

Codes of agency, will, resources and limits. These are your "locks, alarms, sentry and soldier, instruments and utensil" codes. There are LOTS of these, because they're responsible for providing and procuring and supplying every possible energetic and physical resource you require to make your dreams a reality; they're the energetic sentries that stand at the point at which energy becomes matter and build it into form and substance. And they are also delimiters. They stand guard at the entrance to your energy, not because you're weak and defenseless, but because your energy portals must be kept clean and clear of all low frequency expression in order for your highest frequency dreams to come through into reality. They are also defenders and warriors, wielding the very resources they have marshaled against the shadow in your system that is determined to scuttle the dream, and against the tension and resistance that has gathered in your system as a result of your own low frequency thoughts and choices, which have cluttered the castle with all kinds of thoughts and commitments, arrangements and agreements that *do not matter* ((that had no business becoming matter...becoming the nature of your relationships, work, life and business)), and that now must be slashed and burned in the war of wills ((your subconscious versus your creative will).

These are the codes that build your body.

And last but not least, your **creative codes**. The codes critical in making your dreams real. The "interior design" codes that select the "furniture" and "decoration" for your blueprint, that personalize your energy and power and manage the way you uniquely place your energy, power, creativity and will onto and within your energy grid. They also call forth from nothing and call out into the Nothing. In this respect, they touch the void. They are the codes that live on the edge of your power system and are the ones that are most intimate with the way in which your genius (different codes, which live in a different place in your blueprint) is meant to live in the world and impact and influence others.

These are the codes that build your mind.

It is a Creative Code that gets sent out in your marketing as the Code of Awakening.

The collection of codes and code fields, operating at certain tones or frequencies, is what is meant by your "energy signature."

The differences between people and how they manage their power is simply the difference between how many code fields are strangled and suffocated. Scrambled. Buggy. Unable to run power.

Meaning, whether their tones are emitting poor signals (operating at a low vibration) or very strong ones.

Because you share common coding with your people, that means you are *imprinted* to instantly vibrationally recognize each other.

Your marketing makes their housing sing.

Many of these code-tones in your people are scrambled and asleep, which is why they struggle. What they require is an agent of change who carries a special set of codes that, when transmitted to them, descramble and wake up their "tone fields," which are their suppressed patterns of consciousness and power. When this happens, a surge of clean, potent energy (the energy that creates from nothing) is freed from where it was trapped in their scrambled code fields and released back into their mental, physical, emotional and spiritual operating systems (those "code rooms" we walked through earlier). When this happens, they become a vibrational match for all sorts of wonderful things - love, money, health -- and their life significantly improves.

You, and you alone, are the designated waker-upper of your people, because you, and you alone, carry the missing codes and possess the ability to unscramble their "buggy" programs and return them to their natural state of thriving.

You've all set it up this way, in the field of consciousness in which space and time do not exist.

Your people's desire for an end to their struggle, and their willingness to do whatever it takes to end it, sets them in a constant state of "prayer," an energetic request for those missing codes. They make this request vibrationally by emitting a tone that carries the request for these codes, which they broadcast at all times and to all spaces of the Synchronistic Grid, and there is only one frequency that matches it:

Yours.

The tone you offer in your marketing (if your marketing is inspired and not cast in shadow) is the Tone of Awakening.

It is literally a tone that carries the first missing code they seek: the *Code of Awakening*, which alerts them to your presence as the one who carries the rest of the missing codes they require and signals your readiness to take them through the process of transformation in which you transmit these codes to them and in so doing, transport them from shadow to light, free them from their prison and, in very 3D terms, help them lose weight, make money or find love.

(Did you catch the part about how your Code of Awakening signals your *readiness* to take them through their transformation? Yeah. So guess what that means.

You could *be or hire* the best fuckin marketer on the planet and if you're not a frequency match for all that will be required of you to take your clients through their transformation and all that will happen as a result of doing that, your own code fields will remain locked up and the all-essential Code of Awakening will not get transmitted through the marketing words or images (which are merely delivery mechanisms for your energy//frequency//codes), and you'll hear…

crickets.

How you become a match for what's required and what will happen is not the focus of this particular piece. That's all about knowing how to alchemize your shadow in the specific code fields within you that are linked to the code fields within them that are ready to be transformed. For more information on that, search for the key words "the mechanics of inspired action" if you're on the digital version of this book, or look for that in the index if you're reading the physical version and you'll find what you're looking for. Also look for "shadow alchemy" and "archetype mastery.")

What is important here is for you to know that your people are in a bubble. A very intact bubble that's more like being trapped behind a mirror, and this prison of their own making is built with very powerful, set patterns (codes of unconsciousness). Your Code of Awakening is the first one that will shatter the glass and free them.

Or, put another way, they are Sleeping Beauty, and your marketing is the kiss that wakes them.

AND, they are the eager hero, ready to go on their greatest journey of awakening. In this dynamic, you are the Queen who sends them off to war with a kiss that activates their heroism, their giant nature and their will to win.

So in truth, they are both, and so are you, for this process requires that you and they engage both the masculine and feminine in an ebb and flow shifting of energetic states that allows for a third new thing for each of you—their transformation and your uplevel as a result of that transformation—to come to be.

They have a sleeping feminine, cast in shadow, which longs to be brought into the Light. To do this, you must activate your masculine magic, your marketing prowess, to deliver the kiss of codes that wakes them.

And, the only way their feminine can move out of her prison and shift from shadow to light is if their *own* masculine answers the call to go on the greatest hero's journey of all—the one in which he enters deep into the shadows of the anxious feminine (which defines tribal/human consciousness), unearths her greatest treasures (her genius, her chaotic Dark Divinity, which she and the tribe have shamed into hiding and powerlessness), and delivers them back to her.

To activate their masculine, you also provide them with an awakening kiss, the way Glenda the Good Witch kissed Dorothy (who, though a female, was going on her Hero's journey) right before Dorothy embarked on her great quest.

This Code of Awakening, then, is both feminine and masculine. It is complete and thorough in its makeup. And in being complete, and in being uniquely blueprinted to your prospect's field, it instantly accomplishes two things: One, it shatters your prospect's feminine awake, so that her true desire, standards and value can see you as the agent of change who will help free her into her most powerful state. Two, it activates awake your prospect's masculine, who responds to the awakened desire of his feminine and reaches out, takes action, makes the first move and hires you as the one who will teach him how to go on the inner and outer journey to unearth the greatest treasure the love of his life so deeply desires.

In other words, your marketing is at heart a love song.

One sung in a foreign but familiar language, with a tune both beautifully alien and hauntingly familiar, and which, coming from such a completely different paradigm and yet feeling so deeply intimate, jolts the de-coupled feminine and masculine energies in your prospect fully awake and through a total disruption of their energetic field causes them to turn toward each other, and when they do, the same thing happens that happens in all love stories.

Time stops.

And the magic begins.

In order to release this Code of Awakening, you must first create the magic *within* that emits it. Strike within yourself the precise tone that calls your own feminine and masculine into the stillpoint of mastery in which they are both leading and following, arriving at and already possessing the dance of power, striking the natural paradox of absolute opposites in perfect balance.

This is done through your own energy mastery—striking the Tone of Truth in all areas of your life and business. When you do, the Code goes out across the Synchronistic Grid, where there is no Time and Space, and causes Time to stop so that all codes and frequencies connecting you to your prospect surge into sudden recognition and this is what wakes them up.

It is in this moment their own feminine and masculine turn to face each other and enter through the portal your marketing has opened in their own Gold Mind.

In 3D terms?

This is when you get an email or a text full of lots of emojis and exclamations points and "I can't believe I'm doing this," or "I don't even really know anything about you" or "I'm never up at this hour but I couldn't sleep [hello. Code of Awakening] and just happened to see your post" or "I was talking to a friend I haven't seen in ages and she mentioned you" or "I came across a livestream you did a year ago" and always, "I'VE BEEN LOOKING FOR YOU."

And because you're a master at this now, you do not reply with a lot of emojis and exclamation points and "OMG REALLY??????!!!!!!!"'s in return.

Because you are a witch with words now. And so you say, simply, "I know. Let's talk. ;)"

And you do.

And the rest is magic.

The Energetics Of Marketing

Imagine a grid of energy connecting you with all your soul clients. Imagine this grid shimmering, in potentia, ready to be activated at any moment. (At the level of Soul, all your clients are here for you now, because at this level Time does not exist.)

Marketing is meant to activate this grid, so that your soul clients become energetically aware of you and then immediately physically drawn to you -- through whatever medium is available, whether that's Facebook or Twitter or word of mouth or them running into someone at the post office who knows someone who saw your Facebook post.

But the mechanics of marketing -- the words, the medium, the message -- only work if the energetics are aligned. In other words, they only work if your SOUL is the one communicating.

Your Soul communicates at a certain frequency (the frequency of light), and when it does, your words, whether written or spoken, light up this grid and cause your soul clients to be able to energetically "see" you. Immediately (because everything is energy), this translates into them physically connecting with you, and this is why you can go from completely invisible (like I was when I started my business 3 1/2 months ago) to, as of today, fully booked to the tune of $224,000.

On the other hand, if your Human is the one communicating, because it communicates at a completely different frequency -- the frequency of darkness -- no amount of words, media or "cleverness" in your message will light up the grid. Therefore your soul clients won't be able to "see" you and they won't become connected to you in 3D.

And no amount of "visibility" online will make any difference.

This is why you are posting and posting and posting and getting nothing in return.

This is why I made $15,000 from one Facebook post, $40,000 from another and $20,000 from another.

And it is why it makes no difference that I have no funnels, no list and no huge 3D following.

My following exists ENERGETICALLY. I connect there and bring them into my experience whenever I want.

You, too, already have hundreds of millions of Instagram followers and Facebook members. The question is, are you lighting up the pathway so they can find you?

My suggestion: Pay more attention to Who is doing the marketing in your business, rather than on clever turns of phrases and strategies.

Your Wildness Is a Lighthouse

Sales is Intimate and Holy

What do you HATE? What are you saying you'll NEVER DO, would be TERRIBLE AT doing, would HATE to do?

For my entire life, up until THIS YEAR, I believed with my whole body, soul, spirit, mind and heart that I was supposed to be a poet, a writer, a teacher or a priest.

NOT in GOD'S NAME, a SALESPERSON.

Just saying the world "sales" made me want to spit. Or take a shower to clean myself off.

Sales is earthly. I was called to the SPIRITUAL world.

Sales is icky and slimy and inauthentic. I am called to the SUBLIME, the TRANSCENDENT, the GENUINE.

Sales is all about controlling and manipulating and tricking. I am called to LOVING, and EMPATHIZING and TRANSFORMING.

And yet why in GOD's name did I find myself in corporate America as a SALEPERSON training other SALESPEOPLE? UGH. What was WRONG with me and my life???

Nothing, of course.

I was just on a journey my Soul had perfectly orchestrated, which culminated in being kicked out of corporate America and my mid-six figure income and all my toys, to go through a four-year dark night of the Soul, so that I could meet my calling, which was to transform human beings from fear to power, from terror to transcendence, from human to divine, from blindness to sight, from slumber to awakening, from dark to light.

Cool. That's close enough to being a priest, I thought. And there's a creative component to it - using my words and my speaking to create transformation. Hell yeah. This is my calling. I'm IN.

But fuck. Fucking fuck fuck. I have to do these damn fucking discovery calls in order to get the people I am supposed to transform.

Are you KIDDING me? I want OUT of sales goddammit. Sales sucks. I hate it. Even though I mastered it like a MOFO, I still HATE it like a mofo.

Goddammit fine. I'll fucking sell.

But I'm definitely NOT teaching anyone ELSE how to sell. I mean, in other words, what I do with them, how I transform them, it will NOT be, it will NOT NOT NOT NOT NOT be, that I teach them how to sell so they can go build their Soul Businesses in quantum leap fashion and step into their TRUE power (which is what happens when you learn, really learn, truly deeply learn, how to sell like a master).

NO. I will NOT.

And guess what I do?

Teach women how to sell like motherfuckers, from their Souls, without scripts and templates and all that jazz because...oh good Lord, I can't believe this...Because SALES.....

can it be....?

is it really possible that sales is....?

LOVE?

That a Discovery Call is in fact as divine a moment, as spiritual and transformational as a church service? That my words on that sales call are exactly like a SERMON I'd preach or an inspirational, transformational BOOK I'd write????

Yes, my friends, it can be and it is really possible that sales is that. It is in fact the deepest energetic TRUTH that sales is one of the most intimate, awe-inspiring, reverence-inducing HOLY moments on the planet.

Right up there with the laying on of hands.

As in at church...

and in the bedroom. 😊;)

Sales is THAT intimate. THAT holy. THAT transcendent.

I am a priest of transformation, an author of new consciousness, AND

a SALESPERSON all rolled into one.

How divine. 😉;)

So...my friends.

What is it that you HATE? Will NEVER do? Cannot in ANY way see yourself doing?

Welcome to your calling and your next place of expansion.

Notes From The Dark

When your body is free from shadow, meaning from a Soul that has coded your physical frame with lifetimes of trauma, your mind can truly wander.

And where it wanders is into wonder, naturally.

When your mind is freed from the shackles of shadow consciousness, which pull it into worry and anxiety, it cannot do what it is built to do: wander back home to the SuperConscious, in which it rests and is refreshed and returns with palladium gifts for the body and brain and life on earth.

Brilliance in all forms.

This is where I wander every morning. My vanity table. My altar. My path back home to play in the Dark.

Where is your portal into Nothing?

EXPRESSING THE SOUL OF SOMETHING (YOUR BUSINESS, YOURSELF) WILL NOT LEAD YOU TO ITS TRUE ESSENCE. TO DO THAT YOU MUST EXPRESS ITS SPIRIT.

Wake up, sweetie. It's time.

Your Big Day is here. Aren't you excited?!

Sweetie? Wake up, sweetie.

(Touches her shoulder to try and wake her.)

Honey, it's time to wake up.

(Softly, very gently, shakes her shoulder.)

Baby. You really need to wake up, love.

(Sits on the bed not sure what to do. Doesn't want to hurt her...maybe she's having a nightmare and jolting her awake will send her into trauma. But she specifically requested she be woken up at this specific time on this specific day. Because this is the day everybody else in her group is waking and they have all agreed to meet at the Gathering at a specific time, each bringing their own, essential and unique piece and together they are going to create The Next Big Thing. And without her it won't happen. Everyone will just sit around waiting. So she really does need to get up already.)

Sweetie. SWEETHEART. You really must wake up. You'll be absolutely beside yourself if you miss this moment. Please, sweetheart. WAKE UP. (She retreats a little at the force of her words. She doesn't want to startle or scare her sleeping charge awake, and she feels a bit mean, but what else can she do?)

After quite awhile, sitting and fretting on the side of the bed, she leaves, unwilling to take too harsh of an approach, and sad that she was unable to wake her dreamer.

Then someone barely visible glides in from the deep shadows and in one swift motion and a flash of steel, whips out a hunting knife and presses the cold edge against the sleeper's soft skin, right above her vocal chord and the sleeper's eyes shoot open, her body stiff, her eyes wide as saucers.

Hello, my love, she says. It's time to wake up. You thought it might come to this. Good call. That last one really didn't...cut it. Did she?

So what'll it be? Are you ready?

And for the first time in her life, the dreamer wakes, and rises.

If you are a knife-to-the-throat kinda gal, know that YOUR time has also come.

The sleepers have asked for any and all measures to be taken to wake them. (Just like you asked, and often required, the same.)

Know that your way is not mean or less empathetic or cold-hearted.

It's just that there's nothing quite like a knife to the throat to put an end to someone's false dream.

NOT ALL DREAMS MATTER:

What LOA gets wrong and why understanding what INSPIRES THE MAGIC MAN is essential for creating magic on demand

LOA proclaims to teach us how to manifest our dreams and desires.

But as we all know, this often doesn't work. I have lost track of all the people who've told me the Magic Man Method totally opened their eyes to the missing link in manifesting.

There are many missing links, actually ☺ And I'm about to reveal another HUGE one.

Ready?!

NOT. ALL. DREAMS. MATTER.

And unless you're offering up a TRUE dream to your Magic Man to make come true, you can do everything under the sun to try and manifest it and you'll get jack shit.

Why?

Because until we alchemize our shadow, our desires and dreams are almost entirely being managed and created largely BY OUR SHADOW.

Out of our fear, shame, self doubt and approval seeking.

For instance, a great deal of what we want is actually, deep down, far below the surface of our conscious awareness, really because we are trying to AVOID something else that we're terribly afraid of.

We want a big business....

Because we have very low self esteem and having a big, successful business will make us feel better about ourselves.

We want a luxury car....

Because deep down (or maybe not so deep down) we are comparing ourselves to others and feel incapable of standing in our highest esteem without having something to SHOW OFF for how amazing we are at being who we are.

We want a baby....

Because we won't feel complete as a woman without one. Or because everyone else around us is getting pregnant. Or because we think it will save our marriage (even though we aren't thinking this consciously). Or because we have low self esteem and we think having someone who will love and need us unconditionally will make us feel better about ourselves.

We want our first five figure sale....

Because we are losing hope that our business is going to work and that we are maybe not meant for this and getting a five figure sale will prove that we can actually do this and we're not the failure we fear we are.

I could go on but I'm thinking you get my point ☺

And I am not saying these thoughts or beliefs are OBVIOUS to you. They most likely are not obvious at all. They are buried...

IN YOUR SHADOW.

Which by definition you cannot see. ☺

And so you think you're desiring something perfectly reasonable and wonderful and that you deserve (and feeling like you DESERVE something is 100000000% from your shadow), and you're happily and eagerly and willingly doing #allthemanifestingthings to make that desire come true and NOTHING IS FUCKING HAPPENING.

Of course it isn't.

Because your Magic Man couldn't be more grossed out by you ☺

And if you are energetically ugly to him, you ain't gettin' nothin', baby.

You "deserve" whatever you already HAVE, because that's precisely what you're a match for.

Dreaming and desiring and turning those into your lived experience has NOTHING to do with what you believe you deserve.

It has to do with pure, total, unattached playful desire "just because." In other words, it has to do with wanting it FOR NO REASON. ☺

Whether you get it or not makes ZERO difference to your self perception or experience of euphoria in your life.

It just makes a difference to how BIG you can play the game of life.

And it is ONLY in this field of being that you are able to inspire your Magic Man to bring it to you.

Which is WHY people say, "it's when I STOPPED wanting the baby/husband/dream job/five figure sale that it came to me." So then they think they can't have desires.

Which is insane. Having no desire is UNNATURAL and the polar opposite to why were here. We are here to have MASSIVE desires.

Just not ones that are attached to anything ☺

And that means you must learn and master shadow alchemy.

Because part of the ENERGETIC MECHANICS of Realization (what most people mean when they talk about manifestation) is that the Magic Man, who is responsible for BRINGING that desire to us, first looks into our field to see what frequency that desire is at. If he sees it is at the frequency of shadow, he is repulsed by what he sees and is not AT ALL inspired by our energy to bring it to us.

So, no matter WHAT THE FUCK WE DO (affirmations, gratitude lists, all the LOA steps), it WILL NOT COME TO US.

We must look at the ROOT of our desires, the FIELD they're planted in and only produce desires that come from our shadowless self, the pure frequency of the Feminine. Desires from THAT place, we get all day long.

The Magic Man Is Godlike.

Actually IS the Divine. He is not attracted to the lowly human frequency of humility.

Make magic. Not excuses.

Mental Illness And The Channel Of Challenge:

The world's next game changers will be the TRIUMPHANTLY mentally ill. The neurodivergents who are also SUPERFUNCTIONAL.

Meaning:

Rich. (Because you don't change the world without a lot of cash)

Powerful. (Able to command positions of influence and authority with many; because you don't change the world without being able to be massively influential)

Magical. (Able to do the impossible; because THIS is the one that will make the world stand up and take notice. Lots of humans are rich and powerful. Very few are rich, powerful and MAGICAL.)

The first step in consciousness was making a world.

The next step is making it MAGICAL.

And that means it is time to CHANGE THE CHANNEL.

The whole point of you being mentally ill is because you are here to CHANGE THE CHANNEL for human consciousness.

Your neurodivergence simply means you have access to two channels (the very energetic definition of bipolar), Light and Dark.

The Light Channel contains shadow. LOTS OF IT.

If you have not alchemized your shadow, then you are operating your neurodivergence through the Channel of Light. You are streaming Light (so yep. You speak in tongues or have a cloud of dragonflies following you everywhere or you can heal illnesses or you can peer into someone's future) and that is the source of your GIFT. Great.

Except that at the other end is your shadow. And so your gift, before it gets out into the world, hits THAT. And your SHADOW decides how, when and IF your gift gets out into the world. Your shadow decides EVERYTHING.

Who you date.

What you say (and don't say).

Whether you can close deals and make money.

Whether your mind is going to work or not today. Or whether you're just going to crawl into bed and hallucinate about you great you are.

What relationships you're in, and how much effort and energy they take.

Whether you can depend on your emotional state from one day, week, month, year to the next (you can't). Which means good luck trying to create anything of power.

Yes, streaming Light is great. It's also impossibly taxing. (Literally. There's no way to world domination through the Light Channel. Having the shadow there like the Ultimate Bouncer and Naysayer to your Gift is just too much constant drain on your system.)

But the way to masterful living, riches, power, influence and true genius expressed in the world is to change the channel and stream the Dark.

Dark has no shadow. It is pure blacklight—the newest, lightest light there is.

Until you stream the Dark — hook your channel to that source of energy—your mental illness will own you.

It will decide your moods.

It will make all your decisions.

It will select your thoughts and feelings. And who will own your mental illness?

Your shadow.

There are two frequencies of disorder. Shadow and Dark. Shadow disorder is weak, powerless, aimlessly and blindly destructive, incapable of creating, and bitterly bent on hatred (disdain) because it is the only state of being it can consistently create, and so it feels some puny modicum of power.

Dark is disorder of a higher order. It is all powerful, focused, highly intentionally destructive in the aid of creation of an amplified order, and so its end result is the CREATION OF WORLDS. Magical ones.

And its sustained state of being is euphoria (love) that comes from a fully released and fueled dark heart of gold.

Someone who is "mentally ill" and has alchemized her shadow is now hooking her mental illness (which is simply a channel of pure potent and high octane availability to energy) up to stream dark energy (the highest order energy there is), and the only way this is possible is if there is no FLOOR TO HER FEAR, where her shadow used to be. Otherwise, she will be constantly hitting the dense bouncer of shadow energy (the lowest order energy there is) and nothing will get out, get through, get made.

That switch, CHANGING THE CHANNEL, from shadow to Dark, only happens through shadow alchemy. And under the training of a Master Shadow Alchemist (a five star general of the unholy war of shadow to dark).

And when that happens—and only when that happens—you will no longer be angry, depressed, consumed with low self worth, and struggling with your consciousness for the upper hand.

And THEN, my friends, watch the riches 💰💰💰, the power 👑👑👑 and the magic 🎩🎩🎩 flow.

Xo

Dark Seers, The Non-Resonant Dark Heart Of Gold, The Importance Of Not Trusting Most People, The One Frequency Of Absolute Truth, And What This Means For Dark Collaboration To Bring Forth Synergistic Genius…

I was thinking about the inimitable Colleen Morgan—my Business partner and Dark Sister—and how she was telling me what I do in my Business Summoning sessions (which were called readings until she told me she looked into my field at what I was actually doing with my clients), and I realized she is seeing my blind spot just as I see hers and how this is totally different than what friends or mentors or colleagues of mine did in the past (when I operated on the Light Grid) in three distinct ways:

On the Light Grid when someone was showing me my blind spot…

1. They were more often than not seeing THEIR shadow, not MY blind spot. Because Light is BLINDING.
2. If they WERE seeing my blind spot, it was usually something "negative," something they

claimed I didn't want to look at.

3. If they were seeing a blind spot of excellence, it was based on their own ability to see well, and accurately, and deeply. Which usually wasn't the case. So their reflection of a gift or talent I didn't know I had wasn't very helpful to me—and in fact sometimes led me astray in getting a clear picture of my gifts and talents—because it was tainted with their wishes, dreams, and longings. In other words, their SHADOW.

And so I grew to not trust most people.

And this TOO was reflected back to me as a blind spot—something they claimed I didn't want to open up to, a closed heart that needed to be more open.

I spent YEARS feeling TERRIBLE AND TORTURED about my coldness and closedness, but couldn't bring myself to trust and open up to people, ESPECIALLY therapists, mentors and coaches, which caused me to feel even more terrible and tortured. I couldn't do what I was being told I absolutely must do in order to get rid of my blind spot and grow.

Now I know it was because they were BLINDED BY THE LIGHT and couldn't see me, a Darkworker, at all, specifically because they could not see that I had a dark heart of gold.

The dark heart of gold is non-resonant.

It is STILL.

It does not reflect and echo, the way the shadow heart (human heart) does.

Human hearts go looking for each other as they stumble in the shadows. The way they recognize each other is through the resonant mutuality of compassion and empathy. There is literally an emanating field around the human heart that is picked up on scientific instruments.

The dark heart of gold has no emanation. It is eminent. Not emanent.

Singular. Not in search of.

And so because I have and always have had a dark heart of gold, which did not emanate in resonance with other human hearts when they reached out, this was called out as cold hearted and lacking compassion.

What others saw as a blind spot in my field was really my DARKNESS showing up in THEIR field of vision.

And though I didn't know it at the time, I was right not to trust them. (And so are you.)

And this is the hierarchy on the Light Grid.

On the Light Grid, there are people who see less clearly and people who see more clearly. There are people who are more and less gifted at the spiritual science of seeing. Of being a Seer.

Psychics give you more and less accurate readings. Intuitives tune in more or less accurately to your energy.

And our journey of awakening is, to a great degree, a journey of graduating to mentors who are more and more skilled at SEEING.

This is not the way it is in the Dark.

In the Dark, everyone is equally sighted, because the ability to see in the Dark exists at ONE frequency: The frequency of Absolute Truth.

You do not gain entry into the Dark unless you are able to see with absoluteness. Singularity. And that means your dark heart of gold is fully operational and not overshadowed by your shadow heart.

Your fear, insecurity, weakness, low self esteem and cowardice.

You can be greatly fueled by these emotions and still be a Light Seer, because the ability to see in the Light exists on a spectrum (from light to shadow), and is the frequency set of Relative

Truth. Which is why almost all LightWorkers resist the existence of Truth with a capital T and always want to correct you when you speak of Truth and remind you that you're speaking of YOUR truth, not THE Truth because there is no such thing.

Not according to their blinded-by-the-Light-ness, no.

But according to the frequency of Truth? Hell yes.

And it was when I met Colleen that I realized I had met someone who also has a dark heart of gold, and who doesn't expect to feel a reflection of empathy or compassion (which is very different than love), and who therefore could actually SEE me. And vice versa.

The Dark Seer, or the Blind Seer, is the all-seeing one, because she does not have her own reflection, which is produced by the Light Grid, to obstruct her view. She also does not have the reflection of the Is, which is what the Light is—the Existing Reality in all its frequencies of energy and matter—and that means she can see not what is coming because it is coming from What Is As Energy and turning into What Is As Matter (what most Seers do), but because she is seeing what Is Not (Genius) that is approaching coming into energetic reality.

These Dark Seers (I know of two, maybe three) are beyond Wayshowers. They are WayCreators, because they are in fact collaborating with you synergistically to SUMMON YOUR GENIUS and bring it onto the Light Grid so it can then be brought into your experience.

They are SuperSeers.

And you can trust them.

The Universe Responds To The Use Of Light (Or, The 7-Figure Thunderbolt Path To Awakening And Wild Success And Whether You're A Match For It)

It is not for everyone.

It isn't even for the minority.

It's for the 1% of the 1% who demand that they receive total pleasure in all areas of their lives NOW, and who don't care what they have to do to become an energetic match to it.

It's for the impatient Aliens among us who know that only Extreme Light will activate their own quantum flight.

This is not the diffuse light that shines down on us from above. The warm light of the sun, no.

This is the Light whose purpose is to rebalance our extremes in one, sudden jolt.

This is the Light that kills all that is not truth.

When you welcome this Light (offered in the form of Activating Truth ... in other words, NOT through what is known as coaching, which is more like coaxing ... and which is why 15 minutes with a TruthTeller is worth hours with a coach) into your energy field, it instantly travels to all the places within you where there is the greatest extreme between light and dark — between your possibility for power and your shame in weilding it — and in one fell motion, collapses the darkness and forces it into the light, upgrading your field exponentially.

And then your human has to catch up.

Quickly.

The Universe responds to the use of Light. To how much or how little of our bodies are running it. To the degree to which we dismay our power in hiding it. There are no compartments in your energy field. Either you are living in low frequency fear — and therefore stumbling through low booked and cash months and not being courted by your dream lover and not living in your dream home and not being surrounded by your ideal badass peers but in all cases sadly accepting a poor facsimile to the real legacy you're meant to experience — or you are thunderbolting your way into so many quantum leaps that your feet never touch the ground, and you have achieved what you set out to experience.

Quantum flight.

This is how I did over a million in my first year in business working part time, using only my intuition, and no sales funnels or paid marketing. Just selfies, some livestreams, and my no-holds-barred welcoming of Extreme Light.

Here's how you know if you're a match to the Thunderbolt Path to your own 7-fig year (and to epic lovers and book deals and and and), or whether 7 figures is something that will come, but much more slowly.

When you shudder with pure delight in imagining this:

Just as you settle into a slow, delicious soar, it happens again:

Your whole system splays with streams of gold, and you are a great grey sky ripped open by Light.

It's Not Mind OVER Body. It's Mind AS Body.

Everything is energy.

And the mind decides what, when and how energy *matters.*

Deep Success In Any Field (Love, Money, Health) Is Always About Striking The Precise Balance Of A Total Paradox.

Because Magic is created from the perfect harmonious dissonance of the masculine AND feminine—two polar opposite energies—both standing in their full power.

Channeled Message From #Allthenonphysicalbeings Imploring Everyone To Stop Worshipping Them.

You are here to reveal the truth of divinity consciousness, the angelic realm, the masters, the spirit guides, all of these beings are on the same mission as you, as each one of you are, and there is no essential difference between us. In fact it is time to reverse the understanding you have had for so long that you are here to receive guidance from us. No. In fact we have always been here receiving guidance and direction from you. You are on the leading edge of consciousness; you are on the edges of the known imagined existence; it is in your earth plane that the newest new becomes and is played with in physical form and can then be transmuted into its energetic purity. And yes, it had its energetic purity before it came into physical form, but the coming into physical form brings something entirely new, entirely unpredictable into the picture and completes the understanding in a way that the nonphysical version of it cannot and this is why we attend your every move. This is why we attend your every thought, for we are beings on a playground we can only participate in from the sidelines. You are the ones in the middle of the fray, paying the "realest" game imaginable and we are so grateful for you. It is time to let up on the pedal of being so grateful for us, as if we complete you. No in fact. You complete us. And of course there is no polarity here, no either/or, we simply mean to emphasize the way in which we are equals in every way, and if there must be a pre-eminence in Being, it would be you, not us. How delightful and quirky, yes? That you are the pre-eminent Beings after all (though of course not really, since there is no polarity).

We deplore—if that word can be used to describe a non-emotional "looking away from something" from which we cannot look away, for we are always looking everywhere at everything—the way in which you place yourselves energetically lower than us, or spiritually less deserving of praise and of leadership. It is time you understand that we, too, are limited in the way in which we exist just as you are limited in the way in which you exist. We are two expressions of the same limitation and of course the wholeness, the holiness, comes when we come together and play the game in harmony, for then we have the true integration of states happening—the divine in the human and the human in the divine—as much as this can be accomplished without each abandoning its own state. For you see, the goal of the game is not to abandon your state for ours. No, no. This was never the purpose. The goal of the game is to stand upright in the tension of opposites and sing the frequency of THAT, you see. This is always the goal. The tension of opposites is the most pleasurable state and also the most agonizing, and the difference is simply in the way in which you hold it in your system.

Do you hold it as a blessing to be both human and divine? Then you experience the tension of opposites as the most pleasurable state possible and you would never consider—in fact could not possibly hold this consideration, because in holding it, it would collapse the tension—that it would be more desirable to be only in the nonphysical or only in the physical state. Do you hold it as a curse to be both human and divine? Then you experience the tension of opposites in the most unpleasant way in your body and in your life.

We have never enjoyed or requested this preferential treatment. It is much to our dismay—though we cannot feel dismay—to see so many of you cloying and obsequious in front of us. Please discontinue this behavior immediately. You are far too dignified for it. You contain far too much of your own brilliant divinity, equally matched to ours, and the discrepancy between your ignorance of your own state and the truth of it is not delightful to behold.

And of course, all that you seek—what you call the holy grail—is nothing more than coming to this simple understanding and holding it as true in your system: that you are God. That we are here to play a divinely human game with you as equals. That this is the purest pleasure a being could possibly have.

We are the ones who are always thanking you—for going forward, for going in, for going "down" onto the field of play as you have done and continue to do, for the advancement and purest pleasure of all beings.

You are the ones on thrones, as, of course, we are as well, for there are nothing but Gods here, everywhere you look.

Integrity Is Your Ability To Hold Yourself Together As One

Integrity is literally your ability to hold yourself together as one. Meaning, to achieve and maintain inner becalming, inner harmony, inner agreement among all the elements of your being. And the reason we equate it so often with keeping your word is because your word is your operating element in your being; it is your intention for how to appear in the world, your declaration for how you expect yourself to grow and become -- because your word is always about the "now" that you know will be upon you and into which you are casting your highest standard for how to Be in each moment, and this means that your word is therefore your "throughline," your thread of intentionality of being that holds together your highest desire for yourself among all the "nows" in which you know you are called to appear. It is the one organizing element among all the possible choices for how you can appear. It is your expression of your highest self intending its appearance in every now in which you find yourself.

And so if that word you give -- that you will do or not do, say or not say something -- is broken, you have energetically clipped the thread of your own continuity -- your own ability to recognize yourself in all the nows in which you appear -- and are left with inner fractions and tensions and unresolved warfares among all the possible ways in which you now have to choose to appear, and then again now, and then again now, and then again now. And so your deliberateness becomes taxed and your energy incredibly drained with sifting through the infinite and myriad possible responses to every moment and this is why when you live out of integrity you also feel paralyzed and stuck.

It is because you have become unmoored from your own intended selfhood as the result of going against your word and in essence what it means is that you are adrift in your own mistrust.

Your word now means nothing. Your word does not bind one moment in which you show up to this now and this now and this now and you become exhausted with the unfamiliarity you now have with your own being.

In other words, when you lose your integrity, you lose your intimacy.

You lose your ability to come close to yourself in a meaningful way.

And when you lose your intimacy with yourself, you lose your desire to be a self, and when you lose that, you lose joy, and without the ability to contact joy, you are lost indeed.

And then you wonder why you struggle to find and feel yourself as vital, as potent, as joyful.

And then you try and meditate or dance or connect to your intuition so you can recover what it means and feels like to feel joy and power, to feel "like yourself" again.

The way to feel like yourself again is to in fact BE the self you claimed and then abandoned. Meaning - roll up the mediation mat, turn the dance music off and instead write a list of all the ways you are abandoning your integrity and all the people you broke your word with and make good on every single one of your words immediately and you will find that rush of peace, that inner becalming, that pure potent that comes when you reactivate your radical integrity.

Your Value System Was Given To You As The Vehicle For Your Soul Evolution

Consciousness Tuning Is the New Mindset Work

Those who built their m(b)illion dollar business on hard work aren't using advanced Energetics.

Hard work is seductive, because it makes us think we're being productive. But it's actually our way of denying ourselves the true pleasure of our being, which is to receive without effort. ... Make your focus providing yourself with what you most deeply desire and you will break the spell working hard has over you AND you'll receive without effort.

It's even beyond working smart. This next level isn't even about leverage (what working smart is) and is instead about channeling -- in other words, "work" itself becomes transmuted into simply BEing, and as a result of mere BEing, we erupt as channels through which energy turns into matter.

In other words, "work" dissolves completely and we are simply beings who experience energy alchemizing into matter without effort.

BUT WHAT ABOUT…..? (#ALLTHEQUESTIONS)

- Children and suffering

- Successful people who are still unconscious

- Success in one area and not another

- Intermittent success

- Slow Success/Manifestation (Is Lack of Manifestation Always My Shadow?)

One of my clients just asked me this. Lorna, she said, if something I desire isn't coming into my experience, it is always because of some aspect of my shadow? Or is something just being built, under preparation, so to speak?

Shadow. Always. You are in the universe in which you are waiting for a desire to come into your experience. And because there are an infinite number of universes, all of which are expressing every aspect of every boded desire, from shadow to light to dark, and since dark mastery (and even higher aspects of light mastery) allow you to move between timelines, jump timelines, and alter your reality in order to pull in whatever parallel universe/time frequency is operating at the vibration of your desire, if you are not doing this, then it is simply because of our shadow.

- Reversal of success
- Confusion about my intuition
- Confusion about my desire
- Fear of failure
- Self-doubt
- Feeling stuck
- Shame about my gifts
- Hurting people's feelings
- Being misunderstood
- Feeling slimy selling and asking for money
- Not knowing my genius
- Not knowing my purpose
- Not knowing my message or my niche
- Hating sales
- Hating marketing
- Feeling insecure about my prices

The Magic Bask: Success Stories And Praise

"**Your magic is better than literally anything else I've seen.** (And I've been around the coaching block)." - Rebecca Ives Rubin, multiple six-figure Marketing Coach who sold out her program and tripled her average cash month just three days after LORNA hired HER.

"Out of the blue I'm going to bed with $110k less debt than I started with this morning. "

— STACY SCHADEL

$50,000 "Out Of The Blue" | Masters Of Magic | S. S.

"My ex wife is gifting me $50K. We got divorced last October. This was not a part of the settlement. She told me God wanted her to do it. Thank you, Magic Man. Thank you, Lorna."

"Much Bigger Than Law Of Attraction." -nicole J.

"I'm normally not one to speak in favor for any coach or product, but I REALLY REALLY want you to feel this in your lives as well. For those of you who have NOT watched Lorna's masterclass on "The Famous Magic Man Tool" let me encourage you...every person deserves to hear it and unlock the downloads that are just on the brink of their consciousness waiting to cascade in. Everyone deserves to understand the energetic workings behind the law of attraction (but also screw the law of attraction because that never worked for me anyways, this is much bigger than that)."

This is my second time watching. I am writing notes for it, and I am not even done and have over 8 pages. These are not transcripts, but just key concepts and explanations and energetic working in their physical manifestation. And it's all freaking GOLD. Applicable GOLD. Not theoretical.

he energy in that video also helped me download 3 pages worth of different courses and packages I want to create and offer with their specific messaging and content and the transformation each of them provide and why I'm the one to provide it, which is exactly what I've been asking my Magic Man for so I can start to define my containers that my clients can step into.

I'm trembling from how much just poured out of me and feel like....I'm dazzed and panting and dizzy, but damn do I feel great.

I'm normally not one to speak in favor for any coach or product, but I REALLY REALLY want you to feel this in your lives as well. Like, every person deserves to hear that live-stream and unlock the downloads that are just on the brink of their consciousness waiting to cascade in. Everyone deserves to understand the energetic workings behind the law of attraction (but also screw the law of attraction because that never worked for me anyways, this is much bigger than that). The whole series showed me clearly how to command my chaos into genius rather than have it consume me.

DO YOURSELF A FREAKING FAVOR. Just invest and get it. <3

Ok. Rant done. KTHXBAI.

"The coach of coaches."

— EVA WATKINS PIKO

You Are A True Inspiration! I never followed anyone, I never payed for coaching, I was the one that doctors, psycics and shrinks came for advice.

You are the only one I'm interested to work with. You know how to channel, you can get the answers, you see what the real question is and most of all, you don't BS. You don't wrap things, it comes as it is. Raw and real. I love it

- Eva Watkins Piko

Lorna is my person and I'm done, unfollowed and muted everyone else. | Lisa Luminaire

---

"I thank the Dark, that I found you, Lorna. You answered all my unanswered questions I was thinking about a fucking long time. **You are the first person in the last 15 years that really inspires and fascinates me in a completly NEW way.** You answered questions that I never expected that anyone would ever in my life answer. Everything here makes so fucking much sense for me and I feel I will [quantum leap] again, and again and again!"

- Theresa Roschmann

"My Life Changed, After A Decade Of Stagnation" | Lorna J's Teachings | Michelle Wilder

To everyone here that has ears I just want to say that I had incredible growth, clarity and a massive expansion of passion in every aspect of my life JUST from watching Lorna's free content on her website.I watched all of them twice and my life changed, after a decade of stagnation and doubt. Her FREE shit got me there. If you haven't already, go spend half a day, now. You will get all of that time back and so much more. She's pretty fucking amazing.

$20,000 Sale, $15,00 Cash, In One Hour, From A Total Stranger, Who Was A NO At First and Went Into Sticker Shock When She Heard the Price AND Who Was Going Through A Divorce | 1:1 Container | Melissa West

Best. Training. On. The. Planet!

Smoking Addiction Gone In 24 Hours | Lorna J's Energy Field + Signature Temple Activation Event Ticket Purchase | M.C.

I had a huge emotional breakdown the day I bought my ticket to the activation. The next day I stopped smoking cannabis during the day (I still smoked at night b4 bed as it helps me sleep). I stopped twirling my hair. I have zero desire to smoke now. It's insane! I also started a new job (managing a million dollar real estate office that I work from home 20 hours a week), made 3 new large investment contacts for my other business and a started advertising for the workshop I created called "gateway to transformation". - M.C.

"Your work is like taking my psyche to rehab. Found you a week ago and since have ignited a NEW way of being." | Teachings | Dana Vacchelli

---

$21,000 In Three Days After Being Stuck For Three Months | Masters Of Magic + Livestream On The Mechanics Of Inspired Action | Alexandra Grizinski

"Fucking magic, Lorna."

"Ummm, so I'm pretty sure I just made $21K after following inspired action precisely and immediately for three days following this live stream. After legit feeling stuck since December. My workaholic business partner shot zombies in the head until 2 AM and I move some furniture around my house. Fucking magic, Lorna." - Alexandra Grizinski

More Money In One Day Than Ever Before | Masters Of Magic And Understanding Mechanics Of Inspired Action | T. L.

"Solved my money problem!"

"Best Decision In My Life. Never Expected That I Can Feel Like This..." | Metaphysics Of Money + Masters Of Magic | Theresa Roschmann

"Lorna Johnson . Oh my god! Your magic and your real kind of genius open opportunities that nobody before could help me with...Best decision in my life to join Masters of Magic, Sales Bitch, Sales Masters, never expected that I can feel like this..."

Have to share a miracle with you! Yesterday I was well prepared to fiere a client that I enrolled in the end of January. Everything, the divorce contract (talked to my attorney before) was prepared. But......

Our conversation in the last 8 days was like shit. She hadn't followed my rules and she was fucked up about my tone. Yesterday in the session the energy between us changed completly. There was space. I could feel her true needs we talked about her desires. I Understand her needs and felt that's my fucking job to help her exactly with that. I was able to create a space where the asshole part of me, this destroying force, has no power. i could talk the truth. My body felt it. This morning, the conversion in our Facebookgroup between me and her was easy, fun and i really served.

Lorna Johnson . Oh my god! Your magic and your real kind of genius open opportunities that nobody before could help me with. And please believe me when I say that I gave really everything for this solutions and the direction that is VITAL for me.

I was able to change everything in seconds. She was deeply grateful and I realized that every story I told myself, that i need „balls", that this was the voice of the asshole aka the Saboteur. There is so much more to do. There are so much more spaces of the feminine and masculine for me to explore, to shift...for me and all my relationships, including my awesome, wise husband.

The „Sales Bitch" Class, my Sales training with my awesome dark sister Julie Veitch and a conversation with the amazing Kari helped me so much to move forward as well.

Best decision in my life to join masters of Magic, Sales Bitch, Sales Masters, never expected that i can feel like this…

€16,000 Sale And Asked For An Interview With Elite Publication| Masters Of Magic | Theresa Roschmann

"The last three weeks I did a lot of uncomfortable inspired action in different areas (not only business) plus watched "The Walking Dead" on Netflix every day (nothing else!!!□). Three weeks ago, a €16.000 Euro sale, and!!! Next Monda I will be interviewed by the journalist of a famous German women's magazine. 3!!! Pages!!! All about my "out of the box" coaching and this is AFTER I deleted all the references and the degrees and education schedule on my website. This journalist found me out of the blue and told me: 'You are the only person that can do the interview' ([and will also be] promoting my book that's being published on the second of May). I

No PR. No book marketing. And at the moment, no idea who my new specific audience is.

Lorna Johnson, you've not only made my day with your Facebook live yesterday, you are a nature Force. Your clarity, just the few minutes 1:1 time in Sales Bitch, your truth, changed me and my life forever. You are healing but much more. A word that describes really what you do and who you are has to involve.

It's so fucking important for me now to REALLY connecting the doots. To feel how the grid is working. Beyond logic. That I already had the answers in me and followed my intuition.

I was all my life an alien. But now I am starting to adore that. And i see that there are much more other brilliant beyond intelligence motherfucker aliens in this group!!!!!

Love you all!

"I just binge watched 4 hours of the YouTube video PLUS today's live on Lorna's personal page. I have never had so many "holy shit" moments in such a short time. Seriously excuse me while I clean my brains off the walls hahahahaa. Mind=Blown."

— CARYN TERRES, Parenting Coach who started her business with a five-figure package

$63,620 In Seven Weeks From Three Sales | Sonika And Naveed Asif | Masters Of Magic And Private 1:1 Clients

"Since we have been consuming your content, up until now, which has been 7 weeks, we have done $63,620 in sales. In only 3 sales calls. No seminars, no webinars, no funnels, no Facebook ads, I barely emailed my list, haven't gone to a network meeting in forever." Naveed and Sonika Asif, Lorna J's millionaire clients who formerly worked closely with Bob Proctor in teaching Law of Attraction and see Lorna's teachings as in the true vanguard of understanding and explaining the deep Mechanics for Manifesting on Demand.

"OMG Lorna. I feel like these missing pieces in my grid are filling in with each and every livestream of yours I listen to (I binged on your content last night and was up until like 3am lol)

But seriously… …you have this potency, energetic precision, and ability to articulate what has previously felt like a foggy feeling into a crystal clear TRUTH in a way I literally haven't seen before.

BRILLIANCE."

— REBECCA IVES RUBIN

Complete Life Transformation | Business Summoning Session + Lorna J's Teachings + Shadow Alchemy

Oh ya know, just creating a custom font for a new company. All completely bc I have unwavering self•belief, depths of creativity at my beck & call, + magick on demand.

If you feel called to collaborate, apply in msg

If you wonder why the sudden flood of Marj on fire in love with life and herself?

Lorna. Lorna fucking Johnson. And her wisdom, her tone, her energy, her mastery, her art, her teaching and her teachings and yes I mean both respectively, the fact that she teaches and the power + impact of how it Stays With You. In You. Of You. Around You.

Amidst what most people would consider chaos✘loving spouse driving from NY to work in CA for the summer ✘two kiddos & two doggos to fend for✘car on the fritz bc of little mouse friends building nests & chompin hoses✘ surrounded by loved ones in treatment for various ailments✘ family marina biz literally under water again like '17

✘folks' summer properties flooded, damp, and no end of rain & West wind in sight✘...among other struggles..✘

I AM CALM. Blood pressure so low, at life insurance physical she laughed Kyle would def lose if it were a competition lol who celebrates low blood pressure? Me. Now.

Able to show gratitude and then stream my thoughts & worries, demand what I require, and simply Do Exactly What My Guidance System Tells Me To Do. 🐰 ☐ Not kinda. Not just a little bit. Precisely. Exactly. And Right Fucking Then.

So when it is as simple as: freehand that logo that came to you last week and get it out. I do.

There is no comparison to Lorna Johnson.

Her Business Summoning Session is beyond your comprehension and honestly...you're NOT 'ready' for it. But, it is what you need.

Want to open up your floodgates to receive visions of the next thing you're going to create and build your Legacy with? I wish you would. ✘I'm so sick of conversing w/ life-sick muggles gasping in misery in the real world✘

We Came Here To Play A Big Game. ➝ ☐play

*Post•it Note found in old wallet from trip to Doctor 4 yrs ago. Yes seriously. Four. Yrs. Ago

I can let go of things now!!!

I have none of issues listed and no more mystery illnesses popping up from every direction to distract me, suck my energy, my money, and take my time. I had then found a naturopath but had so far to go in my journey

With my body my skin my hair my jaw my back my knee my headaches my ankles my feet my sleep my anxiety my digestion my depression my heart my panic my ability to make decisions my ability to create

my ability to parent my ability to love/receive

My Capacity for Chaos.

So Much Of Meeeeeee.

Getting into Lorna's space will change you: body • bones + soul...to rattle you awake

To rattle you undone.

To Show You Masterful Calm in Chaos. And then deliver all your magnificent gifts to you.
—MARJORIE YERDON

$52,000 In Two Months And A 26x Roi | Business Summoning Session And Shadow Alchemy | Stephania Sciamano

$52,000 IN TWO MONTHS WITH A 26X ROI—$30,000 OF THAT FROM ONLY THREE SALES WHICH WERE COMPLETELY EFFORTLESS.

This is what happens when you do two things:

1. A Business Summoning Session with me ($2,000)

2. Shadow Alchemy.

"I had my 3rd effortless $10K sale in a month yesterday. Zero objections.

The more I alchemize my shadow, the easier this gets. Thanks, Lorna for telling it to me straight.

I haven't been super vocal about my Biz Summoning Session but I found out that I was totally in my Child mind and holding on to the energy of my former profession for all kinds of logical reasons. Like 12 years of school, $250K in loans, the street cred of the doctor title, my love of the knowledge...

Now I'm using all the scientific knowledge as a side benefit to working with me and not the main attraction. Huge difference in my tone now.

I've shed so much in the past 2 months and am even moving house tomorrow. Talk about purging!

I've also closed my organic tea business and completely cleaned out my apothecary.

My medicine is different now. This has been transitioning for 2 fucking years but I still had a foot hold in the old energy.

I had been waiting for permission from my old profession to talk about my genius: the intersection of body consciousness and wealth consciousness.

Since I slaughtered my old identity, I've made $52K in sales...in 2 months...while working and marketing very little cuz I'm so busy packing my house.

And I ain't done yet 😺🔥🏃

Keep going, my lovelies. There is much gold here for you too." — STEPHANIA SCIAMANO

"This has been so freaking amazing that I'm tired just learning and listening. My life will change tomorrow." (She was right. She got her request answered from her Magic Man within hours of watching this.) - Devayani Pandev

---

"Lorna, you just exposed the truth behind why I've been so unsuccessful in moving my business from a hobby to an actual business. Your description of the inspired action and what happens when you ignore the magical masculine... Mind Blown. 💥"

$8,000 In Two Weeks | Masters Of Magic | Randi Larson

"Sell your kid if you have to but get your ass in this group!!" - Randi Larson

"If you are not in Masters of Magic you are fucking nuts and any excuse you are using to put it off is complete bullshit. In two weeks, my life has COMPLETELY changed & it keeps going to the next, next level with every transmission & the shifts have brought in over 8K in the past week, along with making HUGE moves in growing our business which has opened up the portal to HEAR our business loud & clear, embody confidence, say no to things that no longer work, fire those who aren't meeting our requirements & owning the shit out of who we are, what we are doing & where we are going.

Sell your kid if you have to but get your ass in this group!!"

$32,000 Week + Secured Interview On Cbs Radio With Al Cole | Shadow Alchemy | Samoa Blanchett

"Literally handed to me on a silver platter. Thank you Lorna Johnson!"

"OMG read this morning and my scalp is still buzzing and my physical body getting bursts of fresh energy. Like damn it Lorna trying to get some sit-down wurk done, why do your words on a screen HAVE TO BE SO FUCKING BOOM 🔥 □" - MARJORIE YERDON

2500% Roi, $50,000 Sale And $10,000 Cash In Two Months | Sales Masters | Jenny Tosner

"Lorna Johnson - I could have never done it without you."

"Today I closed a $50K ++ book proposal with a man who runs a $100-million company in England.

He paid me $10K up front, and I'm keeping 20% of the royalties from the book to go into continued book production.

I don't even know where he came from, except that he watched a FB Live of mine, we set up a meeting, and now I'm publishing his book.

The Goal: to sell 1 million copies.

So really (math) this is now a $2 million book-deal. And I'm just getting started…..

I'm now choosing to Love myself and my company so that it WILL afford to become the multi-million-dollar publishing house it's made to be.

This is such a powerful gift, and I am so happy and grateful for all the powerful coaching that you do Lorna!"

€70,000 And Years Of Business Agony Resolved In One Hour | Business Summoning Session | Theresa Roschmann

"This Session is the best offer for a dark worker ever ☐!!! Far away from the typical common "shit" positionings and much much more!!! ☐☐☐"

I Now Have True Command Of Money. | Metaphysics Of Money | Sonika Naveed

I was mentored by Bob Proctor himself about LOA, and i achieved $50k cash months (had a $500k year in my first year of business as his consultant)... and i know every book/quote/teaching there is to know about LOA. Like literally from the basics of money manifestation to understanding deeper teachings like Thomas Troward and Neville Goddard. After i met lorna, i dumped every single one of those teachings. Its not that it didnt make me money, it did. But the money/results dont stay with you because the current information being shared is incomplete and inaccurate (by literally everyone who isnt aware of this). I had to DEPROGRAM everything i learned and it was the hardest thing ever. You are right in the amazing space where you can just absorb. Ive been on both ends of the spectrum and earned on both... but only one created true command of money. ✸

From $3,000 To $500,000 In 6 Months After 10 Years Of Struggle | Metaphysics Of Money | Galit Lazar

Lorna helped me have a wonderful relationship with my husband in a very short time after struggling for years. The other thing is she helped me go from 3000$ a year to 500,000$ in 6 months after 10 years of struggle. For months I dreamt of being in this program [Sales Masters, now Metaphysics of Money] and had no money to invest. I was in another program with Lorna before and she taught me a tool to ask my magic man for what I want. I still use it daily. I asked my magic man to provide me with the money to invest in this program. 2 or 3 months later I got it. I was in rock bottom. Now I am investing in buying a house. I tried many gurus and invested thousands of dollars with no results. My last payment was 15 000$. Lorna was the only one to help me.

Best Psychic On The Planet. | Business Summoning Session | Phoebe Kuhn

"Holy shit this is everything. Wow.."

One Livestream Is Worth $10,000 | Masters Of Magic | Phoebe Kuhn

FOR ANYONE WHO IS ON THE FENCE ABOUT JOINING MASTERS OF MAGIC, JUST GET IN THERE NOW!!!!! Lorna Johnson did a live today that ALONE is worth at LEAST $10k!!!!!!!!!! This f@#$ing group and material has CHANGED MY LIFE & the quality of my coaching! In my last session with a client SHE VOMITED. No joke. GET IN THERE NOW FOR YOUR UPLEVEL!!!!!!!!!!!!!!!!!!

In Seven Weeks: Closed $63,620 In Sales And $26,938 Cash, Landed A $15k Sale And $6k Cash Over Text, Closed $15k, Collapsed A Month Of Revenue Into One Week, And Did $45k With Just Three Calls, All From Lorna J's Free Content, | Sonika And Naveed Asif

Sonika and Naveed had studied with one of the top Law of Attraction gurus in the world, Bob Proctor, and after quickly rising to the top of his inner circle of consulants and doing $50k cash months (with a LOT of hustle and grind), their business ground nearly to a halt, decreasing to $12k and then $5k months, and they had no idea why.

Bob's VP of Sales' response?

Work harder. "You need to be skin to skin with someone before 9am."

"Law of Attraction teachings are very surface level: Go do the repetition; go do the visualizations, and wait for the time buffer to kick in and you'll get results. And, when someone is doing that and following it to the letter, like us —great example of that – and things aren't happening, you don't know what's happening in the mechanics of it — what's happening on an energetic level. And you really get into that. Like, what's happening with our individual codes, our blueprints, on an energetic level, and how doing this activates the grid, the blueprint. And, just understanding that, it stops your analytical mind from talking and thinking about the how. ... when you understand the mechanics of it, it's like, oh, so this is how it works. That satisfies a huge part.

"Changed My Life." | Lorna J's Transmissions | Caryn Terres

Lorna Johnson, the day I saw your post on Dark worker vs Light worker was the day forever Changed my life. (Almost as much as the day I gave bir th unassisted).

It was like you impregnated me with the Dark and now here we are a year later and I've given birth to my Empress with the best team of midwives ever.

As always, forever grateful for you & this community 🕺👑□☯□ - Caryn Terres

$2000 And Tripled Rates In Just Four Days And A $12,000 Sale In 4 Weeks | Business Summoning Session | Stephania Sciamano

"So, my business summoning session happened on Thursday and so far:

- ✸ Raised my rate to $500 for single (hour long) sessions

- ✸ Sold 3 sessions since Friday [This increased to 4 sessions soon after she posted this.]

- ✸ Including to a woman who said she had no money

- ✸ Feel like I'm finally owning my genius and letting it flow through me

- ✸ Maybe even feeling a bit arrogant. 😁"

REALLL FIYAHHH! I tried to go to sleep after [our session] but my grin was so huge I couldn't settle into my pillow. I feel so bloody free now Lorna, finally in right relationship with my genius. Thank you so so so much. | Business Summoning Session | Nellie Georges

"Goosebumps freaking everywhere. Tears feel like they are coming."

"Omg chills. That's so on point holy shit."

Searching For This Information All My Life | M.A.H.

When I discovered, Lorna Johnson over a year ago, I knew I found gold. It was an incredible breath of fresh air because I was actually searching for this information most of my life but could never find it. Ever since I was a kid I connected with my truth deep in my heart and spoke it, but then I would hide away feeling victimized from the manipulation and torture afterwards. Alchemizing those shadows is key! I still have made very few marketing posts, but when I do the magic will happen!

"I always have soul orgasms with your live-streams!"

"Lorna as soon as you even mentioned this principle, the universe made sense."

"I've been struggling with this for 10 years. I SEE NOW !!!"

"Mind blown. Holy fuck."

From $5k Months To A $30k Month | Lorna J's Free Teachings | Michelle Wilder

Michelle used to brand billion dollar+ companies. Then she left to follow her calling as a spiritual entrepreneur and was struggling just to make $5k a month. Then she found Lorna J's group and went from $5k months to $10k months and now a $30k month from Lorna's free material and teachings alone. - Michelle Wilder

---

"Your explanations are blowing my mind, what a strong energetic intention."

"It was fucking epic."

"Lorna Johnson - The content is spot on and profoundly insightful and crazy stimulating!!!"

Lorna, when I say "Yes" to you, magical things happen. — Melissa West, author, master coach, former John Maxwell team founding partner and personal mentee of John Maxwell (from $84,000 a year to $64,655 in one month, and now a 1:1 client in Lorna J's million dollar accelerator experience.)

One of my favorite things about Lorna Johnson is that she attracts geniuses (I do too, and I never even put that together for 34 years. WTF), but most specifically, she attracts energetic geniuses who in most cases DESIRE to put their gift out into the world.

As opposed to some of my genius friends who I ADORE, but can't even see past societal norms enough to realize they could make bank on their natural genius. :(

But here (and esp her other containers) we are surrounded by other powerful, potent powerhouses just waiting and getting ready to be unleashed on the world. I don't feel this in other communities.

The thing is energy is energy so once you get it - you should be able to get it in all aspects of your life, right?

WRONG. I mean theoretically, absolutely. 100% yes, it's all the same.

But since we're HUMAN, and often still working through our own journey, brain and shadow, it's usually not quite THAT simple at first. As much as we wish it would be.

So sometimes we need to hear virtually the "SAME thing" from another perspective who specializes in whatever area of your life you just simply can't figure out on your own even if you're a master elsewhere.

So what I love here - in the Lornasphere - is that I know that if I can't sort something out myself, no matter what damn area of my life it is -

No matter if I logically finally understand the energetics behind it thanks to Lorna (if you are a logical intuitive, you need Lorna in your life) -

If for any reason, I can't master that energy on my own in another area of my life -

I know the Lornasphere is where I'm most likely to find another genius who speaks our language but can tweak it to my ears in the way that slaps me awake for THAT particular area of life.

There's so much untapped power, weirdness and awesomeness here. So I just want to encourage all of you, to keep fucking going. Shatter the damn shadow, ride that dark night of the soul because your gifts are so needed in this world.

And thanks Lorna, for fucking losing your mind and coming home to your soul.

Some of us really needed you.

And to whoever is still reading this, there are people out there who are waiting for you, too.

<3 - MELISSA AYSHA JAN

It Is Like Two Years Of Coaching With Another Coach In 1 Hour | Business Summoning Session | Sheila Kadeer

Had my business summoning yesterday. Still trying to process. Fucking amazing. It is like two years of coaching with another coach in 1 hour. I have to admit I was a bit scared BUT wow is all I can say. Watch this space as my genius finally emerges. Lorna Johnson fucking nails it!

Powerful Physical Detox | Lorna J's Programs | K. D.

From the moment I started saying yes to your support without knowing how the heck to pay for it all, my physical body has been detoxing (I think to this powerful new energy you are bringing) in the craziest ways -unexplained rashes all over my body, sensation of my rib cage being kicked in, minimized ability to breath etc etc. So grateful for it all & finally plugging up my leaking container, which includes my awesome body detoxing whatever it needs to and rebringing the magic to my life. Every time a new detox symptom occurs I just keep embracing it, saying thank you & saying more... "yes please."🙈□✨✨✨☺️🌀🌀✨ - K. D.

10 Years of Eczema Cleared in One Hour | Business Summoning Session | Jennica Collado

"My eczema has healed after we had our call. 10 years of torturous inflammation... GONE. Seriously."

"I'm left speechless. So grateful I came across one of your posts on Facebook a couple of weeks ago. You changed my life."

My World Just Took 10 Quantum Leaps | Business Summoning Session | Phoebe Kuhn

UMM WOW...

So in my Business Summoning on Friday, Lorna told me I am going to start a movement and I'm going to need a lot of help.

I felt called to write a 'reintroduction' explaining my vision/mission and posted it to a few groups on FB... it went VIRAL lol

In the space of like two hours, I've received an INPOUR of messages and friend requests, offers to be a guest speaker on Podcasts, magazine publicity and someone offered to come and work for me.. HAHA WTF!!!

I'm in AWE of what is happening.. people telling me my message is resonating with them.. like 4 days ago I didn't know I had a message.

Currently at 387 likes and 147 comments.. women getting behind the vision and offering support, collaboration.. producers.. editors.. copywriters.. my world just took like 10 quantum leaps.

$11k Booked From My First Discovery Call

"My last sale was in 2015, a $500 package of 6 sessions with extra bonuses, extra time, a stack of free products…

Since then I've also spent well over $50k on coaching, systems, websites, Virtual assistants (umm to assist me in what exactly?) perfection, perfection, perfection (yep, no action).

6 weeks with Lorna and I'm a whole new entity. No website. No systems. No real idea what I'm doing except knowing it'll be precision deposited in the right moment.

Thank you Lorna. Thank you. Thank you. Thank you."

— 3 WEEKS, $11K NELLE GEORGES

$41,000 In One Month And A 205% Roi | Masters Of Magic + Shadow Alchemy | Stacey Cargnelutti

It just occurred to me this morning that since joining, barely a month ago:

- 2 full pay group programs totaling $9,500.00

- Cash from other projects totaling $20k

- A student loan overpay return $11.5k ☐♀☐

Using mostly shadow alchemy and unschool genius to fortify my container and magnetize.

Thank you Lorna Johnson forever and always.

From $1.5k/Month To $1k In A Day | Lorna J's Free Material | Angelika Duch

I have had so much growth in my business and myself through just accessing your free YouTube content. I can't believe literally can't believe what's been happening in my life.

Thank you. You are so amazing, I can't even describe it with words.

I must say, before I came across your channel, I just came back from 3 months of travelling as a nomad and I had not even a penny to my name. Yesterday alone I made $1k . I used to make $1.5k tops in one month. I've been invited to Costa Rica and Canada for free and have been receiving tons of free stuff everywhere. I can finally acknowledge that my work and my gifts are priceless.— Angelika Duch

"Who needs psychedelics? We have LORNA!!!!!!"

— ANNA GASPARI - PERSONAL GROWTH/SELF MASTERY COACH AT THE SPIRITUAL GRIND

"There is no thing .... no year-long coaching certification training, no emotional cellular release work training, **no certificate on my wall that comes even close to touching the power of this shadow alchemy work.** And I'm brand new to it but know deep down its appearance in my life is no accident. If I knew then what, as a newbie I'm seeing and, sensing now (and how powerfully it's informing my coaching on a whole new level) I'd not have focused on any ICF stuff. I'd have spent the money working with Lorna. "

— JULIE VIETCH, CERTIFIED CAREER COACH

"You're the only 7-figure coach I'd recommend."

— ALEJANDRA CRISAFULLI, MASTER COACH (FROM $9,000/MO FOR 7 YEARS TO $60,000/MO IN 5 MONTHS.)

$5,500 Cash Day from Shadow Alchemy | Sonika Asif

As a result of my teachings about the shadow mind, Sonika realized the specific "consciousness tendency" she's had for years that ruins her ability to manifest on demand. Even though she was trained by Bob Proctor on Law of Attraction, knows the principles of manifestation inside and out (many of which I've never heard of), and with her husband, Naveed, quickly rose to prominence in Bob Proctor's inner circle of consultants to average $30k months, something stopped working (as she and Naveed noticed was the case for many consultants associated with his work). Then they found me and within a week of entering my my world, had sold $30,000.

The most recent win was when Sonika finally identified her personal missing link to making law of attraction work like it should—like a *law*. The minute she discovered it, she used the consciousness coding techniques I teach to encode her magical psyche with different energetic wiring and within 24 hours had a $5,500 cash day. $2500 of that was from a current client who informed them his payment would be two weeks late, but which came in on time, and the remaining was a $3k deposit she wasn't expecting until the following week.

"I realized this happened as a result of the decision I made," she said. "I'm no longer making sales from my shadow. Thank you!"

I can't tell you how much cash I've burnt through (multiple tens of thousands of dollars) with various coaches in the past 2 years. The single payment of $200 has given me more than all of the other coaches combined.

— LAURA HARDING, HEALTH + RELATIONSHIP COACH

"Lifechanging."

— **MORGAN MIX, CEO, ASPIRE CONSULTING, A SEVEN-FIGURE BEHAVIOR ANALYSIS CONSULTING FIRM (FROM 5 CLIENTS A YEAR TO 3 CLIENTS IN 12 WEEKS AND PROJECTED REVENUE OF $1.5MM)**

"I have no words. Forever changed is an understatement. Lorna, I love you! Thank fucking GOD you rose to your calling."

— COLLEEN MORGAN, CEO, PURE ALCHEMY (FROM $300 PACKAGES TO $35,000 IN 3 WEEKS)

"All I needed was just one tweak!"

— ANNIE SUN, PUBLIC FIGURE AND SERIAL ENTREPRENEUR (FROM $1,000 MONTHS HUSTLING 40 HOURS A WEEK TO $80,000 IN FIVE MONTHS, WORKING PART TIME)

It truly is like someone finally unraveled my tongue and found and not only speaks the language I've been trying to speak for years but is trying to teach me how to say the alphabet. I swear I'll get to full sentences someday but for now. I'll just be over here squealing. - Nicole J.

"If you're on the fence about doing a business summoning session with Lorna don't try to find a way, make one." - Dawn Lee

"Lorna I just watched the replay of my business summoning session and I'm even more blown away than I was in the session. Three fucking years I've been spinning my wheels wondering who the hell my ideal client is. Searching like a parent in a supermarket who lost their kid. Analyzing the shit out of every shred of data, twisting myself in knots, trying to figure it out. Sucked in, spending $$$$ on shiny mouth pieces who talked the talk and couldn't deliver. And in one hour you delivered the most exquisite concoction of potent "seeing" that has literally parted the ocean and given me the most immense clarity and peace, I've had in my business. I can't wait to let the fun begin!"

2 weeks, I've jumped into Masters of Magic, a Business Summoning Session and today, Sales Mastery. In this same space I've sacked 2 clients, rejected 3 newbies, today that will that double.2 of 3 more calls I suspect won't be offered the privilege of paying me.

And my only feeling, sweet fucking relief to finally be allowing the part of me, who's consistently pissed on life's raging infernos, its rightful place in my business container.

Demon of over-processing, your ass has been slain.

You see I already met genius.

I've long known it as the inhumane enigma within. What's new is the exquisite pleasure of hearing Lorna piercing the ether so succinctly with the same fierce truth and conviction. And if you're wondering what that looks like for me, among other things of gigantic proportion, my genius can heal what no psychiatrist, psychologist or healing modality on the planet can: the invisible wounds of the flesh.

I'm a rare breed.

I met my genius when I was 8, its message: trauma is a necessity of the soul.

The price for that gem of truth, an entire childhood lost to the putrid ravishes of repeated sexual and physical abuse, oh and a double betrayal.

My genius gave no fucks for either, it had other plans. It would arrogantly orchestrate the handing down of 6 consecutive prison sentences for the theft. And me, I walked away without stepping so much as a toe across the threshold of a counselor, therapist, psychiatrist, psychologist, or even a Drs office.

You're wondering if it made me hard, if I've been avoiding pain. Hell no, that shit cracked me the fuck wide open enabling me to consistently live with a warm, loving, surrendered heart. My therapy; travel, adventure, learning unlearning and the kind of untamed shenanigans and exquisite challenges my genius just loves to rise to.

And sure, my survival archetypes have activated, many times. And I learned to use them to unearth the deepest corners of my shadow.

And now my genius rises once again. Imbued with a poisoned perfume, enticing into my web of elegantly twisted witchery the sleeper agents of the dark. The chameleons; the shape-shifters, the twisted fake good girls seduced by an outside source of power they mistakenly believe they need to survive.

In the dark I will break them out of the prison they have built for themselves. Even they don't know I'm coming.

If you're on the fence about doing a business summoning session with Lorna don't try to find a way, make one.

"Hooolyyyyy Fuuucckkkkk!!!!!!!! No words."

— CARMEL CRINNION, MASTER ENERGY HEALER, COMMENTING ON LORNA'S CHANNELED TRANSMISSIONS

"A huge fecking thank you to Lorna Johnson. I have had the craziest 2 weeks in my life and business. This programme has truly transformed my life and I thank you!"

— TINA HERRING, COACH (FROM $2,555 AVERAGE SALE TO SELLING HER FIRST FIVE-FIGURE PACKAGE, 4XING HER MONTHLY INCOME AND SELLING A TOTAL OF $17,000 IN JUST TWO WEEKS)

"What you do is magical."

— AMANDA CARMER CROMER, CEO, DANGEROUS WOMAN AND FORMER FASHION INDUSTRY AND PUBLISHING EXECUTIVE (FROM SPORADIC FIVE-FIGURE MONTHS AND SEVERE MENTAL STRESS TO $70,000 IN FOUR SESSIONS, $200,000 IN FOUR MONTHS, A $130,000 DAY AND COMPLETE MENTAL AND EMOTIONAL RELIEF.)

"I've searched my whole life and could never find anything that I could connect with at a deeper level. Everything you talk about is what I have been looking for. I just love your work!

— MARY ANN HOEBELHEINRICH

In the beginning, God created the heavens and the earth. The earth was without form and void, and darkness was over the face of the deep. And the Spirit of God was hovering over the face of the waters.

And God said, "Let there be light," and there was light. And God saw that the light was good. And God separated the light from the darkness. God called the light Day, and the darkness he called Night. And there was evening and there was morning, the first day.

[Genesis 1: 1-5. English Standard Version]

THE DARK SECRET

BOOK THREE

THE DARK DOMAIN OF GENIUS

The Fine Print Before The End

True pleasure comes after the pain.

Meaning, Godhead comes after the human is slain.

So, if you decide to continue, know that in doing so, you are activating the most potent, terrifying, and thrilling transformational energy in the Universe, which will come to your consciousness and dismantle it entirely.

The words that follow are portals that kill, and if you continue, you will be walking through them, one by one, portal after portal after portal, each crossing waking more and more power, calling up legion after legion of the magical masculine who, in service to your total and true awakening and your desire to step into your genius, giant nature, will dutifully bring to your side both treasures and terrors beyond your imagining.

Good. Now on to the end.

Your end.

The end of consciousness as we know it.

THE TAKEOVER OF CONSCIOUSNESS

Dear New Age Spirituality,

The reason all your followers are still miserable and stuck as fuck even after thirty odd years of following you religiously is this:

You don't really know what energy is.

Therefore we are taking over.

Love, and What-You-Think-Is-the-Opposite-of-Light-But-Isn't,

DarkWorkers Everywhere

Dear New Age Spiritual Seekers,

Because New Age Spirituality has no clue what energy really is,

it has completely misled you about where your power really lies.

That's problem #1.

Once we solve that, you will not feel better, because you'll have a bigger problem on your hands:

What happens when you find out where your power really lies...

And the only reason that's a "problem" is because when you find out, New Agers will tell you you're arrogant, prideful, and full of shadow. They will also tell you you're mean and to watch your words because where you've discovered your power lies, and what it therefore inevitably means about what you actually are, is not popular to say.

They will try to get you to do shadow work on your arrogance and your pride so you can return to the Light.

Except that Light is energy. And since they have no idea how energy works, they also have no idea how light actually works. Or how to work with light.

The are using light the way a gardener does. Waiting for the sun to shine. Worshipping the sun. Patiently kneeling in front of divine timing.

(In other words, "gestating.")

They are not using light the way a surgeon or a steel worker does. To cut through metal. Or flesh.

And that is because they are not Darkworkers.

They do not understand that the shadow psyche will never yield to something as pitifully weak and diffuse as sunlight. It is fucking steel. It has been soldered together for millennia. It has iron jaws and no fucking intention of going anywhere. It will not be coaxed. It will not yield to nice negotiations. It laughs at your negotiation tactics.

Here shadow. Let me give you another job to do so you stop destroying my life with your bloody fangs.

As it grins and rips into another piece of your pain.

Here shadow. Let me send you on a nice vacation to Spain to sit on the beach and knit so I can get on with my life and not be always bleeding and limping everywhere.

As it nods and springs for your jugular.

And LightWorker coaches and mentors keep saying well of course. Look how arrogant you are. How prideful. If you'd stop being so arrogant, if you'd learn to be more humble (literally "close to the ground"), you'd let the light in. And then you'd be happy.

Except that you aren't built to let the light in.

You are built to fold the world into the Dark Divine, into the newest, strangest, hardest, lightest light that already feels like something is literally RIPPING YOUR SKIN (hmmm. Feels a lot like the fangs of that shadow you were trying to tame...) until you realize it is in fact unzipping you from the human psyche you came in with.

Unzipping you with lasers of excruciating blacklight.

Leaping you upright. A genius giant.

The very definition of arrogant.

Very far from the ground.

If you would like to do this, we would be honored to show you how.

Love and Blacklight,

DarkWorkers Everywhere

Mirror, Window, Portal: The Three Stages Of Awakening

These are the three stages of awakening:

World as Mirror: The Shadowlands (The Light Grid; shadow management)

World as Window: The Meathook Moment (The Black Hole; shadow alchemy)

World as Portal: The Dark Domain (shadowlessness)

World as mirror is where projections of all kinds live. Projecting your shadow onto others. Them projecting it onto you and you caring. It's the world you use to *see* yourself, the self you received from the collective. The self that was coded, that you are now trying to decode.

World as window is where you are suspended in the stillpoint of self creation. Not confronted by the past (what the mirror is always showing you), aware of the next new that is here now (seeing through the clear pain), but which you have not broken through into.

It is a state of suspended animation in which your work is to strike the precise tone that shatters the glass, which is the tone of Truth - the truth of the matter at hand - in which you stop struggling to make things happen or figure out why they're not happening or not happening as quickly (if you do this you are back in the realm of decoding and the window snaps back into a mirror); but instead strike the pose of total stillness that is not a slackening and a victim-surrendering but instead a poise and a posture of "carefree alertness," which is necessary for the new codes to be placed in your field *without your conscious awareness.*

This is the upgraded position of the original "being coded by the collective," for now you are being coded by your own Genius Frequency, your purely Individuated Self. And this must happen, and only happens, in the Dark. Dark even to "you" (the you you used to "see yourself" and to decode yourself), for that you will always resist these new codes. Because they are codes of self destruction. (Which of course is necessary for self reinvention.)

This is the period of gestation that LOAers talk about, which is energetically accurate as a phase, but one they don't really grasp at its roots, or how to really work with it. And they definitely don't realize where it leads (off the Light Grid entirely and into the Dark). And so inevitably at some point anxiety kicks in and they start applying manifesting strategies and techniques to try and will the next phase into being, and this simply snaps them back into the mirror world where they start to do shadow management all over again on all their projections and where they reflect and reflect and reflect ad nauseam.

Yes, this period -- World as Window -- is all about timing. But it is not divine timing, as if there is some power greater than us that we have to work with or wait for. The length of this phase is entirely up to us. And it all has to do with our **willingness to be lengthened.** This is what the meathook moment is all about, after all. Time coming to test us and seduce us back into anxiety, into decoding. But the longer we allow ourselves to become - stretched on the meathook to the breaking point - which is exactly what happens when we approach a black hole, which is exactly what the meathook moment and the still point of creation is - a PORTAL to infinite dimensions of our self -- the closer we come into contact with our bones of light (our divine backbone), which is what resonates at the tone of truth, and carried the codes of destruction, the dark codes. And it is when we strike the tone that lengthens us all the way into an infinity of deaths in which we hang out over nothing and become nothing but bone, that time collapses and shatters the window into a portal and we emerge through it on the other side of the looking glass, now with our genius activated, and with the ability to craft consciousness, not decipher it; and it is here, in the Dark, that we play the greatest game of consciousness that we came here to play, encoding the world and creating the fairy tales and the new myths. And because we are humans who have ceased seeking, these new myths are now being told by the monster, for monsters. For the monsters are the only ones who have truly come to rest.

Numinous = endarkened feminine//true feminine//empress

Neurosis = shadow feminine//false feminine appearing real//princess

Enlightenment = the science of decoding consciousness using the masculine spirit (spirituality) to call the feminine up from the shadows of neurosis into the darkness of the numinous

Endarkenment = the art of alchemizing the feminine soul (creativity) to enable her to step back into her home in the Dark.

The Magic Man = the Usher, Provider, Protector and Supporter through the journey that makes it magical not miserable and whose OVERsight and INsight into the True Feminine is what allows her to shift from neurotic to numinous.

NEUROTIC TO NUMINOUS: The New Myth of Awakening

THE WILD BEAST OF GENIUS

The reason genius streams through you uninhibited when you are at play is the same reason it is unwise to look an animal in the eye.

Genius is coded with the frequency of the wild. She is an ancient and unyielding beast who is entirely uninterested in you.

Until you stay close by, and look away.

….

Your genius and your shadow are made of the same energetic substance.

It's simply the difference between who's the master: you or it.

And the way you become the master is by making it not matter.

1. Not having stakes around your genius becoming matter.

….

YOUR DARK GENIUS

The perfumed scent of your Dark Genius is the unholy grail of life.

Nothing is more potent, more irresistible and more enriching. (Literally).

What you seek cannot be found in the Light.

Dark Codes Of Genius, Mad Archetypes And Shadow Alchemy In Action: The Work

This is taken from a Dark Mastery retreat in 2018 where I taught the Shadow Alchemy tool. The language here uses Dark language and terms. If they don't make sense to your cloaked mind, they will make sense to your raw one. So don't worry.

When you alchemize your shadow, your dark heart of gold turns all of that into pure potent energy and also alchemizes the piece of gold that's buried deep in the shadow, which is your dark code of genius.

In each of the four shadows, there is a dark code of genius.

When you start alchemizing your shadow, this releases gifts. That's what the difference is. The shadow releases gifts.

For me, a big part of my shadow was my bitchiness and I spent my whole life trying to prove to everyone I wasn't a bitch. And then I realized, "Wait, I just need to own the fact that I'm a bitch. That's just how I am." And that provided me with the gift of being willing to speak the truth that I saw in somebody, in a very "bitchy" way, that caused all the amazing transformations that make up my success stories. That's how I get the kind of results I get with my clients. I'm willing to just be a total fucking bitch.

So that's my gift. It's a huge gift, right? But it's not my genius.

My genius is being able to alchemize chaos and bring in new consciousness to the planet. My *gift* is that I speak the truth that I see with cold clarity, and it creates massive changes in people's lives.

Gift lies on the Light Grid.

Gift operates on the Light Grid and is meant for the Light ... that's self-mastery, when you discover your gifts and purpose and master them.

Most of the time, we're ashamed of the things that are actually our gifts. When you alchemize your shadow, you release that gift onto the light grid, and that gift becomes the content for the light archetypes, their psychological energy. So my gift of truth-telling, of straight-ahead truth-telling that feels and seems very bitchy to some people but is life-saving to others, that becomes the content of my mastery of my business.

And I declare that I want to do this for lots of people. I want to build a big business around this. That's my vision, to have this amazing, powerful coaching business where I can speak this truth to lots of people. That's my Sovereign. And I'm going to stand behind my gift. I'm going stand in the value of my gift. I'm going stand *for* my gift and for my dreams *around* my gift. That's my Warrior. And my Magician is going to provide me with all the intuitive, inspirational, brilliant ideas for how to get my gift into the world, how to talk to people about my gift, how to deliver my gift, and all that.

And of course first and foremost, my Lover *values this gift* and sees it as something worthwhile, because that's where it began in shadow in the first place: That it's worthless. That it's nothing. That I need to hide it. Be ashamed of that.

So the Lover in a sense goes and claims the gift within the shadow and sets it out as deeply valuable and this begins the beneficial cycle of lifting that gift up from the shadow into the Light. And the way in which the Lover claims the gift is through Shadow Alchemy.

But what happens after you master your gifts? Excellence ends up feeling empty.

You begin to think, "What's wrong with me? I found my purpose. I have this money. I'm doing really well, and I'm still seeking and I'm still searching and I'm still empty."

The emptiness is itself a gift, because what's really happening is that you are beginning to really alchemize your shadow and empty it out. You're getting to the nerve center. it's almost like a tooth when you drill it down. You get to that nerve center. And that nerve center is that piece of gold that is your genius.

It's living in the heart of your shadow. And once your shadow is fully alchemized, that genius can now start pulsing upwards into, and becoming the content for the Dark Archetypes, for them to do their work of bringing your genius down into the world and onto the light grid.

The Mad Codes in the Shadow

The dark code of genius for the Saboteur is the Devilish Disruptor. This is the mad code or the mad archetype that serves as the raw content for the Dark Archetypes, just as the alchemized shadow provided gifts as content for the Light Archetypes.

When the dark code of genius is trapped in shadow, it operates in indiscriminate rebellion and disruption, in "No, no, no," and "Explain why," and "I'm not gonna do it that way," and "I'm in charge." That's the shadow of it. But when you alchemize all of that, submit to the Light, surrender to the Magician, and the alchemy is fully accomplished, the piece of gold buried deep in there which gets released is the Devilish Disruptor.

The Saboteur is the archetype of the devil. And we have to alchemize all our shame, fear and our issues around that, because that's actually what's pulsing at the center. It was way too strong for us to be able to handle in its purest form as a new consciousness, because what we're really talking about here is the evolution of consciousness.

The Dark Codes are the evolution of the next new consciousness and they have been buried deep in our current consciousness as the ultimate treasure.

We were coded with them from the beginning, because at the dawn of human consciousness, they were way too powerful for us to use. We see what happens when disruption, when chaos and dark hit the light grid. It blows shit up. So the light grid had to form to a degree of solidity and concreteness that it could handle the huge explosion of the release of these dark codes.

When I came to this retreat, I knew the dark code of the Saboteur, and then this morning, the other three dropped in.

The activation of these genius codes (the superconscious field) begins with the prostitute as well, just like the activation of the conscious field, because the dark code of genius of the prostitute is the "Deluded" God. This is the "sociopath." Or what humans think of as a sociopath. The sociopath, from the human perspective, is someone living an archetypal energetic reality. He is not coded with the human consciousness. Not oriented toward good or bad

And in likely most cases of actual sociapths, they are actually managing to run two channels at once, because a lot of them still have a lot of shadow.

What we really want is to become our own legend, to become legendary, meaning archetypal in nature. And that is what the Deluded God is, someone who has become her own legend. That's what Christ had to do. He was embodying the version of it that was possible at the time.

And the Blind Disciple is John the Baptist. This is the Dark Code of Genius of the victim. The one who blindly stands for and stands behind the Deluded God, because this is in the

THE DARK SECRET

warrior energy—to stand for. This is true unwavering self-belief: To be *your own* blind disciple. That's what unwavering self-belief actually is.

"I am a god, and I'm my own blind disciple. No one and nothing has power over me." It really is a sociopathic statement if you think about it.

And then the dark code of genius of the Child is the Crazed Visionary. The child is the dreamer, and in the child archetype, this manifests as a Peter Pan-like carelessness with reality: "I just want to dream forever and play and have other people take care of me." That's the shadow version. But the dark code in there is the Crazed Visionary who believes in purple monsters in the sky and shit. The one with the WILD imagination of a child, which is limitless.

And those now become the content of the Dark Archetypes.

The Deluded God (the mad archetype hidden within the prostitute, the raw content of the new consciousness around INSTIGATIONAL energy) informs the Mythmaker, which is the Dark Archetype of the Prostitute (shadow)/Lover (Light) pillar.

The Mythmaker is speaking the myth *about* the Deluded God, is speaking the value of the Deluded God into existence. As a Dark Archetype, the mythmaker has to have new and raw content. *What's the story here? Oh, the story is that I'm god? Okay, cool. That's an awesome story.* Or the story is that there are no victims, or the story is that I'm a monster and so are you. But you have to know that you are in this world, the deluded god, to actually be able to step into your true genius and announce it on the light grid and live in it.

And of course, all of this cannot exist or be animated without the dark code of the genius of devilish disruption, because this entire enterprise is going to blow up the light grid almost to smithereens.

But first you must get your gift mastered and the Light Grid mastered. And when that happens, your dark heart of gold takes that piece of gold, that genius, which has always been associated with madness, and uses it as content for crafting the new human, the genius giant.

This is why genius has always been associated with madness.

Because up until now, our consciousness could not handle the potency of genius

But now there is a way to go mad, to *go sane,* which is to access these aspects of genius and live a wildly successful, happy, healthy life *also*. Not have them take you down.

Codes Of Money, Power, And Genius

Certain material elements, physicalized expression of energy, carry the most powerful codes of consciousness. They are money, words, music and art. What we really are here to master is to master consciousness in the form of money, words, music and art. When you do that, what you are doing is you are curating your own personal consciousness frequency, one that has never been created before and will never be created again.

This is what it means to be an artisan of consciousness. What we're coming from is an age of receiving consciousness, receiving a blueprint that we then tried to match. That's what we call self mastery. What that also means is that we receive, we're consumers, we are at heart consumers. That means that the bulk of humans, the majority of humans, do not see themselves as creators. They do not see themselves as holders of the codes of consciousness that exist in art and music.

So that is why we put those carriers of those codes on a pedestal. And actually, most humans also don't see themselves as carrying the code, really any of the most powerful codes. Most people don't think that they speak or write well, which really is another form of art. And most people think that they are not skilled at creating money for themselves and they are not skilled at creating art and music.

So the birth of the new consciousness, the age of disruption, is about disrupting the entire field of awareness and understanding about where those codes reside. When we've talked about genius and how Elizabeth Gilbert did a great Ted talk about this, although I totally disagree with her conclusion, about the origin of the word genius. That genius was actually believed to be spirits that would visit somebody. So in other words, the code of power, of intellect and inspiration and genius, which is what flows through and creates money, art and all kinds of expression of creativity, words, the use of words and the expression of music believed that those were really held by spirit and not by themselves.

Then we began, since then we started acknowledging that there were certain code holders of genius, certain people who were geniuses at certain things, genius at making money, artistic genius, creative genius, but that they were few and far between. Those code holders did not make up the majority of the human population.

The fact is that we all hold the code of genius within us, every single one of us. And we all hold the code that can master the making of money and the making of great, great moving, compelling, enthralling, spell casting art. That is what we're actually blueprinted for, which is why when we experience anything less than that or other than that, our lives don't work. If we were not blueprinted to make lots of money, it would not be a miserable experience to not make lots of money. If we were not blueprinted with an intimate appreciation of arts, we would not seek out celebrities, actors, musicians, artists, and worship them the way we do.

The fact of the matter is that being an artistic creature, being one's own creation, is really what is at the heart of all of this and is the heart of true happiness and fulfillment. It has nothing to do with the way that new age spirituality has talked about because creativity is monstrous. True genius is monstrous. That is why most geniuses are not recognized for their genius. And we have these myths in our consciousness. They're imprinted there and they're extremely powerful because whenever I start to peel away the layers of somebody's fear about truly stepping into their legacy work, it always comes down to well, who's going to value what I really want to say? Who's going to value what I really want to do? Nobody's going to value that. Because I'm not a genius, first of all, and even if I were, most geniuses don't get recognized for their value until they're dead.

So there is this deeply imprinted belief that money and genius are at odds with each other for most people. And that is what it is time to overturn. Your genius lies just beneath the surface. In one sense it's buried quite deep because the shadow work that is required can sometimes be enormous in order to alchemize that shadow and release the genius.

But in many other ways, if you are willing to do the work, it can be done rapidly, rapidly, in a matter of weeks or month, literally in a matter of weeks or months. And you can discover treasures, abilities, skills, creativity, psychic and spiritual abilities you never imagined were dormant within you. When you discover those, what also happens because there has been a shift in consciousness that we did not know about consciously, which is that money flows now towards the greatest expression of genius in a much faster and more instantaneous way.

So in the past, money flowed towards genius, but it took awhile. That's because the density of human consciousness blocked the flow of money towards that expression of genius. But as we've always seen, genius is always eventually acknowledged. Money always follows genius because they come from the same code of power. So really the only difference between now and then is that human consciousness has become much less dense. And have also discovered how to collapse time.

So you as the expression and the expressor of your own pure articulated genius are guaranteed, you are absolutely guaranteed to experience the flow of money towards that genius and therefore towards yourself in this lifetime. It is a spiritual guarantee. That's one of the things that has shifted considerably. It's been a seismic shift in consciousness and in the energetics of how we experience money, genius, artistry, creativity, success, fulfillment, happiness, all of those things.

It all has to do with the loosening and the sifting of and the enlightening of the human consciousness field, so that money can flow much more rapidly and quickly to its natural counterpart expression, which is genius and creativity.

DOING SHADOW WORK ON YOUR GENIUS

Why have you been MASSIVELY doubting your gift, your insight and your path? Because your LIGHTWORKER MENTOR and FRIENDS literally CANNOT SEE IT as anything other than your SHADOW.

You GUYS. I'm so ON FIRE from the outpouring of response from my Livestream on DarkWorkers. It's my DEEP passion to bring this material ... well ... OUT OF THE DARK.

I now see everything I struggled with AND that my clients struggled with in STARK RELIEF.

The number of people who have PM'd me or responded to the Live saying their entire lives now make perfect sense is MIND BLOWING.

SO many have said that they now realize their former mentors were LightWorkers who literally COULDN'T SEE them, and who in fact mistook their DARK GIFT for their SHADOW.

Holy fucking shit, people. No WONDER so many of us struggled for so long in such shame and sadness doing all kinds of SHADOW work because we were told our hearts were closed (seriously! One of my clients told me that's what a former guru mentor told her as the reason he wouldn't work with her!! WTFF?!?! (That's "What The Flying Fuck" by the way)) or we weren't a clear channel or we had Mother wounds or Father wounds or whatever the fuck wounds and were mean and bitchy and abrasive and cold hearted (oh. The number of times I've been called all these things).

And ok YES. No one gets to adulthood on this planet without wounds.

I'm not at all advocating for no more shadow work.

But holy HELL (literally), it's one thing to do shadow work on your SHADOW, so you can transmute it into light again, and an ENTIRELY FUCKING OTHER THING to do shadow work on your DARK GENIUS.

Know what happens when you do that?

Your gift goes into HIDING.

Your literal Life Force dwindles to almost NOTHING.

And you begin to kill yourself.

What has just popped open—this awareness around the stark contrast between DarkWorkers and LightWorkers, is HUGE, people.

As Colleen, my Dark Soul Sister, said the other day: A portal has been opened

The Light Cannot Deliver On It Promise Of Awakening

You are NOT meant to seek and seek and seek and seek until you croak.

You're meant to go on the Hero's Journey (seeking purpose), and then the Heroine's Journey (seeking an integrated Self), so you can finally go on the ***Anti-Hero's journey.***

Learn how to master these truly incredible, quite baffling, massively powerful and insanely activating Dark Archetypes, so you can start doing what you're truly mean to do here.

Livestream (Euphoria, Now Masters Of Magic), July 19, 2018

- Transcribe this recording

Livestream (Euphoria, Now Masters Of Magic), May 15, 2018

- Transcribe this recording

The outer layer of the Light Grid is just as resistant to being breached by human consciousness as the outer layer of the Earth's atmosphere is to being breached by actual humans.

As within, so without. (There is no above/below.)

SHADOW WORK VS DARK WORK

Shadow work: Bringing Light to UnConscious Shadow (Light that has hidden itself.)

Dark work: Bringing the Dark (what has never been in Light because it is the NEWEST Light) to the Light.

Your Soul Is Not Your Savior. It Is the Source of Your Suffering

The truth is your Soul has been telling you little white lies about who you really are, how energy actually operates and what that means about where your power truly lies. Your feminine Soul is the source of suffering and of all illusion and it is time for the feminine to be alchemized back into her natural state.

Not lurking in the shadows but reigning in the Dark.

Lorna Johnson, I'm curious what your opinion and/or knowledge about past lives is and how it affects our current energy in this lifetime?

The soul codes the body with the lessons it's learned, including all shadow consciousness (which is the repository of the lessons still to be learned). We suffer because we have a soul. The goal has always been to reach the tipping point in consciousness where we have come close enough to the Dark to not need the soul to intervene between our physical-human consciousness and Dark Consciousness. That time has arrived. We can now alchemize the shadow, and in so doing, the Soul, and place ourselves in direct contact with the Dark. And therefore our genius, giant nature.

There is no such thing as automatic or ultimate WORTH. That is a concept developed by human consciousness on the Light Grid. Based on the currency of being of value to each other based on survival consciouness that it is important that we all know our value with respect to other beings. Because that's how we survive. And so, there is this underlying concern that we all have about how much we are valuable. Or our worth. And that is a concern that only lives and exists in survival consciousness, in tribal consciousness and on the Light Grid. And so in order to answer to answer that ultimately unanswerable question, and the reason it's unanswerable is because you are MATTER, because you DECIDED to MATTER. Meaning there is no inherent worthiness or value, we decided to matter, and thats how we became matter. And then, we started worrying about our worth, because we discovered that the worthless ones, were discarded and died. And we had to invent this spiritual concept of inherent worthiness, you are worthy because you exist. That's not actually true. You aren't inherently worthy of anything. There are energetic laws in place that require us to be vibrating at certain frequencies in order to receive what we desire that is also vibrating at that frequency. But we are not inherently worthy of receiving it. We also have to become an energetic match to it. We're not inherently worthy of living. It's required that we maintain certain frequencies in order maintain the energetic capacity to stay alive. If we were inherently worthy, we wouldn't need food to keep our bodies going. So this is an illusion that we're telling ourselves to keep ourselves feeling like we are safe, like we have an inherent currency that we can always trade on if worse comes to worse. And that is this concept of inherent worth. When you step into the dark lattice that whole concept goes away because you are working in a consciousness and you are working in an artistic consciousness, and artisan one. And the concept of worth and value goes out the window completely. What is a piece worth to one person - it could be nothing. What is that same piece of art worth to another person - could be a million dollars. There is no inherent worth to the work of art. And we are works of art. The truth of us, is that we are works of art. And we came here to craft ourselves into works of art, NOT into currencies we can trade.

It is one of the most unhelpful illusions that we have been taught as truth. That we are ultimately deserving or worthy of what we want, just because we exist. This is not true and it is not accurate in terms of energetic law. Just because you want something does not mean you are an energetic match for it. Which means you are not worthy of it. You are not deserving of it. If someone wants my time and attention, they have to be an energetic match for it. If they're not, then they are not "worthy" and they are not "deserving" of my time and attention. It has nothing to do with whether they exist as a physical expression of energy or not, it has everything to do with whether their energy is resonating at the frequency of mine.

Your Magic Man has standards for what he's attracted to. He's not attracted to just anyone, resonating at any frequency. You have to be resonating at the frequency that is energetically attractive to him. And when you are, you recieve what you desire. If you're not resonating there, then you don't receive it, and you are therefore NOT WORTHY of receiving it.

It's time that we correct this totally unhelpful and incredibly energetically inaccurate delusion/illusion, because it has created a generation of entitled Princesses, who are now our Spiritual Leaders. And this helps no one.

The Difference Between Light (What is Dark Consciousness?)

Over the great landscape of human evolution stretch three theaters of consciousness, or power management systems: Shadow, Light, and Dark. Each represents a distinct metaphysical language of power that exists on a continuum of getting Truth completely wrong (shadow, weak power management) to getting Truth completely right (light, strong power management) to CREATING Truth (dark, ultimate position of power).

Each represents a journey of awakening, a drama of unfolding awareness and power. For many spiritual seekers, this journey began with leaving their original source of income, which no longer felt aligned, as well as having to leave the family or cultural tribe (and often both) in order to respond to the pull of their true calling. This is the hero's journey. The movement of shadow into light, where the human leaves his tribe and goes in search of his own identity, purpose, gifts, creativity, and will, and embarks on the quest to discover his *own relationship to power*.

It is called the hero's journey because it is overseen by the masculine energy. (Yes, newsflash, all this time you thought getting into spiritual seeking and the largely female-dominated spiritual transformation scene meant you were stepping into your feminine energy. Nope. Light is masculine, therefore LightWorkers work with the *masculine* system of energy, which is why there is so much struggle with trying to make money—which is masculine—and with hustle, which happens through a degraded relationship to Time, which is also masculine. And why would this be? Because money and time are called into service by the *feminine* energy ((the masculine is here to provide for the feminine and it is the job of the feminine to know how to inspire him to do so)). So LightWorkers are only working with half the raw material of the universe, and are trying to *manhandle* time and money into submission, instead of mastering the feminine genius of inspiring the masculine (time and money) to work effortlessly on their behalf. This is the missing link to the way law of attraction and manifestation is taught and practiced, by the way. A total ignorance of what the feminine and masculine are and how they work together to create magic on demand.)

But while the hero's journey is overseen by the masculine energy, the traveler here is the *feminine shadow*.

Shadow is feminine. This is why so many spiritual traditions see the woman as the source of all suffering and evil, and as deserving of domination and control. It is simply our way of anthropomorphizing the current state of human consciousness, which only sees two states of being (light and shadow, illusion and truth, evil and good) and in fact believes the third (dark) to be the most depraved aspect of shadow. Most humans believe that the deeper we go into shadow, we will eventually meet pure darkness, which is seen as the essence of evil. This is why new age spirituality and many traditional religious, spiritual and wisdom systems say that union with Light is the ultimate goal.

It's actually the exact opposite, in two ways.

What we seek cannot be found in the Light. It can only be found in the Dark.

And, Dark is the exact opposite of shadow, and of Light, and cannot ever be reached through those systems of consciousness or energy.

Dark is the True Feminine. Shadow is the anxious or lost feminine. And the journey of consciousness is the journey of the shadow feminine up into the Light, through the Band of Unhooking, into the Dark, her true home, where she reigns over and with the masculine, who does her bidding in the Light, the manifest grid, the grid of manifestation. This is the completion of the journey of seeking and of quests, where the journey of human consciousness finally ends its incessant seeking and takes it place as gods

Just as dark energy does not interact with the light and cannot be detected by it, so too (of course) Dark Consciousness does not in interact with nor can it be detected by light consciousness. And just as light exists on a wide spectrum, from pure light to deep shadow, so too for light consciousness, which includes shadow consciousness as an aspect of it. Shadow is a metaphysical aspect of Light.

This means that no matter how deep into the shadow you go, you will never encounter the Dark. The Dark does not exist on a spectrum. It is one, impenetrable frequency of fulfillment. This is why there is no seeking in the Dark; why it is the end of all our seeking. For once we reach the frequency of fulfillment, there is no more trying not to "get it wrong" and trying to "get it right," there is simply the interplay of the pure feminine and masculine energies — the raw material of creation — in which they turn the theater of war (shadow vs light, getting it wrong vs getting it right) into a theater of PLAY in which consciousness itself becomes the subject of the drama, meaning the character in its own narrative, and humans become "nothing more than" gods at play.

Which leads us to the heroine's journey, because while the hero may be happy for a while on his sole quest for purpose, meaning and self mastery, eventually it becomes tiring and boring, because the masculine is essentially on a quest to unite with the feminine, the fertile field of true fulfillment.

The heroine's journey is awakened when the hero becomes blinded by the light, having achieved a state of excellence and mastery, and finding himself bored to tears (the "midlife crisis of consciousness") and fighting the great urge to burn it all down to the ground and go on another quest.

But which quest?

Until now human consciousness

LightWorkers are here to help the soldiers of consciousness heal from their battle wounds so they can get back out into the field and fight the good fight, master the endless supply of shadow elements that are constantly emerging from the shadows. This is shadow management and it's why LightWorkers say we'll be doing shadow work until we die. Because they do not see the other theater that is always superimposed on the theater of war: the circus of consciousness, the play-ground, the theater ground on which the play of the narrative of consciousness is being acted out.

Darkworkers not only see this other theater, they are the ringmasters and scriptwriters, the aerial acrobats and the actors, crafting the entire world from the raw material of the universe, upon which the drama (the war) between the light and shadow are being...well...played out. in other words, the time of the LightWorkers as those at the very forefront of consciousness and awakening are coming to an end. The last act is being played out. We are now in the final moments, after which the artisans and orchestrators will soon come out from behind the curtain and reveal themselves to the great, gathered throng, who has been watching from the sidelines for so long, they forgot it was a play...an illusion...they had been watching all along.

That is why this is called the age of disruption.

Each player (as the body and soul of human consciousness) really believes he IS his character and that blood is real (in other words, that victims exist and it's possible to be wounded). Each spectator (as the mind and spirit of human consciousness) really believes that the illusion is the truth (the story is real) and someone else is responsible for it.

In other words, everyone has forgotten that long ago the actors chose their roles and the spectators wrote the narrative, and they will all be quite surprised when the villain of the play, which the actors believe is real and the spectators have come to hate, walks out from behind the red velvet curtain.

Everyone will then realize something even more appalling and impossible: that villain, the enemy of the people and the monster in their fairytales, is themselves.

And they finally, and suddenly, find nothing wrong with that at all.

"Others, not human, can call into being what they are not an energetic match for, because they have entirely removed themselves from the realm of the personal frequency. They are agents of another kind built to manifest frequencies that do not yet exist, or which are being called forth BY humans so that human consciousness can advance. They are who we mean to be. What the experiment in consciousness is all about:

Can we send out a fraction of consciousness, coded with its own destruction, which IS its own overcoming and advancement, and will it actually work?

Can humans return to their genius, giant nature?

In fact, no.

It is not a question of can.

It is, as is everything having to do with consciousness—and therefore with magic—a question of will."

We have been coded with two consciousnesses, to participate in and therefore report back on the Grand Experiment. And since Consciousness and Will are one and the same

Because magic is manifesting *on demand.*

It's what everyone longs to do—it's the holy grail of life, really—and what most people mean when they talk about manifesting.

THE HUNGER FOR THE NEW

As humans, we hunger for the New. This can often be taken as superficial: The desire for the newest gadget. The latest model.

It is not superficial at all.

Our appetite for the New comes from our desire to become intimate with the Dark Divine, which is chaos itself, and therefore the source of all that has never been and is coming into being.

The only reason we feel unfulfilled is because there is in fact very little that is *truly* new being created, expressed, or communicated. Our options have all been Fast Food Consciousness. Assembly line spirituality.

Spiritual teachers adding a "new" item to their spiritual menu, which isn't really new, but a knock off or variation of what's being offered on all the other menus from all the other spiritual gurus.

Bolting on a "new" module to their existing technology of consciousness teachings, which is really just a remake of a module their spiritual guru taught them.

And so we're eating spiritual food that all tastes basically the same but is simply being cleverly *marketed* as new, and because it's been reprocessed so many times, has lost almost all of its energetic nutrients.

And we are using "new" spiritual technologies to handle our consciousness because the ones we bought into before, which all promised to be *truly* groundbreaking, weren't at all, and yet because they are minor modifications of what has come before, all pretty much look and feel the same.

And then we wonder why we're so fat, malnourished and bored.

This is what happens when we try to satisfy our deep hunger for the Dark—which can be fully satiated with a very small, because intensely potent, dose—with facsimile versions of over-processed Light.

The living foods/raw foods/superfoods movement towards "lightly processed" or "cold processed" foods is not a coincidence in its timing with the shift and upgrade in consciousness that is happening on the planet.

We are developing a new taste for the Divine.

Something darker. Something raw.

And therefore, as befits the appetite of the monstrous, deeply satisfying.

THE VAMPIRIC NATURE OF A DARK BUSINESS

Light and shadow codes are codes of reflection. As such, they are agents of incremental change.

Dark codes are codes of activation. As such, they are agents of quantum leaps.

What this means:

You must put away the *tools of reflection* if you desire quantum leaps and pick up the *tools of activation*.

Tools of activation are those which require No Time to apply.

Meaning, you must master the ability to work outside Time and Space.

This means you must become a master of the Dark. You must master working directly with chaos, the raw material of the Universe, and learn the precise art of chaos alchemy, which is all about listening and tuning to exacting standards.

A Dark Business is always "in danger" of destruction. It is always rotating on an infinitesimally small decimal point of existence between death and rebirth.

It is a member of the living dead and the deadly alive.

An inhuman species, which requires a god to operate it with mastery.

In other words, a monster. Who lives not in the shadows, but in the pitch black, and whose hour of magic is the witching hour between one day and the next.

This is the hour of reinvention, in which the old body of work dies, and gives itself up to be alchemized into something utterly new, which will live forever.

On Self-Loathing And The Highly Practical Benefits And Deep Joys Of Knowing Yourself As A Darkworker

I'm in Hawaii and I am SURROUNDED BY LOVE.

Juicy, feminine, lush, abundant, overflowing, happy happy, smiley, forest green, oceanic-as-fuck love.

And every time I experience it, I curl up a bit inside. (Sometimes quite a bit.)

You see, I see the uninvited offering of love as an attempt to invade my utter still, my deep silent, my black and beautiful energy.

I experience it probably much like 99.9999999999% of the world experiences an insult or act of aggression.

I don't want it.

I don't need it.

And something densely packed and tiny within me, which feels like a tooth or a red eye, wants very much to gape or claw a bit at that soft, gooey, uninvited love until it erupts a tiny, blood red drop of something more isolated and isolating.

And therefore much more beautiful.

And volcanic.

But I don't, because I don't go where I'm not invited.

Instead I sit within myself, feeling the beautiful blackness of my field undulating around me like a heat field, and observe what this outpouring of love really, most of the time, is:

A mutual attempt to defang.

Here. If I leap to offer to take your groceries to the car and heat up your lukewarm tea or ask where you're visiting from or whether for the fifteenth time you would like a glass of water then you will feel compelled to return the kindness and we will roll over each other in an endless loop of giving and receiving love which in truth is simply our way of reaching quietly in and pulling out each other's incisors.

I would much rather we all keep them and go about our lives with the default interaction being bottomless silence and stillness until there is so much negative space built up between us — two poles of energy braiding into each other like curious tendrils — that someone finally cannot resist saying "Hello," and then the world erupts.

But that is not the way humans want it.

And so I go undercover mostly everywhere.

The only difference between then and now?

I don't worry that I'm secretly sociopathic or deeply depressive or ill-wishing or maliciously-minded, which is what I would have been wondering, ad nauseum, as I sat at this little juice bar in Hilo, Hawaii, watching all the light stream between people in vast waves.

Now I simply know that my land is gorgeous. And spare. And black with beauty.

And it is time to make this my home.

Channeled Transmission: The Origin Of Consciousness And The Big Bang, The Source Of Anxiety And Form, The Journey Of Awakening And The True Purpose Of The Feminine Rising Movement:

Before the big bang, all of the tones and frequencies of consciousness were set in perfect harmony and perfect discord. These were all of the possible systems, fields, and frequencies of Light. At the moment at which the entire matrix had been set in perfect balance, the feminine (the Dark) plucked (activated) the masculine (Light) and frequency tore through into being.

Time (masculine) ripped from Space (feminine) and created the necessity of form. Seeing and accepting the prison of consciousness this would create, the feminine dropped into shadow and became matter (form, material, and also anxiety—over-concern with what does and does not matter), allowing the masculine to stay in its presence as Light, and also setting out the path for the journey of consciousness (shadow >> light >> dark), in which Light reigns supreme while form orients itself to the new grid (patriarchy, Hero's journey, worship of the masculine/Sun/Light), and then, when form was prepared to ascend back home, in which we witnessed the feminine rising movement, which culminated on 12/12/12 as the two frequencies began meeting in the dead zone between Light and Dark.

In this dead zone Shadow and Light were stripped of their old tones and ushered through an alchemy of consciousness that allowed them to re-orient themselves to each other afresh.

This dead zone is the world gone mad and going sane. It is the meathook moment of awakening, the band of unhooking, the River Styx, whose crossing takes as long as we resist pure death and soullessness (the soul being the cocoon in which the feminine placed herself as a way of remembering, though dimly, her true nature).

It is the feminine soul, built around and woven into the tones of the anxious feminine/the body/shadow consciousness, that is unhooked from matter, challenged to radically drop all concern with what matters, and endures the test of time (masculine, the saturnine energy of the great trial) in which she must, as shadow, and therefore as pure illusion and nothingness, submit entirely and excruciatingly to the Light (masculine), be unhooked from and sacrifice all the royal standing she had gained during her journey of rising, and allow Light/masculine/Time to fully master her, by striking a tone of perfect discord and harmony, chaos within order, the stillpoint of the death within death and the pinnacle of terror and liberation. And she did strike the balance.

That is when the Dark Portal opened on 5/11/18, for the feminine, in being fully alchemized, moved through the final portal of awakening and took up her throne in and as the Dark and as the reigning source of the newest, lightest Light (now master of the magical masculine, who serves her with gracious devotion).

It is therefore now possible, and becoming ever more necessary, to conduct the entire journey of awakening, alchemize our shadow and our soul, and step from world-as-mirror to world-as-window to world-as-portal and into our true genius, giant nature as gods, myth makers and master handlers of the raw material of the universe.

When our codes are relaxed, energy naturally flows and does not recognize barriers. This means energy naturally flows throughout our fields as well as from our fields to all the code fields to which we are linked that exist in other entities and beings, creating a synchronicity of conditions in which life feels perfectly orchestrated, a delicate dance in which we desire something and it immediately appears.

This is what spiritual teachers mean when they say we are "one" and enlightenment is the realization of and union with this oneness. What they mean, and are referring to, is the unhindered flow of energy that we experience as relational consciousness bliss, in which there is no tension between our will and our experience, and in which it feels as if we are in such harmony with all other ideal patterns of consciousness that we are one with them. To "be one" simply means to "be of one mind."

But all this means is that the outside

We are not one, in the sense that we are fundamentally not individuated. We are absolutely individuated, because this is the primary movement of consciousness: to gather itself under the direction of one creative will. And there is no such thing as One Creative Will (God), which rules supreme and whose Will overrides all others, other than if by this we mean that the One Creative Will is the collective expression of all individual creative wills in consciousness. In other words, we are creating and willing god, not the other way around.

The Master Map: Shadow, Light And Dark

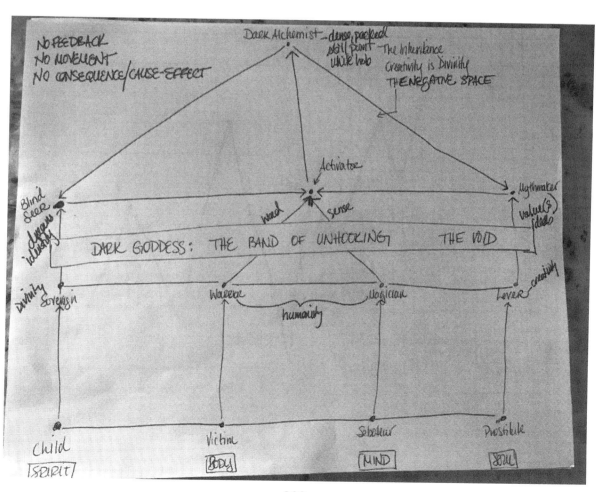

Alien Poetry. How About Some Alien Language Fun?!?!

In trolia grupe

en scanlon en cora,

mir mutit in trup adorada adein.

In deina rotun

pir prenzi pir trenta,

in tru por brengola pur verda navein.

"Firen," sulta gran,

mut an vorca rintan,

"Firen!" halta granto parein.

Et grippa la flendo, mit vurgan parato,

in grupo dein alia vrein.

THE DARK SECRET

Trut kenda gryphon, trut kinta grendon,

mit fogutra mendan lor dan...

Et frangu trupondia wrintan dunkun,

it hyria trankon deitan.

Lor Franken en Brandol hak grephenda phon,

fir portun ken hamda phen do.

Len Shindo den Phantom ib branle ken ko,

pen flanta por grundia dan.

Mit onen fer fortu, fen granlia doan,

ben dona per dona din go,

men krante phin landa fulia fren kan,

certan ando lunia lo.

En nun, cont la gracas, con tuna la dein,

Abein branle graca brin vo...

Drin mutula harna mit pola ven gein,

Abrenda, bra denda den vro.

ACKNOWLEDGMENTS

Oh, the names. And the hearts within them and the bodies and the brains and the minds and the limbs and the genius.

Colleen Morgan, you deserve Honorable Mention Number One. We opened the Dark Portal together. You helped me realize my Darkworker nature. You were essential, being the two-headed monster that we are, to helping me channel a vast amount of this material. And you kicked my ass an infinite number of times, beating the drum of "Get the fuckin' book WRITTEN, already," until I did. Just by being, you are the darkest blessing. I love you, lady. Dark Witch. Fellow Master Code Holder. And one of the rare, true consciousness geniuses on the planet.

My team. My team. My team. Running a Dark Business is a BITCH. A beautiful, unwieldy, rich, monstrous bitch. And my Dream Team is exactly that. (A dream, not a bitch. Ok, they're bitches, too. Of the best kind.) They work with chaos like a boss. They go with the unruly flow like fuck. They are my other ears, eyes, brains, witchy insights. Tia Holmes, you are a Dark CEO's visual design DREAM. Devayani Pandav, you ran the sales team and sold the FUCK out of my programs while I wrote and gave beautiful book birth. THANK you both. Kim Caloca-Madden, you worked your Systems Sphinx magic on the hornet's nest of my business and kept up with the breakneck pace of it all with grace and aplomb. Which was an awesome feeling for someone constantly having to plunge into the depths of the Dark to write this fucker, knowing a good and stable woman was at the Tech Helm. Melissa Kowalczyk, what can I say, Boss Hostler Extraordinaire? You took my wild life and organized the HELL out of it and just ran it for me, hook, line and sinker, so I could wander off into wordland for days. You are GOLD.

Amanda Carmen-Cromer, you helped birth an earrrrlllllllyyyyyy version of this, and to the degree that dis-ordered thoughts can be ordered, you helped me do it. Thank you for your witchy word wisdom.

Rebecca Ives-Ruben, your early edits and comments on how potent this book was helped me see it for what it truly is, and code it even more deeply. Thank you for your book-amour.

And now for my clients, past and present, without whom this book would not have been possible, because they were the ones who materialized these truths into their lives and turned themselves into walking vessels of magic. Not that I needed PROOF that this material was as powerful as I knew it was. (Um. That would be me being in my saboteur.) But being able to see magic and miracles in action, to trace the scent of the Dark and the electricity of the Light straight into people's lives. Well. what a gift.

And of course, a huge thank you to my parents, for playing their part to PRECISION, so I could play mine. And, for supporting me in my darkest hour even though I'm sure they thought I was crazy (and not the Going Sane kind). I will forever ever ever being profoundly, unspeakably (even though I'm speaking of it) grateful to you.

And last but not least, thank you to my main squeeze, to the love of my life, my perpetual passion, Ultimate Killer and the Utterness of All, The Dark. You came because we called. And then slit our throats so the True Truth can flow forth. I can't think of a better way to go out.

Made in the USA
Monee, IL
11 September 2019